A Vietnam War Chronology

ISBN: 1-58898-959-3

To order additional copies, please contact us.
BookSurge, LLC
www.booksurge.com
1-866-308-6235
orders@booksurge.com

A Vietnam War Chronology
According to Military Assistance Command Vietnam (MACV)

Randall M. Romine

2003

A Vietnam War Chronology

This book is dedicated to all those who served in Vietnam and especially those that made the ultimate sacrifice.

Preface

Established in Saigon on February 8, 1962, the US Military Assistance Command Vietnam (MACV) operated as a subordinate unified command under the Commander in Chief, Pacific Command. The MACV was responsible for advising the US ambassador to South Vietnam, controlling all US military operations, commanding all US Army elements, assisting and advising the South Vietnam armed forces, coordinating US intelligence operations and providing oversight to the many allied units and agencies in the RVN. The subordinate commands to the MACV included the US Army Vietnam, the 7th Air Force, the US Naval Forces Vietnam and the 3rd Marine Amphibious Force.

The MACV was the primary source of information on the progress of the war during 1962-1973 and I consider the information in the MACV collection to have been extremely helpful in my research of the Vietnam conflict over the years. However, the collection is quite voluminous and the time required to conduct meaningful research was excessive. In addition, I spent too much time on research trips to the National Archives to review and extract information from the collection. Most of my research consisted of verifying combat incidents that occurred within certain time periods so I decided to create a chronology utilizing only MACV records. I have found this chronology to be extremely helpful and so I decided to make it available to others interested in the significant events of the Vietnam War. Most researchers, and other interested personnel, do not have the time or resources to conduct their own research at the National Archives, so this book will be helpful in their studies. All the information in this book is extracted entirely from MACV unit records and I consider this work to be a history that will stand up through the ages.

Forward

After reviewing all the collections of various books on the Vietnam War there is no reference book quite like this one. This is required reading, both by the student and by the person who simply likes to learn about the US involvement by the Military Assistance Command, Vietnam (MACV). MACV was responsible for the planning, combat analysis and the execution of the overall conduct of the war in South East Asia. Until now, no one had the dedication or the wherewithal to methodically comb the MACV operational reports by day, month and year to record the Vietnam War on a daily basis. Here at last is a book that describes the day-to-day events of the war, beginning in 1964 and ending in the eventual pullout of US troops in March 1973. This book will assist the serious researcher and the novice in better understanding the US military role in South Vietnam and the events that eventually led to the US withdraw.

Randy's dedication and lifelong study of the Vietnam War comes from his twenty year commitment as a member of the US Navy who also served aboard ship in the contiguous waters of Vietnam. Also, Randy has worked as a military researcher of

Agent Orange exposure inquiries and Post Traumatic Stress Disorder (PTSD) claims while assigned to the US Armed Services Center for Unit Records Research.

If there is an important collection of MACV papers or notes that would appear to shed a light on the overall conduct of the war that he has not examined, it would be hard for me to name it. Mr. Romine has reviewed, analyzed and read every document or report that was created by MACV that exists at the National Archives in College Park, Maryland.

Randy has crammed each page with lucid facts, important information and thousands of combat incidents that occurred during one of the most trying periods in our nation's history.

A book of this nature has been needed for a long time, but up to now no one has provided the meticulous details of what happened in South Vietnam as recorded by MACV. This book belongs in the hands of anyone interested in knowing the military history of MACV and its role in fighting the war. No bookshelf would be complete without a copy of this work. Randy has taken on a project that was enormous in scope and has succeeded in providing a resource that can be used by everyone interested in learning about the daily combat operations of the US military.

Donald C. Hakenson

MAY 7, 1954

- Dien Bien Phu fell, ending French military influence in Asia.

JULY 21, 1954

- Geneva agreements ended Indochina hostilities, partitioned Vietnam at 17th Parallel and set national elections for 1956.

SEPTEMBER 8, 1954

- The Southeast Asia Defense Treaty was signed at Manila.

OCTOBER 10, 1954

- The North Vietnam Communist regime formally took control in Hanoi.

OCTOBER 23, 1954

- President Eisenhower offered US military aid to Diem.

JANUARY 1, 1955

- The US began direct aid to Vietnam.

JANUARY 20, 1955

- The US took over training of the SVN Army from the French.

JULY 7, 1955

- Communist China signed an aid agreement with Hanoi.

JULY 18, 1955

- The USSR signed an aid agreement with Hanoi.

APRIL 28, 1956

- The MAAG officially assumed responsibility for training the Vietnamese Army.

APRIL 28, 1956

- The French Military High Command in Vietnam was dissolved.

MAY 1, 1957

- The French responsibility for training the Vietnamese Navy and Air Force terminated.

MAY 1959

- At the request of the GVN, CINCPAC directed that US advisors be provided to infantry regiment, artillery, armored and separate Marine battalion level units. The CINCPAC also took steps to obtain Special Forces mobile training teams from the USARPAC and CONUS sources to assist in training RVN Ranger companies for counter guerrilla warfare.

FEBRUARY 5, 1960

- The GVN requested the US double the MAAG strength to 685.

MAY 5, 1960

- The US announced that the MAAG was being increased to 685.

MAY 30, 1960

- A US Special Forces team arrived in the RVN to conduct training.

JANUARY 31, 1961

- The MAAG was authorized to detail advisors down to all battalion headquarters and to serve at command posts at lower levels when required.

FEBRUARY 1961

- The RVNAF estimated the total Viet Cong strength at 10,000.

MAY 5, 1961

- President Kennedy said the US was considering use of US military forces to help the RVN.

MAY 11-12, 1961

- Vice-President Johnson pledged US aid to RVN forces.

AUGUST 2, 1961

- The GVN ordered all men between 25 and 35 to report for military duty.

AUGUST 11, 1961

- The increase of RVNAF was up to 200,000 authorized.

OCTOBER 1961

- The RVNAF estimated Viet Cong strength at 17,500.

OCTOBER 11, 1961

- President Kennedy announced the dispatch of General Maxwell D. Taylor to Southeast Asia.
- President Diem asked for a bilateral defense treaty and for the dispatch of US troops to Vietnam.

OCTOBER 18, 1961

- President Diem declared a nationwide state of emergency, assumed special powers, and asked for US combat troops.

OCTOBER 26, 1961

- President Kennedy sent a personal message assuring President Diem of continued US support.

DECEMBER 4, 1961

- President Kennedy informed President Diem that the US was prepared to participate in increased joint effort with the RVN. US uniformed forces would participate in operational missions with RVN forces.

DECEMBER 11, 1961

- Two US Army helicopter companies, the 8th and the 57th Transportation Companies, arrived as the first complete US military units sent to the RVN.

DECEMBER 14, 1961

- A President Kennedy letter to President Diem agreed to increase US aid to the RVN.

DECEMBER 17, 1961

- A US Army logistical support team from the 9th Logistical Command on Okinawa deployed to the RVN.

JANUARY 9, 1962

- The ARVN increased from 170,000 to 200,000.

JANUARY 31, 1962

- Viet Cong strength was estimated between 20,000 and 25,000, divided into three categories: full-time guerrillas, part-time guerillas and village para-military.

FEBRUARY 1, 1962

- US Special Forces personnel joined the CIDG program as advisors to create an irregular anti-Viet Cong, para-military force.

FEBRUARY 8, 1962

- The DOD announced creation of the MACV under General Paul D. Harkins. The US Army Ryukyu Islands (USARYIS) Support

Group (Provisional) organized to provide administrative and logistical support to US Army combat support units in the RVN.

FEBRUARY 14, 1962

- President Kennedy stated that US troops in the RVN were instructed to fire to protect themselves if fired upon, but were "not combat soldiers in the generally understood sense of the word."

MARCH 22, 1962

- The first clear and hold operation was initiated in Binh Duong Province.

APRIL 8, 1962

- The Viet Cong executed two wounded prisoners of war near An Chau in Central Vietnam. Each, with hands tied, was shot in the face. They could not keep up with their captors.

SEPTEMBER 1962

- The GVN successes forced Ho Chi Minh to change his timetable. In 1959 he predicted the defeat of the GVN in one year and revises estimate to 15-20 years. The main targets of the Viet Cong were strategic hamlets.

FEBRUARY 22, 1963

- The DOD stated US pilots were flying many Vietnamese Air Force operational missions and were authorized to make tactical strikes.

APRIL 17, 1963

- An Amnesty Program was proclaimed for Viet Cong defectors.

JUNE 3, 1963

- A Buddhist demonstration was renewed in the city of Hue. The GVN imposed martial law in Hue.

JUNE 11, 1963

- The first Buddhist monk committed suicide in Saigon.

JUNE 27, 1963

- President Kennedy announced the appointment of Henry Cabot Lodge as Ambassador to the RVN.

AUGUST 21, 1963

- Martial law was proclaimed throughout the RVN. Curfew and censorship was imposed.

NOVEMBER 1-2, 1963

- President Diem and Nhu were overthrown and slain in a military coup led by Major General Duong Van (Big) Minh. The Military Revolutionary Council suspended the constitution and dissolved the National Assembly.

JANUARY 4, 1964

- Cambodian forces attacked an RVNAF unit in the An Gian Sector.

JANUARY 17, 1964

- The RVN dissolved the special Saigon command and put the capital under III Corps.

JANUARY 18, 1964

- The largest heli-lift of war to date consisted of 115 helicopters carrying 1100 troops into Zone D. The Viet Cong avoided contact.

JANUARY 21, 1964

- A USN team fought a cholera epidemic in Saigon.

JANUARY 30, 1964

- Major General Nguyen Khanh replaced Minh in a non-violent coup.

FEBRUARY 3, 1964

- In Kontum city the MAAG compound was attacked with grenades, with one US wounded and one building burned.

FEBRUARY 7, 1964

- The Playboy Bar was bombed resulting in five US killed.

FEBRUARY 9, 1964

- Pershing Field bleachers were bombed resulting in two US killed and 25 wounded.

FEBRUARY 11, 1964

- The Capitol Kinh Do Theater was bombed resulting in three US killed and 50 wounded.

FEBRUARY 27, 1964

- Supposedly trapped, a Viet Cong battalion fought through a 2,500-man ARVN ring in the Dinh Tuong Sector.

MARCH 3, 1964

- RVN airborne troops killed 110 Viet Cong out of an estimated enemy battalion near the Cambodian border in the Kien Phong Sector

MARCH 8, 1964

- Secretary of Defense McNamara visited Vietnam.

MARCH 14, 1964

- Three hundred Viet Cong were captured in an operation in Kien Phong Sector.

MARCH 20, 1964

- RVN forces mistakenly hit the Cambodian town of Chantreau.

MARCH 23, 1964

- *Operation Phuong Hoang* 13-14/10, Kien Phong Sector, finds a Viet Cong battalion in a fortified village and killed 126.

APRIL 7, 1964

- General Khan made Saigon a special zone and split III Corps.

APRIL 13, 1964

- The District Capital of Kien Long (near U Minh Forest) was overrun and about 300 ARVN were killed and 200 civilian casualties.

APRIL 25, 1964

- An ARVN ambush near Plei Ta Nag killed 84 Viet Cong.

MAY 2, 1964

- A Viet Cong shaped charge in Saigon River damaged the aircraft ferry, USNS CARD.

MAY 3, 1964

- A Viet Cong bombing at the USNS CARD dock injured eight US.

MAY 7, 1964

- Cambodians charged that a GVN armored troop attacked the village of Taey two miles inside the border. The RVN claimed that Cambodia interfered with the hot pursuit of Viet Cong.

MAY 10, 1964

- A terrorist plot to explode a bridge along the Secretary of Defense's route was discovered and foiled.

MAY 12, 1964

- The Secretary of Defense visited Vietnam. Two Cambodian jets strafed RVN units in Tay Ninh Province.

MAY 25, 1964

- Other Free World assistance began.

JUNE 5, 1964

- The RVN bombed and burned a 20-mile strip on Vai Co Orient River along the Cambodian border.

JUNE 23, 1964

- Ambassador Lodge resigned and General Taylor was named to replace him.

JUNE 24, 1964

- *Operation Thang Lang-Hai Yen 79* on the Dinh Tuong-Kien Phong Sector border, killed 99 Viet Cong.

JUNE 25, 1964

- A successful attack on a Viet Cong training camp in Quang Ngai killed 50 Viet Cong.

JUNE 29, 1964

- The New Zealand Army Engineers Detachment arrived.

JULY 4, 1964

- The Special Forces camp at Polei Krong was overrun, which resulted in 50 friendly killed. The DRV charged that RVN guerrillas were attacked in Laos on June 27, 1964 and the DRV coast on June 30, 1964.

JULY 6, 1964

- The Nam Dong Special Forces camp was hit resulting in 58 friendly killed, of which, two were US and one was Australian.

JULY 15, 1964

- Secretary of Defense McNamara informed press conference that no PAVN units were operating in the RVN.

JULY 20, 1964

- The 9th Regiment, PAVN 304th Division, was cut up in battalion encounters with the ARVN in Thua Thien, Quang Nam and Quang Tri Sectors.

JULY 27, 1964

- The Pentagon announced that several thousand additional advisors would be going to Vietnam.

AUGUST 2, 1964

- Three DRV PT boats attacked the USS MADDOX on patrol in Gulf of Tonkin.

AUGUST 5, 1964

- US carrier planes hit PT pens and Vinh oil tanks in the DRV.

AUGUST 19, 1964

- The Viet Cong inter-province headquarters in the Mekong Valley was bombed. The Viet Cong began effective 20mm anti-aircraft fire.

AUGUST 21, 1964

- A Viet Cong ambush in a previously cleared area of the Mekong Delta disturbed the US.

AUGUST 26, 1964

- Rioters attacked a US supported hospital in Da Nang when a guard shot over their heads.

SEPTEMBER 5, 1964

- Four Cambodian jets cross the border and fired on RVN aircraft and missed.

SEPTEMBER 6, 1964

- One Cambodian aircraft fired on a Chu Muong outpost.
- 150,000 Buddhists took part in a parade in Saigon at a funeral for victims of Buddhist-Catholic rioting.

SEPTEMBER 12, 1964

- The US State Department announced no plans for international negotiations on Vietnam.

SEPTEMBER 15, 1964

- Khanh arrested five coup leaders.
- *Operation Tu Luong 134* near Quang Ngai City resulted in 80 Viet Cong killed.

SEPTEMBER 18, 1964

- A second Tonkin Gulf incident occurred. DRV PT boats attacked the DDs USS EDWARDS and USS MORTON.

SEPTEMBER 20, 1964

- Centering in Bon Sai Pa Special Forces Camp, Quang Duc Sector, Montagnard soldiers began a rebellion against the RVN authority.
- *Operation Lam Son 129*, Quang Tri Sector, resulted in 77 Viet Cong killed.

OCTOBER 3, 1964

- An Xuyen *Operation Dan Chi 73* resulted in 150 Viet Cong killed.

OCTOBER 4, 1964

- Riot police dispersed workers in Saigon.
- Viet Cong killed one US and 40 Vietnamese 18 miles from Saigon.

OCTOBER 11, 1964

- Three Viet Cong battalions and RVN forces engaged near Go Gau Ha, which resulted in heavy losses.

NOVEMBER 1, 1964

- The Viet Cong shelled Bien Hoa Air Base with 81mm mortars, which killed four US and two Vietnamese soldiers.

NOVEMBER 4, 1964

- Typhoon Iris hit Central Vietnam causing widespread disruption of communications and destruction of crops.

NOVEMBER 17, 1964

- US Overseas Mission (USOM) allocated flood relief supplies and Marine helicopters began shuttling supplies from the USS PRINCETON.

NOVEMBER 21, 1964

- *Operation Thang Long 27*, Dinh Tuong Sector, wrested Ba Dua from Viet Cong control and killed 136 Viet Cong.

NOVEMBER 22, 1964

- *Operation Phong Hoai,* Tay Ninh Sector, concluded with the destruction of a Viet Cong base area and arms factory. The Viet Cong suffered 157 killed.

DECEMBER 6, 1964

- *Operation Dan Chi 92,* IV Corps, resulted in 138 Viet Cong killed.

DECEMBER 7, 1964

- The Viet Cong overran the battalion command post on Hill 193, which threatened An Lao Subsector headquarters and stayed in the area to fight. Two companies of ARVN were missing.

DECEMBER 9, 1964

- RVN forced the retake of Hill 193 and secured An Lao Subsector headquarters. The Viet Cong attacked the 3rd Regiment headquarters and artillery positions in Quang Tin Sector. The RVN reaction forces killed 162 Viet Cong.

DECEMBER 25, 1964

- The Brink Bachelor Officers Quarters (BOQ) was bombed resulting in two US killed and 108 US and Vietnamese wounded.

DECEMBER 28, 1964

- An RVN reaction force ran into two to four hard core Viet Cong battalions in Ba Xuyen Sector, killing 87 Viet Cong, making the largest capture of enemy weapons to date, including two 75 recoilless rifles and four .50-caliber anti-aircraft machine guns.

JANUARY 1, 1965

- As the fifth year of US involvement in the war began, American military strength in Vietnam totaled 23,000 men, primarily advisory personnel. For the RVNAF, January 1966 was the most successful month since the beginning of the counterinsurgency effort. All eight major operations involving battalion-size forces or larger were government victories. Viet Cong losses were the highest for any month since 1961.

- US military strength in Vietnam 23,000

FEBRUARY 7, 1965

- In its first major action of the year against American forces, the Viet Cong attacked a US compound at Pleiku and nearby Camp Holloway. Friendly casualties were eight killed and 108 wounded. Eighteen aircraft were destroyed or damaged.
- US aircraft were ordered to strike the North Vietnam for the first time. USN planes hit the Dong Hoi military barracks north of the 17th parallel. One A-1 aircraft was lost and the pilot was killed.

FEBRUARY 8, 1965

- President Johnson ordered the evacuation of all US dependents from Vietnam, which started almost immediately.

FEBRUARY 9, 1965

- The first US troop unit entered the country when elements of the USMC Light Anti-Aircraft Missile Battalion became operational in the Da Nang area.

FEBRUARY 10, 1965

- The Viet Cong blew up a four-story hotel in Qui Nhon occupied by US enlisted men. After days of digging through the rubble 30 feet high, final casualties were announced as 23 US dead, 21 injured and 14 Vietnamese injured.

FEBRUARY 16, 1965

- Eighty tons of Viet Cong weapons were found near and aboard a supply ship that was attacked and sunk in shallow water off the coast of Vung Ro Bay.

FEBRUARY 19, 1965

- The first US jet aircraft used in operations in South Vietnam were F-100s and B-57s, which carried out interdiction strikes against Viet Cong targets around Phuoc Tuy, 40 miles east of Saigon.

MARCH 4, 1965

- The first US aircraft were shot down by MIGs over North Vietnam. Two USAF F-105 Thunderchief aircraft were downed on a mission over the Ham Ron Bridge near Thanh Hoa, 85 miles south of Hanoi.

MARCH 9, 1965

- The first US ground offensive unit to enter the country was the 3rd Battalion, 9th Marines, 3rd Marine Division, Fleet Marine Force, which landed at Da Nang.

MARCH 30, 1965

- A Viet Cong car filled with explosives heavily damaged the US Embassy in Saigon. Two Americans and 11 VN were killed and 143 persons were injured.

APRIL 1965

- There were no significant news events this month. The period was without major battles and was one of general Viet Cong inactivity. ARVN operations brought generally light contacts.

MAY 5, 1965

- The first American paratroopers entered the country when the 173rd Airborne Brigade began landing and immediately went into tactical bivouac at the Bien Hoa Air Base north of Saigon.

MAY 7, 1965

- US Marines and Seabees began landing at Chu Lai, south of Da Nang. Security deployment was quickly carried out and construction of a new airfield got underway.

MAY 11, 1965

- The Viet Cong launched a heavy attack on the provincial capital of Song Be. Friendly casualties were 56 killed, including five US. Thirteen US were wounded, while 297 Viet Cong were killed.

MAY 16, 1965

- A series of accidental explosions at Bien Hoa Air Base killed

24 Americans and injured 105. More than 40 aircraft were destroyed or damaged.

MAY 29-JUNE 3, 1965

- In a weeklong battle around Quang Ngai City, the ARVN suffered about 500 casualties and Viet Cong casualties were estimated at 825.

JUNE 1, 1965

- US military strength in Vietnam was 52,000

JUNE 8, 1965

- The first Australian combat troops entered the country when the 1st Battalion, Royal Australian Regiment arrived.

JUNE 9, 1965

- Some 2,500 US Army combat engineers began construction of a major base including an airfield, logistics and port facilities at Cam Ranh Bay, Khanh Hoa Province.

JUNE 9-12, 1965

- Both sides suffered heavy losses in a four-day battle at Dong Xoai, about 55 miles northeast of Saigon. Friendly casualties were estimated at 650, including seven US killed, 15 wounded and 11 missing. An estimated 700 Viet Cong were killed.

JUNE 16, 1965

- A 10-20 pound charge was exploded at the civilian passenger terminal of Saigon's Tan Son Nhut Airport. There were 46 persons injured, including 34 US.

JUNE 17, 1965

- Two F-4 Phantom II aircraft from the aircraft carrier USS MIDWAY shot down the first MIGs of the war, about 50 miles south of Hanoi. The Phantoms were on a strike mission against the Yen Phu barracks when they were attacked by four MIGs. Two of the surviving MIGs fled north.

JUNE 18, 1965

- Twenty-seven B-52 bomber aircraft hit a Viet Cong concentration north of Ben Cat in Binh Duong Province of South Vietnam. This raid, with high explosive and general-purpose bombs, was the first of the war by B-52's.

JUNE 25, 1965

- The Viet Cong set off two claymore mines at the My Canh floating restaurant in Saigon. Of the 44 persons killed, 14 were US. The 81 injured also included 16 US.
- The Viet Cong launched a multi-battalion attack on an ARVN battalion at Duc Hoa in Hau Nghia Province. Friendly casualties were 87, while Viet Cong casualties were estimated at 137.

JULY 7, 1965

- About 8,000 men of two US Marine battalion landing teams and combat support elements of the III MAF landed and deployed at Da Nang and Qui Nhon.

JULY 12-16, 1965

- The 2nd Brigade, 1st Infantry Division, and the 1st Logistical Command landed at Cam Ranh Bay, Vung Tau and Qui Nhon.

JULY 15, 1965

- MACV confirmed that US Army Sergeant First Class (SFC) Isaac Cammancho had escaped after nearly 20 months of imprisonment by the Viet Cong.
- MACV announced it accepted as confirmed the presence in South Vietnam of the complete PAVN 101st Regiment with three battalions. MACV acknowledged as probable the presence of the PAVN 18th Regiment and as possible the presence of the 95th Regiment.

JULY 17, 1965

- B-52 bombers were used in support of a ground operation in South Vietnam for the first time, when about 30 aircraft bombed a suspected Viet Cong troop area in the Mang Yang Pass along Highway 19.

JULY 24, 1965

- The first US plane was shot down by a surface-to-air missile over North Vietnam. A USAF F-4C aircraft was shot down about 40 miles west of Hanoi, while in support of a strike on the Lang Chi explosive plant. The pilot was presumed lost.

JULY 27, 1965

- US aircraft hit surface-to-air missile sites in North Vietnam for the first time. A flight of 46 F-105s struck two sites and the Phu Nhien Barracks 40 miles northwest of Hanoi.

JULY 29, 1965

- The first elements of the 1st Brigade, 101st Airborne Division landed at Cam Ranh Bay.

JULY 30, 1965

- US military strength in Vietnam was 80,000

AUGUST 9, 1965

- The US presented four B-57 aircraft to the VN Air Force. Premier Ky accepted these first jets for his Air Force and flew one himself after ceremonies at Tan Son Nhut.

AUGUST 14-15, 1965

- 6,400 Marines, including the 3rd Battalion, 9th Marines Regiment, arrived at Da Nang and Chu Lai.

AUGUST 18-24, 1965

- Marines carried out the largest US action of the war to date, *Operation Starlight.* The combined surface and air regimental strength assault south of Chu Lai resulted in 614 Viet Cong killed.

AUGUST 24, 1965

- A Viet Cong mortar attack on Bien Hoa Airfield damaged 26 US and 23 VN aircraft. Friendly casualties were light.

SEPTEMBER 7-10, 1965

- US Marines joined VN Marines and soldiers in *Operation Piranha,* an amphibious/heli-borne assault, in the Batangan Peninsula south of Chu Lai. The coordinated operation netted 178 Viet Cong killed, 69 captured, 168 suspects detained and 24 weapons captured. Friendly casualties were light.

SEPTEMBER 18, 1965

- Elements of the US Army's 1st Cavalry Division (Airmobile) landed at Qui Nhon and were headquartered at An Khe in Binh Dinh Province.

SEPTEMBER 18-21, 1965

- Elements of the 101st Airborne carried out *Operation Gibraltar* near An Khe. There were 226 Viet Cong killed.

SEPTEMBER 23-30, 1965

- On a weeklong battle for the Phu Co outpost along Highway 1 northwest of Qui Nhon, the ARVN killed an estimated 700 Viet Cong. Friendly casualties were moderate in the action, which involved an overall Viet Cong force estimated at regiment size.

OCTOBER 8, 1965

- The first elements of the Capitol ROK Division arrived in South Vietnam.

OCTOBER 10, 1965

- The first elements of the US Army's 1st Infantry Division arrived in Vietnam.

OCTOBER 17, 1965

- Five USN jet aircraft from the aircraft carrier, USS INDEPENDENCE, destroyed what was believed to be the first operational surface-to-air missile installation, located 52 miles northeast of Hanoi.

OCTOBER 19-31, 1965

- The month-long battle for and around the Plei Me Special

Forces Camp began October 19, 1965. The first phase involved the Viet Cong attack and subsequent relief of the camp by friendly forces and ended October 31, 1965 with 317 Viet Cong killed and 70 believed killed and carried away. Friendly casualties were 117 killed, including 12 US and 246 wounded, including six US.

OCTOBER 27, 1965

- The Viet Cong launched simultaneous mortar and suicide squad attacks against US Marine air installations at Marble Mountain (Da Nang East) and Chu Lai. Friendly casualties were light while 39 Viet Cong were killed. In the two attacks, 18 helicopters and two A-4 Skyhawk aircraft were destroyed and 22 helicopters and five A-4s damaged.

NOVEMBER 1-12, 1965

- The 1st Brigade of the 1st Cavalry Division battled the Viet Cong west of Plei Me. The Viet Cong lost 216 killed and 117 captured. US losses were 55 killed and 194 wounded.

NOVEMBER 8, 1965

- The 173rd Airborne Brigade clashed with a large Viet Cong force 30 miles northeast of Saigon in War Zone "D". Viet Cong losses were 391 killed and friendly casualties were moderate.

NOVEMBER 10-12, 1965

- *Operation Blue Marlin,* north of Chu Lai, involved the first combined US and VN Marine amphibious landing against the Viet Cong. Losses on both sides were light.

NOVEMBER 14-19, 1965

- In the biggest US engagement of the war to date, the 1st Cavalry Division's 3rd Brigade fought the battle of the Ia Drang Valley through the week of November 14, 1965. The Viet Cong lost 1,238 killed and 20 captured. US losses were 250 killed and 358 wounded. For the entire Plei Me-Ia Drang Campaign. Total figures: Viet Cong 1,771 killed and 138 captured; US 317 killed and 558 wounded; ARVN 105 killed and 248 wounded.

NOVEMBER 27, 1965

- On November 27, 1965, an estimated Viet Cong regiment overran the ARVN 7th Regiment at the Michelin Plantation in Binh Duong Province. Friendly casualties were heavy.

DECEMBER 1, 1965

- In the week ending December 1, 1965, a total of 1,098 Viet Cong incidents were reported, the highest weekly figure of the war to date.

DECEMBER 2, 1965

- The nuclear-powered aircraft carrier USS ENTERPRISE went into combat for the first time, launching 118 sorties against Viet Cong targets in South Vietnam

DECEMBER 4, 1965

- A Viet Cong panel truck carrying explosives was set off at the Metropole Bachelor Enlisted Quarters (BEQ) in Saigon. Eight persons were killed and 137 injured.

DECEMBER 15-22, 1965

- On December 15, 1965, USAF F-105 aircraft struck the Uong Bi thermal power plant 14 miles from Haiphong. Jets from the carrier USS KITTY HAWK hit the plant again on December 20, 1965, and the plant was practically destroyed December 22, 1965, in a third day raid by Navy planes from the USS ENTERPRISE, USS KITTY HAWK and USS TICONDEROGA.

DECEMBER 19, 1965

- The extensive search and destroy *Operation Harvest Moon* carried out by US Marines and ARVN south of Da Nang ended with 419 Viet Cong killed, 53 captured and 314 suspects detained.

DECEMBER 24-26, 1965

- Between 1800 hours, December 24, 1965 and 0600 hours, December 26, 1965, the Viet Cong initiated 84 hostile actions, despite its own and the US/South Vietnam announced Christmas ceasefires.

DECEMBER 29, 1965

- Elements of the 3rd Brigade, 25th Infantry Division began arriving at Pleiku, RVN from Hawaii.

DECEMBER 31, 1965

- US military strength in Vietnam was about 181,000 men.

JANUARY 1, 1966

- *Operation Marauder.* Initiated in Hau Nghia Province by the 173rd Airborne Brigade and the 1st Battalion, Royal Australian Regiment.
- *Operation Jefferson.* Initiated in Phu Yen Province by ROK and ARVN forces.

JANUARY 2, 1966

- The enemy bombed the 5th Special Forces Headquarters at Nha Trang.

JANUARY 4, 1966

- This is the first confirmed enemy use of 120mm mortars in the RVN during a mortar attack on Khe Sanh Special Forces Camp in Quang Tri Province with 25-75 rounds of 120mm mortar fired.
- *Operation Jefferson.* Friendly forces used riot control agents.

JANUARY 5, 1966

- The first elements (advance partillery) of 2nd Brigade, 25th Infantry Division arrived in the RVN.

JANUARY 6-7, 1966

- The Viet Cong detonated a claymore at the Tan Son Nhut main gate killing two persons and injuring 12.

JANUARY 8, 1966

- *Operation Crimp.* Initiated in Hau Nghia and Binh Duong

Provinces by the 1st Battalion, Royal Australian Regiment and 1st Infantry Division units.

- Two Viet Cong junks were beached and ammunition was recovered after a firefight off Go Cong Province.

JANUARY 9, 1966

- *Operation Flying Tiger VI.* Initiated in Binh Dinh Province by a Capitol ROK Infantry Division unit.

JANUARY 10, 1966

- The first C-130 cargo drop occurred in the RVN (Special Forces camp near Dalat).

JANUARY 12, 1966

- Terrorists bombed the Non-Commissioned Officer (NCO) Club at Da Nang.
- *Operation Buckskin.* Initiated in Hau Nghia Province by 1st Infantry Division units.

JANUARY 14, 1966

- USN Swift boats moved from An Thoi to Da Nang.

JANUARY 16, 1966

- *Operation Jefferson.* Terminated in Phu Yen Province. Final results were 391 enemy killed and 14 enemy captured. Friendly casualties were light.

JANUARY 17, 1966

- Elements of the 1st Marine Regiment arrived in the RVN from Okinawa. The regiment landed at Chu Lai.
- The main body of the 2nd Brigade, 25th Infantry Division arrived in the RVN. The division landed at Vung Tau and was positioned at Bien Hoa.
- The Viet Cong overran the CIDG outpost at Bien Hep in Long An Province. Friendly casualties were heavy.

JANUARY 19, 1966

- *Operation Van Buren.* Initiated in Phu Yen Province by the 1st Brigade 101st Airborne Division and 2nd ROK Marine Brigade. This was a rice harvest security operation.
- The Viet Cong bombed a military billet at Can Tho.

JANUARY 20, 1966

- The cease-fire over the Lunar New Year (TET) holiday commenced at 1200 hours. The enemy-initiated incidents of violation of the cease-fire totaled: 106 (77 against US and FWF and 29 against RVNAF units). Friendly losses over the period were: 13 killed, 36 wounded, and one missing. The holiday saw the climax of an intensive US-GVN psychological warfare campaign to encourage enemy defections under the Chieu Hoi program.

JANUARY 21, 1966

- A USAF helicopter, USS NICHOLAS and VN Navy units rescued the crew of the Panamanian merchant ship BRIGHT STAR that was grounded near Chu Lai.
- *Operation Van Buren.* Terminated in Phu Yen Province. The final results were 679 enemy killed and 49 enemy captured. Friendly casualties were light.

JANUARY 22, 1966

- Terrorists bombed an Army billet in Saigon.

JANUARY 24, 1966

- The end of Tet stand down occurred at 1800 hours.
- *Operation Masher.* Initiated near Bong Son in Binh Dinh Province by the 3rd Brigade, 1st Cavalry Division (Airmobile) and a battalion of the Capitol ROK Infantry Division.

JANUARY 25, 1966

- The Viet Cong attacked Da Nang airfield and nearby I Corps Headquarters with 120mm mortars, inflicting minor damage and light casualties.
- A USAF C-123 aircraft crashed near An Khe and all 46 aboard were killed. This was the worst air crash in the RVN, to date, involving US troops.

JANUARY 28, 1966

- *Operation Double Eagle I.* Initiated in Quang Ngai Province by US Marines.

JANUARY 31, 1966

- US aircraft resumed bombing in North Vietnam after a 37-day lull.
- The Viet Cong detonated charges at the US Bachelor Enlisted Quarters (BEQ) in Dalat resulting in one US killed, 10 US wounded, one US missing and one VN wounded.

FEBRUARY 3, 1966

- The USS BRINKLEY BASS and USS WADDELL received NVN shore battery fire during an effort to rescue a downed pilot. There was no damage.

FEBRUARY 4, 1966

- *Operations Masher/White Wing. Operation Masher* entered the second phase and renamed *Operation White Wing.* Final results of *Operation Masher* were enemy losses 697 killed and 131 captured. Friendly casualties were light.

FEBRUARY 5, 1966

- Terrorists detonated a claymore in a bar in Vinh Long City resulting in seven killed (two US, five VN), 16 wounded (six US, 10 VN), one Viet Cong killed and two suspects detained.

FEBRUARY 13, 1966

- The number of USN Swift boats in RVN reached 22.

FEBRUARY 14, 1966

- *Operation Market Time.* A Viet Cong mine sank a USN Swift boat 15 miles NW of Rach Gia off Keng Giang Province resulting in four USN killed and two USN wounded.

FEBRUARY 15, 1966

- B-52s struck a major enemy command center in Tay Ninh Province.

FEBRUARY 17, 1966

- *Operation Double Eagle.* Phase I terminated.

FEBRUARY 19, 1966

- *Operation Double Eagle* I. Terminated in Quang Ngai Province. Final results were 312 enemy killed and 19 enemy captured. Friendly casualties were light.

FEBRUARY 20, 1966

- The enemy mortared the 1st Cavalry Division (Airmobile) base camp at An Khe, which resulted in light friendly casualties, light aircraft damage, and seven Viet Cong killed.

FEBRUARY 23, 1966

- Nine US Coast Guard Cutters (USCGCs) arrived in the RVN bringing the total to 26.

MARCH 4, 1966

- The seaplane tender USS SALISBURY SOUND arrived at Cam Ranh Bay with a squadron of seaplanes.
- *Operation Utah.* Initiated in Quang Ngai Province by Task Force D (USMC).
- MIGs attacked US aircraft over North Vietnam. This is the first MIG attack since resumption of strikes on North Vietnam.

MARCH 6, 1966

- *Operation White Wing.* Terminated in Binh Dinh Province. Final results were 1,047 enemy killed, 445 enemy captured, 226 individual weapons and 28 crew-served weapons captured. Friendly casualties were light.

MARCH 7, 1966

- *Operation Silver City.* Initiated along Song Be River in Binh Duong and Long Khanh Provincial border area by the 1st Brigade 1st Infantry Division, 173rd Airborne Brigade and 1st Battalion, Royal Australian Regiment.

MARCH 8, 1966

- *Operation Utah.* Terminated in Quang Ngai Province. Final results were 358 enemy killed and four enemy captured. Friendly casualties were light.

MARCH 9, 1966

- An estimated NVA Regiment attacked the A Shau Special Forces Camp in Thua Thien Province, which consisted of three days of heavy fighting.
- The USCGC POINT WHITE intercepted, rammed, and sank a 25-foot Viet Cong motor junk in Rung Sat Special Zone near the mouth of the Vam Sat River resulting in seven Viet Cong killed.

MARCH 10, 1966

- USN units began river minesweeping operations in the RVN.

MARCH 11, 1966

- Friendly forces evacuated the A Shau Special Forces Camp in Thua Thien Province. The three-day battle resulted in heavy friendly casualties and unknown enemy losses.
- A terrorist threw a grenade into a US Army truck in Saigon injuring four US and three VN.

MARCH 13, 1966

- The enemy mortared Vung Tau airfield.

MARCH 14, 1966

- The first USAF squadron arrived at the newly activated Phan Rang Air Base.
- A USAF F-4 aircraft was downed by ground fire over Hon Me Island 30 miles SSE Thanh Hoa North Vietnam. During a rescue effort, a HU-16 Albatross seaplane was hit by NVN shore

fire and sank. The USS BERKELEY and the USS ISBELL took shore positions under fire. USN helicopters rescued six of the total eight USAF personnel from the two aircraft.

MARCH 15, 1966

- Field Force Vietnam (FFV) was redesignated I Field Force Vietnam (IFFV) and remained at Nha Trang. II Field Force Vietnam (IIFFV) was activated at Bien Hoa.

MARCH 19, 1966

- *Operation Texas.* Initiated in Quang Ngai Province by 1st Marine Division units to assist the ARVN recapture of An Hoa outpost from Viet Cong main force units.

MARCH 21, 1966

- The first 11 USN PBRs arrived in the RVN.

MARCH 23, 1966

- *Operation Maeng Ho 5.* Initiated in Binh Dinh Province by Capitol ROK Infantry Division units.
- *Operation Silver City.* Terminated in Long Khanh and Binh Long Provinces. Final results were 336 enemy killed and one enemy captured.

MARCH 24, 1966

- The USCGC POINT CYPRESS sank a Viet Cong junk at the mouth of the Soi Rar River.

MARCH 25, 1966

- *Operation Lincoln.* Initiated in Pleiku, Darlac and Phu Bon Provinces by the 1st Cavalry Division (Airmobile) and 3rd Brigade, 25th Infantry Division.
- *Operation Fillmore.* Initiated.
- *Operation Jack Stay.* Initiated. The southernmost large-scale employment of US units to date.

MARCH 26, 1966

- *Operation Jack Stay.* US Marines of the Special Landing Force conducted an amphibious assault on Long Thanh Peninsula in Rung Sat Special Zone.

- *Operation Jack Stay.* Nine Usages and six Swift boats participated in *Operation Jack Stay.* The TF-115 "river flotilla" acted as a blocking force with the command center aboard the USS BELLE GROVE (LSD-2).
- *Operation Su Bok.* Initiated in Binh Dinh Province by the Capitol ROK Infantry Division.

MARCH 27, 1966

- *Operation Maeong Ho 5.* Terminated in Binh Dinh Province. Final results were 349 enemy killed and 281 enemy captured. Friendly casualties were light.

MARCH 29, 1966

- The Headquarters, 1st Marine Division was established at Chu Lai relieving the 3rd Marine Division of Chu Lai tactical area of operations responsibility (TAOR).

APRIL 1, 1966

- At 0510 hours, the Viet Cong detonated an estimated 450 pounds of explosives at the entrance of the Victoria Bachelor Officers Quarters (BOQ) in Saigon/Cholon. The first three floors were extensively damaged, upper floors and surrounding buildings were moderately damaged. Friendly casualties were six killed (three US, three VN) and 116 wounded (107 US, three AUS, six VN).

APRIL 2, 1966

- Some US vehicles were damaged in a wave of Saigon demonstrations.

APRIL 4,1966

- US dependents were evacuated from Dalat where demonstrators burned a radio station and clashed with police. A US jeep was burned in continued Saigon demonstrations. Martial law was declared in Nha Trang. Demonstrators threatened US installations.

- Converted seaplane tender, the USS CORPUS CHRISTI BAY, arrived at Cam Ranh Bay to provide a floating aviation maintenance facility for US Army helicopters.

APRIL 8, 1966

- *Operation Lincoln.* Terminated in Pleiku, Darlac and Phu Bon Provinces. Final results were 453 enemy killed and 12 enemy captured. Friendly casualties were light.

APRIL 10, 1966

- The USN introduced PBRs into service in the RVN.

APRIL12, 1966

- B-52s struck in North Vietnam for the first time, striking Yu Gia Pass.

MID-APRIL 1966

- US strength in RVN exceeded 240,000 making MACV the second largest command of the US armed forces outside CONUS. Of this number. 146,000 were US Army, 48,600 USMC, 32,000 USAF and 12,600 USN. Only the US European Command with strength in excess of 300,000 was larger.

APRIL 13, 1966

- The enemy shelled Tan Son Nhut Air Base with about 157 rounds of 82mm mortar/75mm recoilless rifle fire, inflicting light casualties and moderate materiel damage.

APRIL 16, 1966

- The first elements of the ROK 26th RCT arrived in RVN, landing at Qui Nhon, and assigned in II Corps area.

APRIL 17, 1966

- USAF aircraft hit surface-to-air missile sites 15 and 17 miles from Hanoi in the closest strikes to Hanoi to date. USAF pilots cut a Phu Ly railroad bridge 35 miles south of Hanoi and USN pilots cut Hai Duong bridge 21 miles NW of Haiphong.

APRIL 18, 1966

- USN pilots struck the Uong Bi thermal power plant 14 miles NNE of Haiphong. It was previously hit December 1965.

APRIL 20, 1966

- An estimated 15 Viet Cong penetrated An Khe airfield inflicting light aircraft damage with satchel charges.
- The first elements of the Royal Australian Army Task Force arrived in the RVN.

APRIL 22, 1966

- The Viet Cong mortared and infiltrated the New Pleiku Airfield causing light casualties and damage.

APRIL 23, 1966

- MIG-21s engaged US aircraft for first time in the conflict, unsuccessfully attacking a mission support aircraft during an F-105 strike against the Bac Giang railroad bridge 25 miles NE of Hanoi. F-4C escort aircraft countered the two MIG-21s and eight MIG-17s. USAF pilots downed two of the MIG-17s.

APRIL 26, 1966

- USAF F-4C pilots over North Vietnam shot down the first MIG-21 to be shot down in this conflict. The MIG was downed in a brief engagement involving two F-4C aircraft and two MIG-21s 65 miles NNW of Hanoi. A sidewinder missile downed the MIG with the pilot ejecting. The F-4Cs were undamaged.

APRIL 27, 1966

- B-52s struck for the second time in North Vietnam. The strike was on Mu Gia Pass.

APRIL 29, 1966

- USAF F-4 pilots shot down two MIG-17s.

- The 1st Brigade, 25th Infantry Division arrived in the RVN, completing the deployment of the 25th Infantry Division. The brigade landed at Vung Tau.

APRIL 30, 1966

- A USAF F-4 pilot shot down a MIG-17.

MAY 2, 1966

- The first three USN patrol air cushion vehicles (PACV) arrived in the RVN.

MAY 4, 1966

- *Operation Davy Crockett.* Initiated in Binh Dinh Province by the 3rd Brigade 1st Cavalry Division (Airmobile) and ARVN units.

MAY 5, 1966

- B-52s struck in support of *Operation Birmingham.*

MAY 10, 1966

- *Operation Paul Revere I.* Initiated in Pleiku Province by the 3rd Brigade, 25th Infantry Division.
- A 120-foot steel-hulled enemy trawler was detected, attacked and heavily damaged by the USCGC POINT GREY, US and VN Air Force planes along the east coast of Ca Mau Peninsula. Salvage operations yielded 15 tons of weapons and ammunition manufactured in Communist China in 1965, movie projectors, film, and other propaganda material.
- In confused firing after the Viet Cong detonated a mine near the Brink Bachelor Officers Quarters (BOQ) in Saigon, five VN civilians were killed, 21 VN wounded and eight US wounded.

MAY 11, 1966

- USN jets struck a surface-to-air missile site 10 miles from Haiphong, the closest strike to Haiphong to date.

MAY 12, 1966

- A USAF F-4 downed a MIG.

- The III MAF reported that major action resulted in 175 enemy killed.

MAY 16, 1966

- *Operation Davy Crockett.* Terminated in Binh Dinh Province. Final results were 374 enemy killed and 82 enemy captured. Friendly casualties were light.
- *Operation Crazy Horse/Bun Khe 66-7.* Initiated in Binh Dinh Province by the 1st Brigade, 1st Cavalry Division (Airmobile) and the Capitol ROK Infantry Division.

MAY 17, 1966

- Headquarters Support Activity, Saigon (HSAS) officially disestablished and the Naval Support Activity (NSA) Saigon simultaneously established to provide support to US Naval Forces in II, III and IV Corps Tactical Zones (CTZs) and coastal waters.

MAY 18, 1966

- The Viet Cong attacked Soc Trang Airfield in Ba Xuyen Province.

MAY 23, 1966

- A USN Swift boat was sunk by enemy recoilless rifle fire in the Rung Sat Special Zone.

MAY 30-31, 1966

- US pilots attacked Yen Bay facilities in North Vietnam. This was the largest strike against a single target in North Vietnam to date. Two US planes were downed by ground fire.

JUNE 1, 1966

- Struggle force mobs in Hue sacked and burned the US Consulate and several residences and seized a large number of weapons. US Army aircraft were evacuated to Phu Bai. US personnel were confined to the Hue MACV compound.

JUNE 2, 1966

- *Operation El Paso II.* Initiated in Binh Long Province by the 1st and 3rd Brigade, 1st Infantry Division.

JUNE 3, 1966

- *Operation Hawthorne.* Initiated in Kontum Province by the 1st Brigade, 101st Airborne Division.

JUNE 5, 1966

- The 1st Australian Task Force became operational under the II FFV.
- *Operation Crazy Horse/Bun Khe 66-7.* Terminated in Binh Dinh Province. Final results were 478 enemy killed, 27 enemy were captured and light friendly casualties.

JUNE 6, 1966

- The enemy attacked An Khe Airfield.

JUNE 9, 1966

- Buddhist altars halted US and ARVN troop movements through Hue.

JUNE 11, 1966

- *Operation Hawthorne.* USMC jets killed 79 of the enemy. B-52s struck in support of *Operation Hawthorne.*

JUNE 12, 1966

- *Operation El Paso.* The day's results were 93 enemy killed.
- A USN F-8 Crusader aircraft downed a MIG-17.

JUNE 13, 1966

- *Operation Hawthorne.* B-52 bombers struck in support of *Operation Hawthorne.*

JUNE 14, 1966

- A USN F-4B aircraft engaged an enemy aircraft NE of Thanh Hoa in a night encounter. One enemy aircraft was probably destroyed.

JUNE 16, 1966

- A USMC reconnaissance platoon held off an enemy battalion.

JUNE 18, 1966

- USCGCs engaged three enemy junks.

JUNE 19, 1966

- A USMC company thwarted an enemy attempt to blow up ESSO fuel tanks.
- *Operation Nathan Hale.* Initiated in Phu Yen Province by the 1st and 3rd Brigades, 1st Cavalry Division (Airmobile).

JUNE 20, 1966

- *Operation Hawthorne.* Terminated in Kontum Province. Final results were 531 enemy killed and 22 enemy captured.
- *Operation Market Time.* USCGC POINT LEAGUE shadowed and forced a 100-foot enemy trawler aground near the mouth of the Co Chien River and Vinh Binh Provinces. The trawler was captured intact with 100 tons of cargo including more than 2,300 weapons, many of Chinese Communist manufacture.

JUNE 21, 1966

- A USN F-8 aircraft was downed by a MIG-17. Also, a USN F-8 aircraft shot down a MIG-17.

JUNE 22, 1966

- The enemy attacked Soc Trang Airfield for the sixth time in a nine-month period with an estimated 20 rounds of 75mm recoilless rifle fire resulting in light friendly casualties.

JUNE 23, 1966

- A USMC company was heli-lifted into the former A Shau Special Forces camp and destroyed a large enemy ammunition cache there.

JUNE 29, 1966

- USAF and USN aircraft struck the POL facilities 3½ miles NE of Hanoi (USAF) and 2½ miles WNW of Haiphong (USN) for the first time inflicting heavy damage. Four MIG-17s were encountered and one probably destroyed by USAF F-105 aircraft. No surface-to-air missiles were sighted. USN pilots struck a Do Son POL facility 10 miles SSE of Haiphong.

JUNE 30, 1966

- USAF pilots hit Viet Tri and Nguyan Khe POL in North Vietnam. USN pilots hit Bac Giang POL and Kep radar in North Vietnam.

JULY 1, 1966

- A flight of F-100 aircraft attempted to jettison ordnance in the ordnance jettison area. The ordnance hung up and hit the village of Tan Nyen near Bien Hoa, killing five civilians and wounding 43 civilians.
- *Operation Nathan Hale.* Terminated in Phu Yen Province. Final results were 459 enemy killed, 36 enemy captured and light friendly casualties.
- A PBR captured an enemy sampan two miles E of My Tho. Five enemy were killed.
- A C-141 aircraft made the first USAF medical evacuation flight from the RVN direct to the US with 60 patients aboard from Tan Son Nhut to Travis Air Force Base, California.
- The USN sank three NVN PT boats in Tonkin Gulf and picked up 19 of the PT crewmen.
- Five US aircraft were downed over North Vietnam.

JULY 2, 1966

- *Operation El Paso II*: Heavy contact resulted in 78 enemy killed.
- An estimated two enemy companies attacked Plei Djereng Special Force Camp with light friendly casualties.
- US military personnel casualties in Vietnam cumulative from January 1, 1961: 4,129 dead, 22,791 wounded, 267 missing or captured.

JULY 3, 1966

- *Operation Paul Revere I.* Heavy contact occurred between a

25th Infantry Division company and an estimated two enemy companies.

- USAF F-4C and B-57 aircraft hit two 20-truck convoys near Dong Hoi destroying 29 trucks, causing 22 secondary explosions and leaving 31 fires burning.

JULY 4, 1966

- Marine units fought in a battle near Thu Bon River 17 miles SW of Da Nang in Quang Nam Province. Enemy losses were 60 killed.
- USMC jets attacked a battalion-size force near Tra Bong River SW of Chu Lai resulting in 45 enemy killed.
- *Operation Macon.* Initiated in Tua Thien and Quang Nam Provinces by the 3rd Marine Division.

JULY 5, 1966

- US pilots over North Vietnam report 29 surface-to-air missiles fired at them during the day, the highest number reported for any previous day.

JULY 7, 1966

- USN jets attacked four NVN PT boats near Hon Gay Island 30 miles ESE of Haiphong. The strike sank two boats, heavily damaged the third boat, and left the fourth boat beached and burning. USN A-4 and F-8 aircraft struck the Haiphong POL storage area two miles NW of Haiphong. Pilots reported four POL tanks destroyed, four probably destroyed, two pump houses destroyed, and a secondary explosion with a 1,000-foot fireball and heavy black smoke visible from 80 miles.
- Two MIG-21s using missiles attacked a flight of F-105 aircraft near Hanoi with no damage. USMC A-4 aircraft hit an enemy company position destroying three .50-caliber machine guns and 10 anti-aircraft positions.
- *Operation Hastings.* Initiated in Quang Tri Province. Conducted by Task Force D (USMC).

JULY 8, 1966

- The enemy attacked Binh Tuy Airfield in Phuong Binh Province with 40 rounds 75mm recoilless rifle fire shortly after midnight, which resulted in light casualties and light equipment and structure damage.

JULY 9, 1966

- *Operation El Paso II.* Heavy contact occurred between 1st Infantry Division units and an estimated reinforced Viet Cong regiment. Enemy losses were 238 enemy killed.
- Two USN Swift boats approached a junk 40 miles N of Qui Nhon and received fire. They returned fire capsizing the junk and capturing eight Viet Cong, one rifle and four bayonets.

JULY 10, 1966

- Two USMC A-4 aircraft from Chu Lai sank an armed motorized enemy sampan that was heading toward two downed USAF crewmen awaiting rescue in the water eight miles N of the DMZ.

JULY 11, 1966

- USN pilots attacked about 200 barges and junks in North Vietnam, destroying or damaging at least 55.

JULY 12, 1966

- USAF aircraft dropped more than three million leaflets over Thanh Hoa and Vinh. USN A-4 aircraft struck Dong Nahm POL storage area 16 miles NW of Haiphong. Three flights of USMC F-4Bs and USAF A-1Es struck an enemy troop concentration 38 miles N of Qui Nhon. Enemy losses were 71 killed.

JULY 13, 1966

- *Operation El Paso II.* Terminated in Binh Long Province. Final results were 855 enemy killed, 37 enemy captured and over 1,500 tons rice. Friendly casualties were light.
- Four USN F-4Bs engaged six MIG-17s 38 miles SE of Hanoi destroying one.

JULY 14, 1966

- USAF F-4C aircraft scoring with sidewinder missiles downed two MIG-21s 30 miles NW of Hanoi. Three USN F-8s engaged two MIG-17s 28 miles SSE of Hanoi. One MIG and one F-8 were damaged.

JULY 15, 1966

- USAF pilots struck 31 storage and staging areas in the southern panhandle of North Vietnam, setting off 22 secondary explosions and more than 50 fires.
- An estimated 75 enemy using recoilless rifles, 60mm mortars and small arms attacked a USMC company outpost 10 miles S of Chu Lai in a two-hour pre-dawn attack. Enemy losses were 27 killed and Marine casualties were moderate. A USMC reconnaissance team 20 miles S of Da Nang directed artillery and air strikes on an enemy force estimated at 300 men. Enemy losses were 30 enemy killed. An estimated enemy company attacked a USMC company position at 2000 hours. The attack was repulsed at 0045 hours. Enemy losses were 35 killed and friendly casualties were light.
- *Operation Deckhouse II.* A Special Landing Force Battalion landing team landed in an amphibious assault in Quang Tri Province 40 miles N of Hue.

JULY 18, 1966

- The enemy attacked a 4th Marine company in Quang Tri Province. The attack lasted over five hours. Enemy losses were 138 enemy killed and friendly casualties were light.
- *Operation Deckhouse II.* Terminated. The BLT commenced role in *Operation Hastings.*
- *Operation Hastings.* Near Cam Lo, a large NVA force, from 1500 to 1900 hours, attacked two Marine rear-guard platoons. The two platoons had heavy casualties.

JULY 19, 1966

- USAF and USN pilots sighted 29 surface-to-air missiles over North Vietnam.
- USAF F-104 aircraft arrived in Southeast Asia.
- An estimated multi-company Viet Cong main force unit in Hau Nghia Province heavily engaged a 2nd Brigade, 25th Infantry Division company. Enemy losses were 55 killed and friendly casualties were heavy.
- An encounter between USAF F-105 and MIG-17 aircraft occurred 20 miles NW of Hanoi. One F-105 was downed and three MIG-17s damaged.

- Two USN River PBRs sank a 30-foot junk on the Co Chien River. When challenged, the junk fired on the PBRs. A USN Swift boat and ocean minesweeper engaged the evading junk/sampan force near Chu Lai. They destroyed a 30-foot junk, damaged another, and damaged three sampans. There were no friendly casualties.

JULY 20, 1966

- USN jets in North Vietnam attacked more than 240 cargo barges, 100 trucks, and 65 railroad cars, destroying or damaging 135 barges, 24 railroad cars, 21 trucks and two railroad engines.

JULY 21, 1966

- *Operation Hasting.* The enemy attacked a 1st Marine command post shortly after midnight with 50 rounds of 81mm mortar fire resulting in light friendly casualties. The 1st Marine battalion blocked a large enemy unit moving W out of the *Operation Hastings* area. The contact was heavy and lasted over four hours. Marine casualties were light. A 19-man Marine reconnaissance patrol N of Chu Lai engaged an enemy force and killed 24. Marine casualties were light. An enemy squad using grenades and satchel charges attacked Marine artillery positions near Quang Ngai airfield. Friendly casualties were moderate and light equipment damage. A surface-to-air missile impacted in the village of Ha Gia, 19 miles N of Hanoi.
- *Operation Fillmore.* Terminated in Phu Yet Province. Final results were 373 enemy killed and 73 enemy captured. The operation protected the Tuy Hoa rice harvest and was extremely successful.
- *Operation Game Warden.* US Army armed helicopters from the USS TORTUGA received fire from, and struck, several junks and sampans.
- Three MIG-17 aircraft attacked a flight of F-105s, 65 miles WSW of Hanoi. The MIGs fired four rockets but missed.

JULY 22, 1966

- A USN pilot escaped communist captors and returned to US control in the RVN.
- *Operation Hastings.* A 5th Marine unit was involved in a five-

hour battle resulting in 25 enemy killed and moderate friendly casualties.

JULY 23, 1966

- *Operation Hastings.* An opposing enemy force identified as the 324B NVA Division was involved in a one-hour battle with a 1st Infantry Division multi-battalion force 25 miles N of Saigon.
- A USN PBR engaged a 30-foot enemy sampan 40 miles SSW of Saigon resulting in eight Viet Cong killed. The sampan was captured and contained one weapon, numerous documents, mines and ammunition. There were no friendly casualties.
- The enemy attacked the Marble Mountain Air Facility outside Da Nang with an estimated 75 rounds of 81/82mm mortar fire resulting in light friendly casualties and light equipment damage.
- The enemy attacked Trai Ri Special Forces Camp 15 miles NW of Tay Ninh City with 100 to 200 rounds of 81mm/82mm mortar fire resulting in light friendly casualties and light equipment and structure damage.

JULY 24, 1966

- *Operation Hastings.* Enemy losses reached 618 enemy killed, 10 enemy captured and 157 weapons captured. Friendly casualties remained light.
- USAF F-4C aircraft struck a fortified position 20 miles SE of Hue resulting in 59 enemy killed.
- Units of the 5th Marine engaged an estimated 100 NVA attempting to move NE in an operation area resulting in 17 enemy killed and light friendly casualties.
- The enemy mortared a 4th Marine battalion with light friendly casualties.
- The first tactical air strike occurred in the DMZ.

JULY 25, 1966

- USAF F-4C Phantom aircraft crews set off more than 20 secondary explosions and started a large fire in an enemy staging area 15 miles S Vinh.

JULY 26, 1966

- The enemy attacked the 25th Infantry Division base camp at Cu Chi, 18 miles NW of Saigon twice during the night with mortar and recoilless rifle fire. The attacks resulted in light friendly casualties and light equipment and structure damage.
- The enemy attacked Soc Trang airfield 35 miles SW of Can Tho in Ba Xuyen Province with 20 rounds of mortar fire. There were no friendly casualties or damage.

JULY 27, 1966

- A record 542 strikes were flown in the RVN by US aircraft.

JULY 28, 1966

- Lieutenant Junior Grade (LTJG) Dieter Dengler, a USN pilot, escaped communist captors and returned to US control.
- In Binh Dinh Province on Highway 1, ARVN troops found 90 enemy killed as a result of a USAF F-100 aircraft strike 39 miles NNW of Qui Nhon. Ground follow-up of a B-52 strike in Binh Duong Province found heavy damage to tunnels, bunkers, and supply structures, a Viet Cong truck destroyed, six tons rice, 150 documents, individual weapons and ammunition.
- *Operation Hastings.* A USMC reconnaissance team directed artillery and air strikes on an estimated 200 enemy spotted 20 miles W of Dong Ha, resulting in 65 NVA killed.

JULY 30, 1966

- The first B-52 aircraft struck the DMZ. The target was in the S half of DMZ.

JULY 31, 1966

- A USAF C-47 aircraft on a classified mission is missing over North Vietnam since July 29, 1966, with a crew of eight.
- *Operation Paul Revere I.* Terminated in Pleiku Province. Final results were 546 enemy killed and 68 enemy captured. Friendly casualties were moderate.

AUGUST 1, 1966

- *Operation Paul Revere II.* Initiated in Pleiku Province by the 3rd

Brigade, 25th Infantry Division and a Capitol ROK Infantry Division battalion.

- *Operation Paul Revere II.* 3rd Brigade, 25th Infantry Division units took heavy enemy fire in Pleiku Province. Friendly casualties were light. The 2nd Brigade, 25th Infantry Division units discovered an arms cache containing 90,000 rounds small arms and other munitions in Binh Duong Province.
- Seven US aircraft were down over North Vietnam.

AUGUST 2, 1966

- *Operation Paul Revere II.* 25th Infantry Division, 3rd Brigade Task Force units engaged an estimated enemy battalion shortly after noon in Pleiku Province. The engagement resulted in 100 enemy killed and moderate friendly casualties.

AUGUST 3, 1966

- *Operation Paul Revere II.* 1st Cavalry Division (Airmobile) units joined the operation, which increased the operation to multi-brigade size. The operation continued under the 1st Cavalry Division (Airmobile) control with the 3rd Brigade, 25th Infantry Division role continuing.
- *Operation Hastings.* Terminated in Quang Tri Province. Final results were 882 enemy killed and 15 enemy captured. Tactical air sorties were 1,209. Friendly casualties were moderate.
- *Operation Prairie.* Initiated in Quang Tri Province by Task Force Delta (USMC)

AUGUST 5, 1966

- *Operation John Paul Jones.* ROK Marines engaged a fleet of enemy sampans at 2210 hours, 18 miles SE of Tuy Hoa. The engagement resulted in 17 enemy killed, seven sampans destroyed and no friendly casualties.
- A 9th Marine company found 12 VN bodies (four men, four women and four children) that had been murdered in a village by the Viet Cong.
- USAF F-4C aircraft hit a 40-truck convoy on Route 1A just N of the DMZ. The attacks resulted in 26 secondary explosions and 25 secondary fires.
- USN jets from the carrier USS CONSTELLATION attacked

a POL storage area at Do Son, 13 miles SSE of Haiphong, destroying three large oil tanks and damaging another. There were three USN carriers on Yankee station.

AUGUST 6, 1966

- USN A-4 and A-6 aircraft destroyed four NVN PT boats and damaged one at two locations 40 and 50 miles ENE of Haiphong.
- Elements of the 4th Infantry Division arrived at Qui Nhon, RVN from Fort Lewis, Washington.

AUGUST 7, 1966

- Seven US strike aircraft were downed by enemy action over North Vietnam: Five USAF F-105s, one USAF F-101 and one USN A-1H. A USAF F-105 hit a 20-car train 67 miles NW of Hanoi and another 50 miles NE of Hanoi. The engine and all 20 boxcars were damaged at the NW location. The engine and all 20 boxcars were destroyed at the NE location.

AUGUST 8, 1966

- The pilot of an F-101 aircraft was downed over North Vietnam August 7, 1966, was picked-up by a USAF HH-43 rescue helicopter, 100 miles NW of Hanoi. The pilot evaded capture for 26 hours.
- *Operation Paul Revere II.* A 1st Cavalry Division (Airmobile) company engaged an estimated three enemy companies in a two-hour battle 10 miles W of Plei Me. The Cavalry unit was reinforced. The engagement resulted in 90 enemy killed. There were heavy casualties in the first friendly company engaged and overall moderate friendly casualties.

AUGUST 9, 1966

- Two USAF F-100 aircraft under forward air controller control expended bombs and 20mm rounds on targets along a canal bank near Truong Thanh eight miles W of Can Tho in Phong Dinh Province. The pilots hit the target as directed; however, 24 civilians were killed and 82 civilians wounded.
- *Operation Paul Revere II.* An estimated reinforced enemy battalion attacked a Capitol ROK Infantry Division company just before midnight. Three hours later the ROK company,

reinforced by other ROK units and US armor elements, launched a counterattack. The enemy broke contact at 0540 hours. The attack resulted in 170 enemy killed and light friendly casualties.

AUGUST 10, 1966

- USAF F-100 aircraft struck a staging area near the coast 47 miles S of Saigon, resulting in 71 sampans destroyed or damaged.
- *Operation Colorado.* 5th Marine units engaged a multi-battalion enemy force five miles W of Tam Khe resulting in 121 enemy killed and moderate friendly casualties.
- A Military Police detail suffered two killed and 17 wounded from an enemy mine explosion at Binh Tri Dong pistol range SW of Saigon.
- The USCGC POINT WELCOME was struck by US aircraft off mouth of Cua Viet River, 35 miles up coast from Hue. Strike casualties were two US Coast Guard killed, three US Coast Guard wounded, one VN translator wounded, and one newsman (UK subject) wounded. The cutter proceeded to Da Nang under own power.

AUGUST 12, 1966

- *Operation Colorado.* Two Marine command posts were hit by enemy mortar, recoilless rifle and small arms fire 18 miles NW of Chu Lai in Quang Tin Province. The attacks resulted in light friendly casualties and light equipment damage.
- A flight of F-105 aircraft engaged two MIG-17s, 60 miles NW of Hanoi, which resulted in two MIGs damaged, and one F-105 slightly damaged. The MIGs disengaged. A ground follow-up of area struck by US aircraft 22 miles WSW of Hue found 34 enemy killed.

AUGUST 13, 1966

- USAF jets destroyed or damaged 33 POL storage areas in North Vietnam along with 32 other enemy storage facilities, which resulted in 130 secondary explosions and 133 secondary fires.
- USN A-4 pilots from the USS ORISKANY destroyed two PT boats 25 miles ENE of Haiphong.

AUGUST 15, 1966

- USN A-4 aircraft hit Tuc Tranh POL area three miles S of Thanh Hoa causing smoke to 6,000 feet, visible 30 miles away.
- *Operation Paul Revere II.* A 1st Cavalry Division (Airmobile) battalion heavily engaged an estimated enemy battalion in S portion Chu Phong Mountains, 18 miles SW of Plei Me resulting in 175 NVA killed and light friendly casualties.
- A 1st Infantry Division command post near Lai Khe, 27 miles NNW of Saigon, received 82 rounds of 82mm mortar and small arms fire from 2315 to 0050 hours resulting in light friendly casualties.
- Two MIG-17 aircraft attacked a flight of USN A-4s over North Vietnam. The MIGs broke-off. There was no aircraft damage.

AUGUST 16, 1966

- A surface-to-air missile fired at a USN jet in Haiphong area missed and detonated in a populated area one to two kilometers E of Haiphong. A fire was observed in the area after impact.
- *Operation Deckhouse III Phase I.* Initiated when a USMC BLT landed in Binh Tuy Province 35 miles NW of Vung Tao.

AUGUST 17, 1966

- An enemy unit mortared a USMC tank and amphibian tractor command post area five miles SSW of Da Nang resulting in light damage. A reaction force killed 10 Viet Cong. Friendly casualties were light.
- A USMC F-8E aircraft crashed on take-off from Da Nang into a village ¾ mile S of the end of runway. The pilot ejected uninjured. The ordnance on the plane detonated on impact. Casualties in the village were 30 killed and 15 injured.
- At 0242 hours, an enemy force mortared a 1st Australian Task Force command post in Phuoc Tuy Province.
- An enemy force using anti-tank rockets and grenades attacked the 1st Logistical Command Motor Pool at 2115 hours. Friendly losses were light casualties and light damage.
- VN Air Force A-1 and USAF F-100 aircraft struck the enemy 90 miles NNE of Saigon in Phuoc Long Province resulting in 103 enemy killed.
- At 1710 hours, Marines observed a group of an estimated

60 enemy 15 miles S of Da Nang. Air strikes were called in and swept area resulting in 37 enemy killed and no friendly casualties. A USMC reconnaissance patrol engaged an estimated enemy platoon 22 miles SW of Da Nang. Directed supporting tank fire and air strikes resulted in 21 enemy killed and friendly light casualties.

- An enemy force hit a CIDG unit at 1400 hours 35 miles SW of Pleiku. The CIDG unit was reinforced. Contact later established with an estimated reinforced enemy battalion. Enemy losses were six killed. Friendly losses were heavy in a CIDG unit.

AUGUST 18, 1966

- Two MIG-17 aircraft attacked four USAF F-105s 25 miles N of Hanoi. One MIG-17 was downed by 20mm cannon fire and the other MIG disengaged.
- *Operation Smithfield.* Initiated in Phuoc Tuy Province by the 1st Australian Task Force.

AUGUST 19, 1966

- B-52s struck in N half in the DMZ.

AUGUST 20, 1966

- A large enemy force assaulted a USMC reconnaissance platoon a few miles NW of Chu Lai. Mortars supported the enemy. The Marines repulsed the assault resulting in 11 enemy killed.
- Two terrorists threw three grenades in Da Nang in a Non-Commissioned Officer (NCO) Club, wounding eight US servicemen and four others. One terrorist was shot and killed and another terrorist captured. Three suspects were arrested.
- The 5th Battalion, 7th Cavalry arrived RVN to join the 1st Cavalry Division (Airmobile). The unit arrived at Qui Nhon from Fort Carson, Colorado.

AUGUST 21, 1966

- *Operation Market Time.* A USN Swift boat was fired on from the shore at 0900 hours 165 miles SW of Saigon. The Swift returned fire with .50-caliber machine guns and 81mm mortar, obtaining two secondary explosions and silencing the enemy fire. There were no friendly casualties.
- *Operation Smithfield.* Terminated in Phuoc Tuy Province. Final

results were 245 enemy killed and three enemy captured. Australian casualties were 17 killed and 22 wounded.

- B-52s bombed a supply and storage area just N of the DMZ.

AUGUST 22, 1966

- *Operation Deckhouse III Phase II.* Initiated 0800 hours with USMC air and sea assault 50 miles SE of Saigon in Phuoc Tuy Province.

AUGUST 23, 1966

- USN A-4 aircraft destroyed a NVN PT boat and damaged two others 25 miles ENE of Haiphong.
- The MSTS BATON ROUGE VICTORY was mined at 0910 hours in Long Tau River 22 miles SE of Saigon. The ship was badly damaged and grounded near the bank. One person was wounded and seven missing and presumed dead. The channel, which is the main channel to Saigon, was restricted by the mined ship but not blocked.
- A USMC company engaged an estimated enemy platoon 16 miles SW of Da Nang. Enemy losses were 23 enemy killed.
- *Operation John Paul Jones.* The 2nd ROK Marine Brigade terminated participation.

AUGUST 24, 1966

- *Operation Game Warden.* USN PBRs killed two Viet Cong and captured 91 classified documents in an enemy sampan in a firefight with an enemy force attempting to cross the My Tho River at night, seven miles W of My Tho. The PBRs received fire from the banks but suffered only light boat damage. There were no friendly casualties.

AUGUST 25, 1966

- *Operation Paul Revere II.* Terminated in Pleiku Province. Final results were 809 enemy killed. Friendly casualties were light.

AUGUST 26, 1966

- US pilots flew 156 missions in North Vietnam.
- *Operation Allegheny.* The number of the enemy killed rose to 98 as a result of enemy bodies found in an area of previous fighting 15 miles SW of Da Nang.

- *Operation Prairie.* 4th and 12th Marine units repulsed an early morning attack on their perimeter. Enemy losses were 73 killed and 40 individual weapons.
- *Operation Amarillo.* A 1st Infantry Division battle occurred on August 25-26, 1966 with an estimated reinforced Viet Cong battalion 28 miles N of Saigon in Phu Loi area. Enemy losses were 93 killed.
- *Operation Toledo.* 173rd Airborne Brigade units uncovered a major enemy resupply area and base camp area in N Phuoc Tuy Province.

AUGUST 28, 1966

- The enemy attacked Vinh Long Airfield 62 miles SW of Saigon with 10 to 12 rounds of recoilless rifle fire. Friendly losses were light equipment damage and no friendly casualties.
- *Operation Game Warden.* The Viet Cong attacked a USN PBR with a mine attempt and automatic weapons fire on the Co Chien River 55 miles SSW of Saigon. There were no friendly casualties or PBR damage.

AUGUST 29, 1966

- US jets destroyed two RVN PT boats and damaged two others about 55 miles ENE of Haiphong. A USN MSB was jarred by an explosion and companion MSB taken under enemy fire on Long Tau River. There were no MSB casualties.

AUGUST 30, 1966

- USN jets destroyed a NVN PT boat and damaged another 55 miles ENE of Haiphong.
- The mined merchant vessel BATON ROUGE VICTORY broke loose from salvage moorings shortly after midnight in a flood tide, causing Long Tau River to be closed temporarily. The ship was towed to Vung Tau, clearing the mouth of the river at 1318 hours.

SEPTEMBER 1, 1966

- *Operation Amarillo.* Terminated in Binh Duong Province with 102 enemy killed and six enemy captured. Overall friendly casualties were light; however, casualties in battalion-size force most heavily engaged were moderate.

SEPTEMBER 3, 1966

- *Operation Macon.* A 9th Marine unit directed air strikes and artillery on group of 50 enemy 16 miles S of Da Nang resulting in 32 enemy killed.
- A 1st Cavalry Division (Airmobile) support area at An Khe was hit by about 40 rounds in a 10-minute 82mm mortar attack. The attack resulted in moderate damage to aircraft, light damage to airfield and light friendly casualties.

SEPTEMBER 5, 1966

- *Operation John Paul Jones.* Terminated in Phu Yen Province. Final results were 262 enemy killed and 39 enemy captured.
- USN A-4 and F-8 aircraft attacked 34 boxcars and 18 tank cars 47 miles NNE of Thanh Hoa. Enemy losses were 25 boxcars destroyed, 10 heavily damaged and 15 slightly damaged.
- The first major elements of the 9th ROK Infantry Division (White Horse Division) arrived in the RVN at 0900 hours at Nha Trang.
- A US Army CV-2 aircraft crashed in a village 21 miles NW of Tuy Hoa resulting in three US injured, four VN civilians killed and 20 to 25 VN civilians injured.
- *Operation Macon.* 9th Marine units attacked a battalion-size enemy force 15 miles SSW of Da Nang resulting in 73 enemy killed.

SEPTEMBER 7, 1966

- The Vanguard 11th Armor Cavalry Regiment arrived in the RVN in Vung Tau from Fort George G. Meade, Maryland.

SEPTEMBER 8, 1966

- The Viet Cong unsuccessfully attempted to mine a USN MSB on Long Tau River 17 miles SE of Saigon.

SEPTEMBER 9, 1966

- *Operation Amarillo.* A MACV spokesman announced on record that US casualties from the napalm strike on August 25-26, 1966 battle were three killed and 19 wounded.
- USN A-4 and A-6 aircraft sank a NVN PT boat and damaged two others.

SEPTEMBER 11, 1966

- US pilots flying 171 missions over North Vietnam, destroyed 25 barges and damaged 82 others, obtained over 70 secondary explosions and 60 secondary fires. USAF pilots hitting in the DMZ reported fifty-five of the secondary explosions.
- The enemy attacked Phan Thiet Airfield 93 miles E of Saigon with mortar and small arms fire. The attack resulted in light aircraft damage, no friendly casualties and no airfield damage.
- Shortly after midnight, the enemy launched attacks by fire on four 5th Marine positions about five miles W of Chu Lai. Friendly casualties were light.

SEPTEMBER 12, 1966

- The 2nd Battalion, 34th Armor Cavalry Regiment arrived in the RVN. The regiment landed at Vung Tau.

SEPTEMBER 14, 1996

- USN A-4, A-6 and F-4C aircraft destroyed or damaged 35 to 40 boxcars, 31 miles NNE of Thanh Hoa. The targets were two trains of 30 and 50 boxcars respectively.
- An enemy platoon attacked a combined USMC and Popular Forces patrol 13 miles SE of Da Nang resulting in five enemy killed and heavy friendly casualties.
- The enemy attacked a 1st Marine command post with 100 rounds of 81mm mortar fire three miles WNW of Hoi An in Quang Nam Province. Friendly casualties were light.

SEPTEMBER 15, 1966

- *Operation Deckhouse IV.* Initiated when BLT 1/26 landed in an amphibious operation in Quang Tri Province. The BLT reconnaissance team met an estimated enemy company, was heavily engaged at close range, and was extracted with moderate casualties. Enemy losses were nine killed.

SEPTEMBER 16, 1966

- A USAF F-4C aircraft firing a sidewinder missile, downed a MIG-17, 45 miles NE of Hanoi during a clash between three F-4Cs and four MIGs. Two MIGs fled following a brief encounter with four USAF F-105s.

- *Operation Baton Rouge.* In a 30-minute action, two enemy sampans were sunk and 11 enemy killed.
- *Operation Prairie.* Three 4th Marine companies heavily engaged in a battle 2½ miles N of "Rockpile" resulting in 171 enemy killed.
- USN jets destroyed or damaged 50 trucks and 35 railroad cars in attacks on Ninh Binh and Thanh Hoa railroad yards and adjacent areas.

SEPTEMBER 17, 1966

- *Operation Golden Fleece 7-1.* The battalion-size rice harvest protection operation initiated in Quang Ngai Province by the 7th Marines.
- *Operation Seward.* A US paratrooper company and an estimated enemy battalion fought a one-hour battle 15 miles N of Tuy Hoa. Friendly casualties were light.
- *Operation Thayer I.* US air cavalry troops uncovered two enemy munitions factories and an arms cache.
- *Operation Prairie.* A 4th Marine company outflanked and assaulted an enemy ambush force 10 miles W of Cam Lo.

SEPTEMBER 18, 1966

- USN pilots hit Ninh Binh railroad yards for the third straight day. Of 80 boxcars in the yard, 70 were hit hard. Sixty trucks attempting to unload the railroad cars also were hit with over half destroyed or damaged.
- *Operation Deckhouse IV.* An estimated enemy company attacked BLT 1/26 unit. Marines called in Naval gunfire support resulting in 52 enemy killed.
- *Operation Prairie.* BLT 1/26 was added to Prairie Task Force upon termination of *Operation Deckhouse IV.*
- *Operation Prairie.* A 4th Marine unit in close contact with an enemy force requested and received extremely close supporting air strike resulting in three friendly killed and four friendly wounded from the strike. Enemy casualties are unknown.
- USAF F-105 aircraft had two separate MIG-17 encounters

with MIGs making single firing passes. There was no aircraft damage.

SEPTEMBER 19, 1966

- *Operation Prairie.* In three significant contacts, enemy losses were 63 killed.

SEPTEMBER 20, 1966

- A USN A-6 aircraft sank a NVN PT boat 52 miles ENE of Haiphong.
- B-57s hit two ammunition dumps and triggered nine secondary explosions 17 miles S of Dong Ha.

SEPTEMBER 21, 1966

- The enemy mortared Chu Lai airstrip with 10 to 12 rounds, which resulted in light damage to aircraft and light friendly casualties.
- USN jets pounded Thanh Hoa railroad yards, ferry junction and flak sites, which resulted in 16 buildings destroyed, four secondary explosions, numerous fires, heavy smoke, and seven anti-aircraft sites silenced. Of 89 railroad cars in the area, 66 received total or heavy damage and 10 others suffered moderate damage.
- USAF pilots reported nine MIG sightings or encounters NE of Hanoi. USAF F-15s 35 miles NE of Hanoi downed two MIG-17s and probably destroyed another. Another MIG-17 and MIG-21 were damaged.
- *Operation Prairie.* Heavy fighting 10 miles NW of Dong Ha resulted in 51 NVA killed.
- *Operation Thayer I.* A 1st Cavalry Division (Airmobile) company engaged an enemy company nine miles S of Bong Son in a prolonged fight.
- *Operation Prairie.* The enemy mortared a 4th Marine Battalion command post 25 miles WNW of Quang Tri. A Marine reaction force killed 14 enemy. Friendly casualties were light.

SEPTEMBER 22, 1966

- A 1st Infantry Division unit working in a minefield 38 miles N of Saigon had seven killed and 14 wounded from accidental mine detonations.

- *Operation Su Bok.* Terminated in Binh Dinh Province. Final results were 299 enemy killed and 33 enemy captured. Friendly casualties were light.
- The enemy attacked two USN MSBs on Long Tau River with fire from both banks and recoilless rifle or rocket fire from W bank. One MSB took a hit in the pilothouse resulting in heavy casualties. The other MSB was not hit.

SEPTEMBER 23, 1966

- The enemy attacked Hammond airstrip with mortar, automatic weapon and small-arms fire. The attack resulted in light friendly casualties and light damage to the airstrip and aircraft.
- Enemy losses were 151 as a result of Naval gunfire, artillery and Marine patrol action since September 17, 1966 in the coastal plain area S of Quang Ngai City.
- *Operation Maeng Ho 6.* Initiated in Binh Dinh Province by the Capitol ROK Infantry Division.

SEPTEMBER 24, 1966

- Two flights of USAF B-57 aircraft struck a fortified enemy camp destroying or damaging 54 military structures and setting the area on fire.
- *Operation Seward.* A 1st Brigade, 101st Airborne Division unit located 12 VN who have been abandoned 40 minutes before by Viet Cong captors. The Viet Cong had withdrawn with 46 VN prisoners. Of the 12 left behind, one was dead and 11 in poor condition. A 7th Marine outpost called naval gunfire and artillery on an estimated enemy company 11 miles from Quang Ngai resulting in 25 enemy killed.
- *Operation Prairie.* Two 7th Marine companies heavily engaged an estimated enemy battalion for several hours resulting in 58 enemy killed and moderate friendly casualties. A Marine reconnaissance team 17 miles S of Dong Ha engaged a 30-man enemy force resulting in 18 enemy killed. The team was extracted with light casualties.

SEPTEMBER 25, 1966

- *Operation Prairie.* The BLT1/26 returned to the operational control of the Naval Task Force Afloat. The 4th Marine company engaged an entrenched reinforced enemy platoon 15 miles WNW of Dong Ha. Enemy losses were 12 killed.
- USN A-4 aircraft destroyed a PT boat 50 miles ENE of Haiphong.

SEPEMBER 26, 1966

- Nine USAF F-100 aircraft hit a large enemy camp 30 miles WSW of Dalat, destroying or damaging 82 military structures.
- Three separate naval gunfire and artillery firing missions during past two days in Quang Ngai Province resulted in 33 enemy killed.
- *Operation Maeng Ho 6.* Moderate contact. The 1st Brigade, 25th Infantry Division unit captured an enemy rice cache 65 miles NW of Saigon.
- A 2nd ROK Marine Brigade company 12 miles N of Quang Ngai engaged an enemy force resulting in 22 enemy killed.

SEPTEMBER 27, 1966

- A 7th Marine outpost 11 miles S of Quang Ngai directed artillery fire on an estimated 300 enemy in an open area resulting in 27 enemy killed.
- USN A-6 aircraft hit a NVN PT boat 25 miles ESE of Haiphong.
- Sixty officers and men of the PHILCAGV arrived in the RVN at Tan Son Nhut from Philippines.
- The 29th Regiment, 9th ROK (White Horses) Division arrived in RVN at Nha Trang.
- While conducting an air strike, two USMC A-4 aircraft from the 1st Marine Air Wing dropped ordnance on a village killing 28 civilians and wounding 17 civilians.
- *Operation Golden Fleece 701.* Terminated in Quang Ngai Province. Final results were 244 enemy killed and one enemy captured. A VN work force harvested 7,620 tons rice under the

protection of this 7th Marine battalion operation and ARVN forces. Marine casualties were light.

SEPTEMBER 28, 1966

- *Operation Prairie.* Heavy fighting 2½ miles N of "Rock Pile" resulted in 50 NVA killed.
- USN A-4 aircraft hit a NVN PT boat 25 miles ESE of Haiphong.

SEPTEMBER 29, 1966

- *Operation Prairie.* Marines found 51 enemy killed in an enemy regimental command post area containing bunkers, tunnels, spider holes, and graves.

SEPTEMBER 30, 1966

- About 2,500 troops of the 4th Infantry Division arrived in the RVN. The division landed at Qui Nhon after a 23-day trip from Tacoma, Washington.
- USAF B-57 aircraft surprised 200-300 enemy in a camp 13 miles WNW of Quang Ngai resulting in 53 enemy killed.

OCTOBER 2, 1966

- *Operation Irving.* Initiated in Binh Dinh Province by the 1st Cavalry Division (Airmobile).
- A 1st Brigade, 101st Airborne Division unit liberated 23 prisoners from a Viet Cong camp in the jungle 17 miles SW of Tuy Hoa in Phu Yen Province. The airborne unit was led to the camp by VN liberated a week ago from another camp in the same area.

OCTOBER 3, 1966

- A USAF F-100 aircraft was downed by enemy ground fire 35 miles W of Can Tho in RVN. The pilots were rescued.

OCTOBER 4, 1966

- *Operation Irving.* At 1530 hours, a 1st Cavalry Division (Airmobile) multi-company force engaged an enemy force near a downed helicopter in a mangrove swamp just E of Nuoc Ngot Bay 25 miles NW of Qui Nhon. The contact terminated at

1845 hours. Enemy losses were 43 killed, 60 captured and 208 surrendered. Friendly casualties were light.

- *Operation Game Warden.* Two USN PBRs intercepted and captured a Viet Cong sampan at 2029 hours on the Co Chien River 50 miles SW of Saigon. Enemy losses were three Viet Cong killed and three individual weapons. There were no friendly casualties.
- A CV-2 aircraft crashed on Hong Kong Mountain 3½ miles NW of An Khe at 1545 hours. The two-engine aircraft had a four-man crew and was on an administrative flight with 27 passengers. Causalities were 12 killed and 19 injured.
- B-52s struck in Quang Tri Province.

OCTOBER 5, 1966

- *Operation Maeng Ho 6.* ROK infantry troops inflicted 77 enemy killed, three enemy captured and 35 enemy surrendered in heavy contact.
- The first troops of the 1st Brigade, 4th Infantry Division arrived in the RVN. The brigade landed at Nha Trang at 1020 hours.
- *Operation Irving.* Enemy losses were 45 killed and 31 captured.

OCTOBER 6, 1966

- *Operations Irving and Maeing Ho 6.* Both operations continued with moderate contact in Binh Dinh Province. A MACV spokesman announced that major elements of the 12th Regiment, 610th NVA Division were identified in the operations. A 3rd Marine Division unit observed 11 of the enemy, 21 miles SW of Da Nang, and directed artillery on them resulting in 11 enemy killed.
- A Marine unit destroyed an enemy battalion headquarters area in *Operation Prairie.*
- *Operation Irving.* A 7th Cavalry company burned a small Viet Cong hamlet 22 miles NNW of Qui Nhon and obtained a secondary explosion.
- *Operation Maeng Ho 6.* At 1715 hours, a 26th ROK Regiment company found three natural caves on the N side of the Phu Cat Mountains 35 miles N of Qui Nhon. Bitter hand-to-hand fights took place with the Viet Cong in the caves. Result were 50 Viet Cong killed and friendly casualties were light.

- A B-57 aircraft was downed by enemy fire eight miles NW of Dong Ha in the RVN. The pilot was rescued.
- B-52 aircraft bombed Route 103 in North Vietnam.

OCTOBER 7, 1966

- A 1st Marine unit found two Viet Cong caves 10 miles S of Da Nang. The Viet Cong threw grenades from the caves. The Marines attacked. Enemy losses were nine Viet Cong killed and one Viet Cong captured. There were no friendly casualties.
- *Operation Market Time.* Junks received enemy small arms fire while supporting a Marine company 16 miles SSE of Da Nang. Air strikes were called-in. Enemy losses were 26 killed.
- *Operation Seward.* Fourteen enemy boats were sighted on the Cai River 17 miles NNW Tuy Hoa. Artillery fire sank 12 of the boats.
- B-52 aircraft struck an enemy base camp in Binh Dinh Province.

OCTOBER 8, 1966

- B-52s struck infiltration routes in the DMZ. The raid was on the Demarcation Line.
- USAF F-105 pilots reported five MIG sightings and two encounters N of Hanoi.

OCTOBER 9, 1966

- *Operation Prairie.* A 4th Marine unit found 25 enemy killed in fresh graves four miles N of Thon Son Lam outpost 16 miles W of Dong Ha.
- A 5th Royal Australian Regiment, 1st Australian Task Force company uncovered a Viet Cong administrative headquarters 10 miles NW of Phuoc Le in Phuoc Tuy Province.
- *Operation Irving.* A 1st Cavalry Division (Airmobile) company chased a Viet Cong group into a cave at the tip of Hung Lac Peninsula. Forty-six Viet Cong captured, of which, one was a female nurse. 9th Cavalry helicopter gunships accounted for an additional 12 Viet Cong killed, three Viet Cong captured.
- 1st Brigade, 1st Cavalry Division (Airmobile) units conducted helicopter assaults on two small islands 33 miles N of Qui Nhon off the N coast of Hung Lac Peninsula. Viet Cong were in caves

with underwater entrances. Enemy losses were two Viet Cong killed and 40 Viet Cong captured.

- A USN F-8 pilot downed a MIG-21. A USN A-1 pilot downed a MIG near Phu Ly. The USN A-1 pilot was credited with a probable downing.

OCTOBER 10, 1966

- A series of unit moves were made in the III MAF to enhance combat posture. The 3rd Marine Division Headquarters moved from Da Nang to Phu Bai. 3rd Marine Division elements deployed to Quang Tri and Thua Thien Provinces. The 1st Marine Division Headquarters and some units moved from Chu Lai to Da Nang.
- The 4th Battalion, 503rd Infantry, 173rd Airborne Brigade moved from II FFV to Da Nang.
- B-52 crews struck targets in North Vietnam.

OCTOBER 11, 1966

- A 1st Cavalry Division (Airmobile) unit was led to a Viet Cong camp 33 miles NNW of Qui Nhon by five VN males who had been prisoners at the camp. The camp contained the bodies of 12 VN males shot and killed with hands tied behind their backs and an old man unable to walk because of burned feet.
- USAF pilots struck enemy positions 25 miles SE of Ban Me Thuot for the third day. Results of three day's attacks were 28 secondary explosions and over 500 structures destroyed or damaged.

OCTOBER 12, 1966

- The last contingent of the 4th Infantry Division (4,000 men of the 3rd Brigade) arrived in the RVN. The contingent landed at Vung Tau at 0600 hours after a 19-day voyage aboard the USS WALKER from Seattle, Washington.
- Two USAF F-100 aircraft were downed in Chuong Thien Province 32 miles SSW of Can Tho. The crews were rescued.
- USAF pilots located and destroyed a surface-to-air missile site 15 miles NW of Dong Hoi. The site contained four missiles and one radar van. All targets were destroyed.

OCTOBER 13, 1966

- *Operation Irving.* A Cavalry company located an enemy medical center. The center included mess facilities and fighting and protective bunkers. Viet Cong were spotted moving W from the area.
- *Operation Seward.* A 1st Brigade, 101st Airborne Division company engaged 7-10 Viet Cong at 1030 hours near My Phu 2 Hamlet 11 miles SSE of Tuy Hoa. Armed Viet Cong used 15 VN civilians from the hamlet as shields during the action, and then fled. Two of the civilians were wounded. Enemy casualties are unknown and there were no friendly casualties.
- US pilots flew 173 missions over North Vietnam.

OCTOBER 14, 1966

- *Operation Attleboro.* Terminated in Tay Ninh Province with 12 enemy killed and no enemy captured.
- *Operation Tulsa.* A 1st Infantry Division company located and destroyed a 230-yard tunnel complex 31 miles NNW of Saigon.
- *Operation Prairie.* Three separate actions occurred near the DMZ. Enemy losses were 27 NVA killed. Friendly casualties were light.
- A 1st Marine Division unit apprehended nine Viet Cong surrenderees and found about 40,000 NVN piasters in a house near Chu Lai.
- US pilots flew 174 missions over North Vietnam.

OCTOBER 15, 1966

- A Mission spokesman announced the arrival in Tay Ninh of 239 PHILCAGV officers and men. Also, announced was over 1,000 more to arrive next few days.
- *Operation Attleboro.* Initiated in Tay Ninh Province.
- *Operation Irving.* A CIDG company engaged an enemy force at 1500 hours in a two-hour battle in Binh Dinh Province. Enemy casualties were unknown and friendly casualties were light. At 1635 hours, a few miles to the SW, a 1st Cavalry Division (Airmobile) unit engaged an estimated enemy company. Enemy casualties were unknown and friendly casualties were

light. The day's results were seven enemy killed and 47 enemy captured.

- A camera was found that belonged to Mr. Sam Casten, a senior editor of LOOK Magazine killed during *Operation Crazy Horse* in May 1966.
- B-52s struck in S half of the DMZ.

OCTOBER 16, 1966

- Marines, five miles S of Da Nang, threw a cordon around the Viet Cong inhabited Tra Khe Village. The day's results were 20 Viet Cong killed and four Viet Cong captured. There were no friendly casualties.
- *Operation Irving.* A 5th Cavalry, 1st Cavalry Division (Airmobile) company engaged a Viet Cong company in a seven-hour battle. The day's results were 41 enemy killed and 29 enemy captured.

OCTOBER 17, 1966

- In Binh Thuan Province at 0035 hours a Viet Cong threw several hand grenades at the Phan Rang Beach Pumping Station causing light US casualties and light equipment damage. The Viet Cong escaped.
- In Gia Dinh Province at 0630 hours, Viet Cong detonated a claymore mine in front of the Ky Son Bachelor Enlisted Quarters (BEQ) in Saigon. The incident resulted in one US killed, seven US wounded (all military), one VN civilian killed (woman) and two VN civilians wounded.
- *Operation Irving.* A 5th Cavalry company found two enemy weapons caches. The day's results were 40 enemy killed and 19 enemy captured.
- Eighty-five missions were flown in North Vietnam.

OCTOBER 18, 1966

- At 0625 hours near Tien Bachelor Officers Quarters (BOQ) near Tan Son Nhut, a terrorist grenade explosion caused five US wounded (four slight).
- The enemy attacked a 173rd Airborne Brigade command post just N of Bien Hoa, using claymores, small arms and grenades.

The attack commenced at 2215 hours and terminated at 2230 hours. Enemy casualties are unknown. Friendly casualties were light. There was also light aircraft damage and light equipment damage.

OCTOBER 19, 1966

- At 1230 hours, USN Swift boat sighted an 87-foot trawler beached four miles SE of Tam Ky in Quang Tin Province. The trawler was an RVN vessel beached due to engine trouble. Forty Viet Cong had boarded, taken away five of the eight crewmembers and were unloading cargo. The Swift fired a warning shot, received return fire, and called for an air strike, which was delivered by two USMC A-4 aircraft. A USMC rifle company heli-lifted in and swept the area. Enemy losses were one Viet Cong killed, six Viet Cong captured, one Viet Cong surrendered and three individual weapons captured. The trawler, partially unloaded, and with 60 percent damage from strike, was recovered.
- *Operation Irving.* Enemy losses were 21 killed, 19 captured and 18 tons salt captured. Improved weather over some areas of North Vietnam enabled US pilots to fly 77 missions.

OCTOBER 20, 1966

- *Operation Paul Revere IV.* At 1040 hours, a 3rd Brigade, 25th Infantry Division company engaged an enemy force 22 miles W of Pleiku City. Another 3rd Brigade company reinforced the friendly company. Enemy losses were four killed. An air strike during action resulted in nine US slightly injured from 20mm fragments.
- A 1st Marine squad patrol found about 390,000 piasters (about US $3,305) in a cave eight miles SW of Da Nang.

OCTOBER 21, 1966

- The enemy attacked a 5th Marine unit six miles W of Chu Lai airstrip with mortar rounds, grenades and small arms fire. Enemy losses were one killed and friendly losses were light casualties.
- *Operation Attleboro.* A 196th Light Infantry Brigade unit uncovered an enemy cache 21 miles NNW of Cu Chi in Tay Ninh Province. The cache contained 13 tons rice, ½ ton salt,

over one ton peanuts and 750 pounds fish. There were no friendly casualties.

- *Operation Queanbeyan.* 5th Royal Australian Regiment units captured an enemy high-powered radio transmitter/ receiver and power unit on a mountain 17 miles N of Vung Tau in Phuoc Tuy Province.

OCTOBER 21, 1966

- USN pilots sighted and struck 300 barges in the inland waterways and coastal area of North Vietnam. The pilots reported 125 barges damaged or destroyed.

OCTOBER 22, 1966

- *Operation Irving.* 1st Cavalry Division (Airmobile) units captured 155 tons salt, 28 miles NW of Qui Nhon.

OCTOBER 23, 1966

- *Operation Paul Revere IV.* A 3rd Brigade, 25th Infantry Division company engaged an estimated enemy platoon 1310 to 1835 hours about five miles NE of Plei Djereng. Enemy losses were 13 enemy killed and two enemy captured. Friendly casualties were light.
- *Operation Maeing Ho 6.* Enemy losses were 10 killed and 13 captured.
- *Operation Thayer I.* Terminated in Binh Dinh Province. Final results were 230 enemy killed and 66 enemy captured.
- At 1500 hours, a 9th Marine element directed artillery fire on an estimated 200 enemy 27 miles SSW of Da Nang resulting in 25 enemy killed.

OCTOBER 24, 1966

- *Operation Irving.* Terminated in Binh Dinh Province. Final results were 681 enemy killed, 690 enemy captured, over 60 tons rice and 267 tons salt. Friendly casualties were light.
- At 0230 hours, the enemy attacked a 173rd Airborne Brigade unit eight miles NW of Da Nang airfield with 15 rounds of mortar fire. Friendly casualties were light.
- *Operation Prairie.* At 0145 hours, the enemy attacked a 7th Marine command post seven miles NNW of Dong Ha with 30-40 rounds of 60mm mortar fire. Friendly casualties were light.

OCTOBER 25, 1966

- At 1355 hours, a USN MSB discovered and disarmed an enemy mine in a Saigon main shipping channel 17 miles from Saigon. The mine was rigged for command detonation.
- *Operation Seward.* Terminated in Phu Yen Province. Final results were 239 enemy killed and 34 enemy captured.
- *Operation Byrd.* A 1st Cavalry Division (Airmobile) company engaged an estimated enemy company in a two-hour firefight 16 miles NE of Phan Thiet. Enemy losses were 48 killed and two enemy captured. Friendly casualties were light.
- USN ships commenced surveillance of the southern North Vietnam coast.
- While the USS HANSEN and USS MANSFIELD were patrolling off S coast North Vietnam, NVN shore batteries fired on them and they returned fire. During the morning, there were two exchanges and during the afternoon, one exchange. Enemy losses are unknown. There were no friendly casualties or damage.

OCTOBER 26, 1966

- US President Lyndon B. Johnson visited Cam Ranh Bay.
- A fire broke out aboard the USS ORISKANY (CVA-34), which resulted in 43 killed, three seriously injured and 35 minor injured.
- *Operation Paul Revere IV.* A 2nd Brigade, 4th Infantry Division company engaged an estimated NVA company nine miles NNW of Plei Djereng. Enemy losses were 17 enemy killed and four enemy captured. Friendly casualties were light.
- A 1st Marine company detained 163 enemy surrenderees during a search of the tunnel and cave area 11 miles SSW of Da Nang.

OCTOBER 27, 1966

- *Operation Paul Revere IV.* At 0010 hours, an estimated NVA company attacked a 12th Infantry company from 0010 to 0215 hours. Enemy losses were 17 killed and friendly casualties were light.
- *Operation Allentown.* At 0414 hours, a 1st Infantry Division ambush patrol eight miles N of Saigon was approached by

group of persons during curfew hours without lights or noises. VN National policeman with the ambush advised that the group must be Viet Cong. The patrol opened fire resulting in eight VN civilians killed, seven VN civilians wounded, all women and children.

OCTOBER 28, 1966

- *Operation Macon.* Terminated in Thua Thien and Quang Nam Provinces. Final results were 507 enemy killed, five enemy captured and friendly casualties were moderate.
- *Operation Paul Revere IV.* An estimated NVA company attacked a 35th Infantry company 1855 to 2040 hours about six miles NW of Plei Djereng. Enemy losses were eight enemy killed, one enemy captured and friendly casualties were light.
- *Operation Shenandoah.* 1st Infantry Division units in afternoon battle near Michelin Plantation 41 miles NNW of Saigon. Enemy losses were 74 enemy killed, two enemy captured and friendly casualties were light.
- In Bien Hoa Province at 2045 hours, 13 miles NE of Saigon, the Viet Cong attacked a USARV ammunition dump near Long Binh with mortar fire and demolitions. The attack resulted in light friendly casualties. A pallet of 8-inch howitzer ammunition detonated.
- A US Army CV-2 aircraft crashed into a ridgeline 10 miles E of An Khe at about noon, which resulted in one killed, 20 injured and one missing.
- An F-100 aircraft was lost in the RVN to gunfire.

OCTOBER 29, 1966

- *Operation Paul Revere IV.* An estimated enemy reinforced company attacked an 8th Infantry company at 0230 to 0445 hours and an estimated enemy reinforced company attacked another 8th Infantry company at 0315 to 1030 hours. Enemy losses were 41 enemy killed, one enemy captured and friendly casualties were light.
- *Operation Shenandoah.* Enemy losses were 75 enemy killed and two enemy were captured.

- *Operation Attleboro.* 196th Light Infantry Brigade units found a large enemy rice and salt cache 45 miles NW of Saigon.

OCTOBER 31, 1966

- *Operation Attleboro.* Nineteen enemy tunnels were destroyed and 271 tons rice captured.
- A Navy UH-1B helicopter and PBRs sunk 43 sampans and seven junks on the My Tho River 47 miles SW Saigon while stopping Viet Cong crossing the river.

NOVEMBER 1, 1966

- *Operation Thayer II.* Moderate contact with an estimated enemy battalion. Enemy losses were 38 enemy killed and 50 tons rice captured. Friendly losses were light casualties.
- *Operation Attleboro.* A US infantry battalion operating 203 miles NW of Dau Tieng conducted saturation patrolling and captured 55 tons rice and other supplies.
- *Operation Lam Son II.* 2nd Brigade, 1st Infantry Division units engaged an enemy force in a sweep of a suspected Viet Cong base camp area eight to 10 miles NE of Saigon. There were also other scattered actions. Enemy losses were 19 enemy killed and six enemy captured. Friendly casualties were light.
- At 0710 hours, The Viet Cong fired 14 rounds of long-range 75mm recoilless rifle fire at a National Day parade in Saigon. Four rounds were duds. The attack resulted in one US killed, two US wounded, six VN killed, 39 VN wounded and light damage to buildings. At 0845 hours, the Viet Cong again fired 14 rounds long-range 75mm recoilless rifle fire at the parade. Three rounds were duds. The attack resulted in two US civilians wounded, one VN wounded and light damage to buildings. The parade continued.
- At 0420 hours, the Viet Cong detonated a mine on the Long Tau River 14 miles SE of Saigon sinking a USN MSB with heavy casualties to the six-man crew. A companion MSB attempted immediate rescue and received heavy small arms and automatic weapons fire from the riverbank.
- The weather cleared in North Vietnam. US pilots flew 122 missions in North Vietnam, hitting in the southern panhandle, Haiphong and Hanoi areas. Targets were lines of communication, military areas, and staging and storage areas.

USN flew 66 missions, USAF 48, USMC eight. USN pilots hit a surface-to-air missile site near Haiphong destroying two surface-to-air missiles and a radar van.

NOVEMBER 2, 1966

- US pilots flew 165 missions over North Vietnam (USN 86, USAF 66, USMC 13). Targets were lines of communication, surface-to-air missile sites and military areas. USAF pilots reported three MIG sightings, but no contact.

NOVEMBER 3, 1966

- *Operation Attleboro.* At 1148 hours, a US infantry company engaged an enemy force four to five miles NW of Dau Tieng. The enemy were dug-in and used small arms, hand grenades and claymores. At 1040 hours, a US infantry company engaged an estimated enemy platoon in fortified positions five to six miles NW of Dau Tieng.
- US pilots flew 165 missions in North Vietnam (USN 85, USAF 66, USMC 14). The targets were in the southern panhandle, Hanoi and Haiphong areas.

NOVEMBER 4, 1966

- *Operation Attleboro.* At 0208 hours, the 196th Light Infantry Brigade base camp near Tay Ninh received a 20-minute mortar attack (approximately 150 rounds 60mm and 82mm). The camp was hit again at 0540 hours (11 rounds). Friendly losses were light casualties and light damage. The brigade continued the operation with units becoming heavily engaged. The 1st Battalion, 27th Infantry was operating six to seven miles NW of Dau Tieng in the dense jungle. At 1315 hours, Company C, of that battalion and a company from another battalion became heavily engaged with an estimated Viet Cong battalion. During the battle, the Viet Cong attempted a company-size assault. The Viet Cong assault was thrown back with heavy losses. The 1st Battalion, 27th Infantry established a defensive position. The contact continued and reaction forces moved into the area. Another US company captured 215 tons rice. The day's results were significant enemy losses and friendly casualties light overall.
- Destroyers USS PERKIN and USS BRAINE were fired on by

NVN shore batteries while patrolling off the NVN coast 35 miles SE Dong Hoi. Both ships returned fire and called in air strikes. Results were two enemy guns damaged, two large secondary explosives and three large fires ashore. There were no friendly casualties.

- At 1745 hours, a fire broke out on the USS FRANKLIN D. ROOSEVELT. The fire lasted until 1801 hours. The fire resulted in eight men killed and 14 injured. The ship suffered minor fire and smoke damage to the lower deck storage and supply areas.

NOVEMBER 5, 1966

- *Operation Attleboro.* Control of the 196th Light Infantry Brigade with *Operation Attleboro* shifted from the 25th Infantry Division to the 1st Infantry Division. The operation reinforced and heavy contact continued.
- USAF F-4C aircraft downed two MIG-21s 100 miles NNW of Hanoi.
- Five US aircraft were down over North Vietnam.

NOVEMBER 6, 1966

- *Operation Attleboro.* Friendly forces committed to the operation totaled 11 infantry battalions, heavy artillery support, and numerous support units. The operation continued under the operational control of II FFV. Units participating were from the 1st Infantry Division, 25th Infantry Division, 173rd Airborne Brigade, 3rd Brigade 4th Infantry Division and 11th Armored Cavalry Regiment. At 1930 hours, a 3rd Brigade, 1st Infantry Division company adjusted artillery fire on 150 Viet Cong moving S on trail 15 miles NE Tay Ninh. Results were 70 Viet Cong killed.

NOVEMBER 7, 1966

- *Operation Thayer II.* A 7th Cavalry company engaged an estimated NVA company 1435 to1930 hours in N Cay Giep Mountains. Tactical aircraft supported the Cavalry company and Cavalry armed helicopters. Enemy losses were 55 enemy killed. Another 7th Cavalry company had significant contact.
- *Operation Attleboro.* At 1101 hours in the main area of contact, a 2nd Brigade, 1st Infantry Division company located a battalion-

size Viet Cong base camp of 50 bunkers and destroyed it. Search of the battlefield produced 54 Viet Cong bodies. At 1400 hours, a 196th Light Infantry Brigade company was engaged by an enemy force. The enemy employed three claymore mines and intense small arms causing light friendly casualties. Heavy artillery fire and aerial suppressive fires were called in.

- At 0530 hours, the 5th Battalion Royal Australian Regiment (+) conducted cordon and search of Long Phuoc Hoa in Phuoc Tuy Province. Search completed at 1306 hours. Results were 497 suspects evacuated to sector headquarters at Ba Ria for investigation.

NOVEMBER 8, 1966

- *Operation Attleboro.* At 0625 hours, an estimated two Viet Cong battalions attacked a 3rd Brigade, 1st Infantry Division battalion 13 miles NNW of Dau Tieng. The initial enemy assault came from NW with fire spreading down W side of the friendly perimeter. At 0642 hours, a Viet Cong company attacked from SW and was repulsed. At 0720 hours, another Viet Cong company attacked from NW and was beaten back by massive air strikes and artillery fire at 0731 hours. At 0755 hours, a final Viet Cong attack was launched from N and continued until 0916 hours. Results of the attacks were 293 Viet Cong killed. Elsewhere in the operation, there were numerous small contacts. A Viet Cong tunnel complex was located which contained 4,000 grenades and other weapons and equipment. One arms cache contained 1,299 tear gas grenades of CHICOM manufacture.
- *Operation Hayman.* Operation initiated in Phuoc Tuy Province (Long Son Island).

NOVEMBER 9, 1966

- *Operation Maeng Ho 6.* Terminated in Binh Dinh Province. Final results were 1,161 enemy killed, 518 enemy captured. 454 individual weapons, 43 crew-served and 67 tons rice captured. Friendly casualties were light.
- *Operation Hayman.* Continued on Long Son Islands. At 0720 hours, 23 boats loaded with civilians were intercepted leaving the island. Two hundred suspects were evacuated to Ba Ria. At 0800 hours, three Viet Cong were captured. At 0900 hours, 60

Viet Cong surrendered. At 0930 hours, several well-constructed bunkers destroyed. At 1235 hours, 15 Viet Cong surrendered. At 1500 hours, three camouflaged sampans intercepted. At 1520 hours, six sampans (four with inboard engines) intercepted. At 1545 hours, three camouflaged sampans intercepted. At 1625 hours, a patrol engaged five Viet Cong. There were no friendly casualties.

- *Operation Attleboro.* Shortly after noon, a 2nd Brigade, 1st Infantry Division battalion conducted an airmobile assault nine to ten miles NNW of Dau Tieng. Armed helicopters covering the assault received small arms fire and called in air strikes in response. By 1300 hours, the battalion had located extensive fortifications on SW side of the LZ. Fresh blood trails were prevalent throughout the area. At 1038 hours, a 3rd Brigade, 1st Infantry Division battalion located battalion-size Viet Cong base camp. Another 3rd Brigade battalion located a bunker containing 85 Viet Cong bodies. At 1020 hours, a company of that battalion located a Viet Cong base camp S of Suoi Tre. The camp contained a mine factory with 450 claymores. At 1100 hours, the battalion located seven Viet Cong bodies and another base camp containing large amount of munitions and supplies. Another 3rd Brigade, 1st Infantry Division battalion located two large enemy base camps in the same general area. Cumulative results for *Operation Attleboro* were 875 enemy killed and nine enemy captured. Friendly casualties were light. The number of tactical air sorties flown in support of the operation exceeded 500.

NOVEMBER 11, 1966

- At 0900 hours, near An Trach Village 708 miles SSW of Da Nang, a 3rd Marine patrol engaged an estimated 25 Viet Cong, called in artillery and air. Results were 16 Viet Cong killed, 40 Viet Cong surrendered and one-ton rice captured.
- *Operation Paul Revere IV.* Ten NVA were killed, one NVA captured and friendly casualties were light. Three UH-1B helicopters were downed by enemy ground fire W of Plei Djereng with heavy casualties to crews.
- *Operation Geronimo I.* Sporadic contact 16 miles of NW Tuy Hoa. Enemy losses were nine enemy killed and 27 enemy captured.
- *Operation Byrd.* 30 tons of rice were captured.

NOVEMBER 12, 1966

- In Thua Thien Province at 0130 hours, a 1st Marine platoon at An Trac village seven to eight miles SSW Da Nang was infiltrated and attacked by a Viet Cong force using small arms, grenades and satchel charges. Enemy losses were three killed. Enemy losses were heavy casualties.
- *Operation Paul Revere IV.* A 2nd Brigade, 4th Infantry Division multi-company force engaged an estimated two enemy battalions 17 miles W of Plei Djereng in Kontum Province. Enemy mortar fire of 500-600 rounds received. Enemy losses were 76 enemy killed and two enemy captured. Friendly casualties were light.
- *Operation Attleboro.* The Viet Cong mortared the base camp area of the 25th Infantry Division and 196th Light Infantry Brigade at Tay Ninh and the airfield and 25th Infantry Division operating base at Dau Tieng. Friendly casualties were light and equipment damage light in both attacks. Fire was returned.
- *Operation Hayman.* Terminated. Final results were 10 enemy killed, eight enemy captured, 23 enemy surrendered and 23 sampans destroyed. Friendly casualties were light.

NOVEMBER 13, 1966

- *Operation Paul Revere IV.* At 1305 hours, a 3rd Brigade, 25th Infantry Division company engaged an estimated enemy platoon 18 miles W Plei Djereng. The contact terminated at 1330 hours. Enemy losses were eight enemy killed and friendly casualties were light. At 1530 hours, the same friendly company engaged an estimated NVA battalion NE of the previous contact. Friendly ground reinforcements, air strikes and artillery supported. The contact terminated 1700 hours. Enemy losses were 26 enemy killed. Friendly casualties were heavy in the company making initial contact and overall friendly casualties light. At 1445 hours, another 25th Infantry Division company engaged an enemy force 12 miles NW of Plei Djereng. The contact terminated at 1500 hours. Enemy losses were five enemy killed. There were no friendly casualties.
- *Operation Attleboro.* Light contact. There were scattered engagements 14 miles ESE Tay Ninh. The 1st Brigade, 1st Infantry Division units found three separate Viet Cong rice

caches, totaling 358 tons, seven miles NW of Dau Tieng. A 2nd Brigade, 1st Infantry Division battalion and VN national police killed one Viet Cong and captured 27 Viet Cong in the village of Ben Oui II. The day's results were 14 enemy killed and 28 enemy captured.

- Two USN River PBRs from Sa Dec provided fire support for an ARVN outpost under attack on the My Tho River 85 miles W of Saigon. Two USN PBRs from Can Tho provided medical evacuation support for the ARVN outpost at Tra On, evacuating five ARVN wounded to Can Tho.

NOVEMBER 14, 1966

- Light scattered contact. At 0205 hours, the Viet Cong detonated a satchel charge against a generator bunker near the quarters of the Commanding General (CG) III MAF at Da Nang East. There were no friendly casualties. The generator bunker and adjacent armory were destroyed, nearby storage building extensively damaged and minor damage to other buildings.
- *Operation Attleboro.* Scattered light contact. 1st Infantry Division units captured 10 tons of rice. 25th Infantry Division units captured 20 tons rice and a rice-milling machine.
- At 1400 hours, the USS JOHN R. CRAIG and USS HAMNER were fired on by NVN shore batteries, while patrolling off North Vietnam in international waters 25 miles NNW of Dong Hoi. The ships took evasive action and called in air strikes. The ships made a neutralization pass and received no more fire. Numerous secondary explosions with smoke to 1,000 feet was observed. There were no friendly casualties or damage.

NOVEMBER 15, 1966

- *Operation Attleboro.* Light scattered contact. A 1st Infantry Division battalion was airlifted from Soui Da to LZ NNW of Suoi Tre. The battalion received heavy automatic weapons fire while going into the LZ. Three UH-1D helicopters were downed by enemy ground fire. Air strikes and artillery were employed to neutralize the enemy fire. Contact terminated at1615 hours. A large Viet Cong base camp was uncovered. Fifteen Viet Cong bodies found in the area the next day. The three helicopters were extracted. Friendly casualties were light in the action.

- Tuy Hoa Air Base opened.
- USMC and USAF pilots flew 322 sorties in the RVN. USN, USMC and USAF pilots flew 25 missions over North Vietnam.

NOVEMBER 16. 1966

- *Operation Prairie.* At 0730 hours, a 9th Marine company engaged by an NVA company and another 9th Marine company reinforced. The Marine company first engaged assaulted with tanks. A third 9th Marine company was heli-lifted in. All companies were in contact until 2230 hours. The location was 10½ miles SW Dong Ha. Enemy losses were 28 enemy killed, one enemy captured and friendly casualties were light.
- *Operation Lam Son II.* The Viet Cong attacked a US infantry company at 0200 hours. The attack was beaten back by artillery and small arms fire. The contact was sporadic by 0240 hours. Enemy losses were 43 enemy killed and one enemy captured. Friendly losses were moderate casualties. In Long Khanh Province seven miles S of Xuan Loc from 2015-2025 hours, the enemy attacked the 11th Armored Cavalry Regiment tactical command post with 37 rounds of mortar, estimated 82mm, and 16 rounds recoilless rifle fire. Fire was returned. Friendly casualties were light.
- *Operation Attleboro.* More rice caches uncovered. Total rice seized in *Attleboro* reached 2,217 tons, a new high for any one operation. Previous high was *Operation Birmingham* with 2,103 tons.

NOVEMBER 17, 1966

- *Operation Attleboro.* Light contact. A Viet Cong base camp was destroyed and several rice caches discovered.

NOVEMBER 18, 1966

- At 0115 hours, the Viet Cong attacked Long Binh Ammunition Supply Point 13 miles NE of Saigon with 203 rounds mortar fire and two satchel charges. One satchel charge did not detonate. Fire was returned. There were no friendly casualties and light damage.

- *Operation Attleboro.* Scattered light contact. A 3rd Brigade, 1st Infantry Division company found 40 Viet Cong bodies in a recently dug grave.
- *Operation Market Time.* USCGC POINT BANKS on patrol off coast Ca Mau Peninsula fired on two junks and six sampans with 26 rounds 81mm mortar. Two sampans were damaged. The POINT BANKS then came under automatic weapons fire from an enemy position at the river mouth. The POINT BANKS returned fire with .50-caliber machine guns and 82mm mortar, damaging a camouflaged junk and obtaining five secondary explosions.
- About 0900 hours, the Seventh Fleet destroyers USS JOHN R. CRAIG and USS HAMNER fired five-inch naval guns on a NVN fire control radar located two miles N of DMZ. The radar was tracking the ships. Several secondary fires were in the target area. About 1000 hours, the ships observed 12 cargo craft beached along the coast near the radar site. The ships destroyed three boats and damaged three.

NOVEMBER 19, 1966

- In Quang Nam Province at about 2200 hours, the enemy attacked with 30 rounds of mortar fire on the 9th Marine Battalion command post 23 miles SW of Da Nang. Friendly casualties were light.
- *Operation Paul Revere IV.* At 1205 hours, a CIDG company and two 3rd Brigade, 25th Infantry Division companies engaged an estimated NVA company due W of Plei Djereng two kilometers from the border. Moderate contact continued until 1815 hours and sporadic contact until 1945 hours. Enemy losses were 166 enemy killed and friendly casualties were moderate.
- Seventh Fleet destroyers USS HAMNER and USS JOHN R. CRAIG on patrol 25 miles NNW of Dong Hoi observed two groups of enemy logistics craft and engaged with five-inch naval guns. A NVN coastal battery opened fire at the destroyers but received direct hits when the destroyers returned fire. Three were large secondary explosions in the short battery area. Five enemy logistics craft were destroyed, 15 damaged and no friendly damage.

NOVEMBER 20, 1966

- A Viet Cong battalion attacked a ROK Marine company resulting in a 2½-hour battle near the central coast eight to nine miles NW of Quang Ngai City. Enemy losses were 91 enemy killed, one enemy captured and friendly casualties were light.

NOVEMBER 21, 1966

- At 1110 hours, a 1st Marine platoon combat patrol received heavy enemy small arms fire seven miles SSW of Da Nang. Fire was returned and artillery called in. Thirteen of the enemy were killed. At 0945 hours, a Marine squad from a combined action company found two VN women and one VN boy injured from a booby-trapped table in a market place three miles SE of Hue. The injured were evacuated to Phu Bai.
- *Operation Paul Revere I.* At 1010 hours, a 2nd Brigade, 1st Cavalry Division (Airmobile) company(-) made heavy contact with an estimated enemy battalion 23 miles SSW of Plei Djereng. During the fight, a cavalry platoon was overrun by an estimated 150-200 enemy who deliberately shot several US wounded as they overran the platoon. Heavy contact continued until 1545 hours and sniper fire until 1800 hours. The enemy broke contact and withdrew NW. Cavalry blocking forces made light contact. Results of this engagement were 146 enemy killed and friendly casualties were heavy to the company(-). Elsewhere in *Operation Paul Revere IV*, the 2nd Brigade, 4th Infantry Division units killed 48 of the enemy.
- *Operation Attleboro.* In light contact, 19 of the enemy were killed.
- At 1020 hours, an estimated 75-100 Viet Cong attacked a supply convoy of 11th Armored Cavalry Regiment unit on Highway 1 about 28 miles NE of Saigon. Fire was exchanged for nearly an hour. Artillery, armed helicopters and air strikes were called in. Results were 28 Viet Cong killed, one Viet Cong captured and a 57mm recoilless rifle captured. Friendly casualties were light.
- *Operation Ingham.* Light contact. Two battalion-size Viet Cong base camps and a small base camp were destroyed.
- US pilots flew 473 sorties in the RVN. USAF pilots flew 293 (new high) sorties.

NOVEMBER 22, 1966

- *Operation Rio Blanco.* Several small unit contacts. Enemy losses were 22 killed, one captured and four surrendered.
- At 0600 hours, a 7th Marine combined action company squad patrol engaged 20 Viet Cong 11 miles ESE of Chu Lai. A reaction squad reinforced and the contact continued. Artillery, naval gunfire and air strikes employed. At 1045 hours, a 5th Marine company was heli-lifted into the area and engaged an estimated 100 Viet Cong. Enemy losses were 25 enemy killed, seven individual weapons and three crew-served. Friendly casualties were light.
- *Operation Attleboro.* Sporadic light sniper contacts. Search operations continued. Between 2150-2200 hours, CIDG and US artillery units at the Soui Da FSB received 20 rounds of 81/82mm mortar fire. Friendly casualties were light. Earlier, between 0205-0210 hours, the 2nd Brigade, 25th Infantry Division command post 22-23 miles N of Tay Ninh received 20 to 30 rounds of 81/82mm mortar fire. Friendly casualties were light.

NOVEMBER 23, 1966

- *Operation Thayer II.* Scattered contact. Enemy losses were 26 killed and three tons salt captured. Four US troops were wounded by a short 500-pound bomb dropped by an F-100 aircraft.
- *Operation Ingham.* Australian units destroyed two Viet Cong battalion base camps, three Viet Cong company base camps, and located over six tons rice. The rice was paddy rice in US Agency for International Development (USAID) bags.
- The destroyers USS WARRINGTON and USS MULLANY sighted 60 cargo barges off the coast of North Vietnam just N of Dong Hoi. The destroyers were engaged with naval gunfire. Results were 47 barges damaged or destroyed.
- US pilots flew 377 sorties in the RVN.
- USN pilots struck a Can Thon POL storage area (40 miles NW of Hanoi).

NOVEMBER 24, 1966

- *Operation Thayer II.* Light contact throughout the day four miles

W of Bong Son between the 7th Cavalry unit and a scattered Viet Cong force. Results were 32 Viet Cong killed, 57 grenades and 56 bangalore torpedoes. Friendly casualties were light. During an action four miles W of Bong Son, five US were wounded when an armed helicopter overshot a target.

- Two OH-13 helicopters were downed by enemy ground fire seven miles W of Bong Son. Both aircraft were destroyed. One US was killed and one US injured.
- *Operation Paul Revere IV.* A 3rd Brigade, 25th Infantry Division company found 66 enemy bodies and 90 destroyed enemy bunkers in and around a cave complex 14 miles W of Plei Djereng in Kontum Province. B-52 aircraft had struck the area five days before. The infantry units destroyed 204 enemy bunkers with demolitions during the ground sweep.
- Near Dalat in Tuyen Duc Province, at 0730 hours, an estimated Viet Cong platoon attacked an eight-vehicle construction convoy of 54 workers and seven US military. The workers were all civilian employees of Page Communications Company. One US military, one US civilian and seven foreign nationals were. Six US military, one US civilian and three foreign nationals were wounded. Two vehicles were destroyed and other vehicles damaged. The contact terminated at 1000 hours.
- In Hau Province 28 miles NW of Saigon a 2nd Brigade, 25th Infantry Division unit ambushed a Viet Cong ox cart convoy at 1848 hours. A search the next morning revealed 15 oxen killed, four carts, two individual weapons, a radio and documents.

NOVEMBER 25, 1966

- Eleven VN arrived at USMC camp at Phu Bai. They were part of group of 125 captured by enemy in battle of A Shau last March 1966. They stated that the enemy had released 59. Ten more arrived the next day and three more arrived on November 27, 1966. The last three were so weak they required hospitalization. All showed ill effects of their captivity.
- *Operation Rio Blanco.* At 0950 hours, an estimated 100 Viet Cong attempted break through a 7th Marine battalion blocking force. Marines returned small arms and mortar fire. Enemy

losses were 23 enemy killed, five enemy captured and friendly casualties were light.

- *Operation Attleboro.* At 2345 hours, US elements at Dau Tieng received 30-50 rounds of 81mm mortar fire. Fire was returned. Results were friendly casualties light and light damage.
- *Operation Attleboro.* Terminated at 2400 hours with final results of 1,106 enemy killed, 44 enemy captured, over 2,384 tons rice, 44 tons salt and many tons other equipment and supplies. It was the largest US operation of the war to date. Air support sorties 2,448. TAC sorties 1571.
- *Operation Paul Revere IV.* Eighty-two bunkers were destroyed.
- *Operation Ingham.* Scattered light contact. Nearly 47 tons rice captured and four base camps destroyed.

NOVEMBER 26, 1966

- At 1919 hours, a USAF C-47 aircraft with four crew members and 23 US military passengers crashed one mile N of Tan Son Nhut due to mechanical failure shortly after take-off. There were no survivors.
- In the afternoon, a USAF C-123 aircraft carrying 32 US troops crash-landed due to enemy ground fire just after take-off from Dau Tieng in Tay Ninh Province. The crash resulted in 14 injured (one serious).

NOVEMBER 30, 1966

- *Operation Bismarck.* At 0845 hours, an air strike on 80 Viet Cong 14 miles NNE of Bien Hoa resulted in 39 Viet Cong killed. At 0900 hours, a patrol contact resulted in 11 Viet Cong killed. There were no friendly casualties. At 0915 hours, a patrol contact resulted in five Viet Cong killed. There were no friendly casualties.
- The GVN announced that allies in the RVN would undertake no offensive military actions against the Viet Cong/NVA during the periods December 24-26, 1966, December 31, 1966, January 2, 1967-February 12, 1967. The GVN stated that RVNAF and allied military forces have standing orders to take, if necessary, any appropriate measures for self-defense during the periods.

DECEMBER 1, 1966

- *Operation Thayer II.* A 1st Cavalry Division (Airmobile) platoon engaged an enemy force at 1040 hours. Cavalry units reinforced. The enemy broke major contacts at 1945 hours. Sporadic contact continued until 2130 hours. The day's results were 78 enemy killed, 17 tons rice captured. Friendly casualties were light.
- The US Army Engineer Command, Vietnam was established, the successor to the18th Engineer Battalion.

DECEMBER 2, 1966

- *Operation Mississippi.* A 7th Marine company escorted 1,221 refugees from one area to another about 25 miles SSW of Da Nang. The Marines arranged for food and shelter.
- *Operation Paul Revere IV.* At 0955 hours, a 2nd Brigade 4th Infantry Division company engaged an estimated NVA company while on patrol in Kontum Province 18 miles WNW or Plei Djereng. Artillery and air strikes called in and another 2nd Brigade company reinforced. The day's results were 17 NVA killed and friendly casualties were light.
- *Operation Geronimo I.* A 1st Brigade, 101st Airborne Division company engaged an NVA platoon 22 miles WNW of Tuy Hoa in Phu Yen Province. Results were 15 NVA killed, one NVA captured and friendly casualties light. In other contacts, four NVA were killed.
- *Operation Atlanta.* At 1640 hours, a Viet Cong battalion attacked a five-vehicle 11th Armored Cavalry Regiment convoy in Long Khanh Province 48 miles ENE of Saigon. The convoy was reinforced, air strikes and artillery called in, and blocking forces employed. The Viet Cong succeeded breaking major contact at 1750 hours with sporadic contact continuing until 1950 hours. AC-47 aircraft provided flares and suppressive fire. Enemy losses were 93 Viet Cong killed. Captured enemy weapons included a 75mm recoilless rifle, two heavy machine guns, three light machine guns and a rocket launcher. Friendly casualties were light.
- USN pilots struck the Van Dien Vehicle Depot five miles S of Hanoi. USAF pilots struck the Ha Gia POL depot 14½ miles N of Hanoi. Eight US aircraft were downed over North Vietnam.

DECEMBER 3, 1966

- *Operation Ingham.* Terminated in Phuoc Tuy Province. Final results were 10 enemy killed, one enemy captured, 19 enemy surrendered, 11 individual weapons, 65 tons rice captured, 11 base camps and 22 bunkers destroyed. Friendly casualties were light. The operation was supported by tactical air sorties.
- US Army armed helicopters killed 33 enemy in three separate attacks on enemy groups spotted in Hau Nghia Province.
- US pilots flew 59 missions over North Vietnam (USAF 37, USN 18, USMC four). USAF pilots reported three sightings of MIG-17/MIG-21 aircraft.

DECEMBER 4, 1966

- At 0218 hours, an estimated enemy company attacked Tan Son Nhut Air Base. An estimated 30 enemy penetrated the base perimeter NW of main runway under cover of mortar fire from positions 2½ kilometers N and another four kilometers W of the base. About 30 mortar rounds total were fired onto the base. Flare ships illuminated. Armed helicopters, VN Air Force A-1H air strikes and counter-mortar fire were employed. USAF Air Police and sentry dogs detected the enemy inside the perimeter and engaged them. Results were 18 Viet Cong killed, six Viet Cong captured (two of the Viet Cong captured later died of wounds). Contact terminated about 0430 hours. An ARVN reaction force swept enemy mortar positions areas. Friendly losses from the attack were light friendly casualties, light equipment damage, and light aircraft damage.
- At 2015 hours, an enemy unit attacked Tan Son Nhut Air Base with small arms fire near the rear gate near W end of runway. Armed helicopters and flare ships supported the defense. US Air Police swept the area until 0348 hours, December 5, 1966. Ten Viet Cong were killed. An Air Police unit killed another Viet Cong at noon, December 5, 1966 just N of the intersection of the two main runways. Friendly casualties were light in the attack. Final Viet Cong casualties in the two Tan Son Nhut attacks December 4-5, 1966 were 31 Viet Cong killed, four

Viet Cong captured. In Saigon at 0455 hours, the Viet Cong detonated an explosive charge on the roof of the PsyOps temporary quarters (former Ding Do Capital Theater) at 83 Le Van Duyet Street. The building was in use as an office and quarters by the 6th Psychological Warfare Operations Battalion. Twelve US were injured and heavy damage to building.

- USAF pilots struck the Yen Vien Railroad Yard six miles NE of Hanoi and Ha Gia POL area 14½ miles N of Hanoi. USAF pilots had four MIG encounters during strikes in Hanoi area. F-105s downed a MIG-17 and probably downed another.

DECEMBER 5, 1966

- *Operation Atlanta.* Scattered actions. At 1100 hours, an 11th Armored Cavalry Regiment unit engaged an estimated enemy platoon 36 miles ESE Saigon. Enemy losses were four Viet Cong killed, 41 Viet Cong captured, 278 enemy surrendered, over eight tons rice and over one ton peanuts.
- USMC UH-34 helicopter downed by enemy ground fire S of Da Nang. There were no friendly casualties and there was heavy damage to the helicopter.
- The destroyer, USS INGERSOLL, while patrolling in international waters 11 miles NNW of Dong Hoi, was fired on at 1040 hours by NVN shore batteries. The USS INGERSOLL returned fire and continued the patrol.
- USAF pilots hit Yen Bay railroad yard 76 miles NNW of Hanoi.
- In Binh Duong Province at 2145 hours, the Viet Cong placed mortar fire on a bivouac position of a US 8th Infantry unit 18 miles NNW of Saigon. At 2340 hours, the Viet Cong attacked that position. Friendly casualties were light.
- At Tan Son Nhut Air Base at 1630 hours, a 62-pound satchel charge was found in an ammunition storage area. The charge was disarmed by an EOD team.
- In Tay Ninh Province at 0930 hours, 15 miles NW of Tay Ninh City, multi-company CIDG force found 30,000 Viet Cong uniforms – khaki and black pajama type, in follow-up of B-52 strike.
- At Tan Son Nhut Air Base at 0945 hours, another 62-pound satchel charge was found in an ammunition storage area. The charge was disarmed by an EOD team.

- In the Rung Sat Special Zone at 1142 hours, 16 miles SE of Saigon, The MSTS charter ship SS PHOENIX ran aground while proceeding N on the Long Tau River. There were no casualties. Security and tugs were provided.
- At 1040 hours, the destroyer, USS MANLEY (DD-940), while engaged in naval gunfire support off III MAF area had 5"/54 round explode in the forward mount which resulted in one wounded and minor damage.
- US pilots flew 405 sorties in RVN (USAF 284, USMC 119, USN two).
- Two F-5 aircraft crashed in the RVN. One loss 25 miles NE of Saigon. The pilot ejected but died of injuries. The second crashed causes unknown 30 miles N of Saigon. The pilot was killed.

DECEMBER 8, 1966

- A USAF B-57 aircraft was downed by ground fire in the RVN on Ca Mau Peninsula 25 miles S of Ca Mau City. USN Swift boats rescued both pilots.
- USAF F-105 aircraft encountered MIG-17 and MIG-21 aircraft N of Hanoi. The MIGs fired air-to-air missiles. No damage was reported.

DECEMBER 9, 1966

- First increment of the 199th Light Infantry Brigade arrived in RVN, at Vung Tau.

DECEMBER 10, 1966

- *Operation Prairie.* The enemy attacked the 4th Marine base camp 10 miles NW of Dong Ha with 50 rounds of 60mm mortar fire at 0005 hours. The Marines returned fire with 81mm mortars. Friendly casualties were light.
- *Operation Prairie.* At 1245 hours, two USMC A-4 attack planes dropped six 250-pound bombs on a NVA concentration NNW of the Rock Pile, 17 miles W of Dong Ha. Two bombs went over the edge of a ridge landing in USMC company positions resulting in 17 USMC killed and 11 USMC wounded.
- At 0300 hours, artillery or mortar fire hit an area five miles W of Bien Hoa City in Bien Hoa Province, killing one VN and wounded three VN. A US 4.2-inch mortar platoon had received

permission from sector chief and were firing harassing and interdiction missions.

- In Long Binh Ammunition Dump, 13 miles NE of Saigon, an ammunition pad exploded at 0030 hours. The guards received small arms fire just prior to the explosion. Another pad exploded at 0050 hours. On a third pad, a satchel charge was discovered before it exploded. Friendly casualties and damage were light.
- A U-10 utility aircraft was downed by ground fire 0950 hours 20 miles SW of Long Xuyen in An Giang Province. The crew was rescued. There were no friendly casualties. Damage to plane unknown.
- *Operation Pickett.* Located an enemy arms cache containing 59 individual weapons.
- An enemy cache discovered 25 miles SE of Tay Ninh City containing 46 tons rice.
- At 1120 hours, 10 miles NE of Tay Ninh City, a 3rd Brigade, 1st Infantry Division platoon encountered an enemy force during a TAOR operation. Results were 26 Viet Cong killed, one AK-47 rifle seized. Friendly casualties were heavy in the platoon and light in the operation.

DECEMBER 10, 1966

- *Operation Game Warden.* In Dinh Tuong Province, USN PBRs and a light fire team killed 15 enemy, destroyed 28 sampans one structure and obtained an secondary explosion, in action eight miles W of My Tho (43 miles SW of Saigon).
- Two 7th Fleet ships fired naval gunfire in North Vietnam and silenced a radar site 12 miles NNW of Dong Hoi (December 10-11, 1966), destroyed one junk, damaged two junks 30 miles NNW of Dong (December 11, 1966).

DECEMBER 12, 1966

- *Operation Charleston.* At 1545 hours, in Bien Hoa Province, 11 miles SE of Nha Be (16 miles SE of Saigon) a 2nd Brigade, 1st Infantry Division unit located an enemy grenade factory. There was no contact.
- *Operation Ala Moana.* At 1330 hours, 15 miles SE of Tay Ninh City, an infantry company located and destroyed 50 enemy bunkers and a trench system.

- Between 2130 hours, December 11, 1966 and 0130 hours, December 12, 1966, armed helicopters from the 334th Armed Helicopter Company sank 42 sampans and destroyed three enemy structures 17 miles S of Saigon (20 miles E of Tan An) in Long An Province.

DECEMBER 13, 1966

- *Operation Pawnee III.* At 2010 hours, A USMC F-4B aircraft dropped a bomb 1600 meters short of intended target hitting a village 34 miles SE of Hue in Thua Thien Province. The incident resulted in five VN civilians killed and three VN civilians wounded.
- At 2230 hours, four rounds of undetermined origin impacted five miles E of Saigon in Gia Dinh Province, which resulted in three VN civilians, killed and two VN civilians wounded.
- USAF pilots reported four MIG sightings in Hanoi area. One engagement with MIG-21s. There was no damage to either side.

DECEMBER 14, 1966

- At 0245 hours, a 5th Marine platoon outpost four miles S of Chu Lai came under heavy attack by an estimated enemy platoon. At 0630 hours, the enemy broke contact. Results were friendly casualties heavy and enemy casualties unknown.
- At 0920 hours, a terrorist threw a grenade into a 2½-ton US Army truck near 506 Ben Hom Tu Street in Cholon resulting in one US wounded. The suspect was apprehended by VN police.
- Numerous MIG sightings were reported by US pilots over North Vietnam. Three US aircraft were downed over North Vietnam. A USAF F-105 was downed by enemy air action with the pilot rescued. A USN A-4 and an F-8 aircraft were downed by enemy ground fire with the pilots missing.

DECEMBER 15, 1966

- An 11th Armored Cavalry Regiment unit destroyed an enemy base camp in Binh Tuy Province about 71 miles NE of Saigon.

DECEMBER 16, 1966

- *Operation Thayer II.* The 1st Brigade, 1st Cavalry Division

(Airmobile) assumed conduct of *Operation Thayer II* relieving the 3rd Brigade, 1st Cavalry Division (Airmobile).

- At 2055 hours, two rocket rounds were fired in the vicinity of a Tan Son Nhut military gate. There were no friendly casualties. An EOD team reported accidental discharge of ARVN multiple rocket launcher (mobile) due to static electricity.
- An 11th Armored Cavalry Regiment unit discovered a rice cache containing 34-45 tons rice in Binh Tuy Province 73 miles NE of Saigon.

DECEMBER 17, 1966

- *Operation Thayer II.* Heavy contact occurred between the 1st Brigade, 1st Cavalry Division (Airmobile) battalion (reinforced) size force and an estimated NVA battalion, 1019 hours to1800 hours in Highway 506 Valley, about 38 miles NNW of Qui Nhon. The Cavalry companies surrounded the enemy battalion. The enemy was dug in with overhead cover. Results were 116 NVA killed, three NVA captured and friendly casualties moderate.
- *Operation Ala Moana.* 2nd Brigade, 25th Infantry Division units discovered three closely situated rice caches containing a total of 24 tons rice, 30 miles NW Saigon.

DECEMBER 18, 1966

- I FFV. A US Artillery unit had a breech explosion in a 155mm howitzer at 1200 hours, which resulted in one US killed and 11 US wounded.

DECEMBER 19, 1966

- Elements of the 3rd Brigade, 9th Infantry Division arrived in the RVN. The brigade landed at Vung Tau.
- *Operation Garden Warden.* Two USN PBRs engaged an enemy sampan 2000 hours at the mouth of the My Tho River in Go Cong Province. Enemy losses were two enemy killed, five enemy captured and friendly losses was one US wounded.
- Naval Gunfire. A 7th Fleet destroyer fired on 20 enemy logistics watercraft off S coast North Vietnam near Cap Lay resulting in four destroyed and 10 damaged.

DECEMBER 20, 1966

- *Operation Thayer II.* At 0917 hours, 1st Cavalry Division (Airmobile) units sighted an estimated enemy company 11 miles SSW Bong Son. Air and artillery was called in. Enemy losses were 14 killed and there were no friendly casualties.
- At 2005 hours, the enemy mortared Plei Me Special Forces camp 26 miles SSW Pleiku City. Artillery and AC-47 aircraft fired at suspected enemy mortar positions. Forward Air Controllers directed air strikes. There were no friendly casualties or materiel damage.
- In Bien Hoa Province at 1345 hours, the Viet Cong mined one truck and one passenger bus two kilometers N Di An. Results were one civilian killed, two US injured and two civilians injured.
- Naval Gunfire. A 7th Fleet destroyer fired Naval gunfire in North Vietnam damaging four enemy cargo junks 38 miles SE Dong Hoi, N of Cap Day.

DECEMBER 21, 1966

- At 0400 hours in Thua Thien Province 15 miles NW Hue, an estimated two enemy companies attacked two companies (reinforced) of the 26th Marines. The enemy fired 82mm mortars and small arms. Enemy losses were 54 enemy killed, four enemy captured and friendly casualties were light.
- Light to moderate contact. 7th Marine units supported by artillery killed 26 enemy and captured one in engagement with an estimated enemy company in Quang Ngai Province 12 miles SSE Quang Ngai City. 1st Marine units supported by artillery killed 10 enemy in Quang Nam Province 12 miles SSW Da Nang.
- Naval Gunfire. Four destroyers and a guided missile cruiser fired Naval gunfire in the RVN.
- The USS LONG BEACH tracked two slow-moving aircraft by radar early in morning 25 miles ENE Thanh Hoa. The USS KITTY HAWK launched two F-4 aircraft, which intercepted and fired air-to-air missiles at the aircraft. The enemy aircraft then disappeared from the radar.

DECEMBER 22, 1966

- *Operation Chinook.* The 26th Marine regained contact with an enemy force in Thua Thien Province 16 miles NW Hue. Enemy losses were 110 enemy killed.
- *Operation Thayer II.* Enemy losses were 23 killed and 12 captured.
- At 2143 hours, 13 miles NW Dong Hoi off the coast of North Vietnam, a 7th Fleet destroyer damaged five enemy logistics watercraft.
- MACV spokesman announced the presence of 25-50 North Korean pilots in North Vietnam.

DECEMBER 23, 1966

- Naval Gunfire. At 1100 hours, The USS O'BRIEN on patrol off the coast of North Vietnam 25 miles NNW of Dong Hoi suffered two hits port side and numerous minor fragment holes from enemy shore battery fire. The DD maneuvered and returned fire. The USS KITTY HAWK A-4 aircraft struck an enemy battery position.
- At 0030 hours, a 7th Fleet destroyer damaged 15 enemy logistics watercraft in two Naval gunfire missions in North Vietnam, four and 8½ miles NNW of Dong Hoi off coast.
- B-52s struck twice in North Vietnam (both raids were about 33 miles S Dong Hoi, seven and nine kilometers N of the DMZ).

DECEMBER 24, 1966

- At 1445 hours, a 5th Marine company received small arms, automatic weapons and mortar fire from an enemy force. Artillery fire called in and company reinforced. Friendly casualties were light.
- At 1916 hours, a CL-44 Flying Tiger cargo aircraft crashed 1½ kilometers from the runway while on ground control approach (GCA) to Da Nang Air Base. The plane crashed into the village of Binh Thai in Hoa Vang District in Quang Nam Province.

Results were 107 VN killed, four crew killed (entire crew), 18 VN injured, 13 VN missing and 66 houses destroyed.

- At 0205 hours, a Military Police (MP) at Armed Forces Radio and Television Service (AFRTS) at 9 Hung Thap Tu in Saigon received fire from across street. The MP returned fire. There were no friendly casualties.

DECEMBER 25, 1966

- In Hau Nghia Province 20 miles NW Saigon (two kilometers from Cu Chi and ¾ mile from Bob Hope's Show), a 25th Infantry Division patrol received fire from three of the enemy. US returned fire. There were no friendly casualties. Enemy losses were two enemy killed, two individual weapons and one Russian made radio.
- In Binh Duong Province 13 miles NNW Saigon (less than two miles N of Bob Hope's Show at 1st Infantry Division Headquarters at Di An), a 1st Infantry Division reconnaissance squad received small arms fire from a platoon-size enemy force. The US returned fire. Friendly casualties were heavy and one enemy killed.
- At 0600 hours, in Saigon Port, 5,000 dockworkers began a general strike in response to a call issued by the Port Worker's Union on Sunday. Thirty-four US ships and several military transports were affected.
- In Quang Ngai Province 15 miles SSW Quang Ngai City, a Marine reconnaissance team spotted an estimated 100 enemy at 1200 hours and directed artillery, armed helicopter and Naval Gunfire. Enemy losses were 23 enemy killed and there were no friendly casualties.
- *Operation Paul Revere IV.* Seventeen miles N of Pleiku City, a 3rd Brigade Task Force 25th Infantry Division unit captured 14 enemy near a village.
- At 1530 hours, in Tay Ninh Province 12 miles SE Tay Ninh City (40 miles NW Saigon), enemy attacked a 196th Light Infantry Brigade unit with six to 12 mortar rounds. Armed helicopters supported the unit. Friendly casualties were light.
- Between 2330 and 2345 hours, in Binh Duong Province 16 miles N of Saigon, the enemy attacked the 1st Infantry Division base camp with 30-50 rounds 81mm mortar fire. Counter

mortar fire returned. Two USAF AC-47 aircraft supported. Friendly casualties were light and equipment damage light.

- At 1345 hours, in Phuoc Tuy Province 45 miles SE Saigon, ARVN and 1st Australian Task Force engaged an enemy company. Artillery and air strikes called. Enemy losses were 27 killed, 105 individual weapons, two submachine guns one 82mm mortar and unspecified number of mines. There were no friendly casualties.

DECEMBER 26, 1966

- B-52s struck twice in Bien Hoa Province and in the DMZ straddling the demarcation line 16 miles WNW Dong Ha.

DECEMBER 27, 1966

- Scattered actions near Da Nang and S of Quang Ngai City. Enemy losses were 27 enemy killed.
- *Operation Thayer.* In Binh Dinh Province 12 miles SW Bong Son, an estimated enemy battalion assaulted a 1st Cavalry Division (Airmobile) unit at an LZ from 0106 to 0300 hours. Results were 49 NVA killed, five individual weapons, four crew-served. Friendly casualties were heavy and there was moderate equipment damage.
- In Long An Province 14-16 miles SSE Saigon, the 334th Armed Helicopter Company destroyed 110 enemy sampans during the night of December 26-27, 1966.
- Naval Gunfire. Seventh Fleet destroyers fired gunfire in I, II and IV Corps areas.

DECEMBER 28, 1966

- At 1815 hours in Bien Hoa Province 27 miles E Saigon, a UH-1B helicopter gunship was downed by enemy ground fire. Five US were injured and the helicopter was destroyed.
- In action ending at 0250 hours in Long An Province 14-16 miles SSE Saigon, the 334th Assault Helicopter Company destroyed 64 enemy sampans.

DECEMBER 29, 1966

- At 1836 hours, in Gia Dinh Province six miles NE Saigon, the enemy detonated claymores against a patrol from the 2nd Brigade, 1st Infantry Division. Patrol casualties were heavy.

- A USAF A-1E aircraft was downed by enemy ground fire in Binh Tuan Province 22 miles NE Phan Thiet. The pilot was rescued.

DECEMBER 30, 1966

- *Operation Byrd.* Light contact. Twenty-one dead Viet Cong were uncovered in fresh graves at three locations.
- A USAF A-1E aircraft passing over an aerial observer was downed by enemy ground fire, crashed in Lake Ban Trang and sank. The pilot parachuted into the lake and was rescued by a Cavalry helicopter.

DECEMBER 31, 1966

- *Operation Paul Revere IV.* Terminated. Final results were 977 enemy killed, 90 enemy captured and friendly casualties were light.
- The first elements of the 1st Brigade, 9th Infantry Division arrived in the RVN. The brigade landed at Vung Tau.

JANUARY 1, 1967

- US military strength in the RVN was 395,000.
- New Year's stand-down observed, started 0700 hours, December 31, 1966.
- *Operation Market Time.* Swift boats intercepted a steel-hulled trawler SW of Vung Tau; the trawler beached and burned.
- *Operation Game Warden.* USN PBRs captured a 30-foot junk on Soi Rap River with one light machine gun, 15 rounds B-40 anti-tank, rounds 75mm recoilless rifle, 500 grenades and 40,000 rounds small arms.
- Elements of the 4th and 25th Infantry Division launched *Operation Paul Revere V/Sam Houston,* a 95-day search and destroy operation in Pleiku and Kontum Provinces. Friendly losses were 172 killed, 767 wounded and one missing. Enemy losses were 773 killed, two retained, 305 detained, 162 individual weapons and 47 crew-served weapons.
- 1st Cavalry Division (Airmobile) search and destroy *Operations Byrd* in Binh Thuan Province, launched on August 25, 1966, and *Dazzlem* in Binh Dinh Province, launched on October 1, 1966, continued into 1968.

JANUARY 2, 1967

- The New Year's 48-hour stand-down period ended at 0700 hours. USMACV reported 111 incidents during period, of which 24 were significant.
- USAF F-4 aircraft shot down seven MIG-21s over Red River Valley. Total MIG kills rose to 34.

JANUARY 3, 1967

- *Operation Thayer II.* The 3rd Brigade, 25th Infantry Division transferred from operational control 4th Infantry Division to operational control 1st Cavalry Division (Airmobile).
- *Operation Maeng Ho 8.* Initiated. The 26th ROKA Regiment launched the 60-day search and destroy operation in Phu Yen and Binh Dinh Provinces. Friendly losses were seven killed and 17 wounded. Enemy losses were 211 killed, 375 prisoners of war, 699 detained, 145 individual weapons and 34 crew-served weapons.

JANUARY 4, 1967

- Long Kanh Province. Two American engineers and a Filipina were released by the Viet Cong after seven months as prisoners. The prisoners arrived at the MACV Compound in the vicinity of Xuan Loc City.
- USN A-4 and F-4 aircraft were downed by enemy ground fire over North Vietnam. The crews were rescued.

JANUARY 5, 1967

- *Operation Glen Burnie.* Announced and terminated.
- *Operation Niagara Falls.* Initiated.
- *Operation Seine.* Launched by the 2nd ROKMC Brigade and was a nine-day search and destroy operation in Quang Ngai Province. Friendly losses were 37 killed and 56 wounded (two US). Enemy losses were 140 killed, 71 detained, 15 Ralliers and four individual weapons.

JANUARY 6, 1967

- *Operations Song Than/Deckhouse V.* Initiated. The first US assault in the Mekong Delta as Marines of BLT 1/3 of the SEVENTHFLT Amphibious Ready Group/Special Landing

Force go ashore in Kien Hoa Province in *Operation Deckhouse V.*

- USAF F-4 aircraft downed two MIG-21s 100 miles W Hanoi, raising total to 36.

JANUARY 7, 1967

- The enemy attacked Camp Holloway Airfield four kilometers E Pleiku City with a ground assault supported by mortar fire. The enemy attacked Pleiku Air Force Base and Lac Trung Sub-section at the same time. 207 rounds mortar from 10 mortar positions were received within Camp Holloway. Pleiku Air Force Base received 60mm round of mortar fire near ammunition dumps. The enemy penetrated the center of Camp Holloway with satchel charges and grenades. Friendly losses were light casualties, light equipment and aircraft damage.
- First units of the Mekong Delta Mobile Riverine Force arrived in-country.
- *Operations Song Than/Deckhouse V.* A VN Marine Brigade landed by surface and helicopter over the beach of the Co Chien River.
- The enemy mortared Binh Thuy Air Base.

JANUARY 8, 1967

- *Operation Cedar Falls.* Initiated. 25th Infantry Division, including ARVN units, launched *Operation Cedar Falls,* an 18-day Search and Destroy operation in Binh Duong, Tay Ninh, Hau Nghia Provinces to clear the Iron Triangle/Than Dien Forestry Reserve area. Friendly losses were 72 killed and 337 wounded. Enemy losses were 720 killed, 213 prisoners of war, 512 detained, 555 individual weapons and 23 crew-served weapons.
- *Operation Duck.* Announced. Initiated December 17, 1966.

JANUARY 9, 1967

- *Operation Niagara Falls.* Announced and terminated.
- Rung Sat Special Zone. Dinh Tuong Province. On the Mekong River, Viet Cong mined the US RMK-BRJ dredge, JAMAICA BAY, sinking the dredge in 20-foot water. Results were three US civilians killed and one wounded. There were no ARVN

casualties. The JAMAICA BAY is the world's fourth largest dredge.

- Naval Forces. Forty-eight Chinese fishermen from Hainan rescued by the USN when in distress in early December 1966, were flown to Hong Kong by USAF C-130 for repatriation.

JANUARY 10, 1967

- *Operation Maeng Ho 8.* Announced.
- *Operation Cedar Falls.* Large quantities of rice was discovered the last few days. Twenty-two rounds of US 105mm artillery landed in the position of a US infantry unit. Results were two US killed and 14 US wounded. Captured were 151 small arms and 543 tons rice.
- US engineer, signal and security units prepared the base at Dong Tam, Dinh Tuong Province.

JANUARY 11,1967

- A USMC reconnaissance patrol picked up seven VN, Thua Thien Province 26 kilometers SE Hue who appeared to be A Shau Special Forces camp personnel released by the enemy. All were in poor physical condition.
- *Operation Cedar Falls.* A tactical air strike in a forest reserve area resulted in 18 secondary explosions, 103 CHICOM gas masks and 782 tons rice.

JANUARY 12, 1967

- *Operation Cedar Falls.* Enemy losses were 48 killed, 11 detained and 440 tons of rice captured, located in three enemy concrete buildings. One was a three-story building partly underground.
- An enemy force attacked Binh Thuy airfield, Phong Dinh Province, with 50 rounds of mortar and recoilless rifle fire resulting in light damage to airfield, buildings and aircraft.

JANUARY 13, 1967

- *Operation Cedar Falls.* Enemy losses were 49 killed, 13 detained and 133 tons rice. Friendly casualties were light. A 1st Infantry Division unit was hit by 10 rounds of 155mm supporting fire. Results were eight US killed and 34 wounded.

- *Operation Song Than/Deckhouse V.* VN Marine Corps found a claymore factory, 2,500 pounds iron, anti-tank, anti-personnel mines, grenades and small arms ammunition.
- Elements of the 9th Infantry Division set up first US base camp in the Mekong Delta region (Dong Tam).

JANUARY 14, 1967

- Quang Nam Province. A 1st Marine company conducted a heliborne raid on an enemy hamlet. Enemy losses were 61 enemy killed and one detained. Friendly casualties were moderate.
- Rung Sat Special Zone. A USN minesweeper collided with the merchant ship MUI FINN in the Long Tau River. Results were two US killed, one seriously injured, one minor injured and one missing. There was light damage to the MUI FINN.
- USN announces SEAL (Sea-Air-Land) units in operation in RVN.

JANUARY 15, 1967

- *Operation Song Than/Deckhouse V.* Terminated.
- *Operation Game Warden.* Dinh Tuong Province. Two USN PBRs intercepted two large, heavy loaded sampans in the My Tho River. Enemy losses were nine killed, nine sampans sunk, 17 enemy structures damaged and 17 destroyed. Friendly casualties were light. One PBR suffered light damage.

JANUARY 16, 1967

- Binh Duong Province. A US Infantry unit pursued the enemy who used riot control gas to hinder pursuit.
- US announced resumption of air strikes in the Hanoi area.

JANUARY 17, 1967

- North Vietnam. Thai Nguyen railroad yards were hit by USAF pilots.

JANUARY 18, 1967

- *Operation Paul Revere V.* Operation re-named *Operation Sam Houston* retroactive January 1, 1967.
- US announced use of bases in Thailand in support operations in Vietnam.

JANUARY 19, 1967

- *Operation Pickett.* Terminated. Units of the 101st Airborne Division terminated *Operation Pickett,* a 42-day search and destroy operation in Kontum Province that commenced December 8, 1966. Friendly losses were 23 killed and 104 wounded. Enemy losses were 63 killed, 18 prisoners of war, 14 detained, 108 individual weapons and one crew-served weapon.
- *Operation Cedar Falls.* US units located an enemy tunnel complex three levels deep and 300-600 meters long.
- *Operation Silver Lake.* Terminated.
- *Operation Dan Chi 275/B.* One-day search and destroy operation in An Xuyen Province. Friendly losses were 22 killed and 43 wounded. Enemy losses were 181 killed, seven prisoners of war, three detained and 30 individual weapons.
- Naval Gunfire. Two radar sites were taken under fire by the DDs USS STODDARD and the USS KEPPLER N of Vinh on Hoi Thong Peninsula and Hon Matt Island.
- A USN A-6 aircraft was downed over North Vietnam due to unknown causes. A USAF F-4 aircraft was downed due to unknown causes. Both two-man crews are missing.

JANUARY 20, 1967

- Long An Province. Two 199th Light Infantry Brigade companies conducted a heli-borne raid on an enemy supply depot and received heavy small arms, automatic weapons and recoilless rifle fire. PBRs, PCs, LCMs, RAGs and helicopter gunships supported. Enemy losses were four enemy killed and 320 detained. Ten cases of TNT and 45 tons rice was captured. Friendly casualties were light.
- Naval Gunfire-North Vietnam. The DDs the USS STODDARD and the USS BENNER attacked 40-60 enemy barges. The DDs came under NVN coastal fire SE Vinh. The DDs returned fire, silencing shore batteries and destroyed or damaged five barges.
- North Vietnam. USN pilots hit Dong Phong Thuong railroad complex and bridges. USAF pilots hit Ha Gia railroad bridge.

JANUARY 21, 1967

- Naval Gunfire-North Vietnam. The DD USS STODDARD destroyed or damaged four watercraft NNW Dong Hoi at the mouth of the Song Giang River. Later, the DD fired on two watercraft off-loading onto seven trucks. One craft and two trucks were destroyed. One truck was damaged and burning. A secondary explosion was observed. The DD USS BENNER damaged a 40-foot watercraft NNW Dong Hoi.
- *Operation Ma Doo I.* Launched. A 17-day search and destroy operation in Phu Yen Province. Friendly losses were three killed and 14 wounded. Enemy losses were 160 killed, 57 prisoners of war, 162 individual weapons and five crew-served weapons.
- *Operation Sierra.* The 7th Marine Regiment units terminated operation, a 40-day search and destroy operation in Quang Ngai Province that commenced December 12, 1966. Friendly losses were 10 killed and 50 wounded. Enemy losses were 111 killed, 10 prisoners of war, 66 detained, seven retained and 36 individual weapons.
- North Vietnam. USAF F-4 and F-105 aircraft reported MIG sightings. F-105 and MIG-17 aircraft exchanged cannon fire. There was no reported damage to either aircraft. USN pilots hit the Ninh Binh complex. USAF pilots hit Bac Giang bridge.

JANUARY 22, 1967

- North Vietnam. USN pilots hit Ninh Binh. USAF pilots hit Thai Nguyen railroad bridge. F-105 aircraft engaged four MIG-17s NW Hanoi. No damage was reported either side.

JANUARY 24, 1967

- *Operation Tuscaloosa.* Initiated.
- *Operation Cedar Falls.* US troops searched a 2,100 meters tunnel complex, which was 600 meters long with 10 branches.
- *Operation Tuscaloosa.* Announced.
- *Operation Cedar Falls.* Terminated.

JANUARY 25, 1967

- A Soviet mine was found in Saigon River. This the first Russian mine found in war.

JANUARY 26, 1967

- *Operation Farragut.* The 56-day search and destroy operation was launched by the 1st Brigade, 101st Airborne Division in Binh Thuan Province. Friendly losses were 14 killed and 128 wounded. Enemy losses were 115 killed, four prisoners of war, 155 detained and 80 individual weapons.
- *Operation DeSoto.* A 71-day search and destroy operation in Quang Ngai Province was launched by units of the 7th Marine Regiment. Friendly losses were 69 killed and 556 wounded. Enemy losses were 383 killed, 247 detained and 28 individual weapons.

JANUARY 27, 1967

- North Vietnam. A USAF F-4 was downed by ground fire. The crew was rescued.
- Newport, Saigon officially opened as a military port terminal facility.

JANUARY 28, 1967

- *Operation Tuscaloosa.* Terminated.
- *Operation Colby.* Terminated.
- *Operation Iola.* Reinitiated.

JANUARY 29, 1967

- The 2nd Brigade, 9th Infantry Division arrived the RVN at Vung Tau, Phuoc Tuy Province.
- *Operation Peng Mai I.* Operation launched by elements of the 28th, 29th and 30th ROKA Regiments. The 35-day search and destroy operation occurred in Nhanh Hoa Province. Friendly losses were 19 killed and 35 wounded. Enemy losses were 394 killed, 40 detained, 271 individual weapons and 34 crew-served weapons.
- North Vietnam. USN pilots hit Than Hoa transshipment point and USAF pilots hit Thai Nguyen railroad yard.

JANUARY 30, 1967

- *Operation White Horse I (Baek Ma I).* Announced.

JANUARY 31, 1967

- *Operation Prairie.* Terminated by elements of the 3rd and 4th Marine Regiments. The 181-day search and destroy operation in Quang Tri Province commenced August 3, 1966. Friendly losses were 225 killed, 1,159 wounded and one missing. Enemy losses were 1,397 killed, 27 prisoners of war, 110 detained, 298 individual weapons and 15 crew-served weapons.
- Quang Nam Province. Twenty kilometers SSW Da Nang, a group of VN civilians came to the 1st Marine battalion command post with 14 bodies of VN civilians. A medical examination indicated many shot at close range and/or bayoneted. Villagers stated enemy told them to bring bodies and say they were killed by artillery and air strikes.

FEBRUARY 1, 1967

- US military strength in RVN was 410,000.
- *Operation Prairie II.* Initiated. Elements of the 3rd Marine Division launched the 46-day search and destroy operation in Quang Tri Province. Friendly losses were 93 killed, 483 wounded and one missing. Enemy losses were 693 killed, seven prisoners of war, 569 detained, 114 individual weapons and 23 crew-served weapons.
- *Operation Independence.* Initiated. Elements of the 9th Marine Regiment launched the nine-day search and destroy operation in Quang Nam Province. Friendly losses were nine killed, 35 wounded and three CIDG wounded. Enemy losses were 145 killed, 31 prisoners of war, 100 detained, 15 individual weapons and one crew-served weapon.
- *Operation Big Spring.* Initiated SW part War Zone “D”.

FEBRUARY 2, 1967

- *Operation GADSDEN.* Elements of the 4th and 25th Infantry launched the 19-day search and destroy operation in Tay Ninh Province. Friendly losses were 29 killed and 107 wounded. Enemy losses were 161 killed, 21 detained, 24 individual weapons and one crew-served weapon.

FEBRUARY 3, 1967

- USAF pilots hit a Thai Nguyen railroad yard with 20 railroad cars destroyed.
- The first PBR (*Operation Game Warden*)was lost to hostile fire.
- Twenty-eight prisoners of war were repatriated to North Vietnam at the Ben Hai River crossing, DMZ.

FEBRUARY 4, 1967

- *Operation Farragut.* Announced
- North Vietnam. USAF pilots report sighting two MIG-17 and six MIG-21 aircraft with one engagement. A USAF B-66 aircraft was downed by ground fire over North Vietnam with the crew missing. A USN F-4 aircraft was downed to causes unknown. The crew is missing.

FEBRUARY 5, 1967

- DMZ. The first defoliation mission was flown in DMZ (S half).
- North Vietnam. USAF F-4 aircraft attacked two flights of MIG-17s. Fire was exchanged with no damage reported to either side.

FEBRUARY 6, 1967

- North Vietnam. USAF pilots hit Phu Le Army Camp. USAF O-1 and CH-3 aircraft were downed by ground fire. One CH-3 crewman was rescued. The O-1 pilot and a remainder of the CH-3 crew are missing.

FEBRUARY 7, 1967

- *Operation Thayer II.* Binh Dinh Province. An enemy force attacked a 1st Cavalry Division battalion and ARVN regiment at English airfield. Friendly casualties and damage were light.
- The enemy mortared Binh Thuy Air Base.
- *Operation Ma Dco* I. Terminated.

FEBRUARY 8, 1967

- At 0700 hours, allied forces commenced observance of a four-day period of curtailed military operations for TET.
- Bien Hoa Air Base experienced an explosion and fire in the napalm storage area. There was no friendly casualties and no aircraft damage.

- *Operation Lam Son II.* Terminated. A combined US Army/ ARVN 259-day security operation in Binh Duong Province (commenced May 23, 1966. Friendly losses were 70 killed and 339 wounded. Enemy losses were 251 killed, 198 prisoners of war, 1,450 detained, 49 individual weapons and eight crew-served weapons.
- At 0700 hours, Allied forces commenced observance of four-day cease fire for TET. The truce period was marked by 183 minor and 89 significant cease-fire violations.
- North Vietnam. A USAF RF-101 aircraft was downed by ground fire prior to 0700 hours. The pilot was rescued.

FEBRUARY 9, 1967

- *Operation Independence.* Terminated.

FEBRUARY 11, 1967

- *Operation Pershing.* Elements of the 1st Cavalry Division (Airmobile) launched a search and destroy operation in Binh Dinh Province, which continued into 1968.

FEBRUARY 12, 1967

- The four-day TET period curtailment military operations in the RVN terminated at 0700 hours. Normal military activity resumed. During the period, 272 incidents involving US or other FWMAF were recorded which were 89 were significant. Friendly losses were 18 US killed and 158 wounded. Enemy losses were 112 enemy killed and 75 detained.
- *Operation Stone.* Initiated.
- *Operation Thayer.* Terminated. ARVN and elements of the 1st Cavalry Division terminated the operation, a combined US Army/VNMC 111-day search and destroy operation in Binh Dinh Province (commenced October 24, 1966). Friendly losses were 208 killed, 876 wounded and two missing. Enemy losses were 1,757 killed, 132 prisoners of war, 3.952 detained, 161 retained, 426 individual weapons and 52 crew-served weapons.
- *Operation Pershing.* Initiated.
- A USAF F-100 aircraft crashed during a bomb run in Phuoc Tuy Province, with the cause unknown. The pilot was killed.

FEBRUARY 13, 1967

- *Operation Baek Ma I.* The name is changed to *Peng Ma I.*
- *Operation Lanakai.* Terminated. Elements of the 25th Infantry Division terminated the 152-day search and destroy operation in Long An Province, which commenced September 14, 1966 Friendly losses were 16 killed and 44 wounded. Enemy losses were 94 killed, 12 prisoners of war, 135 detained, 15 individual weapons and three crew-served weapons.
- *Operation Beaumaris.* Initiated.
- One of four mortar rounds (81mm) directed at MACV 1 compound hit an ARVN truck at Phan Than Gian Street. The MACV compound was not hit and there were no US casualties. This is the first firing of enemy mortars within Saigon/Cholon. The enemy escaped.
- US military court-martial jurisdiction over all civilian personnel serving with or accompanying US forces was announced.

FEBRUARY 14, 1967

- *Operation Enterprise.* Initiated.

FEBRUARY 15, 1967

- Quang Ngai Province. Elements of the 2nd ROK Marine Brigade was attacked by an estimated three enemy battalions. The enemy used flamethrowers against Republic of Korea Marine Corps bunkers. The enemy broke contact and withdrew to S. Enemy losses were 243 enemy killed, two detained. 36 individual weapons, 10 crew-served weapons, 350 CHICOM grenades, 6,000 rounds small arms ammunition and a quantity of bangalore torpedoes captured. Friendly casualties were moderate.
- *Operation Gatling II.* Terminated.
- Ten US Army UH-1 helicopters were downed by ground fire in Chuong Thien Province in support of an ARVN operation. Two US were killed and seven wounded.
- The Viet Cong attacked USN MSBs on Long Tau River, which resulted in two friendly killed, 16 missing, one MSB sunk and two MSBs damaged.

FEBRUARY 16, 1967

- *Operation Chinook I.* Terminated.
- *Operation Deckhouse VI.* Initiated.
- *Operation Big Spring.* Terminated.
- *Operation River Raider One.* River Flotilla One and the 3rd Battalion, 47th Infantry, 2nd Brigade, 9th Infantry Division units conduct initial combat operations.
- *Operation Deckhouse VI.* SEVENTHFLT Special Landing Force/ Amphibious Ready Group launched the 15-day search and destroy operation in Quang Ngai Province. Friendly losses were six killed and 117 wounded. Enemy losses were 280 killed, 21 detained and one individual weapon.
- *Operation Chinook II.* Elements of the 4th Marine Regiment (Reinforced) terminated the 47-day search and destroy operation in Thua Thien Province. Friendly losses were 12 killed and 111 wounded. Enemy losses were 104 killed, 226 detained and 20 individual weapons.
- B-52s struck seven times in the RVN, five in support of *Operation Sam Houston* and once in Binh Duong and Thua Thien Provinces.

FEBRUARY 17, 1967

- *Operation Chinook II.* Initiated and announced.

FEBRUARY 18, 1967

- North Vietnam. A USAF F-105 aircraft was downed by ground fire. The crew is missing.

FEBRUARY 19, 1967

- Naval Gunfire-North Vietnam. The DD USS STRAUSS sank a large steel-hulled cargo craft SE Vinh.

FEBRUARY 20, 1967

- *Operation Prairie II.* A 3rd Marine unit discovered an enemy cache (two 82mm mortar, 48 rounds 82mm mortar, 24 CHICOM artillery rockets, 375 CHICOM grenades and 250 pounds explosives).

- *Operation Deckhouse VI.* Operational Command changed from Commander, Seventh Fleet to III MAF.
- *Operation Sam Houston.* A US company discovered an enemy cache (three 60mm mortar, four light machine guns, 6,000 rounds small arms ammunition, 27 rounds 57mm recoilless rifle, 360 pounds explosives, seven bangalore torpedoes and miscellaneous equipment).
- Naval Gunfire-RVN. The DD USS MADDOX hit an enemy ammunition dump in the vicinity of the mouth of the Cau Dai River, Kiem Hoa Province, resulting in two large fires that triggered several secondary explosions. A 40-foot enemy sampan and one bunker were destroyed.

FEBRUARY 21, 1967

- *Operation Chinook II.* Dr. Bernard B. Fall, author and authority on Vietnam, was killed by an enemy mine at 1640 hours while covering USMC operations 19 kilometers NW of Hue in Thua Thien Province.
- *Operation Gadsden.* Terminated.
- *Operation Tucson.* Terminated.
- *Operation Junction City.* 4th, 9th and 25th Infantry Division units launched the 81-day search and destroy operation in Tay Ninh Province. Friendly losses were 282 killed and 1,574 wounded. Enemy losses were 2,728 killed, 97 detained, 137 retained, 491 individual weapons and 100 crew-served weapons. D-Day saw 845 paratroopers dropped into LZs in northern Tay Ninh Province.

FEBRUARY 22, 1967

- *Operation Stone.* Terminated.
- *Operation Giant Dragon.* Terminated.
- *Operation Junction City.* Initiated in War Zone "C" Tay Ninh Province by a multi-division search and destroy operation. Conducted by units 1st, 4th and 25th Infantry Divisions, 196th Light Infantry and 173rd Airborne Brigades and 11th Armored Cavalry Regiment, 2nd Battalion, 503rd Airborne Infantry. The 173rd Airborne Brigade made the first US combat parachute jump in the RVN. Four other brigades assaulted by ground and heli-lift to form a horseshoe blocking force. Initial enemy contact was scattered.

- Kien Hoa Province. ARVN Operation *Cuu Long 55* search and destroy, day's results included the capture of 316 individual weapons, four crew-served weapons, 12 mines, 200 blocks TNT and eight 75mm pack howitzers.
- US pilots flew 573 tactical air sorties in the RVN (new high).

FEBRUARY 23, 1967

- *Operation Junction City.* The 11th Armored Cavalry Regiment and the 2nd Brigade, 25th Infantry Division elements attacked into the open end horseshoe set by blocking forces. Results to date: 19 enemy killed, eight individual weapons, 39 tons rice, 200 tires captured. 415 tactical air sorties and five B-52 raids supported.
- Two US Army men (Sergeant Womack and Private First Class Cfrats) were released by the enemy and returned to US control at Lai Khe in Binh Duong Province.

FEBRUARY 24, 1967

- USMACV announced the use of artillery based in the RVN against military targets in and N DMZ to supplement air strikes against military targets in the DMZ area.
- *Operation Junction City.* A 173rd Airborne unit located an enemy base camp containing two mess halls, three sleeping huts, five shelters, clothing and utensils.
- A USAF F-4 aircraft crashed from unknown causes. The pilots ejected and walked to a Special Forces camp. The aircraft was destroyed.
- North Vietnam. USN pilots hit Hon Gai and Bac Giang Thermal Power Plants.

FEBRUARY 25, 1967

- *Operation Junction City.* A Regiment or larger size enemy base camp was discovered.
- North Vietnam. USN A-6 aircraft re-struck Hon Gia and Bac Giang Thermal Power Plants.

FEBRUARY 26, 1967

- *Operation Junction City.* 25th Infantry Division units discovered and destroyed five enemy base camps, 192 fortified positions destroyed and 25 tons rice captured.

- Naval Gunfire-North Vietnam. USMACV announced in order to supplement air strikes against military targets; US surface ships in the Gulf of Tonkin were attacking military targets in North Vietnam.
- The first river minefield was laid in North Vietnam by TF-77 aircraft.

FEBRUARY 27, 1967

- USMACV announced that the US was emplacing air-delivered non-floating mines in selected river areas S part of North Vietnam. The action posed no danger to deepwater maritime traffic.
- An estimated 51 rounds of 140mm rockets hit Da Nang Air Base with some rounds hitting Ap Do village near the base. This was the first time the 140mm rocket was used in the RVN.
- *Operation Deckhouse VI.* Quang Ngai Province, USMC units of the Special Landing Force extracted from Sa Huynh February 26, 1967, landed over beaches 17 hours later, 25 kilometers N Sa Huynh extending operation. After an amphibious assault, other Special Landing Force units came ashore in a heli-borne assault from the Amphibious Assault Ship (Helicopter) (LPH) USS IWO JIMA.
- *Operation Enterprise.* Announced.

FEBRUARY 28, 1967

- *Operation Junction City.* A 1st Infantry Division squad engaged an enemy company. Artillery and tactical air supported, with heavy reinforcements committed. Results were 167 enemy killed and friendly casualties light. A 173rd Airborne Brigade unit found an enemy base camp including extensive bunker system, 30'x 60' mess hall, 18 huts with underground bomb shelters, 40' x 40' training hut, one fully equipped photo darkroom, one gas generator, one electric pump and miscellaneous equipment and papers. Other scattered action located 115 tons rice and three enemy base camps.

- North Vietnam. A USAF F-105 aircraft was downed by ground fire N Mu Gia Pass. The pilot was rescued.
- For the first time, radar-guided US jets bombed military sites in the panhandle and SE of Hanoi.
- The Mobile River Force (TF-117) was activated under command of COMNAVFORV.

MARCH 1, 1967

- US military strength in the RVN was 418,000.
- DOD stated that military court-martial jurisdiction would not apply to newsmen.
- North Vietnam. USN A-6 aircraft hit Chi Ne Army barracks twice resulting in heavy damage with numerous fires.
- Naval Gunfire-North Vietnam. The USS CANBERRA received 57mm fire resulting in light damage.

MARCH 2, 1967

- North Vietnam. USN A-4 aircraft hit Sam Son Army barracks resulting in damage to the barracks area.
- *Operation Prairie II.* Two USMC companies engaged an estimated NVA company WNW Dong Ha in the vicinity of Hill 124. The contact was heavy until enemy broke contact at 2200 hours. Enemy losses were 40 killed and friendly casualties light. The day's results were 109 enemy killed and 27 individual weapons captured. Friendly casualties were light.
- Quang Tri Province. USAF F-4 aircaft struck Lang Vei 2 Village. Eighty three VN civilians were killed, 176 VN civilians injured and 10 VN civilians missing.
- Dinh Tuong Province. A US artillery unit fired 11 rounds of 105mm hitting Trung Luong Village. Five VN civilians were killed and 24 VN civilians wounded. Twenty-four homes damaged or destroyed.

MARCH 3, 1967

- *Operation Prairie II.* An aerial observer observed an estimated 250 enemy on a trail in NW Quang Tri City and 50-60 more enemy one kilometer W. Artillery and air strikes called on both groups. Results were 70 enemy killed and no friendly casualties.

MARCH 5, 1967

- USMACV announced new procedures for reporting US casualties numerically for significant actions instead of light, moderate, heavy.

MARCH 6, 1967

- North Vietnam. USN A-6 aircraft hit Thanh Hoa railroad yard and Loi Dong POL storage area.
- Quang Tin Province. The enemy attacked Chu Lai Airfield with 30-35 round 82mm mortar fire. There was light aircraft damage.
- Camp Carroll was attacked by 102mm rockets. This is the first use by enemy of this type of rocket.

MARCH 7, 1967

- Naval Gunfire-North Vietnam. The USS CANBERRA , USS KEPPLER and the USS INGERSOLL, hit 17 enemy targets in the Ha Thinh area.
- *Operation Oh Jac Kyo I.* Elements of the 26th and 27th ROKA Regiment launched the 40-day search and destroy operation in Phu Yen Province. Friendly losses were 23 killed and 115 wounded. Enemy losses were 831 killed, 418 detained, 630 individual weapons and 29 crew-served weapons.

MARCH 8, 1967

- *Operation Game Warden.* In the Long Tau River, a USN PBR was rammed and cut in half by the British Merchant Ship DENY GRANGE.

MARCH 9, 1967

- The President acknowledged US jets based in Thailand were bombing North Vietnam.

MARCH 10, 1967

- North Vietnam. USAF F-105 aircraft hit the Thai Nguyen steel fabrication plant for the first time. Two MIGs were shot down. USN pilots flew strikes against Hon Gai thermal power plant.

- *Operation Junction City.* The Battle of Prek Klok II resulted in 197 Viet Cong killed, five detained. Friendly losses were one killed and 31 wounded.
- Ninh Thuan Province. A C-47 aircraft disintegrated in the air with 25 personnel aboard killed.

MARCH 11, 1967

- North Vietnam. USAF pilots hit the Thai Nguyen steel fabrication plant. USN pilots hit the Bac Giang thermal power plant.

MARCH 12, 1967

- North Vietnam. USAF F-105 and F-4 aircraft hit the Viet Tri thermal power plant (first strike this target).

MARCH 14, 1967

- *Operation Market Time.* The USN and USCG intercepted a 100-foot enemy steel-hulled trawler. The trawler beached NE Quang Ngai City. The trawler was destroyed by several explosions. Captured were 1,150 CHICOM carbines, 25 heavy machine guns, 29 light machine guns, 1-57mm recoilless rifle, 18 bolt action rifles, 7,000 rounds. 7.62 ammunition and 12 claymores.

MARCH 15, 1967

- A USN F-8 and USMC A-4 aircraft were downed in North Vietnam. The F-8 pilot is missing and the A-4 pilot rescued.
- Quang Nam Province. The enemy attacked Da Nang Air Base with over 10 rounds of 140mm Russian spin-stabilized rockets. Sixteen US were wounded. Aircraft and runway damage was negligible. Reaction forces located 23 launchers, 11 rockets in bush E bank Yen River, 11 kilometers SW of the Air Base.
- Phuoc Tuy Province. 1st Australian Task Force. Royal Australian Air Force Caribou and Iroquois aircraft conducted their first air strike in the conflict.

MARCH 16, 1967

- North Vietnam. USN A-6 aircraft hit Bac Giang thermal power plant.
- Rung Sat Special Zone. Long Tau River, the enemy attacked

the US cargo ship the SS CONQUEROR with 75mm recoilless rifle with six hits. The ship proceeded under own power.

MARCH 18, 1967

- North Vietnam. USN A-6 aircraft hit Thai Nguyen steel fabrication plant.
- *Operation Kitty Hawk.* Elements of the 9th Infantry Division launched the search and destroy operation in Long Khanh Province. This operation continued into1968.

MARCH 19, 1967

- North Vietnam. USAF F-105 aircraft hit the Thai Nguyen and Viet Tri Thermal Power Plants. USN A-6 aircraft hit the Thai Nguyen steel fabrication plant.
- A USMC F-4 aircraft was downed by ground fire. Both pilots are listed as missing. A USAF C-123 aircraft detonated a mine while taxiing at Vo Dat airfield, Binh Tuy Province. The nose wheel and under fuselage were damaged. There were no friendly casualties.
- *Operation Prairie III.* Elements of the 3rd Marine Division launched the 30-day search and destroy operation in Quang Tri Province. Friendly losses were 55 killed and 529 wounded. Enemy losses were 252 killed, 164 detained, one retained, 117 individual weapons and 11 crew-served weapons.

MARCH 20, 1967

- North Vietnam. USN A-6 aircraft hit the Thai Nguyen steel fabrication plant.
- *Operation Beacon Hill I.* A Search and destroy operation in Quang Tri Province with Marine units amphibious assault from 7th Fleet Special Landing Force. Marine units heli-assaulted to near Gio Linh Village, Quang Tri Province. Friendly losses were 29 killed and 230 wounded. Enemy losses were 334 killed, four detained, 29 individual weapons and three crew-served weapons.
- *Operation Prairie III.* A 3rd Marine unit located 136 rounds 102mm rockets with three launchers 27 kilometers WNW Quang Tri City. Rockets were the CHICOM version of the US 4.5-inch rocket.

- *Operation Junction City.* Battle of Bau Bang II resulted in 227 killed, three detained, three killed and 63 wounded.

MARCH 21, 1967

- North Vietnam. USN A-6 aircraft hit the Thai Nguyen steel fabrication plant.
- The enemy attacked Gio Linh with more than 720 mortar, rocket and artillery rounds. Friendly casualties were 49 wounded. There was light damage to the installation and equipment.
- *Operation Junction City.* Battle of Suoi Tre. A 3rd Brigade, 4th Infantry Division battalion engaged five enemy battalions (3,000 men). The US reinforced the battalion. At mid-morning the enemy began to withdraw to the NE and SE. Artillery and tactical air supported against the retreating enemy. Enemy losses were 654 Viet Cong killed, 135 individual weapons, 43 crew-served weapons, 580 RPG rockets and 1,900 stick grenades. Friendly losses were 31 killed and 187 wounded. The USAF supported the operation with 117 direct support sorties.

MARCH 22, 1967

- *Operation Junction City.* Enemy losses were 198 killed.
- *Operation New Castle.* Elements of the 5th Marine Regiment launched the three-day search and destroy operation in Quang Nam Province. Friendly losses were five killed and 55 wounded. Enemy losses were 118 killed, 35 detained and three individual weapons.
- USAF F-4 and F-100 aircraft attacked a large enemy troop concentration at Quang Ngai City resulting in 160 enemy killed.

MARCH 23, 1967

- North Vietnam. USN A-6 aircraft hit the Thai Nguyen thermal power plant.
- Da Nang Air Base. A USAF C-141 and USMC A-6 aircraft collided on E runway which resulted in five USAF killed, two USMC injured, one USAF injured. Both aircraft were destroyed.
- *Operation Sam Houston.* Ninety-four enemy bodies were found.

MARCH 25, 1967

- North Vietnam. USN A-6 aircraft hit the Bac Giang thermal power plant and Thai Nguyen steel plant.
- *Operation Prairie III.* A 9th Marine company located a grave with 31 enemy bodies (including two females) dressed in NVA uniforms NW Quang Tri City.
- Naval Gunfire-RVN. The DD USS OZBOURN was hit twice by enemy shore fire with no friendly casualties and light damage.

MARCH 26, 1967

- North Vietnam. One MIG-17 was downed by F-105.

MARCH 27, 1967

- *Operation De Soto.* SE Quang Ngai City. A USMC helicopter observed and attacked 30 enemy hiding in shallow water with bamboo breathing tubes, 26 enemy killed, four detained and no friendly casualties.

MARCH 28, 1967

- Thirteen USMC were killed and one injured during an accidentally detonated M-16 in a mine warfare class.

MARCH 31, 1967

- *Operation Junction City.* A major contact estimated NE Tay Ninh City by 1st Brigade, 1st Infantry Division elements. The contact continued.
- The Australian destroyer, HMAS HOBART, arrived and joined US Naval forces off the coast of North Vietnam.
- Phu Cat's new 10,000-foot jet capable airfield opened.

APRIL 1, 1967

- *Operation Beacon Hill I.* Terminated.
- *Operation Boone.* Announced.
- *Operation Junction City.* Battle of Ap Bu resulted in 608 Viet Cong killed, five detained, 47 individual weapons and six crew-served weapons. Friendly losses were 11 killed and 77 wounded.
- US military strength in the RVN was 443,000.

APRIL 2, 1967

- The first medical evacuation (medevac) mission to the US was flown from Da Nang.
- *Operation Adams.* Elements of the 1st Brigade, 4th Infantry Division terminated the 59-day crop protection and search and destroy operation in Phu Yen Province that commenced October 25, 1966. Friendly losses were 46 killed and 278 wounded. Enemy losses were 491 killed, 2,046 detained and 33 retained.

APRIL 3, 1967

- *Operation Summerall.* Announced.
- *Operation Portsea.* Announced.

APRIL 4, 1967

- *Operation Chinook II.* Terminated.
- *Operation Oh Jak Kyo.* Fifty-eight enemy were killed, 31 individual weapons and 31 radios captured.

APRIL 5, 1967

- North Vietnam. USN pilots hit thermal power plant 32 kilometers NE Hanoi.
- *Operation Oh Jak Kyo.* Seventy-eight of the enemy killed and 95 individual weapons captured.
- *Operation Francis Marion.* Elements of the 4th and 25th Infantry Divisions launched the 190-day search and destroy operation in Pleiku Province. Friendly losses were 183 killed, 843 wounded and 10 missing. Enemy losses were 1,203 killed, 1,092 detained, 11 retained, 299 individual weapons and 66 crew-served weapons.

APRIL 6, 1967

- An unknown number of Viet Cong attacked the Quang Tri Province jail and released 220 prisoners (enemy guerrillas and cadre). Friendly losses were 99 killed and 138 wounded. Enemy losses were 77 killed.
- *Operation Canyon.* Announced.
- *Operation Francis Marion.* The enemy attacked the 4th Infantry

Division with light concentration riot control agent (powdered gas dispensed from packets and bottles).

APRIL 7, 1967

- North Vietnam. USN pilots night attacked at Thai Nguyen steel complex.
- Naval Gunfire-North Vietnam. The USS TURNER JOY received a hit from an enemy shore battery SSE Thanh Hoa on the after-part main deck which resulted in minor damage and one USN wounded.
- *Operation Oh Jak Kyo.* Results were 52 enemy killed and 15 detained. Seventy-one individual weapons and three crew-served weapons were captured.
- *Operation Wailua.* Terminated.
- *Operation Le Jeune.* Elements of the 5th Cavalry and 7th Marine Regiment launched the 15-day search and destroy operation in Quang Ngai Province. Friendly losses were 17 killed and 65 wounded. Enemy losses were 181 killed, 17 detained, 15 individual weapons and one crew-served weapon.

APRIL 8, 1967

- *Operation Oh Jak Kyo.* Results were 62 enemy killed, 38 individual weapons and four crew-served weapons captured.
- *Operation Portsea.* A 9th Infantry Division company found a large tunnel complex containing two light machine guns, 23 submachine guns, 10 rifles, three AR, 12 carbines, one revolver, 201,000+ pounds grenades, 3,000+ pounds TNT and 16 bangalore torpedoes.

APRIL 10, 1967

- North Vietnam. USN pilots night attacked Thai Nguyen.
- *Operation Big Horn.* Announced.
- *Operation Canyon.* Terminated.
- The USS SANCTUARY (hospital ship) arrived at Da Nang.
- The first B-52 aircraft land at U Tapao, Thailand.

APRIL 11, 1967

- *Operation Enterprise.* Contact continued from April 9, 1967 SW Saigon with 207 enemy killed and one US.

- Last operational flight of the P5M Marlin seaplane from Cam Ranh Bay Seadrome.

APRIL 12, 1967

- The enemy attacked Chu Lai airstrip with 30-40 rounds of 82mm mortar fire. Results were two US killed and 45 wounded. Light aircraft and equipment were damaged.
- Nha Trang harbor. British POL tanker SS AMASTRA had an external explosion below the waterline with the stern resting on bottom in 60 feet of water. There were no casualties.
- Task Force Oregon. Consisting of the 3rd Brigade, 25th Infantry Division and the 196th Infantry Brigade, activated to reinforce the III MAF units in the I CTZ.

APRIL 13, 1967

- A 75-foot span of Nam O Bridge over Cu De River collapsed by unknown size explosion.
- Cam Ranh Bay. A USAF C-141 crashed into the bay on take-off with two injured and seven missing.

APRIL 14, 1967

- The 196th Light Infantry Brigade, under operational control 1st Marine Division, completed air movement from Tay Ninh Province to Chu Lai.

APRIL 15, 1967

- Binh Dinh Province. NW Qui Nhon, two F-100 aircraft on a preplanned night radar control mission dropped ordnance off target. ARVN casualties were 35 killed and 69 wounded.
- *Operation Portsea.* The 1st Brigade, 9th Infantry Division terminated their portion of the operation.
- Kien Hoa Province. In the vicinity of Truc Giang, an F-100 aircraft accidentally bombed Chieu Hoi Village. Results were 14 killed, 25 wounded, five houses destroyed or damaged.
- The GVN announced a plan to evacuate 20,000 civilians from the area close to the DMZ to allow construction of a fortified barrier.
- USCGCs BARATARIA, BERING STRAIT AND GRESHAM

arrived off the RVN to replace the Seventh Fleet DERs on *Operation Market Time* patrol.

APRIL 16, 1967

- *Operation Lejeune.* Announced.
- *Operation Portsea.* Terminated.
- *Operation Junction City.* Terminated Phase II. Phase III initiated.

APRIL 17, 1967

- Cholon. At 0610 hours, two grenades exploded at a bus stop in front of the Colosseum Annex Bachelor Enlisted Quarters (BEQ), 10 USN wounded. A claymore mine was found 20 meters away and an EOD team disarmed.

APRIL 18, 1967

- North Vietnam. USAF F-105 and F-4 aircraft hit Thai Nguyen railroad yard and steel complex.
- *Operation Oh Jak Kyo.* Phase I terminated. The 26th and 28th ROKA Regiment units launched the 43-day search and destroy operation in Phu Yen Province. Friendly losses were 21 killed and 50 wounded. Enemy losses were 109 killed, 17 detained, 28 retained and 51 individual weapons.
- *Operation Harvest Moon.* Announced.

APRIL 19, 1967

- North Vietnam. USAF reported 17 MIG engagements with one MIG-21, three MIG-17s were downed by F-105s.
- *Operation Prairie III.* Terminated.
- Eight Australian Canberra (B-57) bombers of Squadron Number 2 arrived at Phan Rang Air Base to make Australia the second country to support the RVN with a tri-service contingent.

APRIL 20, 1967

- North Vietnam. USN pilots hit Haiphong W and E power plants. USAF F-4 aircraft destroyed a 60-car train.
- Quang Tri Province. A Marine reconnaissance element found a weapons cache (200 rounds of 82mm mortar, 100 CHICOM

grenades, 25 individual weapons with additional ammunition and fuses).

- Rung Sat Special Zone. Long Tau River SE Saigon, the enemy attacked a USN LST with 75mm recoilless rifle fire. The ship was hit in the superstructure. The LST proceeded to Nha Be under own power.
- The 7th Royal Australian Regiment arrived RVN at Nui Dat.
- *Operation Union.* Elements of the 1st, 3rd and 5th Marine Regiment launched the 26-day search and destroy operation in Quang Nam and Quang Tin Provinces. Friendly losses were 110 killed and 473 wounded. Enemy losses were 865 killed, 351 detained, 64 individual weapons and eight crew-served weapons.
- Operation Prairie IV. Elements of the 3rd Marine Division launched the 41-day search and destroy operation in Quang Tri Province. Friendly losses were 164 killed and 1,240 wounded. Enemy losses were 764 killed, 94 detained, 128 individual weapons and 22 crew-served weapons.
- Seventh Royal Australian Regiment arrived in the RVN at Nui Dat.
- USN aircraft struck inside the 10-mile restricted zone of the port city of Haiphong for the first time. An electric power plant was destroyed and the entire city was left in darkness.

APRIL 21, 1967

- *Operation Big Horn.* Terminated.
- *Task Force Oregon.* Joined III MAF units in I CORPS. Under operational control of the III MAF.
- *Operation Lejeune.* Terminated.
- *Operation Makalapa.* Terminated.

APRIL 22, 1967

- *Operation Grand.* Announced.
- *Operation Prairie IV.* Announced.
- A USAF B-57 aircraft was downed by ground fire SE Saigon. The pilot was killed and the navigator rescued.
- CG Task Force Oregon located at Chu Lai, I CTZ, assumed

operational control of the 3rd Brigade, 25th Infantry Division and the 196th Light Infantry Brigade.

- *Operation Manhattan.* Elements of the 25th Infantry Division launched the 46-day search and destroy operation in Binh Duong Province. Friendly losses were 47 killed and 327 wounded. Enemy losses were 191 killed, 370 detained, 28 retained, 614 individual weapons and 14 crew-served weapons.
- *Operation Shawnee.* Elements of the 4th Marine Regiment launched the 30-day search and destroy operation in Thua Thien Province. Friendly losses were 13 killed and 139 wounded. Enemy losses were 128 killed, 60 detained and 80 individual weapons.

APRIL 23, 1967

- North Vietnam. USAF F105 and F4 aircraft hit the Thai Nguyen steel mill coke production and foundry.
- USAF F-4 aircraft downed one MIG-21 and one probable.
- *Operation Beacon Star.* Announced.

APRIL 24, 1967

- USN A-4, A-6, F-8 aircraft hit Kep airfield. USAF F-4 aircraft hit Hoa Lac airfield. USN F-4s downed two MIG-17s.
- *Operation Shawnee.* Announced.
- *Operation Manhattan.* Initiated.

APRIL 25, 1967

- North Vietnam. USAF pilots hit railroad repair yards ENE Hanoi, transformer site N Hanoi. USN pilots hit a cement plant 1/8 kilometers W Haiphong. A MIG-17 was downed by USN A-4 aircraft.

APRIL 26, 1967

- USAF pilots hit railroad/highway bridge six kilometers NE Hanoi, and main transformer site 11 kilometers N Hanoi. USN pilots hit POL storage area 3.2 kilometers SW Haiphong.
- *Operation Grand.* Terminated.
- CG 1st Marine Division turned over responsibility for defense of the Chu Lai installation to CG Task Force Oregon.

APRIL 27, 1967

- *Operation Manhattan.* Three supply caches were found consisting of 71 tons rice, 50 CHICOM rifles, seven Browning Automatic Rifles, seven machine guns, two .30-caliber machine guns, and 45,000 rounds small arms.
- *Operation Puckapunyal.* Initiated.

APRIL 28, 1967

- North Vietnam. USAF pilots reported 21 MIG sightings with six engagements. Two MIG-17s were downed by F-105 aircraft.
- The enemy attacked a 9th Marine command post NW Quang Tri City with 50 rounds 40mm rocket fire. Marine units found 30 firing positions with 50 rocket rounds. Results were nine US killed and 51 wounded.
- *Operation Beaver Cage.* Initiated. The Special Landing Force launched the 15-day search and destroy operation in Quang Tin Province. Friendly losses were 56 killed and 183 wounded. Enemy losses were 181 killed, 66 detained, 10 individual weapons, one crew-served weapon.
- *Operation Manhattan.* The 1st Infantry Division found enemy caches (25 30-pound mines, 900 grenades, 200 rounds 60/82mm mortar and 300 mortar fuses).

APRIL 29, 1967

- North Vietnam. US pilots, Naval gunfire and long range Army artillery destroy surface-to-air missile complex 10 kilometers N of the DMZ. This was furthest south surface-to-air missiles have been located to date.
- *Operation Summerall.* Terminated.

APRIL 30, 1967

- North Vietnam. A USAF F-105 aircraft downed a MIG-17.
- NW Khe Sanh, two 3rd Marine battalions engaged an entrenched enemy on Hill 881. Interim results were 180 enemy killed. The contact continued.
- USS GALLUP (PG-85), the first of a new class of high speed,

diesel-turbine powered gunboats, arrives at Cam Ranh Bay for *Operation Market Time* duty.

MAY 1, 1967

- US military strength in the RVN was 460,000.
- North Vietnam. USN pilots hit Kep airfield. Three MIG-17s were destroyed, one damaged on the ground. Two MIG-17s were destroyed, two damaged in air by USN F-8 and F-4 aircraft. USAF pilots hit Hoa Lac airfield. Five MIG-17s were destroyed on the ground, one MIG-17 was downed by USAF F-4 aircraft. This was the first attack against NVN airfields.
- The Battle of Khe Sanh, Quang Tri Province resulted in 160 enemy killed and 26 bunkers destroyed. The contact continued.
- *Operation Beaver Cage.* To operational control III MAF.
- *Operation Francis Marion.* A 2nd Brigade, 4th Infantry Division company+ fought a daylong battle with an enemy battalion. 75,000+ rounds small arms ammunition captured.
- *Operation Puckapunyal.* Announced and terminated.
- US strike pilots flew 625 tactical air sorties in the RVN (new high). USAF F-100 aircraft downed by ground fire, crew rescued.

MAY 2, 1967

- North Vietnam. A USAF F-105 aircraft was downed by ground fire, pilot rescued.
- *Operation Palm Beach.* A 3rd Brigade, 9th Infantry Division battalion was in heavy contact with a 514th Viet Cong battalion. The 199th Light Infantry Brigade moved to reinforce. Enemy losses were 181 killed. Contact continued.

MAY 3, 1967

- North Vietnam. USAF pilots hit Hoa Lac airfield with four to six MIG-17s destroyed or damaged on ground.
- Battle of Khe Sanh, Quang Tri Province. Enemy losses were

111 enemy killed, 29 individual weapons and nine crew-served weapons were captured. Friendly losses were 20 US killed.

- *Operation Manhattan.* 1st Infantry Division elements found cache (3,500 60/82 mortar rounds, 40 rounds 57mm recoilless rifle, 500 rifle grenades, 400 hand grenades, 270 mines, 100+ pounds TNT, 297,625 rounds small arms, 1,600 mortar primer rounds, 100 time bombs, 220 mausers, 147 CHICOM carbines and 20 tons rice captured).
- *Operation Palm Beach.* Contact continued from May 1, 1967, terminated 1130 hours. Results were 195 enemy killed and 19 US. Seventeen individual weapons and crew-served weapons were captured.
- USS GALLUP, a new design patrol gunboat, begins *Operation Market Time* patrols.

MAY 4, 1967

- North Vietnam. A USAF F-4 aircraft downed a MIG-21. A USN A-4 aircraft was downed by ground fire. The pilot is missing.
- Battle of Khe Sanh. Elements of the NVA 325th Division believed to have been in action against Marines at Hill 881. Enemy losses were 561 killed. Friendly losses were 133 US killed and 383 US wounded.

MAY 5, 1967

- North Vietnam. USAF pilots hit a surface-to-air missile transporter with three surface-to-air missiles 51 kilometers SSE of Dong Hoi. The transporter and two surface-to-air missiles were destroyed. There were six secondary explosions. USMC jets destroyed a surface-to-air missile transporter.
- *Operation Panhandle.* Three USAF F-105 aircraft were downed by ground fire with the crews missing.
- USMC BLT 2/3 took Hill 881 near Khe Sanh.

MAY 6, 1967

- North Vietnam. A USN A-4 aircraft was downed by ground fire with the pilot missing.
- *Operation Union.* Announced. Results to date were 327 enemy killed.

MAY 7, 1967

- The enemy attacked Binh Thuy airfield with mortar fire. Moderate aircraft and installation were damaged. There were no friendly casualties.

MAY 8, 1967

- North Vietnam. A USAF F-105 aircraft was downed by ground fire, pilot missing, USAF hit Hoa Lac Airfield.
- *Operation Prairie IV.* Heavy contact Hill 158. Interim casualties: 198 enemy killed and 115 weapons captured. Friendly casualties were 44 killed, 110 wounded. CIDG casualties were light.
- The enemy launched coordinated attacks at Dong Ha (25 rounds 140mm rocket fire, five US wounded), Gio Linh (150 rounds of 81/82mm mortar and 105mm artillery fire, 10 US wounded with light damage), Camp Carroll (102mm rocket fire, five US wounded).
- *Operation Lismore.* Announced and terminated.

MAY 9, 1967

- Khe Sanh. A 3rd Marine company located 203 NVA bodies in graves.

MAY 10, 1967

- North Vietnam. USN pilots hit Kien An airfield, Haiphong thermal power plant E, and Haiphong thermal power plant W. A USN A-4 aircraft was downed by ground fire in the vicinity of Kien An airfield, pilot missing.
- *Operations Union/Beaver Cage.* Both operations combined for the day. A 3rd Marine company reinforced with 5th Marine companies engaged a multi-company NVA force Hill 110. The Hill was secured. Results were 211 enemy killed. Friendly casualties were 33 killed and 133 wounded.
- *Operation Malheur.* Elements of the 101st Airborne Division launched the 28-day search and destroy operation in Quang Ngai Province. Friendly losses were 51 killed and 285 wounded. Enemy losses were 392 killed, 305 detained, 151 individual weapons and 11 crew-served weapons.
- A USAF F-100 aircraft was downed by ground fire. The pilot

was killed. A USMC A-4 aircraft was downed by ground fire over the DMZ. The pilot was rescued.

- Naval Gunfire-RVN. The USS HUNTERDON COUNTY (LST) destroyed an enemy vessel S Phu Vinh.

MAY 11, 1967

- RVN. A USMC A-4 aircraft was downed by ground fire with the pilot rescued.

MAY 12, 1967

- North Vietnam. A USAF F-4 aircraft was downed by a MIG-17, two F-105 aircraft downed (one by ground fire, one by unknown causes), pilots missing.
- *Operation Union.* 1st Battalion, 5th Marine multi-company force engaged the enemy in the vicinity of Hill 110. The contact continues.
- *Operation Prairie IV.* A Marine company located a suspected guidance system for a Russian surface-to-air missile 2.4 kilometers SW Con Thien. Dimensions: 9' long, 2' diameter. Item was forwarded to the US for evaluation.
- *Operation Beacon Star.* Terminated.
- The enemy attacked Bien Hoa airfield with 125 rounds of 122mm rocket, 82mm mortar and 75mm recoilless rifle fire. Results were six US killed and 85 US wounded. There was also moderate damage to installation, equipment and aircraft.

MAY 13, 1967

- North Vietnam. USAF pilots downed seven MIG-17s.
- *Operation Union.* Contact occurred in the vicinity of Hill 110 from May 12, 1967. Enemy losses were 138 enemy killed.
- *Operation Malheur.* Announced.
- *Operation Beaver Cage.* Terminated.
- A New Zealand troop increment arrived in the RVN at Nui Dat.
- *Operation Crocket.* Elements of the 26th Marine Division launched the 64-day search and destroy operation in Quang Tri Province. Friendly losses were 53 killed and 255 wounded. Enemy losses were 206 killed, five detained, 23 individual weapons and three crew-served weapons.
- *Operation Kole Kole.* Elements of the 25th Infantry Division

launched the 208-day search and destroy operation in Hau Nghia Province. Friendly losses were 92 killed, 640 wounded and 12 individual weapons. Enemy losses were 645 killed, 1,232 detained, 30 retained, 286 individual weapons and five crew-served weapons.

MAY 14, 1967

- North Vietnam. USAF F-4 aircraft downed three MIG-17s in the vicinity of Hanoi. A USAF F-105 aircraft was downed by ground fire and the pilot rescued. A USN F-4 aircraft was downed by unknown causes with the crew missing. Ha Dong Army barracks and Kien An airfield were struck.
- *Operation Union.* Seventy-three of the enemy killed bodies were uncovered.
- *Operation Junction City.* Terminated.
- *Operation Ala Moana.* Units of the 2nd Brigade, 27th Infantry terminated the 165-day search and destroy operation in Hau Nghia Province, which commenced November 30, 1966. Friendly losses were 47 killed and 158 wounded. Enemy losses were 382 killed, 666 detained, 93 individual weapons and five crew-served weapons.
- *Operation Harvest Moon.* Terminated.
- A USAF F-100 aircraft was downed by ground fire S Bien Hoa with the pilot rescued.

MAY 15, 1967

- North Vietnam. A USAF F-105 aircraft was downed by ground fire with the two-man crew missing.
- *Operation Union.* Final results of the action in the vicinity of Hill 110: 381 enemy killed, 41 US. 150 US were wounded.

MAY 16, 1967

- *Operation Prairie IV.* Two kilometers E Con Thien, a 26th Marine company plus engaged a company in prepared positions. Enemy losses were 73 enemy killed. Friendly losses were 15 killed and 60 wounded.
- *Operation Barking Sands.* Elements of the 1st Brigade, 25th Infantry Division launched the 204-day search and destroy operation in Binh Duong Province. Friendly losses were 152 killed, 1,060 wounded, four individual weapons and one crew-

served weapon. Enemy losses were 304 killed, 2,036 detained, five retained, 209 individual weapons and 18 crew-served weapons.

- The 11th Marine NW Da Nang received 11 rounds of 140mm rocket fire, 31 rocket launchers, 16 rocket rounds captured. Friendly casualties were two wounded.
- A USMC F-4 aircraft was downed by friendly fire during a bombing run. The two-man crew was rescued.

MAY 17, 1967

- North Vietnam. The USN struck Kep airfield. A USN F-8 aircraft was downed by unknown causes with the pilot missing.
- *Operation Union.* Terminated.
- *Operation Hickory.* Units of the 9th Marine Regiment launched the 11-day search and destroy operation in Quang Tri Province. Friendly losses were 119 killed and 811 wounded. Enemy losses were 367 killed, 36 detained, 86 individual weapons and 22 crew-served weapons.
- *Operation Diamond Head.* Elements of the 3rd Brigade, 25th Infantry Division launched the 204-day search and destroy operation in Binh Duong Province. Friendly losses were 80 killed, and 605 wounded. Enemy losses were 237 killed, 459 detained, four retained, 104 individual weapons and two crew-served weapons.
- Naval Forces. Three 311-foot USCGCs arrived and serving with Operation *Market Time* forces. US Coast Guard in-country strength now is 800+.
- VNN PCE-12 begins *Operation Market* time patrol in the Second Coastal Zone.

MAY 18, 1967

- North Vietnam. A USN A-4 aircraft downed by ground fire with the pilot missing.
- *Operations Hickory/Beau Charger/Lamson 54.* Initiated. A search and destroy operation S of the DMZ. This is the first US entry into the DMZ in force.
- *Operation Thunder Dragon.* The 2nd Brigade, ROKMC launched the nine-day search and destroy operation in Quang Ngai

Province. Friendly losses were 15 killed (one USMC) and 45 wounded. Enemy losses were 147 killed, six detained, seven individual weapons and two crew-served.

- The enemy attacked positions Gio Linh with 200 rounds 82mm mortar, 30 rounds 120mm mortar and 58 rounds artillery fire. Friendly casualties were one killed and 12 wounded. The enemy attacked the 3rd Marine Division base Dong Ha with 400 rounds 140mm rocket and 122mm artillery fire. Moderate damaged structures with light damaged vehicles and aircraft. Friendly casualties were 11 killed and 91 wounded.
- 9th Marine elements found 27 enemy bodies NNE Con Thien, 177 rounds 82mm mortar, five machine guns, four AK-47s, seven carbines, three rocket launchers and 125 grenades.

MAY 19, 1967

- North Vietnam. USN F-8 aircraft downed four MIG-17s, damaged one. Five USN F-8s and A-1s lost over North Vietnam with the pilots missing. USN pilots struck Hanoi thermal power plant. USAF pilots hit Hoa Lac and Kep Army barracks.
- *Operation Hickory.* 4th Marine units discovered an eight-ton ammunition cache and 10 tons of rice.
- Naval Gunfire-RVN. The cruisers USS ST PAUL and USS BOSTON, DDs USS SUMNER, USS STRAUSS, USS FLECHTELER and HMAS HOBART hit enemy artillery and gun positions in the DMZ.

MAY 20, 1967

- North Vietnam. USAF F-4 aircraft downed six MIGs. F-4 and RF-101 aircraft downed over North Vietnam with the crews missing. The USN damaged Haiphong thermal power plant and Bac Giang thermal power plant.
- First O-2 aircraft, twin-engine Cessna successor t the O-1 "Birddog" forward air controller aircraft, arrives in-country in Nha Trang.
- *Operation Lam Son 54.* NE Con Thien ARVN forces engaged an enemy battalion in a daylong battle resulting in 250 enemy killed.

MAY 21, 1967

- North Vietnam. USN pilots hit a Hanoi thermal power plant and Kep airfield. Three MIGs were burning on the ground. USAF pilots hit Hoa Lac airfield. USN F-4 aircraft and HS-3 rescue helicopter were downed by ground fire. All crews were rescued.
- *Operation Shawnee.* Terminated.
- B-52 aircraft struck six times in the RVN.

MAY 22, 1967

- North Vietnam. USAF F-4 aircraft downed two MIG-21s, and hit Hanoi transformer site. Two USAF F-4s and O-1 were downed by ground fire with one pilot rescued.
- *Operation Dallas.* Announced.
- *Operation Wellington.* Announced and terminated.
- A USAF F-100 aircraft was downed by ground fire with the pilot missing.

MAY 23, 1967

- Buddha's birthday, stand down 0001-2400 hours. Summary of truce incidents: total 71 incidents, 32 friendly casualties, 12 killed and 57 wounded, 51 enemy killed and 16 detained.

MAY 24, 1967

- North Vietnam. USAF B-57 aircraft hit an ammunition storage area S Dong Hoi with 25 secondary explosions reported. A USN A-4 aircraft was downed by ground fire with the pilot rescued.

MAY 25, 1967

- North Vietnam. USAF pilots attacked Kep, VA Chua, Bac Le railroad yards NE Hanoi, USN pilots hit Phu Ly railroad yard. A USN A-1aircraft was downed by unknown causes, pilot killed.
- In Quang Tri Province, 9600 refugees from Gio Linh were at Cam Lo settlement. VN and USMC elements provided necessities for refugees.
- *Operation Crockett.* Announced.
- *Operation Choctaw.* Announced.
- *Operation Dallas.* Terminated.
- *Operation Union II.* Elements of the 5th Marine Regiment

launched the 11-day search and destroy operation in Quang Nam and Quang Tin Provinces. Friendly losses were 110 killed and 241 wounded. Enemy losses were 701 killed, 40 detained, 19 individual weapons and 12 crew-served weapons.

- Naval Gunfire-RVN. The cruiser USS PROVIDENCE was hit by an enemy shore battery fired from the DMZ receiving superficial damage to main mast and no casualties. Fire was returned and the batteries silenced.

MAY 26, 1967

- North Vietnam. USN hit Kep airfield, a Haiphong thermal power plant W and Uong Bi thermal power plant. Three MIGs were damaged at Kep. USAF pilots hit Hoa Lac airfield. A USN A-4 aircraft was downed by ground fire, pilot missing.
- *Operation Union II.* Announced. The 5th Marines were engaged in heavy contact. Results were 171 enemy killed and 28 friendly.
- *Operation Beau Charger.* Terminated.
- *Operation Francis Marion.* In the vicinity of Hill 521, a 1st Brigade, 4th Infantry Division company killed 98 NVA, captured 28 individual weapons and 10 crew-served weapons. Friendly casualties were 10 killed and 54 wounded.

MAY 27, 1967

- North Vietnam. A USAF F-105 aircraft was downed by ground fire with the pilot missing.
- *Operation Lam Son 54.* Terminated.
- *Operation Thunder Dragon.* Announced. Terminated.
- *Operation Diamond Head.* Announced.
- *Operation Barking Sands.* Announced.
- Naval Gunfire-RVN. The DD USS EDSON was hit off the coast of the DMZ with one round, resulting in damage to radar and antenna. Ten US were wounded, none serious.

MAY 28, 1967

- *Operation Hickory.* Terminated.

MAY 30, 1967

- North Vietnam. USAF pilots hit Hoa Lac airfield. USN pilots destroyed a Phu Ly railroad bridge. USAF F-4 aircraft was downed by ground fire with the crew rescued. A USN A-4 aircraft was downed by ground fire with the pilot missing.

- The 2nd Royal Australian Regiment relieved the 6th Battalion, Royal Australian Regiment.
- A USMC A-4 aircraft was downed by ground fire W Tam Ky with the pilot killed.

MAY 31, 1967

- North Vietnam. USN pilots hit Cong My and Loi Dong POL storage and transshipment areas three to five miles NW Haiphong. USAF pilots hit Kep Army barracks and railroad yards. A USN A-4 aircraft was downed to unknown causes, pilot missing.
- *Operation Oh Jak Kyo II.* Terminated.
- *Operation Prairie IV.* Terminated.
- *Operation Hop Tac.* The 3rd Brigade, 9th Infantry Division launched the search and destroy operation in Dinh Tuong Province.
- *Operation Cimarron.* Elements of the 3rd, 4th, 9th, and 26th Marine Regiments launched the 32-day search and destroy operation in Quang Tri Province. Friendly losses were 38 killed and 470 wounded. Enemy losses were 245 killed, 176 detained, 58 individual weapons and 10 crew-served weapons.

JUNE 1, 1967

- US military strength in RVN was 484,000.
- The VN Air Force received a squadron of F-5 Freedom Fighter aircraft.
- North Vietnam. USN pilots hit Do Xa transshipment and storage area.
- *Operation Cimarron.* Initiated.
- *Operation Palm Beach.* Terminated.
- *Operation Coronado.* Elements of the 2nd Brigade, 9th Infantry Division and TF-117 launched the 54-day day search and destroy operation in Dinh Tuong Province. Friendly losses were 40 killed, 173 wounded, 41 individual weapons and one crew-

served weapon. Enemy losses were 478 killed, 526 detained, 75 retained, 52 individual weapons and five crew-served weapons.

JUNE 2, 1967

- North Vietnam. A USAF F-105 aircraft was downed by ground fire. An F-4 aircraft was downed by unknown causes with three crewmen missing.
- *Operation Union II.* Twenty kilometers NW Tam Ky, a 5th Marine multi-battalion force engaged an enemy force in fortified positions. The day's results were 117 enemy killed. Contact continued.
- *Operation Bear Bite.* Initiated.

JUNE 3, 1967

- North Vietnam. USAF pilots hit a Bac Giang railroad yard. An F-105 aircraft was downed two MIG-17s. A USAF B-57 aircraft was downed from unknown causes. A two-man crew was missing.
- *Operation Union II.* Contact continued from June 2, 1967. Contact broke at 1530 hours. Results were 54 enemy killed and 73 US in two-day battle.

JUNE 4, 1967

- North Vietnam. A USAF F-105 aircraft was downed by ground fire with the pilot rescued.

JUNE 5, 1967

- North Vietnam. USAF F-4 aircraft downed three MIG-17s. A USN F-8 aircraft was downed by ground fire with the pilot missing.
- *Operation Union II.* Terminated.
- *Operation Matu II.* The 28th ROKA Regiment launched the 15-day search and destroy operation in Phu Yen Province. Friendly losses were light. Enemy losses were 139 killed, 12 detained, 78 individual weapons and 12 crew-served weapons.

JUNE 6, 1967

- North Vietnam. A USN F-8 aircraft was downed by ground fire, pilot rescued.
- At English airfield, fire broke out in a support area. Light

damaged aircraft with heavy loss POL, ammunition and rations. Results were two US killed and 39 injured. The cause was unknown.

- *Operation Bluefield.* Announced.
- *Operation Hoptac.* Announced.
- *Operation Game Warden.* Vinh Long Province. Two USN PBRs engaged seven enemy sampans. Results were nine enemy killed, seven sampans destroyed. There were no friendly casualties.

JUNE 7, 1967

- North Vietnam. USN pilots hit Kep airfield, destroyed one MIG, and damaged four on the ground. USN pilots hit a surface-to-air missile storage area SW Hanoi, destroyed nine loaded missile transporters, one radar van, one POL truck, one oxidizer truck. There were numerous secondary explosions.
- *Operation Manhattan.* Terminated.
- *Operation Malheur II.* Elements of the 1st Brigade, 101st Airborne Division launched the 56-day search and destroy operation in Quang Ngai Province. Friendly losses were 30 killed, 260 wounded, four individual weapons, one crew-served weapon. Enemy losses were 488 killed, 589 killed, 589 detained, six retained, 141 individual weapons and seven crew-served weapons.

JUNE 8, 1967

- North Vietnam. USAF F-4 aircraft was downed by ground fire with the two-man crew missing.
- *Operation Malheur.* Terminated
- *Operation Malheur II.* Initiated.

JUNE 9, 1967

- North Vietnam. USAF pilots hit Kep and Bac Le railroad yards. A USAF F-4 aircraft was downed by ground fire with the two-man crew rescued.
- *Operation Bluefield.* Terminated.
- North Vietnam. A B-57 aircraft crashed SW Cam Ranh Bay with the crew missing.

JUNE 10, 1967

- North Vietnam. USN pilots hit a Hanoi thermal power plant.

USAF pilots hit Kep and Bac Le railroad yards. USN F-8 and A-4 aircraft were downed by ground fire with the pilots missing.

- Thirty enemy were killed in a battle to secure area of the B-57 aircraft crash June 9, 1967 with the crew killed. The wreckage was secured.
- Quang Tri Province. A USMC CH-46 helicopter exploded in air from unknown causes with 12 US killed.

JUNE 11, 1967

- North Vietnam. USN pilots hit Kep airfield (destroyed two MIGs, damaged two on ground) and Uong Bi thermal power plant. USAF pilots destroyed or damaged 90-100 railroad cars. A USN F-8 and a USAF A-1 aircraft downed by friendly fire, crew rescued.
- *Operation Colgate.* Terminated.

JUNE 12, 1967

- North Vietnam. USN pilots hit a Than Hoa thermal power plant. A USAF F-4 was downed by friendly fire with the crew rescued.
- *Operation Billings.* Elements of the 1st Infantry Division launched the 14-day search and destroy operation in Binh Long, Phuoc Long and Binh Duong Provinces. Enemy losses were 347 killed, two detained, four individual weapons and four crew-served weapons.

JUNE 13, 1967

- North Vietnam. USAF pilots hit Kep airfield (destroyed or damaged six MIG-17s on ground) and Kep railroad yard (destroyed or damaged 15-20 railroad cars). Forty-five railroad cars were destroyed or damaged in two other strikes.
- *Operation Chapman.* Terminated.
- A USAF F-100 aircraft was downed by unknown causes with the pilot killed.

JUNE 14, 1967

- North Vietnam. A USAF F-4 aircraft was downed by ground fire with the two-man crew missing.
- *Operation Billings.* Announced.
- VN Air Force attack aircraft and US Army gunships supported

ARVN Rangers and Armed Forces forces in a major battle in Phong Dinh Province. Results were 202 enemy killed.

- General Westmoreland presented the Presidential Unit Citation to the ARVN 37th Ranger Battalion; the 934th Regional Forces Company; and the 2nd Platoon, Battery B, 21st Artillery Battalion, the 2nd ARVN Infantry Division artillery, for extraordinary heroism during battle with a Viet Cong Regiment November 22, 1965.

JUNE 15, 1967

- North Vietnam. A USAF F-105 aircraft was downed by ground fire, pilot missing.
- *Operation Arizona.* Announced.
- *Operation Adair.* Initiated.
- *Task Force Oregon.* Highway 1 between Duc Pho and Chu Lai (98 kilometers) returned to government control by the 11th Armored Cavalry Regiment and a US Army Engineer battalion.
- *Operation Geraldton.* Initiated.
- *Operation Broken Hill.* Announced.

JUNE 16, 1967

- North Vietnam. A USAF F-105 aircraft was downed by ground fire, pilot rescued.
- *Operation Angry Dragon II (No Roying II).* Announced and terminated.
- *Operation Horsehead II (Matu II).* Announced.
- The enemy attacked the Dak To Special Forces camp with 60 rounds of 120mm rocket/mortar fire. Results were seven US killed.
- *Operation Great Bend.* Announced.

JUNE 17, 1967

- North Vietnam. US pilots hit railroad yards and destroyed or damaged 107-112 railroad cars. The attack resulted in 21 secondary explosions and 61 fires reported.
- A USAF C-130 aircraft with 55 personnel aboard attempted to

abort take-off from An Khe airfield, ran off runway, exploded and burned with 34 killed.

- *Operation Billings.* In Phuoc Long Province, two companies 1st Infantry Division in LZ engaged a 9th Viet Cong Division battalion in a 4½ hour fight. Results were 222 enemy killed and 33 US.
- *Operation Greeley.* Elements of the 503rd Airborne Infantry, 173rd Airborne Brigade launch the 117-day search and destroy operation in Kontum Province. Friendly losses were 129 killed and 210 wounded. Enemy losses were 191 killed, 17 detained, three retained, 88 individual weapons and 16 crew-served weapons.

JUNE 18, 1967

- *Operation Brown.* Initiated.
- *Operation Beach Torch.* Initiated by an amphibious and helicopter assault supported by 7th Fleet units.
- *Operation Akron.* Announced.
- *Operation Coronado.* Announced.

JUNE 19, 1967

- North Vietnam. USAF pilots hit Bac Giang thermal power plant and railroad yard.
- *Operation Enterprise.* Heavy contact by the 9th Infantry Division and USN River Assault Force with a 5th Viet Cong LF battalion. Interim results were 169 enemy killed and 28 US. Contact continued.

JUNE 20, 1967

- *Task Force Oregon.* Duc Pho Province. Ammunition and lumber storage areas were heavy damaged and an LCU light damaged by fire. Twenty-four personnel were injured.
- *Operation Enterprise.* Contact continued from June 19, 1967. Final results of the two-day battle were 250 enemy killed and 48 US.
- *Operation Great Bend.* Terminated.

JUNE 21, 1967

- North Vietnam. A USAF RF-101 aircraft was downed with the pilot rescued.

- Capital Military District. A VN man and woman on a red motorcycle shot a USAF Sergeant in the vicinity of the 3rd Field Hospital. The Sergeant was in good condition and the assailants escaped.

JUNE 22, 1967

- North Vietnam. USN pilots hit Nam Dinh thermal power plant. A USN A-4 aircraft was downed with the pilot missing.
- *Operation Arizona.* Terminated.
- *Operation Brown.* Terminated.
- *Operation Greeley.* A 173rd Airborne Brigade company+ engaged an enemy force in Kontum Province. Sporadic action continued. Results were 106 enemy killed and 76 US.
- *Operation Geraldton.* Announced.
- Capital Military District, Gia Dinh Province, A Military Airlift Command (MAC) C-121 chartered aircraft and a USAF RF-4C aircraft had a mid-air collision resulting in seven US civilians in the C-121 killed. The USAF crew ejected and hospitalized with minor injuries.

JUNE 23, 1967

- North Vietnam. USN pilots hit a Nam Dinh thermal power plant.
- *Operation Greeley.* Announced.

JUNE 24, 1967

- *Operation Adair.* Terminated.
- The enemy attacked Dau Tieng airfield with 100 rounds of mortar fire. Results were 40 US wounded and moderate damaged aircraft.

JUNE 25, 1967

- *Operation Calhoun.* Initiated.
- A 26th Regiment ROK Infantry Division multi-platoon force engaged an enemy force in Phu Yen Province. Results were 43 enemy killed, 28 individual weapons and four crew-served weapons captured. There were no friendly casualties.
- *Operation Market Time.* In An Xuyen Province, a USN SWIFT boat was hit by 57mm recoilless rifle. The boat sank in shallow water and one crewmember was wounded.

JUNE 26, 1967

- *Operation Malheur II.* Forty tons of rock salt were captured.
- *Operation Billings.* Terminated.

JUNE 27, 1967

- North Vietnam. USN pilots hit a Nam Dinh thermal power plant. USAF pilots hit railroad facilities and destroyed or damaged 48 railroad cars and one locomotive.
- *Operation Crockett.* The enemy attacked the 26th Marine elements in the vicinity of Khe Sanh with 70 rounds of mortar and 50 rounds of 120mm rocket fire. Results were nine US killed and 125 wounded.

JUNE 28, 1967

- North Vietnam. USAF pilots hit a Thai Nguyen thermal power plant and iron ore processing plant. A USN F-4 aircraft was downed, two-man crew missing.

JUNE 29, 1967

- North Vietnam. USN pilots hit the Loi Dong POL area and Cong My transshipment point. USAF pilots hit Kep airfield and damaged one MIG on ground.
- The Viet Cong detonate a mine against the side of the USS COCONINO COUNTY, offloading cargo at the Cua Viet Ramp. At Cua Viet Port, explosives caused moderate damage to the LST and resulting in one US wounded.
- *Operation Akron.* Terminated.

JUNE 30, 1967

- North Vietnam. Two USN A-4 aircraft were downed with the pilots missing.

JULY 1, 1967

- North Vietnam. Eighty railroad cars were destroyed or damaged, 40 secondary explosions and 95 fires were reported.
- *Operation Calhoun.* Terminated.
- *Operation Cooparoo.* Announced and terminated.

JULY 2, 1967

- North Vietnam. 42 secondary explosions and 131 fires initiated. Two USAF F-105 aircraft downed with pilots rescued. A USN A-4 aircraft downed with pilot missing.
- *Operation Cimarron.* Terminated.
- *Operation Buffalo.* Initiated. Elements of the 3rd Marine Division launch the 12-day search and destroy operation in Quang Tri Province. Friendly losses were 159 killed, 885 wounded, and one missing. Enemy losses were 1,281 killed, 14 detained, 79 individual weapons and 20 crew-served weapons.
- *Operation Beacon Torch.* Terminated.
- *Operation Pershing.* 1st Brigade, 1st Cavalry Division companies in heavy contact with two enemy companies fortified positions. Results were 79 enemy killed and 19 US.
- *Operation Enterprise.* 9th Infantry Division elements located 29 individual weapons, one 60mm mortar, 10 boxes small arms ammunition, 10 20-inch mines, and one radio in cache.
- Fifty-five enemy killed by USMC pilots.

JULY 3, 1967

- North Vietnam. USAF pilots hit Thai Nguyen and Thai Hop military barracks areas.
- *Operation Buffalo.* USMC 105mm artillery killed 75 of the enemy.
- In the Capital Military District. Two US suffered minor wounds by hand grenades, Tran Hung Dao Street, Saigon. US Army gunships sank 148 sampans in Quang Tri Province.

JULY 4, 1967

- USN pilots hit Kep airfield.
- *Operation Buffalo.* The enemy attacked Con Thien, Gio Linh and Dong Ha base areas with artillery/mortar fire. Con Thien received three ground probes. Results were 15 US killed and 51 wounded.

JULY 5, 1967

- North Vietnam. USN pilots hit the Don Son POL area. The

pilots destroyed or damaged 37 railroad cars and 15 trucks. Three USAF F-105s, one F-4 were downed, pilots missing.

- *Operation Buffalo.* The enemy attacked the Con Thien and Dong Ha base areas with 425 rounds of rocket/artillery/ mortar fire. Results were seven US killed and 54 wounded.
- *Operation Elliot.* Initiated.
- *Operation Kole Kole.* Announced.

JULY 6, 1967

- North Vietnam. USAF pilots hit a Thai Nguyen thermal power plant. A USMC A-4 aircraft was downed with crew rescued.
- *Operation Buffalo.* A 9th Marine battalion engaged 400 enemy in a day-long battle. Results were 155 enemy killed and three US
- *Operation Elliot.* Terminated.
- Major General W.J. Crum and five others were killed when B-52s collided 80 kilometers SE Saigon and crashed into South China Sea. Seven crewmen were rescued. Other B-52s struck seven times in the RVN (Thua Thien Province five times).
- Hanoi radio announced the death of a four-star NVA General Nguyen Chi Thanh, reputed to be in charge of Viet Cong operations in the RVN.

JULY 7, 1967

- North Vietnam. USAF pilots hit Kep airfield with 55 secondary explosions. Seventy-five fires were reported over North Vietnam.
- *Operation Bearclaw.* Announced.
- *Operation Beaver Track.* Announced.
- *Operation Buffalo.* An aerial observer observed a large enemy group and called in artillery/air strikes resulting in 200 enemy killed. A 9th Marine company observed 200 enemy and engaged with small arms and automatic weapons fire. Results were 150 enemy killed. In Con Thien, the enemy attacked with 12 rounds of artillery fire (first confirmed use of 152mm artillery).
- *Operation Malheur II.* Elements of the 1st Brigade, 101st Airborne Division, launched the 26-day search and destroy operation in Quang Ngai Province. Friendly losses were 30 killed, 260 wounded, four individual weapons and one crew-

served weapon. Enemy losses were 488 killed, 589 detained, six retained, 141 individual weapons and seven crew-served.

- Secretary of Defense McNamara, Under Secretary of State Katzenbach and Chairman, Joint Chief of Staff Wheeler arrived in the RVN for a four-day visit.

JULY 8, 1967

- North Vietnam. USN pilots hit the Ban Ten Army barracks and missile storage area.
- Da Nang Air Base. A B-52 with electrical failure and two engines out attempted an emergency landing and ran off S end of runway adjacent minefield and burned. Results were five crewmembers killed and one survivor.
- *Operation Hong Kil Dong.* ROK units launched the 49-day search and destroy operation in Phu Yen Province. Friendly losses were 27 killed and 68 wounded. Enemy losses were 638 killed, 184 detained, 34 retained, 359 individual weapons and 94 crew-served weapons.

JULY 9, 1967

- North Vietnam. USN pilots hit the Loi Dong POL area and Haiphong POL area with 84 secondary explosions and 78 fires were reported in North Vietnam.
- *Operation Choctaw.* Terminated.
- *Operation Fremont.* Elements of the 4th Marines launched the 114-day search and destroy operation in Thua Thien Province. Friendly losses were 17 killed and 260 wounded. Enemy losses were 123 killed, 192 detained and 39 individual weapons.
- Viet Cong detonated a claymore mine at the Capital Bachelor Enlisted Quarters (BEQ) in Saigon and scattered sniper fire breaks out after the explosion. Results were 17 US wounded, two VN civilians killed and 19 civilians wounded.

JULY 10, 1967

- North Vietnam. USN pilots hit the My Xa POL area. USAF pilots hit the Phu Tho Army barracks. Seventy-two secondary explosions and 120 fires were reported in North Vietnam.

- *Operation Buffalo.* Dong Ha airfield was attacked by artillery or rocket fire. Results were 12 US wounded and light damage.
- *Operation Fremont.* Initiated.
- An enemy concentration in Dinh Tuong Province was hit by artillery fire resulting in 50 enemy killed.

JULY 11, 1967

- North Vietnam. USN pilots hit the Tram Bang POL area. Forty-eight secondary explosions and 54 fires were reported in North Vietnam.
- *Operation Market Time.* A 120' olive green steel-hulled trawler with no flag or name was under surveillance in international waters.

JULY 12, 1967

- North Vietnam. USAF pilots hit Hoa Lac airfield. Sixty-nine secondary explosions and 62 fires were reported in North Vietnam. A USN A-4 aircraft was downed by ground fire with the pilot rescued.
- *Operation Francis Marion.* A 2nd Brigade, 4th Infantry Division company engaged an enemy battalion. Two US companies reinforced. Results were 110 enemy killed and 44 US.
- *Operation Paddington.* Announced.
- A USAF F-100 aircraft was downed by ground fire, pilot missing.
- *Operation Market Time.* A trawler was under surveillance in international waters.

JULY 13, 1967

- North Vietnam. USAF pilots hit Thai Hop military barracks. USN pilots hit Don Son POL area. A NVN village burst into flames when hit by a surface-to-air missile. Seventy-seven secondary explosions were reported in North Vietnam.
- A USAF A-1 aircraft was downed by ground fire in the vicinity of Khe Sanh. A VN Air Force helicopter rescued the pilot.
- *Operation Market Time.* A trawler was under surveillance in international waters.
- The Secretary of Defense and COMUSMACV meet with the President at the White House, and announced a troop increase for the RVN. Precise figures were not announced.

- B-52s struck three times in the DMZ.

JULY 14, 1967

- North Vietnam. USN pilots hit a Thanh Hoa railroad ferry complex and damaged 15 cars. Sixty-three secondary explosions and 106 fires were reported in North Vietnam. A USN A-4 aircraft was downed by ground fire with the pilot missing.
- *Operation Buffalo.* Terminated.
- *Operation Hickory II.* Initiated.
- *Operation Market Time.* A 120-foot steel-hulled trawler was challenged when it entered RVN waters. The challenge was ignored and the trawler fired on a Swift boat. The contact continues.
- An unknown number of Viet Cong attacked Hoi An in Quang Nam Province and Hoi An Prison. Friendly losses were four Regional Forces killed, one National Police killed, four civilians killed, six Regional Forces wounded, five National Police wounded, 29 civilians wounded. Enemy losses were five killed and six individual weapons. Escapees: 30 killed, 206 recaptured and 960 escape.

JULY 15, 1967

- North Vietnam. 64 railroad cars, one locomotive, 20 trucks destroyed or damaged. Fifty-two secondary explosions and 87 fires were reported in North Vietnam.
- USN A-4 and A-1 aircraft were downed by ground fire with one pilot missing and one rescued.
- Da Nang Air Base was attacked with an estimated 50 rounds of 122mm rocket fire. Results were 10 aircraft destroyed, 41 damaged, W runway cratered. Eight USAF were killed, 138 USAF wounded (40 hospitalized), 37 USMC wounded. The bomb storage area was heavily damaged, airfield moderate damaged and 13 barracks destroyed.
- *Operation Hickory II.* Announced.
- *Operation Barking Sands.* A 25th Infantry Division company found two 100-volt generators, 30 rounds of 2.7 inch rocket in cache.

- *Operation Market Time.* A trawler ran aground in the vicinity of Cape Batangan 18 kilometers NE Quang Ngai City.
- Units of TF-115 intercept ed and beached a NVN trawler as it attempted to land at Cape Batangan. Friendly losses were: 44 ROK killed and six ROK wounded. Enemy losses were 23 killed, 1,169 individual weapons, 23 crew-served weapons, 394-560 rounds of 7.62mm incendiary, 311,520 rounds of 7.62mm ball, 1,960 anti-personnel mines, 1,734 hand grenades, 5,750 rounds of 12,7mm ammunition, 43 rounds of B-40 rockets, 996 rounds of 82mm mortars, 6,880 pounds of C-4 plastic explosives, 5,148 pounds of TNT, 900 non-electric detonators and 444 electric detonators.

JULY 16, 1967

- North Vietnam. USN pilots hit a Thanh Hoa railroad ferry complex. A USN F-8 aircraft was downed by ground fire, pilot rescued.
- *Operation Crockett.* Terminated.
- *Operation Paddington.* Terminated.
- *Operation Kingfisher.* Elements of the 3rd Marine Division launched the 107-day search and destroy operation in Quang Tri Province. Friendly losses were 340 killed and 3,085 wounded. Enemy losses 1,117 killed, 142 detained, 126 individual weapons and 29 crew-served weapons.

JULY 17, 1967

- North Vietnam. USN pilots hit the Don Son POL area. USAF pilots hit Kep railroad yard. A USAF F-105 aircraft was downed by ground fire, pilot missing.
- *Operation Hickory II.* Terminated.
- *Operation Ardmore.* Elements of the 3rd Marine Division launched the 106-day search and destroy operation in Quang Tri Province. Friendly losses were 10 killed, 29 wounded. Enemy losses were 113 killed, six detained, nine individual weapons and one crew-served weapon.

JULY 18, 1967

- North Vietnam. USN pilots hit the Thi Liet POL area. USAF pilots hit a Mo Trang railroad yard, destroyed, or damaged 20-25 railroad cars. A USAF F-4 aircraft was downed by ground fire, crew rescued.

JULY 19, 1967

- North Vietnam. USN pilots hit the My Xa POL area. 44 railroad cars, 20 trucks destroyed or damaged. USAF F-4 aircraft engaged eight MIG-17s with no aircraft losses.
- A ROKMC squad ambush platoon killed 33 enemy in Quang Ngai Province.
- *Operation Malheur II.* The 1st Brigade, 101st Airborne Division found a Viet Cong prison compound and hospital complex with 22 personnel (19 men, three women).
- Twenty-five secondary explosions and 25 fires were observed in strikes in the RVN.

JULY 20, 1967

- North Vietnam. Thirty-seven secondary explosions and 61 fires were reported in North Vietnam.
- *Operation Bear Chain.* Initiated.

JULY 21, 1967

- North Vietnam. USN F-8 aircraft downed three MIG-17s, one probable downed. Fifteen railroad cars, six trucks were destroyed or damaged.
- Naval Gunfire-North Vietnam. The DD USS STODDERT destroyed one watercraft, damaged seven on a beach in the vicinity Dong Hoi.
- *Operation Kingfisher.* Announced.
- *Operation Ardmore.* Announced.
- *Operation Beacon Guide.* Initiated.
- The ROK 26th Infantry Regiment multi-light force killed 47 enemy in Phu Yen Province.

- *Operation Emporia.* An 11th Armored Cavalry Regiment troop engaged a Viet Cong 275th Regiment battalion. Results were 93 enemy killed and 15 US.
- The GVN ceased censorship of VN press.

JULY 22, 1967

- *Operation Emporia.* Announced.

JULY 23, 1967

- North Vietnam. USN pilots hit the Ben Thuy thermal power plant. USMC pilots hit a Thai Nguyen thermal power plant resulting in 75 trucks, 24 railroad cars, and 14 watercraft destroyed or damaged.
- *Operation Francis Marion.* A multi-company 4th Infantry Division force engaged a multi-company NVN force. Results were 124 enemy killed and 20 US.
- *Operation Hong Kil Dong.* Announced.
- *Operation Game Warden.* Two USN PBRs received fire from sampans and shore, Vinh Long Province. Fire was returned. Results were six enemy killed, two secondary explosions, nine sampans destroyed or damaged. There were no friendly casualties.

JULY 24, 1967

- North Vietnam. USN pilots hit the Ben Thuy thermal power plant resulting in 43 secondary explosions. Fifty-three fires were reported in North Vietnam.
- Naval Gunfire-North Vietnam. The cruiser USS ST PAUL, supported by DDs USS BARNEY and USS BLUE, hit the Ben Thuy thermal power plant.

JULY 25, 1967

- North Vietnam. Thirty-three secondary explosions and 63 fires were reported in North Vietnam. A USAF F-4 aircraft was downed by unknown causes, two-man crew missing. A USN A-4 aircraft was downed by ground fire, pilot missing.

- *Operation Coronado.* Terminated.

JULY 26, 1967

- The first A-37 light attack aircraft arrived Southeast Asia for evaluation.
- North Vietnam. Eighteen secondary explosions and 68 fires were reported in North Vietnam. A USAF F-4 aircraft was downed by unknown causes with the two-man crew missing.
- *Operation Bear Chain.* Terminated.
- Operation Southport. Announced. Terminated.
- B-52s struck twice in North Vietnam (11 and 14 kilometers N Con Thien).

JULY 27, 1967

- North Vietnam. A USAF F-4 aircraft encountered two MIG-21s, probably downed one. Sixty-seven watercraft, 35 trucks destroyed or damaged, 30 secondary explosions and 89 fires reported in North Vietnam.
- *Operation Hong Kil Dong.* A Capitol ROK Infantry Division company killed 32 enemy, captured 24 individual weapons and two crew-served weapons. There were no friendly casualties.
- *Operation Rang Dong.* A 199th Light Infantry Brigade company found a 10-foot enemy sampan with seven individual weapons, 142 rounds 60mm mortar, 224 grenades, 220 pounds TNT, 134 detonators, 2000-foot wire, and 2000 rounds assorted small arms ammunition.
- *Operation Coronado II/Song Thang III.* Elements of the 9th Infantry Division and the 25th Infantry Division and ARVN units launched the joint seven-day search and destroy joint operation in Binh Tuong Province. Friendly losses were 10 US killed, 61 ARVN killed, 65 US wounded, and 220 ARVN wounded. Enemy losses were 441 killed, 780 detained, one retained, 33 individual weapons and eight crew-served individual weapons.
- The enemy attacked the Phuoc Vinh base camp and airfield with 137 rounds 122mm rocket and 82mm mortar fire. Results were two enemy killed and 12 US killed and 72 US wounded. There was light equipment and materiel damage.

JULY 28, 1967

- North Vietnam. USAF pilots hit the Son Tay Army barracks; USN pilots hit Loi Dong storage area.
- Naval Gunfire-North Vietnam. Cruiser USS ST PAUL hit two military areas NE Vinh. Two secondary explosions were observed. The DD USS BARNEY hit coastal batteries, three secondary explosions.
- *Operation Kingfisher.* Marine elements entered S. half DMZ on a search and destroy operation.
- US strike pilots killed 51 enemy, destroyed or damaged 49 sampans and 23 secondary explosions.

JULY 29, 1967

- The USS FORRESTAL, Gulf of Tonkin. Fuel ignited on the flight deck just prior to the morning launch. Bombs and rockets on aircraft detonated. Results were 131 killed, 62 injured, three missing, 25 aircraft destroyed and 42 aircraft damaged.
- North Vietnam. USAF pilots hit Trai Thon barracks area. USN pilots hit Loi Dong barracks area.
- The enemy attacked the US Army Aviation Brigade base camp at Phu Loi with 200 rounds 122mm rocket and 82mm mortar fire. Results were two US killed and 22 wounded.
- The enemy attacked the 2nd Brigade, 1st Infantry Division base camp at Lai Khe with 68 rounds 122mm rocket and 82mm mortar fire. Results were one US killed and three wounded. Light damage reported both camps.
- MACV staff began the relocation to new headquarters near Tan Son Nhut.

JULY 30, 1967

- North Vietnam. USN pilots hit the Bac Giang transshipment area and Mong Duong transformer station.
- USAF pilots hit a missile transporter 40 kilometers SSE of Dong Hoi.
- Naval Gunfire-North Vietnam. The DD USS AULT received superficial shrapnel holes in the superstructure when the enemy was attacked by a shore battery. There was no major damage and no personnel casualties.

- *Operation Kingfisher.* 9th Marine units completed sweeps at 1200 hours.
- *Operation Game Warden.* USN gunners and the USS HUNTERDON COUNTY hit an enemy ammunition and fuel storage area in Kien Hoa. Province in the vicinity of the mouth of the Ham Luong River and reported large secondary explosions and fires.

JULY 31, 1967

- North Vietnam. Thirteen railroad cars and seven trucks were destroyed or damaged. Sixteen secondary explosions and 31 fires were reported. A USN F-8 aircraft was downed by ground fire, pilot missing. A USAF F-4 aircraft was downed by unknown causes, pilot missing.
- *Operation Beacon Guide.* Terminated.
- *Operation Coronado II.* Announced.
- *Operation Pike.* Elements of the 1st Marine Division launched the three-day search and destroy operation in Quang Tin and Quang Nam Provinces. Friendly losses were eight killed and 60 wounded. Enemy losses were 100 killed, 58 detained and four individual weapons.

AUGUST 1, 1967

- US military strength in the RVN was 485,000.
- North Vietnam. USAF pilots hit a Bac Giang thermal power plant. 37 watercraft, 22 trucks destroyed or damaged. Thirty-three secondary explosions and 128 fires were reported. A USAF RF-101 aircraft was downed due to unknown causes, pilot missing. A USN A-4 aircraft was downed by ground fire, pilot rescued.
- *Operation Pike.* Initiated.
- *Operation Kangaroo Kick.* Initiated.
- The 3rd Brigade, 4th Infantry Division, redesignated the 3rd Brigade, 25th Infantry Division, at Dau Tieng in Binh Duong Province. At the same time, the 3rd Brigade, 25th Infantry Division, was redesignated the 3rd Brigade, 4th Infantry Division.
- The SS BIENVILLE arrived in Da Nang, inaugurating containership service in the RVN.

- The 3rd Naval Construction Brigade HQ shifted from Saigon to Da Nang.
- The DOD announced that the USS NEW JERSEY (BB-62) is to be recommissioned.
- The A-37, the first light attack counterinsurgency aircraft, arrived in the RVN at Bien Hoa Air Base, for combat evaluation.

AUGUST 2, 1967

- North Vietnam. USAF pilots hit a Thai Nguyen thermal power plant. Twenty-three watercraft, 46 trucks were destroyed or damaged.
- Naval Gunfire-North Vietnam. The cruiser USS ST PAUL was hit by enemy shore fire which resulted in light damage and one crewman wounded.
- *Operation Pike.* Announced.
- *Operation Kangaroo Kick.* Announced.
- *Operation Malheur II.* Terminated.
- *Operation Emporia.* Terminated.
- *Operation Cairns.* Announced. Terminated.

AUGUST 3, 1967

- North Vietnam. Seventy-two watercraft, 161 trucks destroyed or damaged. 82 secondary explosions and 307 fires were reported. USAF pilots hit a troop concentration 35 kilometers SSE Dong Hoi, destroyed two half-tracks, one tank, three artillery pieces and destroyed or damaged five trucks.
- *Operation Pike.* Terminated.
- *Operation Kangaroo Kick.* Terminated.
- *Operation Emporia II.* Initiated.
- *Operation Coronado II.* Terminated.
- Capital Military District. An unknown VN threw TNT with a watch and battery fusing in the vicinity of US Army Bachelor Enlisted Quarters (BEQ) Gia Dinh Province. A VN boy reported the package. The EOD located and disarmed the bomb.
- The enemy attacked the Naval Support Activity Detachment (NSAD) Nha Be and 199th Light Infantry Brigade elements in the vicinity of the POL tank farm with 30-40 rounds mortar, recoilless rifle and small arms fire. Results were light damage

NSA and boats, POL drum storage area and 199th positions. Results were 24 USN wounded, six US Army, one USAF wounded, three VNN wounded, 44 civilians wounded, eight Regional Forces wounded, 1,000 55-gallon drums of mogas destroyed, 5,000 55-gallon drums of mogas damaged, one PBR and one MSB destroyed, two PBRs and two MSBs damaged).

- The White House announced a 45,000-man increase in personnel for the RVN.

AUGUST 4, 1967

- North Vietnam. Forty-six watercraft, 20 railroad cars, 41 trucks were destroyed or damaged. Thirty-eight secondary explosions and 144 fires were reported. USN pilots hit the Khe Sat storage area.
- *Operation Ballarat.* Initiated.

AUGUST 5, 1967

- North Vietnam. Fifty-eight watercraft, 23 trucks were destroyed or damaged. Eighty-nine secondary explosions and 181 fires were reported. USN pilots hit Ben Thuy thermal power plant and the Ninh Binh military headquarters area.
- Naval Gunfire-North Vietnam. The cruiser USS ST PAUL and DD HMAS HOBART hit a boat repair facility ENE Thanh Hoa. Fourteen boats were destroyed or damaged. Repair facilities suffered heavy damage.

AUGUST 6, 1967

- North Vietnam. Forty-two trucks, three PT boats were destroyed or damaged and 190 secondary explosions and 162 fires were reported.
- Naval Gunfire-North Vietnam. The cruiser USS ST PAUL and DD HMAS PERTH hit a radar site on Hon Matt Island.
- An explosion occurred aboard an LCU anchored in the Dong Ha stream. Satchel charges were the suspected cause. Results were two US Army wounded and the LCU light damaged.
- *Operation Emporia II.* Announced.
- *Operation Kole Kole.* A 25th Infantry Division company found a munitions factory-tunnel complex.

AUGUST 7, 1967

- North Vietnam. USN pilots hit A Loi Dong storage. 28 watercraft, 125 trucks, eight railroad cars destroyed or damaged. Sixty-one secondary explosions and 162 fires were reported. A USAF F-4 aircraft was downed by ground fire, two-man crew missing.
- Naval Gunfire-North Vietnam. The cruiser USS ST PAUL with DDs USS BLUE and HMAS PERTH hit Thanh Gia military installation.
- *Operation Beacon Gate.* Initiated.
- Two enemy companies overran the 16th VNN Coastal Group Base Camp in Quang Ngai Province. Friendly losses were one US killed, 14 VN Navy killed, three civilians killed, two US wounded, 35 VN Navy wounded, one VN Navy missing, two individual weapons, seven crew-served weapons, one ¼-ton truck, fuel dump, and all but one building within compound destroyed. Enemy losses were 11 killed.
- Brigadier General J.F. Freund, CG 199th Light Infantry Brigade was slightly wounded when Brigade and ARVN Rangers engaged the enemy in Gia Dinh Province. Five helicopters were downed by ground fire.

AUGUST 8, 1967

- North Vietnam. Forty-one secondary explosions and 125 fires were reported. USAF pilots hit Bac Giang railroad yard and bridge.
- Naval Gunfire-North Vietnam. The DD USS RUPERTUS received light damage when hit by shore fire. There were no personnel casualties.
- *Operation Beacon Gate.* Announced.
- *Operation Ballarat.* Announced.
- *Operation Barking Sands.* A 25th Infantry Division company landing from a ARVN RAG boat received RPG and small arms fire. Results were four US killed and 30 wounded.

AUGUST 10, 1967

- North Vietnam. A USN F-4 aircraft shot down two MIG-21s.

USAF pilots hit Kep and Thai Nguyen railroad yards, 45 railroad cars were destroyed or damaged.

- US Army gunships killed 59 enemy and destroyed 69 sampans.

AUGUST 11, 1967

- North Vietnam. USAF pilots dropped the center span of Doumer bridge. USN pilots hit Phu Ly transformer station.
- *Operation Cochise.* Elements of the 1st Marine Division launched the 18-day search and destroy operation in Quang Nam and Quang Tin Provinces. Friendly losses were 10 killed and 93 wounded. Enemy losses were 156 killed, 138 detained and 41 individual weapons.
- A USMC A-4 aircraft was downed by ground fire with the pilot killed. A US Army U-1A was downed by ground fire with the aircraft destroyed. There were no casualties.

AUGUST 12, 1967

- North Vietnam. USAF pilots damaged the center and NE sections of Canal des Rapides bridge. USN pilots hit Kien An airfield and barracks area. USMC pilots hit Viet Tri barracks. USAF pilots engaged MIG-17s seven times. No aircraft were downed. USAF RF-4 and F-105 aircraft were downed by ground fire with three crewmen missing.
- Naval Gunfire-North Vietnam. DDs USS RUPERTUS and USS PORTERFIELD hit coastal defense sites NNW Dong Hoi with two secondary explosions observed.

AUGUST 13, 1967

- North Vietnam. USAF pilots hit Lang Dong railroad siding, destroyed or damaged 55 railroad cars; Lan Gian railroad yard, destroyed or damaged 55 railroad cars; Lang Son railroad yard, destroyed or damaged 30-40 railroad cars. USN pilots dropped the center span of Lang Son highway/railroad bridge. A USN RA-5C aircraft was downed by ground fire, two-man crew missing.
- Naval Gunfire-North Vietnam. The cruiser USS BOSTON and

DD HMAS HOBART with a USN A-1 aircraft spotter aircraft supporting, destroyed or damaged 63 watercraft E Vinh.

- *Operation Hood River.* Terminated.
- *Operation Benton.* Elements of the 101st Airborne Brigade and the 196th Light Infantry Brigade launched the 21-day search and destroy operation in Quang Tin Province. Friendly losses were 41 killed and 263 wounded. Enemy losses were 397 killed, nine detained, 150 individual weapons, eight crew-served weapons.
- The USAF revealed officially, for the first time, that American war planes have been bombing communist targets in Laos since May 1964.
- US planes bomb a railroad yard and bridge 10 miles from the Red Chinese border and hit two other nearby rail centers in the closest American raids to China since the Korean War.
- B-52s struck three times in the DMZ.

AUGUST 14, 1967

- North Vietnam. Thirty-four trucks were destroyed or damaged and 73 secondary explosions reported. USN pilots dropped S span Lang Son railroad bridge by-pass. USMC pilots hit Hon Gia Port facilities.
- *Operation Benton.* Announced.
- *Operation Cochise.* Announced.
- *Operation Portland.* Initiated. Announced.

AUGUST 15, 1967

- North Vietnam. Sixty-three watercraft, 46 trucks were destroyed or damaged. Sixty-seven secondary explosions were reported. USN pilots hit a Ben Thuy thermal power plant.
- A multi-battalion 41st ARVN Infantry Regiment engaged two NVA companies in Binh Dinh Province. US 1st Cavalry Division elements moved to surround. Results were 65 enemy killed, one killed US and ARVN casualties light.
- B-52s struck three times in the DMZ.

AUGUST 16, 1967

- North Vietnam. Forty-five watercraft, 13 trucks were destroyed or damaged. Sixty-four secondary explosions and 122 fires were reported.

- *Operation Kingfisher.* A 9th Marine company found 127 rounds recoilless rifle, mortar, RPGs and one 102mm rocket; 33 anti-tank and anti-personnel mines; 30 grenades in cache. Eleven enemy bodies were found in graves.
- *Operation Ballarat.* Announced. Terminated.

AUGUST 17, 1967

- North Vietnam. Forty watercraft, 34 trucks, six railroad cars were destroyed or damaged. Nineteen secondary explosions and 52 fires were reported. USMC pilots hit Vinh railroad yard. A USAF F-105 aircraft was downed by ground fire, pilot rescued.
- *Operation Benton.* A 101st Airborne Division company found five tons rice and one ton rock salt, 146 rounds mortar and recoilless rifle ammunition and penicillin.
- *Operation Shelby.* Initiated.
- *Operation Emporia II.* Terminated.
- A combination tear-nausea gas was dropped from Marine helicopter gunships for the first time in RVN.
- General Omar N. Bradley, General of the Army, arrived in the RVN for a 13-day orientation visit.

AUGUST 18, 1967

- North Vietnam. A USAF pilot logged 105 armed reconnaissance missions over North Vietnam (record). Destroyed or damaged were 108 watercraft, 29 trucks and 12 railroad cars. Thirty-nine secondary explosions were reported. USN pilots hit Ben Thuy thermal power plant.
- Naval Gunfire-North Vietnam. The cruiser USS BOSTON hit Ben Thuy ferry crossing and cave storage complex.
- B-52s struck North Vietnam and the DMZ.
- Naval Forces. A USN SEAL team killed one chief of enemy military section and one head of the local armory and printing factory 70 miles S Saigon. The SEALS were led to the area by Hoi Chanh.
- Coastal Squadron THREE (PGs) was commissioned at CRB.

AUGUST 19, 1967

- North Vietnam. USN pilots hit a Ben Thuy cave storage area and Long Dan transshipment point.

- US Army gunships killed 58 enemy. A US Army UH-1 helicopter was downed by ground fire with four US killed.

AUGUST 20, 1967

- North Vietnam. USAF pilots destroyed or damaged 25 railroad cars Huong Vi railroad yard. A MIG in pursuit was hit by surface-to-air missile in the vicinity of Ha Gia. USN pilots destroyed one dredge and damaged one ESE Haiphong.
- *Operation Coronado IV.* Elements of 9th Infantry Division launched the 20-day search and destroy operation in Long An Province. Friendly losses were three killed, 27 wounded, one helicopter damaged and one individual weapon. Enemy losses were 101 killed, 148 detained, 165 individual weapons and 15 crew-served weapons.

AUGUST 21, 1967

- North Vietnam. A USAF pilot destroyed or damaged 25 railroad cars Prung Quan railroad yard, set off 25-30 secondary explosions; destroyed 10-12 railroad cars and 102 locomotives Yen Vien railroad yard. USN pilots hit a Hanoi thermal power plant; set off nine secondary explosions Port Wallut Naval Base; destroyed or damaged two biplanes Kep Ha airfield. Two USAF F-105 aircraft were downed by ground fire, three A-6 aircraft were downed (two apparently over Communist China), crews missing.
- A USN F-4 aircraft was downed, pilot rescued.
- *Operation Kingfisher.* The enemy attacked a USMC truck convoy. Two 3rd Marine companies with tanks reinforced. Results were 109 enemy killed and five US.
- *Operation Portland.* Terminated.
- *Operation Coronado IV.* Announced.
- B-52s struck DMZ. Eleven RVN policemen were killed as the result of a strike.

AUGUST 22, 1967

- North Vietnam. USAF pilots hit Canal des Rapides bridge; Thang Quang railroad yard. USN pilots dropped three spans of Co Trai railroad bridge, hit Nam Dinh POL transshipment area and Hai Yen boat yard and ferry.
- Naval Gunfire-North Vietnam. Cruiser USS BOSTON and DD

USS BERKELEY destroyed or damaged five 90-foot barges NNE Vinh.

- *Operation Kingfisher.* The enemy attacked 9th Marine elements with 100 rounds of mortar fire. Results were two US killed and 16 wounded.
- B-52s struck twice in the DMZ.
- *Operation Game Warden.* USN gunships destroyed one large junk and 63 sampans on the Co Chien River in Kien Hoa Province.

AUGUST 23, 1967

- North Vietnam. An F-105 aircraft pilot shot down two MIG-17s. USAF pilots hit Bac Giang railroad yard and Hoang Mai siding, 30 railroad cars destroyed and 20 damaged in Yen Vien railroad yard. Two USAF F-4s were downed by MIG-21s, one F-105 was downed by ground fire. A USN F-4 was downed from unknown causes. One pilot was rescued.
- *Operation Cochise.* A 3rd Marine company found 230 rounds 82/60mm mortar, 24 grenades, 34 cases mortar detonators and 27 cases mortar fuses in ammunition cache.
- *Operation Atherton.* Terminated.
- Capital Military District. A US Army enlisted man was shot and killed by two unknown VN civilians on a Honda, in the vicinity of El Paso Bachelor Enlisted Quarters (BEQ) in Cholon.

AUGUST 24, 1967

- North Vietnam. USAF pilots destroyed or damaged 29 railroad cars at Kep railroad yard. USN pilots hit Port Wallut Naval Base and Kep Ha airfield, and Hai Duong railroad/highway bridge. USMC pilots hit Hoa Lac airfield and Long Con military area.
- Naval Gunfire-North Vietnam. The cruiser USS BOSTON and DD USS BERKELEY destroyed or damaged 28 watercraft NNE Vinh.
- *Operation Shelby.* Terminated.

AUGUST 25, 1967

- North Vietnam. USN pilots hit Port Wallut Naval Base.
- *Operation Kingfisher.* The enemy attacked 9th Marine elements with 175 rounds 60/82mm mortar fire and 60 grenades.

AUGUST 26, 1967

- North Vietnam. USAF pilots hit Mo Trang railroad bridge, Quang Kien railroad causeway and Huong Vi railroad yard.
- A USAF F-4 aircraft was downed to unknown causes with the two-man crew missing. An F-100 aircraft was downed to ground fire with one crewman rescued.
- A 2nd Brigade, 9th Infantry Division battalion discovered 16 individual weapons, one automatic weapon, 200 rounds small arms, 1,000 rifle grenades, 100 hand grenades, 39 M-79 rounds, 20 booby traps and 30 pounds explosions in cache.
- B-52s struck in the DMZ.

AUGUST 27, 1967

- North Vietnam. USN pilots hit Chau Cau Army barracks and Nam Dinh railroad yard.
- An aerial observer directed USMC air strikes and artillery missions against the enemy in Quang Tri Province. Results were 83 enemy killed. Four secondary explosions and seven fires were reported.
- *Operation Belt Drive.* Initiated.
- *Operation Cochise.* Terminated.
- *Operation Akron II.* Terminated.
- IV CORPS. The enemy, with 57 recoilless rifle and 82mm mortar rounds, hit Province and ARVN Hospital, MACV compound and city. Forty-six VN civilians were killed and 222 wounded. Five US were wounded and light ARVN casualties.
- *Operation Market Time.* USCGC HALF MOON killed 11 enemy and destroyed or damaged 18 fortified positions in An Xuyen Province.

AUGUST 28, 1967

- North Vietnam. USAF pilots destroyed or damaged 15 railroad cars Vu Chua and Cau Nung railroad yards. USN pilots hit Bai Thuong airfield.
- *Operation Kingfisher.* The enemy attacked the operation area with 287 rounds artillery/mortar/rocket fire. Results were six US killed and 30 wounded. Elements participating in *Operation Kingfisher* at Gio Linh in Quang Tri Province received artillery

airbursts. This was the first time the enemy employed airburst shells.

- The enemy attacked Marble Mountain Air Facility with 10 rounds 140mm rocket fire. Results were four US killed and 80 wounded. There was light material damage.
- An enemy squad shot six VN civilians in Phuoc Long Province.
- B-52s struck the DMZ.
- Naval Gunfire-RVN. The DD USS DU PONT received hits from an enemy shore battery N part DMZ. Results were one US killed nine wounded. There was light damage to the ship. The DD remained on station.

AUGUST 29, 1967

- North Vietnam. USAF pilots hit Kep railroad yard and Kep Army barracks. USMC A-4 aircraft was downed by ground fire with the pilot missing.
- *Operation Coronado IV.* A 2nd Brigade, 9th Infantry Division company found 2000 rounds .30 caliber ammunition, 2,000 rounds 9mm ammunition, 13 rounds M-79, six pounds TNT and one sniper scope in a supply cache in Long An Province.
- Capital Military District. A VN sailor was shot and killed by an unknown terrorist in the vicinity of the racetrack in Saigon.
- B-52s struck three times in the DMZ.

AUGUST 30, 1967

- North Vietnam. USAF pilots hit Hoa Lac airfield. Aircraft silhouettes were painted in revetment and bomb craters painted on runways. USN pilots hit Ninh Dinh railroad siding and railroad by-pass bridge, and destroyed Cam Pha railroad bridge. A USN A-1 and an A-4 aircraft were downed by ground fire, A-1 pilot rescued and A-4 pilot missing.
- B-52s struck three times in the DMZ.

AUGUST 31, 1967

- North Vietnam. USN pilots hit Vinh airfield and Army barracks. Twenty-seven secondary explosions and 31 fires were reported in North Vietnam. Three USN A-4 aircraft were downed by ground fire, three pilots missing.
- VN Air Force A-1 and USAF A-4 aircraft supported ARVN

Rangers battalion S Da Nang killed 38 enemy and destroyed 53 positions. Twenty secondary explosions and 29 fires were reported.

- B-52s struck three times in the DMZ.

SEPTEMBER 1, 1967

- US military strength in RVN was 492,000.
- North Vietnam. USN pilots hit Vinh POL area and Vinh Army barracks.
- Naval Gunfire-North Vietnam. The cruiser USS ST PAUL was hit on the starboard bow by an enemy shore battery fire. There were no personnel casualties.
- The enemy attacked the USMC base camp at Phu Bai with 60mm and 80mm mortar fire. Three USMC and one US Army were killed, 49 USMC and US three US Army wounded.
- *Operation Beacon Point.* Initiated.
- *Operation Belt Drive.* Terminated.
- *Operation Benton.* Terminated.
- B-52s struck three times in the DMZ.

SEPTEMBER 2, 1967

- North Vietnam. USAF pilots hit Huong Vi railroad yard. USMC pilots hit Uong Bi thermal power plant. USN pilots hit Thanh Hoa railroad yard. A USAF F-105 aircraft was downed to unknown causes with the pilot missing.
- *Operation Kingfisher.* The enemy attacked the operation area with artillery/rocket/mortar fire. Results were two US wounded and 27 missing.
- *Operation Cook.* Initiated.
- The USMC Force Logistical Command complex at Da Nang was hit with 22 rounds 122mm rocket fire. Results were one US killed and 61 wounded. The Installation received minor damage. Da Nang Air Base was hit with four to six 140mm rockets. There was minor damage to aircraft (no fighter aircraft). Four US were wounded.
- B-52s struck three times in the DMZ.

SEPTEMBER 3, 1967

- North Vietnam. USAF pilots hit Kep airfield, Cam Pha barracks area, and Kep Ha barracks area. USN pilots hit Thanh Hoa railroad/highway bridge and Thanh Hoa railroad complex. A USAF F-105 aircraft was downed by ground fire with the pilot missing.

- *Operation Kingfisher.* The enemy attacked the operation area with 120 rounds of artillery/mortar/rocket fire. Results were 44 US wounded.
- *Operation Beacon Point.* Terminated.
- B-52s struck three times in the DMZ.

SEPTEMBER 4, 1967

- North Vietnam. USAF pilots hit Kep Ha barracks area and mobile surface-to-air missile site 25 kilometers SSE Dong Hoi.
- *Operation Kingfisher.* The enemy attacked the operation area with 87 rounds artillery and recoilless rifle fire. Results were two US wounded.
- *Operation Swift.* Elements of the 1st Battalion, 5th Marines launched the 11-day search and destroy operation in Quang Nam and Quang Tin Provinces. Friendly losses were 127 killed and 352 wounded. Enemy losses were 571 killed, 66 detained, 70 individual weapons and 15 crew-served weapons.
- *Operation Coronado IV.* A 2nd Brigade, 9th Infantry Division platoon found 4,000 rounds 9mm, 2,050 rounds 7.92mm, 680 rounds .30 caliber, 20 rounds 60mm mortar and eight pounds TNT in an ammunition cache.
- B-52s struck twice in the DMZ.

SEPTEMBER 5, 1967

- North Vietnam. USMC pilots hit Hon Gai storage area.
- *Operation Cook.* Announced.
- *Operation Swift.* 5th Marine units engaged two enemy battalions. Results were 160 enemy killed. The contact continued.
- *Operation Dragon Fire.* Elements of the 2nd Brigade ROKMC launched the 55-day search and destroy operation in Quang Ngai Province. Friendly losses were 46 ROK killed, two US killed, and 200 ROK wounded. Enemy losses were 541 killed, 138 detained, 38 individual weapons and seven crew-served weapons.
- A 1st Brigade, 9th Infantry Division eight-man platoon lost radio contact Bien Hoa Province. A search was underway for the patrol.

- B-52s struck twice in the DMZ.

SEPTEMBER 6, 1967

- *Operation Swift.* Results of the contact on September 5-6, 1967: 180 enemy were killed and 54 US killed. 5th Marine elements engaged a regiment-sized enemy force. The contact continued. Twenty-four individual weapons and six crew-served weapons were captured and 23 personnel detained.
- The ARVN killed 219 of the enemy in the vicinity of Tam Ky, 29 detained, 195 weapons captured. ARVN casualties were light.
- The eight-man patrol that was lost on September 5, 1967 was located in Bien Hoa Province. All were killed.
- B-52s struck twice in the DMZ.

SEPTEMBER 7, 1967

- *Operation Swift.* Results of the September 6-7, 1967 contact were 170 enemy killed and 41 US.
- *Operation Kingfisher.* The enemy attacked a 3rd Marine convoy on Highway 9 and the 3rd Marine force reinforced. Results were 92 enemy killed and five US.
- The Secretary of Defense announced the decision to construct a wire and electronic barrier across the RVN south of the DMZ.
- B-52s struck twice in the DMZ.

SEPTEMBER 8, 1967

- North Vietnam. USAF pilots hit Lang Dang rail siding, Cao Nung railroad bridge, Bac Giang railroad and highway bridge. USN pilots destroyed a Thuong Hoa bridge and damaged a Thoi Thanh Xom highway bridge. USMC pilots hit Cham Phuong railroad yard.
- *Operation Kingfisher.* The enemy attacked the operation area with 20 rounds of 140mm rocket fire. Results were 40 US wounded.
- On Highway 13 from Di An to Quan Loi, 240 vehicles (101 ARVN) made the four-hour trip.
- *Operation Coronado IV.* A 9th Infantry Division company found 95 individual weapons, eight machine guns, 162 grenades, 65 pounds TNT, 30 rounds 60mm mortar, 50 rounds 75mm recoilless rifle and 23,500 rounds small arms in cache. Another

company found an enemy hospital complex; 2½ tons rice, 35 black uniforms and a large quantity of medical supplies.

- B-52s struck North Vietnam and the DMZ.

SEPTEMBER 9, 1967

- North Vietnam. USAF pilots destroyed three MIG-17s on the ground Kep airfield, destroyed one anti-aircraft site. One MIG engagement with no damage reported. USN pilots hit Nam Dinh POL area and railroad yard, Dong Lo transshipment point. USMC pilots hit the Uong Bi thermal power plant.
- *Operation Swift.* A 5th Marine company found 152 rounds 60mm mortar, 28,800 rounds 7.72mm small arms, 1,190 rounds 12.7mm machine gun ammunition, 59 rounds 82mm mortar, 19 rounds 75mm artillery, 36 rounds 57mm recoilless rifle, 458 CHICOM grenades and 18 rounds B-40 anti-tank in cache.
- *Operation Coronado IV.* Terminated.
- B-52s struck four times in the DMZ.

SEPTEMBER 10, 1967

- North Vietnam. USN pilots hit Cam Pha port facilities. USMC pilots hit Song Dong Army barracks.
- *Operation Kingfisher.* 26th Marine elements engaged an estimated enemy regiment. Results were 140 enemy killed and 34 US.
- *Operation Cook.* Terminated.
- B-52s struck North Vietnam.

SEPTEMBER 11, 1967

- North Vietnam. USN pilots hit the Haiphong warehouse area, railroad yard; highway bridge; railroad/highway bridge, with direct hits on both bridges. USMC pilots hit Long Con military area. USN A-1aircraft observed two surface-to-air missiles explosions in the vicinity of three ships anchored SE Haiphong. A B-57 aircraft was downed by ground fire, two-man crew missing.
- *Operation Wheeler.* Elements of Task Force Oregon launched the 61-day search and destroy operation in Quang Tin Province (combined with *Operation Wallowa* to become *Operation Wheeler/Wallowa* on November 11, 1967).

SEPTEMBER 12, 1967

- *Operation Kingfisher.* SE Con Thien, the enemy attacked operation area with 150-170 rounds artillery/mortar fire. Results were four US killed and 101 wounded.
- *Operation Swift.* Elements of the 5th Marines killed 71 in the enemy day's action. Six AK-47s, one heavy machine gun, one B-40 rocket and 14 individual weapons captured. Results were four US killed.
- *Operation Coronado V.* Elements of the 9th Infantry Division and TF-117 launch the 26-day search and destroy operation in Dinh Tuong Province. Friendly losses were 35 killed, 175 wounded. Enemy losses were 350 killed, 253 detained, one retained, 16 individual weapons and two crew-served weapons.
- *Operation Neutralize.* A 41-day coordinated massive air operation to neutralize the threat to Dong Ha, Gio Linh, Camp Carroll and Con Thien originating from the area in and near the DMZ, was initiated.
- B-52s struck three times DMZ.

SEPTEMBER 13, 1967

- North Vietnam. USN pilots dropped Thuong Quang Tien railroad bridge, Phuc Tang highway bridge and damaged Xom Thai Xa bridge and Khe Thi highway bridge. USMC pilots hit Uong Bi thermal power plant.
- Naval Gunfire-North Vietnam. The DD USS ROBISON hit by enemy coastal defense site NNW Dong Hoi. No casualties reported and light damage.
- *Operation Wheeler.* Announced.
- *Operation Coronado V.* Numerous enemy contacts. Ground forces and air killed 151 enemy, seven US killed.
- *Operation Ainslie.* Announced.
- B-52s struck twice DMZ.

SEPTEMBER 14, 1967

- *Operation Kingfisher.* 4th Marine elements received 137-147 rounds rocket/mortar/recoilless rifle fire. Results were 15 US killed and 58 wounded.
- B-52-s struck North Vietnam and twice in the DMZ.

SEPTEMBER 15, 1967

- North Vietnam. USAF pilots dropped Lang Lau railroad bridge; destroyed six railroad cars, Thai Nguyen railroad yard and highway damaged Ha Gia railroad bridge.
- *Operation Swift.* Terminated.
- *Operation Coronado V.* Elements of the 2nd Brigade, 9th Infantry Division engaged the enemy. Heavy fighting resulted: 69 enemy killed and five US. The Mobile Riverine Force forces run into a large enemy force in Ba Rai Creek, Dinh Tuong Province during the operation. Results were 18 boats damaged. The 3rd Battalion, 47th Infantry, 9th Infantry Division engages the enemy who suffer 213 killed.
- B-52s struck North Vietnam and DMZ.

SEPTEMBER 16, 1967

- North Vietnam. USAF pilots hit Thang Quang railroad siding and Mo Trang railroad yard. USAF F-101 aircraft was downed by a MIG, pilot missing.
- *Operation Ballistic Charge.* Initiated.
- B-52s struck North Vietnam and twice in the DMZ.

SEPTEMBER 17, 1967

- North Vietnam. USN pilots hit Haiphong railroad/highway bridge. USAF pilots hit That Khe highway bridge (11 kilometers W Chinese Border).
- Satchel charge exploded at Neptune Non-Commissioned Officer (NCO) Club Nha Trang. One VN civilian was killed, two VN civilians wounded and 29 US wounded. The club was heavily damaged.
- *Operation Fortress Sentry.* Initiated.
- B-52s struck twice North Vietnam.

SEPTEMBER 18, 1967

- North Vietnam. USN pilots hit Haiphong railroad/highway bridge; highway bridge; railroad yard and warehouse area. USAF pilots hit Huong Vi railroad yard.
- *Operation Fortress Sentry.* Announced.

- *Operation Barking Sands.* Elements of the 1st Brigade, 25th Infantry Division found an enemy ammunition shop: 120 pounds rice, 10 pounds rock salt, 50 pounds explosions, five pounds documents, three Mauser rifles, 10 grenades, assorted hand tools and uniforms.
- *Operation Arkansas City.* Initiated.
- B-52s struck in the DMZ.

SEPTEMBER 19, 1967

- North Vietnam. USAF pilots damaged Lang Son railroad bridge.
- *Operation Kingfisher.* The enemy attacked the operation area with 494 rounds rocket and mortar fire. One US was killed and 88 wounded.
- *Operation Bolling.* Elements of the 173rd Airborne Brigade and 1st Cavalry Division launched the search and destroy operation in Phu Yen Province. This operation continued into 1968.
- Enemy terrorists detonated 20-30 pounds of explosives contained in a suitcase in the passport office of the Embassy of the Republic of China in Saigon. Sniper fire was simultaneously received. Friendly losses were one civilian killed, 26 civilians wounded, 1/3 of the Embassy building was destroyed. Enemy losses were three detained.
- B-52s struck twice in the DMZ.
- *Operation Kingfisher.* The enemy attacked the operation area with 545 rounds rocket/artillery/mortar fire. Results were six US killed and 69 wounded.
- *Operation Arkansas City.* Announced.
- B-52s struck three times in the DMZ.

SEPTEMBER 20, 1967

- The first Armored Support Patrol Boats (ASPD) arrive at Vung Tau.

SEPTEMBER 21, 1967

- North Vietnam. USN pilots hit Kien An highway bridge and Haiphong railroad/highway bridge. An RF-8 aircraft was downed by ground fire, pilot missing.
- *Operation Kingfisher.* Battalion attacked area with 585 rounds

rocket/artillery/mortar fire. Results were three US killed and 88 wounded.

- A 2,300 Queen's Cobra Regiment of the RTAFV Regiment arrived at Saigon's Newport to be stationed at Bear Cat.
- B-52s struck North Vietnam.
- Naval Gunfire-RVN. Seventeen enemy were killed, 36 positions destroyed and two secondary explosions by the USS ST FRANCIS RIVER NNE Quang Ngai City.

SEPTEMBER 22, 1967

- North Vietnam. USMC pilots hit Nam Dinh railroad yard.
- Naval Gunfire-North Vietnam. The cruiser USS BOSTON and DD USS COLLETT hit Ben Thuy cave storage area.
- *Operation Kingfisher.* The Battalion attacked operation area with 304 rounds rocket/artillery/mortar fire. Results were six US killed and 56 wounded.
- *Operation Bolling.* Announced.
- Task Force Oregon was redesignated Americal Division.
- US strike pilots killed 60 enemy, 25 secondary explosions and 20 fires were reported.
- B-52s struck the DMZ.

SEPTEMBER 23, 1967

- *Operation Kingfisher.* The enemy attacked operation area with 241 rounds rocket/artillery/mortar fire. Results were 17 US wounded (medevac), 60 wounded (treated and returned to duty).
- Camp Holloway. Explosions in POL area resulted in moderate damage. There were no casualties reported.
- *Operation Bluefield II.* Initiated.
- *Operation Arkansas City.* Terminated.
- Official communiqué from Moscow announced the signing of USSR/North Vietnam military assistance agreement whereby the USSR would furnish "airplanes, antiaircraft and rocket equipment, artillery and small arms, ammunition and other military equipment..."
- B-52s struck North Vietnam.

SEPTEMBER 24, 1967

- *Operation Kingfisher.* The enemy attacked operation area with

295 rounds rocket/artillery/mortar fire. Results were five US wounded (medevac), 43 wounded (treated and returned to duty). Four US were killed.

- *Operation Bolling:* The Brigade found five tons rice, 100 rounds 60mm mortar, 150 rounds 57mm recoilless rifle, 15 rifle grenades and small quantity assorted small arms ammunition in a cache.
- B-52s struck three times the DMZ.

SEPTEMBER 25, 1967

- North Vietnam. USAF pilots hit Kep Ha Army barracks.
- Naval Gunfire-North Vietnam. The DD USS MANSFIELD was hit by a shore battery fire in the vicinity of Dong Hoi. Results were one crewmember killed and two wounded. Light damage was reported.
- *Operation Kingfisher.* The enemy attacked operation area with approximately 1,000 rounds artillery/mortar/rocket fire. Results were two US killed, 50 US wounded (evacuated), 152 wounded (treated and returned to duty).
- *Operation Pershing.* Elements of the 3rd Brigade, 1st Cavalry Division found a cave containing two 75mm recoilless rifle with 50 rounds ammunition, two 57mm recoilless rifle, three 81mm mortar, four 60mm mortar, two 12.7 machine guns, one M-60 machine gun, 15 individual weapons, 20 rifle grenades, 28 bangalore torpedoes, three cases small arms ammunition.
- *Operation Barking Sands.* Elements of the 1st Brigade, 25th Infantry Division found a cache: two CHICOM carbines, one M-1 rifle, 250 pounds small arms ammunition, 30 pounds clothing, 22 rounds 82mm mortar, 104 grenades, 200 detonators, 200 rounds small arms ammunition, 60 pounds documents and 4600 pounds rice.
- B-52s struck three times DMZ.
- Naval Gunfire-RVN. The DD USS MORTON set-off seven secondary explosions in the DMZ.

SEPTEMBER 26, 1967

- North Vietnam. USN pilots hit Haiphong railroad/highway bridge and Kien An highway bridge. USAF pilots hit Lang Dang railroad siding. An F-4 aircraft was downed by ground fire with pilot missing, one rescued.

- *Operation Kingfisher.* The enemy attacked operation area with 227 rounds of artillery/mortar fire. Results were three US killed, 10 wounded (treated and returned to duty).
- B-52s struck North Vietnam.
- The HMAS PERTH joined Naval Gunfire Support replacing the HMAS HOBART, to become the second Australian ship to operate with the Seventh Fleet.

SEPTEMBER 27, 1967

- North Vietnam. USAF pilots hit a Hon Gai ammunition storage area. USN pilots hit a Nam Dinh Army barracks. Seventy-four watercraft and 33 trucks destroyed or damaged in North Vietnam.
- *Operation Kingfisher.* The enemy attacked operation area with 87 rounds artillery/mortar fire. No damage or casualties.
- *Operation Fortress Sentry.* Terminated.
- US Army gunships demonstrating support of infantry units hit a group of spectators in Phuoc Tuy Province. Two personnel of the 1st Australian Task Force killed and eight wounded.
- B-52s struck three times in the DMZ.

SEPTEMBER 28, 1967

- North Vietnam. USN pilots hit a Haiphong railroad/highway bridge. 144 watercraft, one locomotive and 18 trucks destroyed or damaged in North Vietnam.
- *Operation Bluefield II.* Terminated.
- B-52s struck twice DMZ.

SEPTEMBER 29, 1967

- North Vietnam. USAF pilots hit Hoa Lac airfield. USN pilots hit a Haiphong highway bridge (SSE). An F-4 aircraft was shot down by ground fire, two-man crew rescued.
- The enemy attacked Dong Tam base camp, Dinh Tuong Province with 35 rounds of mortar fire. Results were 16 US wounded.
- *Operation Shenandoah II.* Elements of the 1st Infantry Division launched the 51-day search and destroy operation in Binh Duong Province. Friendly losses were 107 killed, 322 wounded and four armored personnel carriers destroyed. Enemy losses

were 956 killed, 63 detained, two retained, 71 individual weapons and 30 crew-served weapons.

- B-52s struck North Vietnam and twice in the DMZ.

SEPTEMBER 30, 1967

- North Vietnam. USAF pilots hit Kep airfield and Kep Ha Army barracks. USN pilots hit Long Doi transshipment point. USMC pilots hit Kien An airfield.
- *Operation Kingfisher.* Six rounds artillery containing leaflets exploded over Con Thien. Leaflets were not recovered due to the wind.
- B-52s struck three times in the DMZ.

OCTOBER 1, 1967

- US military strength in the RVN was 476,000.
- North Vietnam. USAF pilots hit Kep airfield and Kep railroad yard. USN pilots hit Cam Pha railroad/highway bridge and Hai Duong railroad bridge.
- *Operation Shenandoah II.* Announced.
- B-52s struck twice in the DMZ.

OCTOBER 2, 1967

- *Operation Kingfisher.* Three rounds of artillery containing leaflets exploded over Con Thien base area. None of the leaflets were recovered.
- The 3rd Brigade, 1st Cavalry Division deployed to Chu Lai and commenced operations in Quang Tin and Quang Nam Provinces as a part of the Americal Division.
- B-52s struck North Vietnam and in the DMZ.

OCTOBER 3, 1967

- North Vietnam. USN pilots hit a Hon Gai thermal power plant and Loc Binh highway bridge. USAF pilots hit Long Giai railroad yard and damaged 12-15 railroad cars and one locomotive. A USN A-4 aircraft was downed by ground fire, pilot rescued. A USAF F-105 aircraft downed by ground fire, pilot missing.
- B-52s struck North Vietnam and twice in the DMZ.

OCTOBER 4, 1967

- North Vietnam. USAF pilots hit Lang Son railroad bridge, Ha Gia railroad/highway bridge, destroyed or damaged 25 railroad cars Kep railroad yard and Thai Nguyen railroad yard. USN pilots hit Hai Duong military barracks area and Ban Muc barracks area. USMC pilots hit Hoa Loc and Kien An airfield. A USN A-4 aircraft was downed to unknown causes, pilot missing.
- *Operation Wallowa.* Elements of the 3rd Brigade, 1st Air Cavalry Division launched the 37-day search and destroy operation in Quang Nam and Quang Tin Provinces (becomes *Operation Wheeler/Wallowa* on November 11, 1967). This operation continued into 1968.
- B-52s struck North Vietnam and twice in the DMZ.

OCTOBER 5, 1967

- North Vietnam. USN pilots hit Haiphong POL Storage area; destroyed a Haiphong highway bridge. USAF pilots damaged a Lang Son railroad bridge and Lang Lau railroad bridge and bypass bridge. USMC pilots hit a Uong Bi thermal power plant and Hoa Loc airfield. A USAF F-105 aircraft downed by ground fire. Pilot missing.
- *Operation Barking Sands.* A 1st Brigade, 25th Infantry Division company found one CHICOM machine gun, three .30 caliber automatic weapons, two Browning automatic weapons, two Japanese machine guns, six individual weapons, one 60mm mortar, one 81mm mortar tube, 10 CHICOM claymore mines, 43 rounds 75mm recoilless rifle ammunition, 4,100 rounds .50 caliber ammunition and 400 pounds clothing in cache.
- *Operation Sea Wolf* crews destroyed or damaged 17 loaded enemy sampans beached in a restricted area of Kien Hoa Province.
- B-52s struck North Vietnam and DMZ.

OCTOBER 6, 1967

- North Vietnam. USN pilots dropped Doc Binh highway bypass bridge and hit Yen Bac military storage area and a Nam Dinh thermal power plant. USAF pilots hit Mo Trang railroad yard and bridge. USMC pilots hit a Hon Gai fuel storage area. A USN F-8 aircraft was downed with the pilot missing.

- *Operation Coronado V.* 3rd Brigade, 9th Infantry Division companies engaged an enemy force. Results were 94 enemy killed and nine US.
- USN SEAWOLF crews observed a group of the enemy off loading ammunition from junks and sampans in Kien Hoa Province. Eight junks and eight sampans destroyed and four sampans damaged.
- B-52s struck in the DMZ.

OCTOBER 7, 1967

- North Vietnam. USAF pilots hit the Cu Van POL storage area, Lang Dang railroad yard and Kep railroad yard. Two Russian-built MI-6 and MI-4 helicopters were destroyed on the ground W Hanoi. USN pilots hit Ha Thon railroad/highway bridge. USMC pilots hit Hoa Lac airfield. A USAF F-4 and an F-105 aircraft were downed by ground fire and USN A-4 was downed by ground fire, all crews missing.
- B-52s struck twice in North Vietnam.

OCTOBER 8, 1967

- North Vietnam. USN pilots hit Cat Bi airfield (first time) and Kien An airfield. USAF pilots dropped Cao Bang highway bridge. USMC pilots hit Ninh Dinh highway bridge.
- *Operation Wheeler.* The 1st Brigade, 101st Airborne Division hit an unknown number of the enemy attempting a two-pronged assault to cut off and encircle a platoon. Results were 60 enemy killed and 17 US. One crew-served weapon and 21 individual weapons captured.
- *Operation Akron III.* A US Army Engineer found one 82mm mortar, one British machine gun, four French machine guns, 12 US submachine guns, one French automatic weapon, seven US carbines, one 75mm recoilless rifle, one German machine gun, two machine guns of unknown origin, three Browning automatic weapons and one Bren Gun in weapons cache.
- *Operation Coronado V.* Terminated.
- A C-130 departing Hue for Da Nang, was reported overdue with a crew of five and 18 passengers.

- The new Huey Cobra, designed especially for ground support in the RVN, was used for the first time in a combat operation.
- B-52s struck twice in North Vietnam and twice in the DMZ.

OCTOBER 9, 1967

- North Vietnam. USN pilots hit a large military barracks area SE Haiphong (first time). USAF pilots hit Yen Bai railroad yard. USMC pilots hit Yen Bai military storage area. A USAF F-105 aircraft was downed by a MIG with the pilot missing.
- *Operation Akron III.* Elements 5th Cavalry found one M-60 machine gun, one .50 caliber machine gun, two French machine guns, 12 CHICOM type 53 machine guns, five12.7mm heavy machine guns, five unknown type machine guns, one anti-aircraft weapon. Two unknown type automatic weapons, six French M1924/M29 automatic weapons, two 81mm mortar, one 82mm mortar, two 57mm recoilless rifle, one homemade recoilless rifle, one M-1, one carbine, one US M-1917 and four .45 caliber submarine guns in the cache.
- *Operation Kenmore.* Announced.
- B-52s struck twice in North Vietnam.

OCTOBER 10, 1967

- North Vietnam. USN pilots hit Cat Bi airfield.
- *Operation Pershing.* The 2nd Brigade, 1st Cavalry Division (Airmobile) swept area of seven tactical air sorties found 37 enemy killed, 23 individual weapons and 11 crew-served weapons captured. There were no friendly casualties.
- A C-130 aircraft was found on the side of a mountain 38 kilometers SW Hue. Twenty-three personnel aboard were killed.

OCTOBER 11, 1967

- North Vietnam. USMC pilots hit Hoa Lac airfield.
- *Operation Medina.* Initiated.
- *Operation Shenandoah II.* 3rd Brigade, 1st Infantry Division elements found 22 tons rice, 15 75mm recoilless rifle rounds, 20 booby traps, three claymore mines and four boxes detonator cord in cache.
- *Operation Kenmore.* Terminated.
- *Operation Coronado VI.* Initiated.

- US Army gunships killed 82 of the enemy and destroyed 18 sampans.
- B-52s struck twice in North Vietnam and in the DMZ.

OCTOBER 12, 1967

- North Vietnam. USN pilots hit Thuong Ly shipyard and Lach Tray boatyard and Cat Bi airfield and Uong Bi thermal power plant. USMC pilots hit Thai Nguyen Army barracks. A USAF F-4 aircraft was downed by unknown causes with the two-man crew missing.
- *Operation Francis Marion.* Terminated.
- *Operation Greeley.* Terminated.
- *Operation MacArthur.* Elements of the 4th Infantry Division launched *Operation MacArthur* (combination of *Operations Francis Marion and Greeley*), a search and destroy operation in Pleiku Province. This operation continued into 1968.
- A light fire team fired on a suspected enemy location with permission. Ten VN civilians were killed and six wounded.
- B-52s struck in North Vietnam.

OCTOBER 13, 1967

- North Vietnam. USAF pilots hit Kep airfield and Kep Ha Army barracks. USMC pilots hit Hoa Lac airfield. A USMC F-4 aircraft was downed by ground fire, two-man crew missing.
- *Operation Kingfisher.* The enemy attacked a 4th Marine battalion with small arms and automatic weapons and 130 rounds mortar fire. The enemy used smoke and tear gas. Results were 24 enemy killed and 21 US.
- *Operation Coronado VI.* Announced.
- B-52s struck in North Vietnam.

OCTOBER 14, 1967

- North Vietnam. USN pilots hit Haiphong shipyard (W); Haiphong storage area; Haiphong highway bridge and Kien An radar site. USAF pilots hit Xom Trai and Hoa Loan boatyards and Kep railroad yard.
- *Operation Akron III.* 9th Infantry Division elements discovered an enemy weapons tunnel complex containing: four 57mm

pack howitzers, 3 57mm recoilless rifle, one 75mm weapon, three .32 caliber pistols, eight bolt action rifles, one automatic weapons, two AK-47 rifles, 32 9mm automatic pistols and six sniper scopes, five .30 caliber machine guns receivers and 17 barrels.

- B-52s struck in the DMZ.

OCTOBER 15, 1967

- *Operation Kingfisher.* A US aircraft had bomb fell short, hit three Marine positions resulting in three US killed and nine wounded.
- *Operation Akron III.* 9th Infantry Division continued to uncover enemy caches. To date, weapons captured total 1,003.
- B-52s struck twice in North Vietnam.

OCTOBER 16, 1967

- North Vietnam. USN pilots hit Kien An highway bridge.
- *Operation Pershing.* Two of the enemy surrendered to a helicopter crew. The enemy later led helicopter troops to a heavy jungled base camp area. Six NVA wounded were found. All eight enemy were detained.
- *Operation Akron III.* 3rd Brigade, 9th Infantry Division elements found 30 graves with one enemy body in each.
- B-52s struck the North Vietnam and in the DMZ.

OCTOBER 17, 1967

- North Vietnam. USAF pilots hit Lang Giai railroad yard, Lang Son railroad bridge, Dep Cau railroad yard; USMC pilots hit Kien An airfield. Three USAF F-105 and USN A-4 aircraft were downed by ground fire with the pilots missing.
- Naval Gunfire-DMZ. The DD DU PONT damaged an enemy radio and radar site N half DMZ.
- *Operation Medina.* Announced.
- *Operation Shenandoah II.* 1st Brigade, 1st Infantry Division companies made contact with an enemy battalion. Results were 103 enemy killed and 58 US.
- *Operation Akron III.* 9th Infantry Division elements discovered 640 mortar and recoilless rifle rounds, 21,600 rounds small arms ammunition and miscellaneous mortar and machine guns parts in cache.

- Australia and New Zealand announced troop increases for the RVN from 6,300 to 8,000 and 376 to 546, respectively.
- B-52s struck the NVN and in the DMZ.

OCTOBER 18, 1967

- North Vietnam. USAF pilots destroyed or damaged 20 railroad cars Lang Dang railroad siding. USN pilots hit Lach Tray boatyard. A USN A-4 aircraft was downed by ground fire with the pilot missing.
- Naval Gunfire-North Vietnam. The DD HMAS PERTH was hit from an NVA shore battery. Results were four crewmen wounded (two medevac). The ship suffered minor damage and returned to the line.
- The 5th Special Forces Group with VN CIDG forces killed 64 Khanh Hoa Province. There were no friendly casualties.
- B-52s struck in the DMZ.

OCTOBER 20, 1967

- *Operation Medina.* Terminated.
- *Operation Lam Son 138.* Quang Tri Province. ARVN 1st Infantry Division elements engaged in a three-hour fight: Results were 105 enemy killed and 16 ARVN.
- B-52s struck twice in the DMZ.

OCTOBER 21, 1967

- North Vietnam. USN pilots dropped Phat Diem bridge. USMC pilots hit Ninh Binh highway bridge and Thai Binh highway bridge.
- M-26 grenades exploded behind a stage performance at An Khe. Three Korean performers and one civilian were minor wounded.
- *Operation Riley.* Announced.
- *Operation Akron III.* Terminated.
- B-52s struck in North Vietnam.

OCTOBER 22, 1967

- North Vietnam. USN pilots hit Haiphong railroad yard and the Nui Ong Bang Naval dispersal area. A USN A-4 aircraft was downed by ground fire with the pilot missing.

- The 198th Light Infantry Brigade joined the Americal Division.
- The 3rd Battalion, 503rd US Airborne Infantry arrived in the RVN at Qui Nhon in Binh Dinh Province with their base camp located at Camp Radcliff in Binh Ding Province.
- B-52s struck in North Vietnam and in the DMZ.

OCTOBER 23, 1967

- North Vietnam. USN pilots hit Haiphong railroad yard and highway bridge. USAF pilots destroyed or damaged one locomotive and 8-10 railroad cars at Thanh Moi railroad yard and Hoa Lac airfield. USMC pilots hit Nam Dinh railroad yard.
- *Operation Wallowa.* 1st Cavalry Division elements engaged in heavy contact with the enemy. Results were 98 enemy killed and 15 US.
- The first C-130 landed at Quang Tri Airfield, eight days ahead of the scheduled operational date.
- B-52s struck in North Vietnam.
- Naval Gunfire-RVN. USS CARRONADE destroyed or damaged 144 support buildings and 21 sampans and triggered 15 secondary explosions E Quang Ngai City.

OCTOBER 24, 1967

- North Vietnam. Phuc Yen MIG airfield was damaged by the first combined strike of USN, USAF and US Marine Corps pilots. USAF pilots hit Kep airfield. USN pilots hit Haiphong railroad yard. USAF F-105, USN A-4 and two F-4 aircraft downed by ground fire. F-4 crews were missing, the other crews rescued.
- *Operation Wallowa.* Fifty additional enemy bodies were found as a result of action on October 23, 1967.
- *Operation MacArthur.* Announced.
- *Operation Shenandoah II.* 1st Infantry Division unit found 78 RPG rounds, five 122 rockets, 21 82mm mortar rounds, five 122mm rocket warheads and 59 60mm rounds mortar in a cache.
- *Operation Barking Sands.* A 1st Brigade, 25th Infantry Division company found 20,000 rounds small arms ammunition,

48 pounds C-4 explosions, 17 rounds 57mm recoilless rifle ammunition and 500-pound bomb in a cache. The ammunition was destroyed.

- B-52s struck DMZ.

OCTOBER 25, 1967

- Americal Division formally activated (formerly Task Force Oregon).
- North Vietnam. USN pilots hit Phuc Yen airfield. USAF pilots dropped two spans of Doumer bridge. USMC pilots hit Uong Bi thermal power plant. Two USAF F-105s and a USN A-4 aircraft were downed by ground fire with the crews missing.
- B-52s struck the North Vietnam.

OCTOBER 26, 1967

- North Vietnam. A MIG-21 downed by USN F-4, three MIG-17s downed by USAF F-4 aircraft. USAF pilots hit Thai Nguyen railroad yard. USN pilots hit Hanoi thermal power plant. USMC pilots hit Phuc Yen airfield and Hoa Lac airfield. Two USN A-4s and an F-8 aircraft downed by ground fire, all three pilots missing.
- General Westmoreland presented Silver Star Medal on behalf of the President of the US to Colonel Nguyen Van Toan, Commanding Officer, 2nd ARVN Infantry Division.
- A 5th ARVN infantry battalion 115 kilometers NNE Saigon with ARVN artillery and combined with US artillery support killed 134 enemy. Friendly casualties light. Fifty-four AK-47 weapons, six CHICOM light machine guns, 10 RPG launchers, five flame throwers, two Russian rifles, 35 rounds RPGs and two launchers captured.
- USN gunships killed 73 enemy and destroyed 39 sampans.
- B-52s struck North Vietnam.

OCTOBER 27, 1967

- North Vietnam. USAF pilots dropped two spans of Canal des Rapides highway/railroad bridge. USN pilots damaged the Uong Bi thermal power plant; USMC hit Yen Bai storage area. A MIG-17 was downed by a USAF F-105. Two USAF F-105s and F-4 were downed by ground fire with the pilots missing.

- *Operation Kingfisher.* The enemy attacked the operation area with 170 rounds mortar fire. Results were seven US killed and 41 wounded in the operation.
- *Operation Wallowa.* 3rd Brigade, 1st Cavalry Division elements contact an estimated two NVA battalions. Results were 78 enemy killed and 10 US.
- B-52s struck North Vietnam.

OCTOBER 28, 1967

- North Vietnam. USAF pilots damaged the center span of Canal des Rapides railroad/highway bridge. USN pilots hit Doumer bridge. USAF F-105 aircraft was downed by ground fire with the pilot missing.
- Terrorists explode devices in a restaurant in Nha Trang resulting in one US killed, 13 US military, four US civilians, and two VN wounded.
- The 7th Battalion, 17th Air Cavalry arrived at Qui Nhon aboard the USNS WALKER and sets up base camp at Camp Enari in Binh Dinh Province under the operational control of the 4th Infantry Division.

OCTOBER 29, 1967

- North Vietnam. USN pilots hit Cat Bi airfield, Chi Lai transshipment point and Kien An barge repair yard. USAF pilots hit Phu Lo railroad bridge. USMC pilots hit Yen Bai airfield.
- The NVN fire the first surface to air missiles at US B-52 aircraft (near DMZ).
- The enemy attacked Loc Ninh Subsector Headquarters Compound and CIDG Compound. 2nd Brigade, 1st Infantry Division troopers, CIDG and ARVN soldiers killed 160 enemy. Three US were killed. ARVN and CIDG casualties were light.
- B-52s struck twice in North Vietnam.

OCTOBER 30, 1967

- North Vietnam. USAF pilots cratered Kep airfield and destroyed or damaged 1,015 railroad cars Kep railroad yard. USN pilots hit Ken An airfield, destroyed Uong Bi bypass bridge and damaged Uong Bi thermal power plant. USMC pilots hit Yen Bai airfield and Nam Dinh Army barracks. A MIG-17 was downed by a USN F-4.

- The enemy continued the battle in Loc Ninh. Eighty-three enemy were killed and four US. ARVN and CIDG casualties were light.
- Vice President Humphrey arrived in the RVN for the presidential inauguration and tour of the country.

OCTOBER 31, 1967

- North Vietnam. USN pilots hit Tri Chi highway bridge and Yen My Army barracks area. A USMC pilot hit Canal des Rapides bridge. A USMC A-6 aircraft was downed by unknown causes with the pilot missing.
- Naval Gunfire-North Vietnam. Mui Ron radar site damaged by the DD USS DAMATO.
- *Operations Kingfisher, Ardmore and Fremont.* Terminated.
- *Operations Scotland, Kentucky and Lancaster.* Initiated.
- Enemy attempts to capture Loc Ninh resulted in 126 enemy killed and four US. ARVN and CIDG casualties were light. Casualties of the three-day battle were 369 enemy killed and seven US, light casualties ARVN and CIDG.
- Enemy terrorists mortar the Presidential Palace in Saigon with four rounds of 60mm mortar fire. Friendly losses were one civilian killed, two civilians wounded and one building minor damage. Enemy losses were: one killed. Vice President Humphrey inside Palace when first round landed.

NOVEMBER 1, 1967

- US military strength in the RVN was 487,000.
- *Operation Neosho.* Elements of the 3rd Marine Division launch the search and destroy operation in Thua Thien Province. This operation continues into 1968.
- *Operation Kentucky.* Elements of the 3rd Marine Division launch the search and destroy operation in Quang Tri Province. This operation continues into 1968.
- *Operation Scotland.* Elements of the 3rd Marine Division launch the search and destroy operation in Quang Tri Province. This operation continues into 1968.
- *Operation Lancaster.* Elements of the 3rd Marine Division launch

the search and destroy operation in Quang Tri Province. This operation continues into 1968.

- B-52's struck North Vietnam.

NOVEMBER 2, 1967

- North Vietnam. USMC pilots hit Yen Bai airfield. A USN A-4 downed by ground fire, pilot missing.
- Naval Gunfire-North Vietnam. The DD USS BLUE returned to duty off coast of North Vietnam.
- *Operation Coronado IX.* Elements of the 9th Infantry Division launch the search and destroy operation in Dinh Tuong Province. This operation continues into 1968.
- *Operation Sante Fe 1.* Elements of the 9th Infantry Division launch the 64-da6 search and destroy operation in Long Khanh and Binh Tuy Provinces. Friendly losses were two US killed, three AUG killed, one ARVN killed, 13 US wounded and nine AUS wounded, 13 ARVN wounded, two tanks, one Rome Plow, and two trucks destroyed. Enemy losses were 126 killed, six by ARVN, 86 by US, 32 detained, 119 individual weapons and 20 crew-served weapons.
- Viet Cong burned 300 homes in Dai Loc Hamlet Quang Nam Province. In a series of attacks, four enemy killed and 10 US. Nine VN civilians killed.
- Early morning battle Loc Ninh resulted in 463 enemy killed and eight US. ARVN and CIDG casualties light.
- B-52s struck DMZ.

NOVEMBER 3, 1967

- North Vietnam. USN pilots hit the Hai Duong railroad siding.
- Total casualties in Loc Ninh battles since October 28, 1967: 860 enemy killed and 11 US. ARVN and CIDG casualties light.
- The fire support base of the ARVN 2nd Brigade, 4th Infantry Division, 40 kilometers NNE Ban Me Thuot, Darlac Province, received a mortar and ground attack. The Battle of Dak To commenced in *Operation MacArthur* area.
- B-52s struck in the DMZ.

NOVEMER 4, 1967

- North Vietnam. USN pilots hit Nam Dinh railroad yard.
- Naval Gunfire-North Vietnam. The HMAS PERTH shelled Mui Dat boatyard SSE Vinh.
- *Operation Coronado IX.* Announced.

NOVEMBER 5, 1967

- North Vietnam. USAF pilots hit Phuc Yen airfield. Two MIG-17s estimated to be damaged on ground. A USAF F-105 aircraft downed by ground fire, pilot rescued. One hundred seventeen secondary explosions and 54 fires.
- *Operation MacArthur.* 1st Brigade, 4th Infantry Division elements made contact with enemy force in well fortified post in heavily jungled ridge line.

NOVEMBER 6, 1967

- North Vietnam. A USAF F-4 aircraft crew downed two MIG-17s. The USAF hit Gia Thuong storage area (first time) and Kep railroad yard. An F-105 aircraft was downed by ground fire with the pilot missing.
- *Operation Essex.* Initiated.
- *Operation MacArthur.* Dak To action continues with 104 enemy killed and 16 US.
- An estimated enemy company kidnaps 245 Montagnard civilians, nine kilometers W of An Khe in Binh Dinh Province (one civilian killed and 245 civilians kidnapped).

NOVEMBER 7, 1967

- North Vietnam. USAF pilots hit Lang Dang railroad complex. USN pilots hit in Ninh Ngoai shipyard and repair facility and Uong Bi barge yard and highway bridge. A USAF F-105 and an F-4 aircraft downed by ground fire, three pilots missing.
- *Operations Wheeler/Wallowa.* Merged.
- *Operation Shenandoah II.* 1st Infantry Division companies

contact with an estimated enemy battalion in the Loc Ninh area. Results were 66 enemy killed and 18 US.

- US Army gunships killed 89 enemy, estimated 27 sampans.
- B-52s struck North Vietnam and DMZ.
- Naval Gunfire-RVN. 53 supply and storage buildings NNE Quang Ngai City destroyed by DD USS KYES.

NOVEMBER 8, 1967

- North Vietnam. USAF pilots hit Lang Kay railroad bridge, Yen Bai airfield supply area and Dai Loi railroad bridge. USN pilots hit Dong Lo transshipment point, Phuong Dinh bridge complex and Ninh Xa railroad bridge. An F-105 aircraft downed by ground fire, pilot missing. A USAF F-4 downed by a MIG-21, one pilot rescued, one missing.
- The 10-day battle of Loc Ninh, which commenced October 29, 1967 terminates. Friendly losses were 29 US killed, 21 ARVN killed, 123 US wounded, and 111 ARVN wounded. Enemy losses were 851 killed and 15 detained.
- *Operation Essex.* Announced.
- *Operation Santa Fe I.* Announced.
- *Operation MacArthur.* Heavy contact Dak To battle with 232 enemy killed and six US.
- B-52s struck DMZ.

NOVEMBER 9, 1967

- Naval Gunfire-North Vietnam. The DD USS BLUE set off numerous secondary explosions and fires reported at an NVA fuel depot area.
- Gia Dinh Province (Saigon). An ammunition barge was sunk in Saigon River 90-foot water. One ARVN and Two US wounded. A Viet Cong frogman was believed killed by ARVN guard.
- Naval Gunfire-RVN. The USS WHITE RIVER, USS ST FRANCIS RIVER, USS CLARION RIVER, CARBONADE destroyed 78 apartment buildings and nine bunkers and set off two secondary explosions SE Da Nang.

NOVEMBER 10, 1967

- North Vietnam. USN pilots hit Nam Dinh Army barracks and Dong Thuong railroad bridge. Two USAF F-4s were downed to unknown causes with both crews missing.
- *Operation MacArthur.* Contact continued Dak To. Thus far casualties: 424 enemy killed and 48 US.
- Phu Loi base camp received an unknown number mortar rounds resulting in one US killed and 32 wounded treated and returned to duty and four wounded medevac.
- B-52s struck the DMZ.

NOVEMBER 11, 1967

- North Vietnam. USMC pilots hit Yen Bai railroad yards, Hon Gai storage areas and Vinh railroad yards.
- *Operation MacArthur.* Contact continued at Dak To. Results thus far: 527 enemy killed and 76 US.
- *Operation Wheeler/Wallowa.* Elements of the Americal Division launched the search and destroy operation in Quang Tin Province. This operation continued into 1968.

NOVEMBER 12, 1967

- North Vietnam. USMC pilots hit the Uong Bi thermal power plant.
- Naval Gunfire-North Vietnam. The DD USS GOLDBOROUGH was hit by a shore battery NNE Dong Hoi. There was no casualties and light damage reported.
- *Operation MacArthur.* Dak To battle results thus far: 635 enemy killed and 92 US.

NOVEMBER 13, 1967

- Major General B.A. Hocmuth, The Commander of the 3rd Marine Division was killed in a helicopter explosion near Dong Ha in Quang Tri Province.
- *Operation Osceola.* Announced.
- *Operation Foster.* Elements of the 7th Marines launched the 17-day search and destroy operation in Quang Nam Province. Friendly losses were 21 killed and 137 wounded. Enemy losses were 125 killed, 79 detained, 10 individual weapons and two crew-served weapons.

- *Operation MacArthur.* Action continued at Dak To. Results were 639 enemy killed and 102 US since November 1, 1967.
- B-52s struck North Vietnam.

NOVEMBER 14, 1967

- North Vietnam. USMC pilots hit the Trai Hop military barracks area.
- *Operations Wheeler/Wallowa.* A UH-1 helicopter hit by enemy automatic weapons fire resulted in eight US killed.
- *Operation Foster.* Announced.
- *Operation MacArthur.* Action Dak To reported light.

NOVEMBER 15, 1967

- North Vietnam. USAF pilots hit Hoa Lac and Kep airfield. USMC pilots hit Nam Dinh Army barracks and Hai Duong railroad bypass bridge. USN pilots dropped S span Phuong Ding railroad bypass bridge.
- *Operation Osceola.* A 1st Marine Regiment platoon detained three 14-year olds and two 10-year olds with two grenades, 140 rounds of 5.56 ammunition.
- *Operation Foster.* 7th Marine Regiment forces found 107 tons rice.
- *Operation MacArthur.* The Dak To airfield was attacked four times. Casualties were reported light.
- The 25th Infantry Division base at Cu Chi received approximately 99 rounds mortar/75mm recoilless rifle fire. Enemy casualties were unknown. Friendly losses were five US killed and 12 wounded (medevac) and 13 wounded (treated and returned to duty).
- B-52s struck North Vietnam.

NOVEMBER 16, 1967

- North Vietnam. USN pilots hit Haiphong shipyard #2 (first time). USMC pilots hit Song Dong Army barracks, Kien An airfield and Hon Gai storage area. A USN F-4 aircraft was downed by ground fire with the crew missing.
- *Operation Kentucky.* Marine mortar crews had seven rounds of

81mm impact within the 3rd Marine positions with one Marine killed and nine wounded.

- *Operation MacArthur.* Dak To airfield was hit with 43 rounds of mortar fire. There were no casualties.
- Naval Forces. A Nationalist Chinese merchant ship was damaged by enemy fire SE Saigon. Damage was reported light. There were no casualties.
- B-52s struck the DMZ.

NOVEMBER 17, 1967

- North Vietnam. USAF pilots hit Hanoi Bac Mai airfield (first time). USN pilots hit Hanoi barge yard (first time). A USAF F-105, USN A-4 aircraft were downed by ground fire, crews missing.
- *Operation Essex.* Terminated.
- *Operation MacArthur.* Dak To battle continues. The 4th Infantry Division made contact with an enemy force in well dug-in positions.
- *Operation Kien Giang.* Initiated.
- *Operation Strike/Uniontown.* Elements of the 199th Light Infantry Brigade launch the 30-day search and destroy operation in Bien Hoa Province. Friendly losses were 34 killed and 127 wounded. Enemy losses were 100 killed, eight detained, seven individual weapons and one crew-served weapon.
- US Army gunships killed 47 enemy and destroyed 57 sampans.

NOVEMBER 18, 1967

- North Vietnam. USN pilots damaged Haiphong ordnance department and Doan Lai storage area. USMC pilots hit an ammunition storage area NW Hanoi. A USAF F-105 aircraft was downed by a MIG and two F-105s were downed by ground fire with the crews missing.
- *Operations Wheeler/Wallowa.* Americal Division elements found 30 rounds 60mm mortar, 10 rounds 81mm mortar, 14 rounds 82mm mortar, five rounds 57mm recoilless rifle ammunition, five hand grenades, 1,750 rounds small arms ammunition, 200

pounds explosions, one mortar plate and two machine gun barrels in cache.

- *Operation MacArthur.* The battle continued at Dak To. 173rd Airborne Brigade companies engaged an enemy force. Results thus far to date were 800 enemy killed and 139 friendly.
- *Operation Kien Giang.* Announced.
- Two explosions at the Non-Commissioned Officer (NCO) club at Nha Trang resulted in four US military, two US civilians, one VN Air Force, two VN police, one ROK military and one Filipino wounded.
- Korean civilian workers at Cam Ranh Bay started a two-day riot over working conditions.
- The SS BUCHANAN was attacked and hit 19 times by recoilless rifle and machinegun fire on the Saigon River 15 miles N of Vung Tau resulting in no US casualties. Reaction forces killed 16 Viet Cong.

NOVEMBER 19, 1967

- North Vietnam. USAF pilots hit a Hanoi concrete plant and Thuy Phuong barge yard and transshipment point (first time) and Yen Vien railroad yard. USN pilots hit Haiphong railroad/ highway bridge bypass, destroyed or damaged 45-55 railroad cars at My Coi railroad yard and Ninh Binh railroad yard. USMC pilots hit Kien An airfield, Dong Cuong railroad yard, Nam Dinh railroad siding and Phu Ly railroad bridge. Two F-105 and two USN F-4 aircraft were downed by ground fire, crews missing.
- *Operation MacArthur.* Battle Dak To continues. Results since November 1, 1967: 868 enemy killed and 229 US (by US only).
- RVN. An F-100 aircraft was downed in Binh Long Province by ground fire, pilot missing.

NOVEMBER 20, 1967

- North Vietnam. USAF pilots destroyed 40-50 railroad cars at Duc Noi railroad yard and damaged Lang Lau railroad bridge. USN pilot hit Cat Bi airfield and Haiphong railroad highway bridge. USMC pilots hit Song Dong Army barracks. A USAF F-4 aircraft was downed to unknown causes, pilots rescued. An F-105 aircraft was downed by a MIG-21, pilot missing.

- *Operation MacArthur.* Light action reported at Dak To. Results to date: 1,143 enemy killed, 234 US and ARVN casualties light.
- *Operation Cove.* Announced.
- B-52s struck DMZ.

NOVEMBER 21, 1967

- *Operation Cove.* Terminated.
- *Operation Atlanta.* Announced.

NOVEMBER 22, 1967

- North Vietnam. USN pilots hit Tho Cac Ba transshipment point.
- *Operation MacArthur.* US and ARVN troops killed 1,377 enemy since November 1, 1967 at Dak To. US casualties were 274 and ARVN casualties light.
- US Army gunships killed 54 enemy and destroyed 37 sampans.
- B-52s struck North Vietnam.

NOVEMBER 23, 1967

- North Vietnam. A USAF F-4 aircraft was credited with probably downing a MIG-21.
- *Operations Wheeler/Wallowa.* In Quang Tin Province 26 kilometers NW Tam Ky, 91 enemy were killed by Americal Division elements in an 11-hour battle. Seven US were killed.
- *Operation MacArthur.* Battle Dak To continues. Hill 875 occupied.
- *Operation Atlanta.* The 2nd Brigade, 25th Infantry Division discovered 65 CHICOM carbines, one Mauser rifle and two submachine guns in cache.
- Battle of Dak To, Hill 875 taken. Friendly losses were 325 killed and 1,137 wounded. Enemy losses were 1,243 killed.

NOVEMBER 24, 1967

- North Vietnam. USMC pilots hit Nam Dinh railroad yard and Song Dong Army barracks.
- *Operation Ballistic Arch.* Initiated.
- *Operation Kien Giang.* Terminated.

NOVEMBER 25, 1967

- North Vietnam. USN pilots hit Dong Phong Thuong railroad bridge.
- Nha Trang Air Base, attacked with 130 rounds 82mm mortar fire and ground attack resulted in six Special Forces troopers wounded. One mortar round landed downtown Nha Trang resulting in one VN civilian killed.

NOVEMBER 26, 1967

- North Vietnam. USMC pilots hit Co Trai railroad/highway bridge. USN pilots hit Qui Vinh railroad bridge.
- *Operation MacArthur.* Dak To battle continues. 1,641 enemy killed to date, 287 US killed, ARVN casualties were reported light.
- Elements of the 199th Light Infantry Brigade found 30 carbines, 100 grenades, 14 boxes of small arms ammunition, two radios and two typewriters in cache.
- B-52s struck North Vietnam.

NOVEMBER 27, 1967

- North Vietnam. USN pilots hit Kien An airfield. USAF pilots hit Yen Bay airfield. USMC pilots hit Hoa Binh military installation.
- *Operation Atlanta.* Elements of the 2nd Brigade, 25th Infantry Division found 72 tons rice in past two days.
- The enemy attacked Soc Trang airfield resulting in one US killed and two wounded. Moderate damage was reported.
- B-52s struck North Vietnam.

NOVEMBER 28, 1967

- North Vietnam. USN pilots hit Haiphong railroad yard (W) and railroad/highway bridge.
- A PBR intercepted a large motorized sampan in Vinh Binh Province. The vessel beached. Captured were 150 rounds antibiotics and other medicines, 310 rounds small arms ammunition, three grenades, one gas mask, 25 pounds medical dressings and other miscellaneous equipment. The

sampan and motor were destroyed by the PBR crew. There were no casualties reported.

NOVEMBER 29, 1967

- The Phouc Dong Province District Headquarters Compound in Bo Duc was attacked by an estimated battalion of enemy force. Results were 78 enemy killed, one VN civilian killed, ARVN casualties were light and no US casualties.
- President Johnson announced that Secretary of Defense McNamara would resign to head the World Bank.
- B-52s struck DMZ.

NOVEMBER 30, 1967

- North Vietnam. USMC pilots hit the Hon Gai storage area.
- Explosives were set off a fire in the Long Binh storage area. There were no injuries reported.
- In Phuoc Long Province the enemy attacked 1st Division battalion positions at Bu Dop 140 kilometers NNE Saigon. The enemy fired 125 rounds of 60/82mm mortar fire into friendly positions. Results were 31 enemy killed and five US.
- *Operation Foster.* Terminated.
- B-52s struck North Vietnam and Thua Thien Province (14 secondary explosions).

DECEMBER 1, 1967

- US military strength in the RVN was 480,000.
- North Vietnam. USAF pilots hit Yen Bai airfield. USMC pilots hit Ninh Binh highway bridge.
- *Operation Forrest.* Announced.
- *Klamath Falls.* Elements of the 101st Airborne Brigade launched the 38-day search and destroy operation in Lam Dong, Binh Thuan and Binh Tuy Provinces. Friendly losses were 28 killed and 138 wounded. Enemy losses were 156 killed, 11 detained, 74 individual weapons and three crew-served individuals.

DECEMBER 2, 1967

- PBR Mobile I with 10 PBRs arrives at Da Nang (10 PBRs follow on December 5, 1967). This was the second time that PBRs have been located in the I CTZ.

DECEMBER 3, 1967

- Naval Gunfire-North Vietnam. The DD USS OZBORN was hit by an enemy shore battery NNE Dong Hoi resulting in five crewmen injured. The ship remained on line.
- Bien Hoa Province. One barge was sunk and one on fire by enemy recoilless rifle fire. There were no friendly casualties.

DECEMBER 4, 1967

- North Vietnam. USAF pilots hit the Thai Nguyen railroad and Yen Bai airfield and storage area. USMC pilots hit Nam Dinh railroad yard and Kien An airfield.
- *Operation Coronado IX.* Binh Tuong Province, elements of the Mobile Riverine Force (2nd Brigade, 9th Infantry Division and USN TF-117 and VN 5th Marine Battalion), made contact with an enemy force. Results were 235 enemy killed and 13 US. VN Marine casualties were light.
- In Bien Hoa Province, fire broke out storage area near Long Binh Base. An estimate of damage is not available.
- A squadron of 14 A-7A, the new Corsair II aircraft, join the Vietnam conflict for the first time in a bombing raid over North Vietnam.
- USN Patrol Air Cushion Vehicles (PACV) return to Vietnam as part of TF-117 (Mekong Delta Mobile Riverine Force). These vehicles were previously in the RVN in 1966 as part of TF-115, Coastal Surveillance Force (*Operation Market Time*).

DECEMBER 5, 1967

- In Quang Tri Province, 38 Hoi Chanhs, believed to be members of the same Viet Cong unit, turned themselves in to representatives of the RVN.
- An unknown number of the enemy, supported by 82mm mortar fire, attacked Dak Son Village, two kilometers NE of Song Be in Phuoc Long Province. Friendly losses were two Popular Forces killed, four RD killed and wounded, 151 civilians wounded, 400

civilians missing, 1,382 refugees and nine individual weapons. Enemy losses were five killed and two Individual weapons.

DECEMBER 6, 1967

- *Operation Kentucky*. Quang Tri Province. A Marine position was hit by a bomb dropped from a Marine aircraft resulted in five US killed and two wounded. The enemy attacked the operation area with 276 rounds of artillery and mortar fire. Results were seven US killed, 58 wounded (medevac) and 19 wounded (treated and returned to duty).
- *Operation Pershing*. Binh Dinh Province. Two companies from the 1st Brigade, 1st Cavalry Division (Airmobile) engaged an estimated reinforced enemy company. Action continues.
- Phuoc Long Province. An AP photographer was wounded in both legs.

DECEMBER 7, 1967

- *Operation Kentucky*. The enemy attacked the operation area with 31 rounds artillery/mortar fire resulting in seven US killed, 60 wounded (medevac) and 11 wounded (treated and returned to duty).
- *Operation Kole Kole*. Terminated.
- *Operation Barking Sands*. Terminated.
- *Operation Diamond Head*. Terminated.
- *Operation Pershing*. Action continues from December 6, 1967. The two-day battle results were 210 enemy killed and light casualties US. Action continues.
- B-52s struck North Vietnam (30 kilometers WSW Dong Hoi).

DECEMBER 8, 1967

- North Vietnam. USAF pilots hit Kim Lang Army barracks. USAF F-4 aircraft engaged two MIG-21s. There was no damage to aircraft of either side.
- *Operation Klamath Falls*. Announced.
- Binh Dinh Province. Elements of the Capitol ROK Infantry Division reported 67 enemy killed during a cordon operation initiated December 7, 1967. ROK casualties were light.
- *Operation Yellowstone*. 260 tons polished rice was captured.

- Chuong Thien Province. ARVN troops killed 390 of the enemy, the highest kill one day by ARVN.
- The 3rd Brigade, Task Force, 101st Airborne Division arrived in the RVN.
- B-52s struck the DMZ.

DECEMBER 9, 1967

- North Vietnam. USMC pilots hit Hoa Binh military barracks area and Nam Dinh Army barracks.
- *Operations Wheeler/Wallowa.* Quang Nam Province. Two companies from the 3rd Brigade, 4th Infantry Division and one company from the 3rd Brigade, 1st Cavalry Division (Airmobile) engaged an enemy force in a nine-hour battle. Results were 103 enemy killed and two US.
- *Operation Yellowstone.* Announced.
- Binh Long Province. 1st Infantry Division troops engaged an enemy force. Results were 124 enemy killed and one US.
- Chuong Thien Province. Elements of the 21st ARVN Infantry Division and Ranger elements have killed 439 enemy in the two-day battle. Friendly casualties were 67 killed and 103 wounded.
- US Army gunships killed 170 enemy.
- B-52s struck the DMZ.

DECEMBER 10, 1967

- North Vietnam. USMC pilots hit Kien An airfield and Nam Dinh railroad yard.
- *Operation Pershing.* In Binh Dinh Province, the 1st Cavalry Division (Airmobile) have killed 254 enemy since December 6, 1967. Twenty-eight US were killed.
- Long An Province. The enemy attacked the 9th Infantry Division camp at An Nhut Tan, Tan Tru District Compound and Engineer positions at Rach Kien. Results were 15 enemy killed, seven US killed and 46 US wounded.
- A USAF F-4 aircraft was downed in the RVN by ground fire with the two-man crew rescued.
- B-52s struck the DMZ.

DECEMBER 11, 1967

- North Vietnam. USMC pilots hit Son Tay Army barracks.
- *Operation Pershing.* Binh Dinh Province. Action since December 6, 1967 results were 471 enemy killed (304 by US and 167 by ARVN). Friendly casualties were 33 US killed and 147 wounded, 30 ARVN killed and 71 wounded.
- Mark II PBR combat patrols commenced.
- Senator C.H. Percy (R-Ill) was caught in Viet Cong fire at Dak Song (III CTZ) and evacuated to Song Be, while on inspection trip.
- B-52s struck the DMZ.

DECEMBER 12, 1967

- North Vietnam. USMC pilots hit Nam Dinh railroad yard.
- Bien Hoa Province, 101st Airborne Division welcomed by General Westmoreland.
- B-52s struck the DMZ.

DECEMBER 13, 1967

- *Operation Saratoga.* Announced.
- The command elements of the US Army's 101st Airborne Division arrived in the RVN in the largest and longest aerial troop deployment in the history of modern warfare. US troops strength in the RVN surpassed the number in the Korean War.
- B-52s struck North Vietnam (14 kilometers NNE Gio Linh).

DECEMBER 14, 1967

- North Vietnam. USAF pilots hit Doumer railroad/highway bridge. A MIG-21 engagement was reported by F-4 crews. There was no damage to aircraft on either side. A USN F-8 aircraft was downed by a wMIG-17. USMC pilots hit Nam Dinh Army barracks. A USAF F-105 aircraft was downed to unknown causes with the pilot missing.
- *Operation Kentucky.* The enemy attacked the operation area with 287 rounds of mortar and artillery fire. Results were four US killed and 21 wounded (medevac) and 10 wounded (treated and returned to duty) in the operation.
- Binh Dinh Province. The enemy overran an ARVN Regional

Forces platoon observation post. An ARVN and US mechanized infantry company moved into the area of contact. Results were 115 enemy killed and three US. ARVN casualties were light.

- Kien Hoa Province. A bomb dropped off target by a USAF pilot resulted in three VN civilians killed.
- B-52s struck North Vietnam.

DECEMBER 15, 1967

- North Vietnam. USN pilots hit Haiphong railroad yard, highway bridge (dropped center span). USAF pilots damaged N end of the Can des Rapides railroad/highway bridge and one MIG-17 Hoa Lac airfield.
- Quang Tri airfield received 50 rounds of mortar fire resulting in one US killed and 18 wounded (medevac) and 12 wounded (treated and returned to duty).
- Quang Nam Province. Marine units were accidentally hit by one round of 81mm mortar fire resulting in 23 US wounded (medevac).
- *Operation Citrus.* Initiated.
- *Operation Pershing.* In Binh Dinh Province, 1st Cavalry Division and ARVN Infantry units engaged an enemy force. Contact continues.
- B-52s struck in the DMZ.

DECEMBER 16, 1967

- North Vietnam. USAF pilots dropped two spans Canal des Rapides railroad/highway bridge and hit Yen Vien railroad yard. USN pilots destroyed or damaged 45 railroad cars in the panhandle. A USAF aircraft was downed by MIG-21 with the crew missing.
- Quang Tri Province. The enemy attacked positions N part Quang Tri Province with 243 rounds enemy fire. Results were five US killed and 31 wounded (medevac).
- *Operation Fairfax.* Elements of the 199th Light Infantry Brigade terminated the 381-day search and destroy operation in Gia Dinh and Long An Provinces, which commenced on November 30, 1966. Friendly losses were 118 killed, 725 wounded, 30 individual weapons and two crew-served weapons. Enemy losses

were 1,043 killed, 2,529 detained, 40 retained, 321 individual weapons and five crew-served weapons.

- *Operation Pershing.* Binh Dinh Province. Contact continued from December 15, 1967. 1st Cavalry Division and ARVN forces have killed 128 in two-day contact. US losses were 22 killed and 52 wounded. There were no ARVN casualties.
- US Army gunships killed 118 of the enemy.

DECEMBER 17, 1967

- North Vietnam. USAF pilots hit Kep airfield and Phuc Yen airfield. USN reported Hai Duong highway unserviceable. USMC pilots hit Nam Dinh railroad yard.
- A US Army soldier was hit in his right leg by small arms in Saigon and admitted to the 3rd Field Hospital.
- *Operation Camden.* Elements of the 25th Infantry Division launched the 14-day search and destroy operation in Hau Ngia Province. Friendly losses were 25 killed, 118 wounded, and one crew-served weapon. Enemy losses were 101 killed, 26 detained, one retained, 22 individual weapons and two crew-served weapons.
- A USAF F-4 aircraft was downed by ground fire in the RVN with one crewman killed and one rescued.
- B-52s struck twice in the DMZ.

DECEMBER 18, 1967

- North Vietnam. USAF pilots dropped three spans and damaged another of Doumer bridge. USN pilots hit and damaged Hoang Xa bridge. USMC pilots hit Nam Dinh Army barracks.
- Naval Gunfire-North Vietnam. The USS McCORMICK received superficial shrapnel damage. No injuries were reported.
- *Operation Citrus.* Announced.
- *Operation Manchester.* Initiated.
- B-52s struck North Vietnam and the DMZ.

DECEMBER 19, 1967

- North Vietnam. USAF F-105 pilots downed two MIGs and another MIG probable down by F-4 crew. USAF pilots downed eight spans of Doumer bridge, heavy damaged Dai Loi railroad bridge, hit Hanoi railroad car repair shop and storage area.

USN pilots hit Ha Thon railroad/highway bridge. USMC pilots hit Co Trai railroad/highway bridge.

- *Operation Manchester.* Announced.
- *Operation Yellowstone.* 1st Brigade, 25th Infantry Division base camp received 200 rounds mortar fire and a ground attack resulting in 23 enemy killed and three US.
- B-52s struck North Vietnam and the DMZ.

DECEMBER 20, 1967

- In Binh Dinh Province, the 11th Infantry Brigade arrived Qui Nhon and will join the Americal Division.
- Thien Ngon Special Forces and CIDG camp received 300 rounds mortar fire and ground attack resulting in six US wounded (medevac). CIDG casualties were light.
- In field positions, a Royal Thai Regiment company received mortar, small arms and automatic weapons fire. The Thai forces returned fire. Enemy losses were 64 enemy killed and Thai casualties were light.
- A terrorist threw grenades in Binh Vinh Bar (Saigon) resulting in three USAF, one US Army and nine VN civilians wounded.
- B-52s struck the DMZ.

DECEMBER 21, 1967

- *Operation Fortress Ridge.* Initiated.
- Fire from unknown causes in ammunition dump in the vicinity Lai Khe resulted in two US soldiers killed and 20 injured.
- Pan American World Airways indigenous employees went on strike for 30 percent wage increase.
- B-52s struck the DMZ.

DECEMBER 22, 1967

- North Vietnam. USAF pilots hit Kep airfield. USMC pilots hit Yen Bai storage area.
- The USN *Operation Market Time* facility at Qui Nhon was attacked by an enemy force using satchel charges. A Swift boat crew discovered and removed the charge without incident. An attack against an enlisted men's billet caused moderate damage, three enemy killed and two US.
- The first significant contact by 3rd Brigade, 101st Airborne Division since arrival resulted in 14 enemy killed and no US.

- The SS SEATRAIN TEXAS was mined at anchor in the Nha Be River 15 kilometers SE of Saigon and proceeded under own power to Saigon. No casualties were reported.
- Terrorists riding a motorbike threw grenades in the vicinity of the Montana Bachelor Enlisted Quarters (BEQ) resulted in two US wounded (treated minor wounded and released) and three admitted to the 3rd Field Hospital.
- B-52s struck the DMZ.
- Air America indigenous employees strike for 40 percent wage increase.

DECEMBER 23, 1967

- North Vietnam. USN pilots destroyed a Binh Lang highway bridge. USAF pilots hit Yen Bai airfield and storage area.
- *Operation Citrus.* Terminated.
- *Operation Atlanta.* Terminated.
- US Army gunships killed 72 enemy and destroyed 80 sampans.
- President Johnson made a brief Christmas visit to US troops at Cam Ranh Bay.
- B-52s struck the DMZ.

DECEMBER 24, 1967

- A 24-hour Christmas stand-down was observed from 1800 hours, December 24, 1967 to 1800 hours, December 25, 1967. At the end of the truce period a total of 40 major incidents (i.e. casualties) and 78 minor incidents were recorded.
- *Operation Fortress Ridge.* Terminated.
- *Operation Camden.* Announced.
- The 11th Light Infantry Brigade arrived at Duc Pho in Quang Tin Province and joined the Americal Division for future operations in the I CTZ.
- B-52s struck the DMZ and reported 10 secondary explosions nine kilometers NE Con Thien.

DECEMBER 25, 1967

- North Vietnam. After 1800 hours, pilots hit truck convoys in the panhandle area included one seven-mile 150-truck convoy. 100 trucks were destroyed or damaged.
- US/RVNAF/FWMAF curtailed offensive operations from 1800

hours, December 24, 1967 to 1800 hours, December 25, 1967. During the ceasefire, 118 incidents were reported during the 24-hour period. Forty were significant which resulted in two US killed, 24 wounded and 33 enemy killed.

DECEMBER 26, 1967

- North Vietnam. Twenty trucks were destroyed, 10 secondary explosions and 17 fires in the panhandle.
- *Operations Wheeler/Wallow.* Americal Division troops discovered 83 individual weapons and 37 crew-served weapons in cache.
- *Operation Badger Tooth.* Initiated.
- The main body of the 3rd Battalion, Royal Australian Regiment arrived at the 1st Australian Task Force base camp at Nui Dat.
- B-52s struck twice in the DMZ and reported 26 secondary explosions.

DECEMBER 27, 1967

- USAF pilots hit Mo Trang railroad siding. Thirty-one trucks were destroyed. Eight secondary explosions and eight fires were reported in the panhandle.
- *Operation Badger Tooth.* Announced. The 1st Marine Regiment engaged two enemy companies in fortified positions in a village. Enemy losses were 27 known killed. Friendly losses were 48 US killed and 81 US wounded.
- *Operation Bolling.* 173rd Airborne Brigade elements engaged an estimated two enemy companies resulting in 33 enemy killed and 12 US.
- The enemy attacked the base camp of the 25th Infantry Division in Binh Duong Province with 180 rounds of mortar fire. Results were 15 US wounded (medevac) and 24 US wounded (treated returned to duty). One US Red Cross was minor wounded.
- Four UH-1 helicopters were downed by ground fire in the RVN resulting in four crewmen killed and three wounded. One CH-47 helicopter crashed and burned resulting in seven US killed and 25 injured.
- B-52s struck North Vietnam and the DMZ.

DECEMBER 28, 1967

- North Vietnam. USMC pilots hit Haiphong highway bridge (SSE). USAF pilots hit Hoa Lac airfield.

- *Operation Auburn.* Initiated.
- In Bin Thuan Province, two USAF B-57s accidentally strafed part of a CIDG unit with 20mm cannon and .50 caliber machine gun fire resulting in four CIDG killed, 34 wounded (two of which were US).
- US Army gunships killed 92 enemy and destroyed 32 sampans.
- B-52s struck the DMZ.

DECEMBER 29, 1967

- North Vietnam. A USN F-4 aircraft was downed by ground fire. The crew was rescued.
- *Operation Pershing.* A CIDG company and two Popular Forces platoon engaged an enemy force and reinforced by 1st Cavalry Division units. Enemy losses were 48 killed and light casualties of the RVNAF. There were no US casualties.
- In Binh Duong Province the 2nd Brigade, 101st Airborne Division had a 4.2 inch mortar short round hit positions resulting in four US killed and 10 wounded.
- B-52s struck the DMZ.

DECEMBER 30, 1967

- North Vietnam. USAF pilots hit Yen Bai railroad yard. A USAF F-100 aircraft was downed by ground fire, two-man crew rescued.
- *Operation Auburn.* Announced.
- *Operation Yellowstone.* 25th Infantry Division troops discovered four rice caches (215 tons rice total).
- Four UH-1 helicopters downed by ground fire resulting in one US killed and three wounded.

DECEMBER 31, 1967

- North Vietnam. USAF pilots hit Thai Nguyen highway bridge. A USN A-6 aircraft was downed to unknown causes, two crewmen missing.
- A USAF F-4 aircraft was downed by ground fire in the RVN, crew rescued.
- *Operation Camden.* Terminated.
- A 36-hour New Year's stand-down was observed from 1800

hours, December 31, 1967 to 0600 hours, January 2, 1968. At the end of the truce period a total of 63 major incidents (i.e. casualties) and 107 minor incidents were recorded.

JANUARY 1, 1968

- US military strength in the RVN was 486,000 (US Army – 320,000; USN – 31,000; USMC 78,000; USAF – 46,000; and, US Coast Guard – 452).
- FWMAF strength in the RVN was 48,739 ROK; 6,811 Australia; 516 New Zealand; 2,020 Republic of the Philippines; and 2,205 Thailand.
- US/FWMAF curtained offensive operations from 1800 hours, December 31, 1967 to 0600 hours, January 2, 1968. As of 1500 hours today, 43 incidents were reported (16 significant). Results were 15 US wounded, one CIDG killed, eight CIDG wounded and 16 enemy killed.
- In reconnaissance missions flown over North Vietnam, USMC and USAF pilots observed numerous convoys moving S. Trucks not attacked. USN pilots reported over 200 trucks, 130 railroad cars and 100 barges from N Than Hoa S. Vinh. None were attacked.

JANUARY 2, 1968

- US and FWMAF curtailed offensive operations from 1800 hours, December 31, 1967 to 0600 hours, January 2, 1968. At 0600 hours today, 110 incidents were reported, 37 significant. Results were 27 US and CIDG killed, 205 US and nine CIDG wounded and 387 enemy killed.
- US pilots flew 142 missions over North Vietnam (USN 64, USAF 44, USMC 34) USN pilots destroyed or damaged over 80 cars, 70 watercraft and 30 trucks and dropped two spans railroad bridge and damaged four other bridges. USAF pilots damaged 12 supply and storage structures, destroyed or damaged eight barges and silenced six guns positions. A USN F-8 aircraft was downed to unknown causes, pilots rescued.
- *Operation Badger Tooth.* Terminated. (III MAF).
- In Tay Ninh Province, the 3rd Brigade, 25th Infantry Division Base camp, received another attack. Helicopter light fire teams, tactical air and artillery supported. Enemy losses were 382 enemy killed. Friendly losses were 23 US killed. Enemy

elements were identified as the 271st and 272nd Viet Cong Main Force Regiments.

- A 36-hour New Year's stand-down ends at 0600 hours, January 2, 1968. Sixty-three major (casualties incurred) and 107 minor enemy violations were recorded.

JANUARY 3, 1968

- US pilots flew 106 missions over North Vietnam (USAF 49 USMC 35 USN 22, USN pilots hit Hung Yen boatyard 51 kilometers SE Hanoi; made two direct hits on Hai Duong railroad/highway bridge 34 kilometers WNW Haiphong; damaged Kien An highway bridge three kilometers SW Haiphong. USAF pilots claimed downing two MIG-17s in the vicinity of Hanoi. Other USAF pilots hit Trung Quan railroad yard 11 kilometers NE Hanoi; interdicted runway Kep airfield 95 kilometers ENE Hanoi and hit Lang Dang railroad 103 kilometers NE Hanoi. USMC pilots hit Hoa Binh Army barracks 48 kilometers SW Hanoi. A USN A-4 aircraft was downed by ground fire, pilot missing. A USAF F-105 aircraft was downed to MIG-21, pilot missing.
- *Operation Wheeler/Wallowa* (Quang Nam Province). Americal Division elements engaged 3rd /21st Regiments 2nd NVA Division 17 kilometers SSE An Hoa. The enemy attacked LZs Leslie and Ross in wave formations and mortar fire. Three other positions were attacked at the same time. Losses were 196 enemy killed and 17 US.
- *Operation Auburn.* Terminated. Final results were 37 enemy killed and five US.
- *Operation Pershing* (Binh Dinh Province). The 2nd Brigade, 1st Cavalry Division continues. *Operation Dam Trao Lake* area 20 kilometers SE Bong Son. After tactical air strike, units swept area after January 2, 1968, battle. Light and sporadic contact made during sweep. Results of the two-day battle were 79 enemy killed and six US.
- B-52s struck North Vietnam (15 kilometers NW Gio Linh), Quang Nam Province (20 kilometers SW Da Nang) and Tay Ninh Province (90 kilometers SW Saigon).

JANUARY 4, 1968

- US pilots flew 135 missions over North Vietnam (USN 46,

USN 46, USAF 46, USMC 43). USN pilots hit Hanoi railroad/highway bridge five kilometers N Hanoi; hit Phu Thi ferry 19 kilometers SSE Hanoi; Haiphong highway by-pass ferry destroyed and reported direct hits Yen Ha transshipment point 53 kilometers NE Thanh Hoa. USAF pilots heavy damaged Ha Gia railroad/by-pass bridge 32 kilometers N Hanoi; hit Lang Son railroad/highway bridge 128 kilometers NE Hanoi. USMC pilots hit Xinh Yen Army barracks, Vinh cave storage area and reported secondary explosions at Son Tra railroad yard 131 kilometers NW Hanoi.

JANUARY 5, 1968

- US pilots flew 104 missions North Vietnam (USAF 59, USMC 27, USN 18). USAF pilots destroyed Lang Son railroad bridge 131 kilometers NE Hanoi; cratered Kep airfield 60 kilometers NE Hanoi. USN pilots reported numerous secondary explosions Thanh Hoa transshipment point and hit Thanh Hoa railroad yard three kilometers SW Thanh Hoa. Two USAF F-105 aircraft were downed over North Vietnam, pilots missing.
- *Operation Fargo* (Binh Long/Phuoc Long Provinces). Announced and initiated December 22, 1968.

JANUARY 6, 1968

- US pilots flew 144 missions over North Vietnam (USAF 61, USMC 42, USN 41). USAF pilots hit Bac Giang railroad yard 45 kilometers NE Hanoi and 30 railroad cars near Lang Giai railroad yard 120 kilometers NE Hanoi. USN pilots destroyed or damaged four locomotives, 34 railroad cars and 36 watercraft near Thanh Hoa. USMC pilots hit Co Trai railroad/highway bridge, Phu Ly railroad by-pass bridge and Kep Ha airfield.
- Thua Thien Province. The enemy attacked Allied positions in and near Phu Loc 24 kilometers ESE Phu Bai. The enemy attacked with heavy mortar, small arms, automatic weapons and ground attacks. Artillery and helicopter gunships supported. Fire was returned. Losses were 91 enemy killed and 15 US. RVNAF casualties were reported light.
- *Operation Santa Fe 1.* Terminated. Final results were 86 enemy killed and two US.

JANUARY 7, 1968

- US pilots flew 81 missions over North Vietnam (USAF 40, USMC 29, USN 12). USAF pilots hit Kep airfield 60 kilometers NE Hanoi. USN pilots hit a highway bridge 26 kilometers SE Vinh and a railroad bridge 16 kilometers SSW Thanh Hoa. USMC pilots hit an Army barracks 70 kilometers NW Hanoi.
- *Operation Wheeler/Wallowa* (Quang Tin Province). Two Americal Division companies engaged an unknown size enemy force with small arms and automatic weapons fire. The enemy used heavy mortar and recoilless rifle fire. Artillery and gunship supported. A UH-1 helicopter was hit by ground fire while on the ground making a re-supply mission. The aircraft was destroyed. Results of day's action were 147 enemy killed and eight US.
- An estimated enemy company attacked the Phu Loc district Headquarters in Thua Thien Province. Enemy losses were 91 killed, 13 individual weapons and three crew-served weapons. Friendly losses were 16 US killed, 10 ARVN killed, seven Popular Forces killed, one civilian killed, 68 US wounded, nine ARVN wounded, Two Popular Forces wounded and one civilian wounded.
- B-52s struck the DMZ (nine kilometers NNE Con Thien), Kontum Province (26 kilometers WSW Dak To and twice Tay Ninh Province (both 95 kilometers NW Saigon).

JANUARY 8, 1968

- US pilots flew 76 missions over North Vietnam (USAF 34, USMC 31, USN 11). USMC pilots set off two secondary explosions at Cat Bi airfield five kilometers SE Haiphong. USAF pilots hit Thai Nguyen railroad yard 56 kilometers N Hanoi.
- Thua Thien Province. A USMC CH-53 helicopter downed resulting in 41 killed.
- *Operation Klamath Falls.* Terminated. Final results were 156 enemy killed and 28 US.

JANUARY 9, 1968

- US pilots flew 85 missions over North Vietnam (USAF 45, USMC 23, USN 17).
- USAF pilots hit Kep airfield 60 kilometers NE Hanoi and Yen

Bai airfield and storage area 125 kilometers NE Hanoi. USN pilots cratered a runway at Haiphong Cat Bi Airfield

JANUARY 10, 1968

- US pilots flew 75 missions over North Vietnam (USAF 37, USMC 27, USN 11). USAF pilots hit Cao Nung railroad siding 89 kilometers NE Hanoi. USMC pilots Hoa Binh barracks 48 SW Hanoi. A USAF F-4 aircraft was downed by ground fire with the crew missing.
- *Operation Saratoga* (Hau Nghia Province). 25th Infantry Division elements engaged an enemy force making an abortive attempt to overrun a battalion command post 39 kilometers NW Saigon. Artillery, tactical air supported. Enemy losses were 103 killed and friendly losses were five US killed and 28 US wounded. A UH-1 aircraft was downed by ground fire during the action resulting in two US killed, two wounded and the helicopter destroyed.

JANUARY 11, 1968

- US pilots flew 82 missions over North Vietnam (USAF 47, USMC 27, USN eight). USAF pilots hit Yen Bai railroad yard 122 kilometers NW Hanoi. USN pilots hit Cam Pha mining region 48 kilometers ENE Haiphong, destroyed a steam shovel and heavy damaged a truck. USMC pilots hit Phu Ly bypass bridge and a railroad yard 130 kilometers NW Hanoi.
- *Operation Akron V* (Bien Hoa Province). Initiated by a multi-battalion force 1st Brigade, 9th Infantry Division and 2nd and 7th Royal Australian Regiment Battalions 47 kilometers E Saigon.
- B-52s struck the DMZ (six kilometers NNW Con Thien), Tay Ninh Province twice (four kilometers SW and seven kilometers E Bo Tuc) and Kontum Province (60 kilometers NNE Dak To).

JANUARY 12, 1968

- US pilots flew 91 missions over North Vietnam (USAF 43, USN 29, USMC 19). USMC pilots hit Yen Bai airfield and a storage area 125 kilometers NW Hanoi.

JANUARY 13, 1968

- US pilots flew 98 missions over North Vietnam (USAF 45, USMC 37, USN 16). USAF pilots hit Hoa Lac airfield. USMC pilots hit Co Trai railroad/highway bridge 32 kilometers S Hanoi, Hoa Binh military installation 50 kilometers SW Hanoi and My Trach highway ferry 19 kilometers S Thanh Hoa.
- *Operation Akron V* (Bien Hoa Province). Announced and initiated by a multi-battalion force 1st Brigade, 9th Infantry Division and 2nd and 7th Battalions, Royal Australian Regiment 47 kilometers E Saigon. New Zealand troops attached to the Royal Australian Regiment found two enemy caches which included 1,000 pounds of rice, during sweep missions.

JANUARY 14, 1968

- US pilots flew 83 missions over North Vietnam (USAF 41, USMC 26, USN 16). USAF pilots hit Yen Bai airfield 125 kilometers NW Hanoi. An F-105 aircraft was downed by a MIG-21 NW Hanoi with pilots missing.
- The 786th US warplane was lost over North Vietnam as a MIG-21 downed an Air Force F-105 (38th US air-to-air loss of the war).

JANUARY 15, 1968

- US pilots flew 121 missions over North Vietnam (USAF 61, USMC 33, USN 27). USAF pilots hit Thai Nguyen fabrication plant 60 kilometers N Hanoi. USN pilots hit Nam Dinh railroad yard, Dong Phuong Thoung railroad siding and Chau Cau barracks area.
- *Operation Muscatine* (Quang Ngai Province). Announced and initiated on December 19, 1967 15 kilometers N Quang Ngai City by 11th and 198th Infantry Brigade of Americal Division.
- US District Judge George L. Hart (Washington, D.C.) ruled that wartime provisions of the UCMJ apply to US civilians in the RVN (J.H. Latney vs US).

JANUARY 16, 1968

- US pilots flew 117 missions over North Vietnam (USN 40, USMC 39, USAF 38). USN pilots hit Da Chong Barge repair facility 61 kilometers ENE Haiphong and dropped Thuc Hoa highway/bypass bridges 77 kilometers SSW Haiphong. USAF pilots destroyed one mile track Mo Trang railroad yard 62 kilometers NNE Hanoi and hit Son Bai barracks area 69 kilometers WNW Hanoi. USMC pilots hit Hoa Binh military installation 50 kilometers SW Hanoi. A USAF F-4 aircraft was downed by ground fire, crew rescued. A USAF F-4 was downed by unknown causes, one crew rescued, one missing.

JANUARY 17, 1968

- US pilots flew 82 missions over North Vietnam (USAF 35, USMC 30, USN 17). USMC pilots hit the Hon Gai ferry complex 32 kilometers NE Haiphong and railroad yard 30 kilometers S Hanoi. USN pilots hit a railroad bypass bridge 21 kilometers NW Vinh. USAF pilots damaged three barges 1.6 kilometers N Dong Hoi and hit two anti-aircraft positions 10 kilometers S Dong Hoi.
- *Operation Muscatine* (Quang Ngai Province). Americal Division units engaged an enemy force 17 kilometers NNE Quang Ngai City. A US Army helicopter gunship supported. A 198th Light Infantry Brigade company was inserted into an area to set up blocking positions and made contact with the enemy. The enemy employed small arms fire and fire was returned. Losses were 80 enemy killed and two US wounded.

JANUARY 18, 1968

- US pilots flew 112 missions over North Vietnam (USAF 47, USN 34, USMC 31). USAF pilots hit Bac Giang thermal power plant 45 kilometers NE Hanoi and Kep Ha airfield. USN pilots dropped the center span of Dong Phong Thuong railroad bypass bridge and cratered both approaches of Ky Anh highway bridge 85 kilometers NNW Dong Hoi. A MIG-17 was downed by a USAF F-4. Two USAF F-4 aircraft were downed due to unknown causes with the crews missing.
- *Operation Kentucky*. 4th Marine Regiment, 3rd Marine Division elements engaged an enemy force in a six-hour battle. On a mission three kilometers NE Con Thien, small arms and automatic weapons fire were exchanged with enemy force. Artillery and gunships supported the ground forces. Enemy

losses were 162 enemy killed. Friendly losses were eight US killed and 39 wounded (medevac).

- *Operation Coronado IX* (Dinh Tuong Province). Terminated. Final results were 259 enemy killed and 35 US.
- *Operation Coronado X* (Kien Hoa Province). Initiated by the USN TF-117 and US Army 9th Infantry Division, 66 kilometers SSW Saigon.

JANUARY 19, 1968

- US pilots flew 126 missions over North Vietnam (USAF 48, USN 46, USMC 32). USN pilots destroyed Thi Long railroad bridge and railroad bypass bridge 32 kilometers S Thanh Hoa and downed northern and center spans Dong Phong Thuong highway bridge 19 kilometers NNE Thanh Hoa. USAF pilots heavy damaged 50-truck convoy, 10-15 railroad cars 15-56 kilometers NNE Thanh Hoa.
- *Operation Byrd* (Binh Thuan Province). Terminated. Final results were 849 enemy killed and 34 US killed.
- *Operation Naresuan* (Bien Hoa Province). Announced and initiated October 21, 1967 by the RTAFV Regiment 32 kilometers ESE Saigon.

JANUARY 20, 1968

- US pilots flew 94 missions over North Vietnam (USMC 37, USAF 29, USN 28). USN pilots hit Hon Gai TPP 43 kilometers ENE Haiphong. USAF pilots hit Cao Nung railroad siding 89 kilometers NE Hanoi and Yen Bai airfield 125 kilometers NW Hanoi.
- *Operation Osceoia.* Final results were 76 enemy killed and 17 US.
- Quang Tri Province. A Popular Forces platoon made contact with an estimated 150-200 enemy with small arms and automatic weapons fire exchanged. ARVN reinforcements and an Amphibious Tractor (AMTRAC) force from the 3rd Marine Division reinforced units in contact. US Army artillery supported. Enemy losses were 50 enemy killed. Friendly losses were two US killed and 17 US wounded (medevac). ARVN casualties were light.
- *Operation Lancaster.* Terminated. Final results were 46 enemy killed and 22 US.

- *Operation Coronado X* (Kien Hoa Province). Announced and initiated January 18, 1968, SSW Saigon by USN TF-117 and US Army 2nd Brigade, 9th Infantry Division forces.

JANUARY 21, 1968

- US pilots flew 100 missions over North Vietnam (USAF 39, USN, 33 USMC 28). USN pilots cratered both approaches to the highway ferry 74 kilometers NNW Vinh. USAF pilots hit Yen Bai airfield 125 kilometers NW Hanoi.
- *Operation Saratoga.* (Binh Duong Province). 1st Brigade, 25th Infantry Division elements in the vicinity of Lai Khe made contact with an enemy force 37 kilometers NNW Saigon. US Army helicopter gunships and artillery supported the ground forces. Enemy losses were 63 killed. Friendly losses were one US killed, eight wounded (medevac) and seven light wounded (treated and returned to duty).
- *Operation Fargo* (Binh Long Province). Terminated. Final results were 49 enemy killed and six US killed.
- *Operation Akron V* (Bien Hoa Province). Terminated. Final results were 47 enemy killed and four US killed.

JANUARY 22, 1968

- US pilots flew 75 missions over North Vietnam (USAF 37, USN 21, USMC 17). USN pilots hit Hai Duong railroad yard 37 kilometers NNW Haiphong and Nam Dinh railroad yard 72 kilometers SW Haiphong.

JANUARY 23, 1968

- US pilots flew 52 missions over North Vietnam (USAF 29, USMC, 17 USN six). USAF pilots hit Dong Hoi airfield S panhandle.
- *Operation Pershing* (Binh Dinh Province). The 2nd Brigade, 1st Cavalry Division (Airmobile) made contact with an enemy force five kilometers E Phu My. The enemy was in an open area near Highway 8. US Army helicopter gunships and artillery and USAF tactical air supported. Enemy losses were 128 enemy killed in the eight-hour battle. Friendly losses were four US killed and 19 wounded (medevac).
- The Viet Cong released two US servicemen (USMC Corporal and US Army Private) near Tam Ky, Quang Tin Province.

JANUARY 24, 1968

- US pilots flew 59 missions over North Vietnam (USN 31, USMC 16, USAF 12). USN pilots heavy damaged a railroad siding 24 kilometers SSW Thang Hoa.
- Binh Dinh Province. In action, 10 kilometers SSE Phu Cat involving CRID and 2nd Brigade, 1st Cavalry Division (Airmobile) elements in past two days have resulted in 179 enemy killed. Contact continues.

JANUARY 25, 1968

- US pilots flew 69 missions over North Vietnam (USMC 26, USAF 22, USN 21). Strikes were limited to the panhandle region. Pilots reported 18-23 trucks, seven watercraft and four structures destroyed or damaged and six secondary explosions, two fires. A USN A-4 aircraft downed by ground fire. The pilot was rescued.
- Binh Dinh Province. Contact continued from January 24, 1968 action, 10 kilometers SSW Phu Cat. Capital Republic of Korea Infantry Division (CRID) forces and 2nd Brigade, 1st Cavalry Division (Airmobile) units engaged an enemy force, identified as the 9th Battalion, 18th NVA Regiment. Action continued during the day. Enemy losses were 61 killed. Total since January 22, 1968 were 240 enemy were killed in the three-day action.
- President Johnson ordered the call-up of 14,000 Air Force and 600 Navy Air Reservists in response to the Pueblo Crisis.
- The first sighting of enemy artillery occurred in the Khe Sanh area, Quang Tri Province (nine kilometers NNW of Khe Sanh).

JANUARY 26, 1968

- US pilots flew 60 missions over North Vietnam (USN 24 USAF 20 USMC 16). Pilots limited strikes to the panhandle region. Twelve watercraft were destroyed or damaged.

JANUARY 27, 1968

- North Vietnam. US pilots flew 65 missions over North Vietnam (USAF 33, USN 17, USMC 15). USAF pilots hit Hoa Lac airfield 32 kilometers W Hanoi and damaged approach, one abutment and dropped two spans of highway bridge six kilometers S Dong Hoi. USN pilots hit Vinh Loc railroad/highway bridge 59 kilometers SSW Thanh Hoa and heavy damaged transshipment point 56 kilometers SW Haiphong. Pilots reported 47 watercraft, 17 structures, one bridge destroyed or damaged and one secondary explosion and five fires set off during strikes.

JANUARY 28, 1968

- US pilots flew 90 missions over North Vietnam (USAF 39, USN 32, USMC 19). USAF pilots hit Thanh Hoa railroad/highway bridge three kilometers N Thanh Hoa. USN pilots hit Vinh transshipment point and highway bridge three kilometers S Vinh reported bridge heavy damaged or destroyed and five watercraft heavy damaged.
- *Operation Lancaster II.* Announced and initiated January 21, 1968 by a multi-battalion force 4th Marine Regiment, 3rd Marine Division in Quang Tri Province.
- *Operation Coburg.* Announced and initiated January 24, 1968, by a multi-battalion force 1st Australian Task Force in Bien Hoa Province.
- *Operation San Angelo.* Announced and initiated January 16, 1968 by the 101st Airborne Division's 1st Brigade in Phuoc Long/Quang Tri Provinces.

JANUARY 29, 1968

- US pilots flew 90 missions over North Vietnam (USAF 58, USMC 18, USN 14). USN pilots cratered runway in three places Vinh airfield eight kilometers N of city. USAF pilots destroyed or damaged 52 barges, seven railroad cars, and 31 trucks Mu Gia Pass and Dong Hoi regions.
- US and FWMAF curtailed offensive operations at 1800 hours in the RVN with the exception of I Corps, and North Vietnam with exception of area up to Vinh. (Announced to last for 36 hours to 0600 hours, January 31, 1968).
- The Viet Cong declared a seven-day TET truce from 0100 hours, January 27, 1968 to 0100 hours, February 3, 1968.

JANUARY 30, 1968

- The TET truce cancelled at 0930 hours by the VN. US and

FWMAF ended their defensive posture after repeated violations of the truce by NVA and Viet Cong forces in the RVN. However, the truce still remained in effect N of Vinh in North Vietnam – no air strikes would be conducted there.

- As of 1500 hours, there were 40 incidents reported by US and FWMAF occurring before the termination of the truce at 0930 hours. There were 15 considered significant in which casualties occurred. Friendly losses were 18 US killed and 41 wounded. Enemy losses were 50 enemy killed and eight detained.
- The enemy attacked major cities, airfields and military installations throughout the RVN. Attacks included: (III MAF) Da Nang Air Base, Marble Mountain Airfield, and I Corps HQ; (I FFV) Ban Me Thuot, Pleiku, Tan Canh, Kontum, Qui Nhon, Tuy Hoa, Ninh Hoa, Nha Trang cities. Khanh Hoa Sub-sector HQ; (II FFV) none; (IV Corps) none.
- The GVN cancelled the TET cease-fire and the USMACV followed suit, resuming operations due to Viet Cong/NVA commencement of a general offensive throughout the RVN.

JANUARY 31, 1968

- The enemy attacked major cities, airfields, and military installations in the RVN. Attacks included: (III MAF) airfields at Marble Mountain, Phu Bai, Chu Lai and rocket/mortar attacks against Quang Tri and MACV compound at Hue. Heavy fighting in the city of Hue; (I FFV) city of Phan Thiet, again in Ban Me Thuot, Pleiku, Kontum, Qui Nhon cities; (II FFV) cities of Saigon, Long Binh, Bien Hoa. Tan Son Nhut Air Base, US Embassy, Phu Tho racetrack area maintenance attacks (IV Corps) action heavy Chuong Thien and Phong Dinh Provinces. IV Corps Headquarters at Can Tho attacked by the enemy using B-40 rockets/small arms. Vinh Long city and airfield, Ben Tre City and MACV compound heavy attacked, Chau Doc City hit hard, Ca Mau capital city attacked, Soc Trang had sniper fire, and My Tho hardest hit by ground and mortar attack.
- RVN. Enemy casualties from 1800 hours, January 29, 1968 to 2400 hours, January 31, 1968, were 4,959 killed and 1,862 detained. Friendly casualties the same period were 535 killed and 1,698 wounded. Breakdown of friendly casualties were US 232 killed and 929 wounded: ARVN 300 killed and 747 wounded: FWMAF three killed and 22 wounded.

- President Thieu declares martial law throughout RVN, to include a 24-hour curfew and press censorship.

FEBRUARY 1, 1968

- From 1800 hours, January 29, 1968 to February 1, 1968, over 10,000 NVA and Viet Cong killed. Allied casualties: 917 killed (US 281; ARVN 632; FWMAF 4), 2,817 wounded (US 1,195; ARVN 1,588; FWMAF 34).
- US pilots flew 70 missions over North Vietnam USAF 42, USMC 16, USN 22). Pilots hit targets in the panhandle area. USAF pilots reported 52 support craft and19 structures destroyed or damaged.
- Pleiku Province. Twenty-three kilometers SW Pleiku City 1140 hours, Tan An defended by Regional Forces/Popular Forces elements received intense mortar and ground attack from unknown size end force. Reaction force reinforced; tactical air, artillery and gunship supported. Results were 208 enemy killed and 203 detained. One Popular Forces was wounded.
- Binh Duong Province. Four kilometers NE Phu Cuong, 0945 hours elements 1st Brigade, 1st Infantry Division made contact with an unknown size enemy force. Helicopter gunships supported. The enemy broke contact at 1830 hours. Enemy losses were 197 killed and friendly losses were five killed. Eight kilometers SW Phu Cuong, 1400 hours, Air Cavalry gunships fired on an unknown size enemy force. Enemy losses were 93 enemy killed and friendly losses were one wounded.
- At 1830 hours, elements of a VN Marine battalion engaged an enemy force three kilometers N Tan Son Nhut Air Base, casualties unknown. Activity throughout Saigon and Cholon area characterized by small lightly armed enemy bands engaged in sniper activities as they were forced to break up into small groups by US and ARVN forces sweeping area.
- Light contact reported throughout Corps IV Corps area, mainly in Kien Hoa, Vinh Long and Kien Tuong Province.
- B-52s struck twice Thua Thien Province (both 13 kilometers NW Khe Sanh).
- US military strength in RVN was 510,000.
- The GVN declares martial law throughout the country, imposing a 24-hour curfew. MACV follows suit in respect to curfew.

FEBRUARY 2, 1968

- Casualties reported from 1800 hours, January 29, 1968 to 2400 hours, February 2, 1968 were: 12,704 enemy killed; 3,567 enemy detained; 1,814 individual weapons and 545 crew-served weapons captured; 983 friendly killed (318 US; 661 ARVN; four FWMAF) and 3,483 friendly wounded (1,639 US; 1,792 ARVN; 52 FWMAF). Ratio of enemy to friendly killed: 12.9 to one.
- US pilots flew 69 missions over North Vietnam (USAF 36, USMC 29, USN four).
- USAF pilots struck an Army barracks 69 kilometers WNW Hanoi and another Army barracks area 88 kilometers NW of the city.
- Fighting continues at Hue with the VN Air Force tactical air strikes conducted on enemy strong points in Hue-Citadel compound. Ground fighting heavy throughout day. House-to-house sweeps conducted during the day. At 2230 hours, only the northern portion of the Citadel complex occupied by an enemy forces and over 300 enemy were killed by Allied air and ground units.
- At 2230 hours Kontum City reported quiet with only sporadic light sniper fire at airfield. Sporadic actions continue at Phan Thiet.
- At 2400 hours, February 1, 1968, small arms fire received at N gate at Tan Son Nhut Air Base. At 0100 hours base security and ARVN reinforced repelled enemy fire. Casualties not reported. At 0400 hours a mortar and RPG attack occurred on a US supply company depot in the vicinity of the dock area in Saigon. US and ARVN forces reacting, forcing the enemy from the area. Damage and casualties unknown. Thu Duc National Police district headquarters came under light mortar and small arms attack. The National Police drove off the enemy. Casualties were unknown and there was no report of damage.
- An estimated two enemy battalions attacked artillery positions N Ben Tre City 1930 hours. The enemy repulsed at 2330 hours with AC-47s supporting defenders. Light sniper fire still reported in city. My Tho reported quiet with light sporadic sniper fire occurring. The enemy attacked the cities of Vinh Loi, Vinh Long, Cao Lanh but were repulsed and light sporadic sniper fire continues.

- Capital Military District. Fighting sporadic throughout the day. Between 0900 and 1700 hours US elements engaged an estimated enemy reinforced battalion. Helicopter gunships and tactical air supported units in contact five kilometers NE Tan Son Nhut. The enemy attempted escape along Saigon River to NE and engaged by ARVN force.
- B-52s struck three times in the vicinity of Khe Sanh (12 kilometers ESE, five kilometers SE and 21 kilometers NW).

FEBRUARY 3, 1968

- Casualties reported from 1800 hours, January 29, 1968 to 2400 hours, February 23, 1968. Enemy losses were 14,997 killed; 4,156 detained; 3,055 individual weapons and 646 crew-served weapons captured; Friendly casualties were 1,116 killed (367 US; 738 ARVN; 11 FWMAF) and 4,171 wounded (2,063 US; 2,059 ARVN; 79 FWMAF).
- US pilots flew 61 missions over North Vietnam (USAF 31, USMC 26, USN four). USAF pilots hit Army barracks 104 kilometers NW Hanoi, no BDA.
- In Hue, fighting continues. NE and SE portions of the Citadel remain occupied with heavy contact continuing. Estimated two enemy companies fleeing over SW wall at noontime. Results thus far were 514 enemy killed.
- Contact terminated with in the city of Phan Thiet with only occasional harassing small arms and mortar fire being received. In Dalat, only sporadic sniper fire has been received in the town. No contact with the enemy has been reported. Airfield now secured. The cities of Ban Me Thuot and Pleiku reported as quiet with no contact with enemy forces.
- IV CORPS. All cities reported quiet, with only light sporadic sniper fire occasionally.
- B-52s struck three times in the vicinity of Khe Sanh (six kilometers NE, 10 kilometers W and 10 kilometers WNW).
- Joint US-Vietnam National Recovery Committee established under the direction of Vice President Ky in order to aid civilian victims of the Viet Cong TET offensive.

FEBRUARY 4, 1968

- HQ MACV. Casualties from 1800 hours, January 29, 1968 to 2400 hours, February 4, 1968: 16,976 enemy killed; 4,131 detained; 4,220 individual weapons and crew-served weapons captured; 1,477 Allied killed (471 US; 993 ARVN; 13 FWMAF); 6,075 wounded (2,744 US: 3,229 ARVN; 102 FWMAF).

- US pilots flew 117 missions over North Vietnam (USAF 65, USMC 40, USN 12). USAF pilots radar bombed Hoa Lac airfield and Thai Nguyen steel complex. Other US Air Force, US Marine Corps and USN pilots hit ferries, storage areas and truck convoys in the panhandle. No BDA due to bad weather.
- Hue fighting continues. A Marine company received fire from a built-up area. Marines attacked and killed 15 enemy with one US killed and two wounded (medevac).
- B-52s struck five times in the vicinity of Khe Sanh (four kilometers NE, five kilometers ENE, 14 kilometers S and 14 kilometers W).
- *Operation Tran Hung Dao.* A 33-day search-and-destroy operation launched to eliminate enemy opposition in Saigon, involving five ARVN Airborne Battalions, five VN Marine Corps Battalions and five Ranger Battalions. Enemy losses were 1,666 killed, 1,861 detained, 701 individual weapons and 129 crew-served. Friendly losses were 216 killed, 605 wounded, one missing, 20 individual weapons and five crew-served weapons.

FEBRUARY 5, 1968

- Casualties reported from 1800 hours, January 29, 1968 to 2400 hours, February 5, 1968: 21,330 enemy killed/1,729 Allied killed (546 US; 1,169 ARVN; 14 FWMAF); 7,185 Allied wounded (3,084 US; 3,995 ARVN; 106 FWMAF).
- US pilots flew 72 missions over North Vietnam (USAF 28, USMC 27, USN 17). Poor weather limited BDA as pilots hit airfields, storage areas, weapons positions and lines of communication N of DMZ and in the panhandle. A USAF F-4 aircraft claimed MIG-21 down. An F-105 aircraft downed to MIG-21 NW Hanoi.
- Quang Nam Province. At 0445 hours, elements of the 51st ARVN Regiment made contact with an enemy force 11 kilometers S Da Nang. US Army helicopter gunships and artillery supported. Elements of the 1st Marine Division moved into blocking positions. Artillery, tactical air and gunship fire directed onto enemy positions. The enemy broke contact at 2000 hours. Enemy losses were 187 killed and friendly

losses were six US killed and 14 wounded (medevac). ARVN casualties were reported light.

- B-52s struck three times in the vicinity of Khe Sanh (seven kilometers SE, 10 kilometers SW and 13 kilometers WNW).

FEBRUARY 6, 1968

- Casualties results from 1800 hours, January 29, 1968 to 2400 hours, February 6, 1968: 22,748 enemy killed; 4,914 detained; 5,107 individual weapons and 790 crew-served weapons captured; 1,768 Allied killed (614 US; 1,130 ARVN; 24 FWMAF); 7,358 wounded (3,408 US; 3,821 ARVN; 129 FWMAF).
- US pilots flew 63 missions over North Vietnam (USAF 24, USN 15). Bad weather again hampered BDA as USAF and USN pilots hit airfields, barge repair facilities and railroad sidings NW Hanoi and Haiphong. USMC pilots hit the panhandle area. A USAF F-4 crew downed a MIG-21 W Hanoi.
- *Operation Scotland* (Quan Tin Province). Lang Vei Special Forces camp and Khe Sanh base attacked by enemy mortar and artillery fire of unknown caliber and type. Action continues.
- Thua Thien Province. Fighting continues in Hue with a small pocket of resistance along a wall in extreme SW corner Citadel.
- *Operation Jeb Stuart* (Quang Tri/Thua Thien Province). Announced and initiated January 22, 1968 by the 1st Cavalry Division (Airmobile) and 101st Airborne Division. Since beginning, 578 enemy killed, 15 detained and 70 individual weapons and 19 crew-served weapons captured. US casualties: 23 killed and 144 wounded.
- US Mission announces US will release three NVN seamen captured by the USN off the coast of North Vietnam in July 1966, as a reciprocal gesture for three US fliers released in January 1968 by Hanoi.
- B-52s struck 12 kilometers NW of Khe Sanh.

FEBRUARY 7, 1968

- Cumulative results since 1800 hours, January 29, 1968 to 2400 hours, February 7, 1968 were: 24,662 enemy killed; 4,996 detained; 5,572 individual weapons and 872 crew-served weapons captured; 2,043 Allied killed (703 US; 3,303 ARVN;

37 FWMAF); 8,376 wounded (3,729 US; 4,493 ARVN; 154 (FWMAF).

- US pilots flew 83 missions over North Vietnam (USAF 46, USMC 25, USN 12). Pilots struck targets above the DMZ, but BDA unavailable.
- Fighting continues in Hue. Marines reported captured five pockets of the enemy and sweep operations continues. Thus far 2,036 of the enemy were killed in and around Hue, 46 detained and 508 individual weapons and crew-served weapons captured.
- *Operation Scotland.* Action continues from 1840 hours, February 6, 1968 Lang Vei Special Forces camp and Khe Sanh base area. Main base continues received artillery and rocket fire throughout night ceasing at 1047 hours. Airfield Khe Sanh cratered but fully operational, 1030 hours, Lang Vei Special Forces camp received heavy ground attack by an unknown size enemy force supported by nine armored vehicles (Soviet Model PT-76 tanks), heavy artillery and mortar fire. Heavy contact ensued with continual artillery and tactical air support. An aerial observer observed the enemy employing flamethrowers. Heavy contact continues in the vicinity of Lang Vei until 1100 hours when it was evacuated by defenders. No casualties or material damage assessment reported. This was the first employment of tanks in South Vietnam by the enemy.
- *Operation Hoptac.* Terminated. Final results were 273 enemy killed and 40 US killed.
- B-52s truck three times in the vicinity of Khe Sanh (seven kilometers NNW, eight kilometers N and 11 kilometers NW).

FEBRUARY 8, 1968

- Cumulative results since 1800 hours, January 29, 1968 to 2400 hours, February 8, 1968 were: 26,621 enemy killed; 4,872 detained; 6,232 individual weapons and 1,003 crew-served weapons captured; 2,295 Allied killed (810 US; 4,995 ARVN; 227 FWMAF).
- US pilots flew 63 missions over North Vietnam (USAF 32, USMC 25, USN six). Strikes ranged from Hanoi to the DMZ hitting Phuc Yen airfield, storage areas, railroad sidings and weapons positions and water traffic.
- *Operation Scotland.* An aerial observer from the 3rd Marine

Division observed four enemy tanks 10 kilometers SW of Khe Sanh. Tactical air directed against tanks with two reported disabled. At the same time, 20 vehicles observed 14 kilometers WSW of Khe Sanh. Tactical air strikes left at least two trucks burning.

- Quang Nam Province. At 1300 hours, elements of the 198th Light Infantry Brigade, responded to attack by 200-300 of the enemy six kilometers S Da Nang. Two more companies from the 198th Light Infantry Brigade inserted into the area 1400 hours S of the enemy force. At 1500 hours, USMC elements of the 1st Marine Division moved to make contact with an enemy force from the N. Another company from the 198th Light Infantry Brigade inserted at 1800 hours to reinforce. Artillery, helicopter gunship and tactical air missions supported ground troops. Contact lost at dark. Enemy losses were 152 killed and friendly losses were 15 US killed, 57 wounded (medevac) and six light wounded (treated and returned to duty).
- *Operation Scotland* (Quang Tri Province). Three kilometers NNW Khe Sanh, elements from the 3rd Marine Division received an unknown number of 60mm mortar and RPG rounds followed by ground attack. The enemy was repulsed. Enemy losses were 124 killed. Friendly losses were 21 US killed and 27 US wounded.
- *Operation Coburg.* Announced and initiated January 24, 1968 by US and ARVN units in the Saigon/Bien Hoa area.
- The ARVN 23rd Ranger Battalion completed a sweep of Dalat City, encountered only light sporadic resistance during the day. The city declared clear by ARVN forces.
- B-52s struck three times in the Khe Sanh area (twice 14km WNW and once 13 kilometers SW).

FEBRUARY 9, 1968

- Cumulative results since 1800 hours, January 29, 1968 to 2400 hours, February 9, 1968 were: 27,706 enemy killed; 5,019 detained; 6,298 individual weapons and 1,063 crew-served weapons captured; 2,707 Allied killed (920 US; 1,733 ARVN; 54 FWMAF); 11,519 wounded (4,561 US; 6,721 ARVN; 237 FWMAF).
- US pilots flew 84 missions over North Vietnam (USAF 32,

USMC 30, USN 22). USN pilots hit Cat Bi airfield six kilometers SE Haiphong and USAF pilots hit Kep airfield 61 kilometers NE Hanoi.

- Elements of the 25th Infantry Division reinforced by Cavalry units and supported by USAF tactical air and US Army helicopter gunships engaged an enemy force 16 kilometers NNW Saigon in two separate engagements. Enemy losses were 278 killed and friendly losses were three US killed and 30 US wounded.
- *Operation Wheeler/Wallowa.* Americal Division elements received fire from an estimated 300 enemy supported by mortar 10 kilometers SW Hoi An. The unit supported by helicopter gunships and two more companies reinforced during afternoon. Contact terminated just before dark. Enemy losses were 173 killed and friendly losses were 12 US killed, 12 US wounded (medevac) and 31 wounded (treated and returned to duty).
- In Hue, Marine forces cleared southwestern part of the city within 200 meters of Song Phu Cam. Contact still continues.
- *Operation San Angelo.* Terminated. Final results were 63 enemy killed and 12 US killed.
- *Operation Haverford.* Announced and initiated January 13, 1968 by elements of the 199th Light Infantry Brigade Gia Dinh/ Long An Provinces. Terminated February 2, 1968 with final results of 33 enemy killed and eight US killed.
- B-52s struck four times in the Khe Sanh area (twice nine kilometers NW, once seven kilometers NW and 12 kilometers E.

FEBRUARY 10, 1968

- US pilots flew 76 missions over North Vietnam (USMC 35, USAF 34, USN seven). USN pilots hit a radio communications receiver station 16 kilometers S Hanoi (first time). USAF pilots hit Phuc Yen airfield and the Thai Nguyen thermal power plant around Hanoi.
- Thua Thien Province. In Hue at 1430 hours, in the SE portion of the city, USMC elements came under small arms and automatic weapons fire from unknown size enemy force. Fire returned and Marines secured the area. Enemy losses were

11 known killed and friendly losses were two US wounded (medevac).

- *Operation Pershing* (Binh Dinh Province). The operation terminated January 19, 1968. Final results were 5,401 enemy killed and 600 US killed.
- Long An Province. Tan An City received an enemy attack from an unknown size force at 0300 hours including 250 rounds mixed 60 82mm mortar fire followed by a ground attack against the city and headquarters US Army 3rd Brigade, 9th Infantry Division. Friendly forces supported by US Army artillery and helicopter gunships and AC-47s. Contact terminated at 0600 hours. Enemy losses were 123 enemy killed. Friendly losses were four US killed, 11 US wounded, ARVN casualties reported light, 25 civilians killed and 200 wounded.
- *Operation Saratoga.* Elements of the 25th Infantry Division in conjunction with US ground Cavalry elements made contact with an unknown size enemy force three kilometers NE Hoc Mon, 17 kilometers NNW Saigon. US forces supported by artillery and helicopter light fire teams. USAF tactical air strikes directed on enemy positions. Contact lost at 1900 hours. Enemy losses were 105 killed and friendly losses were five US killed and 31 wounded. First sighting of Soviet- built IL-28 (Beagle) twin jet bombers was made at Phuc Yen Airfield, near Hanoi.

FEBRUARY 11, 1968

- US pilots flew 75 missions over North Vietnam (USAF 39, USN 20, USMC 16). USAF pilots hit Kep airfield 60 kilometers NE Hanoi, Yen Hai airfield 125 kilometers NW Hanoi and destroyed a 30-40 foot barge, truck, and seven military structures in the panhandle region. USN pilots destroyed or damaged several trucks at scattered locations in the panhandle.
- Bien Hoa Air Base received 10-20 rounds 122mm rocket fire at 0001hours. A light fire team employed on suspected launch site reported one fire and two secondary explosions. Friendly losses were one US killed and 36 wounded. Enemy casualties are unknown.
- B-52s struck five times in the vicinity of Khe Sanh (eight kilometers S and SW, six kilometers W, 12 kilometers NW and nine kilometers WNW).

- Intense TET Offensive countrywide action tapers off. Cumulative results from1800 hours, January 29, 1968 through 2400 hours, February 11, 1968. Enemy losses were 31,754 killed; 5,821 detained; 17 returned; 7,505 individual weapons; and 1,276 crew-served. Friendly losses were 1,001 US; 2,082 ARVN; 60 Free World Force; killed (Total – 3,143); and wounded were: US 7,806; ARVN 7,806; and FW 244 (Total – 13,137).

FEBRUARY 12, 1968

- US pilots flew 64 missions over North Vietnam (USAF 40, USMC 18, USN six). A USAF F-4 crew downed a MIG-21 N Hanoi with air-to-air missile. USN pilots hit Ninh Binh railroad yard.
- *Operation Muscatine.* Elements of the Americal Division engaged an unknown size enemy force 16 kilometers NE Quang Ngai City. Artillery and helicopter gunships supported friendly troops throughout the contact. The enemy employed 60 and 82mm mortar, 50 caliber machine guns and anti-tank weapons against the attacking infantry. Enemy losses were 78 enemy killed and friendly losses were one US killed and four wounded.
- B-52s struck five times in the vicinity of Khe Sanh (eight and nine kilometers NW, three kilometers E, four kilometers SSW and nine kilometers SW).

FEBRUARY 13, 1968

- US pilots flew 67 missions over North Vietnam (USAF 31, USMC 27, USN nine).
- USN pilots hit Kien An airfield 10 kilometers SW Haiphong and runway Bai Thuong airfield 35 kilometers NW Thanh Hoa. USAF pilots radar bombed Vinh airfield. USAF F-4 crews downed two MIG-17s NW Hanoi.
- *Operation Coronado X.* Terminated. Final results were 344 enemy killed and 12 US killed.
- Pentagon announces *Operation Ivy Tree*, the movement of an additional 10,000 men to RVN to counter expected "second round" Communist city offensive and assault on Khe Sanh Combat Base (one Airborne Brigade Task Force of 82nd Airborne Division and one USMC regiment (Regimental Landing Team 27 (-) (Reinforced) were units designated).

- B-52s struck once in the vicinity of Khe Sanh and twice in the vicinity of Saigon (16 and 17 kilometers NNW.)

FEBRUARY 14, 1968

- US pilots flew 95 missions over North Vietnam (USAF 54, USMC 24, USN 17). USAF pilots hit the Can des Rapides railroad/highway bridge, Thai Nguyen thermal power plant, Phuc Yen and Hoa Loc airfields. USN pilots hit Cat Bi airfield and Port Redon boat facility 19 kilometers NNE Haiphong. USMC pilots hit Kep airfield. A USAF F-105 and a USN F-8 aircraft downed by ground fire, pilots missing.
- *Operation Saratoga.* Elements of the 25th Infantry Division engaged an unknown size enemy force eight kilometers SE of Cu Chi from 0850 to 1830 hours. Ground units supported by helicopter light fire teams, artillery and tactical air. Enemy losses were 91 enemy killed and friendly losses were four US killed and 48 wounded. In the same area, elements of the 3rd Brigade, 25th Infantry Division engaged an unknown size enemy force at 1035 hours. Artillery supported Infantry in contact. Enemy losses were seven enemy killed and friendly losses were nine US wounded. Results of the two fights were 98 enemy killed, four US killed and 57 wounded.
- *Operation Coronado XI.* Initiated by 9th Infantry Division four kilometers SSW Can Tho.
- B-52s struck five times in the vicinity of Khe Sanh (four and seven kilometers SE, 11 kilometers S, five kilometers NE and 10 kilometers NNW).

FEBRUARY 15, 1968

- US pilots flew 85 missions over North Vietnam (USAF 61, USMC 15, USN nine). USN pilots damaged Kien An airfield. USAF pilots hit Kep airfield, out road N of Vinh and hit other lines of communications in the panhandle area. A USN F-4 and a USAF F-4 downed to unknown causes and ground fire (respectively), crews missing.

- A USAF F-4 Phantom lost over North Vietnam, marking 800th US loss in the three-year air war over North Vietnam.
- B-52s struck seven times in the vicinity of Khe Sanh (twice five kilometers S, 11 kilometers S, five kilometers SW, twice 15 kilometers SSE and six kilometers SSE.

FEBRUARY 16, 1968

- US pilots flew 62 missions over North Vietnam (USAF 31, USMC 22, USN nine). USAF pilots reported hits S end main runway Hoa Lac airfield. USN pilots hit Uong Bi thermal power plant, no BDA.
- *Operation Kentucky.* Three enemy tanks were sighted in the northern part of the DMZ, seven kilometers N Con Thien, taken under fire with unknown results.
- No change in activity in Hue as Allied forces continues clearing operations in the Citadel. The enemy still holds southern half W wall and all S walls.
- *Operation Coronado XI.* Announced and initiated on February 14, 1968, four kilometers SSW Can Tho by a 2nd Brigade, 9th Infantry Division multi-battalion.
- Three US pilots were released by North Vietnam and were flown to Vientiane, Laos, by International Control Commission (ICC) aircraft.
- B-52s struck four times in the vicinity of Khe Sanh (three kilometers SSE, four kilometers SE, 11 kilometers NNW and 14 kilometers NW).

FEBRUARY 17, 1968

- US pilots flew 77 missions over North Vietnam (USAF 38, USMC 29, USN 10). USAF pilots hit Phuc Yen airfield and USN pilots hit Cam Pha transformer station. USMC pilots hit Vinh airfield.
- I FFV. The enemy made wide-scale attacks on military installations. Kontum City airfield received 50 rounds mortar fire. A Popular Forces observation post 11 kilometers W Kontum City received a mortar and ground attack. Helicopter gunships and AC-47 aircraft supported. No results reported. An observation post 18 kilometers S Phu Cat, Binh Dinh Province, received a mortar attack. Nine areas in Quang Duc

Province attacked by mortar fire, four areas Vic Gia Nghia, two areas in the vicinity Nhon Co, and three areas in the vicinity of Duc Lap. No results reported. Di Linh District Headquarters, Lam Dong Province, received a mortar and automatic weapons attack. A CIDG observation post, Tuyen Suc Province, eight kilometers S Dalat received mortar and small arms fire. No results reported. A power plant 23 kilometers SE Dalat received a mortar attack. No results reported. Phan Thiet, Binh Thuan Provinces, received light ground probes and mortar attacks from an estimated enemy battalion E of city. Helicopter gunships, KC-47s and Naval Gunfire supported. No results reported.

- II FFV. (Hau Nghia Province) – 35 kilometers W Saigon, a forward air controller, 9th Infantry Division located 166 enemy sampans. During six-hour action, 79 sampans destroyed and 23 secondary explosions reported.
- *Operation Manchester.* Terminated. Final results were 456 enemy killed and 37 US killed.
- B-52s struck five times in the vicinity of Khe Sanh (twice seven kilometers N, nine kilometers SW, 20 kilometers NW and 19 kilometers SSW).

FEBRUARY 18, 1968

- US pilots flew 79 missions over North Vietnam (USAF 38, USMC 22, USN 22). USN pilots cut runway at Cat Vi airfield and hit the revetment area at Bai Thuong airfield. USMC pilots hit Phuc Yen airfield and USAF pilots hit Yen Bai airfield.
- Province towns and cities throughout South Vietnam and military installations were hit by enemy mortar and rocket fire during early morning hours.
- Phan Thiet received a ground attack during which the enemy employed mortars in support at 0230 hours. An estimated enemy battalion attacked the city and by 0915 hours the enemy held 1/5 of the city. An estimated 500 prisoners released from jail. The Viet Cong captured the provincial hospital. ARVN, Regional Forces/Popular Forces, CIDG and US Army battalion elements attacked the enemy to eject them from city. Jail retaken and an unknown number of prisoners recaptured. At 2330 hours, contact reduced to light and sporadic actions.

Enemy losses were 102 killed and friendly losses were two US civilians killed.

- Gia Dinh Province. Tan Son Nhut received the first rocket attack during conflict. At 0110 hours, The Air Base attacked by an estimated 100 rounds of 122mm rocket fire. Eight rounds impacted the MACV HQ compound. Materiel damage light. US casualties at Tan Son Nhut, one killed, 19 wounded (medevac) and 41 light wounded (treated and returned to duty).

FEBRUARY 19, 1968

- US pilots flew 65 missions over North Vietnam (USMC 29, USAF 25, USN 11). USAF pilots hit Phuc Yen and Yen Bai airfields. Other pilots hit targets in the panhandle area.
- *Operation Jeb Stuart.* A company from the 2nd Brigade, 101st Airborne Division found three mass graves containing 110 NVA soldiers 10 kilometers E Quang Tri City. 1st Cavalry Division elements made contact with an enemy force six kilometers NE Quang Tri City. Artillery and tactical air supported. Results were 51 enemy killed, two US killed and seven wounded (medevac).
- Tan Son Nhut continues to receive sporadic incoming rounds 122mm rocket fire resulting in one USAF airman reported wounded and materiel damage reported light. At 0600 hours, the civilian air terminal received a direct 122mm rocket hit resulting in one US killed and 35 wounded.
- Company C, 2nd Battalion, 14th Infantry, 25th Infantry Division captured 37 rounds of CHICOM 107mm spin stabilized rockets, the first such captured, confirming earlier reports of use of this weapon by the enemy in the III CTZ.
- B-52s struck four times in the vicinity of Khe Sanh (four kilometers S, five kilometers SW, seven kilometers SW and 14 kilometers NW).

FEBRUARY 20, 1968

- US pilots flew 55 missions over North Vietnam (USMC 29, USAF 18, USN eight). Pilots hit targets in the panhandle area with no BDA due to poor weather.

- Gia Dinh Province. At 1115 hours, 1st Infantry Division elements engaged an enemy force with heavy contact. US Army artillery, helicopter gunships and USAF tactical air supported the engagement 10 kilometers NE Saigon. Enemy losses were 123 enemy killed and friendly losses were 15 US killed and 11 wounded.
- B-52s struck four times in the vicinity of Khe Sanh (six and nine kilometers SW, six kilometers NW, and 14 kilometers W).

FEBRUARY 21, 1968

- US pilots flew 54 missions over North Vietnam (USAF 23, USMC 22, USN nine). Poor weather plagued pilots as they hit truck and water traffic near Dong Hoi, a power plant at Ban Thach and military installation SW Hanoi.
- Gia Dinh Province. 11 kilometers W Saigon, an element of the 25th Infantry Division Cavalry squadron made contact with an unknown size enemy force. The cavalry deployed and engaged the enemy force with organic weapons fire. US Army artillery and helicopter gunships and USAF tactical air supported. At 1810 hours, cavalry gunships from the 1st Aviation Brigade, operating in support of the 25th Infantry Division, observed 50-60 enemy in open area. Chopper crews killed 30. the total day's results were 128 enemy killed, three US killed and 21 wounded.
- Gia Dinh Province. At 1635 hours, three 122mm rockets impacted within the perimeter of Tan Son Nhut Air Base. No casualties or damage as result of the attack.
- B-52s struck five times in the vicinity of Khe Sanh (twice nine kilometers SE, 10 and 11 kilometers S and 11 kilometers SW).

FEBRUARY 22, 1968

- US pilots flew 59 missions over North Vietnam (USMC 30, USAF 24, USN five). USAF pilots hit Hoa Lac airfield, radar sites, artillery sites and truck parks. Other US pilots hit in the panhandle targets.
- *Operation Jeb Stuart.* Contact continued from February 21, 1968. After the initial attack, cavalry troops continued to sweep the area and made moderate-heavy contact throughout the day. Cumulative results were 163 enemy killed, 12 US killed and 137 wounded.

- B-52s struck five times in the vicinity of Khe Sanh (11 and 18 kilometers S, eight kilometers E, nine kilometers NE and 11 kilometers WNW).

FEBRUARY 23, 1968

- US pilots flew 60 missions over North Vietnam (USMC 27, USAF 26, USN seven). Pilots continued to bomb targets in the panhandle area.
- In Hue, elements of the 3rd Brigade, 1st Armored Cavalry Regiment, sweeping toward SW corner of Citadel from positions approximately two kilometers SW city, advanced to within 600 meters of the Citadel's wall. Cavalry units encountered light resistance from the enemy during the sweep and killed 10. One US was killed and 44 wounded during the actions. Cumulative results in Hue fighting since 2400 hours, January 31, 1968 were: enemy killed by US 1,548 and 109 detained; enemy killed by ARVN was 2,625 and 54 detained. US casualties the same period were 119 killed and 961 wounded.
- *Operation Muscatine.* Elements of the Americal Division 11th Light Infantry Brigade engaged an enemy force 10 kilometers NE Quang Ngai City. Automatic weapons and small arms fire were exchanged. Tactical air supported the ground troops. Contact was lost at 1900 hours. Enemy losses were 68 enemy killed and friendly losses were two US killed and 13 wounded (medevac).
- B-52s struck four times in the vicinity of Khe Sanh (10 and 14 kilometers NW, eight kilometers SW and 10 kilometers W).

FEBRUARY 24, 1968

- US pilots flew 68 missions over North Vietnam (USMC 32, USAF 27, USN nine). USN pilots hit a Hanoi port facility on the Red River three kilometers SE Hanoi for the first time. USAF pilots hit Kep airfield 45 kilometers NE Hanoi. USMC pilots hit a Hanoi radio station five kilometers W Bac Mai airfield.
- The Black Panther Company of the1st ARVN Division

recaptured Hue Palace grounds. Friendly forces now controlled the riverbank S Palace and extending W.

- *Operation Yellowstone.* Terminated. Final results were 1,254 enemy killed and 135 US.
- An unknown number of enemy attacked at Tan Son Nhut with 26 rounds of 122mm rockets. Results were 15 killed (11 civilians), 32 wounded (nine civilians).
- USMC and ARVN forces had retaken most of Hue Citadel from Viet Cong/NVA forces, virtually ending the 25-day siege and battle of Hue. Enemy losses were approximately 4,200 killed. Friendly losses were approximately 490 killed.
- Hanoi's port, 1.8 miles SE of the center of the city, was hit by A-6 Intruder aircraft from USS ENTERPRISE, the first strike on this 11-acre complex.

FEBRUARY 25, 1968

- US pilots flew 59 missions over North Vietnam (USMC 31, USAF 23, USN five). USN pilots hit Haiphong railroad yard and Bai Thuong airfield.
- In Hue, ARVN and USMC elements conducted a sweep of Imperial Palace grounds and discovered numerous graves, which contained a total 140 NVA bodies.
- B-52s struck three times in the vicinity of Khe Sanh (five kilometers W, 12 kilometers NW and 15 kilometers SW).

FEBRUARY 26, 1968

- US pilots flew 62 missions over North Vietnam (USMC 33, USAF 21,USN eight). Pilots struck in and around the DMZ area, but poor weather prevented BDA.
- Gia Dinh Province. Tan Son Nhut Air Base received 122mm rocket fire. Materiel damage was light.
- *Operation Coronado XI.* The 2nd Brigade, 9th Infantry Division air-assaulted into a hot LZ and engaged an estimated reinforced company. At the same time, a battalion from the 2nd Brigade moved to S of the area of contact in USN TF-117

river craft. At 1245 hours, a company landed from river craft to W and at 1405 hours another company air-assaulted to the E. The engagement continued throughout the day. Heavy small arms and automatic weapons fire was exchanged at 1600 hours. Artillery and tactical air supported the units in contact. Enemy losses were 57 killed and friendly losses were 26 US killed and 51 wounded.

- B-52s struck four times in the vicinity of Khe Sanh (10 and 13 kilometers NW, five kilometers W and 10 kilometers WNW).

FEBRUARY 27, 1968

- US pilots flew 92 missions over North Vietnam (USAF 38, USMC 32, USN 22). USN pilots hit Haiphong railroad yard and touched off secondary explosions at Uong Bi thermal power plant. Other pilots hit targets in the panhandle area.
- *Operation Wheeler/Wallowa.* Ground cavalry elements with the Americal Division contacted an unknown size enemy force four kilometers W Tam Ky. While conducting a sweep of the area, cavalry men became heavily engaged with the enemy in the four-hour battle. Enemy losses were 179 killed. Friendly losses were two US killed and 14 wounded (medevac).
- *Operation MacArthur.* At 0800 hours, 25th Infantry Division elements in night positions were hit by an enemy mortar attack from SW. At 1030 hours, the enemy initiated a ground attack from the same direction. US Army helicopter gunships, artillery and USAF tactical air struck attacking enemy forces. Heavy contact continued until 1930 hours. Enemy losses were 69 killed.
- B-52s struck seven times in the Khe Sanh vicinity (four and 14 kilometers WNW, two kilometers NE, three kilometers SW, five kilometers SE, nine kilometers W, 10 kilometers S).

FEBRUARY 28, 1968

- US pilots flew 70 missions over North Vietnam (USMC 32, USAF 30, USN eight). USAF pilots destroyed 20 30-ft barges S of Dong Hoi. A USAF F-105 aircraft downed by ground fire in the panhandle. Pilot rescued.
- Quang Tri Province. A USMC CH-46 helicopter on a combat

mission 17 kilometers NE Khe Sanh received heavy automatic weapons fire shortly after noon and crashed killing 22 US personnel.

- Gia Dinh Province. Early this morning, several 122mm rocket rounds hit Tan Son Nhut Air Base N. No personnel casualties and material damage was negligible.
- B-52s struck 10 kilometers W Khe Sanh.
- Quang Tin Province. The 3rd Brigade, 82nd Airborne Division, totaling 4,000 men arrived Vietnam. The Brigade began its move to Vietnam based on a 24-hour warning order.
- Quang Nam Province. The 27th Marine Regimental Landing Team, totaling 4,500 men arrived Vietnam. The Regiment began its move to Vietnam on February 15, 1968.
- An enemy trawler was sighted by a *Operation Market Time* P-3U aircraft off Ca Mau Peninsula in IV CTZ and taken under covert surveillance and finally engaged 40 miles ENE of Ca Mau Point, being sunk by gunfire from USCGC WINONA about 0200 hours, March 1, 1968.
- An enemy trawler was sighted by an *Operation Market Time* P-3U aircraft 160 kilometers E of Nha Trang in II CTZ, and taken under covert surveillance. Fire from a VN Navy Patrol Craft Escort (PCE), spooky aircraft and a USN Patrol Craft Fast (PCF) destroyed the trawler after it fled to a cove 10 miles N of Nha Trang at 0231 hours, March 1, 1968.
- An enemy trawler was sighted by an *Operation Market Time* P-3U aircraft and taken under covert surveillance by the USCGC ANDROSCOGGIN. After attempting to evade, the trawler destroys itself near Duc Pho in II CTZ, at 0235 hours, March 1, 1968.

FEBRUARY 29, 1968

- US pilots flew 76 missions over North Vietnam (USMC 30, USAF 28, USN 18). USAF pilots hit a Hanoi motor vehicle maintenance area seven kilometers W Hanoi for the first time. USN pilots hit Ban Thach PP.
- Naval Forces (Quang Ngai Province). At 1541 hours, an unidentified trawler sighted by USN Market Time platoon and tracked to a point 25 miles off the coast of Vietnam. The USCGC ANDROSCOGGIN closed and challenged the trawler as it came into VN waters.

- Naval Forces (Khanh Hoa Province). At 1710 hours, an unidentified trawler sighted 80 miles E Nha Trang heading W toward coast of Vietnam. The ship approached the coast, was challenged and refused to answer. Continued course toward beach. USN Swift Boats and Vietnam Navy platoon craft closed on the vessel.
- Naval Forces (An Xuyen Province). At 2059 hours, USN Operation Market Time units in the vicinity of the mouth of Bo De River sighted an unidentified trawler. Units tracking vessel.
- B-52s struck six times in the vicinity of Khe Sanh (six and 40 kilometers ESE, four kilometers E, 11 kilometers WNW, five kilometers SSE and 20 kilometers NW).
- Naval Gunfire-RVN. A 7th Fleet cruiser was fired on while supported ground troops in the III MAF area. The hostile fire came from enemy shore battery on Cap Lay. The ship was not hit. Another cruiser destroyed five fortifications 11 kilometers SSE Gio Linh. A 7th Fleet DD destroyed six enemy emplacements and started numerous fires at an enemy site nine kilometers SSE Gio Linh.
- *Operation Patrick.* Initiated by a battalion+ force 3rd Brigade, 4th Infantry Division Binh Dinh and Quang Ngai Provinces.
- Refugees as a result of the TET Offensive now total 599,858 (I CTZ 121,518; II CTZ 101,454; III CTZ 94,766; IV CTZ 109,441; Saigon/Cholon/Gia Dinh 172,679). 68,099 homes were reported destroyed and 19,457 civilians wounded.
- Casualties from the TET Offensive (1800 hours, January 29, 1968 through 2400 hours, February 29, 1968) were: Enemy losses were 45,005 killed; 7,417 detained; 40 retained; 11,027 individual weapons, and 1,726 crew-served. Friendly losses were 1,825 US, 3,557 ARVN, and 92 FWF killed (Total 5,474); wounded: 9,854 US; 12,806 ARVN; and 349 FWF (Total 23,009).
- *Operation NAPOLEON,* which began on November 5, 1967 in Quang Tri Province, combined with *Operation Saline,* which began on January 30, 1968 in Quang Tri Province, to form *Operations Napoleon/Saline.*

MARCH 1, 1968

- US Military strength in RVN was approximately 520,000.
- US pilots flew 69 missions over North Vietnam (USAF 27, USMC 27, USN 15). The USN hit Hanoi port facilities and Haiphong railroad/highway bridge. The USAF pilots silenced two radar sites in the panhandle.
- *Operation Saline.* Elements of the 1st Marine Division sweeping area seven kilometers NE Dong Ha engaged an unknown size enemy force. The first contact made at 0645 hours with sporadic contact throughout the day. Contact lost at 2000 hours. Enemy losses were 81 enemy killed. Friendly losses were 22 US killed and 87 wounded.
- Naval Forces (Quang Ngai Province). A trawler observed on February 29, 1968 made a run for the beach at 0120 hours and taken under fire after refusing to answer challenge. The trawler beached in the surf eight kilometers SE Duc Pho. US Army helicopter gunships took the ship under fire at 0210 hours and a company from the Americal Division inserted into the area. The trawler attempted to employ self-destroying equipment and initially 25% successful. The enemy completed self-destruction at 0235 hours.
- Naval Forces (An Xuyen Province). An unidentified trawler observed February 29, 1968 taken under fire by the USCGC WINONA when refused to reply challenge at 0145 hours. The trawler hit with 5" round from WINONA'S main gun, and two secondary explosions observed blowing ship apart. The WINONA hit by fire from the trawler. No damage or casualties reported.
- Naval Forces (Khanh Hoa Province). An unidentified trawler sighted and challenged on February 29, 1968 taken under fire by US/Vietnam Navy patrol boats at 0040 hours. AC-47s also engaged the trawler. The trawler turned N and forced into cove 20 kilometers NNE Nha Trang. At 0230 hours, Swift boats hit the trawler with five 81mm mortar rounds and the ship blew up.
- *Operation Coburg.* Terminated. Final results were 180 enemy killed and 19 US killed.
- Gia Dinh Province. Tan Son Nhut hit with several 122mm

rockets. Personnel casualties light and materiel damage insignificant.

- B-52s struck nine times in the Khe Sanh Combat Base area (six kilometers W, four kilometers W, 16 kilometers NW, two kilometers NE, one kilometer N and three kilometers SSE), twice in the vicinity of Saigon (35 kilometers NW and 45 kilometers E) and 18 kilometers NNE A Shau.

MARCH 2, 1968

- US pilots flew 62 missions over North Vietnam (USAF 28, USMC 20, USN 14). The USN reported several secondary explosions after strike on the Uong Bi thermal power plant; also hit Haiphong railroad/highway bridge. Other pilots hit targets in the panhandle.

MARCH 3, 1968

- US pilots flew 68 missions over North Vietnam (USAF 35, USMC 19, USN 14). USN pilots hit Hanoi port facilities. USAF pilots destroyed or damaged 34 barges and supply boats in the vicinity of Dong Hoi.
- *Operation Kentucky.* Elements of the 3rd Marine Division engaged an unknown size enemy force at 1310 hours four kilometers NE Con Thien. Contact lost at 1650 hours. Enemy losses were 132 enemy killed. Friendly losses were one US killed and three wounded. At the same time another element of the 3rd Marine Division engaged an unknown size enemy force two kilometers E of the first action. Artillery missions directed into enemy positions. Enemy losses were 21 enemy killed and friendly losses were one US killed and five wounded. The day's results were 153 enemy killed, two US killed and eight wounded.

MARCH 4, 1968

- US pilots flew 71 missions over North Vietnam (USAF 42, USMC 19, USN 10). The USAF hit a boat yard (Ha Dong) 10 kilometers SW Hanoi for the first time. Other strikes were in the panhandle.

- Phu Yen Province. ARVN elements in Tuy Hoa attacked by an unknown number of the enemy. The enemy withdrew and attacked again at 1000 hours. Elements of the 173rd Light Infantry Brigade reinforced the ARVN units and engaged the enemy force. The contact was maintained until 1845 hours. US units reported 137 enemy killed, five US killed and 16 wounded (medevac). ARVN elements were in contact until 2030 hours with 69 enemy killed and ARVN casualties light. Cumulative totals were 206 enemy killed and 16 detained.
- US installations received enemy attacks: In Thua Thien Province, the command post 1st Cavalry Division (Airmobile) received an unknown number of 82mm mortar rounds at 0230 hours; In Quang Nam Province, the Marine communication battalion compound seven kilometers SSW Da Nang received eight rounds of unknown caliber rocket fire from 0100 to 0200 hours; In Quang Nam Province, a Marine tank unit and Marine artillery unit in close proximity four kilometers NW Da Nang received more than 20 rounds of 122mm rocket fire, 0100 hours; in Quang Nam Province, elements of the Marine Corps Force Logistics Command (FLC) nine kilometers NW Da Nang received more than five rounds of unknown caliber rocket fire, 0200 hours; in Quang Ngai Province, the MACV compound Quang Ngai received a few rounds rocket and mortar fire, 0200 hours.
- US installations received enemy attacks: In Kontum Province, the base camp of the 4th Infantry Division received an attack 0130 to 0200 hours of 10 rounds of 82mm mortar fire. All impacted outside the perimeter; Kontum airfield received more than 15 rounds of 122mm rocket fire 0100 to 0200 hours; In Pleiku Province, Camp Enari, 4th Infantry Division's base camp, received more than 10 rounds of 122mm rocket fire 0100 to 0200 hours light damaged runway, and closed for a time.
- *Operation Coronado XI.* Terminated. Final results were 264 enemy killed and 39 US.

- B-52s struck six times in the Khe Sanh Combat Base area (seven and nine kilometers WNW, three kilometers SE, three kilometers NE, seven kilometers NW and seven kilometers NNW, 36 kilometers NW A Shau, and twice in the vicinity of Saigon (45 kilometers E and 75 kilometers SE).

MARCH 5, 1968

- US pilots flew 79 missions over North Vietnam (USAF 39, USN 23, USMC 17). The pilots hit targets in the panhandle region.
- *Operation Kentucky.* 1600 hours, an aerial observer from the 3rd Marine Division sighted two tracked vehicles Ben Hair River, directed artillery missions on vehicles. The aerial observer's surveys of the area, revealed vehicles were wooden decoys.
- The 25th Infantry Division base camp Cu Chi received less than 40 rounds of 82mm mortar fire and several 122mm rocket rounds 2200 hours. Casualties light. Light damage to aircraft. (Following received less than 20 rounds direction from Saigon): Go Dau Ha, 58 kilometers NW; Ba Dong, 66 kilometers NNE; Xuan Loc, 66 kilometers ENE; Phuoc Vinh, 66 kilometers NNE; An locations, 110 kilometers NNE; Phu Loi, 25 kilometers N; LZ Sicily, 47 kilometers NNE; LZ Normandy, 45 kilometers N; Long Binh, 30 kilometers NE.

MARCH 6, 1968

- US pilots flew 83 missions over North Vietnam (USAF 49, USN 19, USMC 15). USN pilots hit Hanoi port facilities, Bai Thuong airfield, Van Dien battery plant, Hai Duong railroad yard and Uong Bi thermal power plant. USAF pilots hit Phuc Yen airfield and Dong Hoi airfield.
- *Operation Kentucky* (Quang Tri Province). The 3rd Marine Division five kilometers NE Con Thien, 1115 hours, contact enemy force unknown size. Artillery and tactical air supported Marines. Contact lost at 1730 hours. Enemy losses were 81 killed and friendly losses were 14 US killed and 29 wounded (medevac).
- Quang Tri Province. At 1600 hours, A USAF C-123 aircraft hit

by ground fire crashed in the Khe Sanh Combat Base area. 44 passengers (43 USMC and USN) and four USAF crewmembers aboard killed.

MARCH 7, 1968

- US pilots flew 109 missions over North Vietnam (USAF 53, USN 41, USMC 15). USN pilots hit a Hanoi radio communications receiving station, Van Dien battery plant. USAF pilots hit Key railroad yard.
- Elements of ARVN troops and the 3rd Marine Division engaged an estimated enemy battalion approximately three kilometers NE Dong Ha, 1200 hours. Allied forces supported by tactical air and artillery missions. Contact terminated at 1900 hours. Enemy losses were 164 enemy killed. Friendly losses were 16 US killed, 83 wounded (medevac) and 30 wounded (treated and returned to duty). ARVN casualties were light.
- *Operation Thuong Cong Dinh.* Initiated by the 9th Infantry Division eight kilometers SE Cai Lay, Dinh Tuong Province.

MARCH 8, 1968

- US pilots flew 57 missions over North Vietnam (USAF 38, USN 11, USMC eight). USN pilots hit Vinh airfield. There were other strikes in the panhandle area.
- *Operation Valley Forge.* Initiated by a multi-battalion force 199th Light Infantry Brigade 45 kilometers NW Saigon in Bien Hoa/ Long Khanh Province.
- III CORPS. *Operation Truong Cong Dinh.* The 7th ARVN Infantry Division joined the US 9th Infantry Division in operation.

MARCH 9, 1968

- US pilots flew 66 missions over North Vietnam (USAF 35, USN 18, USMC 13). USAF pilots hit Lang Giai railroad yard. USN pilots hit Port Redon cargo facility and Ban Thac power plant.
- *Operation Wheeler/Wallowa.* Americal Division elements made contact with an unknown size enemy force 1015 hours, heavy engagement and continued until afternoon. Tactical air,

artillery and helicopter gunships supported the ground forces. Contact was lost at 1930 hours. Enemy losses were 129 enemy killed. Friendly losses were 10 US wounded (medevac) and eight wounded (treated and returned to duty).

MARCH 10, 1968

- US pilots flew 76 missions over North Vietnam (USAF 35, USN 24, USMC 17). USN pilots hit Haiphong highway bridge, Ban Thach power plant, Bai Thuong airfield. USAF pilots hit Thai Nguyen railroad yard.
- *Operation Saratoga.* Terminated. Final results were 3,863 enemy killed and 382 US killed.
- *Operation Enterprise.* Terminated. Final results were 2,107 enemy killed and 253 US killed.

MARCH 11, 1968

- US pilots flew 76 missions over North Vietnam (USAF 35, USN 32, USMC nine). USN pilots hit a Hanoi radio communications receiving station, Thanh Hoa thermal power plant, and Can Pha transformer station. USAF pilots hit Ha Dong Army barracks area and Ken Bai airfield. A USAF F-4 aircraft was downed by unknown causes with the crew missing.
- *Operation Wheeler/Wallowa.* Americal Division forces engaged an enemy force with organic weapons fire 1100 hours, 22 kilometers W Tam Ky. Infantry supported by tactical air until contact terminated 1830 hours. Enemy losses were 78 killed and friendly losses were two US killed, 15 wounded (medevac) and 14 wounded (treated and returned to duty).
- *Operation Pinnaroo.* Announced. Initiated February 27, 1968.
- *Operation Quyet Thang.* Initiated by multi-division forces US 1st, 9th, and 25th Infantry Divisions and 9th and 25th ARVN Infantry Division, ARVN Airborne Division Task Force, Vietnam Marine Corps Task Force, ARVN 5th Ranger Group and National Police in Gia Dinh, Long An, Hau Nghia, Binh Duong, and Bien Hoa Province.

- *Operation Valley Forge.* Announced and initiated March 8, 1968.

MARCH 12, 1968

- US pilots flew 76 missions over North Vietnam (USAF 35, USN 25, USMC 16). USAF pilots hit Kep airfield and boat construction yard. USN pilots hit Haiphong railroad yard, Kien An highway ferry.
- Thua Thien Province. Elements of the 1st Cavalry Division (Airmobile) engaged an enemy force at 1025 hours, 18 kilometers SW Quang Tri Province throughout the day. Enemy losses were 59 enemy killed and friendly losses were one US killed and 20 wounded.

MARCH 13, 1968

- US pilots flew 94 missions over North Vietnam (USN 44, USAF 32, USMC 18). USN pilots hit Haiphong railroad/highway bridge, Kien An highway bridge, Kien An airfield, Cat Bi airfield, Uong Bi thermal power plant, Cam Pha military barracks and Ninh Giang transshipment point. USAF pilots hit Chuc Son Army barracks and Lang Giai railroad yard. USMC pilots continued strikes in the panhandle.
- *Operation Worth.* Initiated by a battalion-sized force 1st Marine Division and US Army cavalry squadron Quang Nam Province.

MARCH 14, 1968

- US pilots flew 86 missions over North Vietnam (USAF 34, USN 29, USMC 23). USN pilots hit Haiphong railroad/highway bridge, Uong Bi thermal power plant and POL areas in the Haiphong area. USAF pilots hit Dong Hoi airfield, cutting the runway in two places and Thai Nguyen thermal power plant.
- Quang Nam Province. A Marine reconnaissance patrol from the 1st Marine Division observed approximately 500 NVA troops six kilometers NE An Hoa, 1900 hours. The patrol

directed artillery missions and tactical air on enemy positions resulting in 101 enemy killed and no US casualties.

- *Operation Ford.* Initiated Thua Thien Province by a battalion force from the 1st and 3rd Marine Division.

MARCH 15, 1968

- US pilots flew 100 missions over North Vietnam (USN 39, USAF 35, USMC 26). USN pilots hit Do Son radio communications station, Dong Trieu Army barracks, Hong Gai barracks area, Hon Gai thermal power plant, Van Dien battery plant, Kien An airfield and Cam Pha POL storage area and transformer station. USAF pilots hit Yen Bai airfield.
- *Operation Quyet Thang.* Troops from the 11th Armored Cavalry Regiment made contact with an estimated enemy battalion at 1005 hours, nine kilometers SW Cu Chi. Tactical air, artillery and helicopter gunships supported ground troops. At 1355 hours, elements of the 25th Infantry Division reinforced cavalry and two units engaged the enemy until 1930 hours, when contact terminated. Enemy losses were 81 killed and friendly losses were 21 US wounded. Other elements of the 25th Infantry Division discovered an enemy grave approximately eight kilometers NE Duc Hoa, containing 18 enemy bodies.

MARCH 16, 1968

- US pilots flew 90 missions over North Vietnam (USN 34, USAF 31, USMC 25). USAF pilots hit Phuc Yen airfield and Phu Tho Army barracks area. USN pilots hit Yen Vien railroad yard, dropped southern two spans of the Kien An Highway bridge, Nam Dinh thermal power plant and Cam Pha transformer station.
- *Operation Kentucky.* Two companies from the 3rd Marine Division, supported by tactical air, engaged an enemy battalion four kilometers W Gio Linh. The enemy withdrew to N with Marines in pursuit. An estimated 100 of the enemy in a trench and bunker complex approximately ½ miles to N fired on advancing Marines. Organic weapons, tactical air, helicopter gunships and artillery missions fired into enemy positions.

Contact terminated at 1530 hours. Enemy losses were 83 killed and friendly losses were two US killed, 11 wounded (medevac) and 15 light wounded (treated and returned to duty).

- *Operation Muscatine.* Elements of the Americal Division, 11th Light Infantry Brigade made contact with an enemy force of an unknown size nine kilometers NE Quang Ngai City. The Infantry was supported by US Army helicopter gunships and artillery. Sporadic contact continued until 1500 hours when contact lost. Enemy losses were 128 killed and friendly losses were two US killed, four wounded (medevac) and six light wounded (treated and returned to duty).
- *Operation Quyet Thang Offensive* (Hau Nghia Province). Elements of the 51st ARVN Ranger Battalion supported by the US Army 11th Armored Cavalry Regiment made joint attack on an estimated reinforced enemy company four miles NE Duc Hoa (26 kilometers NW Saigon). ARVN and US force supported by USAF tactical air and US Army artillery and helicopter gunships. Enemy losses were 135 enemy killed. There were no US casualties and ARVN casualties were reported light.
- *Operation Box Springs.* Initiated by 101st Airborne Division multi-battalion force Binh Duong Province.
- The first reported case of 107mm rockets in I CTZ when the enemy attacked Dong Ha Combat Base, Quang Tri Province.

MARCH 17, 1968

- US pilots flew 59 missions over North Vietnam (USAF 26, USMC 22, USN 11). USN pilots hit Cam Pha military barracks, Ninh Binh railroad siding. A USN A-6 aircraft was downed by unknown cause with the crew missing. A USAF F-4 aircraft was downed by unknown causes, crew rescued.
- *Operation Walker.* Initiated by a 173rd Airborne Brigade battalion-size force in Binh Dinh Province.
- *Operation Valley Force.* Terminated. Final results were 27 enemy killed and one US killed.
- *Operation Combat Lancer.* Six F-111 aircraft deployed to Takhli, Royal Thai Air Force Base (RTAFB), for a six-month combat evaluation.

MARCH 18, 1968

- US pilots flew 71 missions over North Vietnam (USAF 38,

USMC 20, USN 13). USN pilots hit Kien An airfield, Hon Gai thermal power plant. A USAF F-100 aircraft was downed by ground fire WSW Dong Hoi with one crewmember rescued with one missing.

- *Operation Napoleon/Saline.* A company from the 3rd Marine Division, supported by artillery, helicopter gunships and tactical air made contact with an enemy force of unknown size in well-prepared positions. The enemy fired 40 rounds of 140mm rockets on friendly positions as the company attacked. Air strikes were directed onto enemy positions. Marines assaulted enemy positions. Contact terminated at an unknown time. Enemy losses were 67 killed and friendly losses were 12 US killed and 24 wounded (medevac).

MARCH 19, 1968

- US pilots flew 82 missions over North Vietnam (USN 35, USAF 31, USMC 16). USN pilots hit Uong Bi thermal power plant, Nam Dinh railroad yard. USAF pilots hit Dong Hoi airfield.

MARCH 20, 1968

- US pilots flew 119 missions over North Vietnam (USAF 63, USN 38, USMC 18). USN pilots hit Hong Gai thermal power plant and reported destroyed or damaged 55 trucks and 49 supply boats in North Vietnam. USAF pilots hit Phuc Yen airfield and reported destroyed or damaged 75 trucks and setting off 15 large fires and 11 secondary explosions in North Vietnam.
- Quang Tin Province. Cavalry and a troop company from the 11th Light Infantry Brigade made contact with an enemy force of unknown size six kilometers SE Hoi An. Infantry and cavalry force attacked at 1800 hours. Supported by artillery fire. Contact terminated 1905 hours. Enemy losses were 64 killed and friendly losses were eight US wounded.
- *Operation Ford.* Terminated. Final results were 145 enemy killed and 14 US killed.
- *Quyet Thang Offensive* (Hau Nghia Province). Two troops from the 11th Armored Cavalry Regiment and elements of the ARVN 25th Infantry Division made contact at 1140 hours with an estimated enemy battalion nine kilometers NNE Duc Hoa. A battalion from the 25th Division immediately reinforced units in contact. Artillery, helicopter gunships and tactical air

supported. Contact terminated 1920 hours. Enemy losses were 142 enemy killed and friendly losses were one US killed and seven ARVN killed, five US wounded and 16 ARVN wounded.

MARCH 21, 1968

- US pilots flew 108 missions over North Vietnam (USN 47, USAF 44, USMC 17). USN pilots hit Bai Thuong airfield, interdicting runway and individual-weaponry also reported destroyed or damaged 50 trucks heading S Routes 1A, 116, 151. USAF pilots hit Lang Dang railroad yard, Dong Cuong railroad siding and Som Tra railroad yard.
- *Operation Wheeler/Wallowa.* Americal unit from 198th Light Infantry Brigade made contact with an enemy force seven kilometers S Hoi An. Organic weapons fire exchanged and cavalry troop reinforced infantry. Contact terminated with 112 enemy killed and 18 US wounded.
- *Operation Patrick.* Announced. Initiated February 29, 1968 by a battalion force 3rd Brigade, 4th Infantry Division Binh Dinh and Quang Ngai Provinces.
- *Operation McLain.* Announced. Initiated January 20, 1968 by battalion force 1st Brigade, 101st Airborne Division Binh Thuan, Binh Tuy, Lam Dong, Ninh Thuan and Tuyen Dug Provinces.
- *Operation Walker.* Announced. Initiated January 17, 1968 by battalion force, 173rd Airborne Brigade, Binh Dinh Province.
- *Operation Box Springs.* Announced. Initiated March 16, 1968 by elements of the 3rd Brigade, 101st Airborne Division battalion force Binh Duong Province.
- *Operation Harrisburg.* Announced. Initiated March 8, 1968. Marine by battalion force 199th Light Infantry Brigade and 11th Armored Cavalry Regiment Bien Hoa Province.
- *Operation Kitty Hawk.* Terminated. Final results were 193 enemy killed and 69 US killed.

MARCH 22, 1968

- US pilots flew 87 missions over North Vietnam (USAF 44, USN 22, USMC 21). USN pilots hit Uong Bi thermal power plant. USAF pilots hit Long Giai railroad yard.

MARCH 23, 1968

- US pilots flew 93 missions over North Vietnam (USAF 35, USN 32, USMC 26). USN pilots hit Ha Dong military barracks area and Cat Bi and Bai Thuong airfields. Other pilots hit in the panhandle area.
- *Operation Harrisburg.* Terminated. Finals results were 18 enemy killed and seven US wounded.
- US strength in Vietnam passed 525,000 (525,464 including 3,877 men of USMC Special Landing Forces A and B (TG 79.4 and 79.5 from SEVENTHFLT).

MARCH 24, 1968

- US pilots flew 89 missions over North Vietnam (USN 36, USAF 34, USMC 19). USN pilots hit Kinh No railroad yard, POL storage area WNW Haiphong and Bai Thuong airfield. USAF pilots hit Ha Dong Army barracks.
- *Operation Quyet Thang Offensive* (Hau Nghia Province). Two companies from the 1st Brigade 25th Infantry Division on reconnaissance-in-force, supported by armor, contacted an unknown size enemy force 0900 hours, 10 kilometers NE Trang Bang. Automatic weapons and small arms fire were exchanged and armor supported with 90mm fire. Another company of infantry and troop of armor reinforced at 1105 hours. Artillery, helicopter gunships and tactical air supported. Contact terminated. Results were 64 enemy killed, 11 US killed and 36 wounded.

MARCH 25, 1968

- US pilots flew 68 missions over North Vietnam (USAF 33, USN 18, USMC 17). USN pilots hit Hai Duong chemical plant and reported large secondary explosions, damaged Nam Dinh railroad yard and hit Ban Thach power plant. USAF F-111 aircraft flew for the first time over North Vietnam.
- *Operation Jeb Stuart.* Two companies from the 1st Cavalry Division (Airmobile) engaged elements of an enemy regiment 0925 hours seven kilometers SW Dong Ha. Small arms and automatic weapons fire were exchanged. Helicopter gunships

supported. Contact terminated at 1900 hours. Results were 66 enemy killed, 13 US killed and 26 wounded.

- *Operation Worth.* Announced. Initiated March 13, 1968 by a battalion sized force 1st Marine Division and US Army cavalry squadron Quang Nam Province.
- *Operation Ford.* Announced. Initiated March 14, 1968 by a battalion sized force 1st and 3rd Marine Division under operational control of the 1st Marine Division. Terminated March 20, 1968 with final results of 145 enemy killed and 14 US killed.
- F-111 fighter-bombers were employed for the first time in combat missions over the North Vietnam panhandle.

MARCH 26, 1968

- US pilots flew 82 missions over North Vietnam (USAF 37, USMC 27, USN 18). USN pilots hit Cat Bi airfield, caused secondary explosions Hai Duong chemical plant and reported direct hits Yen Vien railroad yard and Nam Dinh thermal power plant. USAF pilots hit Yen Bai and Dong Hoi airfields.
- *Operation MacArthur.* At 0330 hours, an estimated two or three enemy battalions attacked the fire support base 1st Brigade, 4th Infantry Division, 31 kilometers W Kontum City with small arms, automatic weapons, B-40 rockets, 60mm mortar and flame throwers. Part of the enemy force penetrated western portion base's perimeter. Two 1st Brigade companies returned fire while one company counter-attacked at penetration and the perimeter restored at 0710 hours. Two other companies were airlifted into the contact area and set up blocking positions. US Army artillery and USAF tactical air hit enemy positions during attack. Results were 135 enemy killed, 19 US killed and 51 wounded.
- *Operation Quyet Thang Offensive* (Hau Nghia Province). Action continued from March 25, 1968 45 kilometers NW Saigon in the vicinity of Trang Bang. Action terminated at 0530 hours and sweep conducted of area. Results were 284 enemy killed, 10 US killed and 71 wounded. ARVN casualties reported light.
- *Operation Worth.* Terminated. Final results were 167 enemy killed and 27 US killed.

MARCH 27, 1968

- US pilots flew 95 missions over North Vietnam (USAF 37, USMC 31, USN 27). USAF pilots hit Lang Giai railroad yard, Som Tra railroad yard and Ky Dong railroad spur. USN pilots hit Kien An airfield, Ha Dong Army barracks, Cam Pha POL storage area and Vinh airfield. A USAF F-4 aircraft was downed by ground fire with the crew missing.
- *Operation Quyet Thang Offensive* (Hau Nghia Province). Contact continued seven kilometers NE Thang Bang. Action continued throughout the day until 1630 hours when contact terminated. Results were 99 enemy killed, two US killed and 38 wounded.

MARCH 28, 1968

- US pilots flew 114 missions over North Vietnam (USAF 58, USN 33, USMC 23). USAF pilots hit Lang Dang railroad yard and Phuc Yen airfield. USN pilots hit Cat Bi airfield. An F-111 aircraft was reported overdue on a combat mission.
- Tay Ninh Province. Action continued throughout day from March 27, 1968 19 kilometers E Katum and 105 kilometers NNW Saigon. Contact terminated at 1630 hours. Results were 121 enemy killed, 15 CIDG killed and 49 wounded. Five US were wounded.

MARCH 29, 1968

- US pilots flew 106 missions over North Vietnam (USAF 57, USMC 33, USN 16). USAF pilots reported possible downing of a MIG-21 and other pilots hit Ha Dong Army barracks. USN pilots hit Hong Gai thermal power plant and reported secondary explosions at the Cam Pha transformer station.
- *Operation Box Springs.* Terminated. Final results were 106 enemy killed and 24 US killed.
- US Government flew three NVN Naval personnel to Vientiane for release to North Vietnam authorities in a reciprocal gesture for North Vietnam's release of three US pilots in February.

MARCH 30, 1968

- US pilots flew 118 missions over North Vietnam (USAF 44, USMC 42, USN 32). A second F-111 aircraft crashed in SE Asia after an in-flight emergency. Both crewmen were recovered.

USAF pilots hit Chuc Son Army barracks. USN pilots hit Haiphong highway bridge and Cam Pha transformer station.

- *Operation Scotland.* At 0730 hours, a reinforced company-size patrol from the 5th Marine Division left Khe Sanh Combat Base to search enemy out to S at 0830 hours, the patrol engaged an estimated enemy battalion, 1½ kilometers S Khe Sanh Combat Base. Small arms, automatic weapons and mortar fire exchanged with Marines supported by artillery. Contact terminated at 0930 hours and the patrol returned to Khe Sanh Combat Base at noon. Results were 115 enemy killed, nine US killed and 42 wounded (medevac) and 29 wounded (treated and returned to duty).

MARCH 31, 1968

- US pilots flew 95 missions over North Vietnam (USAF 43, USMC 37, USN 15). USN pilots hit Cat Bi airfield, Hanoi radio receiver station and Cam Pha Mining area.
- *Operation Jeb Stuart.* Terminated . Final results were 3,288 enemy killed and 290 US killed.
- *Operation Scotland.* Terminated. Final results were 1,561 enemy killed and 204 US killed.

APRIL 1, 1968

- US pilots flew 105 missions over North Vietnam (USMC 49, USAF 44, USN 12). USN pilots struck transport point and three river crossing sites S of Thanh Hoa. Other USAF, USMC, USN pilots hit targets including lines of communication, storage areas, artillery positions in the vicinity of Dong Hoi, southern panhandle and DMZ.
- A USN P-3V aircraft was downed S Phu Quoc Island resulting in 12 killed.
- B-52s: 5.5 and six miles ENE, six miles E, 2.4 and three miles S, nine miles SSW, three miles ESE of Khe Sanh Combat Base and 16 miles SW of Hue.
- President Johnson in a radio and TV address to the nation announced an immediate bombing pause over portions of North Vietnam north of 20 degrees N latitude plus a 13,500 man troop increase for RVN over presently approved 525,000 man ceiling.

APRIL 2, 1968

- US pilots flew 113 missions over North Vietnam (USMC 40, USAF 39, USN 34). USN pilots hit Vinh and Bai Thuong airfields, transport points near Vinh and Thang Hoa. USAF pilots hit lines of communication and storage areas in the panhandle and destroyed or damaged 25 trucks, numerous secondary explosions and 18 fires. USMC pilots hit lines of communication and weapons positions in southern North Vietnam.
- B-52s struck three and seven miles SE, 1.8 miles W, four miles NW, and 1.2 miles S of Khe Sanh Combat Base.

APRIL 3, 1968

- US pilots flew 109 missions over North Vietnam (USAF 41, USMC 38, USN 30). Pilots struck Vinh airfield, two railroad sidings near Thanh Hoa and lines of communication targets in the panhandle.
- *Operation Pegasus/Lam Son 207.* US Army helicopter gunships of the 3rd Brigade, 1st Cavalry Division engaged an enemy force of approximately 200, two miles SW of Khe Sanh. Results were 20 enemy killed.

APRIL 4, 1968

- US pilots flew 109 missions over North Vietnam (USAF 39, USN 31, USMC 39). USN pilots destroyed or damaged 12 trucks and silenced one surface-to-air missile site. The USAF destroyed or damaged nine trucks and four 30-ft barges. The USMC hit Dong Hoi airfield.
- Gia Dinh Province. Tan Son Nhut received less than 10 rounds of 75mm recoilless rifle fire. Casualties and damage were reported light.
- *Operation Wilderness* (Tay Ninh Province). Announced. Commenced March 11, 1968 14 miles NW of Tay Ninh City by elements of the 1st Brigade, 25th Infantry Division and 199th Light Infantry Brigade. Cumulative results thus far operation: 223 enemy killed, 58 detained. Ten US were killed and 93 wounded.
- The 1st Battalion, 9th Marines made first sortie out of Khe Sanh and seized Hill 471 SE of the combat base.

APRIL 5, 1968

- US pilots flew 86 missions over North Vietnam (USMC 40, USAF 35, USN 11). The USAF hit storage areas located S Dong Hoi. The USN and USMC hit artillery sites and storage areas in the DMZ area, reported three secondary explosions and 11 fires.
- *Operations Pegasus/Lam Son 207.* An estimated enemy battalion attacked Hill 471, 1½ miles S of Khe Sanh Combat Base. An element of the 9th Regiment, 3rd Marine Division supported by tactical air and artillery beat off the attack. Results were 122 enemy killed, two US wounded. 1st Cavalry Division Aerial Rocket Artillery (ARA) gunships sighted and fired on an enemy tank four miles SSE of Khe San Combat Base. The tank withdrew to S undamaged.
- *Operation Wheeler/Wallowa.* An NVA detainee led elements of the 196th Light Infantry Brigade, Americal Division, to an arms cache seven miles S of An Hoa. The cache contained 150 individual weapons and 20 crew-served all in operable condition.
- B-52s hit three miles W and three miles WSW of Khe Sanh Combat Base.

APRIL 6, 1968

- US pilots flew 113 missions over North Vietnam (USAF 41, USMC 38, USN 34). One highway tunnel and seven trucks were damaged. Seventeen support boats, six bridges and four anti-aircraft artillery sites were destroyed.

APRIL 7, 1968

- US pilots flew 134 missions over North Vietnam (USN 49, USMC 44, USAF 41). Targets were in the vicinity of Mu Gia Pass and Dong Hoi. Pilots reported 10 trucks damaged, a large POL fire and several secondary explosions. One highway bridge was destroyed and one damaged.
- Quang Nam Province. A reconnaissance element of the 1st Marine Division engaged an estimated company size force six

miles E of An Hoa. Artillery and tactical air support. Results were 68 enemy killed and no US casualties.

APRIL 8, 1968

- US pilots flew 122 missions over North Vietnam (49 USN, 46 USAF, 27 USMC). Pilots damaged or destroyed nine bridges and 14 vehicles. four fires and three secondary explosions reported.
- The Khe Sanh emergency resupply effort terminated with two air land and six airdrop sorties. A total of 1,152 resupply sorties were flown during the period January 21, 1968 to April 8, 1968, delivering 12,773 tons of cargo. USAF, USN, and USMC flew 24,449 sorties in support of the base. B-52's flew 2,548 sorties dropping over 60,000 tons of bombs. Tactical air delivered over 35,000 tons of bombs.

APRIL 9, 1968

- US pilots flew 131 missions over North Vietnam (USAF 59, USN 52, USMC 20). BDA included 16 bridges, 13 watercraft, 11 trucks, nine automatic weapons positions and eight ferries destroyed or damaged. Numerous secondary explosions and fires were reported.

APRIL 10, 1968

- US pilots flew 116 missions over North Vietnam (USAF 46, USN 45, USMC 25). Pilots reported 15 bridges, three weapons sites, nine trucks, 28 boats destroyed or damaged and eight secondary explosions near Dong Hoi and in the panhandle.
- *Operation Toan Thang* (translation "complete victory"). Announced. Multi-division operation involving RVNAF, US, Australia, NZ and Thai forces. The operation encompassed the entire III Corps area. The operation began on April 8, 1968.
- *Operation Pegasus/Lam Son 207.* Elements of the air cavalry troop, 1st Cavalry Division sighted two unknown type enemy tanks eight miles SW of Khe Sanh. Tanks were engaged with helicopter aerial rockets and dispersed. One tank was destroyed and 15 enemy killed.
- Elements of the 1st Air Cavalry Division reoccupied Lang Vei Special Forces Camp, Quang Tri Province. The enemy overran the camp on February 8, 1968.

APRIL 11, 1968

- US pilots flew 105 missions over North Vietnam (USAF 52, USN 24, USMC 29). Pilots reported eight military storage structures destroyed and three secondary explosions in S panhandle.
- The White House rejected Hanoi's proposal of Warsaw as the place for talks in that it was not an "appropriate site in neutral territory."

APRIL 12, 1968

- US pilots flew 90 missions over North Vietnam (USAF 41, USN 26, USMC 23). Pilots reported destroyed three anti-aircraft artillery positions and three secondary explosions near Vinh S panhandle and DMZ.
- *Operation Norfolk Victory* (Quang Ngai Province). Announced. The operation commenced April 8, 1968 as a multi-battalion sweep by 11th Light Brigade and elements of ARVN 2nd Division.
- *Operation Burlington Trail* (Quang Tin Province). Announced. A multi-battalion sweep near Tam Ky. Commenced April 8, 1968 with elements of the 198th Light Infantry Brigade and ARVN 2nd Infantry Division. Cumulative results thus far: 55 enemy killed and nine US killed.
- Route 9 into Khe Sanh officially reopened.
- USAF F-111A aircraft resumed operations over the North Vietnam panhandle after being grounded since March 30, 1968.

APRIL 13, 1968

- US pilots flew 96 missions over North Vietnam (USAF 51, USMC 33, USN 12). Targets included artillery positions, storage areas and lines of communication in the vicinity of Dong Hoi, S panhandle and DMZ. The weather limited BDA.
- *Operation Carentan II* (Thua Thien Province). Announced. 1st and 2nd Brigade, 101st Airborne Division, and 3rd Brigade, 82nd Airborne Division reconnaissance-in-force SE Quang Tri and Ne Thua Thien. Commenced April 1, 1968. Cumulative results thus far in operation: 503 enemy killed. 57 US killed, 278 wounded.
- Thua Thien Province. Elements of the 27th Marine Regimental

Landing Team engaged an unknown size enemy force five miles E of Hue. Tactical air and artillery supported. Results were 62 enemy killed, 20 US killed and 27 wounded.

APRIL 14, 1968

- US pilots flew 143 missions over North Vietnam (USAF 51, USMC 47, USN 45). Pilots reported three radar sites destroyed 30 miles NNW of Dong Hoi, 16 bridges bombed, 12 trucks destroyed, three fires and seven road cuts N and S of Vinh.
- *Operation Pegasus/Lam Son 207.* Elements of the 26th Marine Regimental Landing Team attacked Hill 881 five miles NW of Khe Sanh Combat Base. Artillery and air supported. Results were 106 enemy killed, six US killed and 12 wounded.

APRIL 15, 1968

- US pilots flew 88 missions over North Vietnam (USAF 45, USN 23, USMC 20). Pilots hit targets in the panhandle region. Two USAF F-105 aircraft were downed by ground fire. One pilot was rescued and one missing.
- *Operation Pegasus.* Terminated. Enemy losses were 1,044 killed. Friendly losses were 92 US killed and 48 ARVN 48.
- *Operation Scotland II. Operations Pegasus/Lam Son 207* re-designated *Operation Scotland II.* Operational control passed from 1st Cavalry Division (Airmobile) to the 3rd Marine Division. Same operation area. Final results were *Operations Pegasus/Lam Son 207*: 1,044 enemy killed and 92 US killed.

APRIL 16, 1968

- US pilots flew 112 missions over North Vietnam (USAF 49, USN 32, USMC 31). BDA included 15 boats, nine trucks and five bridges destroyed or damaged. Eight large secondary explosions and seven fires were reported.
- *Operation Cochise Green* (Quang Ngai/Binh Dinh Province). Announced. Initiated March 30, 1968 by a multi-battalion size force of the 173rd Airborne Brigade.

APRIL 17, 1968

- US pilots flew 118 missions over North Vietnam (USAF 49, USMC 38, USN 31). BDA included 16 trucks, two boats, two warehouses, two bridges destroyed or damaged six secondary explosions and four fires reported.

- *Operation Toan Thang* (Dinh Tuong Province). Elements of the 2nd Brigade, 9th Infantry Division made contact with an enemy force 43 miles SW of Saigon while conducting reconnaissance-in-force. Artillery and tactical air supported unit in contact. Results were 78 enemy killed, four US killed and 15 wounded.
- B-52s struck 13 miles NNW, seven, 12, 14 and 15 miles NNW, 14 miles NNE of A Shau.

APRIL 18, 1968

- US pilots flew 146 missions over North Vietnam (USN 70, USAF 49, USMC 26). Weather slightly improved over North Vietnam. BDA included 14 bridges, 16 supply boats, 13 trucks and 34 fortifications destroyed or heavy damaged. Eleven secondary explosions and five fires were reported.
- *Operation Toan Thang* (Binh Duong Province). Cavalry from the 1st Infantry Division discovered an occupied enemy base camp 30 miles NNE of Saigon. A three-hour battle followed, which resulted in 57 enemy killed and three US killed.
- *Operation Toan Thang* (Binh Hoa Province). Elements of the 199th Light Infantry Brigade engaged an unknown number of the enemy 31 miles NE of Saigon at 1130 hours. Helicopter gunships and tactical air supported the unit in contact. At 1140 hours, another company became engaged in the same area. In the afternoon, two more companies reinforced. Results were 57 enemy killed, eight US killed and 18 wounded.
- B-52s: struck 14 miles NNW 16 miles NNW, 11, 12 and 13 miles NNE, 21 and 24 miles NW of A Shau.

APRIL 19, 1968

- *Operation Delaware/Lam Son 216.* Initiated in A Shau Valley with elements of the 1st Cavalry Division (Airmobile), 101st Airborne Division and 1st ARVN Division.
- US pilots flew 160 missions over North Vietnam (USN 75, USAF 48, USMC 37). BDA included 28 trucks, 26 supply boats, 24 fortifications and seven buildings destroyed or damaged. Many secondary explosions and fires were reported.
- *Operation Norfolk Victory*: Terminated. Final results were 45 enemy killed and six US killed.

- B-52s: 13 miles NNE, 14, 15, 18 miles NW of A Shau.

APRIL 20, 1968

- US pilots flew 92 missions over North Vietnam (USAF 41, USN 26, USMC 25). Weather precluded most BDA. Ground fire described as light to moderate.
- B-52s: struck nine miles NW, and 12 miles and 14 miles NW, 10 miles SW and 12 miles NNW of A Shau.

APRIL 21, 1968

- US pilots flew 151missions over North Vietnam (USN 66, USAF 52, USMC 33). BDA included 54 trucks, five bridges, watercraft, storage structures, weapons positions and lines of communication destroyed or damaged. Numerous fires and secondary explosions were reported.
- Elements of the 1st Air Division, participating in *Operation Delaware,* invaded A Shau Valley, Thua Thien Province, the largest NVA/Viet Cong supply base in I CTZ, marking first time US troops have entered the valley since the enemy overran the A Shau Camp in March 1966.
- B-52s struck seven miles, and 1.2 miles NNW, nine, 10, 21, 22 miles NW of A Shau.

APRIL 22, 1968

- US pilots flew 155 missions over North Vietnam (USN 83, USAF 47, USMC 25). BDA included 32 bridges, 25 trucks, 40 watercraft destroyed or damaged. Numerous fires and secondary explosions were reported. An F-111 aircraft was lost due to unknown causes.
- B-52s: six, seven, nine, 11 and 19 miles NW, 1.2 miles S, and two and five miles NNW of A Shau.

APRIL 23, 1968

- US pilots flew 111 missions over North Vietnam (USAF 47, USN 46, USMC 18). BDA included 12 watercraft, five trucks, two radar sites, numerous secondary explosions and fires.
- *Operation Truong Cong Dinh* (Dinh Tuong Province). In a day-long engagement 25 miles N of Can Tho, the 2nd VNMC Battalion, ARVN 47TH Infantry and US 2nd Brigade, 9th Infantry Division elements supported by US Army barge-

mounted artillery, helicopter gunships and USAF tactical air. Results were 56 enemy killed, 15 US wounded and ARVN casualties light.
- B-52s hit seven, 17, 25 miles NE and nine miles NNW of A Shau.

APRIL 24, 1968
- US pilots flew 116 missions over North Vietnam (USN 45, USAF 43, USMC 28). BDA included 31 trucks, one ferry, two bridges and 12 watercraft destroyed or damaged. Seven secondary explosions and five fires were reported. A USAF F-4 aircraft was downed by unknown causes. The crew was missing.
- B-52s struck three, 11, NNW, 17 miles NW of A Shau.

APRIL 25, 1968
- US pilots flew 110 missions over North Vietnam (USN 58, USAF 39, USMC 13). BDA included 43 trucks, 56 supply craft, 14 bridges and three railroad cars destroyed or damaged. Eight secondary explosions and seven fires were reported.

APRIL 26, 1968
- US pilots flew 96 missions over North Vietnam (USN 42, USAF 37, USMC 17) BDA included three bridges, 21 trucks, 14 boats destroyed or damaged. Thirteen fires and 18 secondary explosions were reported. A USAF F-4 aircraft was downed by unknown causes. The crew was missing.
- *Operation Kentucky* (Quang Tri Province). A squad from a combat patrol from 3rd Marine Division engaged an enemy force of unknown size one mile W of Con Thien. Two platoons from the 4th Regiment reinforced while tanks and artillery supported. Contact lost at 1500 hours. Results were 72 enemy killed, nine US killed and 17 wounded.
- B-52s: two and eight miles NW of A Shau.

APRIL 27, 1968
- US pilots flew 93 missions over North Vietnam (USAF 51, USN 24, USMC 18). BDA included two bridges, four trucks, six supply boats and 25 structures destroyed or damaged. Numerous fires and secondary explosions were reported.
- The USN employed P-3V Orion aircraft in the RVN for the

first time, replacing the P-2V Neptune on *Operation Market Time* surveillance patrols.

APRIL 28, 1968

- US pilots flew 106 missions (USN 58, USAF 34, USMC 14). BDA included three surface-to-air missile sites, 12 watercraft, 12 trucks, one ferry, three bridges, 16 anti-aircraft artillery sites and one radar site destroyed or damaged. Twenty-seven secondary explosions and 11 fires were reported. A USN F-4 and A-4 aircraft was lost in the vicinity of Vinh. The F-4 crew was rescued and the A-4 pilot was missing.
- *Operation Toan Thang* (Hau Nghia Province). ARVN Regional Forces/Popular Forces soldiers engaged an estimated reinforced enemy company four miles W of Cu Chi at 1020 hours. Elements of the 1st Brigade, 25th Infantry Division reinforced RVNAF units shortly after noon. US Army artillery, helicopter gunships and USAF tactical air supported. Contact was lost at 1630 hours. Results were 76 enemy killed (22 by US and 54 by RVNAF forces). Seven US were killed, 31 wounded and RVNAF casualties reported light.
- B-52s struck 12 miles NW of A Shau.

APRIL 29, 1968

- US pilots flew 99 missions over North Vietnam (USAF 54, USN 29, USMC 16). BDA included two bridges, 23 trucks, and 11 support boats destroyed or damaged. Eight secondary explosions and 14 sustained fires reported.
- Quang Tri Province. While on combat sweeps two miles NW of Dong Ha, the 2nd ARVN Regiment engaged an estimated two to three enemy battalions along Route #1. A mechanized force USMC reinforced ARVN units while another US company deployed to a prepared position in the vicinity of the Dong Ha bridge. Action began at 1735 hours and terminated at 2310 hours. Results were 130 enemy killed, four USMC killed, 22 wounded and ARVN casualties reported light.
- *Operation Carentan II* (Thau Thien Province). An ARVN Black Panther company from the 1st Infantry Division made contact with an enemy force of unknown size four miles NW of Hue in hamlet. Small arms and automatic weapons fire exchanged until elements of the 2nd Brigade, 101st Airborne Division

reinforced the ARVN unit. Airborne units cordoned off area by blocking possible enemy escape route. Contact heavy throughout afternoon. Heavy support by tactical air, artillery and helicopter gunships. ARVN unit moved into the hamlet. Contact was lost at dark. Results were 352 killed (199 by US and 102 by ARVN forces). Eight friendly killed and 37 wounded.

APRIL 30, 1968

- US pilots flew 88 missions over North Vietnam (USAF 52, USN 26, USMC 10). BDA included one bridge, four trucks destroyed or damaged. Three secondary explosions were reported.
- *Operations Napoleon/Saline* (Quang Tri Province). Elements of the 3rd Marine Division engaged an enemy battalion in a well-fortified bunker complex two miles NE of Dong Ha at 0905 hours. Other elements of the 3rd Marine Division reinforced the unit in contact and heavy pressure was maintained on the enemy position throughout the day. Artillery and tactical air strikes supported the ground units. Contact was lost at 2200 hours. Results were 92 enemy killed, 12 US killed and 92 wounded.
- *Operation Hoptac I.* Terminated. Final Results were 343 enemy killed and 51 US killed.

MAY 1, 1968

- US pilots flew 104 missions over North Vietnam (USAF 47, USN 35, USMC 22). BDA included destroyed or damaged 13 buildings, 39 boats, 12 bridges, seven trucks, two weapons positions and three boatyards. Three fires ignited and one surface-to-air missile site silenced.
- *Operation Carentan II* (Thuan Thien Province). At 0830 hours, a Popular Forces platoon made contact with an estimated enemy battalion three miles W of Hue. Elements of the 101st Airborne Division committed to the area as a reaction force. The Airborne unit attacked the enemy position supported by tactical air and artillery. Results were 121 enemy killed, four US killed and 18 wounded.
- *Operation Carentan II* (Thuan Thien Province). Elements of the 101st Airborne Division cavalry squad 10 miles NW of Hue engaged an estimated enemy platoon at 0918 hours. The enemy withdrew and the airborne unit pursued and

engaged an estimated reinforced enemy company in bunkers. Other cavalry unit reinforced troops in contact at 1540 hours. Tactical air, artillery and helicopter gunships supported and cavalry units overran the enemy position. Contact lost at 1945 hours. Results were 82 enemy killed, one US killed and eight wounded.

- B-52s struck SE A Shau.
- USAF 120th Tactical Fighter Wing (Tactical Fighter Wing), formerly a part of the Colorado Air National Guard (ANG) and the first ANG unit to deploy to a war zone since WW II, arrived at Phan Rang Air Base to become a part of the 35th Tactical Fighter Wing.

MAY 2, 1968

- US pilots flew 92 missions over North Vietnam (USAF 58, USN 21, USMC 13). BDA included destroyed or damaged two watercraft, six bridges, one surface-to-air missile site and eight structures. Eight secondary explosions and one fire were reported.
- *Operations Napoleon/Saline* (Quang Tri Province). Action continued two miles NE of Dong Ha with elements of the 3rd Marine Division and 196th Light Infantry Brigade battling an estimated enemy battalion. After repulsing an enemy counterattack at 1910 hours, the enemy force continued light probing attacks until 2130 hours, when contact was lost. Cumulative totals were: 255 enemy killed, 39 US killed and 238 wounded.
- B-52s struck A Shau area (one mile SSE and two mile SE);

MAY 3, 1968

- US pilots flew 108 missions over North Vietnam (USAF 52, USN 46, USMC 10). BDA included destroyed or damaged six watercraft, 31 trucks, six bridges and five anti-aircraft sites. 12 secondary explosions reported. A USMC A-6 aircraft downed by unknown causes, crew missing.
- *Operation Napoleon/Saline* (Quang Tri Province). At 1223 hours, four miles SE of Gio Linh, a battalion from the 196th Light Infantry Brigade received small arms, 82/120mm mortar

and artillery fire from an unknown size enemy force in well-fortified positions. The Infantry employed fire throughout the afternoon and supported by tactical air and artillery. Three companies maintained contact during the day and the action became light and sporadic. Results were 67 enemy killed, two US killed and 22 wounded.

- *Operation Toan Thang* (Hau Nghia Province). Elements of the US and ARVN 25th Infantry Divisions engaged an estimated enemy battalion four miles SW of Cu Chi. Gunships from the US 25th Infantry Division observed an estimated 200 enemy and engaged with rocket and machine gun fire. At 1100 hours, two companies from the 1st Brigade, 25th Infantry and the ARVN 25th Infantry Division inserted SW of area of contact and immediately engaged an estimated enemy company. Another battalion from the ARVN 49th Infantry inserted to the S and also became engaged immediately. At 1640 hours, an armored battalion from the US 25th Infantry Division reinforced friendly units in contact. US Army helicopter gunships, artillery, tactical air and AC-47 aircraft supported friendly units. The enemy counterattacked and attempted to overrun the position of a battalion from the 1st Brigade, US 25th Infantry Division. The counterattack was repelled and the enemy withdrew. Action terminated on May 4, 1968. Cumulative results: Enemy killed 69, US one killed and 23 wounded.
- B-52s struck, 12 miles NW of A Shau.
- Terrorists explode a taxi loaded with explosives outside of the Saigon AFRTS studios resulting in three civilians killed and 30 wounded (five US). Broadcast service momentarily disrupted.

MAY 4, 1968

- US pilots flew 109 missions over North Vietnam (USN 57, USAF 45, USMC seven). BDA included destroyed or damaged 38 watercraft, five railroad cars, 12 trucks, six bridges, 12 bridge approaches, 10 road segments, two surface-to-air missile sites, 13 anti-aircraft sites. Nine secondary explosions and 11 fires reported.
- *Operation Toan Thang* (Bien Hoa Province). At 0945 hours, an infantry company from the 2nd Brigade, 1st Infantry Division fired on by an unknown size enemy force while conducting a

sweep three miles NNW of Di An. The enemy employed small arms and RPG fire. Fire returned with organic weapons and unit reinforced with a cavalry troop from the 2nd Brigade. Contact continued throughout the day and tactical air supported ground forces. Contact lost at 2040 hours. Results were 236 enemy killed, seven US killed and 27 wounded.

- *Operation Allen Brook* (Quang Nam Province). Initiated seven miles ENE of An Hoa by a multi-company 7th Marine Regiment, 1st Marine Division.

MAY 5, 1968

- US pilots flew 103 missions over North Vietnam (USN 52, USAF 45, USMC six). BDA included destroyed or damaged 24 watercraft, 11 trucks, eight bridges and two anti-aircraft sites. 16 secondary explosions and eight fires reported.
- *Operation Toan Thang* (Binh Duong Province). At 1330 hours, a company from the 4th Cavalry engaged three of the enemy in the open. An unknown size enemy force using small arms and RPG fire immediately fired upon the Cavalry. The Cavalry then attacked the enemy force with US Army helicopter gunships and USAF tactical air supported. The engagement lasted throughout the afternoon and contact was lost at dusk. Friendly losses were 14 US wounded and enemy losses were 137 killed.
- *Operations Napoleon/Saline* (Quang Tri Province). Elements of the 3rd Regiment, 3rd Marine Division and ARVN 2nd Regiment, 1st Infantry Division killed 202 NVA soldiers in the vicinity of Dong Ha. At 1300 hours, two miles NNE of Dong Ha, a Marine battalion in position of the village of Dai Do, received an enemy attack from an estimated 200 of the enemy. An aerial observer on station directing air strikes reported enemy reinforced their elements with an unknown number troops from N during initial engagement. USMC tactical air and artillery and USN gunfire missions supported. ARVN elements made contact at the same time approximately two miles NW of Dai Do with an unknown size enemy force. ARVN troops also received support from Marine artillery and tactical air and USN missions. An ARVN unit reported light casualties and reported killing 51 of the enemy. Contact lost unknown time.

Results were 151 enemy killed. 10 US killed and 64 wounded (medevac). Total 202 enemy killed.

- *Operation Cochise Green* (Binh Dinh Province). At 1145 hours, five miles N of Phu My a mechanized infantry platoon from the 173rd Airborne Brigade was surrounded by an enemy force employing small arms and RPG fire. Several armored personnel carriers hit and caught fire. Troops dismounted and continued fight. US Army helicopter gunships supported units in contact with artillery missions being directed onto enemy positions. At 1530 hours, two companies of mechanized infantry, one company armor and elements airborne battalion reinforced the platoon and attacked enemy position. Contact continues. Results were 34 enemy killed. Seven US killed, 117 wounded. Materiel damaged vehicles heavy. UH-1 helicopter hit by ground fire, crashed and destroyed.
- *Operation Toan Thang* (Long Khanh Province). At 0400 hours, ARVN elements in the village of Cam My received an enemy RPG and mortar attack 44 miles E of Saigon. Elements from the 11th Armored Cavalry moved toward the village and became heavy engaged with an estimated enemy battalion. The action continued throughout the morning while helicopter gunships, tactical air and artillery supported friendly forces. Contact lost at 1210 hours. Results were 107 enemy killed, three US killed, 21 wounded. ARVN casualties reported light.
- *Operation Toan Thang* (Bien Hoa Province). At 1530 hours, elements of the 3rd Brigade, 1st Infantry Division and 11th Armored Cavalry Regiment engaged an enemy force in a bunker complex 21 miles NNE of Saigon. Tactical air strikes, helicopter gunships and artillery supported action. Contact lost at 1930 hours. Results were 67 enemy killed and two US wounded.
- *Operation MacArthur* (Kontum Province). Elements of the NVA 174th Regiment ambushed a 4th Infantry Division truck convoy eight miles S of Kontum City on Highway 14 at 0940 hours. The enemy ambushed trucks from both sides with small arms, B-40 rockets and mortar fire. At 0950 hours, the enemy launched ground attack from tree lines along the road. Tanks of the ARVN 3rd Armed Cavalry reacted immediately and began firing into the ambush. ARVN armored personnel carriers arrived at 1100 hours, forcing their way into the tree line on

W side of road and overran the enemy command post. ARVN Rangers and CIDG troopers reinforced the ground action. US Army helicopter gunships and US and VN Air Force tactical air strikes and artillery supported the ground contact. Contact lost at 1430 hours. Results were 121 enemy killed, 12 US killed, 28 US wounded. ARVN casualties reported light. Materiel damage to convoy reported moderate.

- *Operation Carentan II* (Thua Thien Province). At 0745 hours, a company from the 3rd Brigade, 82nd Airborne Division engaged an enemy force of unknown size 11 miles SW of Hue. two hours later, a second company from the 82nd reinforced. Throughout the action, ground forces supported by artillery and tactical air strikes. At 1600 hours, contact lost. Results were 82 enemy killed, eight US killed and seven US wounded (medevac).
- Gia Dinh Province. Saigon attacked in several widely scattered spots by sporadic mortar fire. None of the attacks consisted of more than 10 rounds.
- B-52s struck 15 miles N of A Shau.
- Viet Cong infiltrators kill three Australian and one British newspaperman in Cholon, Saigon. Viet Cong in Saigon also kill First Secretary of the West German Embassy.
- Tan Son Nhut Air Base Commander Colonel Luu Kim Cuong was killed leading a counter-attack against Viet Cong units attempting to enter base.

MAY 6, 1968

- US pilots flew 109 missions over North Vietnam (USAF 59, USN 42, USMC eight). BDA included destroyed or damaged four watercraft, 43 trucks, eight bridges, four road segments and two surface-to-air missile sites. 12 secondary explosions and four fires reported.
- Naval Gunfire-North Vietnam: The DD USS THEODORE E. CHANDLER was fired on and hit by an NVA coastal defensive site. Damage and personnel injuries reported extremely light. Ship remains operational and continues her tasks.
- *Operational Cochise Green* (Binh Dinh Province), Action continues from May 5, 1968 five miles N of Phu My. Elements of the 173rd Airborne Brigade fought the enemy throughout May 5, 1968 and into May 6, 1968. Contact lost at 1500 hours.

A sweep of the area continued into early evening. Cumulative totals of the two-day action: 144 enemy killed, 20 US killed and 124 US wounded.

- *Operations Napoleon/Saline* (Quang Tri Province). Elements of the 196th Light Infantry Brigade conducting offensive sweep operation made contact with an estimated enemy company at 1340 hours, three miles SE of Gio Linh. Contact remained heavy throughout the day and was lost at 1730 hours. Ground troops supported by tactical air and artillery fire. Results were 72 enemy killed, seven US killed and 19 US wounded.
- *Operation Toan Thang* (Gia Dinh Province). At 1230 hours, approximately 15 rounds 60mm mortar fire hit Tan Son Nhut Air Base in far SW corner. Materiel damage and personnel casualties very light. No fatalities and no aircraft damage.
- *Operation Toan Thang* (Binh Duong Province). At 1255 hours, a troop from the 4th Cavalry supported by a troop from the 1st Air Cavalry and two infantry platoons from the 2nd Brigade, engaged an enemy force of unknown size 15 miles NNE of Saigon. Small arms fire exchanged and helicopter gunships, artillery and tactical air supported ground forces in contact. Contact lost at 1900 hours. Results were 124 enemy killed, four US killed and two wounded.
- *Operation Toan Thang* (Hau Nghia Province): At 2030 hours, 21 miles NW of Saigon, an estimated enemy regiment attacked the position of a mechanized infantry battalion from the 2nd Brigade, 25th Infantry Division and position of a ARVN 51st Ranger battalion. The enemy force made ground attack against positions under support of mortar fire. Friendly units supported by helicopter gunships, tactical air, artillery and AC-47s. Contact lost at 1300 hours. Results were 60 enemy killed, no US casualties, ARVN casualties reported light. One VN civilian wounded during attack.
- B-52s struck Dak To (16 and 17 miles WNW) three miles WNW of A Shau.

MAY 7, 1968

- US pilots flew 117 missions over North Vietnam (USN 56, USAF 51, USMC 10). BDA included destroyed or damaged 114 trucks, 13 bridges, two railroad segments, 12 road segments, one surface-to-air missile site and five anti-aircraft sites, 37 fires and 15 secondary explosions reported.

- *Operation Toan Thang* (Gia Dinh Province). At 1600 hours, elements of the ARVN 30th, 33rd and 35th Ranger Battalions supported by elements of the 4th Cavalry, US 25th Infantry Division made contact with an estimated two enemy platoons four miles W of Palace. Fixing the enemy with organic weapons fire, friendly units were supported by ARVN artillery, VN Air Force and USAF tactical air and US Army helicopter gunships fire directed onto enemy positions. Contact lost at 2200 hours. Results were 71 enemy killed and no friendly casualties reported.
- *Operation Toan Thang* (Gia Dinh Province). A company from the 2nd Brigade, 25th Infantry Division supported by a troop of 4th Cavalry engaged an enemy force 11 miles NW of Saigon at 0910 hours. At 1030 hours, another company reinforced the company in contact. The enemy employed small arms, RPG and mortar fire against friendly units. Artillery and helicopter gunships supported the troops in contact. The contact continues throughout the day and into the darkness. Results were 134 enemy killed, four US killed and 21 wounded.
- More than 10 rounds of 122mm rocket fire impacted Tan Son Nhut Air Base, materiel damage reported negligible and no reported personnel casualties.
- B-52's struck three Dak To area (11, 12 and 16 miles WNW); A Shau area (20 and 22 miles NW).
- The GVN imposes a 24-hour curfew on the Cholon section (6th, 7th, and 8th precincts) of Saigon due to heavy fighting.

MAY 8, 1968

- US pilots flew 105 missions over North Vietnam (USN 62, USAF 33, USMC 10). BDA included destroyed or damaged seven watercraft, 53 trucks, four anti-aircraft sites and two road segments. Seven secondary explosions and nine fires were reported.
- Naval Gunfire-North Vietnam. The DD USS THEODORE E. CHANDLER and cruiser USS ST. PAUL were fired on by coast defensive sites SW of Dong Hoi. Neither ship was hit.

- *Operation Toan Thang* (Gia Dinh Province). Action began May 7, 1968 five miles NE of Palace and terminated at 0800 hours today. Elements of the 2nd Brigade, 1st Infantry Division supported by helicopter gunships, artillery and tactical air reported 65 enemy killed. Friendly losses were nine US killed and 14 wounded.
- More than 10 rounds of 122mm rocket fire impacted Tan Son Nhut Air Base. Materiel damage and personnel casualties were reported light.
- At approximately 0530 hours, one rocket round of unknown caliber impacted Saigon at Cong Ly and Nguyen Cong Tru St one mile SE of Palace. One civilian was killed and five wounded.

MAY 9, 1968

- US pilots flew 104 missions over North Vietnam (USAF 48, USN 45, USMC 11). BDA included destroyed or damaged three watercraft, 29 trucks, three bridges, one surface-to-air missile site, four anti-aircraft sites and eight road segments. 100 secondary explosions and two fires reported.
- Quang Tri Province. Elements of the 1st Brigade, 1st Cavalry Division made contact with an unknown size enemy force four miles N of Dong Ha at 0820 hours. Heavy contact continues throughout morning and into the early afternoon with cavalry troops being supported by helicopter gunships and tactical air. One UH-1 helicopter shot down by ground fire during action. At 1300 hours, the enemy tried to disengage and US forces pursued enemy as they fled. The contact lost at an unknown time. Results were 143 enemy killed, 14 US killed and 40 wounded.
- *Operation Toan Thang* (Gia Dinh Province). At 1230 hours, two companies from the 1st Brigade, 9th Infantry Division on a combat sweep operation three miles SSE of Saigon received small arms and RPG fire from an unknown size enemy force. Helicopter gunships supported engagement as two more companies reinforced, making contact with the enemy force at 1500 hours. At 1750 hours contact lost. Results were 87 enemy killed, eight US killed and 48 US wounded.

- B-52s struck twice Dak To area (12 and 14 miles WNW), A Shau area (21 and 25 miles NW).

MAY 10, 1968

- US pilots flew 113 missions over North Vietnam (USN 61, USAF 42, USMC 10). BDA included destroyed or damaged 15 trucks, eight bridges, 17 road segments, five trucks and four anti-aircraft sites. Fifteen fires and four secondary explosions were reported.
- *Operations Napoleon/Saline* (Quang Tri Province). At 2340 hours last night, the enemy probed the night position of a battalion from the 196th Light Infantry Brigade six miles N of Dong Ha. A heavy firefight ensued. Tactical air strikes supported the ground force in contact. Contact was lost in the morning. A sweep of the battlefield early in morning resulted. Enemy losses were 159 enemy killed. There were no US casualties reported.
- *Operation Allen Brook* (Quang Nam Province). Announced. Initiated May 4, 1968 by a multi-company force from the 7th Marine Regiment, 1st Marine Division seven miles ENE of An Hoa.
- Less than 20 rounds of 122mm rocket fire impacted on Tan Son Nhut Air Base. There were no personnel casualties or materiel damage.
- B-52s struck in the Dak To area (21 and 24 miles WNW).

MAY 11, 1968

- US pilots flew 124 missions over North Vietnam (USN 67, USAF 50, USMC seven). BDA included destroyed or damaged 21 watercraft, 38 trucks, six bridges, five railroad segments, one structure and 14 anti-aircraft sites. 10 secondary explosions and 27 fires reported.
- *Operation Cochise Green* (Binh Dinh Province). At 1355, two companies from the 173rd Airborne Brigade on a sweep operation made contact with an estimated enemy battalion employing small arms and B-40 rocket fire two miles NW of Phu My. Helicopter gunships and artillery supported ground forces in contact. Another company reinforced at 1700 hours. At 1800 hours, the infantry pulled back to allow tactical air strikes to be called onto enemy positions. After sweep of area,

the infantry found 60 enemy killed, three US killed and 34 US wounded.

- *Operation Toan Thang* (Gia Dinh Province). Elements of the 9th Infantry Division engaged an enemy force of unknown size 2½ miles SSW of Saigon at 1120 hours. At 1245 hours, two more companies reinforced the company in contact. Heavy tactical air, artillery missions directed onto the enemy position with helicopter gunships and air cavalry troop from III Corps supported ground forces in contact until contact lost at 2115 hours. Results were 98 enemy killed, 13 US light wounded.
- Rung Sat Special Zone (Gia Dinh Province): At 0921 hours, the 469-ft SS FAIRLAND, an MSTS charter ship, was hit with four rounds RPG fire and some scattered small arms fire. No personnel casualties and light materiel damage reported. The incident happened 24 miles SE of Saigon.
- B-52s struck Dak To area (15 and 16 miles W).

MAY 12, 1968

- US pilots flew 122 missions over North Vietnam (USN 69, USAF 43, USMC 10) BDA included destroyed or damaged 25 watercraft, 21 trucks, one bridge, two railroad segments, nine road segments, seven surface-to-air missile sites and three anti-aircraft sites. Four secondary explosions and eight fires reported.
- Quang Tin Province. The Khan Dug CIDG camp, 47 miles W of Tam Ky, evacuated by air to avoid encirclement and to enable tactical air and B-52s to strike the sizeable enemy force in the area uninhabited by friendly elements. The camp relocated to a new site in I Corps. One USAF C-130 aircraft hit by ground fire during the evacuation and crashed while lifting off Kham Duc airfield. Seven USAF crewmembers and estimated 150 CIDG and ARVN killed in the crash. Results in vicinity of the CIDG camp since May 10, 1968: Over 300 enemy killed. 19 US killed, 89 wounded. CIDG casualties not reported.
- Capital Military District (Gia Dinh Province). Cumulative casualties figures from 0400 hours, May 5, 1968 to 0600 hours, May 12, 1968: 2,982 enemy killed. 67 US killed, 333 wounded. 760 ARVN killed, 303 wounded. Eight Regional Forces/ Popular Forces killed, 73 wounded. 65 National Police killed, 270 wounded.

- Gia Dinh Province. At 0400 hours, two separate attacks enemy fired more than 30 rounds 75mm recoilless rifle fire into Nha Be tank farm complex. No materiel damage. two US personnel light wounded (treated and returned to duty).
- B-52s struck Dak To area (12, 14 and 19 miles WNW), 40 miles SW of Saigon.

MAY 13, 1968

- US flew 102 missions over North Vietnam (USAF 51, USN 41, USMC 10). BDA included destroyed or damaged 31 watercraft, seven trucks, four bridges, three road segments and two structures. Seven secondary explosions and four fires reported.
- *Operation Toan Thang* (Binh Duong Province). At 0145 hours, a fire support base 25 miles NNE of Saigon occupied by elements of the 1st and 3rd Royal Australian Regiments attacked by an enemy force employing small arms and RPG fire. Artillery, helicopter gunships and tactical air supported the friendly unit in contact. Contact lost at 0630 hours. Fifty-four enemy killed. Australian casualties reported light. B-52s struck six times in a two miles radius of the Kham Duc Special Forces camp.
- MACV announces that of the 26 Viet Cong/NVA battalions trying to enter Saigon since May 5, 1968, only elements of eight actually reach the city's fringes. Results were 2,500 killed in city and over 5,200 killed in III CTZ, plus 1,951 individual weapons and 572 crew-served weapons.
- The USS HENRY B. WILSON (DDG-7) engages and sinks an enemy 75-foot steel-hulled trawler 26 miles SW of Phu Vinh, Vinh Binh Province.

MAY 14, 1968

- US pilots flew 101 missions over North Vietnam (USAF 47, USN 39, USMC 15). BDA included destroyed or damaged 18 watercraft, 22 trucks, three bridges, three surface-to-air missile sites and 16 fortifications. One secondary explosion and three fires were reported.
- *Operation Kentucky* (Quang Tri Province). Dong Ha combat base received more than 45 rounds of 122mm artillery fire.

US casualties and materiel damage were reported as light. The airfield remained operational.

- Capital Military District (Saigon). At 2135 hours, unknown type explosions device command-detonated in front of the tailor shop next to Metropole Bachelor Enlisted Quarters (BEQ), Nguyen Cu Trinh and Tran Hung Doa Streets. Extensive damage was caused to the tailor shop but there was no damage to the Bachelor Enlisted Quarters (BEQ). There were no personnel injuries.
- B-52s struck the Dak To area (15 and 16 miles WSW, and 17 miles WNW).

MAY 15, 1968

- US pilots flew 111 missions over North Vietnam (USAF 38, USN 63, USMC 10). BDA included destroyed or damaged 27 watercraft, 28 trucks, 19 bridges, three anti-aircraft sites, one surface-to-air missile site and numerous fortifications. Twelve fires and eight secondary explosions were reported.
- Rung Sat Special Zone (Gia Dinh Province). Merchant ship TRANSGLOBE was hit by enemy fire 12 miles SE of Saigon, There was no damage or casualties.
- *Operation Toan Thang* (Hau Nghia Province). Elements of the US 25th Infantry Division cavalry squadron engaged an unknown size enemy force eight miles NE of Trang Bang (18 miles NW of Saigon). Enemy losses were 82 killed and three detained. Friendly losses were five US killed and 20 wounded.
- MACV announced the release of two Viet Cong prisoners from Quang Ngai prison camp as a reciprocal gesture for the release of two US soldiers freed by the Viet Cong in Quang Tin Province (USMC Corporal J.A. Santos and US Army Private First Class L.O. Rivera) on January 23, 1968.

MAY 16, 1968

- US pilots flew 108 missions over North Vietnam (USN 59, USAF 39, USMC 10). BDA included destroyed or damaged 22 watercraft, 25 railroad cars, 13 trucks, 10 bridges, 22 surface-to-air missile sites and six anti-aircraft artillery sites. Seventeen secondary explosions were reported.

- *Operation Allen Brook* (Dang Nam Province). Elements of the 7th Regiment, 1st Marine Division engaged an estimated enemy battalion nine miles NE of An Hoa. Enemy losses were 131 enemy killed. Friendly losses were 26 US killed and 37 wounded.
- B-52s struck the Dak To area (12 and 14 miles WNW, and 13 miles ENE).

MAY 17, 1968

- US pilots flew 128 missions over North Vietnam (USAF 57, USN 56, USMC 15). BDA included destroyed or damaged eight watercraft, four railroad cars, 29 trucks, 12 bridges, three anti-aircraft artillery sites, eight structures and rail and road segments. Twenty secondary explosions were reported.
- *Operations Delaware/Lam Son 216* (Thua Thien Province). Terminated. Cumulative results were 739 enemy killed, 2,504 individual weapons and 138 crew-served weapons captured. Friendly losses were 142 US killed, 696 wounded (medevac) and 152 wounded (treated and returned to duty.
- *Operation Carentan II* (Thua Thien/Quang Tri Provinces). Terminated. Cumulative results: 2,096 enemy killed, 157 detained, 488 individual weapons and 93 crew-served weapons captured. Friendly losses were 156 US killed and 717 wounded.

MAY 18, 1968

- US pilots flew 120 missions over North Vietnam (USAF 42, USN 65, USMC 13). BDA included destroyed or damaged 17 watercraft, 27 trucks, seven bridges and 18 anti-aircraft artillery sites. Twelve secondary explosions were reported.
- Quang Nam Province. Reconnaissance elements of the 1st Marine Division observed five groups of armed enemy two, six and nine miles NW of An Hoa and 13 miles NW of Da Nang during the day. Artillery fire resulted in a reported 149 enemy killed (99 of the enemy killed were counted at the location two miles of An Hoa).
- B-52s struck Dak To Area 11 miles NW and 15 WNW.

MAY 19, 1968

- US pilots flew 136 missions over North Vietnam (USN 61, USAF

58, USMC 17). BDA included 10 watercraft, four railroad cars, 41 trucks, five bridges, two surface-to-air missile sites, eight structures, and two anti-aircraft artillery sites. nine secondary explosions reported.

- *Operation Scotland II* (Quang Tri Province). Elements of the 1st Regiment, 1st Marine Division engaged an unknown size NVA force SE of Khe San Combat Base. Results were 66 enemy killed, 26 individual weapons and one crew-served weapon captured. Eight US killed, 34 wounded (medevac).
- Rung Sat Special Zone (Gia Dinh Province). The British tanker ANCO QUEEN received enemy small arms and RPG fire 13 miles SE of Saigon. Minor damage reported. US helicopter gunships and USN PBRs attack enemy positions. Regional Forces troops swept area. Enemy losses were 11 killed. Friendly losses were five US wounded. Popular Forces casualties reported extra light.
- B-52s struck Dak To area (13 and 15 miles W).
- The enemy commences campaign of nightly rocket attacks against Saigon. 22 rockets land in Saigon, about 150 houses destroyed near Central Market (three National Police and three civilians killed, 32 civilians and one US wounded).

MAY 20, 1968

- US pilots flew 128 missions over North Vietnam (USN 63, USAF 56, USMC nine). BDA included 18 trucks, seven watercraft, one bridge, five anti-aircraft artillery sites, one structure and one radar site destroyed or damaged. Ten secondary explosions were reported.
- The Philippine tug BREAM with two US Military Police (MP) security guards on board while enroute from Vu Tau to Can Tho via the Mekong and Bassac Rivers lost their way and strayed over the Cambodian border. The tug and all aboard were taken into custody and escorted to Phnom Penh. The MPs were released on June 10, 1968 to Australian authorities in Phnom Penh and flown to Bangkok.

MAY 21, 1968

- US pilots flew 131 missions over North Vietnam (USN 60, USAF 57, USMC 14). BDA included three watercraft, 18 trucks, five bridges, and one anti-aircraft artillery site destroyed or damaged. Twelve secondary explosions were reported.

- *Operation Jeb Stuart III* (Quang Tri/Thua Thien Province). Announced. The 1st Cavalry Division operation commenced May 17, 1968 in an area 10 miles SE of Quang Tri City.
- B-52s struck five times in the Dak To area (13, 14, 15, 16 miles W, and 15 miles WNW).

MAY 22, 1968

- US pilots flew 135 missions over North Vietnam (USN 77, USAF 48, USMC 10). BDA included 38 trucks and four bridges destroyed or damaged. Seventeen secondary explosions reported.
- *Operation Nevada Eagle* (Thua Thien Province). Elements of the 1st Brigade, 101st Airborne Division captured five 85mm artillery pieces (two on May 19, 1968) 21 miles SW of Hue near Route 547A. They also captured 2½-ton trucks and artillery ammunition.
- B-52s struck Dak To area (13, 14, 15 miles WNW).

MAY 23, 1968

- US pilots flew 129 missions over North Vietnam (USN 80, USAF 40, USMC nine). BDA included 20 watercraft, 42 trucks, six bridges and five anti-aircraft artillery sites destroyed or damaged. Eight secondary explosions reported.
- *Operation Kentucky* (Quang Tri Province). Elements of the 3rd, 4th and 9th Regiments, 3rd Marine Division engaged an estimated two enemy battalions tentatively identified as elements of the 52nd and 64th Regiments, 320th NVA Division two miles ENE of Con Thien. Enemy losses were 203 killed. Friendly losses were 23 US killed and 86 US wounded.
- *Operation People'* (Dinh Tuong Province). Incorporated into *Truong Cong Dinh Offensive.* From March 7, 1968 to May 23, 1968 cumulative results were 237 enemy killed, 414 detained, and 86 individual weapons and six crew-served weapons captured.
- B-52s struck eight times in the Dak To area (14, 15 and 16 miles WNW, 12 and 16 miles W, and 12 miles NW).

MAY 24, 1968

- US pilots flew 136 missions over North Vietnam (USN 79, USAF 41, USMC 16). BDA included 15 watercraft, 26 trucks, three bridges, five anti-aircraft artillery sites and several enemy positions destroyed or damaged.
- *Operation Mameluke Thrust* (Quang Nam Province). Announced. Multi-battalion operation with elements of the US 7th Regiment, 1st Marine Division and US 26th Regimental Landing Team commenced May 19, 1968 in the area 24 miles WSW of Da Nang. Cumulative results thus far: Enemy losses were 76 killed and 28 detained. Friendly losses were 16 US killed, 77 US wounded (medevac) and five wounded (treated and returned to duty).
- B-52s struck seven times in the Dak To area (two times 13 miles W, 12 and 14 miles W, and three times 12 miles NW to 12 miles W).

MAY 25, 1968

- US pilots flew 123 missions over North Vietnam (USN 60, USAF 51, USMC 12). BDA included 10 watercraft, 19 trucks, four bridges, 11 surface-to-air missile sites, one anti-aircraft artillery site, four structures and two radar sites destroyed or damaged. Twenty secondary explosions were reported.
- Quang Tri Province. The USN facility at Cua Viet received more than 100 rounds of mixed 100mm, 130mm and 152mm artillery rounds. Personnel casualties light. No materiel damage was reported.
- *Operations Napoleon/Saline* (Quang Tri Province). Elements of the 4th Regiment, 3rd Marine Division engaged 15-20 enemy in fortified positions seven miles NW of Dong Ha. Tactical air supported and enemy withdrew. The US air-assaulted to regain contact with an estimated enemy battalion. Results were 241 enemy killed. 16 US killed, 33 wounded. An aerial observer estimated from aerial body count 75-100 additional enemy killed by support arms.
- B-52s struck Dak To area (12 and 13 miles WNW).

MAY 26, 1968

- US pilots flew 120 missions over North Vietnam (USN 72, USAF 41, USMC seven). BDA included 17 watercraft, 43 trucks, seven bridges, 16 anti-aircraft artillery sites and two structures destroyed or damaged. Twenty-five secondary explosions were reported.
- *Operation Kentucky* (Quang Tri Province). Elements of the 3rd Regiment, 3rd Marine Division engaged approximately 100 enemy from an ambush position. Results were 92 enemy killed. Friendly losses were 11 US killed and 31 wounded.
- B-52s struck six times in the Dak To area 11, 13, and 14 miles NW, strike 12 miles W).
- USAF jets damaged or destroyed 16 100mm anti-aircraft guns emplacements between Dong Hoi and the DMZ. 100mm were largest enemy anti-aircraft weapons in use to date.

MAY 27, 1968

- US pilots flew 127 missions over North Vietnam (USN 74, USAF 38, USMC 15). BDA included 21 trucks, six bridges, one surface-to-air missile site and 14 anti-aircraft artillery sites destroyed or damaged. Nine secondary explosions reported.
- *Operation Toan Thang* (Gia Dinh Province). Elements of the 1st Brigade, 25th Infantry Division pursued an estimated enemy battalion, which attacked night defensive positions. Cavalry elements of the 25th Infantry Division reinforced when contact established. Results were 218 enemy killed, 17 individual weapons and four crew-served weapons captured. Six US killed, 32 wounded. The enemy identified as a battalion of the 273rd Regiment, 9th NVA/Viet Cong Division.
- B-52s struck five times in the Dak To area (three strikes 13 miles W, and 14 and 15 miles WSW).

MAY 28, 1968

- US pilots flew 108 missions over North Vietnam (USAF 57, USN 40, USMC 11). BDA included one watercraft, four railroad cars, 13 trucks, two bridges, one anti-aircraft artillery site and two structures destroyed or damaged. Five secondary explosions were reported.
- *Operation Scotland II* (Quang Tri Province). Elements of the 3rd Regiment, 3rd Marine Division in night defensive positions

attacked by an unknown size enemy force. Tanks and artillery reinforced. Engagement continued all day. Results were 230 enemy killed, 58 individual weapons and crew-served weapon captured. 13 US killed, 44 wounded.

- Saigon. four rounds of rocket fire impacted in Saigon area during early morning, identified as 122mm rockets. One VN killed and 10 VN civilians wounded.
- Gia Dinh Province. Three unidentified rounds hit Phu Lam communication site four miles WSW center of Saigon. No casualties or damaged.
- Gia Dinh Province: two rounds of unknown caliber hit Phu Lam communications site four miles WSW of center of Saigon. Light damage and no US casualties. ARVN casualties very light. Mission of facility not impaired.
- B-52s struck eight times in the Dak To area (14 and 15 miles WSW, 15 miles W, 39 miles NNE, and three times 16 miles WNW).

MAY 29, 1968

- US pilots flew 129 missions over North Vietnam (USN 72, USAF 50, USMC seven). BDA included five watercraft, 54 trucks and four bridges destroyed or damaged. Eighteen secondary explosions were reported.
- B-52s struck eight times in the Dak To area (14, 15 and 16 miles WNW, 29, 30, 31 and 34 miles NNW, and 38 miles N).

MAY 30, 1968

- US Pilots flew 116 missions over North Vietnam (USN 69, USAF 37, USMC 10). BDA included six watercraft, 28 trucks, five bridges, one anti-aircraft artillery site, seven structures and numerous positions destroyed or damaged.
- *Operation Nevada Eagle* (Thua Thien Province). Cavalry and Infantry elements of the 101st Airborne Division and elements of the ARVN 3rd Regiment engaged and cordoned an estimated enemy company seven miles E of Hue. Enemy losses were 142 killed. Friendly losses were five US wounded and ARVN casualties were reported very light.
- B-52s five times in the Dak To area (27, 28, 31, 33 and 37 miles NNW); five times Khe Sanh area (four times six miles SE and once seven miles SE).

MAY 31, 1968

- US pilots flew 95 missions over North Vietnam (USAF 32, USN 53, USMC 10). BDA included four watercraft, five trucks, seven bridges, three anti-aircraft artillery sites and four structures destroyed or damaged. Seven secondary explosions were reported.
- *Operation Scotland II* (Quang Tri Province). Elements of the 3rd Regiment, 3rd Marine Division in night defensive positions received a mortar and ground attack from an unknown size enemy force. Enemy losses were 83 killed and 44 individual weapons captured. US losses were six killed, 32 wounded (medevac), 34 wounded (treated and returned to duty).
- B-52s struck eight times in the Dak To area (six times 15-17 miles W, and twice 31 miles NNW).
- *Operation Toan Thang* (Phase I) (III CTZ/II FFV). Administrative termination (Continued with Phase II effective June 1, 1968). Cumulative results: 11,397 enemy killed, 2,050 detained, 3,318 individual weapons and 874 crew-served weapons captured. Friendly losses were 587 US killed, 3,719 wounded. 694 ARVN killed and 2,183 wounded.

JUNE 1, 1968

- US pilots flew 81 missions over North Vietnam (USAF 31, USN 40, USMC 10). BDA included destroyed or damaged two boats, one road segment, one secondary explosion and six fires reported.
- *Operation Toan Thang*: Phase I Shifted to Phase II at 0001 hours this morning.
- Prisoners of war recaptured from the enemy by ARVN troops 12 miles E of Hue. Corporal Frank C. Iodice and Sergeant Albert J. Totter captured two months ago were in good physical condition
- The 4th Battalion, Royal Australian Regiment closes the RVN for operations with the 1st Australian Task Force at Nui Dat, Phuoc Tuy Province. The 2nd Battalion. Royal Australian Regiment departed the RVN.

JUNE 2, 1968

- US pilots flew 100 missions over North Vietnam (USAF 51, USN

39, USMC 10). BDA included destroyed or damaged seven watercraft, nine trucks, one bridge, eight rail and eight road segments, one anti-aircraft artillery site and radar positions. Four secondary explosions and two fires were reported.

- Saigon. Between 0140 and 0325 hours, 13 rounds of indirect fire were received in the city. Two rounds were 122mm rockets. Results were five VN civilians killed, 17 VN civilians wounded, and three houses destroyed.
- Six high-ranking VN military and police officers were killed in Cholon when a US helicopter fired a rocket, which malfunctions.

JUNE 3, 1968

- US pilots flew 125 missions over North Vietnam (USAF 46, USN 67, USMC 12). BDA included 69 boats, 11 trucks, seven bridges, 13 road cuts, and three anti-aircraft artillery sites destroyed or damaged. A total of 23 secondary explosions and nine fires were reported.
- *Operation Truong Cong Dinh* (Dinh Tuong Province). At 1430 hours, an element of the 1st Brigade, US 9th Infantry Division engaged an estimated enemy battalion seven miles NE of Cai Lay. Reinforcement made by an element of the 3rd Brigade. Contact lost at 2300 hours. One UH-1 helicopter was hit by enemy ground fire and forced to land. Results were 187 enemy killed, US 18 killed, 42 wounded, and 50 individual weapons and nine crew-served weapons were captured.
- Naval Gunfire-North Vietnam. The DD USS HENRY B. WILSON was hit by NVN shore guns N of Dong Hoi. Results were US one wounded. The USS ST. FRANCIS RIVER destroyed or damaged 46 enemy structures and 14 sampans yesterday and today 26-27 miles SSW of Rach Gia. The DD USS BUCHANAN destroyed or damaged 72 enemy structures and six bunkers near Hue and in Quang Ngai City yesterday and today in RVN.

JUNE 4, 1968

- US pilots flew 119 missions over North Vietnam (USAF 57,

USN 43, USMC nine). BDA totaled 21 watercraft, 11 trucks, seven barges, and three anti-aircraft artillery sites destroyed or damaged. A total of 23 secondary explosions, nine fires and 13 road cuts were reported.

- Gia Dinh Province. Forty rounds of indirect fire were received between 0103 and 0145 hours. Twelve VN civilians were wounded and two ships (SS GRETNA VICTORY AND SS STEEL APPRENTICE) received minor damage.
- Gia Dinh Province. Eighteen rounds of an unknown type ordnance hit in Saigon. Results were five VN killed and 21 wounded.
- The enemy fired rockets and mortars into Saigon and suburbs. A cargo ship and Cho Quan power station in south-central Saigon were hit.

JUNE 5, 1968

- US pilots flew 130 missions over North Vietnam (USAF 46, USN 75, USMC nine). BDA included 57 support boats, five bridges, seven railway and 27 road cuts, six anti-aircraft artillery sites and 10 structures destroyed or damaged. Eleven secondary explosions and 20 fires were reported.

JUNE 6, 1968

- US pilots flew 131 missions over North Vietnam (USAF 49, USN 75, USMC seven). BDA included 62 barges, 19 trucks, six bridges, and two railway and nine road cuts. There were 23 secondary explosions and 15 fires reported.
- Saigon. Last night and this morning six rounds of an unknown type ordnance impacted Saigon/Cholon. Eleven VN civilians were killed and 23 wounded. At 1315 hours in Saigon, an estimated 200 pounds of C-4 explosions destroyed the Chinese National Newspaper Building and damaged two other buildings. Five VN civilians were killed. At 1530 hours, 10 rounds 82mm mortar hit Gia Dinh area killing two VN civilians and injuring two.

JUNE 7, 1968

- US pilots flew 131 missions over North Vietnam (USAF 47,

USN 67, USMC 17). BDA included destroyed or damaged 21 barges, 19 trucks, six bridges, nine anti-aircraft artillery sites and 15 road cuts. There were 18 secondary explosions and 35 fires reported along with damage to seven structures and one radar site.

- Saigon. At 0300 hours, 13 rounds of indirect fire (believed to be rockets) impacted in Saigon. Results were two VN civilians killed and four injured.
- *Operation Mameluke Thrust* (Quang Nam Province). Three companies and a 26th Marine Regiment platoon engaged an unknown size enemy force 15 miles WSW of Hoi An. The enemy employed small arms and RPGs. The Marines employed small arms, artillery, helicopter gunships, and tactical air. The enemy withdrew at 1800 hours. Results were 64 enemy killed, 13 individual weapons captured. Friendly losses were US 15 killed, 37 wounded.
- An undetermined number of enemy rockets hit Saigon, killing some 20 civilians and wounding 40 others.

JUNE 8, 1968

- US pilots flew 134 missions over North Vietnam (USAF 72, USN 55, USMC seven). BDA reported damaged or destroyed eight watercraft, five trucks, six bridges, four rail yards and 16 road cuts, three sampans and 13 anti-aircraft artillery sites. Also, 18 secondary explosions and 41 fires were reported.
- Saigon. 22 rounds, believed to be 82mm mortar, hit SE section of city and dock area. Casualties are unknown.

JUNE 9, 1968

- US pilots flew 124 missions over North Vietnam (USAF 68, USN 46, USMC 10). BDA included destroyed or damaged six watercraft, three trucks, two bridges, 22 road cuts, 15 anti-aircraft artillery sites, and caused 13 fires and eight secondary explosions.
- Gia Dinh Province. At 0300 hours, three rounds of unknown mortar rounds hit near Newport Bridge. There was no casualties or damage.

- Saigon. Four rounds of unknown mortar hit near Cha Va Bridge at 2330 hours injuring two police.
- *Operation Truong Cong Dinh* (Dinh Tong Province). In a 12-hour battle near Cai Lay 19 miles NW My Tho, two companies and two battalions of the 9th Infantry Division supported by helicopter gunships, tactical air, and artillery was attacked by an undetermined size enemy force. Results were 61 enemy killed, two detained and 12 individual weapons captured. Friendly losses were US three killed, 17 wounded.

JUNE 10, 1968

- US pilots flew 129 missions over North Vietnam (USAF 56, USN 62, USMC 11): BDA: six watercraft, one rail yard cut, one rail car, two trucks, two barges, four road cuts, two sampans, two anti-aircraft artillery sites and three structures. Eight secondary explosions and 28 fires were reported.
- Saigon. Ten rounds of 122mm rockets hit Saigon from 0205 to 0210 hours. Seven VN civilians were killed and 23 wounded.
- *Operation Muscatine.* Initiated on December 19, 1967, was terminated. Its mission was search and clear the coastal plain between Chu Lai and Quang Tri City. Operations were conducted by elements of the 11th Light Infantry Brigade, Americal Division. Enemy losses were 1,129 enemy killed, 590 enemy detained, and 338 individual weapons and crew-served weapons captured. Friendly casualties were 86 US killed and 501 wounded.

JUNE 11, 1968

- US pilots flew 137 missions over North Vietnam (USAF 59, USN 68, USMC 10). BDA reported seven watercraft, three rail cars, 22 trucks, nine bridges, 12 road cuts, 17 anti-aircraft artillery sites and three structures destroyed or damaged. There were 17 secondary explosions and 20 fires.
- In central Saigon, 25 rounds of 122mm rockets impacted between 0615 and 0625 hours. Nineteen VN civilians were killed and 67 wounded.

JUNE 12, 1968

- US pilots flew 135 missions over North Vietnam (USAF 55, USN 72, USMC eight). BDA included destroyed or damaged

40 watercraft, 24 trucks, four bridges, 17 anti-aircraft artillery sites and 12 road cuts. A total of 40 secondary explosions and 91 fires were reported.

- Saigon. Tan Son Nhut Air Base received 10 rounds of 122mm rockets. Results were two US civilians killed, four VN civilians killed and 24 wounded.
- The enemy rocketed Tan Son Nhut Air Base with 14 rounds of 122mm (one VN killed, 26 VN wounded).

JUNE 13, 1968

- US pilots flew 136 missions over North Vietnam (USAF 56, USN 72, USMC eight). BDA included destroyed or damaged 27 watercraft, five railroad cars, nine trucks, five bridges, seven anti-aircraft artillery sites and cut 19 roads and two railways. There were 27 fires, 12 secondary explosions and three structures destroyed or damaged.
- B-52s, in 12 missions, struck II Corps and DMZ locations 27-30 miles NW Dak To, 17 miles N Kontum City, and 3-4 miles NW and NE Gio Linh.

JUNE 14, 1968

- US pilots flew 82 missions over North Vietnam (USAF 59, USN 12, USMC 11). BDA included destroyed or damaged one bridge, one watercraft, 12 trucks, and cut four roads. There were 15 secondary explosions and 22 fires.
- The enemy rocketed Tan Son Nhut Air Base, Gia Dinh Province (one killed).

JUNE 15, 1968

- US pilots flew 130 missions over North Vietnam (USAF 52, USN 67, USMC 11). BDA included destroyed or damaged 10 watercraft, one radar site, three structures, 17 trucks, 11 bridges, eight anti-aircraft artillery sites, and cut 19 roads. There were 57 secondary explosions and 35 fires reported.
- Gia Dinh Province. At 0115 hours, 20 rounds of unidentified mortar impacted in SW portion of Saigon. Two national policemen and three VN were wounded.
- *Operation Mameluke Thrust* (Quang Nam Province). At 1145 hours, a battalion from US 26th Marine Regimental Landing

Team supported by artillery, helicopter gunships and tactical air, made contact with an estimated enemy company 10 miles W of Hoi An. The team was conducting search and clear operations. Results were 84 enemy killed, US seven killed and 15 wounded.

- *Operation Scotland II* (Quang Tri Province). At 0600 hours, elements of the 4th Regiment, 3rd Marine Division, engaged an unknown size enemy force seven miles SSE of Khe Sanh Village. The enemy employed small arms, RPGs and mortar. Marine tactical air, helicopter gunships and artillery supported. The engagement ended at 1630 hours when the enemy withdrew. Results were 219 enemy killed, 11 suspects detained, 23 crew-served weapons and 55 individual weapons captured. US casualties were 16 killed and 61 wounded.

JUNE 16, 1968

- US pilots flew 142 missions over North Vietnam (USAF 64, USN 72, USMC six). BDA included destroyed or damaged eight watercraft, two railway cars, 79 trucks, three bridges, 10 anti-aircraft artillery sites, two structures, and cut 16 roads and two railways. There were 19 secondary explosions and 54 fires.
- *Operation Nevada Eagle* (Thua Thien Province). A company from the 1st Brigade, 101st Airborne Division, discovered three 1½-ton Russian trucks 20 miles SW of Hue.
- *Operation Toan Thang* (Gia Dinh Province). At 0250 hours, an element of the 2nd Brigade, 25th Infantry Division, in night defensive positions received heavy (mortar) and ground attacks by an estimated enemy battalion. The infantry returned enemy fire with organic weapons and were supported by artillery, helicopter gunships and AC-47 gunship fires. The contact continued until 0940 hours when the enemy withdrew. Results were 52 enemy killed, 21 individual weapons and four crew-served weapons captured. Friendly losses were US three killed and 32 wounded.
- A Navy F-4 Phantom aircraft from the USS AMERICA was downed NW of Vinh and S of the 19th parallel by an air-to-air missile from a MIG-21. Two crewmen are missing.

JUNE 17, 1968

- US pilots flew 142 missions over North Vietnam (USAF 74, USN 58, USMC 10). BDA included destroyed or damaged four watercraft, 12 trucks, two bridges, 14 anti-aircraft artillery sites, 12 structures and cutting 29 roads. There were 15 secondary explosions and 51 fires.
- *Operation Cong Dinh* (Dinh Tuong Province). An element of the US 3rd Brigade, 9th Infantry Division, engaged an undetermined size enemy force at 1230 hours seven miles NW of My Tho. The contact was contained until 2000 hours. Results were 64 enemy killed, six US killed and 25 wounded.
- At 0313 hours in action off Gulf of Tonkin, two men aboard the Australian destroyer HMAS HOBERT were killed. Initial reports indicated weapon may have been US air-to-air rocket called "Sparrow."

JUNE 18, 1968

- US pilots flew 122 missions over North Vietnam (USAF 58, USN 56, USMC eight). BDA included destroyed or damaged eight watercraft, three railway cars, 30 trucks, one bridge, eight anti-aircraft artillery sites, 12 structures, and cuts 32 roads. There were 15 secondary explosions and 51 fires.
- *Operation Scotland II* (Quang Tri Province). Elements of the US 4th Regiment, 3rd Marine Division, in night defensive positions nine miles S Khe Sanh Combat base, received mortar fire and ground probe between 0300 and 0600 hours. Artillery, tactical air, helicopter gunships supported. The enemy withdrew. The Marines pursued and contact was lost at 1645 hours. Results were 128 enemy killed, 29 individual weapons, nine crew-served weapons captured, Friendly losses were US 11 killed, 30 wounded.
- Reports of radar sightings of unidentified aircraft in the vicinity of the eastern end of the DMZ and N of the Ben Hai River during the nights of June 15 and 16, 1968 received. The sightings occurred at night; therefore, no visual confirmation. The low flying aircraft were suspected to be enemy helicopters and were taken under fire by naval vessels and US aircraft in the

area. Daylight reconnaissance missions were being conducted to ascertain damage.

- B-52's marked the end of the third year of participation in the war. USMC elements in defensive positions 14 kilometers SSE of Khe Sanh Combat Base were attacked by an unknown size enemy force for 11 hours. Enemy losses were 128 killed and friendly losses were: 11 killed and 30 wounded.

JUNE 19, 1968

- US pilots flew 125 missions over North Vietnam (USAF 58, USN 57, USMC 10). BDA included 14 watercraft, two railway cars, 42 trucks, two bridges 15 anti-aircraft artillery sites and 11 road cuts. There were 33 secondary explosions and 72 fires.
- B-52s, in 10 missions, bombed six locations 32-36 miles N of Saigon and four targets in the DMZ three miles N of Gio Linh, and 6-12 miles NW of Con Thien.

JUNE 20, 1968

- US pilots flew 129 missions over North Vietnam (USAF 56, USN 58, USMC 15). BDA included 12 watercraft, 35 trucks, six bridges, one radar and five anti-aircraft artillery sites destroyed or damaged. There were 20 secondary explosions, 17 fires, and 11 rounds and six rail roads cut.
- Saigon. At 2339 hours, five enemy rounds of 122mm rockets impacted in Gia Dinh on N edge of Saigon. One round landed on the Tan Son Nhut Air Base. No US casualties were reported, seven VN civilians were reported killed and 14 wounded.

JUNE 21, 1968

- US pilots flew 134 missions over North Vietnam (USAF 81, USN 40, USMC 13). BDA included destroyed or damaged nine watercraft, eight railway cars, 29 trucks, four bridges, 14 anti-aircraft artillery sites, eight structures, and cut 21 roads. There were 22 secondary explosions and 56 fires.
- Saigon. At 0015 hours, five rounds of 107mm rocket impacted on the Tan Son Nhut Air Base at the northern edge of Saigon. Results of 10 rounds of rocket fire received last night and this morning were six VN killed (civilians) and 14 wounded. No US

casualties were reported. Damage at the air base was negligible. One civilian house was damaged. ARVN casualties were light. Enemy fire came from eight miles of center of Saigon.

- B-52s bombed four targets in the DMZ N of Gio Linh miles and NW of Con Thien.
- The Viet Cong rocketed the northern outskirts of Saigon with at least 10 rockets which resulted in six VN killed and 20 wounded.

JUNE 22, 1968

- US pilots flew 126 missions over North Vietnam (USAF 58, USN 58, USMC 10). BDA included 18 watercraft, 59 trucks, five bridges, 10 anti-aircraft artillery sites, eight structures, and two roads cut. There were 173 secondary explosions and 111 fires.
- Saigon. At 0215 hours, eight rounds of indirect fire ordnance impacted in the Saigon dock area three miles SE center of city. Six rounds of an unknown type impacted in the river and adjacent to the river. One round hit the British merchant ship, LONDON STATESMAN, causing minor damage. One VN civilian in a junk next to the ship was killed. One round, a dud, also landed on the ship. The round was identified as a 105mm Howitzer shell. The origin of the fire is unknown.
- Eight rounds impacted on the SE side of the city. Six rounds fell into the Saigon River or adjacent swamp, two hit a British merchantman, causing negligible damage and one VN killed.

JUNE 23, 1968

- US pilots flew 127 missions over North Vietnam (USAF 58, USN 62, USMC seven). BDA included six watercraft, 78 trucks, 10 bridges, 10 anti-aircraft artillery sites, one structure, three radar sites, and cut 45 roads and four railways. There were 89 secondary explosions and 90 fires.

JUNE 25, 1968

- US pilots flew 128 missions over North Vietnam (USAF 59, USN 63, USMC six). BDA included destroyed or damaged five watercraft, 13 trucks, seven bridges, two surface-to-air missile sites, two anti-aircraft artillery sites, three structures, two radar sites, and cut 23 roads. There were 38 secondary explosions and 63 fires.

- *Operation Allen Brook* (Quang Nam Province). At 1215 hours, a reconnaissance element of the US 1st Marine Division observed an estimated 100 enemy 11 miles W of Hoi An. The enemy wore khakis and black pajamas and carried packs and weapons moving W. Artillery and tactical air were directed onto the enemy. Sixty-four of the enemy were killed.
- Bien Hoa Province. At 0755 hours, two US Army UH-1 helicopters collided in mid-air and exploded four miles W of Bear Cat 16 miles ENE of Saigon. The explosion damaged and downed a third UH-1 helicopter flying close by. Twelve US Army personnel, 16 Thai soldiers and one ARVN soldier were killed. Weather was poor with 200-300 foot ceiling and ½ mile visibility.

JUNE 26, 1968

- US pilots flew 131 missions over North Vietnam (USAF 67, USN 50, USMC 14). BDA included destroyed or damaged three watercraft, seven trucks, 17 bridges, one anti-aircraft artillery site, four structures, and cutting six roads and one rail yard.

JUNE 27, 1968

- US pilots flew 138 missions over North Vietnam (USAF 72, USN 50, USMC 16). BDA included destroyed or damaged 12 watercraft, 13 trucks, eight bridges, six anti-aircraft artillery sites, two structures, and cutting 59 roads. There were 26 secondary explosions and 42 fires.
- USMACV announced that Khe Sanh Combat Base, Quang Tri Province, would be abandoned, in a shift to more mobile operations.
- Elements of the ARVN 25th Infantry Division find 76 122mm and 50 107mm rockets 13 miles NW of Saigon while participating in *Operation Quyet Thang.*

JUNE 28, 1968

- US pilots flew 136 missions over North Vietnam (USAF 77,

USN 47, USMC 12). BDA included destroyed or damaged five watercraft, two railway cars, 23 trucks, four bridges, one surface-to-air missile site, eight anti-aircraft artillery sites, two structures, and cut 73 roads. There were 123 secondary explosions and 24 fires.

- *Operation Jeb Stuart III* (Quang Tri Province). Elements of the 1st Cavalry Division swept the area of yesterday's contact and discovered 147 enemy killed. Cumulative total: 152 enemy killed, 36 suspects detained, 17 individual weapons and one crew-served weapon captured. Friendly losses were US three killed and 36 wounded.
- A Viet Cong Sapper squad attacked the Ton Tra refugee hamlet six miles S of Chu Lai, Quang Tin Province, killing 88, of whom 73 were civilians, and wounding 103 others. Eighty-five percent of the hamlet was burned to the ground, leaving 4,000 homeless.

JUNE 29, 1968

- US pilots flew 142 missions over North Vietnam (USAF 77, USN 47, USMC 18). BDA included 10 watercraft, four railway cars, 12 trucks, two bridges, five anti-aircraft artillery sites, 76 road cuts and one structure destroyed or damaged.
- Elements of the US 3rd Brigade, 9th Infantry Division, find a large enemy arms cache near Moc Hoa, Kien Tuong Province. (29 tons of TNT, 297,000 AK-47 rounds; 1,142 mortars; 8,783 grenades; and 401 weapons).

JUNE 30, 1968

- US pilots flew 139 missions over North Vietnam (USAF 80, USN 45, USMC 14). BDA included destroyed or damaged 16 watercraft, 13 trucks, three bridges, 35 road cuts, one railway cut, four anti-aircraft artillery sites and one structure. There were 30 secondary explosions and 55 fires.

JULY 1, 1968

- US pilots flew 131 missions over North Vietnam (USAF 55,

USN 47, USMC 29); BDA included destroyed or damaged eight weapon positions, nine watercraft, two bridges, 11 trucks and surface-to-air missile site. 38 road cuts, 20 secondary explosions and 108 fires reported.

- *Operation Scotland II* (Quang Tri Province). At 0530 hours, a company from the US 4th Regiment, 3rd Marine Division, engaged an unknown size enemy force three miles SE of Khe Sanh Combat Base. Marine aviators engaged another estimated 60 enemy nearby. Results were 169 enemy killed, two US killed, 11 wounded.
- *Operation Chattahoochee Swamp*. Announced. Commenced June 19, 1968 by elements of the Americal Division in Quang Ngai Province and terminated June 29,1968. Cumulative results were two US killed and 18 wounded. Enemy losses were 23 killed, 15 detained and 17 individual weapons captured.
- B-52s flew 13 missions. Ten of the missions were in and just above the northern half of the DMZ.
- The 1st Cavalry Division (Airmobile) was redesignated 1st Air Cavalry Division, and 101st Airborne Division redesignated 101st Air Cavalry Division.

JULY 2, 1968

- US pilots flew 149 sorties over North Vietnam (USAF 68, USN 51, USMC 30). BDA included 23 road cuts, and five trucks, one surface-to-air missile site, seven anti-aircraft artillery positions, four watercraft, and four rail cars destroyed or damaged. There were 78 fires and seven secondary explosions reported.
- Gia Dinh Province. A terrorist booby trap of plastic TNT detonated at 2100 hours in front of the American Bachelor Enlisted Quarters (BEQ) in the center of Saigon which resulted in one VN civilian killed and minor damage to a nearby water pipe.
- An A-1 Skyraider aircraft assisting in rescue operations was downed in the northern half of the DMZ. Pilot missing.
- B-52s struck targets in the northern DMZ and North Vietnam (five miles N of Gio Linh, four missions seven, nine, 12 and 14 miles NW of Con Thien, and five missions 10, 11, and seven miles NW, and seven and nine miles NNW of Con Thien).

JULY 3, 1968

- US pilots flew 135 missions over North Vietnam (USAF 63, USN 48, USMC 24). BDA included destroyed or damaged four surface-to-air missile sites, six anti-aircraft artillery positions, two radar sites, seven supply craft, and three freight trains. There were 114 fires and 27 secondary explosions reported.

JULY 4, 1968

- US pilots flew 141 missions over North Vietnam (USAF 61, USN 54, USMC 26). BDA included destroyed or damaged eight structures, two bridges, six supply craft, 20 trucks, 10 anti-aircraft artillery sites and 34 road cuts. There were 69 fires and 15 secondary explosions reported.
- B-52s flew five missions, hitting base camps and storage areas 11 and 12 miles NWN of Con Thien, and similar targets 24 miles SW of Tuy Hoa. One mission was in the RVN and four were in North Vietnam.

JULY 5, 1968

- US pilots flew 136 missions over North Vietnam (USAF 59, USN 44, USMC 33). BDA included destroyed or damaged eight trucks, two flak sites, six structures, two bridges 16 supply craft, one surface-to-air missile site and cut 28 roads. There were 53 fires and 18 secondary explosions reported.
- *Operation KENTUCKY* (Quang Tri Province). At 0725 hours, elements of the US 3rd Regiment, 3rd Marine Division, engaged an unknown size enemy force two miles SE of Gio Linh. The enemy employed small arms, mortar rounds and artillery fire. Tanks, artillery and tactical air supported the friendly forces. Results were 78 enemy killed, two suspects detained. Friendly losses were US four killed, 40 wounded.
- Two USAF F-4 Phantom aircraft were downed in North Vietnam. All crew members are missing.
- The last USMC units departed the Khe Sanh Combat Base, Quang Tri Province

JULY 6, 1968

- US pilots flew 138 missions over North Vietnam (USAF 68, USN 36, USMC 34). BDA included destroyed or damaged 11 trucks, nine supply craft, five anti-aircraft artillery sites and two railway cars. Eighteen secondary explosions and 59 fires were reported.

- *Operation Kentucky* (Quang Tri Province). Cumulative total of two-day battle involving units from US 3rd Regiment, 3rd Marine Division, three miles SE of Gio Linh: 134 enemy killed, six suspects detained. Friendly losses were US five killed, 64 wounded (52 evacuated).
- *Operation Pocahontas Forest.* Commenced by elements of Americal Division (*Task Force Cooksey*) in Quang Nam/Quang Tin Provinces.
- B-52s flew nine missions, four missions in the RVN and five missions in North Vietnam. One mission was 19 miles W of Saigon, two missions 50 and 58 miles NW of Saigon, three missions 10-12 miles N of Con Thien in northern DMZ and North Vietnam, and two missions 13 and 14 miles NNW of Con Thien in North Vietnam.

JULY 7, 1968

- US pilots flew 133 missions over North Vietnam (USAF 67, USN 39, USMC 27). BDA included destroyed or damaged 10 structures, seven trucks, 18 supply craft, two bridges, cut 47 roads, and started 50 fires and 33 secondary explosions.
- B-52s flew 10 missions with two strikes 13 miles SW of Saigon and 27 miles WNW of Nha Trang; two strikes 74 and 75 miles N of Saigon in Binh Long Province; two strikes 45 and 48 miles NNW of Saigon in Binh Duong Province, and two strikes 10 and 11 miles NNE of Con Thien in North Vietnam.
- *Operation Scotland II* (Quang Tri Province). Inactivation of Khe Sanh Combat Base was completed. US forces continued operations throughout area using mobility concept.

JULY 8, 1968

- US pilots flew 140 missions over North Vietnam (USAF 79, USN 44, USMC 17). BDA included destroyed or damaged 11 structures, nine trucks, five bridges, 30 supply craft, 28 anti-aircraft sites and cut 60 roads. There were 16 secondary explosions and 125 fires

JULY 9, 1968

- US pilots flew 136 missions over North Vietnam (USAF 74, USN 47, USMC 15). BDA included destroyed or damaged 10 structures, 87 trucks, 18 watercraft, four anti-aircraft artillery sites, three rail yards, and cut 57 roads. There were 188 fires and 58 secondary explosions.
- *Operation Kentucky* (Quang Tri Province). Elements of the US 9th Regiment, 3rd Marine Division, credited with 15 enemy killed two miles N of Con Thien. There were no friendly casualties. Another element from the 9th Regiment destroyed 242 bunkers during a search and destroy mission N of Con Thien. A sizable weapons cache was found containing 26,000 rounds of 7.62 ammunition, 12 crew-served weapons (included a 60mm mortar), 300 rounds of 82mm mortar ammunition, 700 rounds of 60mm mortar ammunition, 120 grenades, 91 RPG rounds, 55 anti-personnel and tank mines, 40 gas masks, 175 combat packs and 6,200 pounds of rice.
- A Navy F-8 Crusader aircraft downed a MIG-17 11 miles SW of Vinh.

JULY 10, 1968

- US pilots flew 127 missions over North Vietnam (USAF 78, USN 32, USMC 17). BDA included destroyed or damaged 23 trucks, 115 supply craft, one rail yard, two bridges, two structures, and cutting 22 roads. There were 80 fires and 25 secondary explosions reported.
- A Navy F-4 aircraft from the USS AMERICA (CVA-66) 16 miles W of Vinh downed a MIG-21.

JULY 11, 1968

- US pilots flew 120 missions over North Vietnam (USAF 58, USN 49, USMC 13). BDA included destroyed or damaged 109 trucks, seven freight trains, eight anti-aircraft artillery sites, eight bridges, seven supply craft, and cutting 36 roads. There were 75 secondary explosions and 158 fires.

JULY 12, 1968

- US pilots flew 134 missions over North Vietnam (USAF 75,

USN 41, USMC 18). BDA included eight enemy killed and destroyed or damaged 18 trucks, two freight trains, two anti-aircraft artillery sites, seven bridges, 10 supply craft, and cutting 49 roads. There were 97 fires and 31 secondary explosions reported.

JULY 13, 1968

- US pilots flew 134 missions over North Vietnam (USAF 67, USN 55, USMC 12). BDA included destroyed or damaged 23 supply craft, 24 freight trains, 15 trucks, six structures, six bridges, one rail yard, 32 anti-aircraft artillery sites, 51 road cuts, and 53 fires and 15 secondary explosions reported.

JULY 14, 1968

- US pilots flew 121 missions over North Vietnam (USAF 58, USN 52, USMC 11). BDA included destroyed or damaged 12 supply craft, 44 trucks, three structures, six bridges, 16 anti-aircraft artillery sites, and cut 27 roads. There were 48 fires and 25 explosions.

JULY 15, 1968

- US pilots flew 120 missions over North Vietnam (USAF 71, USN 33, USMC 16). BDA included destroyed or damaged 29 trucks, three freight trains, 22 supply craft, two bridges, nine anti-aircraft artillery sites, two structures, and 41 road cuts. There were 24 secondary explosions and 63 fires reported.
- *Operations Truong Dong Dinh/Peoples Road* (Vinh Binh Province). Three companies from the US 2nd Brigade, 9th Infantry Division, engaged an unknown size enemy force nine miles NW of Phu Vinh. Results were 55 enemy killed, two suspects detained and 17 US wounded.
- *Operation Toan Thang* (Long An Province). Elements of the US 1st Brigade, 9th Infantry Division, engaged an unknown size enemy force 11 miles NE of Tan An. Results were 76 enemy killed, six individual weapons and six crew-served weapons captured. Friendly losses were seven US killed, 21 wounded.
- An F-105 aircraft was downed by enemy ground fire NW of Dong Hoi. The two-man crew is missing.

JULY 16, 1968

- US pilots flew 122 missions through light-to-moderate anti-aircraft artillery fire of North Vietnam (USAF 56, USN 53, USMC 13). BDA included destroyed or damaged six bridges, three freight trains, eight supply craft, and cut 42 roads. There were 25 secondary explosions and 94 fires reported.
- B-52's flew four missions: 29 and 32 S of Dong Hoi (12 and 15 miles N of DMZ), 31 and 38 miles SE of Dong Hoi (four and 11 miles N of DMZ).

JULY 17, 1968

- US pilots flew 117 missions over North Vietnam (USAF 47 USN 57, USMC 13). BDA included destroyed or damaged 41 trucks, six watercraft, four structures, five anti-aircraft artillery sites, three bridges, and cut 42 roads. There were 99 fires and 29 secondary explosions.
- A US Army LCU-1577 of the 5th Transportation Heavy Boat Company inadvertently crossed into Cambodia while enroute from Vung Tau to Can Tho. Eleven US and one ARVN were taken into custody by the Royal Khmer Government Cambodia.

JULY 18, 1968

- US pilots flew 112 missions over North Vietnam (USAF 60, USN 37, USMC 15). BDA included 11 sampans, one radar site, seven bridges, six anti-aircraft artillery sites, two structures, 39 trucks and cut 42 roads. A total of 117 fires and 31 secondary explosions were reported.
- Quang Ngai Province. A VN farmer led a reconnaissance platoon from the 11th Light Infantry Brigade, Americal Division, to an enemy cache 21 miles WSW of Quang Ngai City. The cache contained four 120mm mortars, 20,000 rounds, small arms and 75 bicycles.

JULY 19, 1968

- US pilots flew 128 missions over North Vietnam (USAF 56, USN 60, USMC 12). BDA included destroyed or damaged 39 trucks, three bridges, 11 watercraft, three anti-aircraft artillery sites, two structures, one radar site, and cut 57 roads. There were 178 fires and 31 secondary explosions reported.

- President Johnson and Thieu met at CINCPAC Headquarters, Honolulu, for two days of discussions.

JULY 20, 1968

- US pilots flew 121 missions over North Vietnam (USAF 64, USN 45, USMC 12). BDA included destroyed or damaged three watercraft, nine trucks, 12 bridges, seven anti-aircraft artillery sites, 14 structures, two freight trains, and cut 20 roads. There were 36 fires and 48 secondary explosions.

JULY 21, 1968

- US pilots flew 119 missions over North Vietnam (USAF 67, USN 36, USMC 16). BDA included destroyed or damaged eight weapons positions, four bridges, one ferry, two freight trains, 31 structures, one rail yard, and cut 52 roads. There were 38 fires and 17 secondary explosions reported.
- Viet Cong terrorists killed five civilians and injured 55 civilians by a blast set off in the Quoc-Thanh Theatre, near National Police Headquarters, Saigon. Four others were killed and 41 wounded as Viet Cong terrorists set off a charge in a restaurant on Vo Tanh Street, 2nd Precinct, Saigon.

JULY 22, 1968

- US pilots flew 92 missions over North Vietnam (USAF 51, USN 30, USMC 11). BDA included destroyed or damaged six cargo craft, six structures, 17 trucks, eight bridges, 48 road cuts. Fifty-six explosions and 60 fires were reported.
- 1,500 Thai infantrymen of the Black Panther Division arrived in Saigon aboard the USS OKANOGAN (APA-220), first of 12,000 to deploy to the RVN. Unit to be stationed at Bear Cat, Bien Hoa Province.

JULY 23, 1968

- US pilots flew 112 missions over North Vietnam (USAF 63, USN 38, USMC 11). BDA included destroyed or damaged three trucks, 10 structures, 14 watercraft, seven freight trains, and cut 63 roads. Nineteen secondary explosions and 28 fires were reported.

- *Operation Swift Play*. Commenced in Quang Nam Province by elements from the 2nd Battalion, 7th Regiment, 1st Marine Division/Task Group of Navy Amphibious Task Force 76.
- Major General Robert F. Worley, Vice-Commander, Seventh Air Force, was shot down and killed in an RF-4C Phantom 65 miles NW of Da Nang, Thua Thien Province. The co-pilot bailed out safely.

JULY 24, 1968

- US pilots flew 104 missions over North Vietnam (USAF 46, 47, USMC 11). BDA included destroyed or damaged 26 supply craft, 17 trucks, four bridges, five anti-aircraft artillery sites, 12 structures, one freight train, and cut 25 roads. Seven secondary explosions and 31 fires were reported.
- *Operation Jeb Stuart* (Thua Thien Province). At 1315 hours, an element of the 2nd Brigade, 1st Air Cavalry Division on a combat sweep 22 miles WSW of Hue, found a significant enemy weapons cache containing 75 rounds of B-40 rocket propelled grenades, 535 rounds of 82mm mortar ammunition, 37 anti-tank mines, 290 rounds of 60mm mortar ammunition, 10 rounds of 57mm recoilless rifle ammunition, 89,760 rounds of 7.62 small arms ammunition, 50 pounds of C-4 explosives, 25 pounds of TNT explosions and 11 individual weapons.
- *Operation Swift Play*. Terminated. Cumulative results were no US casualties and nine enemy killed.
- A Navy A-7 Corsair aircraft from the Commander, Air Wing SIX was downed by enemy ground fire near Dong Hoi. The search and rescue was unsuccessful. The pilot was listed as missing. A Navy F-4 aircraft was downed by enemy fire 10 miles NE of Vinh. The crew was rescued.

JULY 25, 1968

- US pilots flew 107 missions over North Vietnam (USAF 52, USN 44, USMC 11). BDA included destroyed or damaged 80 watercraft, 32 trucks, one bridge, four structures, 25 road cuts, 44 fires and 16 secondary explosions.
- B Company, 5th Battalion, 7th Cavalry, 1st Air Cavalry Division discovered a large enemy hospital complex 38 kilometers W of Hue, Thua Thien Province, including 40' x 40' hut with

underground rooms and a large quantity of medicine and equipment.

JULY 26, 1968

- US pilots flew 119 missions over North Vietnam (USAF 67, USN 36, USMC 16). BDA included destroyed or damaged 12 trucks, 13 watercraft, one bridge, and one railway segment. 19 anti-aircraft artillery sites, two structures, and cut 45 roads. nine secondary explosions and 93 fires reported.
- *Operation Toan Thang* (Binh Long Province). Units from the 1st Brigade, 1st Infantry Division, found a 70-ton rice cache 11 miles ENE of Loc Ninh.
- *Operation Swift Play*. Announced. Commenced July 23,1968 and terminated July 24, 1968. Cumulative results were nine enemy killed and no US casualties.
- Four Viet Cong terrorists blew up the Chinese A CHAN (Daily News) building in Cholon, Gia Dinh Province, at 1315 hours, after evacuating employees. The building was destroyed.

JULY 27, 1968

- US pilots flew 130 missions over North Vietnam (USAF 65, USN 54, USMC 11). BDA included destroyed or damaged 132 watercraft, 46 trucks, three bridges, nine anti-aircraft artillery sites, eight structures, 94 road cuts, 49 fires and 23 secondary explosions.

JULY 28, 1968

- US pilots flew 118 missions over North Vietnam (USAF 56, USN 43, USMC nine). BDA included destroyed or damaged 152 watercraft, 30 trucks, two bridges, one surface-to-air missile site, 11 anti-aircraft artillery sites, one bunker, 44 road cuts, 86 fires and 41 secondary explosions.
- *Operation Toan Thang* (Phuoc Long Province). At 1150 hours a large food cache was found 11 miles ENE of Loc Ninh by elements of the 1st Brigade, 1st Infantry Division. It contained 70 tons of rice in 200-pound bags, 100 five-gallon cans of cooking oil, 200 2½-pound cans of assorted food, 25 one-gallon cans of seasoning, 200 three-gallon cans of powdered food (plus 70 bicycles).

JULY 29, 1968

- US pilots flew 114 missions over North Vietnam (USAF 65, USN 40, USMC nine). BDA included destroyed or damaged 25 watercraft, 32 trucks, one bridge, four anti-aircraft artillery sites, 65 road cuts, 53 fires and 67 secondary explosions.
- An air-to-air missile fired by a Navy F-8 Crusader aircraft 26 miles NW of Vinh downed a MIG-17.
- A 1,800-man contingent of Thai Black Panther Division arrived in Saigon, boosting Thai forces in the RVN to 3,300 of a programmed 12,000.
- Rear Admiral Kenneth L. Veth, Commander, Naval Forces, Vietnam presented the first M16 rifles to the VN Navy at the Vietnam Navy Headquarters, Saigon. The Vietnam Navy CNO Commodore Tran Van Chon attends ceremony.

JULY 30, 1968

- US pilots flew 114 missions over North Vietnam (USAF 63, USN 39, USMC 12). BDA included 87 fires, 67 secondary explosions, 79 trucks, three bridges, four anti-aircraft artillery sites and 66 road cuts.
- The 2nd Brigade, 9th Infantry Division and MR Group Alfa with 4th Battalion, 47th and 3rd Battalion, 60th US Infantry and 5th ARVN Marine Battalion launch a 10-day operation into enemy base area 480, 100 miles SW of Saigon and 37 miles SW of Can Tho, Chuong Thien Province, the first allied penetration of this remote area. Enemy losses were 252 killed, 39 detained, 85 individual weapons and nine crew-served. Friendly losses were four US wounded, three VN Marine Corps wounded.
- *Operation Peoples Road.* Terminated. Cumulative results: Friendly: 28 killed, 205 wounded. 239 enemy killed, 121 detained, 83 individual weapons and six crew-served weapons captured.

JULY 31, 1968

- US pilots flew 109 missions over North Vietnam (USAF 63, USN 34, USMC 12). BDA included destroyed or damaged 20 watercraft, 38 trucks, 11 anti-aircraft artillery sites, six freight trains, four structures and 60 road cuts. five secondary explosions and 40 fires reported.

- Approximately 4,000 troops of the US 1st Brigade, 5th Infantry Division (Mech) completed their move to the RVN. The personnel of the brigade were airlifted to Da Nang in 71 USAF C-141 Starlifters with heavy equipment of the brigade arriving by sea. The 1st Brigade would initially be operating under Provisional Corps Vietnam, in tactical areas of operation conducive to mechanical operations. The remainder of the 5th Infantry Division (Mech), the "Red Diamond" Division, was stationed at Fort Carson, Colorado. The movement of this brigade to Vietnam was part of the programmed commitment of troops previously announced by the DOD earlier this year.
- Admiral John S. McCain, Jr., assumed duties of CINCPAC vice Admiral Ulysses S. Grant Sharp, Jr.
- *Operation Dan Sinh/Cochise Green.* In Binh Dinh Province, 15 kilometers W of Phy My, the E Company, 1st Battalion, 50th Mech while searching a cave complex in the vicinity of Hon Che Mountain discovered one ton of rice, assorted documents, and 935,000$ Vietnam plus $15,000 US in $50 bills.

AUGUST 1, 1968

- US pilots flew 105 missions over North Vietnam (USAF 55, USN 40, USMC 10). BDA included 26 fires, three anti-aircraft artillery sites, 12 watercraft, four railway cars, 24 trucks, four bridges and 37 road segments.
- Two Navy F-8 aircraft 25 miles NW of Vinh downed a MIG-21.
- Arrival of 1st Brigade, 5th Mechanized Infantry Division was announced by MACV. The brigade was deployed to Quang Tri and Thua Thien provinces.

AUGUST 2, 1968

- US pilots flew 112 missions over North Vietnam (USAF 67, USN 35, USMC 10). BDA included 36 fires, 15 secondary explosions, 10 watercraft, 19 trucks, two bridges, 11 anti-aircraft artillery sites, six structures and 50 road cuts.
- North Vietnam releases USAF pilots (Majors James F. Low and Fred N. Thompson and Captain Joe V. Carpenter). The pilots were flown to Vientiane, Laos, in an International Control Commission (ICC) plane in company with three US pacifists.

AUGUST 3, 1968

- US pilots flew 109 missions over North Vietnam (USAF 57, USN 38, USMC 14). BDA included 20 fires, 19 secondary explosions, 48 watercraft, 22 trucks, nine bridges, seven anti-aircraft artillery sites, 31 road segments, five freight trains and 11 structures destroyed or damaged.

AUGUST 4, 1968

- US pilots 100 missions over North Vietnam (USAF 54, USN 35, USMC 11). BDA included 25 fires, 24 secondary explosions, 49 watercraft, eight trucks, eight bridges, 39 road cuts, 18 freight trains, 11 structures destroyed or damaged.
- *Operation Quyet Chien.* Announced and commenced with elements from the 2nd and 3rd Brigades, 9th Infantry Division (IV CTZ).
- *Operations Somerset Plan/Lam Son 246.* Commenced with elements from the 1st Brigade, 101st Air Cavalry Division/3rd Regiment, in Thua Thien Province.
- *Operation Pocahontas Forest.* Terminated. Commenced July 6, 1968, Cumulative results were four US killed and 58 wounded. Enemy losses were 96 killed, 53 detained, 93 individual weapons and one crew-served weapon.

AUGUST 5, 1968

- US pilots flew 103 missions over North Vietnam (USAF 65, USN 26, USMC 12). BDA included 16 fires, 12 secondary explosions, destroyed or damaged five anti-aircraft artillery sites, 41 road segments, two bridges, 24 trucks and 46 watercraft.
- *Operation Pocahontas Forest.* Announced. A multi-battalion operation with elements of the Americal Division participated as part of *Task Force Cooksey.*

AUGUST 6, 1968

- US pilots flew 109 missions over North Vietnam (USAF 61, USN 37, USMC 11). BDA included 25 fires, 10 secondary explosions, and seven anti-aircraft artillery sites, 15 trucks and 35 watercraft destroyed or damaged and 83 road cuts.
- IV CTZ (Kein Giang Province). A combination US/Delta Blackhawk force discovered a significant enemy ammunition

manufacturing complex 36 miles NW of Rach Gia. The following items were captured or destroyed in place: 22 individual weapons, two flare pistols, 75 mines, 1,750 pounds of TNT, 500 hand grenades, 100 booby traps, 100 rifle grenades, 30 60mm mortar rounds, five Viet Cong uniforms, one 82mm mortar sight, one 1.5 KW generator, one 24-inch drill press, one 16-inch metal lathe, one 60-inch lathe, three grinding wheels, one arc welder, one 500-pound scale, two cauldrons, one cauldron for iron ingots, one cauldron track, two 50 pound forges, 100 sand casts for grenades, 500 empty grenade casings, 28 aluminum grenades, 460 pounds of tools, 1,000 welding rods, seven 75mm recoilless rifle warhead molds.

- Delta Blackhawk troops in Kien Giang Province, 46 kilometers NW of Rach Gia, discovered and destroyed an enemy arms factory including 34 structures, forges, castings, 500 grenade casings, lathes, mines, cauldron, 22 individual weapons and miscellaneous supplies.

AUGUST 7, 1968

- US pilots flew 110 missions over North Vietnam (USAF 64, USN 34, USMC 12). BDA included destroyed or damaged 65 road segments, 12 anti-aircraft artillery sites, two bridges, 12 trucks and one watercraft. Thirteen fires and 27 secondary explosions were reported.
- IV CTZ (Chuong Thien Province). In a combination US Army/ARVN operation 25 miles SSE of Rach Gia, which began July 30, 1968, cumulative results were 252 enemy killed, 30 suspects detained, 68 individual weapons, and seven crew-served weapons captured. US/ARVN losses seven wounded (four ARVN and three US). US unit involved was the 2nd Brigade, 9th Infantry Division. Action supported by artillery and gunships from 12th Aviation Group.
- IV CTZ (Chuong Thien Province). Elements from the 2nd Brigade, 9th Infantry Division, found an enemy weapons cache nine miles SSW of Vi Thanh. The cache contained 17 rifles, one 75mm recoilless rifle, one CHICOM machine gun, 53 mines, 500 pounds of explosions, assorted ammunition, three 2.75-inch rockets, 26 grenades, one box of blasting caps, 50 feet of detonating cord, one 75mm recoilless rifle warhead and tons of rice.

- *Operations Somerset Plain/Lam Son 246* (Thua Thien Province). Elements from the 1st Brigade, 101st Air Cavalry Division found a large cave containing four 2½-ton enemy trucks.

AUGUST 8, 1968

- US pilots flew 118 missions over North Vietnam (USAF 68, USN 37, USMC 13). BDA included destroyed or damaged 35 watercraft. 29 trucks, seven bridges, five anti-aircraft artillery sites and 13 structures. Fifty-nine fires and 22 secondary explosions were reported.
- IV CTZ (Phong Dinh Province). A Mobile Riverine Force (MRF) convoy was ambushed at 2020 hours on the Can Tho River three miles SW of Can Tho by an estimated Viet Cong company. Enemy fire returned on positions along river bank, some of which passed over enemy positions and entered Cai Rang village, killing one RVNAF soldier and six VN civilians. Eighty-two VN civilians and 15 RVNAF soldiers were wounded. Stray automatic weapons fire from another ambush action also entered Cai Rang. Results were nine VN civilians killed, 23 wounded. Enemy casualties unknown and one boat damaged. The US assisted effort in program.
- *Operation Somerset Plain/Lam Son 246.* Announced with elements from the 1st Brigade, 101st Air Cavalry Division/3rd Regiment (Thua Thien Province).

AUGUST 9, 1968

- US pilots flew 130 missions over North Vietnam (USAF 65, USN 51, USMC 14). BDA included destroyed or damaged three watercraft, eight trucks, seven bridges, 68 road segments, 10 anti-aircraft artillery sites and 26 structures. Seventy fires and 58 secondary explosions were reported.
- *Operation Nevada Eagle* (Thua Thien Province). Elements of the 2nd Brigade, 101st Air Cavalry Division and Vietnam National Police assaulted a coastal area five miles NE of Hue. Navy PBRs and PACV halted enemy attempts to escape by sea. Results were 42 enemy killed, 98 suspects detained (two of which were NVA suspects) and five individual weapons captured. There were no friendly casualties.

- USMC's newest forward air controller aircraft, the OV-10 Bronco, began a combat evaluation period in the RVN by Marine Air Reconnaissance Squadron 2, Marble Mountain, Quang Nam Province.
- A Viet Cong terrorist tossed a grenade into an MP jeep in downtown Saigon, killing one and wounding one in the 3rd Precinct. The terrorist escaped.

AUGUST 10, 1968

- US pilots flew 119 missions over North Vietnam (USAF 68, USN 36, USMC 15). BDA included destroyed or damaged eight structures, five anti-aircraft artillery sites, 34 road segments, 29 trucks and 53 watercraft. 52 fires and 45 secondary explosions reported.
- After one year's service in the RVN the last element of the Royal Thai Volunteer Regiment "Queen Cobras" departed from Saigon for Bangkok.

AUGUST 11, 1968

- US pilots flew 110 missions over North Vietnam (USAF 66, USN 30, USMC 14). BDA included destroyed or damaged 17 watercraft, two bridges, 32 trucks, two radar sites, 10 freight trains, and 40 road segments. Ninety-six fires and 42 secondary explosions reported.
- B-52s flew nine missions and hit targets 34 miles SE of Dong Hoi (North Vietnam), 38 miles SE of Dong Hoi (North Vietnam), eight miles WNW of Con Thien (northern DMZ), 28 miles NW of Tay Ninh, 40 miles SE of Dong Hoi (North Vietnam), six miles W of Con Thien (northern DMZ), two missions four miles S and two miles W of Ben Tre in Hau Nghia Province and 24 miles N of Tay Ninh.

AUGUST 12, 1968

- US pilots flew 90 missions over North Vietnam (USAF 61, USN 19, USMC 10). BDA included destroyed or damaged five freight trains, 61 road segments, three bridges, nine trucks and 13 watercraft. 42 fires and 23 secondary explosions reported.
- *Operation Toan Thang* (Long An Province). Two companies from the 1st Brigade, 9th Infantry Division, engaged an

estimated reinforced enemy platoon five miles S of Can Giuoc, killing 33 enemy, detained eight suspects and captured 11 individual weapons. US casualties two wounded. In another action two miles W of Can Giuoc, another 9th Infantry Division unit engaged unknown size enemy forces, killing 104 enemy, detained 24 suspects and captured 31 individual weapons and five crew-served weapons. US casualties 71 killed and 27 wounded. Both actions supported by artillery and tactical air.

- *Operation Dodge Valley*. Commenced with elements from 7th Regiment, 1st Marine Division (Quang Nam Province).

AUGUST 13, 1968

- US pilots flew 31 missions over North Vietnam (USAF 24, USMC seven). Complete BDA unavailable due to poor visibility resulting from bad weather. USAF and Marine pilots flew only limited missions and the Navy flew none.

AUGUST 14, 1968

- US pilots flew 105 missions over North Vietnam (USAF 59, USN 34, USMC 12). BDA included destroyed or damaged 13 structures, 18 road segments, three bridges, 21 trucks, and nine railway cars, 45 watercraft. 26 fires and nine secondary explosions reported.
- IV CORPS (Kien Phong Province). Elements of the 164th Combat Aviation Group with an ARVN Camp Strike Force destroyed 10 enemy bunkers 11 miles E of Can Lanh. The combined force also captured the following: one metal melting shop, one chemical shop, one sheet metal shop, one blacksmith shop and one booby trap plant. Other items captured or destroyed in place including 4,800 grenades, 50 sheets of 4' x 8' sheet metal, 30 steel one inch x 24 ft rods, one barrel of potassium chloride, one barrel of black powder, two barrels of acid, 1,000 pressure fuses, 1,000 grenade springs, 15 cans of cosmoline, six chemical scales, one melting stove, 60 gallons of crystallized power, 400 hand grenade molds, one blacksmith forge, two anvils, 15 CHICOM anti-tank mines,

300 pounds of charcoal, 80 blasting caps and 40 pounds of propellant mixture and 1,000 pounds of rice.

- Delta Black unit (7th Squadron, 1st US Air Cavalry and Vietnam Special Forces units) 18 kilometers E of Cao Lanh, Kien Phong Province, destroyed three enemy munitions factories (melting, chemical, sheet metal, booby trap, and blacksmith shops; 4,800 hand grenades; 1,600 square feet of sheet metal, chemical stores, etc.).

AUGUST 15, 1968

- US pilots flew 114 missions over North Vietnam (USAF 63, USN 37, USMC 14). BDA included destroyed or damaged nine freight trains, 23 anti-aircraft artillery sites, 31 road segments, three bridges, 24 trucks, and 66 watercraft. 45 fires and 18 secondary explosions reported.
- Quang Tri Province. Infantry from the 2nd ARVN Regiment, 1st Infantry Division, supported by ARVN tanks, anti-personnel carriers and artillery engaged an NVA battalion in bunkers and fortified positions two miles NE of Gio Linh. two platoons of tanks from the 3rd Marine Division, artillery, and tactical air supported ARVN. Results were 165 NVA reported killed in daylong battle, 13 individual weapons, seven crew-served weapons captured. ARVN casualties were light. There were no US casualties.
- PROVCORPSV at Phu Bai, Thua Thien Province, was redesignated as XXIV Corps.

AUGUST 16, 1968

- US pilots flew 96 missions over North Vietnam (USAF 52, USN 33, USMC 11). BDA included destroyed or damaged eight structures, two surface-to-air missile sites, one road segment, and 18 watercraft. eight fires and eight secondary explosions reported.
- *Operation Dodge Valley* (Quang Nam Province). This operation terminated today. Commenced August 12, 1968. Action was light and scattered throughout operation. Total results were three enemy killed, one US wounded. Announced August 16, 1968.
- *Operation Lancaster II* (Quang Tri Province). An element of the

3rd Marine Regiment, 3rd Marine Division, received heavy 60mm mortar fire after air assault into an area four miles NW of Cam Lo. Counter mortar and artillery fire was directed onto suspected enemy positions. Area sweep revealed 10 enemy killed. Marine casualties were four killed and 82 wounded (72 evacuated).

AUGUST 17, 1968

- US pilots flew 92 missions over North Vietnam (USAF 58, USN 26, USMC eight). BDA included destroyed or damaged seven anti-aircraft artillery sites, four surface-to-air missile sites, 24 road segments, three bridges, 45 trucks and 22 watercraft. Twelve fires and seven secondary explosions were reported.
- *Operation Allen Brook* (Quang Nam Province). At 1200 hours, two companies from the 7th Regiment, 1st Marine Division, observed and engaged an estimated 150-200 enemy four miles NE of An Hoa. The action was supported by tactical air from Marine aircraft. Results were 50 enemy killed and US 11 wounded.

AUGUST 18, 1968

- North Vietnam. US pilots flew 102 missions (USAF 51, USN 37, USMC 14). BDA included destroyed or damaged four bridges, 11 road cuts, eight trucks, and 56 watercraft. 15 fires, five secondary explosions reported.
- Kontum Province. The Dak Seang CIDG camp located 13 miles NNW of Dak To received less than 12 rounds of 82mm mortar fire followed by ground attack by an estimated NVA battalion. Attack repelled. Results were 35 enemy killed, 11 suspects detained, 50 individual weapons, 13 crew-served weapons captured. US one wounded. CIDG casualties light.
- *Operation Toan Thang* (Binh Long Province). Regional Forces/ Popular Forces compound two miles of Loc Ninh received ground attack from an estimated enemy battalion using small arms and automatic weapons, mortar and recoilless rifle. Two ARVN Popular Forces companies in the compound repelled

the attack with artillery support. Results were 40 enemy killed, US six wounded, ARVN casualties light.

- *Operation Toan Thang* (Tay Ninh Province). A mechanized element of the 2nd Brigade, 25th Infantry Division, engaged an estimated enemy company 11 miles E of Tay Ninh. Results were 50 enemy killed, five individual weapons, four crew-served weapons captured. US seven wounded.
- Tay Ninh Province. At 0115 hours, the CIDG camp at Katum received a ground attack from an unknown size enemy force employing automatic weapons and RPG fire. Results were 59 enemy killed, 20 individual weapons, seven crew-served weapons captured. US two wounded, CIDG casualties light.
- *Operation Toan Thang* (Long An Province). A company from the 1st Brigade, 9th Infantry Division, inserted into a hot LZ five miles S of Can Giuoc. A UH-1 helicopter was hit by enemy ground fire and destroyed. The other element of the brigade reinforced the company as did other helicopter gunships, artillery and tactical air. Results were 66 enemy killed, 25 suspects detained, 29 individual weapons and eight crew-served weapons captured. US three killed, 22 wounded.
- B-52s flew 11 missions: two missions nine and six miles W of Gio Linh, 19 miles N of Tay Ninh, two missions 29 miles SW and 21 miles W of Saigon, six miles W of Gio Linh, 43 miles WSW of Kontum, eight miles WNW of Gio Linh in N DMZ, 22 miles W of Saigon and seven miles WNW of Gio Linh, seven miles WNW of Gio Linh in N DMZ.

AUGUST 19, 1968

- US pilots flew 126 missions over North Vietnam (USAF 67, USN 40, USMC 19). BDA included destroyed or damaged 40 road segments, one surface-to-air missile site, 14 bridges, 26 trucks, and 45 watercraft. 38 fires, 17 secondary explosions reported.
- *Operation Toan Thang* (Tay Ninh Province). An element of the US 25th Infantry Division engaged an unknown size enemy force four miles E of Tay Ninh. Unit reinforced by a mechanized element of the 1st and 2nd Brigades, 25th Infantry Division. USAF tactical air supported action. Enemy losses were

40 killed, two suspects detained, four individual weapons, one crew-served weapons captured. US losses were five killed, 19 wounded.

- *Operation Lancaster II* (Quang Tri Province). An element from the 9th Regiment, 3rd Marine Division, engaged an unknown size enemy force six miles NE of Cam Lo. Marine artillery and tactical air supported aircraft. Enemy losses were 40 enemy killed, two suspects detained, seven individual weapons and two crew-served weapons captured. Friendly losses were three US killed and 14 wounded.
- *Operation Somerset Plain/Lam Son 246.* Terminated. Friendly losses were 13 US killed, 95 wounded; ARVN: 24 killed, 62 wounded; Enemy losses (by US) 80 killed, one detained, 24 individual weapons, 11 crew-served weapons; Enemy (by ARVN) 53 killed, three detained, 24 individual weapons and one crew-served weapon.
- *Operation Lancaster II* (Quang Tri Province). An element from the 3rd Regiment, 1st Marine Division, discovered a significant enemy weapons cache five miles WNW of Cam Lo. The cache totaled more than eight tons and contained the following: 1,586 82mm mortar rounds, 250 60mm mortar rounds, 129 RPG rounds, 15,000 rounds of small arms, 400 pounds of TNT and five individual weapons.
- B-52s flew 10 missions: 22 miles W of Saigon in Hau Nghia Province, seven miles W of Gio Lingh in S-DMZ, four missions seven miles W of Gio Linh in S-DMZ, two missions five miles N of Con Thien in N-DMZ, and two missions 25 miles W of Saigon in Hau Nghia Province.

AUGUST 20, 1968

- US pilots flew 107 missions over North Vietnam (USAF 52, USN 41, USMC 14). BDA included destroyed or damaged six structures, five anti-aircraft artillery sites, 56 road segments, four bridges, 11 trucks and 17 watercraft. 47 fires and 65 secondary explosions reported.
- *Operation Toan Thang* (Tay Ninh Province). At 0110 hours, an ambush platoon from the 2nd Brigade, 25th Infantry Division, killed 102 enemy seven miles NW of Tay Ninh. The action was

supported by helicopter gunships and artillery. US casualties were light.

- *Operation Jeb Stuart III* (Quang Tri Province). At 1400 hours, an element of the Air Cavalry Squadron from the 1st Air Cavalry Division received heavy automatic weapons fire from an unknown size enemy force four miles NE of Quang Tri. Results were 66 NVA killed, nine suspects detained. US had three killed, 15 wounded.

AUGUST 21, 1968

- US pilots flew 104 missions over North Vietnam (USAF 46, USN 47, USMC 11). BDA included destroyed or damaged 90 structures, 20 road segments, four bridges, 13 trucks and 23 watercraft. 64 fires reported.
- *Operation McClain* (Lam Dong Province). An ARVN force repulsed an enemy battalion sized attack at Di Linh district town, killing 43 enemy, and capturing 12 individual weapons and three crew-served weapons. ARVN casualties were light. An element from the 173rd Airborne Division supported the action. US had three killed, 14 wounded.
- *Operation Toan Thang* (Tay Ninh Province). A mechanized element from the 2nd Brigade, 25th Infantry Division, supported by artillery and tactical air, killed 182 enemy 12 miles E of Tay Ninh.
- Gia Dinh Province. A US Army sergeant was shot to death by two Viet Cong assassins on a Honda while riding in a cyclo on Cong Ly Street in Saigon. An ARVN soldier intervened but was also shot and wounded. Both assassins escaped.

AUGUST 22, 1968

- US pilots flew 117 missions over North Vietnam (USAF 63, USN 41, USMC 13). BDA included destroyed or damaged five anti-aircraft artillery sites, 33 road segments, four bridges, 36 trucks, three railway cars and 15 watercraft. 134 fires and 93 secondary explosions reported.
- Gia Dinh Province. Between 0400 and 0525 hours, Saigon received 20 rounds of 122mm rocket fire. Counter artillery fire was directed onto suspected enemy positions with unknown

results. Fourteen VN civilians were killed and 15 injured. There were no US casualties or damage to installations.

- After a two-month lull, enemy 122mm rockets hit Saigon. Ten fell in the downtown area, six in Cholon and three along the docks (17 civilians killed, 69 civilians wounded). The National Assembly building roof was hit with moderate damage.

AUGUST 23, 1968

- US pilots flew 113 missions over North Vietnam (USAF 54, USN 49, USMC 10). BDA included destroyed or damaged two surface-to-air missile sites, 76 road segments, eight bridges, 74 trucks and watercraft. 120 fires, 58 secondary explosions reported.
- Quang Duc Province. At 0155 hours, the CIDG camp at Duc Lap 29 miles NE of Gia Nghia received an unreported number of 122mm rocket rounds followed by a ground attack from a battalion size enemy force. Attack repulsed. Results were 22 enemy killed, 12 individual weapons, nine crew-served weapons captured. Friendly casualties light. AC-47 flare ships and US Army gunships supported action.
- *Operation Toan Thang* (Binh Long Province). An element from the 1st Brigade, 1st Infantry Division, engaged an unknown size enemy force ½ mile S of Loc Ninh, killing 41 enemy. US casualties one killed, 19 wounded. Artillery, gunships and tactical air supported action.
- The enemy attacks the CIDG Camp, 32 miles NNW of Gia Nghia, Quang Duc Province, and five miles from the Cambodian border. Several days of fighting follows. Enemy losses were 776 killed and friendly losses were 116 killed (two US).

AUGUST 24, 1968

- US pilots flew 113 missions over North Vietnam (USAF 54, USN 50, USMC nine). BDA included destroyed or damaged four surface-to-air missile sites, 28 road segments, six anti-aircraft artillery sites, three bridges, eight trucks and 10 watercraft. 40 fires and 11 secondary explosions reported.
- *Operation Toan Thang* (Tay Ninh Province). At 0200 hours, an element from the 2nd Brigade, 25th Division, attacked by an

unknown size enemy force 11 miles E of Tay Ninh. Results were 62 enemy killed, US two killed and 36 wounded. Action supported by USAF, tactical air, US Army helicopter gunships and artillery.

- *Operation Burlington Trail* (Quang Tin Province). An element from an Air Cavalry Squadron of the Americal Division engaged an unknown size force four miles W of Tam Ky. Results were 223 enemy killed, three suspects detained. 15 individual weapons and six crew-served weapons captured. US 11 wounded. Helicopter gunships supported action credited with killing most of the enemy.
- Quang Nam Province: An enemy force of undetermined size seized the S end of Cam Le Bridge on Route 1 S of Da Nang. An enemy force engaged by the Marine 3rd Military Police Battalion and an element of the 27th Marine Regiment Leading Team. Heavy fighting ensued. Results were 122 enemy killed, 33 individual weapons and 200 kilos of TNT captured. Friendly casualties six killed, 28 wounded.
- *Operation Allen Brook* (Quang Nam Province). This operation began May 4, 1968 and terminated today. Elements were the 7th Regiment, 1st Marine Division; 5th and 27th Marine Regiments. Cumulative results: 1,017 enemy killed, 102 suspects detained, 127 individual weapons, 27 crew-served weapons captured. Marine casualties were 172 killed, 1,124 wounded. The number of tactical air sorties in support of operation were 2,248.

AUGUST 25, 1968

- US pilots flew 112 missions over North Vietnam (USAF 56, USN 46, USMC 10). BDA included destroyed or damaged five anti-aircraft artillery sites, 23 road segments, three surface-to-air missile sites, five bridges, 57 trucks and 24 watercraft. 65 fires and 46 secondary explosions reported.
- *Operation Toan Thang* (Tay Ninh Province). A 25th Infantry Division convoy enroute from Cu Chi to Tay Ninh was ambushed by an unknown size enemy force six miles NW of Go Dan Hau. An Armed Cavalry Squadron reaction force from the division reinforced the contact, supported by US Army

gunships, artillery and tactical air. Enemy losses were 96 killed. US losses were six killed and 51 wounded.

- *Operation Burlington Trail* (Quang Tin Province). Elements from the 1st Squadron, 1st Armed Cavalry, Americal Division and a company from the 11th Light Infantry Brigade, Americal Division, killed 511 enemy in a two-day battle five miles W of Tam Ky. US casualties: seven killed, 47 wounded.
- B-52s flew 13 missions: 28 miles NW of Saigon, two missions one mile E and six miles SE of the Duc Lap CIDG camp, two missions SE of Tay Ninh, six miles SE of Duc Lap CIDG camp, four missions 40 miles W and 48 miles SW of Kontum, three missions 12-13 miles SW of Chu Lai.

AUGUST 26, 1968

- US pilots flew 123 missions over North Vietnam (USAF 59, USN 53, USMC 11). BDA included destroyed or damaged seven anti-aircraft artillery sites, 59 road segments, 14 bridges, 46 trucks and 55 watercraft. 146 fires and 34 secondary explosions reported.
- *Operation Nevada Eagle* (Thua Thien Province). An element of the 3rd Brigade, 82nd Airborne Division, reported 92 enemy killed 16 miles S of Hue in an action supported by artillery and tactical air. US casualties three wounded.
- The 101st Air Cavalry Division and the 1st Air Cavalry Division were redesignated as the 101st Airborne Division Airmobile (Airmobile) and the 1st Cavalry Division (Airmobile).

AUGUST 27, 1968

- US pilots flew 107 missions over North Vietnam (USAF 67, USN 29, USMC 11). BDA included destroyed or damaged nine radar sites, nine bridges, two anti-aircraft artillery sites, 20 trucks, 37 surface-to-air missile sites, 143 structures and 14 watercraft. 61 fires and 11 secondary explosions reported.
- *Operation Toan Thang* (Hau Nghia Province). At 1030 hours, a company from the 3rd Brigade, 101st Air Cavalry Division, reported 103 enemy killed, 22 suspects detained, four individual weapons and two crew-served weapons captured in an action four miles N of Trang Bang. Action supported

against the unknown size engaged force by gunships, artillery and tactical air. US casualties were 16 killed and 25 wounded.

AUGUST 28, 1968

- US pilots flew 121 missions over North Vietnam (USAF 64, USN 47, USMC 10). BDA included destroyed or damaged 32 trucks, one radar site, 132 structures, seven surface-to-air missile sites, 34 road segments, and one bridge. 116 fires and seven secondary explosions reported.
- *Operation Nevada Eagle* (Thua Thien Province). Elements from the 3rd Brigade, 82nd Airborne Division, found a series of enemy caches 16 miles S of Hue. Caches contained 200,000 rounds of small arms ammunition, 100 rounds of 82mm mortar, 500 rounds of 60mm mortar, 150 rounds of 57 recoilless rifle ammunition, 91 RPG rounds, 400 rounds of 7.62mm ammunition, 12 one-pound blocks of TNT, 22 AK-47 rifles, 30 SKS carbines, 41 carbines, one heavy machine gun, three complete 60mm mortars, one Mauser rifle, one .30 caliber pistol, one portable typewriter, three communication radios, one portable tape recorder and two complete field hospitals.

AUGUST 29, 1968

- North Vietnam. US pilots flew 130 missions over North Vietnam (USAF 65, USN 53, USMC 12). BDA included destroyed of damaged seven freight trains, 44 trucks, 40 road segments, and 114 watercraft. 50 secondary explosions and 107 fires reported.
- *Operation Swift Pursuit.* Terminated. Announced August 31, 1968, commenced August 28, 1968. Task Force 76 ship-to-shore movement of BLT 2/26 USMC into *Operation Lancaster II* in Quang Tri Province. There were no friendly or enemy casualties.
- *Operation Sussex Bay.* Commenced with the elements from the 5th Regiment, 1st Marine Division, and two companies from 7th Regiment (Quang Nam Province) in coordination with ARVN *Operation Hung Quang 1065* involving 51st Infantry Regiment and 1st Ranger Group.

AUGUST 30, 1968

- US pilots flew 120 missions over North Vietnam (USAF 61, USN 51, USMC eight). BDA included destroyed or damaged six anti-aircraft artillery sites, 31 trucks and 27 watercraft. 53 fires and 31 secondary explosions reported.
- A Navy A-4 Skyhawk aircraft was downed by enemy ground fire 29 miles WNW of Vinh. Pilot rescued.
- Prisoners at the US Army Long Binh prison stockade riot. One prisoner was killed, 59 prisoners and four guards injured. Heavy damage was done to the stockade. Ten large buildings were burned. Prisoner population was 719 military, one civilian.

AUGUST 31, 1968

- US pilots flew 130 missions over North Vietnam (USAF 75, USN 41, USMC 14). BDA included destroyed or damaged 14 structures, 14 anti-aircraft artillery sites, five bridges, 27 road segments, 26 trucks, and six watercraft. 48 fires and 47 secondary explosions reported.
- *Operation Kentucky* (Quang Tri Province). A company from the 1st Brigade, 5th Infantry Division, engaged an unknown size enemy force in bunkers ½ mile N of Con Thien in an action supported by tactical air and artillery. Enemy losses were 65 NVA killed, 19 individual weapons captured. US losses were two killed and 24 wounded.

SEPTEMBER 1, 1968

- US pilots flew 110 missions over North Vietnam (USAF 57, USN 45, USMC eight). BDA included 26 fires, 26 secondary explosions, 10 anti-aircraft artillery sites, two bridges, 16 trucks, 29 watercraft, six freight trains and 32 structures.

SEPTEMBER 2, 1968

- US pilots flew 121 missions over North Vietnam (USAF 58, USN 54, USMC nine). BDA included 24 fires, 16 secondary explosions, 29 road segments, 28 trucks and 38 watercraft.

SEPTEMBER 3, 1968

- US pilots flew 121 missions over North Vietnam (USAF 73, USN 37, USMC 11). BDA included 24 fires, 11 secondary explosions, 13 freight trains, 45 road segments, 18 trucks and 13 watercraft.
- Two UH-1 helicopters were downed as a result of enemy ground fire. One was hit by enemy ground fire 12 miles NE of Tan An while on a combat assault mission. Three crewmembers were killed and one was wounded. The helicopter was destroyed. The other helicopter was downed 22 miles NNW of Tay Ninh while in process of rescuing two crew members of the Air Force F-4 aircraft that was downed earlier. A USAF HH-43 Husky helicopter rescued three of the four crewmembers. A US Army OH-6 helicopter rescued the other crewmember.
- Viet Cong terrorists explode a grenade in front of the US Agency for International Development (USAID) Headquarters on Le Van Duyet Street in downtown Saigon, wounding seven civilians. Another grenade wounds eight civilians in Saigon dock area.

SEPTEMBER 4, 1968

- US pilots flew 70 missions over North Vietnam (USAF 61, USN three, USMC six). BDA included two anti-aircraft artillery positions, one truck, six road cuts, 12 fires and eight secondary explosions.
- *Operation Champaign Grove.* Commenced. Troops from the 11th Light Infantry Brigade, Americal Division, operation under control of *Task Force Galloway,* were participating in the operation.

SEPTEMBER 5, 1968

- Tropical Storm Bess limited missions flown over panhandle of North Vietnam. No BDA available due to bad weather. US pilots flew only 33 missions (USAF 29, USMC four).
- *Operation Toan Thang* (Hau Nghia Province). At approximately 1215 hours, an element of the US 3rd Brigade, 101st Airborne Division (Airmobile), air assault in a hot LZ three miles E of Trang Bang and engaged an unknown size enemy force. Elements of the Armored Cavalry Squadron of the US 25th

Infantry Division and other paratroopers from the brigade maneuver into blocking positions. Artillery, helicopter gunships and tactical air supported. By 1600, additional elements of the brigade reinforce and took up blocking positions in attempt to cordon the enemy force then estimated at battalion size. Enemy losses were 103 killed, 123 suspects detained, three crew-served weapons and 11 individual weapons captured. US losses were 31 killed and 41 wounded.

SEPTEMBER 6, 1968

- US pilots flew 81 missions over North Vietnam (USAF 47, USN 24, USMC 10). BDA included nine supply craft, seven trucks, seven road cuts, three secondary explosions and eight fires.
- Gia Dinh Province. At 1830 hours, a Viet Cong terrorist explosion occurred at the Vietnam Infantry Center SW of the center of Saigon. Nine VN civilians killed and 30 wounded. It was estimated that 75 pounds of TNT was used to cause casualties and damage.
- Gia Dinh Province. At approximately 2330 hours, the VII Precinct located four miles SW of Saigon received one round of 122mm rocket fire. One VN woman was killed and 11 wounded, including eight children. One civilian house was destroyed and one damaged.
- A USN A-6 Intruder aircraft was downed by enemy ground fire four miles E of Vinh. One crewmember was rescued, but pilot missing.

SEPTEMBER 7, 1968

- US pilots flew 85 missions over North Vietnam (USAF 32, USN 42, USMC 11). BDA included 25 trucks, 17 supply craft, two anti-aircraft artillery sites, eight road cuts, and two bridges. Five secondary explosions, four fires reported.
- Quang Ngai Province. In an action that began September 6, 1968 at 1410 hours, a reconnaissance platoon from the US 11th Light Infantry Brigade, Americal Division, engaged an unknown size enemy force six miles NW of Quang Ngai City. Contact was lost later at an unknown time and while a reconnaissance platoon was waiting for extraction, an aircraft enroute to their site received heavy ground fire and aborted the mission. Two other companies from the brigade effected

an over-land link-up at 2345 hours as helicopter gunships, artillery and AC-47 gunships supported. Contact lost at 0200 hours this morning. Results were 28 enemy killed, US 11 killed, six wounded.

- *Operation Toan Thang* (Long An Province). At 1030 hours, elements of the 1st Brigade, 9th Infantry Division, engaged an estimated enemy battalion in bunkers two miles NW of Can Duoc. Artillery and helicopter gunships supported. Results were 47 enemy killed, 11 individual weapons captured. US casualties were light (five wounded). One suspect was detained.
- B-52s flew two missions four miles and nine miles WSW of Con Thien in the southern half of the DMZ.

SEPTEMBER 8, 1968

- US pilots flew 123 missions over North Vietnam (USAF 53, USN 61, USMC nine). BDA included 16 anti-aircraft artillery sites, 19 watercraft, eight trucks, four radar sites, 15 secondary explosions and three fires. An enemy surface-to-air missile was sighted and successfully evaded by a Navy A-7 aircraft.
- *Operations Binh Tay/MacArthur* (Darlac Province). At approximately 0915 hours, Regional Forces elements engaged an unknown size enemy force while conducting a road operation eight miles NW of Ban Me Thuot. An element of the Armored Cavalry Squadron, 4th Infantry Division, reinforced the VN troops at an unreported time. Helicopter gunships supported. 47 enemy killed while Regional Forces casualties were light. No US casualties.
- *Operation Mameluke Thrust* (Quang Nam Province) At 1845 hours, a reconnaissance team from the US 1st Marine Division observed 145 enemy moving S six miles NNW of An Hoa. The Marines directed artillery, tactical air and an Air Force AC-47 flare ship onto the enemy troops. Results were 45 enemy killed. There were no US casualties.
- An Army UH-1 helicopter was downed by suspected enemy ground fire eight miles NE of Duc Lap. four US Army and two VN personnel were killed. Two other crewmembers were injured. Aircraft was destroyed. Killed was ARVN Brigadier General Truong Quang An, Commanding General 23rd Division.

SEPTEMBER 9, 1968

- US pilots flew 116 missions over North Vietnam (USAF 68, USN 39, USMC nine). BDA included 22 trucks, 60 supply craft, five anti-aircraft artillery sites, one bridge, six automatic weapons positions, six landslides, 27 cuts in roads, 53 fires, and 10 secondary explosions.
- *Operation Scotland II* (Quang Tri Province). At approximately 1500 hours, an element of the US 9th Regiment, 3rd Marine Division, discovered an enemy weapons cache while searching an area six miles WSW of the Rockpile. The cache contained 30 107mm rockets, 204 60mm mortar rounds, 159 82mm mortar rounds, 105 RPGs, 118 mines (anti-personnel and anti-tank), 300 pounds of TNT, 4,400 12.7mm rounds, 1,500 AK-47 rifle rounds, and 2,200 pounds of rice. In addition, miscellaneous medical supplies and clothing of Soviet, Czech and French origin were captured.
- *Operation Sussex Bay* (Quang Nam Province). Terminated. Commenced on August 29, 1968. The operation was conducted by the US 5th Regiment, 1st Marine Division. Results were 65 enemy killed, two individual weapons captured. US six killed, 24 wounded. Marines were supported by 122 tactical air sorties during the operation.
- Viet Cong terrorists set off a 75-pound, charge at the GVN Information Office in Saigon's VI Precinct at 2030 hours, destroying one building and killing nine civilians and wounding 55.

SEPTEMBER 10, 1968

- US pilots flew 130 missions over North Vietnam (USAF 67, USN 52, USMC 11). BDA included 20 trucks, 27 supply craft, eight bridges, 28 road cuts, six anti-aircraft artillery positions, 29 fires, and 12 secondary explosions.
- *Operation Toan Thang* (Long An Province). At approximately 1100 hours, an element of the US 1st Brigade, 9th Infantry Division, was air-assaulted into an area in which helicopter gunships had observed and engaged an estimated 10 enemy earlier in the morning. The infantry engaged an unknown size enemy force near the LZ three miles NNW of Can Duoc and were reinforced by other elements of the 1st Brigade between

1150-1430 hours. As contact continues, another element of the 1st Brigade air-assaulted to join the contact while an element of the 3rd Brigade reinforced at approximately 1930 hours. The action continued into the night with the enemy force estimated to be of battalion size. Tactical air, artillery and helicopter gunships supported. Results were 48 enemy killed, three suspects detained, 18 individual weapons captured. US two killed, one wounded.

- Quang Nam Province: The US 27th Marine Regimental Landing Team, which was sent to Vietnam by Presidential Order last February during bitter TET fighting, departed for the US and involved approximately 700 personnel. Approximately 2,000 Marines have been assigned to other units in Vietnam to complete their 13-month tour. Some 1,500 other Marines have already rotated for various reasons, such as casualties, before being assigned to Camp Pendleton, and were not replaced as they departed.

SEPTEMBER 11, 1968

- *Operation Campaign Grove.* Announced. Commenced September 4, 1968.
- *Operation Comanche Falls.* Commenced. Elements were the 1st Cavalry Division (Airmobile), 1st Regiment, 1st ARVN Division, Regional Forces units (Quang Tri Province).
- US pilots flew 117 missions over North Vietnam (USAF 62, USN 48, USMC seven). BDA included 47 supply craft, three bridges, one structure, one truck, cratered 30 rounds, eight landslides, 10 secondary explosions and 16 fires.
- *Operation Toan Thang* (Binh Duong Province). At approximately 0430 hours, a mechanized element of the US 2nd Brigade, 25th Infantry Division, occupying night defensive positions three miles WSW of Dau Tieng City, received heavy mortar and small arms fire from an unknown size enemy force followed by a ground attack. The infantry employed organic weapons, including their armored personnel carrier weapons, while helicopter gunships and artillery supported. At an unreported time, other mechanized infantry elements of the brigade reinforced and contact continued until 0710 hours when the enemy withdrew. Results were 99 enemy killed, one suspect detained. US six killed, 22 wounded. The following weapons

were captured: 18 AK-47 rifles, five RPD light machine guns, two RPG rocket launchers, two 9mm pistols, one radio, five gas masks and 3,850 small arms rounds.

- *Operation Kentucky* (Quang Tri Province). At 1245 hours, an element of the US 1st Brigade, 5th Infantry Division (Mech), engaged an unknown size NVA force occupying fortified positions one mile NE of Con Thien. Tactical air, tanks and artillery supported. Results were 43 enemy killed, seven suspects detained. One US was wounded (evacuated).
- A USAF F-4 Phantom aircraft was downed by enemy ground fire approximately six miles NNW of Dong Hoi. One crewmember was rescued offshore and the other was missing.

SEPTEMBER 12, 1968

- US pilots flew 107 missions over North Vietnam (USAF 72, USN 25, USMC 10). BDA included 36 supply craft, four trucks, four landslides, two ferry crossings, approaches to six bridges, 20 fires, and seven secondary explosions.
- *Operation Toan Thang* (Binh Long Province). At 0735 hours, elements of the US 1st and 2nd Brigades, 1st Infantry Division, reinforced by a troop from the US 11th Armored Cavalry Regiment, engaged an estimated enemy regiment one to four miles ENE of Loc Ninh. The enemy employed small arms, automatic weapons and RPG fire. US helicopter gunships, artillery, tactical air and AC-47 flare ships supported friendly forces in addition to tanks and armored personnel carriers. Results were 121 enemy killed, three individual-weapon, nine crew-served weapons captured.
- *Operation Toan Thang* (Tay Ninh Province). Between 2300 and 0200 hours, the US 25th Infantry Division Fire Support Base two miles N of Tay Ninh, received heavy mortar and RPG fire followed by a ground attack by an unknown size enemy force. The enemy was reported to have penetrated the NW perimeter but were repulsed later by mechanized infantry elements of the Division's 1st Brigade inside the base. Helicopter gunships, artillery, tactical air and AC-47 flare ships supported the defenders. Results were 76 enemy killed, 22 individual weapons, and 16 crew-served weapons captured. US casualties were light.

- B-52s struck with two missions four to six miles N of Gio Linh in the southern half of the DMZ.

SEPTEMBER 13, 1968

- US pilots flew 114 missions over North Vietnam (USAF 75, USN 30, USMC nine). BDA included 23 supply craft, eight bunkers, two structures, 17 road cuts, four landslides, and cratered the approaches to six bridges and a causeway. 17 fires and seven secondary explosions were reported.
- *Operation Champaign Grove* (Quang Ngai Province). At approximately 1730 hours, an element of the Armed Cavalry Squadron and elements of the 11th Light Infantry Brigade of the Americal Division engaged an unknown size enemy force while sweeping an area four miles W of Quang Ngai City. The infantry, tanks and armored personnel carriers attacked and pursued the enemy soldiers until contact was at 1850 hours. Results were 61 enemy killed, 12 individual weapons and four crew-served weapons captured. US two killed, 22 wounded (18 evacuated).
- *Operation Nevada Eagle* (Thua Thien Province). At 0920 hours, an element of the US 1st Brigade, 101st Airborne Division (Airmobile) conducted an offensive sweep 19 miles SW of Hue, discovered two 1½ ton trucks (one French and one Soviet) and two 23mm anti-aircraft artillery guns.
- *Operation Toan Thang* (Binh Long Province). Major General Keith L. Ware, Commanding General of the 1st Infantry Division was killed when his UH-1 helicopter command and control helicopter crashed and burned three miles SE of Loc Ninh. Cause of crash unknown. seven bodies, including that of General Ware, were recovered and one missing.
- Quang Tri Province. At an unreported time, elements of the US 1st Brigade, 5th Infantry Division (Mech), and the US Marines 3rd Tank Battalion, 3rd Marine Division, conducted a combat sweep operation with elements of the ARVN 2nd Regiment, 1st Infantry Division, against NVA troops occupying fortified positions in the SE portion of the DMZ, two miles NE of Gio Linh. All three elements engaged an unknown size enemy NVA force in a well dug-in bunker complex inside the DMZ. US Naval gunfire, tactical air and artillery supported in addition to the organic tank weapons. Results were 158 enemy

killed, 13 individual weapons and five crew-served weapons captured. US 22 wounded. ARVN casualties were light.

- Ninh Thuan Province. The US 116th Combat Engineer Battalion arrived in Phan Rang. This was the 1st battalion-size Army National Guard unit to serve in RVN. The battalion of approximately 750 men was called to active duty on April 13, 1968 from Idaho Falls, Idaho.
- Major General Keith L. Ware, Commanding General, 1st Infantry Division, was killed along with seven other US in a helicopter crash near Loc Ninh, Binh Long Province. General Ware was the fourth US general killed in the war.

SEPTEMBER 14, 1968

- US pilots flew 114 missions over North Vietnam (USAF 72, USN 32, USMC 10). BDA included 16 trucks, 28 supply craft, five bridges, three anti-aircraft artillery sites, 26 fires, 15 secondary explosions, and 14 rounds, 10 ferry and bridge approaches cratered.
- *Operation Lancaster II* (Quang Tri Province). At 1230 hours, a patrol from the US 9th Regiment, 3rd Marine Division, found an enemy cache seven miles W of the Rockpile. The cache of approximately 10 tons contained: 438 82mm mortar rounds, 171 60mm mortar rounds, 85 RPG rounds, 64 RPD-7 rocket-grenades rounds, five 122mm rockets, 27 anti-tank mines, 650 pounds of TNT, 1,000 blasting caps, 1,000 feet of detonating cord, 5 57mm recoilless rifle rounds and 6½ tons of rice.
- The ARVN uncovered a large ammunition cache 13 kilometers NE of Quang Loi, Phuoc Long Province. It contains 2,742 RPG rounds; 336 grenades; 547,560 AK-47 rounds; 1,701 mortar rounds; 1,969 pounds of CHICOM TNT.

SEPTEMBER 15, 1968

- US pilots flew 131 missions over North Vietnam (USAF 73, USN 51, USMC seven). BDA included 53 supply craft, 20 trucks, seven bridges, 12 anti-aircraft artillery sites, 15 secondary explosions and 38 fires. Twenty-eight rounds were cratered.
- 46th ARVN Regiment, operating south of Saigon in Can Giouc District, Long An Province, finds CHICOM three bank x four tube (total 12) 107mm (barrage) rocket launcher.

SEPTEMBER 16, 1968

- US pilots flew 129 missions over North Vietnam (USAF 74, USN 43, USMC 12). BDA included 40 supply craft, 17 trucks, 180 POL drums, 174 fires and 39 secondary explosions. Roads were cratered in 33 places.
- *Operation Toan Thang* (Tay Ninh Province). At 2300 hours, a US Army 25th Infantry Division Fire Support Base located nine miles NE of Go Dau Ha received an unknown number of 82mm mortar rounds followed by a ground attack. The infantry returned the fire with their organic weapons and artillery. Action continued throughout the early morning of the 17th and terminated at 0630 hours when the enemy withdrew. An element of the 101st Airborne Division (Airmobile) conducting a sweep in the area found 131 enemy bodies. US losses were four killed, 48 wounded. In addition, four suspects were detained, seven individual weapons and five crew-served weapons were captured.
- *Operation Lancaster II* (Quang Tri Province). From 1530 to 1830 hours, an element of the 26th Marine Regimental Landing Team received more than 150 rounds of unknown caliber mortar fire five miles NW of the Rockpile. Later in the evening the element received an unknown number of 60mm mortar rounds and small arms fire, which continued until 0130 hours the following morning. Helicopter gunships, artillery and mortar supported. Results were 27 enemy killed, US 25 killed, 126 wounded (115 evacuated).

SEPTEMBER 17, 1968

- US pilots flew 125 missions over North Vietnam (USAF 70, USN 45, USMC 10). BDA included 28 secondary explosions, 49 fires, 79 supply craft, 16 trucks, five bridges, nine structures, two bunkers, one anti-aircraft artillery site, two ferry boats, and cratered 50 roads.
- *Operation Burlington Trail* (Quang Tin Province). At approximately 1950 hours, a combat construction party consisting of personnel from the Engineer battalion of the Americal Division and Vietnam Popular Forces personnel received small arms fire from an unknown size enemy force 10 miles WSW of Tam Ky. A 16-man reaction force enroute to the

site was ambushed by an unknown number of the enemy. The engineers returned fire and continued until an unreported time before another reaction force from the 198th Light Infantry Brigade began to sweep the area at 0045 hours. 43 enemy bodies were found in the vicinity of the two contacts. US casualties were eight killed, one wounded. No Popular Forces casualties.

- Da Nang. Marine Brigadier General William C. Chip, Commander of Task Force Hotel, Third Marine Division, was injured when his UH-1 helicopter in which he was a passenger crashed 21 miles W of Dong Ha. The cause of crash unknown. One crewmember was missing and all of the four other Marines aboard the helicopter suffered minor injuries.
- B-52s missions included strikes 17 miles NNE of Khe Sanh in the southern DMZ, two missions in the southern panhandle of North Vietnam eight miles NW of Con Thien, two missions five to eight miles NNW of Con Thien in the northern DMZ and North Vietnam.

SEPTEMBER 18, 1968

- US pilots flew 131 missions over North Vietnam (USAF 66, USN 47, USMC 18). BDA included 53 enemy freight trains, 42 supply craft, 18 trucks, nine bridges, 44 secondary explosions, and 31 fires. Roads were cut in more than 45 places. Navy F-8 Crusader aircraft engaged two MIG-21's in the enemy area 40 miles WNW of Vinh with negative results to either side.
- *Operation Champaign Grove* (Quang Ngai Province). While conducting a combat sweep 19 miles W of Quang Ngai City, a company from the 198th Light Infantry Brigade, Americal Division, received heavy small arms fire about 1730 hours from an unknown size enemy force. The Infantry returned fire with organic weapons and engaged the enemy in close combat while helicopter gunships supported. The enemy retreated from the area as the infantry attacked the enemy positions and

contact lost at 2145 hours. Results were 49 enemy killed, US 13 killed, 27 wounded.

- *Operation Lancaster II* (Quang Tri Province). Elements of the 9th Regiment, 3rd Marine Division, while conducting sweep operations seven miles W of the Rockpile found three caches that contained 2,267 rounds of 82mm mortar ammunition, 345 rounds of 60mm mortar ammunition, 10 107mm mortar rockets, one 122mm rocket, 222 rounds of RPG rounds, 6,000 CHICOM grenades, 442 anti-personnel mines, 30 anti-tank mines, 253 rounds of 50 caliber ammunition, 2,400 pounds of TNT, 600 blasting caps, and 8,400 pounds of rice.
- A Navy A-7 Corsair aircraft was downed by enemy ground fire nine miles S of Vinh. The pilot listed as missing.

SEPTEMBER 19, 1968

- US pilots flew 131 missions over North Vietnam (USAF 65, USN 52, USMC 14). BDA included seven enemy freight trains, 30 secondary explosions, 49 fires, 30 supply craft, 25 trucks, 15 bridges, 46 road cuts, four structures, eight anti-aircraft artillery sites, eight landslides and one automatic weapons position. A USN F-8 Crusader aircraft from Carrier Air Wing TEN downed a MIG-21 NW of Vinh using air-to-air missiles. This was the 110th MIG downed since June 17, 1965, the date of the first MIG kill. A second MIG-21 involved in the encounter escaped to the N. The last MIG, also a MIG-21, was downed over the N on August 1, 1968.
- A USAF F-105 aircraft was downed by enemy ground fire SSE of Dong Hoi. An unsuccessful search and air rescue was made and the pilot listed as missing. A Marine F-4 aircraft was downed by suspected enemy ground fire 15 miles SSE of Dong Hoi. The two-man crew is missing.

SEPTEMBER 20, 1968

- US pilots flew 106 missions over North Vietnam (USAF 70, USN 23, USMC 13). BDA included five trucks, 29 supply craft, five bridges, a pier, four anti-aircraft artillery sites, nine structures, seven landslides, cut roads in 26 places, 30 secondary explosions and 50 fires.

- *Operation Lancaster II* (Quang Tri Province). At 1600 hours, a company from the 4th Regiment, 3rd Marine Division, conducting a combat sweep seven miles NNW of the Rockpile, found an enemy cache that contained 450 SKS rifles, one light machine gun, two submachine guns, 300,000 rounds of AK-47 ammunition, 128 cases (21,760 rounds) of .50 caliber ammunition, 168 rounds of 81mm mortar ammunition, and 76 rounds of 82mm mortar ammunition.
- *Operation Lancaster II* (Quang Tri Province). On September 17, 1968, elements of the US 4th and 9th Regiments, 3rd Marine Division, were helicopter-lifted into the southern portion of the DMZ to clear and sweep an area 22 miles WNW of Dong Ha. Since then, the multi-battalion action has accounted for 68 NVA killed and one NVA captured. Friendly casualties have been two killed and 20 wounded. The first significant action was at noon, September 17, 1968, when an element of the 9th Marine spotted and killed 25 NVA with organic weapons and artillery support. There were no Marine casualties in that encounter. Since then contact had been light. Action continued.
- B-52 missions included strikes 17 miles NNW and 14 miles N of Con Thien in North Vietnam, three missions in North Vietnam 13 miles W of Con Thien.

SEPTEMBER 21, 1968

- US pilots flew 72 missions over North Vietnam (USAF 48, USN nine, USMC 15). BDA included 14 supply craft, one structure, one truck, 26 fires, one secondary explosion and cut 17 roads.
- *Operation Lancaster II* (Southern DMZ). At approximately 1600 hours, an element of the US 9th Regiment, 3rd Marine Division, discovered a mass grave containing the bodies of 24 NVA soldiers while sweeping an area nine miles NW of the Rockpile. At 1700, the same unit discovered another mass

grave containing the bodies of 96 NVA soldiers in the same general vicinity. The 120 enemy appeared to have been killed by air strikes four to five days earlier.

- Elements of the 9th Marines found 164 enemy killed in graves NW of the Rockpile, Quang Tri Province, apparently killed by air.

SEPTEMBER 22, 1968

- US pilots flew 76 missions over North Vietnam (USAF 50, USN 18, USMC eight). BDA included 30 supply craft, three storage areas, six highway segments cratered, two anti-aircraft artillery sites, 10 fires, and 12 secondary explosions. The pilot of a Navy F-8 Crusader aircraft reported a surface-to-air missile firing from a location 24 miles NW of Vinh. Evasive tactics were successful and the aircraft was undamaged.

SEPTEMBER 23, 1968

- North Vietnam. US pilots flew 112 missions (USAF 62, USN 44, USMC six). BDA included 41 supply craft, 16 trucks, three structures, 100 meters of trench, two bunkers, two bridges, 21 secondary explosions, 11 fires, one ferry boat, and cuts in 15 segments of road. A fleet of Navy A-4 Skyhawk aircraft reported a multiple surface-to-air missile launch in an area approximately 23 miles NW of Vinh. None of the aircraft received damage.
- A Navy A-4 Skyhawk aircraft was reported downed by enemy ground fire 12 miles NNW of Vinh. The pilot listed as missing.
- MACV announces allied forces in the past two weeks in the DMZ have captured 920 individual weapons, some 15,000 mortar rounds; 5,500 pounds of TNT; over 1,500 miscellaneous rocket rounds; and over 1,000,000 small arms rounds.

SEPTEMBER 24, 1968

- US pilots flew 120 missions over North Vietnam (USAF 57, USN 49, USMC 14). BDA included 23 supply craft, nine trucks, three structures, one ferry boat, one anti-aircraft artillery site, eight landslides, cut six roads and one highway ferry, 32 fires, and 37 secondary explosions.
- *Operation Champaign Grove.* Terminated. Commenced

September 4, 1968 and announced September 11, 1968. Cumulative results: US 43 killed, 172 wounded (156 medevac); enemy 378 killed, 68 detained, and 57 individual weapons and 16 crew-served weapons captured.

- *Operation Burlington Trail* (Quang Tin Province). At 1430 hours, a troop from the Americal Division's armored cavalry squadron engaged an unknown size enemy force four miles SW of Tam Ky. One armored personnel carrier was hit by a RPG round during initial contact and was moderately damaged. Contact was reestablished a short time later one mile W of the first engagement. Three more companies from the division were moved into the area to reinforce the unit in contact. Contact continued until 1930 hours when the enemy force evaded and withdrew. Results were 92 enemy killed, one individual weapon captured. US one killed, 33 wounded.

SEPTEMBER 25, 1968

- US pilots flew 118 missions over North Vietnam (USAF, 57 USN 47, USMC 14). BDA included 16 trucks, 20 supply craft, 11 bridges, two road segments cratered. 25 POL drums, six tents, two structures, 100 meters of trench, one anti-aircraft artillery site, and 46 secondary explosions and 68 fires reported.
- *Operation Burlington Trail* (Quang Tin Province). At approximately 1115 hours, an element of the Armored Cavalry Squadron of the Americal Division, engaged an unknown size enemy force four miles SW of Tam Ky. At an unreported time later, infantry from the division's 198th Light Infantry Brigade also made contact with elements of the same enemy force while sweeping the area. The tanks, armored personnel carriers and infantry supported by helicopter gunships and tactical air attacked the enemy force and action continued until 1430 hours when contact was lost as the enemy evaded. The troops pursued and reestablished contact at an unreported time and action continued until approximately 1800 hours when contact was again lost the enemy successfully evaded and withdrew. Results were 208 enemy killed, and eight crew-served weapons and seven individual-weapon captured. US casualties were three killed and 18 wounded (13 medevac). This raised the two-day total in the area during September 24 and 25, 1968

to 300 enemy killed. Also between August 24 and 26, 1968, Armored Cavalry elements of the Americal Division killed 511 enemy of the 2nd NVA Division in the same general area of Tam Ky.
- ROKFV marks three years of combat in RVN.

SEPTEMBER 26, 1968
- US pilots flew 138 missions over North Vietnam (USAF 59, USN 67, USMC 12). BDA included two ferries, 17 trucks, three structures, 30 supply craft, one anti-aircraft artillery site, 60 fires, 24 secondary explosions and 19 roads cratered. The pilot of an A-6 Intruder aircraft reported observing a surface-to-air missile launch in an area approximately 31 miles NW of Vinh. The missile was successfully evaded and the aircraft was undamaged.

SEPTEMBER 27, 1968
- US pilots flew 119 missions over North Vietnam (USAF 44, USN 57, USMC 18). BDA included 42 supply craft, 12 structures, 17 trucks, seven anti-aircraft artillery sites, one surface-to-air missile site, one bridge, 16 road segments cratered, 16 secondary explosions and nine fires. A Navy A-6 Intruder aircraft from the USS CONSTELLATION fired an air-to-ground missile at a surface-to-air missile site 30 miles NW of Vinh, scoring a direct hit and causing secondary explosions.
- *Operation Comanche Falls.* Announced. The operation was being conducted by elements of the 1st Cavalry Division (Airmobile) to find and eliminate enemy forces and installations, and was centered eight miles SSE of Quang Tri City. The operation commenced September 11, 1968.

SEPTEMBER 28, 1968
- US pilots flew 116 missions over North Vietnam (USAF 52, USN 48, USMC 16). BDA included six structures, five anti-aircraft artillery sites, four bridges, six trucks, 80 feet of trench, cut roads in seven places, 18 fires, and 45 secondary explosions. Air Force pilots were credited with two enemy killed.
- A Navy A-4 Skyhawk aircraft was downed by enemy anti-aircraft

artillery fire approximately 14 miles NE of Vinh. The pilot was rescued and injuries unknown.

- Enemy terrorists exploded a one-to-two-pound TNT charge in a parking area adjacent to Cholon (COFAT) Post Exchange (PX), Saigon, during normally busy Saturday afternoon shopping period. Three vehicles were damaged. There were no personnel injured.

SEPTEMBER 29, 1968

- US pilots flew 77 missions over North Vietnam (USAF 40, USN 29, USMC eight). BDA included four bridges, four supply craft, three anti-aircraft artillery sites, one structure, three fires and three secondary explosions.
- The USS NEW JERSEY arrived off Da Nang, Quang Nam Province.

SEPTEMBER 30, 1968

- North Vietnam. US pilots flew 108 missions against panhandle targets (USAF 57, USN 36, USMC 15). BDA included 52 supply craft, 27 structures, 16 trucks, 30 fires and 12 secondary explosions. Roads were cut in more than 18 places.
- Bien Hoa Province. At 2335 hours, Long Binh Post received approximately 40 rounds of 82mm mortar fire. Helicopter gunships and artillery supported.
- A Navy A-6 Intruder aircraft was reported downed by enemy ground fire approximately 13 miles NW of Vinh. Crewmembers were reported as missing.
- Naval Gunfire. The USS New Jersey in three missions fired approximately 20 rounds of 16-inch ammunition at artillery positions, automatic weapons positions, roads and storage areas in a general area seven miles NNW of Con Thien (Along N DMZ). BDA included four automatic weapons positions; 30 meters of trench line were collapsed. one road cut, one artillery position, and three bunkers destroyed. This was the first battleship action since July 1953.

OCTOBER 1, 1968

- US pilots flew 120 missions over North Vietnam (USAF 57, USN

50, USMC 13). BDA included destroyed or damaged 25 supply craft, eight trucks, five bridges, two roads, one anti-aircraft site, 20 structures, and seven freight trains. Twenty-six explosions and 29 fires were reported. Navy A-7 Corsair aircraft reported a surface-to-air missile launch 19 miles NW of Vinh. The crews successfully evaded the missiles and sustained no damage.

- A Marine A-4 Skyhawk aircraft on a gunfire spotter mission was hit over the N DMZ by enemy ground fire. The crew flew the crippled aircraft over water and ejected. The destroyer USS TOWERS 11 miles E of Gio Linh, three miles offshore in the waters of South Vietnam, picked them up.

OCTOBER 2, 1968

- US pilots flew 130 missions over North Vietnam (USAF 53, USN 56, USMC 21). BDA included destroyed or damaged two watercraft, six trucks, seven bridges, three anti-aircraft artillery sites, five structures, and 36 road cuts. Seventeen secondary explosions and 42 fires were reported.
- *OperationGlDleke* (Quang Nam Province). A multi-company search and clear operation centered 11 miles WSW of Hoi An commenced at 0800 hours. The operation was under the control of the 196th Light Infantry Brigade, Americal Division, and had missions to capture and eliminate enemy forces, installations and material within its area of responsibility.
- A Navy A-4 Skyhawk aircraft was downed by enemy 85 anti-aircraft artillery fire 20 miles N of Vinh. The pilot was listed as missing.

OCTOBER 3, 1968

- US pilots flew 143 missions over North Vietnam (USAF 65, USN 57, USMC 21). BDA included destroyed or damaged 50 supply craft. 31 trucks, three structures, 26 roads, three anti-aircraft artillery sites, six bridges, three anti-aircraft artillery sites and 11 freight trains. Twenty-eight secondary explosions and 20 fires were reported. Seventeen enemy soldiers were killed.
- Thua Thien Province. At approximately 1610 hours, a US Army CH-47 Chinook helicopter collided in mid-air with a US Air Force C-7 Caribou, which had just taken off from Camp Evans. Both aircraft crashed in an area six miles S of Camp

Evans (11 miles NW of Hue) killing all 24 passenger and the crewmembers. Thirteen US personnel, included four Air Force crewmembers, were killed in the C-7 and 11 US personnel, included four Army crewmembers, were killed in the CH-47.

OCTOBER 4, 1968

- US pilots flew 117 missions over North Vietnam (USAF 61, USN 43, USMC 13). BDA included destroyed or damaged 14 watercraft, 21 trucks, nine bridges, four anti-aircraft artillery sites, two radar sites, 25 structures, and two freight trains. There were 93 secondary explosions and 85 fires reported.

OCTOBER 5, 1968

- US pilots flew 131 missions over North Vietnam (USAF 59, USN 59, USMC 13). BDA included destroyed or damaged 50 watercraft, two railway cars, five trucks, three anti-aircraft artillery sites, two radar sites, one structure and seven freight trains. A surface-to-air missile launch was reported by returning A-7 pilots in an area approximately 25 miles NW of Vinh in the Vinh Son area. The pilots successfully evaded and no damage was sustained.
- *Operation Quyet Chien* (Dinh Tuong Province). At approximately 1200-1515 hours, a Cavalry Squad of the US 9th Infantry Division, observed three groups of enemy 15 miles NW of Cai Be. Gunships engaged the enemy and killed 50. At 1540 hours, an element of the division's 3rd Brigade was air-assaulted into the area and made scattered contact. Tactical air, artillery, and helicopter gunships supported the action until 1830 hours when contact was lost as the enemy withdrew. The infantry discovered 90 enemy bodies, 64 killed by gunships. Eight Hoi Chanhs rallied to the troops. Two ChiCom field telephones, three protective masks, three medical kits and a small quantity of miscellaneous ammunition were captured. The sweep continued. There were no US casualties.
- *Operation Scotland II* (Quang Tri Province). Elements of the US 4th Regiment, 3rd Marine Division began a combat sweep in the general vicinity of Khe Sanh with the object of capturing or eliminating NVA units, installations and materiel within the operation area. There was no reported contact to date.

OCTOBER 6, 1968

- US pilots flew 129 missions over North Vietnam (USAF 56, USN 59, USMC 41). BDA included destroyed or damaged 39 watercraft, 19 trucks, two bridges, 40 rounds, 11 anti-aircraft artillery sites and five structures. Reported were 274 fires and 199 secondary explosions.
- *Operation Toan Thang* (Binh Long Province). At approximately 0900 hours, an element of the Cavalry Squad of the US 1st Infantry Division, engaged unknown size enemy forces two miles SW of An Loc. The enemy employed small arms and automatic weapons fire while the cavalry troops returned fire with organic weapons on their armored personnel carriers and tanks. The action continued until 1140 hours. At an unreported time another mechanized element of a Cavalry Squad reinforced and contact was reestablished with unknown size enemy force in the same general area. The action continued until approximately 1645 hours when the enemy evaded and withdrew. Results were 43 enemy killed, US one killed and six wounded. In addition, 13 individual-weapon and four crew-served weapons were captured.
- *Operation Maui Peak* (Quang Nam Province). A multi-battalion search and clear operation centered in an area 11 miles NW of An Hoa commenced at 0900 hours. The combination operation involved elements of the ARVN 51st Regiment and the US 1st Marine Division with a mission to locate and capture or eliminate enemy forces, installations and materiel within the operation area, which encompassed the general vicinity of the CIDG Camp at Thuong Duc.
- A Navy A-7 aircraft was downed by enemy ground fire approximately 17 miles NE of Vinh, five miles offshore. The injury to the pilot was reported as minor.
- USN SEALS and a VN force overran an enemy prisoner of war camp on Con Coc Island, 77 miles SW of Saigon, freeing 23 prisoners of war and killing one Viet Cong.

OCTOBER 7, 1968

- US pilots flew 133 missions over North Vietnam (USAF 69, USN 46, USMC 18). BDA included destroyed or damaged 13 watercraft, seven railway cars, 13 trucks, seven bridges, four anti-aircraft artillery sites and 14 structures. Reported were 217 fires and 114 secondary explosions.

- *Operation Toan Thang* (Binh Duong Province). At approximately 0745 hours, a company from the US 3rd Brigade, 1st Infantry Division, found a base complex and cache containing 1,000 anti-personnel mines, 1,050 hand grenades, 19 individual weapons, 1,550 pounds of medical supplies, 50 72mm recoilless rifle rounds and 87 RPGs.
- *Operation Toan Thang* (Hau Nghia Pro). At approximately 0850 hours, two companies from the US 3rd Brigade, 25th Infantry Division, on a reconnaissance in force mission five miles NE of Trang Bang, engaged an unknown size enemy force. At 1000 hours, additional elements from the 3rd Brigade, 101st Airborne Division, reinforced the contact. Helicopter gunships and artillery supported the infantry. The contact lost at 1930 hours and reestablished at 0045 hours. Enemy losses were 147 enemy killed, seven suspects detained, three individual weapons, one crew-served weapon, 200 rounds of 60mm and 18 rounds of 82mm ammunition captured. US casualties were eight killed and 13 wounded. The enemy unit was tentatively identified as an element from the 101st NVA Regiment.
- *Operation Maui Peak* (Quang Nam Province). At approximately 1500 hours, an element of the US 5th Regiment, 1st Marine Division, engaged an estimated enemy platoon four miles ENE of the Thuong Duc CIDG camp. The Marines returned fire with organic weapons and attacked the enemy force supported by tactical air and artillery. The contact was lost at 1730 hours when the enemy withdrew. The Marines discovered 30 enemy killed by tactical air during the engagement. US casualties were 12 wounded and evacuated.
- *Operation Glake.* Announced. Elements from the Americal Division in Quang Nam Province participated.
- *Operation Maui Peak.* Announced. Elements from the 1st Marine Division in Quang Nam Province participated.
- *Operation Mameluke Thrust* (Quang Nam Province). At 1430 hours, a reconnaissance team from the US 1st Marine Division observed a group of 75 enemy soldiers moving in the area nine miles ENE of An Hoa. Marine Division artillery fire was

directed onto the enemy troops killing 46. There were no US casualties.

OCTOBER 8, 1968

- US pilots flew 129 missions over North Vietnam (USAF 66, USN 46, USMC 17). BDA included destroyed or damaged 36 watercraft, 21 trucks, five bridges, 47 road cuts, six weapon sites and 15 structures. Reported were 110 fires and 49 secondary explosions. An A-6 Intruder aircraft from the USS AMERICA launched an air-to-ground missile at a radar site 28 miles NW of Vinh, and the pilot reported the installation was heavily damaged.

OCTOBER 9, 1968

- US pilots flew 115 missions over North Vietnam (USAF 66, USN 33, USMC 16). BDA included destroyed or damaged 17 watercraft, two trucks, five bridges, an anti-aircraft artillery site, 10 structures, and six freight trains. 59 secondary explosions and 45 fires were reported. A surface-to-air missile was fired at a Navy A-7 Corsair aircraft from N of the 19th parallel. The aircraft evaded the surface-to-air missile that impacted on the ground NW of Vinh.
- *Operation GDuke'* Terminated. Cumulative results were one US killed and three wounded: Enemy losses were 21 killed, 11 detained and 18 individual weapons captured. The operation was announced October 7, 1968 and commenced October 2, 1968.
- *Operation Logan Field.* Announced. The operation under control of the 11th Light Infantry Brigade, Americal Division, and centered in Quang Ngai Province. The operation commenced October 7, 1968.

OCTOBER 10, 1968

- US pilots flew 124 missions over North Vietnam (USAF 69, USN 40, USMC 15). BDA included destroyed or damaged nine watercraft, four trucks, two bridges, 10 anti-aircraft artillery sites, three structures and seven freight trains. Reported were 65 fires and 40 secondary explosions. Flying A-6 Intruders and F-4 Phantoms, Marines reported extensive damage to an enemy supply complex NW of Con Thien and to bunker and storage N of Gio Linh.

- *Operation Lancaster II* (Quang Tri Province). At an unreported time, an element of US 26th Marine Regimental Landing Team discovered nine NVA bodies killed during contact with an estimated NVA platoon on October 8, 1968 eight miles N of the Rockpile (one mile inside the southern edge of the DMZ). Twenty-six total NVA were killed in the action. Marine casualties were two killed and 48 wounded.

OCTOBER 11, 1968

- US pilots flew 120 missions over North Vietnam (USAF 56, USN 51, USMC 13). BDA included destroyed or damaged 25 supply craft, eight trucks, one road, one anti-aircraft artillery site, 10 structures, and one freight train. Reported were 45 fires and 25 secondary explosions.
- Quang Nam Province. At approximately 1530 hours, a Marine CH-34 helicopter and a Marine CH-46 helicopter collided while orbiting seven miles NW of An Hoa. The aircraft crashed and were destroyed. All 12 US military crewmembers and passengers were killed (four crew and four passengers on the CH-34 and crew members in the CH-46).
- *Operation Lancaster II* (Quang Tri Province). At 1100 hours, an element of the US 3rd Regiment, 3rd Marine Division, discovered a bunker complex containing approximately 100 fortified bunkers seven miles NNE of the Rockpile in the southern half of DMZ. In the vicinity of the bunkers, the Marines discovered an unreported number of graves containing 18 NVA soldiers.

OCTOBER 12, 1968

- US pilots flew 100 missions over North Vietnam (USAF 58, USN 34, USMC eight). BDA included destroyed or damaged 43 watercraft, two railway cars, six trucks, seven bridges, 21 structures, and ignited 15 fires and seven secondary explosions.
- *Operation Maui Peak* (Quang Nam Province). At 0400 hours, an element of the US 5th Regiment, 1st Marine Division, in night defensive positions three miles ENE of the Thuong Duc CIDG Camp, received a ground attack by an unknown size enemy

force. The action continued until 0730 hours when the enemy withdrew. The Marines employed organic weapons and were supported by artillery and tactical air. The bodies of 46 enemy were found around the perimeter. In addition, one suspect was detained and 10 AK-47 rifles were captured. US casualties were eight killed and 20 wounded.

- *Operation Logan Field* (Quang Ngai Province). Terminated. The operation commenced at October 7, 1968 and was under control of the 11th Infantry Brigade, Americal Division. Cumulative results: 14 enemy killed, six suspects detained and four individual weapons captured. US casualties were 13 killed, 66 wounded, of whom 42 were evacuated. Seven Naval gunfire missions were fired in support of the infantry. There were no tactical air strikes on B-52 strikes flown in support of the six-day operation.

OCTOBER 13, 1968

- US pilots flew 135 missions over North Vietnam (USAF 62, USN 54, USMC 19). BDA included destroyed or damaged 14 trucks, four bridges, and three structures. Fifty-three fires and 10 secondary explosions were reported.
- A Navy A-6 Intruder aircraft was reported downed to unknown causes approximately 24 miles SE of Vinh. The crew was missing.

OCTOBER 14, 1968

- US pilots flew 118 missions over North Vietnam (USAF 54, USN 59, USMC five). BDA included destroyed or damaged 21 watercraft, seven railway cars, 12 trucks, five bridges, three anti-aircraft artillery sites, one radar site and a freight train. Thirty-two fires and 11 secondary explosions were reported. A radar site was hit with an air-to-ground missile from one of the USS AMERICA's A-6 Intruders and was possibly destroyed 52 miles NW of Dong Hoi according to pilots returning from the mission.

OCTOBER 15, 1968

- Saigon. At 0900 hours, a Navy floating workshop (YR-24), was turned over to the VN Navy in ceremonies at the Vietnam Navy Headquarters. Commodore Tran Van Chon, Chief of Naval Operations (CNO), RVN Navy accepted the ship from Vice Admiral Elmo R. Zumwalt, Jr., Commander US Naval Forces. The YR-24 is a floating shipyard capable of keeping the Vietnam Navy's gunboats in a constant state of readiness and would be manned by a crew of two officers and 135 men. During the past four months, the Vietnam Navy had assumed command of six minesweepers, eight high-speed river patrol boats and four "Swift" boats.

OCTOBER 16, 1968

- US pilots flew 109 missions over North Vietnam (USAF 58, USN 45, USMC six). BDA included destroyed or damaged 18 supply boats, 18 trucks, five bridges, four roads and three structures. 27 fires and 12 secondary explosions were reported.
- American Independent Party Vice-Presidential Candidate General Curtis E. LeMay, USAF (Retired), arrived in RVN for a four-day private "fact-finding" visit.

OCTOBER 17, 1968

- US pilots flew 100 missions over North Vietnam (USAF 48, USN 44, USMC eight). BDA included destroyed 19 supply boats, two trucks, two railway cars, two anti-aircraft artillery sites and six structures. Three fires and nine secondary explosions were reported.
- *Operation Lancaster* (Quang Tri Province). In the afternoon, elements from the US 3rd Regiment, 3rd Marine Division, eight miles N of the Rockpile (two miles N of southern tract of the DMZ) found 333 rounds of 152mm artillery ammunition. The rounds were found in two locations 200 meters apart. Eighty-three artillery rounds were found at one location while the other 250 were found in five bunkers (50 in each bunker).

OCTOBER 18, 1968

- US pilots flew 102 missions over North Vietnam (USAF 55, USN 38, USMC nine). BDA included destroyed or damaged

32 supply craft, four bridges, three structures and four freight trains. One fire and four secondary explosions were reported.

- *Operation Lancaster II* (Quang Tri Province). At an unreported time, an element of the US 3rd Regiment, 3rd Marine Division, discovered a significant NVA ammunition cache while sweeping an area eight miles N of the Rockpile and just inside the S edge of the DMZ. The cache contained 55 rounds of 85mm artillery ammunition.
- *Operation Quyet Chien* (Dinh Tuong Province). In an action that began at 1315 hours, and continued until 0700 hours, October 19, 1968, elements of the US 2nd and 3rd Brigades, 9th Infantry Division air cavalry elements of the division's cavalry squadron killed 12 enemy in an engagement with an estimated company seven miles NW of Cai Be. The Infantry also captured one crew-served weapon and eight individual weapons, and detained three suspects. US casualties were five killed and 32 wounded. While conducting a reconnaissance in force mission in the same general area on October 19, 1968, air cavalry gunships observed and engaged an unknown size enemy force NW of Cai Be at 1150 hours. Contact was lost at approximately 1230 hours when the enemy evaded and withdrew. The infantry found 47 additional enemy bodies in the vicinity of the action (killed by both helicopter gunships and ground fire) raising the total for the two-day sweep to 59 enemy killed. In addition, the troops detained one more suspect and captured 1,287 Viet Cong protective masks and 500 pounds of assorted medical supplies. No additional US casualties.
- *Operation Sea Lords.* Commenced. This was a joint operation under Commander, Naval Forces, Vietnam in IV Corps area.

OCTOBER 19, 1968

- US pilots flew 93 missions over North Vietnam (USAF 53, USN 30, USMC 10). BDA included destroyed or damaged four supply craft, one bridge and a highway ferry. Three secondary explosions and two fires were reported. Total BDA was prevented due to adverse weather over the target area.
- *Operation Maui Peak* (Quang Nam Province). Terminated. The multi-battalion search and clear operation commenced at 0900

hours on October 6, 1968 and was centered in an area 11 miles NW of An Hoa. During the 14-day operation, the Marines and supporting fires killed 202 enemy, detained two suspects and captured two crew-served weapons and 25 individual weapons. US casualties were 28 killed and 148 wounded of whom 79 were evacuated. A total of 147 tactical air sorties were flown in support of the friendly forces.

OCTOBER 20, 1968

- US pilots flew 110 missions over North Vietnam (USAF 64, USN 42, USMC four). BDA included destroyed or damaged one truck, cut roads in six places, 11 sampans, and three weapon positions. two secondary explosions and eight fires were reported.
- An Air Force F-4 Phantom aircraft was downed by enemy ground fire in the vicinity of North Vietnam's Tiger Island (25 miles NE of Gio Linh). While attempting to rescue the two-man crew, the rescue helicopter, an HH-3 Jolly Green Giant, was hit and destroyed by the enemy shore batteries. The four-man crew joined the Phantom crew in the water and two other Da Nang based Jolly Greens retrieved all six.

OCTOBER 21, 1968

- US pilots flew 114 mission over North Vietnam (USAF 47, USN 49, USMC 18). BDA included destroyed or damaged two trucks, one ferry, six supply craft, two freight trains and four bridges. Eleven secondary explosions and two fires were reported.
- Quang Duc Province. At approximately 0600 hours, an Air Force C-47 courier craft assigned to the Tan Son Nhut Air Base and enroute to Da Nang crashed 11 miles SSW of Ban Me Thuot. Initial reports indicated that the aircraft experienced engine failure and the pilot reported that he was unable to feather the propeller.
- A Navy A-4 Skyraider aircraft was reported downed due to unknown causes at a position approximately 50 miles SE of Vinh. The pilot was missing.
- In *Operation Mighty Yankee,* the Seventh Fleet's USS DUBUQUE

(LPA-8) transported 14 NVN sailors from Da Nang to a point 12 miles off Vinh, North Vietnam, where a prisoner of war group was released in a motor whaleboat. The operation was carried off with the concurrence of NVN authorities. The HMAS PERTH and USS BAUSELL escorted the USS DUBUQUE. North Vietnam guaranteed a combat stand-down for the area, as did the US Government when arrangements were made in Vientiane, Laos. Fourteen were the last of a group of 19 who were captured during a NVN PT attack on USN destroyers on July 1, 1966.

OCTOBER 22, 1968

- US pilots flew 120 missions over North Vietnam (USAF 46, USN 57, USMC 17). BDA included destroyed or damaged three trucks, cut roads in four places, 28 supply craft, nine bridges, nine structures, two anti-aircraft artillery sites, and two weapon positions. Four secondary explosions and two fires were reported.
- Quang Nam Province: Between the hours of 1400 and 1800, a 1st Marine Reconnaissance Team, conducting a reconnaissance mission two miles NW of An Hoa observed approximately 114 enemy soldiers in two sightings moving NNE. They were dressed in khakis, black pajamas and shorts and were carrying rifles, machine guns, packs and one rocket round. The Marine directed artillery fire and an aerial spotter called in tactical air onto the enemy positions resulting in 54 enemy killed. Five secondary explosions were also observed. There were no US casualties.

OCTOBER 23, 1968

- US pilots flew 128 missions over North Vietnam (USAF 62, USN 47, USMC 19). BDA included destroyed or damaged five trucks, four ferries, 12 supply craft, seven anti-aircraft artillery sites, 10 freight trains, two bridges, five structures, and four automatic weapons positions. Six secondary explosions and 30 fires were also reported.
- Quang Nam Province. At approximately 1000 hours, a 1st Marine Division Reconnaissance Team sighted 121 NVA soldiers moving ENE in a general location two miles NW of An

Hoa. The enemy soldiers were dressed in khakis with helmets and carrying rifles and heavy packs. One mortar tube was also spotted. The Marines directed artillery fire onto the enemy troops killing 57. One secondary explosion was also observed. This brings the total of enemy killed since October 22, 1968 to 178 in four sightings. 405 enemy soldiers were observed in the four sightings. The groups were wearing varied uniforms and carrying many types of weapons. Sixteen secondary explosions were also observed. There were no US casualties.

- Quang Tri Province. At an unreported time, a combination ARVN Task Force consisting of an element of the 2nd Regiment, 1st Infantry Division, supported by ARVN armored cavalry elements and tanks from the Armor battalion of the US 3rd Marine Division initiated an offensive sweep into the S DMZ. At approximately 1130, the combination force engaged an estimated reinforced NVA company four miles NE of Gio Linh. The action continued into the early afternoon with tactical air and artillery supporting the friendly forces until 1400 hours when contact was lost as the remaining enemy withdrew. Results were 112 enemy killed, one suspect detained, and seven individual weapons, two crew-served weapons, two tons of rice, and 200 rounds of 82mm mortar ammunition captured.
- *Operation Mameluke Thrust* (Quang Nam Province). Terminated. The multi-battalion search and clear operation was conducted by elements of the 1st Marine Division and the 26th Marine Regimental Landing Team and was centered in an area 25 miles WSW of Da Nang. The operation commenced May 19, 1968. Cumulative results: 2,730 enemy killed, 405 suspects detained, and 337 individual weapons and 125 crew-served weapons captured. US casualties were 269 killed and 1,740 wounded of whom 1,419 were evacuated. The operation was supported by 2,015 tactical air sorties.
- *Operation Henderson Hill* (Quang Nam Province). Commenced. The operation was under control of the 5th Regiment, 1st Marine Division, and has the specific missions to capture or eliminate the enemy forces, installations and materiel within

its area of responsibility. The operation was centered six miles E of An Hoa and commenced at 1200 hours.

- At an unreported time, another Air Force O-2 observer aircraft on a reconnaissance mission was downed by enemy ground fire three miles NNE of Con Thien in the S half of the DMZ. The pilot was killed and the aircraft destroyed.

OCTOBER 24, 1968

- North Vietnam. US pilots flew 122 missions (USAF 64, USN 39, USMC 19). BDA included destroyed or damaged three trucks, eight supply craft, three anti-aircraft artillery sites, two freight trains, seven bridges, 17 structures, five weapons positions, 186 meters of trenches and ignited 35 fires and 15 secondary explosions.
- *Operation Kentucky* (Quang Tri Province). During the day, elements of the 1st Brigade, US 5th Infantry Division (Mech), located and attacked small groups of the enemy in a series of six contacts in the S half of the DMZ four miles NE of Con Thien. Artillery and 23 tactical air strikes supported the infantry. Results were 65 enemy killed (27 by tactical air, 31 by artillery and seven by the infantry) and one suspect was detained. There were no friendly casualties.
- An Air Force F-4 aircraft was reported downed by enemy fire 22 miles SW of Dong Hoi. One crewmember was rescued and the second was listed as missing.
- MACV announced that weekly US casualty figures for the seven days ending October 19, 1968 (100 killed) was the lowest figure in 14 months. The previous low was August 12, 1967 when 82 US were killed.

OCTOBER 25, 1968

- US pilots flew 114 missions over North Vietnam (USAF 66, USN 33, USMC 15). BDA included destroyed or damaged seven trucks, nine road segments cut, three supply craft, three anti-aircraft artillery sites, and two structures. Three secondary explosions and 16 fires were reported.
- Khanh Hoa Province. Between 0715 and 1140 hours, elements of the 30th Regiment, 9th ROK Infantry Division, engaged several small groups of enemy soldiers from an unknown size enemy force while conducting a cordon operation six

miles SW of Nha Trang. A total of 36 enemy were killed in the contacts. There were no ROK casualties. The aircraft continued in the afternoon until approximately 1715 hours with Korean infantry engaged several other groups of enemy soldiers within the cordoned area. The enemy employed small arms and automatic weapons fire while the Koreans returned fire with organic weapons supported by artillery and tactical air. The ROK troops found the bodies of 168 more enemy raising the total of enemy killed in the day's fighting to 204. In addition 34 individual weapons and 21 crew-served weapons were captured along with five military radios, five gas masks, one field telephone switchboard and a quantity of assorted ammunition.

- *Operation Kentucky* (Quang Tri Province). Elements of the US 1st Brigade, 5th Infantry Division (Mech) supported by gunships, artillery, tactical air and naval gunfire killed 232 NVA soldiers five miles NNE of Con Thien (one mile N of the S edge of the DMZ). The action started at approximately 1100 hours when a company from the brigade, conducting an offensive sweep, located and engaged an estimated NVA battalion. The enemy employed heavy mortar, small arms and automatic weapons fire while the infantry, supported by tactical air and gunships, returned the fire with their organic weapons. Additional elements, included a tank company reinforced the company as heavy contact continued throughout the afternoon until 1800 hours when the enemy withdrew. Also, six crew-served weapons were captured. US casualties were six killed and 29 wounded. This was the same general area where 65 NVA soldiers were killed by the brigade, and supporting arms on October 24, 1968. The cumulative results for the two-day period were 297 NVA soldiers killed while US losses were six killed and 29 wounded. During a further sweep of the area following the engagement, the troops captured 242 individual weapons and 17 crew-served weapons (included six previously reported) that were left scattered on the battlefield. The crew-served weapons included eight light machine guns, three complete 60mm mortars, two 12.7mm heavy anti-aircraft machine guns, one complete 82mm mortar and three RPG launchers.
- *Operation Garrard Bay* (Quang Nam Province). Commenced. A battalion-size search and clear operation centered nine

miles SSE of Da Nang. It began with an amphibious landing, nicknamed *Operation Eager Hunter*, in which a battalion from the 26th Marine Regimental Landing Team was helicopter and surface assaulted into the operation area from ships of a task group of the Navy's Amphibious Task Force 76. The amphibious operation was terminated about 1530 hours after the Marines had landed and secured their objective areas at which time, the Headquarters, 1st Marine Division, assumed control of the operation. *Operation Garrard Bay* was conducted in coordination with elements of the 1st Regiment, 1st Marine Division, ROK 2nd Marine Brigade, ARVN 51st Infantry Regiment and Vietnam National Police Field Forces operation in the surrounding areas. There was some sporadic contact the first day, however, no significant actions were reported. As of 2400 hours, October 25, 1968, one suspect had been detained. No US Marine casualties reported.

OCTOBER 26, 1968

- US pilots flew 130 missions over North Vietnam (USAF 66, USN 49, USMC 15). BDA included destroyed or damaged 59 supply craft, one ferry, one bridge, eight railway cars, seven trucks, and ignited 14 fires and six explosions.
- *Operation Toan Thang* (Tay Ninh Province). At approximately 0600 hours, an element of the US 1st Brigade, 1st Infantry Division, in night defensive positions 11 miles E of Katum received a mortar and ground attack by an estimated enemy company. The action continued throughout the morning and into the early afternoon when contact was lost at 1330 hours as the enemy withdrew. The infantry and supported fires killed 80 enemy soldiers while US casualties were eight killed and 33 wounded. In addition, 26 individual weapons and six crew-served weapons were captured. In a further sweep around their night defensive positions October 27, 1968, elements of the brigade discovered the bodies of 23 more NVA soldiers killed in the abortive attack raising the total enemy killed for the action to 103. US losses were nine killed and 33 wounded.
- *Operation Nevada Eagle* (Thua Thien Province). A platoon from the US 3rd Brigade, 101st Airborne Division (Airmobile), conducting a combat sweep in an area nine miles S of Hue at approximately 1230 hours, found what appeared to be an

enemy base area. While searching the camp, the infantry found 80 enemy bodies lying above ground.

OCTOBER 27, 1968

- US pilots flew 125 missions over North Vietnam (USAF 61, USN 44, USMC 20). BDA included destroyed or damaged 100 meters of trench line, two ammunition supply caches, 36 supply craft, 11 trucks four road cuts, four freight trains, 15 structures, two weapons positions, and two artillery weapons. Reported were 25 secondary explosions and 30 fires. A surface-to-air missile was fired during a Navy strike NW of Vinh. The crew of an A-6 Intruder aircraft observed the missile as it detonated above the clouds.
- *Operation Henderson Hill* (Quang Nam Province). Announced. The operation was a multi-battalion search and clear operation centered seven miles E of An Hoa and commenced at 1200 hours on October 23, 1968. The operation under the control of the 5th Regiment, 1st Marine Division, and has the specific missions to capture or eliminate enemy forces, installations and materiel within its area of responsibility. As of 2400 hours on October 25, 1968, the Marines had killed 20 enemy and detained 10 suspects while US losses have been one killed and 10 wounded. Thirty-three tactical air strikes had been flown in support of the operation.
- *Operation Garrard Bay* (Quang Nam Province). Announced. The operation was a battalion-size search and clear operation centered nine miles SSE of Da Nang and commenced at 0800 hours on October 25, 1968. The operation, involving the battalion of the 26th Marine Regimental Landing Team, has the mission of capturing or eliminating enemy forces, installations and materiel within the area of responsibility and was conducted in coordination with elements of the 1st Regiment, 1st Marine Division, ROK 2nd Marine Brigade, ARVN 51st Infantry Regiment and Vietnam National Police Field Forces operation in the surrounding areas. As of 2400 hours, October 25, 1968, one suspect had been detained. No US Marine casualties were reported.
- An Air Force F-105 Thunderchief aircraft was downed by enemy ground fire 28 miles W of Dong Hoi. The pilot missing.
- COMUSMACV directed the 1st Cavalry Division (Airmobile) to

relocate from northern I CTZ to northern Tay Ninh Province III CTZ, in *Operation Liberty Canyon.* Movement was by air and 7th Fleet amphibious shipping. The movement starts October 28, 1968 and division move completed to Tay Ninh Province in 1st week of November.

OCTOBER 28, 1968

- US pilots flew 139 missions over North Vietnam (USAF 69, USN 51, USMC 19). BDA included destroyed or damaged 30 meters of trench, a ferry landing, a bulldozer, a road grader, 20 trucks, 19 supply craft, three anti-aircraft artillery sites, four freight trains, one bridge, two structures and ignited 52 secondary explosions and 52 fires.
- An Air Force RF-4C Phantom aircraft failed to return from a reconnaissance mission over the panhandle and was presumed down to suspected ground fire. The last known position of the Phantom was five miles NNW of Dong Hoi. The two-man crew was listed as missing.

OCTOBER 29, 1968

- US pilots flew 134 missions over North Vietnam (USAF 67, USN 47, USMC 20). BDA included destroyed or damaged a steam roller, 60 meters of trench line, two ammunition caches, two artillery sites, 16 trucks, cut roads in two places, three anti-aircraft artillery sites, 17 freight trains, 11 structures, one weapons position and ignited 23 secondary explosions and 35 fires.

OCTOBER 30, 1968

- US pilots flew 126 missions over North Vietnam (USAF 54, USN, 48, USMC 24). BDA included destroyed or damaged one road, a ferry boat, 11 trucks, 47 trucks, 47 supply craft, three anti-aircraft artillery sites, two freight trains, five bridges, one structure, one weapon position and ignited 13 secondary explosions and 20 fires.

OCTOBER 31, 1968

- US pilots flew 125 missions over North Vietnam (USAF 61, USN 41, USMC 23). BDA included destroyed or damaged 20 crates of supplies, 120 meters of trench, a supply area, three trucks, cut roads in 14 places, 33 supply craft, one anti-aircraft artillery site, eight freight trains, one bridge, 12 structures, one weapons position and ignited 45 secondary explosions and 54 fires.

- Gia Dinh Province. At approximately 2130 hours, the enemy fired eight rounds of mixed 122mm and 107mm rockets into the city of Saigon, which impacted at the following locations: three rockets within ½-mile radius of the center of Saigon in the 3rd Precinct (two were duds – one 107mm and one unknown type – while the other was 122mm), four rockets in the 5th Precinct at two locations 1½ miles S and one mile SW of the center of Saigon (all four were 122mm and one was a dud), one rocket impacted in the 1st Precinct 1½ miles E of the center of Saigon. The rocket was a dud of unreported type. Results were two VN civilians were killed and six wounded. two houses were reported damaged. There were no US casualties.
- Between 2125 and 2130 hours, eight rockets (122mm and 107mm) impacted in the city of Saigon. Four were duds and did not explode on impact.

NOVEMBER 1, 1968

- Admiral John S. McCain Jr., CINCPAC, announced the bombing halt of North Vietnam, effective 2100 hours, Saigon time, in accordance with instructions received from the President. (Announcement made by President on October 31, 1968 in Washington).
- Five enemy rockets hit Tan Son Nhut Air Base, causing light damage. This was the first rocket attack on Tan Son Nhut since June 1968. Six rockets hit the southern portion of Saigon, one hitting a Catholic Church on Khanh Hoi Island, killing 21 VN civilians and wounding 64.
- President Johnson ordered a complete cessation of air, ground, and naval bombardment of North Vietnam to begin this date (announcement made on October 31, 1968 in Washington).
- At 0322 hours, three enemy mines detonated between the pontoon and hull on the starboard side of USS WESTCHESTER COUNTY (LST-1167), a Mekong Delta Mobile Riverine Force (MDMRF) support ship, killing 25 (24 US, one Vietnam Navy). The ship was severely damaged, but flooding was controlled.
- US pilots flew 114 missions over North Vietnam (USAF 59,

USN 33, USMC 22). BDA included destroyed or damaged 21 watercraft, two radar sites, five structures, seven freight trains, 42 road segments, four anti-aircraft artillery sites, and an approach to a highway bridge.

- Gia Dinh Province. At approximately 0120 hours, the enemy fired less than five rounds of mixed 107mm and 122mm rockets into Tan Son Nhut Air Base. There were no casualties and light damage. At 0630 hours, the enemy again fired three rockets of undetermined type into the Saigon area. Results were 21 VN civilians killed and 44 wounded.
- A Marine F-4 Phantom aircraft was downed at 1715 hours by enemy ground fire over the southern panhandle of North Vietnam. The aircraft crashed at sea and the Australian destroyer, HMAS PERTH, rescued the two man crew.

NOVEMBER 2, 1968

- *Operation Vernon Lake I.* Terminated. Results were 93 enemy killed, 23 individual weapons and one crew-served weapon captured. One US was killed, four wounded.
- *Operation Vernon Lake II.* Commenced. The operation was a multiple-battalion search and clear operation centered in an area 12 miles S of Quang Ngai City involving an element of the 11th Light Infantry Brigade.

NOVEMBER 3, 1968

- *Operation Sea Lords.* Announced. Operation was under the control of the Commander of Naval Forces, Vietnam and designed to interdict enemy infiltration deep in South Vietnam's Mekong Delta. The operation began October 18, 1968.
- *Operation Jeb Stuart III.* Terminated. Results were 2,014 enemy killed, 251 suspects detained, 1,079 individual weapons and 124 crew-served weapons captured. US 212 killed, 1,512 wounded (1,386 evacuated). Forty-nine enemy returned to the GVN under Chieu Hoi Program. *Operation Jeb Stuart III* terminated with the following results: Enemy losses were 2,114 killed; 261 detained; 60 returned; 1,228 individual weapons; 133 crew-served. Friendly losses were 232 killed; 1,568 wounded and two missing.

NOVEMBER 5, 1968

- *Operation Henderson Hill* (Quang Nam Province). At 0930 hours, an element of the US 5th Regiment, 1st Marine Division, found a five-ton rice cache nine miles ENE of An Hoa. This was enough rice to feed an NVA company for 40 days.

NOVEMBER 6, 1968

- Captured documents indicated that 90% of the 9th Battalion, 18B NVA Regiment, suffered from malaria since moving to the B-3 Front.

NOVEMBER 7, 1968

- *Operation Comanche Falls.* Terminated. Results were 107 enemy killed, 10 suspects detained, 159 individual weapons and nine crew-served weapons captured. US losses were 20 killed, 57 wounded. 11 Hoi Chanhs returned to the GVN.

NOVEMBER 8, 1968

- *Operation Quyet Chien* (Kien Hoa Province): During the period 1045-1815 hours, elements of the US 2nd Brigade, 9th Infantry Division Mobile Riverine Force, engaged an unknown size enemy force in four separate contacts while conducting offensive sweep six miles SE of Ben Tre. The enemy employed small arms and automatic weapons while the infantry returned fire with organic weapons supported by artillery and helicopter gunships. Enemy losses were 51 killed. There were no US casualties.

NOVEMBER 9, 1968

- The US Army's 1st Cavalry Division (Airmobile) completed most of its move from N I CTZ to the II CTZ. The move would be completed and the division would be fully operational in III Corps by mid-November 1968. The move, named *Operation Liberty Canyon,* began on October 28, 1968. The division, with headquarter locations near Phuoc Vinh in Binh Duong Province, would operate initially in the N III Corps area covering portions of Tay Ninh, Binh Long and Long Provinces. The division would be part of II FFV.

NOVEMBER 10, 1968

- DMZ: Between 1030 and 1335 hours, three 3rd Marine Division positions received 75mm artillery and 122mm rocket fire in five attacks from enemy positions in the DMZ, resulting in four Marines killed and 41 wounded. At the first location, Marines received 16 rounds of suspected 75mm artillery fire at 1030 hours resulting in no casualties or damage reported. In three other attacks four miles SW of Con Thien, other elements of the 3rd Marine Division received an unknown number of rocket rounds at 1100, 1120 and 1220 hours resulting in four US killed and 41 wounded (30 evacuated). At the third location four miles SSE of Con Thien, other elements of the 3rd Marine Division received 10 rounds of 122mm rocket fire between 1300 and 1335 hours. There were no casualties or damage reported. An aerial observer S of the DMZ located the two enemy firing positions locations ½ and one mile N of the S tract of the DMZ. Between 1120 and 1130 hours one enemy firing position located three miles W of Con Thien was attacked by Marine aircraft and artillery resulting in one rocket position and 10 bunkers destroyed and one fire ignited. The other enemy firing positions located five miles W of Con Thien were taken under fire with unknown results.
- *Operation Daring Endeavor.* Commenced. The operation was a multi-company search and clear operation centered five miles SW of Hoi An and commenced at 0630 hours. US elements involved in the operation included units from the 7th Regiment, 1st Marine Division and the US Army's Americal Division. The operation commenced with an amphibious and helicopter assault within its area of responsibility. As of 1200 hours, November 13, 1968, 19 enemy soldiers have been killed, 15 captured from enemy and 230 suspects detained. US losses were one killed and 22 wounded.

NOVEMBER 11, 1968

- *Operations Wheeler/Wallowa.* Terminated. The operation commenced September 11, 1967 and centered in an area 16 miles W of Tam Ky. Elements were the 196th Light Infantry Brigade, Americal Division. During the 14-month operation,

10,020 enemy soldiers were killed, 5,195 suspects were detained and 1,724 individual weapons and 392 crew-served weapons were captured. US casualties were 683 killed and 3,599 wounded (2,550 evacuated). 5,552 tactical air sorties and 901 Naval gunfire missions supported the operation.

- *Operation Burlington Trail.* Terminated. The operation, which commenced on April 8, 1968 with elements of the 198th Light Infantry Brigade, Americal Division, killed 1,931 enemy soldiers in an area centered five miles WNW of Tam Ky. In addition, the Infantry detained 1,289 suspects, and captured 441 weapons and 104 crew-served weapons. US casualties were 129 killed and 985 wounded (747 evacuated). The operation was supported by 1,620 tactical air sorties.

NOVEMBER 12, 1968

- Quang Tri Province. At approximately 1330 hours, an element of the ARVN 2nd Regiment, 1st Infantry Division, at a fire support base location four miles ENE of Con Thien, received approximately 10 rounds of enemy 82mm mortar fire resulting in very light casualties. The enemy firing positions to the N of the base were confirmed by visually observing and were locations inside the S half of the DMZ. Counter-artillery fires were directed into the enemy positions with unknown results. Later investigation revealed location was a suspected firing position.
- *Operations Wheeler/Wallowa* terminated in Quang Tin Province with the following results: Enemy losses were 10,020 killed; 5,195 detained; 1,724 individual weapons: 329 crew-served weapons. Friendly losses were 683 killed and 3,599 wounded.

NOVEMBER 13, 1968

- The Air Force announced that the detachment of five F-111 aircraft at Takhli RTAFB, Thailand, had completed their assigned tour of temporary duty, which began in March. Since this temporary tour has ended and because of a requirement to reinforce the wing carry-trough structures, the aircraft were scheduled to return to the US within the next two weeks. The aircraft and crews would return to their permanent station at Nellis Air Force Base, Nevada. While in Southeast Asia, the aircraft flew over 50 combat missions in testing their capability of penetrating a hostile area in a low-level attack mission at night in bad weather. The returning aircraft crews would be used at Nellis to train additional TAC F-111 pilots.

- *Operation Henderson Hill* (Quang Nam Province). At 0900 hours, an element of the US 5th Marine Regiment, 1st Marine Division, while on a search and clear operation, were led by a former enemy soldier to a cache containing 57 tons of rice. The rice will be evacuated and redistributed to VN civilians.
- Elements of Company C, 1st Battalion, 5th USMC participating in *Operation Henderson Hill* discovered a cache containing 57 tons of rice and miscellaneous equipment.

NOVEMBER 14, 1968

- I CTZ (DMZ). Five incidents were reported involving enemy activity in the S portion of the DMZ. Four incidents occurred on November 13, 1968 while one, a delayed report, occurred on November 11, 1968. All incidents occurred between ½ and three miles N of the S edge of the DMZ. There were no US casualties. On November 11, 1968 at 2115 hours, elements from a tank battalion of the US 3rd Marine Division observed an estimated 10 sets of vehicle lights moving S five miles NNE of Con Thien. At 2130 hours, the lights disappeared. The Marines did not engage the targets from their positions S of the DMZ. At 0845 hours, November 13, 1968, an aerial observer flying a reconnaissance mission received anti-aircraft fire from two enemy locations five miles NNW of Gio Linh. The aerial observer directed artillery fire onto the enemy positions with unknown results. At 1100 hours, November 13, 1968 another aerial observer flying a reconnaissance mission received small arms fire from two enemy locations four miles NNW of Gio Linh. The aerial observer directed artillery fire and naval gunfire from the USS DAVIS onto the enemy positions and destroyed numerous bunkers and 15 meters of trench line. At 1600 hours, November 13, 1968, 10 enemy soldiers in the open five miles NE of Gio Linh fired their organic weapons at an aerial observer conducting a reconnaissance mission. The aerial observer directed naval gunfire from the USS CANBERRA onto the enemy soldiers with unknown results. In another incident three miles NNE of Gio Linh at approximately

1800 hours, November 13, 1968, an aerial observer spotted 10 NVA soldiers moving in the open. The spotter directed over 500 rounds of mixed artillery fire from artillery units onto the enemy positions resulting in 34 secondary explosions, large explosion and three fires. Enemy casualties were unknown.

- I CTZ (DMZ). At approximately 0820 hours, a US Army O-1 light observer aircraft, on a visual reconnaissance mission, received small arms fire from an estimated 1,015 enemy soldiers moving in an open area three miles NE of Gio Linh (approximately one mile inside the S edge of the DMZ). The aerial observer directed artillery fire onto the enemy locations resulting in seven secondary explosions. Enemy casualties are unknown and there were no US casualties.
- *Operation Toan Thang* (Binh Duong Province). At 1330 hours, an element of the US 2nd Brigade, 25th Infantry Division, discovered a significant enemy cache while sweeping an area seven miles NW of Phu Cuong. The cache contained approximately 10 tons of polished rice in 385 bags weighing 50 pounds each.
- DMZ. Two additional incidents were reported in the DMZ: (a) At approximately 1440 hours, a US Army aerial observer, on a reconnaissance mission, observed an unreported number of enemy constructing enemy bunkers 10 miles NNW of Camp Carroll in the S half of the DMZ. Artillery fire was directed onto the enemy positions resulting in an unknown number of bunkers destroyed. Enemy casualties are unknown. (b) At approximately 1800 hours, a US Army aerial observer sighted an enemy bunker complex with signs of recent enemy use in an area three miles NE of Gio Linh in the S half of the DMZ. Artillery fire was directed onto the enemy position with large secondary explosion with fire that rose 500 feet in the air.
- *Operation Daring Endeavor*: Announced. The operation commenced on November 10, 1968. The multi-company search and clear operation, centered five miles SW of Hoi An involves elements of the 1st Marine Division and the Americal Division along with Vietnam Regional Forces/Popular Forces troops and Vietnam National Police. The operation commenced with an amphibious assault from ships of the USN Task Force 76. As of 1200 hours, November 13, 1968, 19 enemy had been killed. US losses were one killed and 22 wounded.

NOVEMBER 15, 1968

- DMZ: There were two additional incidents reported involving enemy activity in the DMZ. Both of the incidents occurred between ½ and one mile N of the S edge of the DMZ. There were no US casualties. At approximately 1500 hours, an aerial observer spotted an unknown number of NVA soldiers in bunkers two miles NE of Gio Linh. The aerial observer directed artillery and tactical air onto the enemy positions resulting in 10 secondary explosions and nine bunkers destroyed. The body of one enemy soldier was observed lying in the area following the strike. At approximately 2030 hours, a ground observer S of the DMZ observed a five-vehicle convoy moving on a road two miles NE of Gio Linh. The aerial observer directed artillery fire onto the enemy convoy resulting in 22 secondary explosions and an unknown number of small fires.
- DMZ. At approximately 0800 hours, a US Army aerial observer on a reconnaissance mission observed an unreported number of enemy bunkers and supply three miles NE of Gio Linh in the S half of the DMZ. The aerial observer directed artillery fire and an Air Force F-4 aircraft on the position. One of the strike aircraft was hit and lightly damaged by enemy ground fire from an unknown number of enemy near the bunker complex. The air strikes and artillery resulted in 12 secondary explosions and, following the action, the aerial observer reported the bodies of 32 enemy soldiers lying in the strike area. At approximately 0900 hours, a US Marine aerial observer sighted an unreported number of enemy bunkers and supply five miles NE of Gio Linh in the S DMZ. Artillery and Marine A-4 air strikes were directed onto the enemy position resulting in 12 bunkers destroyed. In addition, the observer reported two enemy killed.

NOVEMBER 16, 1968

- *Operation Toan Thang* (Tay Ninh Province). At approximately 0630 hours, an element of the US 3rd Brigade, 1st Cavalry Division (Airmobile), in night defensive positions 24 miles NNW of Tay Ninh City were attacked by an estimated enemy company employing grenades, automatic weapons and RPG fire. The cavalry troops returned fire with their organic weapons and were supported by helicopter gunships, artillery and tactical air as action continued until 0800 hours when contact was briefly lost as the enemy withdrew. The troops pursued the enemy and reestablished contact with an unknown size force in the same general area at approximately 0825 hours. The enemy employed small arms and automatic weapons fire against the attacking infantry. Some of the enemy were reported killed while firing from hidden positions in trees. The action continued until 1530 hours when the remaining enemy successfully evaded and withdrew. The troops found the bodies of 15 enemy soldiers killed. In addition, one crew-served weapons and three individual weapons were captured. There were no US casualties in the two-hour engagement. At an unreported time on November 18, 1968, an element of the US 3rd Brigade, 1st Cavalry Division (Airmobile) discovered the bodies of eight enemy soldiers and captured eight additional individual weapons while sweeping in the general area of the same unit's nine-hour battle on November 16, 1968 (24 miles) NNW of Tay Ninh City. The eight additional bodies raised the total from 36 to 44 enemy killed. In addition, a total of 19 individual weapons and six crew-served weapons were captured by the troops. US casualties were 11 wounded as a result of the night attack and pursuit action on November 16, 1968. There were no casualties in the sweep action on November 18, 1968.

- DMZ. At approximately 0920 hours, a US Army aerial observer, on a reconnaissance mission, sighted a bunker complex and foxholes occupied by an unknown number of enemy soldiers two miles NW of Gio Linh and approximately ½ miles inside the S edge of the DMZ. Tactical air was directed into the enemy positions resulting in six secondary fires and 14 bunkers destroyed. The aerial observer reported the bodies of eight enemy soldiers lying in the strike area following the action. Immediately following the air strikes, artillery fires were directed onto the enemy positions and the aerial observer reported an additional 13 enemy soldiers killed in the same general area, raising the total to 21 enemy reported killed in the engaged. In addition, the artillery fire destroyed two more bunkers. There were no US casualties.
- DMZ. At approximately 1800 hours, an aerial observer on a reconnaissance mission, observed movement near two enemy anti-aircraft weapons positions. Artillery fire was directed in

the area resulting in two weapons positions and one bunker destroyed and 12 secondary explosions ignited. The area was three miles NW of Gio Linh and one mile above the S edge of the DMZ.

- *Operation Garrard Bay* (Quang Nam Province). Terminated. The battalion size search and clear operation was conducted by elements of the 26th Marine Regimental Team in close coordination with elements of the US 1st Regiment, 1st Marine Division, ROD 2nd Marine Brigade, ARVN 51ST Infantry Regiment and Vietnam National Police Field Forces. During the 22-day operation, the Marines killed 19 enemy soldiers and detained 1,761 suspects. Six individual weapons were also captured. US losses were seven killed and 50 wounded (44 evacuated).

NOVEMBER 17, 1968

- DMZ. At 1155 hours, an aerial observer on a reconnaissance mission observed a bunker complex two miles NW of Gio Linh, ½ miles N of the S edge of the DMZ. Marine A-4, F-4 tactical air strikes were directed onto the target resulting in five enemy killed by air, nine bunkers destroyed and four residual fires ignited.
- *Operation Daring Endeavor.* Terminated. Results were 33 enemy killed, 336 suspects detained, five individual weapons and one crew-served weapon captured. US losses were one killed and 36 wounded (34 evacuated).

NOVEMBER 19, 1968

- *Operation Henderson Hill* (Quang Nam). At approximately 1430 hours, a reconnaissance team from the US 1st Marine Division observed a group of 55 NVA soldiers carrying packs and rifles two miles WNW of An Hoa. The Marines directed artillery fire onto the enemy troop concentration killing 33 NVA soldiers. Approximately two hours later, and in the same general area, the reconnaissance team observed another group of 35 enemy soldiers crossing a rice paddy and directed artillery fire onto the area resulting in 23 enemy killed. There were no Marine casualties in either incident. The 56 enemy killed raised the total to 104 enemy killed by artillery fire from four groups totaling 345 enemy soldiers observed by Marine reconnaissance teams and taken under fire on November 18 and 19, 1968 NW of An Hoa. There were no US casualties during the engagements.

NOVEMBER 20, 1968

- *Operation Meade River* (Quang Nam Province). At approximately 2200 hours, a US Marine aerial observer on a reconnaissance mission sighted 75 enemy soldiers moving in an area nine miles W of Hoi An. The observer directed artillery fire onto the enemy force as an aircraft in the vicinity lighted the area with flares. The observer reported sighting the bodies of 35 enemy lying in the strike area following the action. There were no US casualties.
- *Operation Meade River* (Quang Nam Province). Commenced. US elements involved in the operation included units from all three regiments of the 1st Marine Division under the control of the 1ST Marine Regiment. The operation commenced with a US Marine helicopter assault from USN ships of the 7th Fleet's amphibious Task Force 76. This part of the operation was termed *Operation Swift Move.*

NOVEMBER 21, 1968

- DMZ. There were two incidents reported involving enemy initial action in the DMZ: (a) At approximately 0930 hours, a US Army aerial observer on a reconnaissance mission over the S DMZ received .50 caliber machine gun fire from an NVA position 4½ miles N of Gio Linh near the Ben Hai River in the N Half of the DMZ. The observer directed artillery fire from S of the DMZ onto the locations resulting in one secondary explosion with a large fireball and destroyed the enemy machine gun position. In addition, the aerial observer reported two bunkers and two enemy structures destroyed by the artillery. No US casualties and enemy losses are unknown. (b) Later, at approximately 1110 hours, an aerial observer on a reconnaissance mission over the S DMZ received fire from an NVA anti-aircraft gun position, of unreported caliber, located six miles NNE of Gio Linh near the Ben Hai River in the N half of the DMZ. The observer directed artillery fire from below the DMZ onto the locations silencing the NVA anti-aircraft weapon. No US casualties and enemy losses are unknown.

- *Operation Nevada Eagle* (Thua Thien Province). Between the hours of 0915 and 1200 hours, elements of the US 2nd Brigade, 101st Airborne Division (Airmobile), conducting offensive sweep operations in a general area 14 miles S of Hue, found graves in two locations containing the bodies of 55 enemy soldiers. The bodies were apparently killed by air strikes and artillery fire. The time of death was not reported.

NOVEMBER 22, 1968

- DMZ. An incident was reported involving enemy initial action in the DMZ. At approximately 1345 hours, a USMC aerial observer on a reconnaissance mission over the S DMZ received .50 caliber machine gun fire from an enemy position located six miles NNE of Gio Linh near the Ben Hai River in the N half of the DMZ. The observer directed artillery fire from S of the DMZ onto the locations silencing the machine gun and destroyed a new bunker. There were no US casualties and enemy losses are unknown.
- *Operation Meade River* (Quang Nam Province). Announced. The multi-battalion search and clear operation centered nine miles W of Hoi An commenced on the morning of November 20, 1968.

NOVEMBER 23, 1968

- *Operation Quyet Chien* (Dinh Tuong Province). At 1100 hours, helicopter gunships from the 164th Combat Aviation Group, supported by tactical air on station, engaged an unknown size enemy force two miles NNW of Cai Be. At 1200 hours, an element of the US 1st Brigade, 9th Infantry Division, was inserted into the area and made light and sporadic contact with remnants of the enemy force in the area. Contact was lost at 1830 hours. Enemy losses were 52 killed by helicopter gunships and tactical air, and six killed by the infantry. Fifteen suspects were detained and 55 bunkers and 30 motorized sampans were destroyed. One crew-served weapon and 11 individual weapons were also captured. One US soldier was wounded in the engagement.
- Saigon: A US unarmed reconnaissance plane was lost over North Vietnam. Search and rescue was undertaken by its escort aircraft and by other aircraft called in. The search and

rescue initially for the recovery of the crew of the Air Force RF-4C aircraft was announced as terminated on November 25, 1968. The search and rescue was unsuccessful and the two crewmembers were listed as missing. The aircraft was downed to unknown causes approximately nine miles WNW of Dong Hoi.

- DMZ. At approximately 1600 hours, a US aerial observer on a reconnaissance mission, received automatic weapons fire from two or three enemy soldiers in a tree line four miles NNW of Gio Linh and two miles inside the S half of the DMZ. The observer directed artillery fire onto the enemy position resulting in one secondary explosion and silencing the enemy fire. In addition, one bunker was reported damaged by the artillery fire. There were no US casualties and enemy losses are unknown.
- *Operation Lancaster II* (Quang Tri Province). Terminated. Units involved were from the 3rd Marine Division. The operation was announced January 28, 1968 and commenced January 20, 1968. Cumulative results: US 359 killed, 2,101 wounded (1,714 evacuated). 1,801 enemy killed, 824 individual weapons and 89 crew-served weapons captured.

NOVEMBER 24, 1968

- *Operation Toan Thang* (Tay Ninh Province). At 1130 hours, helicopter gunships from the 12th Combat Aviation Group were conducting an armed reconnaissance flight over an area 15 miles NW of Tay Ninh City when an estimated 200 enemy soldiers opened fire on the aircraft with small arms and automatic weapons. The helicopter maneuvered and attacked the enemy force with machine guns and 2.75-inch rockets and action continued until 1430 hours when contact was lost as the remaining enemy evaded observation and withdrew. Enemy losses were 54 killed. There were no US casualties.
- *Operation Quyet Chien* (Dinh Tuong Province). At approximately 1000 hours, helicopter gunships from the 12th Combat Aviation Group, in support of the US 9th Infantry Division, observed an unknown size enemy force while conducting air reconnaissance operations seven miles W of Cai Lay. The air cavalry troops, employed machine gun and rocket fire, killed 10 enemy soldiers. Later three companies from the 1st Brigade,

9th Infantry Division, supported by helicopter gunships and tactical air, were air-assaulted into the general area of contact. The helicopter gunships continued to engage small groups of Viet Cong as they attempted to evade the ground troops. Two loudspeaker missions were flown and over 100,000 leaflets were dropped in support of the 1st Brigade. Contact was lost at approximately 1530 hours when the remaining enemy evaded the infantry and gunships. The cumulative results: 49 enemy killed (42 gunships, six by tactical air and one by the infantry, nine suspects detained. One crew-served weapon and six individual weapons were captured. There were no US casualties.

NOVEMBER 25, 1968

- *Operation Toan Thang* (Tay Ninh Province). At approximately 0630 hours elements of the US 3rd Brigade, 1st Cavalry Division (Airmobile), while conducting a search and clear operation, engaged an estimated enemy company 21 miles NNW of Tay Ninh City. Contact was lost at 0830 hours and regained at 0900 hours with an estimated 25 enemy located in a nearby tree line. Tactical air and artillery, helicopter gunships and aerial rocket artillery supported the friendly forces. Contact was lost again at 1030 hours. Fifty-two enemy were killed and 20 individual weapons and 17 crew-served weapons were captured. US casualties were five killed and 10 wounded. In a sweep of the area on November 26, 1968, elements of the 3rd Brigade, 1st Cavalry Division (Airmobile) and the VN 5th Marine Battalion swept the area of contact and found 71 additional bodies bringing the total killed by the infantry and supporting teams to 123. The cumulative weapons, equipment and ammunition captured included 20 individual weapons and 17 crew-served weapons, one Soviet radio, three CHICOM radios, four anti-tank mines, 51 CHICOM grenades, 40 RPG rounds, 19 60mm mortar rounds, and 580 rounds of small arms ammunition. US casualties were five killed and 13 wounded. At 0800 hours, November 28, 1968, an aerial reconnaissance team from the US cavalry squadron of the 1st Air Cavalry Division reported an additional 15 bodies that had been killed during the engagement on November 25, 1968. The cumulative totals were 138 enemy killed, six suspects detained, 40 weapons and a small ammunition and equipment cache captured. US losses were five killed 13 wounded.

- DMZ. Three incidents were reported involving enemy initial action in the DMZ: (1) At approximately 0930 hours, three aerial observer aircraft on reconnaissance missions over the S DMZ received .50 caliber machine guns and small arms fire from an enemy position locations four miles N of Gio Linh in the S half of the DMZ (approximately 1.5 miles N of the S tract of the DMZ). One aircraft was hit by .50 caliber rounds and returned to base. There was no damage to the aircraft reported or injuries to personnel. The other aerial observer directed Marine artillery fire, naval gunfire from the USS WADDELL and USAF tactical air onto the enemy position. The .50 caliber machine gun position was destroyed and the small arms fire silenced. One bunker and 25 meters of trench line were destroyed and one other bunker damaged. There were no US casualties and enemy losses are unknown. (b) At approximately 1500 hours, an aerial observer flying a reconnaissance mission S of the Demarcation Line received .50 caliber machine guns fire from an automatic weapons position located five miles N of Gio Linh (1.5 kilometers S of the Ben Hai River). The aircraft took two hits and returned to base. No damage or casualties were reported. Other aerial observers directed tactical air, artillery and naval gunfire onto the weapons position resulting in the .50 caliber machine guns position, one bunker and 50 meters of trench line being destroyed. There were no US casualties and enemy casualties are unknown. (c) At approximately 1650 hours, an aerial observer flying a reconnaissance mission S of the Demarcation Line received .50 caliber machine gun fire from an automatic weapons position locations four miles N of Con Thien in the N half of the DMZ (100 meters N of the Ben Hai River). The observer directed tactical air onto the weapons position destroyed the machine guns. There were no aircraft hit and no US casualties. Enemy casualties are unknown.
- An unarmed US reconnaissance aircraft and an armed US escort aircraft were lost in two separate incidents over North Vietnam. In both cases, suppressive fire was provided by US aircraft in support of search and resulting operations. NVN surface-to-air missiles were fired and a NVN MIG engaged the US aircraft.

NOVEMBER 26, 1968

- DMZ. At approximately 0950 hours, a platoon from the US 3rd Marine Division, engaged an estimated enemy platoon while conducting a reconnaissance mission 2½ miles NNW of Con Thien and about 500 meters inside the S edge of the DMZ. The enemy employed AK-47 automatic weapons fire and .50 caliber machine guns fire from fortified positions in the S DMZ. The patrol returned fire with organic weapons and at approximately 1050 hours, an element of the 3rd Regiment, 3rd Marine Division reinforced the troops in contact. Action continued with artillery and tactical air supporting the Marines until an unreported time in the early afternoon when contact was lost as the enemy evaded and withdrew. Although the patrol reported hearing screams of enemy soldiers apparently wounded by the initial strikes in the area prior to arrival of the reaction force, no bodies were found in a sweep of the enemy positions. Marines found 25 cases of 82mm mortar ammunition with three rounds in each case apparently left by the enemy force. There were no US casualties in the engagement.

NOVEMBER 27, 1968

- *Operation Toan Thang* (Binh Long Province). At approximately 1110 hours, an element of the US 2nd Brigade, 1st Cavalry Division (Airmobile) and an element of the US 11th Armored Cavalry Regiment, engaged an estimated NVA company while conducting a combat sweep four miles N of Loc Ninh. The enemy employed RPGs, automatic weapons and small arms fire while the troops were supported by helicopter gunships and artillery and tactical air in addition to the organic 90mm tank guns and .50 caliber machine guns of the armored personnel carriers. Action continued into the afternoon until 1630 hours when contact was lost as the remaining enemy evaded and withdrew. The results were: 58 enemy killed, and 13 individual weapons, nine crew-served weapons, 12 rounds of 60mm mortar ammunition, 40 B-40 rocket-grenades and 50 CHICOM grenades were captured. US casualties were eight wounded.
- *Operation Toan Thang* (Tay Ninh Province). At approximately 0850 hours, Vietnam Provisional Revolutionary Government (PRG) elements engaged an estimated enemy battalion while

conducting a combat sweep nine miles WNW of Go Dau Ha. The enemy employed small arms and automatic weapons fire in addition to .50-caliber machine gun and 75mm recoilless rifle fire. The Regional Forces troops returned fire with organic weapons supported by Air Force A-37 and F-100 tactical air strike, US Army artillery and ARVN artillery. At approximately noon, other Regional Forces elements reinforced the units in contact and action continued into the afternoon. Elements of the US 1st Brigade, 25th Infantry Division, reinforced the ARVN infantry at approximately 1700 hours and fighting continued into the night on November 28, 1968. Initial reports indicated US and VN casualties were light. Enemy losses were 96 killed, two crew-served weapons and 10 individual weapons captured.

NOVEMBER 28, 1968

- *Operation Toan Thang* (Binh Long Province). At approximately 0900 hours, mechanized elements from the US 3rd Brigade, 1st Cavalry Division (Airmobile) and Infantry from the ARVN 9th Regiment, 5th Infantry Division, engaged an unknown size enemy force while conducting combined sweep operations four miles NNE of Log Ninh. The cavalry troops and infantry were supported by ARVN artillery and US Army artillery and serial rocket artillery gunships until 1030 hours when the contact was lost. At 1315 hours, contact was re-established when the combined force received enemy small arms and RPG fire. Contact continued throughout the afternoon as the friendly forces were supported by tactical air and helicopter gunships. At approximately 1630 hours, contact was lost as the enemy withdrew. Enemy losses were 71 killed. US casualties were four wounded. ARVN casualties were very light. There were no US or ARVN fatalities.
- *Operation Dawson River* (Quang Tri Province). Commenced. The operation was a multi-battalion search and clear operation centered in an area 14 miles S of Cam Lo and was under the control of the US 9th Regiment, 3rd Marine Division.

NOVEMBER 29, 1968

- *Operation Toan River* (Binh Long Province). At approximately 1110 hours, a mechanized infantry element of the US 1st

Infantry Division, under operational control of the 1st Cavalry Division (Airmobile) engaged an estimated NVA battalion while sweeping an area five miles NE of Loc Ninh. The enemy directed small arms, automatic weapons and RPG fire from fortified positions against the troops who returned fire with organic weapons including heavy .50 caliber machine guns mounted on their armored personnel carriers. The action continued into the early afternoon with helicopter gunships, artillery and tactical air supporting the infantry. Contact was lost at approximately 1530 hours when the enemy evaded and withdrew. Enemy losses were 78 killed. US losses were seven killed and 16 wounded.

- *Operation Toan Thang* (Tay Ninh Province). At approximately 1600 hours, an element of the US Army 1st Brigade, 25th Infantry Division, discovered the bodies of 21 enemy soldiers while sweeping an area nine miles NW of Go Dau Ha. The enemy had apparently been killed by supporting fires employed during the action on November 27 and 28, 1968 in which Vietnam Provisional Revolutionary Government (PRG) troops and elements of the brigade supported by ARVN artillery, helicopter gunships, artillery and tactical air killed 96 enemy in an engagement with an estimated enemy battalion in the same general area.

NOVEMBER 30, 1968

- *Operation Quyet Chien* (Dinh Tuong Province). In an action that began approximately 0735 hours, helicopter gunships from the air cavalry squadron of the 12th Combat Aviation Group observed and engaged an unknown size enemy force four miles NE of Cai Be. The gunships employed machine guns and 2.75 inch rocket fire while the enemy returned fire with small arms and automatic weapons. Contact was lost at approximately 0750 hours when the enemy evaded and withdrew. At approximately 0830 hours, an element from the 1st Brigade, 9th Infantry Division was assaulted into the same general area and immediately reestablished contact with an unknown size enemy force. Later in the morning at approximately 1115 hours, another element from the same brigade reinforced the unit in contact as action continued until 1530 hours when the enemy once again withdrew and contact was lost. A sweep of the area was conducted and 70 enemy bodies were found lying about the battlefield. Enemy losses were 70 killed, 20 suspects detained and 14 individual weapons captured. There were no US casualties.

- The GVN released 140 Viet Cong prisoners in simultaneous ceremonies held in Saigon, Pleiku and Da Nang. All prisoners chose to remain in South Vietnam.

DECEMBER 1, 1968

- DMZ. At approximately 1600 hours, two aerial observers flying reconnaissance missions over the S half of the DMZ observed an enemy automatic weapons position four miles N of Gio Linh (approximately 300 meters S of the enemy Hai River) and what appeared to be five 100-pound sacks of supplies in a nearby area. One of the aerial observers received automatic weapons fire from the enemy weapons position and directed tactical air onto the locations resulting in two bunkers, one small structure and 90 meters of trench line were destroyed and one bunker was damaged. In addition, one secondary explosion and one secondary fire were observed. The aerial observers then directed artillery fire onto the supply area and reported the supplies, two large bunkers destroyed, and two secondary explosions with 40-foot fireballs. There were no US casualties and neither aircraft was hit.
- US military strength in the RVN was 538,000.

DECEMBER 2, 1968

- *Operation Hardin Falls* (Quang Nam Province). Commenced. The multi-company search and clear operation involved elements of the US 198th Light Infantry Brigade, Americal Division, the armed cavalry squadron of the division and Vietnam Regional Forces/Popular Forces troops along with National Police elements. The operation area was centered approximately seven miles SE of Hoi An.
- At approximately 1830 hours, an aerial observer flying a reconnaissance mission S of the Ben Hai River received .50 caliber fire from two enemy weapons positions locations five and 5½ miles NNE of Con Thien (one position was located

300 meters N of the Ben Hai River in the N half of the DMZ, the other one was located 100 meters S of the Ben Hai River in the N half of the DMZ. USAF tactical air was directed onto the two positions resulting in one weapons position damaged (N half of the DMZ) and one destroyed (S half of the DMZ). The aircraft were not hit and there were no US casualties.

- *Operation Vernon Lake* (Quang Ngai Province). Terminated. The operation commenced on October 25, 1968. During the eight-day operation, 93 enemy soldiers were killed, 23 individual weapons and one crew-served weapon were captured. US losses were one killed and four wounded.
- The GVN announced it would observe a 24-hour Christmas Truce, commencing at 1800 hours, December 24, 1968.

DECEMBER 3, 1968

- DMZ. At approximately 0830 hours, an aerial observer flying a reconnaissance mission over the S half of the DMZ received automatic weapons fire from an enemy .50 caliber machine guns position locations five miles NNE of Con Thien (150 meters N of the Ben Hai River) in the N half of the DMZ. US Marine tactical air was directed onto the enemy weapons position silencing the gun emplacement. No aircraft were hit in the engagement.
- DMZ. At approximately 0950 hours, an aerial observer flying a reconnaissance mission over the S half of the DMZ received .50 caliber machine gun fire from an enemy weapons position four miles NW of Gio Linh (approximately 200 meters N of the Ben Hai River) in the N half of the DMZ. Marine tactical air and 16-inch Naval gunfire from the USS NEW JERSEY were directed onto the weapons position resulting in the destroying of one bunker and 200 meters of trench line and severe damage to two structures. The enemy weapons position was also silenced. No aircraft were hit in the engagement.
- *Operation Toan Thang* (Phuoc Long Province). At approximately 1025 hours, an element of the US 3rd Brigade, 1st Cavalry Division (Airmobile) was air-assaulted into an area 15 miles WSW of Phuoc Binh. At 1045 hours, the unit received heavy small arms, automatic weapons, RPGs and 82mm mortar fire from an estimated NVA battalion. The heavy fire was followed

by several enemy ground assaults, which were repelled by the cavalry troops employing organic weapons supported by tactical air, artillery and aerial rocket artillery helicopter gunships from the division. The action continued into the afternoon until approximately 1500 hours when contact was lost as the enemy withdrew. US losses in the four-hour battle were 25 killed and 52 wounded. One enemy body was found. During the sweep of the battle area on December 4, 1968, another element of the brigade engaged an unknown size enemy force at about 1510 hours. Tactical air supported the cavalry during the 50-minute firefight, which followed. Contact was lost at 1600 hours as the enemy again withdrew. Thirteen US soldiers were wounded in this engaged. Enemy casualties are unknown.

- *Operation Quyet Chien* (Kien Phong Province). Between 1100 and 1830 hours, F-100 and A-37 tactical aircraft from the USAF 3rd Tactical Fighter Wing attacked elements of an estimated enemy battalion in an area nine miles NE of Cao Lanh while supporting ARVN troops in the 44th SZ. ARVN units moved into the area and conducted a sweep finding 62 enemy bodies killed by the air strikes.

DECEMBER 5, 1968

- *Operation Meade River* (Quang Nam Province). During a cordon and search operation at 1200 hours in an area nine miles W of Hoi An, two companies from the US Marine 26th Regimental Landing Team attacked an unknown size enemy force in well-fortified positions. The Marines attacked the positions after directing tactical air and artillery fire onto the extensive bunker complex. Contact was lost at 1700 hours when the enemy withdrew. Results were 67 NVA soldiers killed, five suspects were detained and 10 individual weapons were captured. There were no Marine casualties.

DECEMBER 6, 1968

- *Operation Hardin Falls* (Quang Nam Province). Announced. Commenced December 2, 1968. The multi-company search and clear operation involved elements of the US Army 198th Light Infantry Brigade, Americal Division, the armed cavalry squadron of the division and Vietnam Regional Forces/ Popular Forces troops along with National Police elements.

The operation was centered approximately seven miles SE of Hoi An and, to date, there had been no significant contacts reported. As of December 5, 1968, 17 enemy have been killed and three suspects detained. In addition, one individual weapon was captured. No friendly casualties were reported.

- *Operation Giant Slingshot* commenced. The operation was centered on the Vam Co Dong and Vam Co Tay Rivers, flowing W from a point S of Saigon around the "Parrot's Beak" section of the Cambodian border. More than 40 USN patrol boats have moved into a "Y"-shaped complex of narrow rivers within 15 miles of Saigon to interdict enemy movement across the W approaches to South Vietnam's capital city. Taking part in the operation were the fiberglass river patrol boats and minesweepers of the Navy's Game Warden River Platoon Force, as well as armed assault support patrol boats, armored troop carriers and "Monitors" of the Navy's River Assault Flotilla One. Neither river had been patrolled regularly by USN Forces.
- DMZ. At approximately 0935 hours, a US aerial observer on a reconnaissance mission over the S DMZ received heavy fire from an enemy .50 caliber anti-aircraft machine guns locations four miles NNW of Gio Linh and about one kilometer from the Ben Hai River in the S DMZ. The observer directed US Marine artillery fire onto the weapons position silencing the enemy weapons. The observer aircraft was not hit and there were no US casualties.
- DMZ. At approximately 1255 hours, a US aerial observer on a reconnaissance mission over the S DMZ observed 31 enemy soldiers two miles NW of Gio Linh (approximately two miles S of the action enemy anti-aircraft machine gun positions reported earlier in the day) in the S half of the DMZ. Artillery fire was directed onto the enemy troop concentration with unknown results as enemy smoke prevented complete assessment of the strike area.
- DMZ. At approximately 1810 hours, a US Marine artillery forward observer located S of the DMZ, observed six enemy soldiers in an open area four miles N of Gio Linh and 300 meters S of the Ben Hai River. The forward observer directed artillery fire onto the enemy troops resulting in one secondary explosion. Enemy casualties are unknown.

- *Operation Henderson Hill* (Quang Nam Province). Terminated. The operation commenced October 23, 1968 under the control of the US 5th Regiment, 1st Marine Division and had the specific mission to capture or eliminate enemy forces, installations and materiel within its area of responsibility. Cumulative results: 700 enemy killed, 94 suspects detained, and 41 individual weapons and five crew-served weapons were captured. Friendly losses were US 35 killed and 273 wounded, of whom, 233 were evacuated. The operation was supported by 818 tactical air sorties.

DECEMBER 7, 1968

- *Operation Taylor Common* (Quang Nam Province). Commenced. The operation was centered in an area 10 miles W of An Hoa, and involved elements of the US 3rd, 5th and 7th Marine Regiments under the control of the 1st Marine Division. As of 2400 hours, December 16, 1968, the Marine and supporting fires had accounted for 123 enemy killed. In addition, 41 suspects have been detained and two crew-served weapons and 18 individual weapons were captured. Marine casualties so far were: 18 killed and 73 wounded. A total of 223 tactical air strikes were flown in support of the ground forces.
- DMZ. At approximately 1215, a US aerial observer on a reconnaissance mission over the S DMZ, observed an enemy anti-aircraft position and two enemy soldiers armed with individual weapons four miles N of Gi Linh and about ½ miles S of the Ben Hai River in the S half of the DMZ. The enemy fired on the observer aircraft and the aerial observer directed artillery fire onto the enemy position resulting in one secondary explosion. In addition, the observer reports one bunker destroyed. Enemy casualties are unknown. The US aircraft was not hit and there were no US casualties in the engagement.
- Company C, 1st Battalion, 5th USMC found a cache in Quang Nam Province of 50-70 tons of rice and 2,000,000 NVN Piasters.

DECEMBER 8, 1968

- *Operation Meade River* (Quang Nam Province). At 1630 hours, elements of the 26th Marine Regimental Landing Team, 5th and 7th Regiments, 1st Marine Division, and an ARVN armored personnel carrier troop, while tightening the cordon in an area nine miles WNW of Hoi An, made contact with an unknown size enemy force in bunker complexes and a tree line. The enemy force was supported by organic weapons included mortar, while artillery and helicopter gunships supported the friendly elements in contact. The action continued until 1915 hours. The remaining enemy avoided contact under cover of darkness. Results were 91 enemy killed, US 16 killed and 37 wounded. One suspect was detained and 15 individual weapons were captured. ARVN casualties were light with no fatalities.

DECEMBER 9, 1968

- *Operation Giant Slingshot* was announced. The operation commenced December 7, 1968 and was centered in the Vam Co Dong and Vam Co Tay Rivers, flowing W from a point S of Saigon around the Parrot's Beak.
- *Operation Toan Thang* (Binh Long Province). At approximately 1045 hours, a company from the US 2nd Brigade, 1st Cavalry Division (Airmobile), conducting a reconnaissance-in-force mission four miles WSW of An Loc engaged an unknown size enemy force. The action continued until 1340 hours when the enemy withdrew to the ESE. The cavalry troops pursued and regained contact a short while later. The action continued until 1630 hours when the remaining enemy evaded and withdrew. Enemy losses were 93 killed, one crew-served weapon, 53 RPGs, 42 CHICOM hand grenades and 34 rounds of 60mm mortar ammunition were captured. US casualties were 14 killed and 16 wounded.
- *Operations Napoleon/Saline* (Quang Tri Province). Terminated. The operation commenced on November 5, 1967 under the control of the 3rd Marine Regiment, 3rd Marine Division. Cumulative Results were 3,495 enemy killed, 549 suspects detained, and 631 individual weapons and 200 crew-served weapons captured. US losses were 395 killed and 2,134 wounded, of whom. 1,680 were evacuated. The operation was supported by 373 tactical air sorties and 197 naval gunfire missions.
- An Air Force RF-4C reconnaissance aircraft was downed by

enemy ground fire approximately 10 miles N of Dong Hoi and four miles off the coast of North Vietnam. Jolly Green Giant helicopters rescued the two-man crew. Both Navy and Air Force aircraft flew cover during the pickup, however no suppressive fire was employed.

- *Operation Meade River* (Quang Nam Province). (a) At approximately 1045 hours, elements of the US 26th Marine Regimental Landing Team, while searching an area nine miles W of Hoi An discovered the bodies of 140 NVA soldiers apparently killed by supporting fires during previous contacts. In addition, the Marine detained eight NVA soldiers apprehended in the search and captured 32 individual weapons and five crew-served weapons, which were found, scattered in the vicinity. Additional items found by the Marine included approximately 1,000 articles of enemy clothing and individual equipment, 372 hand grenades, 42 RPGs and miscellaneous other small arms and automatic weapons ammunition. Company contact was made during the search and there were no Marine casualties. (b) Later, at approximately 1130 hours, elements of the US 26th Marine Regimental Landing Team and the US 5th Regiment, 1st Marine Division, engaged an unknown size enemy force in fortified positions inside a cordoned area nine miles W of Hoi An and 500 meters N of the previous sweeps. Tactical air and helicopter gunships supported the ground troops until contact was lost at approximately 1500 hours when the remaining enemy avoided further engagements. Enemy losses were 39 NVA soldiers killed in the action. One NVA soldier was detained and 14 individual weapons were captured. US losses were two wounded.
- *Operation Meade River* (Quang Nam Province). Terminated. The operation commenced on November 20, 1968 and was centered in an area nine miles W of Hoi An involving elements from the US 1st Marine Division, and in conjunction with ARVN, Korean Marine and Vietnam National Police elements. Cumulative results: 841 enemy killed and detained 2,710 suspects (of whom 71 were Viet Cong Infrastructure personnel). In addition, 100 enemy soldiers were detained and turned over to the ARVNs as prisoners of war's. Also captured were 164 individual weapons and 15 crew-served weapons. US losses were 107 killed and 523 wounded (386 evacuated). Initial

reports indicate that elements of the independent, NVA, 36th Regiment, were trapped within the highly effective cordon and suffered heavy casualties which temporarily rendering the regiment combat ineffective. The 36th NVA Regiment has operated in the N provinces of South Vietnam for almost eight months followed infiltration from North Vietnam into South Vietnam earlier this year.

DECEMBER 10, 1968

- *Operation Marshall Mountain* (Quang Tri Province). Commenced. The operation was a combined operation involving elements of the US 1st Brigade, 5th Infantry Division (Mech) and the ARVN 1st Regiment, 1st Infantry Division. The specific missions were to conduct pacification and offensive operations in an area centered three miles E of Quang Tri City.
- DMZ. At approximately 0920 hours, a US observer aircraft, on a reconnaissance mission over the S DMZ, received .50 caliber machine gun and small arms fire from an unknown number of enemy in fortified positions two miles NW of Gio Linh and about ½ miles inside the S edge of the DMZ. The aerial observer directed artillery fire onto the enemy locations destroyed five bunkers and silenced the enemy fire. The aircraft was not hit by enemy fire and there were no US casualties. Enemy casualties are unknown.

DECEMBER 11, 1968

- DMZ. At approximately 1510 hours, a US aerial observer on a reconnaissance mission over the S DMZ, sighted 10-12 enemy soldiers occupying fortified positions five miles WSW of Con Thien and one mile inside the S edge of the DMZ. The observer directed artillery fire onto the enemy positions resulting in three secondary explosions and destroyed 12 bunkers. There were no US casualties and the aircraft was not hit. Enemy losses are unknown.

DECEMBER 12, 1968

- DMZ. At approximately 0700 hours, a US aerial observer on a reconnaissance mission over the S half of the DMZ observed

15-20 enemy soldiers occupying fortified positions four miles W of Con Thien and approximately one mile S of the Ben Hai River in the S DMZ. The observer directed tactical air strikes onto the enemy positions destroyed four bunkers and igniting one secondary fire. No aircraft were hit by enemy fire and enemy losses are unknown.

- DMZ. At about the same time as the above incident, the same aerial observer sighted another group of 15-20 enemy soldiers in a bunker complex 300 meters to the SE of the fortified positions struck by the Marine jets and also in the S half of the DMZ. Artillery fire was directed onto the enemy locations resulting in one secondary explosion. The observer aircraft was not hit by enemy fire and enemy losses are unknown.
- DMZ. At approximately 1050 hours, a US aerial observer sighted a bunker complex and 15 enemy soldiers four miles W of Con Thien. Artillery fire was directed onto enemy troops resulting in two secondary explosions. Sixteen bunkers were destroyed and 15 damaged by the fire mission.

DECEMBER 15, 1968

- *Operation Dawson River* (Quang Tri Province). Announced. The operation, which commenced on November 28, 1968, was a multi-battalion search and clear operation centered in an area 14 miles S of Cam Lo. The operation was under the control of the US 9th Regiment, 3rd Marine Division and, as of 1800 hours, December 13, 1968, 32 enemy soldiers have been killed and 39 suspects have been detained. In addition, 14 individual and three crew-served weapons have been captured. US losses were two killed and 19 wounded, of whom 15 have been evacuated. 145 tactical air sorties have been flown in support of the Marines.
- *Operation Marshall Mountain* (Quang Tri Province). Announced. The operation was a combined operation involving elements of the US 1st Brigade, 5th Infantry Division (Mech) and the ARVN 1st Regiment, 1st Infantry Division, and was centered three miles E of Quang Tri City. The operation commenced on December 10, 1968. As of 1800 hours, December 13, 1968,

six suspects have been detained while US casualties were nine wounded (three evacuated). There had been no reported ARVN casualties. Four tactical air sorties have been flown in support of the operation.

- *Operation Fayette Canyon* (Quang Nam Province). Commenced. The operation was a multi-battalion search and clear operation and was centered in an area seven miles SSE of An Hoa. The operation, under control of the 196th Light Infantry Brigade, Americal Division, has the specific mission of eliminating enemy forces, base camps and materiel within its area of responsibility.
- *Operation Valiant Hunt* (Quang Nam Province). Commenced. The operation was a battalion cordon and search operation and was centered in an area four miles S of Hoi An. The operation was under the control of the Commander, Task Group 76.4 and involves Marine from the 26th Regimental Landing Team. The operation began with an amphibious and helicopter-borne assault into the area of operations and has as its mission to establish cordons around selected villages in conjunction with Vietnam forces. The object of the combined cordon and search and clear operation was to eliminate Viet Cong local forces and infrastructure units and personnel believed to be operational in the area.

DECEMBER 17, 1968

- *Operation Taylor Common* (Quang Nam Province). Announced. The multi-battalion search and clear operation began on December 7, 1968 and was centered in an area 10 miles W of An Hoa. The operation involved elements of the US 3rd, 5th and 7th Marine Regiments under control of the 1st Marine Division.
- *Operation Toan Thang* (Binh Duong Province). At approximately 1100 hours, a US 25th Infantry Division resupply convoy, enroute from Dau Tieng to Tay Ninh Province, was attacked by an unknown size enemy force four miles WSW of Dau Tieng. Convoy security elements engaged the enemy in positions on both sides of the road and were reinforced by mechanized infantry units from the Division's 3rd Brigade. Tactical air,

helicopter gunships and artillery supported the infantry until contact was lost at 1340 hours as the enemy withdrew. Enemy losses were 73 enemy killed. US losses were five killed and 11 wounded. Several trucks in the convoy were damaged in the initial attack.

- Quang Tin Province. At approximately 1130 hours, a USAF C-123 crashed after takeoff due to unknown causes in an area 1½ miles S of Chu Lai. Of the 44 passengers and crewmembers aboard, initial reports indicated 14 were killed. The aircraft was destroyed.
- DMZ. At approximately 1700 hours, a US aerial observer aircraft, on a reconnaissance mission over the S half of the DMZ, received anti-aircraft fire from an enemy .50 caliber machine gun location four miles NNE of Con Thien and about 100 meters S of the Ben Hai River. The aerial observer directed artillery fire onto the enemy anti-aircraft weapons position silencing the fire. The aircraft was not hit and there were no US casualties. Enemy losses are unknown.

DECEMBER 18, 1968

- Quang Nam Province. At approximately 0900 hours, a company from the US 196th Light Infantry Brigade, Americal Division, while conducting a combat sweep in an area six miles SE of An Hoa, observed an estimated reinforced infantry platoon carrying packs and rifles. The infantry, supported by tactical air and helicopter gunships, attack the enemy force and action continues throughout the morning and afternoon until 1800 hours when contact was lost. Enemy losses were 103 killed. US casualties were three infantry wounded. At 0930 hours, nine enemy bodies, apparently killed by small arms fire, were found approximately eight miles SE of An Hoa. About 30 minutes later, graves containing 11 enemy bodies killed by small arms fire during the action were found in a nearby area. Continuing to search, the infantry at noon discovered another 22 enemy bodies apparently killed by artillery fire.
- *Operation Toan Thang* (Phuoc Long Province). Air troops from the US Army's cavalry squadron of the 1st Cavalry Division (Airmobile), conducted aerial reconnaissance operations in an area 12 miles NE of Phuoc Binh, observed and engaged an estimated enemy battalion. The troops, supported by

helicopter gunships and tactical air killed 41 enemy soldiers. There were no US casualties.

DECEMBER 19, 1968

- DMZ. At approximately 1500 hours, a defensive position occupied by an element of the US 4th Regiment, 3rd Marine Division and locations six miles NNE of the Rockpile, received about 10 rounds of enemy 60mm and/or 82mm mortar fire resulting in no Marine casualties and no reported damage. The Marine position was located one kilometer S of the S edge of the DMZ and the enemy fire came from two mortar position locations by counter-mortar radar 1½ kilometers N and 1½ kilometers NNE of the Marine and 500 meters inside the S half of the DMZ. The Marine directed organic 81mm mortar fire on the enemy positions with unknown results.

DECEMBER 21, 1968

- DMZ. At approximately 1140 hours a command post of the US 4th Regiment, 3rd Marine Division located six miles NNE of the Rockpile (½ mile S of the S edge of the DMZ) received approximately 10 rounds of 60mm mortar fire from two enemy firing position locations one mile N of the S edge of the DMZ and 7½ miles NNE of the Rockpile. Tactical air strikes were directed onto the enemy firing positions resulting in six bunkers destroyed. There were no US casualties or damage reported.

DECEMBER 22, 1968

- Khanh Hoa Province. Early this morning at approximately 0345 hours the HELISOMA, a UK tanker, was hit by an unknown type explosion but believed to be a mine, while moored in the Nha Trang harbor. The explosion occurred on the port side causing an undetermined amount of damage. Oil leaked from the tanker but there was no fire. There were no casualties.
- *Operation Fayette Canyon* (Quang Nam Province). Announced. The operation was a multi-battalion search and clear operation and was centered in an area seven miles SSE of An Hoa. The operation, which commenced on December 15, 1968, was under control of the 196th Light Infantry Brigade, Americal Division,

and had the specific mission of eliminating enemy forces, base camps and materiel within its area of responsibility. As of 0600 hours, December 22, 1968, the infantry and supporting fires had accounted for 220 enemy killed. In addition, two suspects had been detained and 14 individual weapons and six crew-served weapons had been captured. US casualties, to date, were two killed and six wounded (three evacuated). A total of 79 tactical air strikes had been flown in support of the ground forces.

- *Operation Valiant Hunt* (Quang Nam Province). Announced. The operation was a battalion cordon and search operation and was centered in an area four miles S of Hoi An. The operation, which commenced on December 15, 1968, involved Marines from the 26th Regimental Landing Team. The objective of the combined cordon and search and clear operation was to eliminate Viet Cong local forces and infrastructure units and personnel believed to be operation in the area. As of 2000 hours, December 21, 1968, the Marine and supporting fires had accounted for 15 enemy killed, and 940 suspects detained. US casualties, to date, were eight wounded. A total of 74 naval gunfire missions and over 700 helicopter sorties supported the operation.
- *Operation Toan Thang* (Tay Ninh Province). At approximately 0015 hours, elements from the US 3rd Brigade, 25th Infantry Division in night defensive positions seven miles NW of Go Dau Ha received a mortar and ground attack from an unknown size enemy force. USAF AC-47 gunships, tactical air, artillery and helicopter gunships supported the infantry throughout the night until 0635 hours when contact was lost as the enemy force withdrew. At 1000 hours this morning an ARVN Airborne battalion and two companies from the 25th Infantry Division were inserted in the N and W of the infantry's defensive positions. A sweep of the area was conducted and the cumulative totals for the action were as follows: 81 enemy killed, nine light machine guns, 25 AK-47's three 9mm pistols, 164 CHICOM hand grenades, 26 RPG-2 boosters, 31 RPG-7

boosters, 38 RPG-7 rounds, 78 RPG-2 rounds, 19,000 small arms rounds, 59 AK magazines with ammunition, 30 light machine gun clips with ammunition, two CHICOM radios, one back pack and two pounds of documents.

DECEMBER 24, 1968

- The National Liberation Front (NLF) announced a 72-hour cease-fire commencing at 0100 hours. This was not observed by RVN, US and other FWMAF.
- RVN announced a 24-hour cease-fire commencing at 1800 hours. The FWF would also observe this cease-fire.

DECEMBER 25, 1968

- During the 24-hour military stand-down of offensive operations by RVNAF, US and FWF that commenced at 1800 hours, December 25, 1968, 133 incidents were reported. Of these, 47 of the incidents were considered significant (those incidents in which casualties occurred). As a result of the incidents involving US Forces, two US personnel were killed and 36 US personnel were wounded. Enemy losses during the period were 34 killed, one suspect detained, one crew-served weapons and 12 individual weapons captured.
- GVN/US/FWF cease-fire terminated at 1800 hours; 133 violations of cease-fire by enemy noted during 24-hour period.

DECEMBER 26, 1968

- *Operation Toan Thang* (Tay Ninh Province). At approximately 0900 hours, elements of the US cavalry squadron of the 1st Cavalry Division (Airmobile) while conducting aerial reconnaissance operations 12 miles E of Katum observed 60 enemy soldiers. The cavalry troops supported by tactical air and aerial rocket artillery helicopters, killed 41 enemy soldiers while sustaining no casualties.

DECEMBER 27, 1968

- *Operation Toan Thang* (Binh Long Province). At noon, a mechanized infantry company from the US 1st infantry Division, under operational control of the 2nd Brigade, 1st Cavalry Division (Airmobile), while conducting sweep operations six miles NW of An Loc made contact with an estimated NVA company. The mechanized troops, supported by tactical air, artillery and aerial rocket helicopters, were reinforced by another company from the same unit at an unreported time. The NVA troops were wearing green uniforms and pith helmets and employed small arms, automatic weapons and RPG fire. The action continued until 1630 hours when contact was lost as the enemy withdrew from the battle area. Enemy losses were 52 killed, three suspects were detained, and three individual and five crew-served weapons were captured. US casualties were two killed and 27 wounded. Damage to the armored personnel carriers was light.

DECEMBER 28, 1968

- Camp Carroll, a fire support and combat base location in N central Quang Tri Province between Ca Lu and Cam Lo, was inactivated this date. The camp was opened in November 1966 for the purpose of providing security for Route 9 and DMZ surveillance. The inactivation of Camp Carroll was a decision based on taking maximum advantage of our superior firepower and mobility in continuance of the mobile posture adopted in W Quang Tri Province with *Operation Pegasus* in April 1968 and which resulted in the inactivation of Khe San Combat Base late in June 1968. Mobile forces tied to no specific terrain were required to attack, intercept, reinforce or take whatever action was most appropriate to meet an enemy threat. The 3rd Marine Division's concept of mobility required infantry battalions to be constantly conducting search and clear operations throughout the division's area of operations. The need for security units at Camp Carroll required infantry units that could better be utilized in the field for the swift moves into enemy areas. The mobility concept rarely required that major infantry maneuver elements be within the confines of a static combat base. Since the role played by Camp Carroll could be satisfied by other fire support bases in the area with an overall economy of security forces, Camp Carroll had been inactivated. Camp Carroll was named after Captain J.J. Carroll, USMC, who was killed in *Operation Hastings* on October 5, 1966. Captain Carroll was posthumously awarded the Navy Cross for heroism during the action in which he was killed.
- *Operation Toan Thang* (Phuoc Long Province). At approximately

0930, helicopters from the 1st Cavalry Division (Airmobile) Air Cavalry Squadron, conducting aerial reconnaissance operations 22 miles SW of Phuoc Binh, received automatic weapons and small arms fire from an estimated enemy company. USAF tactical aircraft – F100s from the 37th Tactical Fighter Wing and F-4s from the 12th Tactical Fighter Wing – along with US Army helicopter gunships attacked the enemy positions. The helicopters then moved back into the area and the crews reported counting 59 enemy bodies lying in the area of the air strikes. There were no US casualties and no reports of helicopters hit by enemy ground fire.

- DMZ. At approximately 1530 hours, an aerial observer on a reconnaissance mission over the S DMZ spotted seven enemy soldiers and an unreported number of bunkers and trails with signs of recent action locations in the S half of the DMZ seven miles NNE of Gio Linh. The aerial observer called for and received US Marine artillery and US naval gunfire on this target with good coverage resulting in seven enemy reported killed, 15 bunkers destroyed, 11 bunkers damaged and three secondary explosions. The USS ISBELL, a Navy destroyer, provided the naval gunfire support.

DECEMBER 30, 1968

- DMZ. At approximately 0950 hours, a US aerial observer aircraft on a reconnaissance mission over the S DMZ received small arms fire from an unknown number of enemy soldiers in bunkers locations four miles NE of Gio Linh and about one mile S of the Ben Hai River in the S half of the DMZ. The observer directed US Marine tactical air strikes onto the enemy fortifications resulting in one secondary explosion and destroyed six bunkers. No aircraft were hit by enemy fire and there were no US casualties in the action. Enemy losses are unknown.

DECEMBER 31, 1968

- By the end of the year the strength of the Free World Military Forces assisting the RVN totaled over 600,000. (US 538,000; Korea, Australia, New Zealand, Thailand, Philippines, and China 66,000).
- At end of year, US casualties since January 1961 were: killed,

30,614; wounded, 99,787 (hospital care required); missing, 1,238 (includes captured).

- IV CTZ (Kien Giang Province). At approximately 1330 hours, a US Army officer held prisoner by the Viet Cong for over five years was recovered during an operation being conducted by elements of the ARVN 21st Infantry Division in an area 38 miles SSW of Rach Gia near the N edge of the U Minh Forest. The officer was identified as Major James N. Rowe who was captured by an unknown size enemy force that overran a GVN outpost locations 13 miles NE of Ca Mau in An Xuyen Province on the afternoon of October 29, 1963. At the time of his capture, Major Rowe, (then a 1st Lieutenant) was serving on temporary duty from the US with the US 5th Special Forces Group as an advisor. Shortly before his recovery, Major Rowe over-powered an armed enemy guard and escaped. He was reported to be in good physical condition.
- DMZ. At approximately 1630 hours, a US observer aircraft on a reconnaissance mission over the S DMZ received small arms fire from an unknown number of enemy occupying fortified positions four miles N of Gio Linh and about 400 meters S of the Ben Hai River. The aerial observer directed naval gunfire from the USS ISBELL resulting in three secondary explosions and fires and the destroyed of 13 bunkers. The enemy fire did not hit the aircraft and enemy casualties are unknown.

JANUARY 1, 1969

- Free World Military Strength was: US – 537,500; FWMAF – 66,000.
- Three US prisoners of war were released in a battlefield meeting between representatives of the Viet Cong and CG II FFORCEV in Tay Ninh Province.

JANUARY 3, 1969

- An explosion in the mess hall of the 20th Engineer Brigade at Cu Chi Base Camp, results in 15 killed and 26 wounded. The explosive was believed to have been a mine.

JANUARY 6, 1969

- Le Minh Tri, GVN Minister of Education was assassinated in Saigon.

JANUARY 7, 1969

- A Viet Cong command-detonated floating type mine damaged a bridge across Highway 4, 5 kilometers SW of Gia Rai, Bac Lieu Province. Another command detonated mine later destroyed the bridge.

JANUARY 11, 1969

- The 6th Co, ROK Marine Brigade, found 225 tons of rice and small quantities of miscellaneous small arms ammunition and documents 10 kilometers SW of Hoi An, Quang Nam Province.

JANUARY 13, 1969

- An unknown size enemy force attacked Can Tho Airfield with RPGs, heavy small arms, satchel charges, and automatic weapons fire, in addition to succeeding in penetrating a portion of the airfield. Results were five enemy killed and eight US wounded. Damage was reported as light to moderate.

JANUARY 14, 1969

- A 48th Transportation Group convoy was ambushed by an unknown number of enemy in Tay Ninh Province. Enemy losses were 122 killed, and three individual weapons and one crew-served weapon captured. Friendly losses were seven killed and 10 wounded.

JANUARY 14, 1969

- DELTA BLACKHAWK forces contact a large enemy force in Kien Phong and Kien Tuong Provinces, killing 139 enemy, detaining 17, and capturing 66 weapons, and large quantities of ammunition and explosives, including first the 107mm rockets captured in IV CTZ. Friendly losses were five killed and 21 wounded.

JANUARY 21, 1969

- The Vung Tau Army Airfield and dock area received about 10 rounds of 122mm rocket fire. One round penetrated the deck of a USN LST killing one Navy man, wounding 12 others and causing major damage to the ship.

- Elements of the US 2nd Brigade, 1st Cavalry Division, discovered one of the largest caches of the war SE of Kontum. The 30-ton cache consisted of mortar and small arms ammunition, and various explosives.

JANUARY 26, 1969

- The enemy attacked Binh Tien War Office on Phu Dinh Street in the 6th Precinct in Saigon, using 10 RPG rounds, two hand grenades, and small arms. Four civilian Self-Defense cadre were wounded and the building 50% destroyed. This is the first attack within Saigon city limits since May-June Offensive 1968.
- The 1st Cavalry Division (Airmobile) *Toan Thang Offensive* in Tay Ninh Province, found an underground hospital complex under construction 19 kilometers NE of Phu Khuong. A hospital contained five operating rooms, six wards (capacity 15-18 persons each), two mess halls (capacity 200 persons), 12 tunnels each 20 feet deep five feet in diameter, 100-125 bunkers each 10 feet x 15 feet x 6 feet with overhead cover connected to two fighting positions each, two bunkers 15 feet x 150 feet with overhead cover, 45 bunkers 4 x 5 x 8 feet with overhead cover, six additional mess areas.

JANUARY 31, 1969

- The 1st Cavalry Division (Airmobile) participating in *Toan Thang Offensive* Tay Ninh Province found two enemy caches totaling over 69 tons of rice.
- Terrorists attempted to assassinate Major General Nguyen Van Kiem, Chief of Staff, Special Staff, Office of GVN President, four blocks from Presidential Palace. General Kiem suffered a broken leg.

FEBRUARY 9, 1969

- RVN Marines found one of the war's largest munitions and weapons cache in Tay Ninh Province. It contained modified over-caliber 240mm rockets.

FEBRUARY 11, 1969

- Lieutenant General Frederick C. Weyand, US Army, was named as military advisor to the US negotiating team in Paris.

FEBRUARY 14, 1969

- The last contingent of the Thai Black Panthers arrived in RVN. Thai strength in RVN was approximately 11,250.

FEBRUARY 16, 1969

- Phase II of *Operation Toan Thang* Offensive, which began on June 1, 1968, terminated. Phase III of the combined operation involving ARVN and FWMAF in III CTZ commenced. Enemy losses were 25,248 killed; 10,724 detained; 10,285 individual weapons and 2,307 crew-served weapons captured.

FEBRUARY 16, 1969

- The GVN announced temporary cessation of offensive operations from 1800 hours, February 16, 1969 to 1800 hours, February 17, 1969 for TET.

FEBRUARY 17, 1969

- The GVN and FWF 24-hour cessation of offensive operations terminated at 1800 hours. A total of 93 significant enemy-initiated incidents (casualties incurred) during the cease-fire was noted.

FEBRUARY 23, 1969

- The enemy launched a series of indirect fire harassing attacks against more than 100 locations throughout the RVN. Several attacks by fire were accompanied by ground attacks of varying intensity. Seven 122mm rocket rounds impacted in Saigon; the first rocket attack against Saigon since November 1, 1968.

FEBRUARY 23, 1969

- A US Army reaction force made contact with the enemy in the vicinity of the Long Binh Post. Enemy losses were 132 killed. Friendly losses were seven US killed and 30 wounded.

FEBRUARY 26, 1969

- GVN forces pre-empted an attack on Bien Hoa and killed 264 of the enemy. VN casualties were 10 killed and 200 wounded.

FEBRUARY 26, 1969

- Elements of the 9th Regiment, 3rd Marine Division, found

two caches 50 kilometers SSW of Quang Tri City. Caches were estimated to weigh approximately 300 tons, 90 percent of which were new weapons and ammunition.

FEBRUARY 26, 1969

- US military strength in RVN was 542,000.

MARCH 1, 1969

- 1,005 Hoi Chanhs reported for the week ending March 1, 1969, the highest number in one week since March 1967.
- Elements of the 3rd Battalion, 503rd Airborne Infantry, found a cache containing 346 tons of rice 23 kilometers SSE of Bao Loc in Lam Dong Province.

MARCH 3, 1969

- The Ben Het CIDG Camp received a ground attack. Ten tanks (USSR PT-76) and six trucks supported the ground forces. Two tanks were destroyed. This is the first use of armor by the enemy in II CTZ and first use in South Vietnam since February 7, 1968.

MARCH 5, 1969

- Elements of the 9th Marine Regiment discovered another significant enemy munitions cache (55 tons) 30 miles SSW of Quang Tri City. Total amount of weapons and munitions captured by Marines since February 21, 1969 was 435 tons.
- The 2nd Brigade, 25th Infantry Division, made contact with estimated an NVA battalion on March 4, 1969 and an unknown size NVA force on March 5, 1969 eight KM NE of Trang Bang. Enemy losses were 179 killed and 67 weapons captured. Friendly losses were 11 killed and 53 wounded.

MARCH 6, 1969

- Secretary of Defense Melvin R. Laird arrived in RVN for a four-day visit.
- The enemy launched an indiscriminate attack by 122mm rocket fire against Saigon, the third such attack since the start of the current offensive; six rounds impacted into I, IV, and IX Precincts, killing 22 VN civilians and wounding 43.
- Elements of the 1st Brigade, 4th Infantry Division, in a night

defense 42 kilometers W of Kontum City, attacked by an estimated NVA battalion. Enemy losses were 112 killed, 20 individual weapons and three crew-served weapons. There were no friendly casualties.

MARCH 8, 1969

- Elements of the 1st Brigade, 1st Cavalry Division (Airmobile), in a night defense six kilometers NE of Phu Khuong, attacked by an estimated NVA battalion. Enemy losses were 154 killed, 23 individual weapons and eight crew-served weapons. Friendly losses were 11 killed and 30 wounded.
- Marines of the 9th Regiment discovered additional arms and munitions caches 49 kilometers SSW of Quang Tri City. Total amount of weapons and ammunition captured by 9th Marines since February 21, 1969 was 452 tons.

MARCH 9, 1969

- The Viet Cong released Renate Kuhnen, the German nurse captured March 3, 1968 in Kontum.
- Secretary of Defense Laird presented the Presidential Unit Citation to 1st ARVN Division for operations during the period January 1, 1967 to February 25, 1968.

MARCH 12, 1969

- Four US Army airmen were released by the Royal Khmer Government. The Viet Cong captured the men on February 12, 1969.

MARCH 16, 1969

- The enemy conducted 65 mortar and rocket attacks on military installations and population centers in South Vietnam. This was the highest number of attacks since the first day of the current offensive. Seven 122mm rockets landed in the Saigon area.
- Elements of the 196th Infantry Brigade discovered 40 mass graves containing 152 enemy bodies 15 kilometers W of Tam Ky. The enemy had been killed approximately four days earlier by artillery, air strikes, and small arms.

MARCH 22, 1969

- Elements of the 2nd Battalion, 3rd Marine Regiment participating in *Operation Maine Crag* discovered an enemy cache 17 kilometers SE of Khe Sanh. It includes 356 tons of rice, 3.5 tons of salt, 100 pounds of lard, one ton canned food, one ton powered milk, 2.5 tons TNT, 600 meters communication wire, three trucks, 44 122mm rockets, 9,044 rounds 82mm mortar, 587 rounds 60mm mortar, 3,503 rounds RPGs, 7,500 rounds 12.7mm ammunition, 100 rounds 57mm, 55 rounds 75mm, 854,280 rounds small arms ammunition, 339 individual weapons and 13 crew-served weapons.

MARCH 24, 1969

- US killed in the Vietnam war surpasses 33,628, the number of killed in Korean War.

MARCH 27, 1969

- Elements of the 1st Brigade, 5th Infantry Division (Mech) engaged an unknown size NVA force 10 kilometers NW of Cam Lo. Enemy losses were 120 killed, seven individual weapons, three crew-served weapons. Friendly losses were 15 killed and 30 wounded.

MARCH 28, 1969

- Elements of the 1st Brigade, 5th Infantry Division (Mech) engaged an unknown size NVA force 10 kilometers NW of Cam Lo. Enemy losses were 68 killed and 16 individual weapons. Friendly losses were one killed and 30 wounded. Enemy losses in the last two days in this area totaled 188 killed.

MARCH 29, 1969

- 1,043 Hoi Chanhs were reported for the period March 23-29, 1969.

MARCH 31, 1969

- US military strength in RVN was 540,000.

APRIL 1, 1969

- A US Army UH-1 helicopter which was apparently attempting an autorotation because of an in-flight emergency crashed in the vicinity of the Massachusetts Bachelor Officers Quarters (BOQ) near the entrance to Tan Son Nhut Air Base killing all six US personnel aboard. One RVN soldier and one VN civilian near the crash site at the time were injured.

APRIL 2, 1969

- A US Army CH-47 helicopter struck a tree and crashed while extracting Vietnam Regional Forces troops from an LZ in an area 10 kilometers SSE of Khe Sanh. The aircraft was destroyed, 24 personnel (23 Regional Forces and one US) were killed and 53 personnel (49 Regional Forces and four US) were injured.

APRIL 11, 1969

- The MACV and USAF Compounds in Tay Ninh City received less than 10 rounds of 82mm mortar fire and less than five rounds of 107mm rocket fire. Overall materiel damage was moderate-to-heavy. Two VN civilians were killed and 10 others wounded. US casualties were very light with no casualties.

APRIL 15, 1969

- Patrol Base Diamond Number Three 10 kilometers SW of Go Dau Ha in Tay Ninh Province received indirect fire and ground attack. Enemy losses were 198 killed, eight detained, 40 individual weapons and 27 crew-served weapons. Friendly losses were 13 killed and nine wounded.
- An element of the 2nd Brigade, US 101st Airborne Division (Airmobile) found a munitions cache 28 miles S of Hue in Thua Thien Province. The cache was estimated at 4.5 tons and included approximately 2,000 mortar rounds.

APRIL 16, 1969

- An element of the 1st Brigade, 25th Infantry Division in *Operation Toan Thang III* found 93 NVA bodies in an area 22 miles NNW of Tay Ninh City in Tay Ninh Province. The enemy were killed by tactical air strikes about 10 days previously.
- Regional Forces elements, in a one-day sector-controlled operation, discovered a prisoner of war camp five kilometers NW of Vung Liem in Vinh Long Province. Ninety-eight males and 19 female VN civilians were released.

APRIL 17, 1969

- The US Government recognized Cambodia for the first time since 1965. The GVN simultaneously agreed to open discussions on disputed South Vietnam-Cambodian boundaries.

APRIL 21, 1969

- A VN Air Force plane with a number of high-ranking persons aboard crashed and burned on take-off from Vung Tau. The following persons were injured: Tran Ba Phuoc, Vietnam Defense Minister; Paul Edmonds, NZ Ambassador to Vietnam; Anastacio Bartolome, Philippine Charge d'Affaires; and Paul Nur, South Vietnam Minister for Ethnic Minorities.

APRIL 26, 1969

- In ceremonies at Can Tho, the 6th Battalion, 77th Artillery completed turnover of equipment to the 213th ARVN Artillery Battalion. This was first in a series of support and services units, which would go through the same procedures as part of the overall program of upgrading ARVN.
- A fire support base occupied by an element of the 1st Brigade, 25 Infantry Division, 20 kilometers S of Tay Ninh City was attacked by an estimated two enemy battalions. A ground assault preceded by heavy indirect fire attack consisting of about 300 rounds of 82mm mortar and 107mm rocket fire. Army artillery, helicopter gunships, AC-47 and AC-119 gunships and tactical air supported. Enemy losses were 213 killed, six detained, 35 individual weapons and 15 crew-served weapons. Friendly losses were seven wounded.

APRIL 27, 1969

- An estimated enemy battalion assaulted night defense positions of an element of the 2nd Brigade, 25th Infantry Division, 10 kilometers northeast of Tang Bang. Enemy losses were 100 killed, one detained, 32 individual weapons and 23 crew-served weapons. Friendly losses were 10 killed and three wounded.
- An estimated enemy battalion assaulted night defense positions of an element of the 2nd Brigade, 25th Infantry Division. 10 kilometers northeast of Trang Bang. Enemy losses were 100

killed, one detained, 32 individual weapons and 23 crew-served weapons. Friendly losses were 10 killed and three wounded.

- A grass fire started by burning refuse from civilian trash disposal area went out of control at 1045 hours and ignited a quantity of ammunition in an ammunition supply area located two miles SW of Da Nang. Damage to the ammunition supply area was heavy. US casualties were one killed and 14 others wounded and hospitalized. Low casualties were due to prompt action by US forces to evacuate the area.

MAY 5, 1969

- An element of the 1st Brigade, 1st Cavalry Division (Airmobile) in night defense seven miles south of Katum in Tay Ninh Province received a ground attack from an unknown size NVN Army force. An unreported number of the enemy penetrated the perimeter but were driven out. Enemy losses were 101 killed.

MAY 6, 1969

- A US Army CH-47 helicopter transporting ARVN troops crashes three miles SW of Phuoc Binh in Phuoc Long Province, killing 32 ARVN soldiers and injuring 34 others. Two US personnel were killed and one was injured.

MAY 9, 1969

- The GVN announced that it would observe a 24-hour cessation of offensive operations on May 30, 1969 in observance of Buddha's birthday.
- An element of the 5th Regiment, 1st Marine Division, engaged an estimated 400 to 600 enemy in an area six miles NE of An Hoa in Quang Nam Province, supported by artillery and tactical air. Enemy losses were 233 killed, five detained, and 47 weapons captured. Friendly losses were 23 killed and 58 wounded.
- Elements of the 3rd Brigade, 15th Infantry Division, engaged an unknown size enemy force five miles SE of Dau Tieng in Binh Duong Province, killing 102 enemy and capture during a 24-ton rice cache.

MAY 12, 1969

- The number of indirect fire harassing attacks by the enemy greatly increased with 212 attacks reported during the night of May 11-12, 1969. Of these, 105 were considered significant. Ground attacks or probes followed several of the indirect fire attacks against US forces.
- An enemy force 11 miles NE of An Hoa in Quang Nam Province attacked elements of the 39th ARVN Ranger Battalion and 21st ARVN Ranger Battalion. Enemy losses were 116 killed, one detained and 39 weapons captured. Friendly losses were six killed and 15 wounded.
- An element of the 3rd Brigade, 1st Cavalry Division (Airmobile) in night defense at a fire support base 14 miles SE of Katum in Tay Ninh Province received more than 200 rounds of 82 mortar and 107mm rocket fire, followed by a ground assault by an unknown size enemy force. Some of the enemy penetrated a portion of the perimeter but were killed or repulsed. Seventy-two of the enemy were killed.
- A mechanized infantry element of the 3rd Brigade, 9th Infantry Division, engaged an estimated enemy battalion four miles NW of Tan An in Long An Province, and were supported by gunships, artillery, and tactical air. Enemy losses were 83 killed and 18 weapons captured.
- Elements of the 3rd Regiment, 1st ARVN Infantry Division, found 71.6 ton cache 30 miles SE of Khe Sanh. It included one 122mm field gun, 10 tons of mixed small arms ammunition, eight 60mm mortars, eight Molotova trucks, 50 bicycles, and 78 individual weapons.

MAY 14, 1969

- Secretary of State William P. Rogers arrived in the RVN for a three-day visit.

MAY 16, 1969

- Two 82-foot Coast Guard cutters, the POINT LEAGUE and the POINT GARNET, were transferred to the VN Navy in ceremonies in Saigon. These were the first US Coast Guard ships to be turned over to the RVN.

MAY 18, 1969

- An element of the 3rd Brigade, 101st Airborne Division (Airmobile), engaged an unknown size NVA force occupying fortified positions 30 miles WSW of Hue, killing 125 enemy soldiers.
- A Marine F-4 Phantom aircraft collided in-air with a Marine KC-130 refueler transport aircraft refueling two other Marine F-4's over the South China Sea about eight miles NW of Phu Bai. One of the F-4's disengaged and returned safely to base. The other was damaged by fragments from the collision but also disengaged. The crew ejected and was rescued. The KC-130 and the F-4 that collided with it, both crashed.

MAY 20, 1969

- Secretary of the Navy J.F. Chafee arrived in Vietnam for a seven-day visit.
- Elements of the 3rd Brigade, 101st Airborne Division (Airmobile) and an element of the 3rd Regiment, 1st ARVN Infantry Division, seized Hill 937 in A Shau Valley after three major engagements on May 18, 19, and 20, 1969.

MAY 22, 1969

- An element of the 1st Brigade, 9th Infantry Division, engaged an estimated enemy battalion while sweeping an area nine miles west of Cai Be. They were supported by helicopter gunships and artillery and killed 117 of the enemy and captured 21 weapons. US casualties were four wounded.

MAY 23, 1969

- Secretary of the Air Force R.C. Seamans, Jr., arrived in the RVN for a three-day visit.

MAY 24, 1969

- An element of the 1st Brigade, 1st Infantry Division, engaged an unknown size enemy force five miles WSW of An Loc, killing 96 of the enemy and detaining one.
- An element of the 2nd Brigade, 9th Infantry Division, engaged

an estimated enemy company six miles NW of Ben Tre. An infantry element of the Brigade reinforced and helicopter gunships supported. Enemy losses were 91 killed, US casualties were four wounded.

MAY 25, 1969

- The Viet Cong announced a 48-hour cease-fire for Buddha's Birthday, commencing 0700 hours, May 29, 1969.
- An element of the 2nd Brigade, 1st Cavalry Division (Airmobile) discovered a cache 15 miles SE of Katum in Tay Ninh Province. It contained over 60 tons of food and seven tons of ammunition.

MAY 26, 1969

- The 22nd ARVN Ranger Battalion, the 2nd Battalion, 42nd ARVN Infantry, and the 1st and 2nd Special Forces Battalions engaged the enemy in five separate actions during the period June 19-26, 1969, killing 209 of the enemy.
- While sweeping an area six miles SW of Dak to, the 11th ARVN Ranger Battalion attacked an estimated reinforced enemy company. Artillery, gunships, and tactical aircraft supported. Enemy losses were 262 killed and friendly casualties were light.

MAY 30, 1969

- The GVN announced that a 24-hour cessation of operations commenced at 0600 hours.

MAY 31, 1969

- The 6th Battalion, 77th Artillery, which turned its equipment over to the ARVN on April 26, 1969, was deactivated.
- The GVN announced that the 24-hour cessation of offensive operations terminated. A total of 158 incidents (85 significant) were recorded during this period.
- The National Liberation Front (NLF) announced that the 48-hour cease-fire terminated at 0700 hours.
- US military strength in the RVN was 538,500.

JUNE 2, 1969

- One 122mm rocket impacted in Saigon's 4th Precinct and

another in the 9th Precinct, killing two VN civilians, and wounding 25.

- Hoi Chanhs for 1969 reach 18,748 and now exceeded the 1968 total of 18,171.

JUNE 5, 1969

- An element of the 1st Brigade, US 25th Infantry Division, ambushed an enemy force eight miles NW of Go Dau Ha, Tay Ninh Province, and were supported by US Army gunships and artillery and tactical air. Enemy losses were 45 killed and 73 weapons were captured. US losses were one killed and 14 wounded.
- An element of the 2nd Brigade, US 25th Infantry Division, and an element of the 49th Regiment, 25th ARVN Infantry Division, engaged an enemy force six miles NE of Trang Bang, killing 72, detaining three, and capturing 28 weapons. Friendly casualties were seven killed, and 23 wounded.

JUNE 6, 1969

- A mechanized infantry element of the 1st Brigade, 1st Infantry Division, engaged an estimated enemy company three miles NW of An Loc, supported by artillery, helicopter gunships, and tactical air. Enemy losses were 115 killed, nine suspects detained, and 36 weapons captured. Friendly losses were three US killed and 13 wounded.
- An element of the 5th ARVN Airborne Battalion in night defense six miles SW of Tay Ninh City was attacked. Enemy losses were 60 killed, and 31 weapons captured. Friendly casualties were 22 wounded. Elements of the 88th NVA Regiment were identified as the attacking unit.
- FSB Crook, 14 miles NW of Ben Soi in Tay Ninh Province, occupied by an element of the 1st Brigade, 25th Infantry Division was attacked. Enemy losses were 76 killed, two detained, and 17 weapons captured. Friendly casualties were one killed and two wounded.

JUNE 7, 1969

- FSB Crook received a fire attack and ground attack and was supported by US Army gunships, artillery, and tactical air. Enemy losses were 323 killed, 10 suspects detained, and 43 weapons captured. Friendly losses were two wounded. The enemy unit was identified as the 9th Viet Cong Division. This raised to 399 the number of enemy soldiers killed in last two days.

- Mechanized infantrymen of the 1st Brigade, 1st Infantry Division and troopers from the 11th Armored Cavalry Regiment, in tanks and armored carriers, engaged an estimated two NVA companies four miles SW of An Loc in Binh Long Province, killing 95 enemy and capturing 39 weapons. US losses were three killed and seven wounded.
- *Operation Apache Snow* terminated. A multi-regiment operation was centered in an area 32 miles WSW of Hue and involved the 9th Regiment, 3rd Marine Division, and the 3rd Brigade, 101st Airborne Division (Airmobile). An element of the 1st ARVN Division also participated. Enemy losses for the operation were 977 killed, five suspects detained, and 752 weapons captured. Friendly losses were 135 killed, and 733 wounded. There were heavy losses to the 29th NVA Regiment with elements dug in on Hill 937.

JUNE 9, 1969

- President Nixon, President Thieu, and General Abrams arrived at Midway Island for a meeting. This was the seventh meeting between US and GVN heads of state since 1961.
- Elements of the 5th Regiment, 1st Marine Division, made contact with two groups of NVA soldiers NW of An Hoa, Quang Nam Province. Enemy losses were 155 killed, 53 weapons captured. Friendly casualties were three killed and 19 wounded.
- Mechanized infantry troops of the 1st Brigade, 25th Infantry Division engaged an enemy force 11 miles east of Tay Ninh City, killing 51. US losses were three killed and 18 wounded.

JUNE 10, 1969

- President Nixon announced the redeployment of the division equivalent of 25,000 US troops from the RVN.
- Twenty-five river assault craft of River Assault Division 92 were turned over to the Vietnam Navy during ceremonies.

River Assault Squadron 9 and River Assault Division 92 were decommissioned.

- The Viet Cong announced establishment of a government called the "Provisional Revolutionary Government of the Republic of South Vietnam."
- A 4th Infantry Division convoy traveling Highway 14 was ambushed nine miles north of Pleiku. Enemy losses were 42 killed and four weapons captured. Friendly losses were one killed and one wounded.

JUNE 11, 1969

- Prince Sihanouk announced that the Royal Kingdom of Cambodia would reestablish diplomatic relations with the US Government at the Charges d'Affaires level.
- The DOD announced that troops to be redeployed would include combat units as well as support units

JUNE 13, 1969

- The DOD announced that major units departing the RVN would be two brigades of the 9th Infantry Division and the Regimental Landing Team 9 of the 3rd Marine Division.

JUNE 15, 1969

- A fire support base of the 3rd Brigade, 101st Airborne Division (Airmobile) located 28 miles SW of Hue was attacked by an NVA Force. Enemy losses were 52 killed, three detailed, and 14 weapons captured. US losses were seven wounded.

JUNE 16, 1969

- Five rounds of 122mm rocket impacted 1½ miles WNW of Tan Son Nhut Air Base.
- Elements of the Royal Thai Armed Forces at Bear Cat received a fire attack followed by a heavy ground attack from an estimated enemy battalion. Artillery and gunships supported. Enemy losses were 212 killed, one detained and 36 weapons captured. Friendly losses were six killed and 34 wounded.

JUNE 17, 1969

- Admiral J.S. McCain, Jr. CINPAC arrived in the RVN for a two-day visit.
- Elements of the 3rd Regiment, 3rd Marine Division, contacted the enemy in five separate actions in the general area 2½ miles SW of Gio Linh in Quang Tri Province, killing 102 enemy and capturing 33 weapons. US losses were 17 killed and 34 wounded.

JUNE 18, 1969

- B-52's marked the end of their 4th year of participation in the war.

JUNE 19, 1969

- An element of the armored cavalry squadron of the 25th Infantry Division engaged an enemy force five miles SE of Tay Ninh City, supported by gunships and artillery. Enemy losses were 85 killed. US losses were two killed, 13 wounded and one missing.
- A company of the 6th ARVN Airborne Brigade made contact with an unknown size enemy force 5½ miles SW of Tay Ninh City. Two companies of the 6th ARVN Airborne Brigade, one company from the 6th VNMC Battalion, and one company from the 25th Infantry Division reinforced. Enemy losses were 101 killed, 47 weapons captured. Friendly losses were 11 killed and 95 wounded.
- An estimated one to two companies of enemy soldiers entered a northern suburb of Tay Ninh City and was engaged by elements of the Regional Forces and the 8th ARVN Airborne Battalion, supported by artillery and aerial rocket artillery. As a result of enemy action and action taken to dislodge the enemy, 200 houses were destroyed, 75 to 100 homes damaged, five civilians were killed and 73 civilians wounded.

JUNE 20, 1969

- LZ Ike, located 12 miles south of Katum in Tay Ninh Province and occupied by an element of the 1st Brigade, 1st Cavalry Division (Airmobile) received an attack by fire followed by a ground attack by an estimated reinforced NVA battalion. Gunships and artillery supported. Enemy losses were 90 killed, five detained and 54 weapons captured. Friendly casualties were seven killed and 18 wounded.

JUNE 22, 1969

- Admiral J.J. Hyland, CINCPACFLT, arrived in the RVN for a two-day visit.
- Elements of the 21st ARVN Infantry Division operating seven miles NW of Kien Long in Chuong Thien Province contacted an unknown size enemy force. Artillery, gunships and tactical air supported. Enemy losses were 98 killed, five detained and 15 weapons captured. Friendly losses were two killed and three wounded.

JUNE 25, 1969

- Sixty-four USN river boats were transferred to the Vietnam Navy. This represented the largest single turnover of US military hardware thus far in the war.

JUNE 26, 1969

- The Ben Het CIDG Camp was shelled for the 19th consecutive day. A total of 5,539 rounds were received during this period. One rallier stated that the intentions were to destroy the camp to support the Paris Conference. If Ben Het could be occupied, the enemy would claim another Dien Bien Phu type victory.

JUNE 27, 1969

- Elements of the 25th Infantry Division engaged the enemy in two separate contacts eight miles NE of Tay Ninh City. The enemy unit was later identified as the 9th Viet Cong Division. Ninety-four enemy were killed and 32 weapons were captured. Friendly casualties were two killed and 16 wounded.

JUNE 28, 1969

- An element of the 2nd Brigade, 1st Cavalry Division (Airmobile) on a sweep SSW of An Loc in Binh Long Province discovered the bodies of 54 enemy soldiers, apparently killed by artillery one month ago.

- A reconnaissance element of the 1st Marine Division observed an estimated 400 enemy in an area 11 miles east of An Hoa in Quang Nam Province, and called in tactical air strikes, killing 40 enemy.

JUNE 30, 1969

- The USN turned over to the VN Navy the USS COCONINO COUNTY (LST-603) in ceremonies at Guam, Mariana Islands. The ship was renamed VNS VUNG-TAU (HQ-503). This was the 167th naval craft transferred to Vietnam Navy since June 1968.
- Five AC-47 gunships were turned over to the VN Air Force as part of the improvement and modernization program.
- *Project MOOSE* (Move Out of Saigon Expeditiously) terminated. Over 12,000 personnel were moved out of the downtown Saigon area as a result of this program.
- US military strength in the RVN was 538,700.

JULY 1, 1969

- A mechanized infantry element of the 1st Brigade, 25th Infantry Division, operating eight miles NE of Tay Ninh City, engaged an unknown size enemy force. Tactical aircraft, helicopter gunships, and field artillery support. Forty-four enemy were killed and 12 weapons captured.

JULY 2-3, 1969

- An element of the 2nd Brigade, 1st Cavalry Division (Airmobile), six miles east of Phu Khuong, engaged an unknown size enemy force in fortified positions. Tactical aircraft and field artillery support. Enemy losses were 32 killed.

JULY 5, 1969

- River Assault Flotilla One, and the 2nd Brigade, 9th Infantry Division, were awarded the Presidential Unit Citation for outstanding performance during the Tet Offensive Campaign of 1968.

JULY 6, 1969

- Two rockets impacted two miles east of Saigon's center. There was no damage or casualties.
- The Nationalist Chinese-owned merchant ship WELFARE was mined on the Nha Be River, eight miles SE of Saigon, and sank, slightly injuring several crewmen. It was the first ship to be sunk in this area since August 1966.
- A person claiming to be a Viet Cong captain contacted a USN river patrol boat and stated that he had 300 Viet Cong who wanted to "Chieu Hoi." The 44th Special Zone and Border Control Center completed arrangements, and 231 persons crossed with a total of 108 individual weapons and 14 crew-served weapons. The incident occurred in Chau Doc Province 11 miles NW of Tri Ton.

JULY 8, 1969

- The 3rd Battalion, 60th Infantry, 2nd Brigade, 9th Infantry Division, departed the RVN for the US from Tan Son Nhut Air Base. These were the first troops to leave the country as part of the 25,000-troop redeployment announced at the Midway Conference, and which was to be completed by August 31, 1969.

JULY 11, 1969

- GVN President Nguyen Van Thieu called for a national vote to settle the war, and offered participation to all political parties and groups if each renounced violence and pledged to accept the election results.

JULY 13, 1969

- Marines of the 9th Regimental Landing Team departed for Okinawa as part of the 25,000-man troop redeployment.

JULY 19, 1969

- Elements of the 2nd Brigade, US 25th Infantry Division, engaged an enemy force six miles NE of Trang Bang in Hau Nghia Province, and were supported by artillery, helicopter gunships, and tactical aircraft. Forty-seven enemy were killed, 10 were detained, and 27 weapons were captured, with no US casualties. The enemy unit was later identified as an NVA element of the 9th Viet Cong Division.

- Elements of the ARVN 2nd Infantry, 20 miles SW of Quang Tri, found 15 bunkers containing 680 cases of small arms ammunition and 1,950 rounds of mixed recoilless rifle, mortar, and rocket ammunition. The cache, which weighed 36.2 tons, and the bunkers were destroyed.

JULY 21, 1969

- Elements of the 1st ARVN Division, 16 miles SW of Quang Tri, found 118 NVA bodies in a mass grave.

JULY 26, 1969

- A reconnaissance patrol of the 1st Brigade, 4th Infantry Division, found the bodies of 30 enemy soldiers 16 miles NNE of An Khe in Binh Dinh Province. USAF tactical aircraft apparently killed them. The bodies of 25 other enemy soldiers, also killed by aircraft, had been discovered July 25, 1969, raising to 55 the total number of enemy killed by aircraft in this general area.

JULY 27, 1969

- An element of the 2nd Brigade, 25th Infantry Division, engaged an unknown size enemy force four miles NE of Trang Bang in Hau Nghia Province. Twenty-four enemy were killed and 15 weapons captured. There were no US casualties.

JULY 28, 1969

- Infantrymen of the 2nd Brigade, 25th Infantry Division, engaged an unknown size enemy force four miles NE of Trang Bang in Hau Nghia Province. US forces were supported by helicopter gunships and artillery. Enemy losses were 53 killed, three detained, and 33 weapons (five crew-served) captured. US losses were three killed and 14 wounded.

JULY 29, 1969

- CIDG elements engaged an enemy force 15 miles WSW of Duc Hoa in Hau Nghia Province, and were reinforced by elements of the 3rd Brigade, 25th Infantry Division. Enemy losses were 63 killed, and two weapons captured. Friendly losses were 10 killed, 12 wounded.

- The destroyer USS RENSHAW rescued five NVN fishermen from a sinking sampan in international waters 25 miles NE of Dong Hoi. They were taken to Da Nang pending disposition.

JULY 30, 1969

- President Nixon arrived in RVN.
- The destroyer USS MEREDITH rescued five more NVN fishermen from three rafts in international waters two miles north of Dong Hoi.

AUGUST 1, 1969

- A Ranger element from I FFV's Task Force South six miles NE of Song Cau in Binh Thuan Province engaged an enemy force and was reinforced by elements of the RVN 44th Infantry Regiment. Enemy losses were 24 killed.

AUGUST 2, 1969

- Helicopter gunships from an element of the US 4th Infantry Division engaged an unknown size enemy force 12 miles north of An Khe in Binh Dinh Province, killing 23 with aerial machine guns and rocket fire.

AUGUST 3, 1969

- Elements of the 3rd Brigade, 9th Infantry Division, engaged an unknown size enemy force in an exchange of small arms and automatic weapons fire 15 miles west of Duc Hoa in Hau Nghia Province. Helicopter gunships and artillery supported the action, and 39 enemy were killed. US casualties were two wounded and no fatalities.

AUGUST 4, 1969

- Helicopter crewmen of the US 4th Infantry Division directed gunships onto an unknown number of enemy 22 miles north of An Khe in Binh Dinh Province. They killed 24 enemy while suffering no casualties.

AUGUST 5, 1969

- The NVN released three prisoners of war (two sailors and one airman) to a representative of a US anti-war organization in Hanoi.
- An element of the 1st Brigade, US 25th Infantry Division, and an element of the Army of the RVN 2nd Airborne Battalion, in a combined sweep, engaged an unknown number of enemy 11 miles NE of Go Dau Ha in Tay Ninh Province, killing 35.

AUGUST 7, 1969

- A number of satchel charges apparently placed by enemy sappers who infiltrated the area over the beach were detonated within the confines of a US Army convalescent hospital at Cam Ranh. US casualties were two killed (both patients) and 98 wounded. One hospital ward was destroyed and three were heavily damaged.
- Suspected Viet Cong terrorists detonated an estimated 60-pound charge in a small automobile outside the USAF Language School in Saigon's 5th Precinct. The blast killed 12 people (nine VN civilians and three VN military) and wounded 67 (28 USAF). The school was heavily damaged and two nearby houses were destroyed.
- An element of the 1st Brigade, US 25th Infantry Division (Mech) engaged an estimated NVA company four miles WSW of Con Thien in Quang Tri Province, and was supported by helicopter gunships and artillery. Fifty-six enemy were killed, and 26 weapons (three crew-served) were captured. US casualties were three killed and 13 wounded.

AUGUST 8, 1969

- An air cavalry element of the 11th Armored Cavalry Regiment attacked an unknown size enemy force with aerial machine guns and rocket fire nine miles west of An Loc in Binh Long Province, killing 38 NVA. There were no US casualties. Ten miles to the north, helicopter gunships of the US 1st Cavalry Division attacked an estimated nine enemy soldiers and were supported by artillery and tactical aircraft. Another 25 enemy were killed. Again, no US casualties.

AUGUST 9, 1969

- The Department of the Army announced plans for the immediate inactivation of the 9th Infantry Division. The 3rd Brigade, the only brigade of the 9th Infantry Division remaining in the RVN, was to be redesignated.

AUGUST 9-10, 1969

- An element of the 3rd Regiment, 3rd Marine Division, six miles NNW of the Rockpile, received two ground probes by an unknown size enemy force. Thirty-seven enemy were killed, and US casualties were 19 killed, 80 wounded. In action over the past two days in this area, elements of the 9th Regiment, 304th North Vietnam Army Division, had been identified. This marked the first appearance of the regiment in the RVN since the battle of Khe Sanh, which ended in April 1969.

AUGUST 10, 1969

- Helicopter gunships of the 11th Armored Cavalry Regiment engaged an estimated enemy company nine miles NW of An Loc in Binh Long Province, and two miles east of the Cambodian border. Air cavalry troopers from the regiment were air-assaulted into the area, and they were later joined by elements of the air cavalry squadron, 1st Cavalry Division (Airmobile), and troopers from the ARVN 9th Regiment, 5th Infantry Division. Thirty-one enemy were killed, four suspects were detained and four enemy rallied to the GVN. US casualties were five wounded. There were no ARVN casualties.

AUGUST 12, 1969

- Enemy initiated activity increased sharply throughout the RVN. There were 149 attacks by fire recorded throughout the country, of which, 68 were considered significant.
- Elements of the 7th Regiment, 1st Marine Division, engaged an unknown size enemy force four miles NW of An Hoa in Quang Nam Province. A short distance to the east, another element of the same unit engaged an unknown number of enemy. Enemy losses were 169 killed, four suspects detained, and 39 individual

and 13 crew-served weapons captured. Friendly losses were 15 killed and 101 wounded.

- An element of the 11th Armored Cavalry Regiment and an element of the 5th ARVN Infantry Division, in night defense at an LZ four miles WSW of An Loc in Binh Long Province, were attacked by an unknown size enemy force. Seventy-seven of the enemy were killed and two were detained. US casualties were two killed and two wounded.
- A mechanized infantry element of the 3rd Brigade, 1st Infantry Division, providing security to a convoy on Highway 13 enroute from Di An in Bien Hoa Province to Quan Loi in Binh Long Province was attacked by an unknown size enemy force seven miles south of An Loc. Sixty-one of the enemy were killed, two were detained and 12 weapons (three crew-served) were captured. Friendly losses were two killed and two wounded.
- An element of the 1st Brigade, 1st Cavalry Division, in night defense seven miles SE of Katum in Tay Ninh Province, was attacked by an unknown size enemy force. Enemy losses were 59 killed and four crew-served weapons captured. Friendly losses were 13 killed and 39 wounded.
- An unknown size enemy force four miles SW of An Loc in Binh Long Province attacked an element of the 11th Armored Cavalry Regiment. Fifty-three of the enemy were killed. Friendly losses were one killed and three wounded.
- An unknown size enemy force attacked an element of the 196th Brigade, Americal Division 19 miles west of Tam KY. Fifty of the enemy were killed, two detained and five individual weapons were captured. US casualties were four wounded.
- The base camp of Headquarters, 3rd Brigade, 1st Cavalry Division (Airmobile), and elements of the 11th Armored Cavalry Regiment, four miles NE of An Loc in Binh Long Province was attacked by an unknown size NVA force. Forty-eight enemy were killed and seven were detained. US casualties were three killed and 23 wounded. The enemy was later identified as elements of the 271st and 272nd Regiments, 9th Viet Cong Division.

AUGUST 13, 1969

- An element of the 11th Armored Cavalry Regiment contacted and engaged an unknown size enemy force two miles SW of

Loc Ninh in Binh Long Province. Enemy losses were 79 killed, and 27 weapons captured. US losses were two killed and six wounded.

AUGUST 15, 1969

- An element of the 1st Brigade, 25th Infantry Division, and an element of the 25th ARVN Infantry Division, engaged an unknown number of enemy 15 miles west of Tay Ninh City. Thirty-one enemy were killed, and two crew-served weapons were captured. US casualties were one killed, one wounded. No ARVN casualties.

AUGUST 20, 1969

- Secretary of the Army Stanley H. Resor arrived in the RVN for an eight-day visit.
- Elements of the 9th Infantry Division engaged an estimated enemy company five miles N of Can Duoc in Long An Province, killing 35. US casualties were one killed and two wounded.
- An unknown size enemy force attacked elements of the 196th Brigade, Americal Division, 23 miles W of Tam Ky in Quang Nam Province. Artillery, gunships and tactical aircraft supported. Enemy losses were 103 killed. US casualties were two killed and 22 wounded.

AUGUST 24, 1969

- Elements of the 2nd Brigade, 25th Infantry Division, engaged an unknown size enemy force eight miles SW of Ben Cat in Binh Duong Province, killing 48, detaining one, and capturing 21 weapons. US losses were two killed and four wounded.

AUGUST 25, 1969

- The Mobile Riverine Force (MRF) was deactivated. Vietnam Navy Amphibious Task Force 211 will assume the mission and responsibilities of this force on September 1, 1969.
- An element of the 196th Brigade, Americal Division, engaged an unknown size enemy force 23 miles W of Tam Ky in Quang Tin Province, killing 74, and capturing 10 weapons. US casualties were one killed and 49 wounded.
- An ARVN element observed an enemy force of approximately 200 soldiers 17 miles W of Tam Ky in Quang Tin Province and

called for US artillery support. Fifty-two of the enemy were killed. There were no friendly casualties.

- An ARVN element found 100 enemy bodies (killed by air) 17 miles W of Tam Ky in Quang Tin Province.

AUGUST 26, 1969

- An unknown number of terrorists threw four hand grenades into a building in which a hamlet meeting between villagers and a RVN Rural Development cadre was being conducted, five miles NW of Phu Cat in Binh Dinh Province. Twenty-four VN civilians were killed, and 100 others were wounded. In terms of casualties, this was the worst single terrorist action of the year, and one of the worst recorded in the war.

AUGUST 27, 1969

- The number of Hoi Chanhs in 1969 surpassed the 30,000 mark.

AUGUST 28, 1969

- A 1st Marine Division reconnaissance team observed 50 to 60 enemy soldiers six miles ENE of An Hoa and directed tactical aircraft onto the location. Forty-eight enemy were killed.
- An estimated 400-pound, cylindrical water mine detonated near the civilian tanker KENIA (of Netherlands registry) while the ship was discharging cargo at the Nha Be fuel storage facility, seven miles SE of Saigon. The explosion caused heavy damage to the ship, but no casualties.

AUGUST 31, 1969

- US military strength in the RVN was 509,600.

SEPTEMBER 4, 1969

- Radio Hanoi announced the death of North Vietnam President Ho Chi Minh on September 3, 1969.
- The Viet Cong Liberation Radio announced that military forces would observe a three-day cease-fire in observance of

Ho Chi Minh's funeral. The cease-fire would commence at 0100 hours, September 8, 1969.

SEPTEMBER 5, 1969

- Mechanized infantry elements from the 11th Armored Cavalry Regiment engaged an estimated enemy company one mile NW of An Loc in Binh Long Province, killing 63 enemy. Friendly casualties were two killed and15 wounded.

SEPTEMBER 6, 1969

- Elements of the 11th Armored Cavalry Regiment engaged an unknown size enemy force three miles west of Loc Ninh in Binh Long Province, killing 70 of the enemy and detaining five. Friendly casualties were three killed and 31 wounded.
- A 1st Infantry Division convoy, escorted by an element of the 3rd Brigade, 25th Infantry Division and an element of the 2nd Brigade, 1st Infantry Division, was attacked by an unknown size enemy force 12 miles south of An Loc in Binh Long Province. Enemy losses were 55 killed, four detained, and 13 weapons (five crew-served) captured. Friendly losses were one killed and six wounded.

SEPTEMBER 11, 1969

- The Chi Lang ARVN Training Center, located six miles north of Tri Ton in Chau Doc Province, received an attack-by-fire and ground attack by an unknown size enemy force. Friendly forces were supported with artillery and AC-47 and helicopter gunships. Enemy losses were 83 killed, four detained, and four weapons captured. Friendly losses were four killed and 19 wounded.

SEPTEMBER 13, 1969

- A Combined Action Platoon and a Popular Forces unit in night defense 13 miles NW of Quang Ngai received an attack-by-fire followed by a ground attack from an estimated two enemy companies. An unknown number of enemy also attacked nearby An Thong village and three surrounding hamlets, destroying 260 houses. Enemy losses were 116 killed, one detained, and seven weapons captured. US losses were two killed, and three wounded. RVNAF were casualties light.

SEPTEMBER 15, 1969

- A I FFV Ranger element observed an enemy company with RPG launchers and AK-47 rifles 21 miles NNE of Phan Thiet in Binh Thuan Province. An element of the 101st Airborne Division (Airmobile) from Task Force South was air-assaulted into the area and gunships and ground forces engaged the enemy. Enemy losses were 58 killed. There were no US casualties.

SEPTEMBER 16, 1969

- President Nixon announced Phase II Redeployment of US Troops from the RVN. Redeployment was to begin immediately. Authorized troop ceiling would be 484,000, reduced from 524,500.

SEPTEMBER 20, 1969

- An Air Force F-4 aircraft of the 366th Tactical Fighter Wing collided in-air with an Air Vietnam DC-4 approximately two miles NW of Da Nang Air Base. The F-4 pilot landed safely at Da Nang after the navigator ejected safely. The DC-4 crashed one mile NW of the base, killing 75 persons aboard the plane, and two more on the ground.

SEPTEMBER 22, 1969

- The USMC announced that Marine tours in RVN would be reduced from 13 to 12 months.

SEPTEMBER 25, 1969

- ROKV marked four years of combat operations in RVN.

SEPTEMBER 30, 1969

- US Military strength in RVN was 510,500.

OCTOBER 6, 1969

- The Republic of the Philippines President Marcos announced in Manila that the PHILCAGV would "probably be withdrawn from RVN sometime after the Philippine national elections." The elections were scheduled for November 11. 1968.

OCTOBER 9, 1969

- DOD announced that US casualties reported in the past week (September 28-October 4, 1969) were the lowest in nearly three years. Casualties included 64 US killed.

OCTOBER 10, 1969

- USN turned over 80 PBRs to the VN Navy in ceremonies in Saigon. This turnover brought to 229 the number of USN craft turned over since June 1968.

OCTOBER 12, 1969

- An element of the 3rd Brigade, US 82nd Airborne Division, discovered a significant enemy weapons and munitions cache five miles SW of Ben Cat in Binh Duong Province. It contained 90 SKS rifles, 21 light machine guns, 12,500 rounds of small arms ammunition, 200 81mm mortar rounds and nine 60mm mortar rounds.

OCTOBER 15, 1969

- The SS KIN WAH, a 1,260-ton freighter of Panamanian registry, was mined and sunk by the enemy in Nha Trang harbor. The main ship channel was not blocked. Three crew members and two guests aboard were killed.

OCTOBER 18, 1969

- *Operation Sea Lords,* the USN offensive against enemy infiltration in III and IV CTZs marked the end of its first year of operations. Thus far, it has accounted for more than 2,000 enemy killed and more than 550 tons of enemy weapons and supplies captured.

OCTOBER 20, 1969

- Communist forces in I CTZ released Private First Class (PFC) Jesse P. Harris, Jr., of the 101st Airborne Division. PFC Harris was captured June 8, 1969.

OCTOBER 21, 1969

- The 10 NVN fishermen rescued in international waters off the DMZ in July 1968 were returned by sea to North Vietnam.
- A total of 1,310 Hoi Chanhs were reported for the week of October 12-18 1969.

OCTOBER 23, 1969

- US military strength in country dipped below 500,000 to 497,000.

OCTOBER 25, 1969

- DOD announced that US casualties during the week of October 19-25, 1969 resulted in 102 killed. This was the first time in four weeks that American losses exceeded 100 killed.

OCTOBER 26, 1969

- An element of the 3rd Brigade, US 1st Infantry Division, six miles NW of Ben Cat in Binh Duong Province, discovered an enemy cache containing 97 SKS rifles, 31 Soviet small arms, 13 machine guns, 114 rocket-grenades, and 174 57mm recoilless rifle rounds.

OCTOBER 28, 1969

- A Viet Cong terrorist threw a hand grenade into the market place in Hoa Hoi hamlet located two miles north of Phu Cat in Binh Dinh Province, killing eight VN civilians and wounding 47 others. Six suspects were detained, ages 11-14.

OCTOBER 31, 1969

- The GVN freed 88 Viet Cong prisoners of war and President Thieu ordered amnesty for 310 civilian prisoners. Among the civilian prisoners released was Thich Thien Minh, a prominent Buddhist monk.
- An element of the 3rd Brigade, 4th Infantry Division, was attacked by an estimated platoon 16 miles NW of Pleiku City. Enemy losses were 35 killed. Friendly casualties were two killed and 13 wounded.

OCTOBER 31, 1969

- US military strength in RVN was 495,200.

NOVEMBER 3, 1969

- An enemy force attacked LZ Buttons one mile SW of Phuoc Binh in Phu Yen Province. Troops of the 2nd Brigade, 1st Cavalry Division and support forces responded. Sixty-three of the enemy were killed.

NOVEMBER 4, 1969

- President Richard M. Nixon's major Vietnam policy address to the nation was heard live by forces in Vietnam.
- Enemy forces attacked four US positions in III CTZ. Enemy losses were 152 killed.

NOVEMBER 5, 1969

- The 377th Combat Support Company, an Army Reserve unit from Wisconsin, departed RVN to be deactivated at Ft. Riley, Kansas, and reconstituted in Manitowec, Wisconsin.
- Communist troops released three US Army prisoners. This brought to 27 the number of American military personnel released since February 1967.

NOVEMBER 5, 1969

- The Coastal Surveillance Center Qui Nhon in Binh Dinh Province was turned over to the Vietnam Navy in ceremonies conducted this date.

NOVEMBER 6, 1969

- The ARVN 15th Artillery Battalion took over the equipment of B Battery, 6th Battalion, 33rd Artillery, in I Corps.

NOVEMBER 7, 1969

- Major General W.K. Jones, Commanding General of the 3rd Marine Division departed the RVN as Headquarters, 3rd Marine Division redeployed to Okinawa in accordance with Phase II Redeployment.

NOVEMBER 8, 1969

- Governor George A. Wallace arrived in the RVN for a five-day fact-finding visit.

NOVEMBER 10, 1969

- The GVN announced that 1969's Hoi Chanh rate has passed the 40,000 mark.

NOVEMBER 12, 1969

- The first aircraft of a squadron of USAF AC-119K "Shadow" gunships arrived in Vietnam to begin replacement of the AC-47 "Spooky" gunships transferred to the GVN.

NOVEMBER 13, 1969

- The DOD announced that US killed during the week of November 2-8, 1969 were 97. This was the seventh reporting period during 1969 that US killed have been below 100.
- Attacks by elements of the NVA 27th Regiment against the 1st Brigade, US 5th Infantry Division (Mech) near the DMZ in Quang Tri Province over the past three days were repulsed. Enemy losses were 197 killed, two detained and 19 weapons (four crew-served) captured. US casualties were 14 killed and 52 wounded.

NOVEMBER 15 1969

- An unknown number of the enemy penetrated the perimeter of Camp Radcliff at An Khe in Binh Dinh Province and used satchel charges. Security personnel within the compound engaged the enemy. Friendly casualties were one killed and 11 wounded. Enemy losses were unknown.

NOVEMBER 16, 1969

- Deputy Secretary of Defense David Packard arrived in RVN for a five-day orientation visit.

NOVEMBER 20, 1969

- The last National Guard unit departed Vietnam as D Company, 151st Infantry (Ranger), Indiana National Guard departed.

NOVEMBER 20, 1969

- Elements of the 7th Regiment, 1st Marine Division, discovered an arms cache containing four CHICOM flamethrowers, one 12.7mm anti-aircraft artillery machine guns, six rifles, 40,000 rounds of small arms ammunition, 20 NVA uniforms and other miscellaneous munitions.

NOVEMBER 21, 1969

- Henry Cabot Lodge, Ambassador to the Paris Peace Talks, announced his resignation, effective December 8, 1969.

NOVEMBER 22, 1969

- A food cart, pushed to an area across the street from the Hong Kong Bachelor Officers Quarters (BOQ) in Cholon by a group of children explodes, causing minor window damage and slightly injuring a VN child. There were no US casualties. EOD personnel found 100 pounds of unexploded TNT and plastic explosives remaining in the cart.

NOVEMBER 23, 1969

- A Civil Rights Team, headed by L. Howard Bennett, Acting Deputy Assistant Secretary of Defense for Civil Rights, arrived in RVN for a seven-day routine visit.

NOVEMBER 24, 1969

- The Department of the Army announced it has ordered First Lieutenant William L. Calley, Jr., to be tried by General Court-Martial on charges of premeditated murder of 109 VN persons. The alleged killings took place during March 1968 in My Lai Village, Quang Ngai Province.

NOVEMBER 25, 1969

- Final units of the 3rd Marine Division redeployed to Okinawa, bringing to an end nearly five years of combat by the division in 120 major operations in RVN.

NOVEMBER 26, 1969

- The White House announced a decision for a 10 percent cut in American Direct Hire Personnel serving abroad. The approximately 1,500 Direct Hire DOD civilians in South Vietnam would be reduced by at least 10 percent by June 30, 1970.

DECEMBER 3, 1969

- An NVA battalion attacked Tuyen Binh District town, Kien Tuong Province. Regional Forces/Popular Forces defended with unit weapons and assistance from tactical air and helicopters from the 164th Combat Aviation Group. Enemy losses were 160 killed, one detained, 54 weapons (six crew-served) captured, as well as 300 hand grenades, and 200 pounds of TNT. Friendly casualties were light.

DECEMBER 4, 1969

- RVN President Nguyen Van Thieu announced that the RVN would observe a 24-hour suspension of combat actions on both Christmas and New Year's Day, from 1800, December 24 until 1800, December 25 and 1800, December 31, 1969 to 1800, January 1, 1970.

DECEMBER 6, 1969

- CIDG and 1st Cavalry Division (Airmobile) troops engage an unknown number of enemy in two actions 22 miles NE of Tay Ninh City. Enemy losses were 53 killed, 21 weapons captured (two crew-served). Friendly losses were one killed, four wounded.

DECEMBER 9, 1969

- The USCGC POINT ELLIS was turned over to the Vietnam Navy at Cat Lo. This was the sixth US Coast Guard craft to be turned over to RVN.

DECEMBER 10, 1969

- Two Army aviators return to US control after being released as prisoners of war by the enemy. Warrant Officer Peterson and Sergeant Shepard were captured November 2, 1969 after their aircraft was shot down near Bu Prang-Duc Lap.

DECEMBER 11, 1969

- Astronaut Colonel Frank Borman arrived in RVN for 10-day tour.

DECEMBER 12, 1969

- PHILCAGV turned over their base to the 1st Cavalry Division as they prepared to redeploy to the Philippines.

DECEMBER 15, 1969

- President Nixon announced that the Phase III Redeployment would be a reduction of 50,000 in the authorized strength, to be completed by April 15, 1970. This would reduce the authorized grade ceiling to 434,000.
- Elements of the ARVN 5th Infantry Division and the US 11th Armored Cavalry Regiment engaged an estimated enemy company four kilometers SE of Bu Dop in Phuoc Long Province, killing 51 enemy, and capturing 22 weapons (seven crew-served). US casualties were four killed, 18 wounded. ARVN casualties were light.

DECEMBER 16, 1969

- Prime Minister John Gorton of Australia announced that there would be a withdrawal of an unspecified number of Australian troops, which would coincide with US troop redeployment.

DECEMBER 19, 1969

- Less than five 122mm rockets impacted on Tan Son Nhut Air Base in Saigon resulting in light casualties.

DECEMBER 20, 1969

- The Vietnam Navy shipyard launched the first ferro-cement PCF (Swiftboat).

DECEMBER 24, 1969

- US, RVNAF and other FWMAF allies suspended combat operations at 1800 hours for a period of 24 hours.

DECEMBER 26, 1969

- The Allied Command announced 115 enemy-initiated incidents during the 24-hour Christmas period. Enemy losses were 101 killed, 13 detained, and 34 individual weapons captured. US casualties were three wounded.

DECEMBER 27, 1969

- Helicopter gunships of the 11th Armored Cavalry Regiment engaged an estimated two companies of NVA troops and were supported in the action by Regional Forces troops and tactical aircraft. The action, which took place nine miles NW of Loc Ninh in Binh Long Province, saw 79 enemy killed and 40 bunkers destroyed.

DECEMBER 28, 1969

- Lieutenant General William R. Peers arrived in Saigon for a 10-day visit in connection with the investigation of an alleged incident involving the shooting of civilians at My Lai hamlet during March 1968.

DECEMBER 31, 1969

- At 1800 hours, the Allies commence a 24-hour suspension of combat operations.
- At the close of the year, US personnel killed since January 1, 1961, exceeded 40,000. During 1969, US casualties included 9,414 killed and 70,216 wounded (32,940 of these requiring hospitalization). Enemy losses during the year were 156,954.
- US troop strength at year's end stood at 474,400.

JANUARY 1, 1970

- US, RVN and other FWF suspended combat operations from 1800 hours, December 31, 1969, to 1800 hours, January 1, 1970. During the period, 115 enemy initiated incidents were reported by all forces, of which, 61 were considered significant (those incidents in which casualties occurred). As a result of the significant incidents, US casualties were nine killed and 16 wounded. RVN casualties were light. There were light Free World casualties reported. Enemy losses were 167 killed and three detained. In addition, 64 enemy individual and five crew-served weapons were captured.

JANUARY 2, 1970

- Quang Nam Province. At 1910 hours, an element of the 7th

Regiment, 1st Marine Division, eight miles SE of An Hoa, observed 25 enemy soldiers and directed artillery fire onto them, killing 20. There were no US casualties.

- *Toan Thang Offensive* (Tay Ninh Province). At 1950 hours, a patrol from an element of the 1st Brigade, 25th Infantry Division, engaged an estimated 50-70 enemy soldiers six miles NW of Go Dau Ha and two miles from the Cambodian border. The infantrymen used unit weapons and were supported by helicopter gunships and artillery. The enemy returned fire with small arms and automatic weapons. Fighting continued for about five hours when the enemy withdrew leaving 17 of his dead. There were no US casualties.

JANUARY 3, 1970

- *Operation Iron Mountain* (Quang Ngai Province). At 2330 hours last night, an element of the 11th Brigade, 23rd Infantry Division (Americal) in night defensive position five miles south of Duc Pho received about 60 rounds of mixed 60mm and 82mm mortar fire along with heavy small arms and automatic weapons fire from an unknown size enemy force. The infantrymen returned fire with unit weapons and were supported by helicopter gunships and artillery. At 0350 hours, the enemy withdrew without penetrating the perimeter. The bodies of 29 enemy soldiers were found in the battle area and nine individual weapons were captured. US casualties were seven killed and 12 wounded.
- Quang Tri Province. At 1240 hours, helicopter gunships from the air cavalry squadron of the 101st Airborne Division (Airmobile), received heavy automatic weapons fire 11 miles SSE of Khe Sanh and one mile from the Laotian border. The crewmen observed 50-80 North Vietnam Army soldiers and engaged them with aerial machine guns and rockets. At 1700 hours, the enemy withdrew, leaving 19 of his dead. There were no US casualties.

JANUARY 4, 1970

- *Toan Thang Offensive* (Tay Ninh Province). At 2250 hours January 3, 1970, an element of the 3rd Brigade, 25th Infantry Division, engaged an unknown number of enemy soldiers four miles SW of Go Dau Ha and 2½ miles from the Cambodian border. The infantrymen used unit weapons and the enemy fired back with small arms and automatic weapons. US Army helicopter gunships, artillery, and a USAF AC-119 gunship from the 14th Special Operations Wing supported the troops in contact. The bodies of five enemy soldiers were found and four individual weapons were captured. There were no US casualties.

- *Toan Thang Offensive* (Tay Ninh Province). At 1410 hours, an element of the 1st Brigade, 1st Cavalry Division (Airmobile), engaged an unknown size enemy force seven miles SE of Katum and eight miles from the Cambodian border. Small arms and automatic weapons fire was exchanged and the enemy used rocket-grenades. US Army artillery and helicopter gunships supported the troops in contact. The enemy withdrew half an hour later with unknown losses while US casualties were one killed and four wounded.

JANUARY 6, 1970

- *Operation Frederick Hill* (Quang Tin Province). At 1200 hours, elements of the armored cavalry squadron of the 23rd Infantry Division (Americal) and ARVN Regional Forces troops engaged an unknown size enemy force four miles west of Tam Ky. Heavy small arms and automatic weapons fire was exchanged and the combined ground force was supported by helicopter gunships and artillery in addition to the heavy weapons on their tanks and armored personnel carriers. At 1215 hours, a US Army UH-1 helicopter was hit by enemy ground fire and crashed in the vicinity. There were no casualties but the aircraft was destroyed. At 1230 hours, another AH-1 helicopter was hit by enemy ground fire and crashed. The aircraft was destroyed and there were no casualties. As fighting continued, at about 1600 hours, another AH-1 helicopter gunship was hit by enemy machine gun fire and crashed. There were no casualties. At 1825 hours, the enemy withdrew. The bodies of 45 enemy soldiers were found and two individual weapons were captured. US casualties were 18 wounded with no fatalities. There were no Regional Forces or Popular Forces casualties reported.
- Quang Nam Province. At 0200 hours, an element of the 7th Regiment, 1st Marine Division, in night position 10 miles SE of An Hoa, received about 75 rounds of 82mm mortar

fire, followed by an attack from an unknown size enemy force firing small arms and automatic weapons. The Marines fired back with unit weapons and were supported by artillery fire. At an unreported time, the enemy withdrew leaving 38 dead. In addition, 11 individual weapons, five rocket-grenade launchers, 30 satchel charges, 216 CHICOM grenades, and four bangalore torpedoes were captured. US casualties were 13 killed and 63 wounded.

- *Toan Thang Offensive* (Tay Ninh Province). At 0820 hours, elements of the 1st Brigade, 1st Cavalry Division (Airmobile), engaged an unknown size enemy force while operating 20 miles NE of Tay Ninh City and eight miles from the Cambodian border. Heavy small arms and automatic weapons fire was exchanged and the troopers were supported by helicopter gunships, artillery and USAF aircraft from the 3rd and 35th TFWs. Fighting continued until 1615 hours when the enemy withdrew. The bodies of 87 enemy were found in the area and 29 individual and seven crew-served weapons were captured. US casualties were one killed and six wounded.
- Bien Hoa. At 1045 hours, a US Army 2½ ton truck and a Royal Thai Army five-ton truck collided while traveling on Highway 15, seven miles SE of Bien Hoa City. The US truck was carrying VN civilian workers. Fourteen VN civilians were killed and eight injured. Three US personnel were also injured. No Thai injuries were reported.

JANUARY 7, 1970

- *Operation Frederick Hill* (Quang Tin Province). At 0830 hours, armored cavalry troops and infantrymen from the 196th Brigade, 23rd Infantry Division (Americal) received small arms, automatic weapons and rocket-grenade fire from an unknown size enemy force 12 miles NW of Tam Ky. The troopers fired back with unit weapons including the tank guns and heavy machine guns on their armored personnel carriers, and were supported by helicopter gunships and artillery. At 1500 hours, the enemy withdrew, leaving 39 of his dead. Also, 16 individual weapons and seven crew-served weapons were captured. US casualties were five killed and 16 wounded.

JANUARY 8, 1970

- *Toan Thang Offensive* (Tay Ninh Province). At 0750 hours, an infantry element of the 1st Brigade, 25th Infantry Division, reinforced with tanks from the division's armored battalion, engaged an unknown size enemy force seven miles NE of Tay Ninh City. Fighting continued until 1830 hours when the enemy withdrew under cover of darkness. The bodies of 62 enemy soldiers were found in the battle area. Two individual weapons were captured. US casualties were two killed and six wounded.

JANUARY 9, 1970

- Quang Nam Province. At 1500 hours, an element of the 7th Regiment, 1st Marine Division, eight miles east of An Hoa, observed 20 enemy in uniform moving west. The enemy moved into two caves and were kept there overnight by organic weapons fire and artillery. At first light, the Marines assaulted the cave. Fifteen enemy were killed. US casualties were two wounded with no fatalities.
- Quang Nam Province. At 2345 hours, an element of the 1st Regiment, 1st Marine Division, while moving to an ambush post 11 miles west of Hoi An, received small arms fire and grenades from an estimated 15 enemy soldiers. The Marines fired back with unit weapons. Twelve enemy were killed and four more were detained. In addition, four individual weapons were captured. US casualties were two wounded and no fatalities
- Pleiku Province. At noon, an element of the 3rd Brigade, 4th Infantry Division, 17 miles SW of Pleiku, found 30 storage huts containing two tons of rice. It was evacuated to Thanh An District.
- *Toan Thang Offensive* (Tay Ninh Province). At 1000 hours, elements of the 1st Brigade, 25th Infantry Division, received small arms and automatic weapons fire from an unknown size enemy force seven miles NNE of Tay Ninh City. The infantrymen returned fire with unit weapons and were supported by artillery, helicopter gunships and USAF tactical

air strikes. The enemy left 47 of his dead while US casualties were four wounded.

JANUARY 10, 1970

- *Toan Thang Offensive* (Tay Ninh Province). At 1115 hours, an element of the 1st Brigade, 1st Cavalry Division (Airmobile), and RVN CIDG personnel received small arms, automatic weapons and rocket-grenade fire from an unknown size enemy force 10 miles SE of Katum and nine miles from the Cambodian border. The enemy were occupying bunkers and the combined ground troops returned fire with unit weapons and were supported by helicopter gunships, artillery and USAF A-37 and F-100 aircraft. In about 15 minutes, the enemy withdrew, leaving 41 dead. US casualties were three wounded. Later in the same day, at 1740 hours, the same units again received small arms and automatic weapons fire in an area 800 meters to the south of the earlier contact. At 1815 hours, the enemy withdrew, leaving 21 dead and one destroyed crew-served weapon. CIDG casualties were light with no fatalities and there were no US casualties.

JANUARY 11, 1970

- *Toan Thang Offensive* (Tay Ninh Province). At 1310 hours, an element of the 1st Brigade, 1st Cavalry Division (Airmobile), received small arms and automatic weapons fire from an unknown size enemy force 12 miles SE of Katum and eight miles from the Cambodian border. The troopers fired back with unit weapons and were supported by helicopter gunships, artillery and tactical air strikes. At 1325 hours, the enemy withdrew, leaving behind 15 of his dead and two destroyed machine guns. There were no US casualties.

JANUARY 12, 1970

- *Toan Thang Offensive* (Long An Province). At 0830 hours, US Army helicopter crewmen from the 12th Combat Aviation Group observed an unknown number of enemy soldiers five miles SE of Tan An. The enemy were engaged with aerial machine guns and Rangers from the 3rd Brigade, US 9th Infantry Division, on board the helicopters, were air-assaulted into the vicinity and engaged the enemy. Small arms and automatic weapons fire was exchanged and the enemy fired a claymore-type mine. At 1245 hours, an OH-6 light observation helicopter was hit by enemy ground fire while support in the action and crashed. The aircraft was destroyed and one crewman was wounded. Helicopter gunships supported the Rangers until contact was lost at 1325 hours. The bodies of 26 enemy soldiers were found in the battle area, and one individual weapon was captured. US casualties were one killed and seven wounded (including the helicopter crewmen).

- *Toan Thang Offensive* (Hau Nghia Province). At 1010 hours, infantrymen from an element of the 3rd Brigade, US 25th Infantry Division, discovered an enemy munitions cache 10 miles WSW of Cu Chi and 10 miles from the Cambodian border. It contained 75 CHICOM bangalore torpedoes, 13 CHICOM hand grenades and 84 RPGs. The items weighed about 1,200 pounds.

JANUARY 13, 1970

- Quang Nam Province. At 1540 hours, Marines from an element of the 5th Regiment, 1st Marine Division, observed 10-20 NVN soldiers with weapons three miles NW of An Hoa. A helicopter gunship crew in the vicinity engaged the enemy with aerial machine guns and the bodies of 10 enemy soldiers were observed in the area. There were no US casualties.

JANUARY 14, 1970

- *Toan Thang Offensive* (Tay Ninh Province). At 0730 hours, an element of the 1st Brigade, US 1st Infantry Division, engaged an unknown number of enemy soldiers 11 miles NNE of Dau Tieng near the Binh Long-Binh Duong province border. The enemy were engaged with artillery fire and a short while later the infantrymen searched the strike area and engaged two enemy soldiers with small arms fire. The bodies of six enemy were found. There were no US casualties.
- An Xuyen Province. At 1500 hours, helicopter gunship crewmen observed three sampans attempting to evade in an area 21 miles NW of Ca Mau at the southern edge of the U

Minh Forest. The helicopters received small arms fire from an unknown number of enemy in the sampans. The sampans were engaged with aerial machine guns. Enemy automatic weapons fire continued and naval gunfire from the USCGC DALLAS was directed onto the enemy location. In addition, USN OV-10 aircraft and USAF tactical aircraft struck the enemy position. At 1840 hours, contact was lost. The bodies of 13 enemy soldiers were sighted in the area. In addition, eight sampans and 24 structures were reported destroyed or damaged. There were no US casualties.

JANUARY 15, 1970

- *Toan Thang Offensive* (Tay Ninh Province). At 0145 hours, a fire support base 24 miles north of Tay Ninh City and five miles from the Cambodian border, occupied by ARVN airborne troops and an element of the US 11th Armored Cavalry Regiment, received approximately 100 rounds of 82mm or 60mm mortar five, followed by a ground attack by an estimated enemy company firing small arms and automatic weapons. The combined airborne and armored cavalry troopers returned fire with unit weapons and were supported by US and ARVN artillery and helicopter gunships, in addition to the heavy weapons on their tanks and armored personnel carriers. During the fighting, an unknown number of enemy soldiers, using satchel charges, penetrated but were repulsed or killed. Fighting continued until 0300 hours when the enemy withdrew, leaving 19 dead. In addition, six AK-47 assault rifles, four RPG launchers were captured along with a small quantity of miscellaneous munitions. US casualties were one killed and seven wounded. ARVN casualties were light with no fatalities. There was no materiel damage.
- *Toan Thang Offensive* (Tay Ninh Province). At 1810 hours, helicopter gunships from the air cavalry squadron of the 1st Cavalry Division (Airmobile) engaged an estimated 15-20 enemy soldiers with unit weapons 27 miles north of Tay Ninh City and three miles from the Cambodian border. The enemy returned fire with small arms. The action was supported by tactical air and artillery. In about 10 minutes, the

enemy withdrew, leaving nine of his dead. There were no US casualties.

JANUARY 16, 1970

- Quang Ngai Province. At 0030 hours, an estimated 30 enemy soldiers attacked the Chau Thuan hamlet on the Batangan Peninsula nine miles NE of Quang Ngai City. The enemy employed small arms and automatic weapons along with 40 rounds of mixed rocket-grenades and 82mm mortars. The hamlet was defended by infantrymen from the 198th Brigade, 23rd Infantry Division (Americal), a US Marine and RVN Popular Forces Combined Action Platoon (command post), Popular Forces and PSDF. The friendly forces returned fire with unit weapons and were supported by helicopter gunships and artillery. During the fighting, an unknown number of enemy entered part of the hamlet and fired into an unknown number of houses. At an unreported time, the enemy withdrew. Four enemy soldiers were killed and one pistol and one rocket-grenade were captured. US casualties were one killed and one wounded. Fourteen VN civilians were killed and 19 others were wounded. Twenty homes were reported 80% destroyed. Popular Forces casualties were light. All friendly casualties and damage were reported to be the result of the enemy fire, and no friendly supporting fires impacted in the village.

JANUARY 17, 1970

- *Toan Thang Offensive* (Phuoc Long Province). At 1800 hours, an element of the 2nd Brigade, 1st Cavalry Division (Airmobile), discovered the bodies of 24 enemy soldiers killed during the night in two ambushes 25 miles ENE of Song Be near the II-III Corps border. In addition, one CHICOM machine gun and six individual weapons were captured. There were no US casualties.

JANUARY 18, 1970

- Thua Thien Province. On December 24, 1969, a US Marine and Popular Forces combined action platoon entered a village and exhumed the bodies of two US Army servicemen who had been killed. Information from inhabitants in the area notified the Marines a few days earlier, that there were two US and three

VN soldiers buried nearby. They had been captured after the action on August 13, 1966, and later shot to death by their Viet Cong captors. The US servicemen were First Lieutenant David R. Devers and Sergeant First Class John H. O'Neill, both members of MACV Advisory Team #3, with the ARVN 1st Infantry Division. Reports from residents in the area stated the Viet Cong took the US prisoners from village to village for several days, putting them on display before executing them. Lieutenant Devers and Sergeant First Class O'Neill were promoted while in a missing status to Captain and Master Sergeant respectively.

JANUARY 19, 1970

- *Toan Thang Offensive* (Binh Duong Province). At 1415 hours, a mechanized infantry element of the 1st Brigade, 1st Infantry Division, discovered a significant enemy munitions cache weighing about two tons nine miles east of Lai Khe. The cache, in good condition, contained 51,750 rounds of 7.62mm ammunition, 1,350 rounds of 12.7mm heavy machine gun ammunition, 1,825 RPG rounds, 75 pounds of TNT, seventeen 60mm mortar rounds, 14 individual weapons, two 40-pound anti-tank mines, two light machine guns, and one 82mm complete mortar.
- *Toan Thang Offensive* (Tay Ninh Province). At 1120 hours, an element of the 3rd Brigade, US 25th Infantry Division, discovered a significant enemy munitions cache weighing about 1,500 pounds, while operating in an area 18 miles SSE of Tay Ninh City and three miles from the Cambodian border.

JANUARY 20, 1970

- *Toan Thang Offensive* (Phuoc Long Province). At 1230 hours, an OH-6 light observation helicopter was hit by enemy ground fire and crashed two miles south of Bo Duc and two miles from the Cambodian border. Elements of the 11th Armored Cavalry Regiment, in tanks and armored personnel carriers, moved to the area and engaged an unknown size enemy force at about 1530 hours. Heavy small arms and automatic weapons fire was exchanged and the troopers were supported by helicopter gunships, artillery, and USAF tactical aircraft. At 1645 hours, the enemy withdrew, leaving 27 of his dead. There were no US casualties in the ground action. One helicopter crewman was killed and one wounded. The aircraft was destroyed.

- *Toan Thang Offensive* (Tay Ninh Province). At 2350 hours, helicopter gunships from the 1st Cavalry Division (Airmobile), received ground fire from an unknown size enemy force 18 miles NE of Tay Ninh City. The area was illuminated with aerial searchlights and an estimated 30 enemy soldiers were observed. The enemy was engaged with machine gun fire and artillery was directed onto the location. At an unreported time, the enemy withdrew. The bodies of 20 enemy were sighted in the area. There were no US casualties.

JANUARY 21, 1970

- *Toan Thang Offensive* (Binh Long Province). At 0745 hours, an element of the 11th Armored Cavalry Regiment engaged an unknown number of enemy soldiers five miles NNE of Loc Ninh and three miles from the Cambodian border. The enemy returned fire with small arms, automatic weapons and rocket-grenade fire. As fighting continued, other elements of the Regiment and an element of the 2nd Brigade, 1st Cavalry Division (Airmobile), moved to the area and reinforced the troops in contact. The ground elements were supported by helicopter gunships, artillery, and USAF tactical aircraft, in addition to the heavy weapons on their tanks and armored personnel carriers. Action continued into the afternoon until 1600 hours when the enemy withdrew. The bodies of 35 enemy were found in the area. In addition, one 57mm recoilless rifle, one complete 60mm mortar, four rocket-grenade launchers, and seven AK-47 rifles, along with a small quantity of miscellaneous munitions, were captured. One 12.7mm heavy machine gun was destroyed. US casualties were one killed and nine wounded.

JANUARY 23, 1970

- Binh Dinh Province. At 0850 hours, an element of the 1st Brigade, US 4th Infantry Division, discovered a significant enemy weapons cache 18 miles north of An Khe. The cache contained four complete 60mm mortars, two 60mm mortar tubes, three 82mm mortar tubes with sights, two 82mm mortar base plates, one 57mm recoilless rifle, 10 RPG launchers, one light machine gun, one machine gun tripod, and three 82mm mortar rounds.

JANUARY 24, 1970

- *Toan Thang Offensive* (Tay Ninh Province). At 1420 hours, an element of the 1st Brigade, 25th Infantry Division, engaged an unknown number of enemy soldiers 16 miles west of Tay Ninh City and one mile from the Cambodian border. Small arms fire was exchanged and the infantrymen were supported by helicopter gunships and artillery. At 1520 hours, the enemy withdrew, leaving 22 of his dead in the area. There were no US casualties.

JANUARY 25, 1970

- *Toan Thang Offensive* (Phuoc Long Province). At 1230 hours, an element of the 2nd Brigade, 1st Cavalry Division (Airmobile), engaged an estimated enemy platoon nine miles east of Phuoc Binh. Small arms fire was exchanged, and the troopers were supported by artillery and helicopter gunships. At 1315 hours, the enemy withdrew. Ten enemy were killed. US casualties were two killed.

JANUARY 26, 1970

- Pleiku Province. At 1115 hours, a former enemy soldier who rallied to the GVN led infantrymen from the 3rd Brigade, 4th Infantry Division, to a munitions cache 14 miles WSW of Pleiku City and 20 miles from the Cambodian border. The cache contained 130 60mm mortar rounds, 124 RPG rounds, 218 hand grenades, 114 RPG boosters, 220 pounds of plastic-type explosive, 94 anti-tank grenades.
- *Toan Thang Offensive* (Tay Ninh Province). At 1150 hours, an element of the armored cavalry squadron of the 25th Infantry Division discovered a significant enemy weapons and munitions cache nine miles north of Go Dau Ha. The cache, weighing slightly more than four tons, contained the following items: 250,000 small arms rounds, twenty 122mm rockets, forty-three 107mm rockets, sixty-four individual weapons, four light machine guns, twenty-five RPGs, forty CHICOM hand grenades, seven 75mm recoilless rifle rounds, six 57mm

recoilless rifle rounds, five 82mm mortar rounds and four cases of TNT.

JANUARY 29, 1970

- *Operation Frederick Hill* (Quang Tri Province). At 1015 hours, an element of the 196th Brigade, 23rd Infantry Division (Americal), observed an estimated 45-50 enemy soldiers with packs and weapons 13 miles west of Tam Ky. Artillery fire was directed onto the location and the enemy was also engaged by helicopter gunships and tactical air strikes. At an unreported time, the enemy withdrew, leaving behind six of his dead, one individual weapon, nine backpacks, and 450 pounds of rice.

JANUARY 31, 1970

- Quang Nam Province. At 1000 hours, an OH-6 light observation helicopter received small arms fire from an unknown number of enemy soldiers eight miles SW of Da Nang. A short time later, an element of the 1st Regiment, 1st Marine Division, was air-assaulted into the vicinity and engaged an estimated 20 enemy soldiers. The Marines were supported by helicopter gunships and at an unreported time, the enemy withdrew. The bodies of 10 enemy were found in the area, and nine suspects were detained. In addition, seven individual weapons, 50 hand grenades and two satchel charges were captured. US casualties were two killed and 11 wounded.

FEBRUARY 1, 1970

- Quang Nam Province. At 1820 hours, a reconnaissance element of the 1st Marine Division sighted 70 enemy soldiers in green uniforms and carrying packs and weapons moving south on a trail four miles NE of An Hoa. Marine artillery fire was directed onto the location, killing 25 of the enemy. A short time later, another reconnaissance element of the Division sighted 50 enemy soldiers moving SW in an area four miles NNW of An Hoa. Marine artillery fire was directed onto the enemy location and the bodies of 15 enemy were observed. There were no US casualties in either action.
- *Operation Geneva Park* (Quang Ngai Province). At 0100 hours,

an element of the 198th Brigade, 23rd Infantry Division (Americal), in a night defensive position five miles NW of Quang Ngai City, received about 120 mixed 120mm and 82mm mortar, rocket-grenade and grenade rounds along with heavy small arms and automatic weapons fire from an unknown size enemy force. The infantrymen fired back with unit weapons and were supported by artillery and a USAF AC-119 gunship. At 0350 hours, the enemy withdrew, without having penetrated the perimeter. The bodies of 11 enemy soldiers were found in the battle area and one enemy soldier was detained. In addition, one individual and four crew-served weapons, 150 hand grenades, 16 bangalore torpedoes, and two satchel charges were captured. US casualties were two killed and 19 wounded. Popular Forces casualties were very light with no fatalities. Two VN civilians were killed and 11 wounded. The civilians were killed or wounded by fire from an unknown number of enemy who moved into a hamlet near the night defensive positions during the fighting.

- *Toan Thang Offensive* (Phuoc Long Province). At 1025 hours, a helicopter from the air cavalry squadron of the 1st Air Cavalry Division (Airmobile), received 12.7mm anti-aircraft fire from an unknown number of enemy soldiers four miles SW of Bu Dop and three miles from the Cambodian border. The enemy location was engaged with helicopter gunships and tactical aircraft. The bodies of eight enemy were later sighted in the area. Less than a mile to the NNW, and two miles from the Cambodian border, another helicopter from the squadron received small arms and automatic weapons fire from an unknown number of enemy soldiers at 1345 hours. Helicopter gunships and tactical aircraft engaged the enemy location. The bodies of 11 enemy were sighted in the area. There were no US casualties in either action.
- On January 25 and again on January 29, 1970 the US 25th Infantry Division at FSB KOTRC, Hau Nghia Province, RVN, came under enemy-initiated indirect fire attack originating from positions inside the Cambodian territory. In both instances, US forces operating in the area returned fire with artillery. The US Command has previously stated that if fired upon from enemy positions outside the RVN, US forces were

authorized to return fire. This was an inherent right of self-defense against enemy attacks.

FEBRUARY 2, 1970

- Quang Nam Province. At 1155 hours, a forward observer team from the 1st Marine Regiment, observed two enemy soldiers carrying a possible mortar tube into a tree line where an additional 30-40 enemy soldiers were observed, 10 miles NW of Hoi An. The enemy was engaged with artillery. The bodies of 13 enemy were sighted in the strike area. In addition, there was one secondary explosion and one bunker destroyed. There were no US casualties.

FEBRUARY 3, 1970

- *Toan Thang Offensive* (Phuoc Long Province). At 1305 hours, helicopter gunships from the air cavalry squadron of the 1st Air Division (Airmobile) engaged an unknown number of soldiers with unit weapons 12 miles north of Phuoc Binh and five miles from the Cambodian border. The enemy returned fire with small arms. OV-10's and USAF tactical aircraft supported the troopers. At 1830 hours, the enemy withdrew, leaving behind 33 of his dead. In addition, 40 bunkers were reported destroyed, and helicopter gunships that landed in the strike area recovered four packs. No US casualties.
- *Toan Thang Offensive* (Bien Hoa Province). At 1900 hours, helicopter gunships from the 3rd Brigade, 1st Infantry Division, engaged with unit weapons an estimated 100 enemy soldiers in four to five groups in a streambed eight miles north of Bien Hoa. The enemy returned fire with small arms and rocket-grenades. An aerial rifle platoon, also from the same brigade, was inserted into the area and was supported by flare ships and helicopter gunships. At 2015 hours, the enemy withdrew, leaving 23 of his dead in the area. No US casualties.
- *Toan Thang Offensive* (Tay Ninh Province). At 1230 hours, an element of the 1st Brigade, 1st Cavalry Division (Airmobile), while on a ground reconnaissance mission, engaged an unknown number of enemy soldiers six miles SE of Katum and three miles from the Cambodian border. Small arms fire was exchanged and the troopers were supported by helicopter gunships and artillery. At 1700 hours, the enemy withdrew. 19

enemy soldiers were killed and 11 individual weapons were captured. No US casualties.

FEBRUARY 4, 1970

- *Toan Thang Offensive* (Tay Ninh Province). At 0425 hours, an element of the 1st Brigade, 1st Cavalry Division (Airmobile), in night defense at a fire support base 25 miles NNE of Tay Ninh City (four miles from the Cambodian border) was attacked by an unknown size enemy force firing small arms, automatic weapons and rocket-grenades. The troops fired back with unit weapons and were supported by helicopter gunships and artillery. In about an hour, the enemy withdrew. In a search of the battle area at first light, the unit received small arms and automatic weapons fire from an estimated enemy company. Fighting continued throughout the morning until 1215 hours when contact was lost as the enemy again withdrew. The bodies of 44 enemy soldiers were found in the vicinity. In addition, 28 individual weapons, two crew-served weapons, 114 rocket-grenade rounds, 145 mortar rounds, 180 CHICOM grenades, 29 CHICOM claymore-type mines, 3,500 small arms rounds and 140 pounds of plastic-type explosives were captured. Three enemy 60mm mortars and two enemy individual weapons were destroyed. US casualties were four killed and three wounded.
- Binh Dinh Province. At 1900 hours, two US Army helicopter gunships reported receiving .50-caliber machine gun fire from an area six miles north of Qui Nhon. The fire was returned with aerial machine gun fire. On a second pass over the area, one helicopter reported receiving machine gun fire again and the fire was returned with unknown results. It was subsequently determined that Regional Forces troops were test firing a .50 caliber machine gun in the vicinity of a hamlet and that the helicopter gunship return fire impacted on the friendly troops and civilians. Seven VN civilians and one Regional Forces soldier were reported killed and 26 civilians and five Regional Forces soldiers were reported wounded. No aircraft were reported hit and there were no US casualties.

FEBRUARY 5, 1970

- Quang Nam Province. At 2045 hours, a suspected M-26 fragmentation grenade was detonated at the US Marine Force

Logistics Command Enlisted Club near Da Nang. As a result of the explosion, one Marine was killed and 62 were injured. Only one of the wounded was considered in serious condition. The incident was apparently not as a result of enemy action.

FEBRUARY 6, 1970

- US, RVN and FWF suspended combat operations in the RVN from 1800 hours, February 5, 1970, to 1800 hours, February 6, 1970. During that period, 118 enemy initiated incidents were reported by all forces, of which, 78 were considered significant (those incidents in which casualties occurred). As a result of the significant incidents, US casualties were three killed and 22 wounded. Enemy losses were 142 killed and 20 detained. In addition, one crew-served and 26 individual weapons were captured.

FEBRUARY 7, 1970

- *Toan Thang Offensive* (Tay Ninh Province). At 1650 hours, an element of the 11th Armored Cavalry Regiment and an element of the 1st Brigade, 1st Cavalry Division (Airmobile), received small arms, automatic weapons and rocket-grenade fire from an unknown size enemy force 28 miles NNE of Tay Ninh City and three miles from the Cambodian border. The enemy was occupying bunkers. The troopers returned fire with unit weapons and were supported by helicopter gunships and artillery in addition to the heavy weapons on their tanks and armored personnel carriers. Fighting continued until 1750 hours when the enemy withdrew, leaving behind 14 of his dead, one light machine gun and two individual weapons. US casualties were nine wounded, no fatalities.

FEBRUARY 8, 1970

- *Toan Thang Offensive* (Tay Ninh Province). At 0620 hours, elements of the 1st Brigade, 25th Infantry Division, reinforced with tanks from the division's armor battalion, engaged an unknown size enemy force 12 miles north of Tay Ninh City and 11 miles from the Cambodian border. Small arms and automatic weapons fire was exchanged and the enemy employed rocket-grenade fire. The troopers were supported by helicopter gunships and USAF F-100 aircraft, in addition to the heavy weapons on their armored vehicles. Fighting continued until 1620 hours when the enemy withdrew, leaving behind 14 of his dead and one crew-served and six individual weapons, as well as eight RPG rounds and five CHICOM hand grenades. Two enemy soldiers were detained. No US casualties.

FEBRUARY 10, 1970

- *Toan Thang Offensive* (Binh Duong Province). At 1830 hours, troopers from the armored cavalry squadron of the 1st Infantry Division engaged an unknown number of enemy five miles SE of Ben Cat. Small arms fire was exchanged. Helicopter gunships and another element of the squadron, in tanks and armored personnel carriers, reinforced the action. At 1845 hours, the enemy withdrew, leaving behind eight of his dead. There were no US casualties.

FEBRUARY 11, 1970

- Quang Nam Province. At 1415 hours, an air observer in support of the 5th Regiment, 1st Marine Division, observed 30 enemy soldiers carrying packs and weapons moving southeast in an area 17 miles west of Hoi An. US artillery and tactical aircraft were directed onto the enemy location. The bodies of 10 enemy soldiers were sighted in the area following the strike. No US casualties.
- An Army OH-6 light helicopter, operating near the Cambodian border, 22 miles NW of Moc Hoa I Kien Tuong Province, received anti-aircraft fire from Cambodia, exploded in mid-air, and crashed. The two crewmen were missing and presumed killed. Rescue aircraft were sent to the scene and they came under heavy fire originating from gun positions inside Cambodia. US aircraft returned fire with tactical air strikes.

FEBRUARY 13, 1970

- *Toan Thang Offensive* (Hau Nghia Province). At 1100 hours, a mechanized infantry element of the 3rd Brigade, 25th Infantry Division, discovered an enemy munitions cache four miles SW of Trang Bang and seven miles from the Cambodian border. The 700-pound cache contained the following: 84 RPGs, 50 RPG charges, 500 AK-47 small arms rounds, three CHICOM claymore-type mines, three 20-pound mines, 2,000 feet of electric detonating wire, two pair of wire cutters, five hand grenades rigged for booby traps. The items were in good condition.

FEBRUARY 14, 1970

- *Toan Thang Offensive* (Tay Ninh Province). At 1445 hours, elements of the 1st Brigade, 1st Cavalry Division (Airmobile), while reconnoitering the area 14 miles north of Tay Ninh City, received small arms and rocket-grenade fire from an unknown size enemy force. The troopers fired back with unit weapons and were supported by helicopter gunships and artillery. At 1515 hours, contact was lost. While the troopers were sweeping the contact area, they received 10 rounds of 60mm mortar fire and reestablished contact at 1615 hours with an unknown size enemy force. Small arms fire was exchanged. Contact was lost again at 1840 hours when the enemy withdrew. Forty-four enemy soldiers were killed. US casualties were 10 killed and 30 wounded. One tank and one reconnaissance vehicle were destroyed and one tank received moderate damage.

FEBRUARY 15, 1970

- *Operation Geneva Park* (Quang Tri Province). At 1110 hours and 1205 hours, an element of the 23rd Field Artillery Group, 23rd Infantry Division (Americal), observed an unknown size enemy force 10 miles NW of Quang Ngai. Both contacts were engaged by US artillery. The bodies of 16 enemy soldiers were sighted in the strike area. There were no US casualties.
- *Toan Thang Offensive* (Phuoc Long Province). At 1145 hours, an element of the 2nd Brigade, 1st Cavalry Division (Airmobile), found rice cache 10 miles NE of Duc Phong. The cache, which weighed 10 tons, was evacuated to the battalion headquarters.

FEBRUARY 16, 1970

- Quang Nam Province. At 1635 hours, a forward observer with the 26th Regiment, 1st Marine Division, observed 40 enemy soldiers moving east in an area nine miles SW of Da Nang. The enemy were engaged with US Marine artillery. The bodies of 16 enemy soldiers were sighted in the area. There were no US casualties.

FEBRUARY 17, 1970

- *Toan Thang Offensive* (Phuoc Long Province). At 1135 hours, helicopters from the 2nd Brigade, 1st Cavalry Division (Airmobile), received ground fire from an unknown number of enemy soldiers 12 miles NNE of Phuoc Binh and five miles from the Cambodian border. The crewmen returned fire with unit aerial machine guns and, following the first contact, the helicopter again received enemy ground fire into the early afternoon from an unknown number of enemy at five different locations in the same general area. The enemy fire was returned with unit weapons and contact was lost at 1430 hours. The bodies of 45 enemy soldiers were observed in the area following the action. There were no US casualties.

FEBRUARY 18, 1970

- *Operation Iron Mountain* (Quang Ngai Province). At 2030 hours, a forward observer from an artillery element of the 23rd Infantry Division (Americal) sighted an unknown size enemy force in an area 11 miles west of Quang Ngai City. Artillery fire was directed onto the enemy location and the bodies of 21 enemy soldiers were observed lying in the strike area. There were no US casualties.
- Binh Dinh Province. At 1400 hours, an element of the 1st Brigade, 4th Infantry Division, discovered an enemy food cache in a jungle area 35 miles north of An Khe. The cache contained two tons of rice. At 1800 hours, another element of the brigade discovered another significant cache about one mile to the southeast. The cache contained 24 tons of rice, one ton of salt, 1,800 pounds of tobacco, 200 chickens and 15 pigs.

FEBRUARY 19, 1970

- *Toan Thang Offensive* (Long Khanh Province). At 1100 hours, an element of the 199th Light Infantry Brigade discovered a significant enemy weapons and munitions cache 30 miles NW of Xuan Loc. It contained 52 rifles, seven light machine guns, thirty-eight 81mm mortar rounds, twenty-five 57mm recoilless rifle rounds, and 10,000 small arms rounds.

FEBRUARY 20, 1970

- *Operation Frederick Hill* (Quang Tin Province). At 1500 hours, an armored cavalry element of the 196th Brigade, 23rd Infantry Division (Americal) received heavy small arms and automatic weapons fire, along with rocket-grenades, from an unknown size enemy force 12 miles NW of Tam Ky. The troopers returned fire with unit weapons, including tank guns and heavy machine guns, and were supported by artillery and helicopter gunships. As the fighting continued, an infantry element of the brigade was air-assaulted into the vicinity to reinforce the troops in contact. During the action, the enemy also used about 10 rounds of 60mm mortar fire. A USAF AC-119 gunship later reinforced the ground elements. At 1950 hours, the enemy withdrew, leaving behind five of his dead, three individual weapons and a small quantity of ammunition. US casualties were 14 killed and 29 wounded. There was light materiel damage.
- *Toan Thang Offensive* (Tay Ninh Province). At 1930 hours, an element of the 1st Brigade, 25th Infantry Division, engaged an unknown number of enemy soldiers 27 miles NNW of Tay Ninh City and two miles from the Cambodian border. The enemy returned fire with small arms and automatic weapons along with mortar and rocket-grenade fire. The infantrymen were supported by helicopter gunships and USAF AC-119 gunships. At 2050 hours, the enemy withdrew with unknown losses. US casualties were two killed and 13 wounded.

FEBRUARY 22, 1970

- *Operation Frederick Hill* (Quang Tin Province). At 0905 hours, an element of the 196th Brigade, 23rd Infantry Division (Americal), reinforced by troopers from the division's armored cavalry squadron, received small arms, automatic weapons, and rocket-grenade fire from an known size enemy force 14 miles NW of Tam Ky. The troopers fired back with unit weapons including the heavy weapons on their tanks and armored personnel carriers, and were supported by helicopter gunships and artillery. Sporadic fighting continued throughout the day until 1850 hours when the enemy withdrew under cover of darkness. The bodies of 23 enemy soldiers were found in the battle area and one crew-served and 12 individual weapons were captured. US casualties were two killed and six wounded.

- *Toan Thang Offensive* (Phuoc Long Province). At 1730 hours, an element of the 1st Cavalry Division (Airmobile) discovered an enemy weapons cache while operating in an area 37 miles south of Phuoc Binh. The cache contained the following: five SKS rifles, nine sub-machine guns, four light machine guns, two heavy machine guns, one 57mm recoilless rifle, 100 82mm mortar rounds, five 120mm mortar rounds, three 60mm mortar rounds, twenty-five 57mm recoilless rifle rounds, 15 CHICOM hand grenades, and 10,000 small arms rounds. The items were in poor condition.

FEBRUARY 23, 1970

- Quang Nam Province. At 1000 hours, a reconnaissance element of the 1st Marine Division found an enemy base camp nine miles SW of An Hoa. The camp contained 12 huts with a tunnel located in each. The tunnels contained 1,500 pounds of unpolished rice, 1,100 pounds of wheat, and 1,000 pounds of corn. Air strikes were called in on the camp, destroying the food and the huts.
- Binh Dinh Province. At 1313 hours, an element of the 2nd Brigade, 4th Infantry Division, found an ammunition cache weighing approximately seven tons in an area 19 miles NNE of An Khe. The cache contained the following: 26 122mm rocket rounds, 116 82mm mortar rounds, 24,300 small arms rounds, 51 B-40 and B-41 rocket rounds, 5,000 feet of detonator cord, 5,000 blasting caps, 250 pounds of TNT, four anti-tank mines and 4,000 blocks of C-4 explosives.

FEBRUARY 24, 1970

- Binh Dinh Province. At 1045 hours, an element of the 2nd Brigade, 4th Infantry Division, found an ammunition cache weighing approximately four tons in an area 19 miles NNE of An Khe. It contained the following: 224 82mm mortar rounds, 134 B-41 rockets, 17 75mm recoilless rifle rounds, 80,000 small arms rounds, 24 60mm mortar rounds, 11,000 blasting caps, 250 pounds of TNT and 1,500 feet of detonator cord.

- Binh Dinh Province. At 0730 hours, another element of the 2nd Brigade, 4th Infantry Division, found two rice caches containing a total of 7½ tons of rice and 500 pounds of potatoes 19 miles west of Bong Song. The rice was evacuated to battalion headquarters.

FEBRUARY 26, 1970

- It was announced that there would be a ceremony held at the Southwest Cantonment Vung Tau Sub Area Command at 1630 hours, February 27, 1970. At this ceremony, approximately 160 buildings would be turned over to the 3rd Vietnam Army Logistical Battalion, which were to be used by the RVNAF Signal School.

FEBRUARY 27, 1970

- Quang Nam Province. At 1635 hours, a forward observer from the 26th Regiment, 1st Marine Division, observed 50-60 enemy soldiers wearing uniforms and carrying packs and weapons 11 miles WSW of Da Nang. The enemy were engaged with artillery and the bodies of 21 enemy soldiers were later sighted in the strike area. There were no US casualties.
- Saigon. A suspected Viet Cong terrorist placed an estimated 10-pound charge of plastic-type explosive near a wall at the Metropolis Bachelor Enlisted Quarters (BEQ) on Tran Hung Dao Street, one mile SSE of the center of Saigon. The charge detonated, resulting in minor damage to the building, two US personnel and two VN civilians were slightly wounded. The terrorist escaped.
- A formal investigation has been ordered into the circumstances surrounding of the deaths of 16 VN civilians on February 19, 1970 in a village in the Que Son District 27½ miles south of Da Nang. The charges, alleging violation of Article 118, UCMJ, have been preferred against five Marines, members of the combat patrol operating in the area where the bodies were found. Although under the administration of the local refugee village, this area has been known to be visited by enemy forces operating throughout the district. This location has also been

the scene of almost continuous sniper fire and booby trap casualties since Marines commenced operations there.

FEBRUARY 28, 1970

- Binh Dinh Province. At 0850 hours, an element of the 7th Regiment, 4th Infantry Division, discovered an enemy munitions cache 16 miles NE of An Khe. The cache, weighing about two tons, contained the following: 117 82mm mortar rounds, 26 60mm mortar rounds, 26 75mm recoilless rifle rounds and 8,455 small arms rounds.

MARCH 1, 1970

- *Toan Thang Offensive* (Tay Ninh Province). At 1035 hours, an element of the 1st Cavalry Division (Airmobile), found a significant enemy rice cache 32 miles north of Tay Ninh City and one mile from the Cambodian border. The cache weighed about 60 tons. It was evacuated for distribution.

MARCH 2, 1970

- *Toan Thang Offensive* (Binh Long Province). At 1245 hours, an element of the 11th Armored Cavalry Regiment engaged an undetermined size enemy force two miles west of Loc Ninh and five miles from the Cambodian border. Small arms and automatic weapons fire was exchanged and the troopers were supported by artillery and helicopter gunships, in addition to the heavy weapons on their tanks and armored personnel carriers. Fighting continued for 45 minutes, and then the enemy withdrew. The bodies of 27 enemy were found, and 13 individual weapons were captured. One US soldier was wounded. No US fatalities.

MARCH 3, 1970

- *Toan Thang Offensive* (Tay Ninh Province). At 0730 hours, an element of the 1st Brigade, 1st Cavalry Division (Airmobile), engaged an undetermined number of enemy soldiers while searching an earlier night ambush site 30 miles NE of Tay Ninh City and four miles from the Cambodian border. Small arms and automatic weapons fire was exchanged and the troopers were supported by helicopter gunships and artillery. The enemy withdrew, leaving 10 dead and 10 individual weapons. No US casualties.

- *Toan Thang Offensive* (Binh Long Province). At 1700 hours, an element of the 3rd Brigade, 1st Cavalry Division (Airmobile), engaged an undetermined number of enemy soldiers six miles SE of Loc Ninh and 12 miles from the Cambodian border. The troopers fired back with unit weapons and were supported by artillery and helicopter gunships. In about 15 minutes, the enemy withdrew, leaving one dead along with 72 rounds of 60mm mortar ammunition, 60 rounds of 82mm mortar ammunition, 15 anti-tank mines, and 2,200 small arms rounds. No US casualties.
- *Toan Thang Offensive* (Tay Ninh Province). In a continued search of the area 32 miles north of Tay Ninh City and one mile from the Cambodian border, where an element of the 1st Cavalry Division discovered a significant enemy rice cache on March 1, 1970, an additional 36 tons of rice was found and evacuated. The additional rice raises the total to 96½ tons the amount found in the vicinity on March 1, 2, and 3, 1970.

MARCH 4, 1970

- *Operation Geneva Park* (Quang Ngai Province). At 1840 hours, a forward observer of the 198th Brigade, 23rd Infantry Division, sighted 46 enemy soldiers with packs and weapons moving north 10 miles west of Quang Ngai City. The enemy was engaged with artillery, killing 22 of them. No US casualties.
- *Toan Thang Offensive* (Tay Ninh Province). At 0615 hours, an element of the 1st Brigade, 1st Cavalry Division, in night positions 29 miles north of Tay Ninh City and two miles from the Cambodian border, received about 50 rounds of 60mm mortar fire and a ground probe from an estimated 50 enemy soldiers firing small arms, automatic weapons and rocket-grenades. The troopers fired back with unit weapons and were supported by artillery and helicopter gunships. In about five minutes, the enemy withdrew, leaving 37 dead and 12 individual weapons. US casualties were one killed and three wounded.
- *Toan Thang Offensive* (Tay Ninh Province). Troopers from the 1st Brigade, 1st Cavalry Division, evacuated additional bags of rice from the large enemy cache discovered north of Tay Ninh

City and one mile from the Cambodian border on March 1, 1970. The additional rice raises the total weight of the cache from 96½ tons to 126½ tons.

MARCH 5, 1970

- *Toan Thang Offensive* (Tay Ninh Province). At 1150 hours, an element of the 11th Armored Cavalry Regiment engaged an unknown number of enemy soldiers eight miles ESE of Katum and three miles from the Cambodian border. Small arms fire was exchanged and the enemy also employed rocket-grenade and 60mm mortar fire. Artillery, helicopter gunships and USAF A-37 and F-100 aircraft supported the troopers. At 1700 hours, the enemy withdrew, leaving 17 dead. US casualties were six wounded, no fatalities.
- *Toan Thang Offensive* (Phuoc Long Province). At 1615 hours, an element of the 2nd Brigade, 1st Cavalry Division, engaged three to four enemy soldiers 22 miles NE of Song Be and 12 miles from the Cambodian border. Small arms fire was exchanged and the troopers were supported by artillery and helicopter gunships. The enemy withdrew almost immediately with unknown losses. There were no US casualties. In a search of the area, the troopers discovered a significant enemy weapons and munitions cache. It weighed about nine tons and contained the following: 1,100 rounds of 82mm mortar, 450 fuses for 82mm mortar, 225 primers for 82mm mortar, 35 bolt-action rifles, 49 SKS rifles, 220 rifle grenades, 43,000 rounds of small arms ammunition, 2,400 pounds of TNT, 38 cases of plastic explosives, one anti-tank mine, 5,000 feet of detonating cord, 170 anti-tank CHICOM grenades, 340 rounds of rocket-grenades, 1,000 pick axes, and 15 shovels.
- At approximately 1630 hours, March 3, 1970, the District Town of Ha Tien, Tien Giang Province, in close proximity to the Cambodian border, came under enemy-initiated 82mm mortar attack originating from positions inside Cambodia. US tactical air strikes were placed on the enemy firing positions inside Cambodia. The enemy fire was suppressed. The US Command has previously stated that if fired upon from enemy positions outside the RVN, US Forces are authorized to return fire.

MARCH 6, 1970

- *Toan Thang Offensive* (Tay Ninh Province). At 0945 hours, an element of the 11th Armored Cavalry Regiment engaged an undetermined size enemy force seven miles SE of Katum. Small arms fire was exchanged. The enemy returned fire with rocket-grenades and the troopers were supported by helicopter gunships and tactical air strikes. In about 30 minutes the enemy withdrew, leaving 31 dead. US casualties were two wounded.
- *Toan Thang Offensive* (Tay Ninh Province). At 0905 hours, an element of the 1st Brigade, 1st Cavalry Division, engaged an estimated enemy company nine miles WNW of Katum. Small arms fire was exchanged. The troopers were supported by artillery, helicopter gunships and tactical air strikes. At 1205 hours, the enemy withdrew, leaving 21 dead. US casualties were one killed and 19 wounded.

MARCH 7, 1970

- *Toan Thang Offensive* (Binh Tuy Province). At 1230 hours, an element of the 199th Light Infantry Brigade discovered a significant enemy food cache while operating 20 miles north of Ham Tan. At the cache site, the infantrymen engaged an estimated enemy platoon. Small arms and automatic weapons fire was exchanged and the troopers were supported by helicopter gunships, artillery and tactical air strikes. At 1310 hours, the enemy withdrew leaving behind four dead and two individual weapons. The food cache consisted of 300 bags of flour weighing a total of 7½ tons.

MARCH 8, 1970

- *Toan Thang Offensive* (Tay Ninh Province). At 1625 hours, an element of the 1st Brigade, 1st Cavalry Division, engaged an undetermined number of enemy soldiers 29 miles north of Tay Ninh City and two miles from the Cambodian border. Small arms and automatic weapons fire was exchanged and the troopers were supported by artillery, helicopter gunships, and USAF air strikes. In about 25 minutes, the enemy withdrew, leaving behind 29 of his dead. US casualties were three killed and 13 wounded.

MARCH 10, 1970

- *Toan Thang Offensive.* At 1030 hours, an element of the 11th Armored Cavalry Regiment engaged an estimated enemy battalion four miles SW of Loc Ninh and five miles from the Cambodian border. Small arms and automatic weapons fire was exchanged and the enemy used rocket-grenades. Artillery, helicopter gunships, and USAF A-37 aircraft supported the troopers. Fighting continued until noon when the enemy withdrew. The bodies of 54 enemy soldiers were found in search of the battle area, and five enemy soldiers were detained. In addition, 10 crew-served weapons (including one 60mm mortar) and 19 individual weapons were captured, along with one field telephone. US casualties were four killed and 18 wounded. The battalion was later identified as part of the NVA 7th Division.
- *Toan Thang Offensive* (Tay Ninh Province). At 0805 hours, elements of the 11th Armored Cavalry Regiment engaged an estimated enemy battalion 25 miles NNE of Tay Ninh City and four miles from the Cambodian border. Small arms and automatic weapons fire was exchanged and the enemy also used 57mm recoilless rifle and rocket-grenade fire. Helicopter gunships, artillery and USAF F-100 and A-37 aircraft supported the troopers. At 1315 hours, the enemy withdrew, leaving 32 dead. In addition, one 57mm recoilless rifle, two individual weapons and one CHICOM field telephone were captured. US casualties were four killed and eight wounded. The enemy force was identified as an NVA element of the 9th Viet Cong Division.
- *Toan Thang Offensive* (Binh Long Province). At 1825 hours, helicopter gunships from the air cavalry squadron of the 1st Cavalry Division, received small arms fire from an undetermined number of enemy soldiers on a reconnaissance mission nine miles NE of Loc Ninh and one mile from the Cambodian border. The enemy was engaged with aerial machine gun fire and US Army artillery was directed onto the

location. At 1905 hours, the enemy withdrew, leaving 26 dead. No US casualties.

- *Toan Thang Offensive* (Tay Ninh Province). At 1445 hours, elements of the 1st Brigade, 1st Cavalry Division, discovered a significant enemy food cache north of Tay Ninh City and one mile from the Cambodian border. The cache contained 23½ tons of rice and 800 pounds of corn. The bodies of four enemy soldiers and two individual weapons were also found in the vicinity of the cache. The enemy had apparently been killed by an earlier air strike in the area.

MARCH 11, 1970

- *Toan Thang Offensive* (Long Khanh Province). At 1225 hours, an element of the 199th Light Infantry Brigade discovered an enemy food cache 25 miles NW of Xuan Loc. It contained 2,000 pounds of peanuts.

MARCH 12, 1970

- *Operation Iron Mountain* (Quang Ngai Province). Between 1210 and 1750 hours, forward observers from artillery elements of the 11th Brigade, 23rd Infantry Division, observed 47 enemy soldiers 11 miles west of Quang Ngai City. In each case, the enemy was engaged with artillery. 47 of the enemy were killed. No US casualties.
- Quang Tri Province. At 0130 hours, an undetermined size enemy force attacked an element of the ARVN 2nd Regiment, 1st Infantry Division, and a US Army XXIV Corps artillery element company, located at a defensive position five miles west of Cam Lo and six miles south of the DMZ. The enemy used small arms, automatic weapons and rocket-grenade fire along with an undetermined number and caliber mortar rounds. The combined US and ARVN troopers returned fire with unit weapons including 40mm guns on self-propelled artillery pieces. Contact was lost about two hours later when the enemy withdrew. In a search of the battle area, the bodies of 30 NVA soldiers were found. In addition, 15 individual weapons and two rocket-grenade launchers were captured. ARVN casualties were light. US casualties were two killed and five wounded. There was light materiel damage.
- Binh Dinh Province. At 0500 hours, an undetermined type and

size explosive charge, believed to have been placed by enemy sapper personnel, detonated against the port side of the SS AMERCLOUD, a cargo ship at anchor in the harbor at Qui Nhon. The ship was damaged, took on water, and was towed to a nearby sandbar where repairs were completed and unloading continued. There were no reported casualties.

- *Toan Thang Offensive* (Tan Ninh Province). At 0630 hours, an element of the 11th Armored Cavalry Regiment and troopers from the 1st Brigade, 1st Cavalry Division, in night defensive positions 29 miles NNE of Tay Ninh City, and three miles from the Cambodian border, received small arms, automatic weapons and rocket-grenade fire from an undetermined size enemy force. The armored and air cavalry troops returned fire with unit weapons and were supported by helicopter gunships and artillery. Fighting continued until 1030 hours when the enemy withdrew, leaving 29 dead. One enemy soldier was detained and eight individual weapons were captured. US casualties were four killed and 17 wounded.

MARCH 13, 1970

- Kien Giang Province. Between the hours of 1300 and 1700 hours, a combined operation involving helicopter gunships from the 164th Combat Aviation Group and elements of the 33rd Regiment, 21st ARVN Division, engaged an undetermined size enemy force 31 miles SSW of Rach Gia. Forty-five enemy soldiers were killed in addition to six detained. Five individual and one crew-served weapons were captured. ARVN casualties were light. There were no US casualties.

MARCH 14, 1970

- *Toan Thang Offensive* (Tay Ninh Province). At 0600 hours, an element of the 1st Brigade, 1st Cavalry Division, in a night defensive position 29 miles north of Tay Ninh City, and three miles from the Cambodian border, received small arms, automatic weapons and rocket-grenade fire from an undetermined size enemy force. The troopers fired back with unit weapons and were supported by helicopter gunships and artillery. At an unreported time, the enemy withdrew. In a search of the battle area, the bodies of 12 enemy soldiers were found. US casualties were one killed and three wounded. At

0730 hours, during a search of the battle area, a supporting AH-1 helicopter experienced an apparent malfunction in the armament system, which resulted in the firing of several 2.75-inch rockets. The rockets impacted in the vicinity of the troops conducting the search, killing three US soldiers and wounding 19 others.

MARCH 16, 1970

- Quang Nam Province. At 1145 hours, a USN EC-121 Constellation aircraft crashed while landing at Da Nang Air Base due to an apparent mechanical failure. The aircraft struck a hangar, burned and was destroyed. The extent of materiel damage in the vicinity of the crash site was undetermined. Of the 31 US personnel aboard the aircraft, 22 were killed and nine injured. In addition, two other US personnel on the ground were slightly injured.
- *Toan Thang Offensive* (Tay Ninh Province). At 1530 hours, a mechanized infantry element from the 1st Brigade, 25th Infantry Division, received small arms and automatic weapons fire from an undetermined number of enemy soldiers nine miles NE of Tay Ninh City. The troopers returned fire with unit weapons and were supported by helicopter gunships, artillery and tactical air strikes. Fighting continued until 1845 hours, when the enemy withdrew, leaving 25 dead. US casualties were two killed and six wounded.
- Based on guidance from Department of Defense, Military Assistance Command Office of Information was authorized to report daily if air operations were conducted over Laos. The following information was authorized to be reported, when appropriate: That USAF, Navy Marine Corps (as appropriate) aircraft flew interdiction operations along the Ho Chi Minh Trail in Laos. That Air Force, Navy, Marine Corps (as appropriate) aircraft flew combat support missions in Laos for Royal Laotian forces. That B-52's participated in interdiction operations along the Ho Chi Minh Trail in Laos. The Communiqué/Evening Release was authorized to simply state whether or not the above type operations were

conducted. No additional information on air operations over Laos was authorized to be released.

- Quang Tin Province. At 1600 hours yesterday, the UH-1 command and control helicopter of the Commanding General, 23rd Infantry Division, (Americal), Major General Lloyd B. Ramsey, crashed in an area seven miles west of Chu Lai. Of the eight passengers and crewmen aboard, one passenger and one crewman were killed. General Ramsey was hospitalized in good condition and the remaining five personnel were hospitalized in satisfactory to good condition.

MARCH 19, 1970

- *Operation Frederick Hill* (Quang Tin Province). At 0725 hours, an element of the armored cavalry squadron of the 23rd Infantry Division (Americal), and infantrymen from the Division's 196th Brigade, were operating 13 miles NW of Tam Ky, when an armored personnel carrier detonated an enemy mine believed to have been made from a 250-pound bomb. Nine US soldiers were killed and one was wounded in the explosion. The armored personnel carrier was destroyed.
- *Toan Thang Offensive* (Tay Ninh Province). At 1215 hours, troopers from the air cavalry squadron of the 1st Cavalry Division engaged an undetermined size enemy force four miles from the Cambodian border and 20 miles NNW of Tay Ninh City. Small arms and automatic weapons fire was exchanged and the enemy used rocket-grenades. An element of the division's 1st Brigade reinforced the action and troops were supported by helicopter gunships and artillery. At 1330 hours, the enemy withdrew. The bodies of 39 enemy were found in the area. In addition, one rocket propelled grenade launcher and seven AK-47 rifles were captured. There were no US casualties.

MARCH 20, 1970

- Quang Nam Province. At 1715 hours, a US 1st Marine Division artillery element firing a support mission, had one 155mm artillery round detonate prematurely in the vicinity of an element of the 5th Marine Regiment ½ mile north of An Hoa.

Twenty-five Marines were injured in the explosion and one was killed.

- *Toan Thang Offensive* (Phuoc Long Province). At 1115 hours, an element of the 3rd Brigade, 1st Cavalry Division, found a rice cache 14 miles WNW of Phuoc Binh. The eight-ton cache contained 54 bags of rice weighing 220 pounds each. The rice was evacuated to Quan Loi.

MARCH 22, 1970

- *Toan Thang Offensive* (Binh Long Province). At 2345 hours, a helicopter from the 11th Aviation Group, 1st Cavalry Division, engaged 30-40 enemy soldiers eight miles west of Loc Ninh and one mile from the Cambodian border. The bodies of 30 enemy soldiers were sighted in the strike area. There were no US casualties.
- *Toan Thang Offensive* (Phuoc Long Province). At 1205 hours, an element of the 2nd Brigade, 1st Cavalry Division, engaged an undetermined size enemy force 18 miles NE of Phuoc Binh and 15 miles from the Cambodian border. Small arms and automatic weapons fire was exchanged and the troopers were supported by helicopter gunships and artillery fire. In about 20 minutes, the enemy withdrew, leaving behind 17 dead. One US soldier was killed. No US wounded.
- *Toan Thang Offensive* (Phuoc Long Province). At 0840 hours, an element of the 3rd Brigade, 1st Cavalry Division, found a 6½-ton rice cache 14 miles WNW of Phuoc Binh. The cache contained 62 unmarked 220-pound bags of rice in good condition. It was estimated to have been in place one week. The rice was evacuated to Quan Loi for distribution.

MARCH 23, 1970

- *Toan Thang Offensive* (Phuoc Long Province). At 1000 hours, an element of the 3rd Brigade, 1st Cavalry Division, discovered a significant enemy rice cache 15 miles NW of Phuoc Binh and six miles from the Cambodian border. The cache contained 13 tons of rice in unmarked bags. Later, at 1700 hours, while searching the same general area, the troopers found another cache of 25 unmarked bags weighing almost three tons.

MARCH 24, 1970

- *Toan Thang Offensive* (Phuoc Long Province). At 1500 hours, an element of the 3rd Brigade, 1st Cavalry Division, engaged an undetermined size enemy force 13 miles WNW of Phuoc Binh and nine miles from the Cambodian border. Small arms and automatic weapons fire was exchanged and the troopers were supported by helicopter gunships, artillery and tactical air strikes. Fighting continued until 1810 hours when the enemy withdrew, leaving 20 dead. There were no US casualties.
- *Toan Thang Offensive* (Phuoc Long Province). At 1230 hours, infantrymen from an element of the 2nd Brigade, 1st Cavalry Division, discovered an enemy munitions cache in a bunker complex eight miles NW of Phuoc Binh and nine miles from the Cambodian border. The cache, weighing about 1,500 pounds, contained the following: 11,340 small arms rounds, 54 60mm mortar rounds, 49 75mm recoilless rifle rounds and six RPGs.

MARCH 26, 1970

- Quang Nam Province. At 0930 and 1000 hours, an element of the 1st Regiment, 1st Marine Division, discovered two enemy weapons and munitions caches 13 miles WSW of Da Nang. The caches, totaling about one ton, contained the following: five individual weapons, three machine guns, one rocket-grenade launcher, one 60mm mortar (complete), nine cases of AK-47 ammunition, 80 rounds of 60mm mortar, 39 rocket-grenade rounds, eight rounds of 82mm mortar, 500 CHICOM hand grenades, 10 bangalore torpedoes, 70 pounds of medical supplies, two 25-pound shaped charges, 10 cases of 60mm mortar charges, 10 cans of 60mm mortar fuses, seven cases of warheads for bangalore torpedoes.
- *Toan Thang Offensive* (Tay Ninh Province). At 1145 hours, an element of the 1st Brigade, 1st Cavalry Division, engaged an undetermined size enemy force 25 miles NNW of Tay Ninh City and three miles from the Cambodian border. The enemy returned fire with small arms, automatic weapons and rocket-grenades. The troopers were supported by artillery, helicopter gunships and tactical air strikes. As fighting continued, another element of the brigade and troops from the 11th

Armored Cavalry Regiment, in tanks and armored personnel carriers, reinforced the contact. Action continued into the early evening when the enemy withdrew at about 1910 hours. Enemy losses were 88 killed. US casualties were two killed and 22 wounded. There was light materiel damage.

- It was reported that a number of bombs from a B-52 mission flown in an area four miles north of Tri Ton in Chau Doc Province impacted outside the target area. Twelve VN civilians were reported wounded, three seriously, and two houses were damaged.

MARCH 27, 1970

- Thua Thien Province. At 1445 hours, helicopter crewmen from the air cavalry squadron of the 101st Airborne Division, on a reconnaissance mission 28 miles SW of Hue and three miles from the Laotian border, over the A Shau Valley, received heavy small arms fire from an undetermined size enemy force. Tactical air strikes and artillery fire was directed onto the enemy location. The bodies of 21 enemy soldiers were sighted following the engagement and three crew-served weapons were reported destroyed. There were no US casualties.
- Gia Dinh Province. At 0600 hours, two suspected Viet Cong terrorists, wearing fatigues and riding two motorcycles, threw an estimated 12-pound plastic type explosive charge into the parking lot of the Louisiana US Bachelor Enlisted Quarters (BEQ) on Chi Lang Street, two miles north of the center of Saigon. The charge exploded, destroying one parked vehicle. Two other vehicles received minor damage. There were no casualties. The terrorists escaped.
- At approximately 1600 hours, March 24, 1970, ARVN forces operating in northern Kien Tuong Province, received enemy-initiated fire originating from positions inside Cambodia. Tactical air strikes were placed on the enemy positions inside Cambodia with unknown results.

MARCH 28, 1970

- *Toan Thang Offensive* (Phuoc Long Province). At 1300 hours, an element of the 2nd Brigade, 1st Cavalry Division, engaged an undetermined number of enemy soldiers 24 miles NNE of Phuoc Binh, and one mile from the Cambodian border. Small arms and automatic weapons fire was exchanged and the troopers were supported by artillery and tactical air strikes. Fighting continued until about 1520 hours when the enemy withdrew, leaving 23 dead. US casualties were five killed and 10 wounded.

MARCH 29, 1970

- *Toan Thang Offensive* (Tay Ninh Province). At 0450 hours, an element of the 1st Brigade, 1st Cavalry Division, at FSB Jay, 20 miles NNW of Tay Ninh City and four miles from the Cambodian border, received an undetermined number of 107mm rockets, 120mm and 82mm mortar and 75mm recoilless rifle rounds followed by a ground attack by an estimated NVA battalion. The enemy used small arms, automatic weapons and rocket-grenade fire. The troopers returned fire with unit weapons and were supported by artillery fire from within the base, helicopter gunships and a USAF AC-119 gunship. Fighting continued until about 0600 hours when the enemy force withdrew. Sporadic fire continued for about four hours. During a search of the battle area, the air cavalry troops engaged an undetermined number of enemy soldiers. Small arms fire was exchanged and contact was lost at an unreported time. Medical evacuation helicopters received 12.7mm anti-aircraft fire from two enemy locations during the action. The bodies of 74 enemy soldiers were found in the vicinity and three enemy soldiers were detained. In addition, 12 AK-47 rifles and an unreported number of 82mm mortar and 57mm recoilless rifle rounds were captured. Also, one former enemy soldier, serving as a scout, was wounded. Light to moderate materiel damage was reported, and no enemy penetrated the perimeter. The enemy unit was later identified as an element of the 9th Viet Cong Division.

MARCH 31, 1970

- Khanh Hoa Province. At 2330 hours, three satchel charges placed by an undetermined number of enemy sappers, detonated at the Cam Ranh Bay fuel tank farm six miles NNE of Cam Ranh. Materiel damage was light to moderate. There were no US casualties and no reported enemy losses. Explosive ordnance personnel disarmed four other enemy explosive charges found in the fuel storage area.

- *Toan Thang Offensive* (Tay Ninh Province). At 1245 hours, an element of the 11th Armored Cavalry Regiment, in tanks and armored personnel carriers, engaged an undetermined size enemy force 27 miles NNW of Tay Ninh City and a ½ mile from the Cambodian border. The troopers fired unit weapons and were supported by helicopter gunships and artillery. Fighting continued until 1630 hours when the enemy withdrew. The bodies of 30 enemy soldiers were found in the battle area and 16 suspects were detained. In addition, five individual and two crew-served weapons were captured. There were no US casualties.

APRIL 1, 1970

- Thua Thien Province. At 1020 hours, elements of the 3rd Brigade, 101st Airborne Division, air-assaulted into an LZ in an area 24 miles west of Hue. The troopers received small arms and mortar fire after landing from an unidentified size enemy force. The enemy fire was returned with unit weapons and supported by helicopter gunships and artillery. Fighting continued until about 1815 hours when the enemy withdrew. Enemy losses are unknown while US casualties were seven killed and 21 wounded.
- Binh Thuan Province. Between 0040 and 0530 hours, an element of the ARVN 44th Regiment, 23rd Infantry Division, located six miles north of Song Mao, received about 100 rounds of 82mm mortar fire. Artillery and mortar fire was directed against the suspected enemy firing positions and elements of the armored cavalry squadron of Task Force South, in tanks and armored personnel carriers, moved to the area as a reaction force, and along with the ARVN infantrymen, engaged an undetermined size enemy force. Small arms and automatic weapons fire was exchanged and fighting continued until an unreported time when the enemy withdrew. The bodies of 111 enemy soldiers were in the area and six enemy were detained. In addition, the combined US and ARVN troops captured 26 individual and

seven crew-served weapons. US casualties were killed and 21 wounded. ARVN casualties were light. Four VN civilians were also reported killed in the mortar attack. Materiel damage was light.

- *Toan Thang Offensive* (Tay Ninh Province). At 0220 hours, an element of the 1st Brigade, 1st Cavalry Division, at a fire support base 22 miles NNW of Tay Ninh City and five miles from the Cambodian border, received about 200 mixed 120mm mortar and 82mm mortar rounds, 15 mixed 107mm and 122mm rockets and a ground attack by an estimated two enemy companies. The enemy employed small arms, automatic weapons and rocket-grenade fire. The troopers fired back with unit weapons and were supported by helicopter gunships and artillery. As action continued, an element of the 11th Armored Cavalry Regiment, in tanks and armored personnel carriers, moved to the area and reinforced the troops in contact with the enemy. Fighting continued until about 0430 hours when the remaining enemy withdrew. No enemy was reported to have penetrated the perimeter. In a search of the area, the bodies of 62 enemy soldiers were found. In addition, 28 individual weapons were captured. US casualties were 24 killed and 54 wounded. Materiel damage was light to moderate.
- Brigadier General William R. Bond, US Army, Commanding General, 199th Light Infantry Brigade, was fatally wounded in Binh Tuy Province. General Bond landed in a helicopter in the operational area in the morning to assess the combat situation. As the general was talking to the ground troops, an estimated two enemy soldiers opened fire with automatic weapons and also fired one rocket-grenade. The general was hit and fatally wounded by the enemy small arms.

APRIL 2, 1970

- *Operation Iron Mountain* (Quang Ngai Province). At 1800 hours, an element of the 11th Brigade, 23rd Infantry Division, detonated an unknown type enemy booby trap while operating in an area 13 miles SW of Duc Pho. Ten personnel were killed in the explosion, including seven US soldiers, one former enemy soldier serving as a scout, one enemy rallier and one VN civilian. Twenty others were wounded including 19 US soldiers and one VN civilian.

- Quang Nam Province. At 0930 hours, the base camp of the Headquarters, 5th Regiment, 1st Marine Division, at An Hoa, 22 miles SSW of Da Nang, received less than 10 rounds of 140mm rocket fire and about five rounds of rocket-grenade fire. US casualties were light with no fatalities and materiel damage was light. In addition, six VN civilians were reported wounded by enemy fire.
- *Toan Thang Offensive* (Tay Ninh Offensive). At 0845 hours, a reconnaissance element of the US 25th Infantry Division received small arms and automatic weapons fire from an undetermined number of enemy soldiers 10 miles SSE of Tay Ninh City and three miles from the Cambodian border. The troopers returned fire with organic weapons and were supported by helicopter gunships. In about 15 minutes the enemy withdrew, leaving behind 12 dead. US casualties were two killed and seven wounded. About 30 minutes later, at 0930 hours, an element of the Division's 3rd Brigade moved to the area of contact and engaged an undetermined size enemy force. The enemy opened fire with small arms and automatic weapons and the infantrymen returned fire with organic weapons and were supported by helicopter gunships and tactical aircraft. The fighting continued throughout the day until 1840 hours when the enemy withdrew. Twenty enemy soldiers were killed in the engagement. US casualties were eight killed and 11 wounded. Cumulative results for the two actions were 32 enemy killed. US casualties totaled 10 killed and 18 wounded.

APRIL 4, 1970

- Quang Tri Province. At 1125 hours, elements of the 1st Brigade, 5th Infantry Division (Mech), received small arms and automatic weapons fire, and 82mm mortar and 122mm rocket fire from an undetermined size enemy force six miles SW of Con Thien and two miles south of the DMZ. The troopers fired back with organic weapons and were supported by helicopter gunships and tanks. A total of about 70 rounds of mortar fire and 20 rockets were received during the action. Fighting continued into the afternoon until 1445 hours when the enemy withdrew. The bodies of 24 enemy soldiers were found in the battle area. US casualties were two killed and 12 wounded.

- *Toan Thang Offensive* (Phuoc Long Province). At 1400 hours troopers from an element of the 2nd Brigade, 1st Cavalry Division (Airmobile), discovered a significant enemy munitions cache 22 miles NNE of Phuoc Binh and four miles from the Cambodian border. The cache, weighing about one ton, contained 61,200 small arms rounds, 590 pounds of explosives, and two 12.7mm machine gun tripods.

APRIL 5, 1970

- Pleiku Province. At 0100 hours, US Army helicopter crewmen engaged a suspected enemy location, 12 miles west of Pleiku City and 27 miles east of the Cambodian border. It was subsequently reported that the aerial machine gun and rocket fire impacted in the vicinity of an element of the ARVN 47th Infantry Regiment, killing 11 and wounding 30 ARVN soldiers. US Army helicopters evacuated the wounded personnel to US medical facilities by about 0300 hours.
- *Toan Thang Offensive* (Tay Ninh Province). At 1035 hours, an element of the 1st Brigade, 1st Cavalry Division (Airmobile), engaged an undetermined number of enemy soldiers 20 miles NW of Tay Ninh City and three miles from the Cambodian border. Small arms and automatic weapons fire was exchanged and the troopers were supported by helicopter gunships, artillery, and tactical aircraft. In a short while, the enemy withdrew with unknown losses. US casualties were seven killed and four wounded.
- *Toan Thang Offensive* (Phuoc Long Province). At 0930 hours, an element of the 2nd Brigade, 1st Cavalry Division (Airmobile), discovered a significant enemy munitions cache while operating 22 miles NNE of Phuoc Binh and four miles from the Cambodian border. The cache, weighing slightly more than two tons, contained 134,640 small arms rounds, 46 rounds of 82mm mortar ammunition and 15 boxes of TNT. In addition, 13 pairs of wire cutters were found in the cache.

APRIL 6, 1970

- *Toan Thang Offensive* (Phuoc Long Province). At approximately 0800 hours, an element of the 2nd Brigade, 1st Cavalry Division

(Airmobile), discovered a significant enemy munitions cache while operating 24 miles NNE of Phuoc Binh and three miles from the Cambodian border. The cache contained 265,680 small arms rounds, 91 rounds of 82mm mortar ammunition, and 941 pounds of TNT. The munitions weighed over 2½ tons.

APRIL 9, 1970

- Quang Tri Province. At 2300 hours, a trip flare was detonated on the perimeter of the CIDG Camp at Mai Loc (four miles SW of Cam Lo), 97 miles NW of Da Nang, and 10 miles south of the DMZ, alerting personnel in the camp. At 0235 hours, the camp received 75-100 rounds of mixed 82mm mortar and rocket-grenade fire, followed 10 minutes later by a sapper attack from an estimated enemy company firing small arms and automatic weapons and using satchel charges. A total of 60 to 80 enemy were reported to have penetrated the outer perimeter at four locations. The CIDG Troopers, US Special Forces advisors and US artillerymen, on self-propelled twin 40mm guns, returned the fire. Heavy fighting from bunkers was reported inside the camp and several small counterattacks from within the camp repulsed the enemy from portions of the perimeter. The enemy was reported unable to penetrate the camp's inner perimeter where the tactical operations center was located. As fighting continued, an element of the 1st Brigade, 5th Infantry Division (Mech) in trucks and armored personnel carriers, moved to the area and engaged the enemy at about 0340 hours. Helicopter gunships and a VN Air Force gunship supported the contact. The remaining enemy began to withdraw, dragging an undetermined number of bodies at the same time. Contact was lost at 0455. RVNAF casualties were light. US casualties were six killed and 13 wounded. One VN child was reported killed. The bodies of 19 enemy soldiers were found in the vicinity. Materiel damage was light to moderate.
- Quang Tri Province. At approximately 2225 hours last night, an element of the 1st Brigade, 5th Infantry Division (Mech), in night defensive positions four miles SE of Gio Linh and four miles south of the DMZ, engaged 10 to 15 enemy soldiers observed after a flare was tripped near their location. The

enemy employed small arms, automatic weapons and rocket-grenade fire. The troops employed organic weapons and were supported by artillery and helicopter gunships. Contact was lost at about midnight; however, sporadic sniper fire continued until about 0200 hours today when the remaining enemy withdrew. The bodies of nine enemy soldiers were found in the battle area. In addition, one crew-served and six individual weapons were captured. US casualties were 15 wounded with no fatalities. One former enemy soldier, serving as a scout, was also wounded.

- Gia Dinh Province. At 0545 hours, an estimated 20-pound explosive charge detonated outside the US Le Lai Bachelor Enlisted Quarters (BEQ) near the Railroad Station one mile SE of the center of Saigon. Two US military personnel were slightly injured in the explosion and light damage to the Bachelor Enlisted Quarters (BEQ) was reported. Three vehicles were also damaged. The charge was believed to have been placed by a suspected Viet Cong terrorist. The terrorist escaped.

APRIL 10, 1970

- *Toan Thang Offensive* (Tay Ninh Province). At 0530 hours, a mechanized infantry element of the 1st Brigade, 25th Infantry Division, in night defensive positions 15 miles NW of Tay Ninh City and six miles from the Cambodian border, received rocket-grenade fire from an undetermined number of soldiers. The troopers returned fire with organic weapons, including heavy machine guns on their armored personnel carriers, and were supported by artillery. In about one hour the enemy withdrew, leaving behind 12 dead, one rocket-grenade launcher and 12 rocket-grenade rounds. US casualties were two killed and five wounded.

APRIL 11, 1970

- Quang Nam Province. At 1900 hours, a reconnaissance element of the 1st Marine Division sighted 20 enemy soldiers moving east in an area five miles NW of An Hoa (21 miles SW of Da Nang). Artillery fire was directed onto the enemy location and the bodies of 11 enemy soldiers were observed lying in the strike area. The remaining enemy evaded further observation. There were no US casualties.

- *Toan Thang Offensive* (Tay Ninh Province). At 1120 hours, a mechanized element of the US 25th Infantry Division, 18 miles NNW of Tay Ninh City and two miles from the Cambodian border, engaged an undetermined number of enemy soldiers with organic weapons. The enemy returned fire with small arms, automatic weapons, and rocket-grenade fire. Helicopter gunships, artillery, and tactical aircraft supported the troopers. At 1320 hours, the enemy withdrew. Contact was reestablished at 1610 hours but terminated at 1640 hours when the remaining enemy again withdrew. Twenty-six enemy soldiers were killed. In addition, seven individual and four crew-served weapons, 15 CHICOM gas masks, 800 pounds of rice, and 120 rifle grenades were captured. US casualties were two killed and three wounded. Light material damage was also reported.

APRIL 13, 1970

- Quang Tri Province. At 0245 hours, FSB Nancy, located nine miles SE of Quang Tri City (75 miles NW of Da Nang), and occupied by an element of the ARVN 1st Regiment, 1st Infantry Division, along with US Army XXIV Corps artillery unit, received about 20 rounds of undetermined caliber mortar fire. The indirect fire was followed at about 0350 hours by a ground attack from an estimated reinforced sapper company, employing small arms, automatic weapons, and rocket-grenade fire in addition to satchel charges. The combined US and ARVN troops returned fire with unit weapons and were supported by artillery fire. During the action, several enemy soldiers penetrated the perimeter but were killed or detained. The enemy withdrew at an unreported time. At first light, ARVN infantrymen from the 1st Regiment made sporadic contact with an undetermined number of enemy soldiers while searching the battle area, small arms and automatic weapons were captured. US casualties were four killed and 34 wounded. ARVN casualties were light with no fatalities. Light materiel damage was reported.
- *Toan Thang Offensive* (Tay Ninh Province). At 1215 hours, an element of the 11th Armored Cavalry Regiment engaged an undetermined size enemy force 29 miles NE of Tay Ninh

City and two miles from the Cambodian border. Small arms and automatic weapons fire was exchanged and the enemy employed rocket-grenade fire. Artillery, helicopter gunships, and tactical aircraft, in addition to the heavy weapons on their tanks and armored personnel carriers, supported the troopers. Fighting continued until 1600 hours when the enemy withdrew, leaving behind 31 of his dead, and one 60mm mortar, one RPG launcher, and one individual weapon. There were no US casualties. Light materiel damage was reported.

- *Toan Thang Offensive.* (Tay Ninh Province). At 1520 hours, helicopters from the air-cavalry squadron of the 1st Cavalry Division (Airmobile) received heavy small arms and automatic weapons fire from an undetermined number of enemy soldiers 22 miles NE of Tay Ninh City and nine miles from the Cambodian border. The enemy were engaged with organic aerial machine guns and rockets, causing three secondary explosions. Contact was lost almost immediately. The bodies of 28 enemy soldiers were sighted lying in the strike area following the engagement. In addition, one light machine gun was reported destroyed. There were no US casualties.
- Gia Dinh Province. At 2330 hours, the enemy fired four 122mm rockets into the city of Saigon, three of the rockets impacted in the 1st and 2nd Precincts, ½ half mile SE, ½ half mile east and one mile ENE of the center of Saigon. The fourth rocket impacted in the Saigon River, two miles east of the center of the city. One of the rounds hit the Olympic Theater, one round impacted in the Cercle Sportif tennis court area and the third hit a VN school near Thong Nhut and Hai Ba Trung Streets. Two VN civilians were reported killed and 41 wounded in the indiscriminate attack. RVNAF casualties were very light with no fatalities. ARVN artillery fire was directed on the suspected enemy firing positions, six miles to the SE, with unknown results. There were no US casualties.

APRIL 15, 1970

- *Operation Iron Mountain* (Quang Ngai Province). At 1300 hours, a 105mm artillery round, rigged as a booby-trap, was detonated by an element of the 11th Brigade, Americal Division, two miles south of Duc Pho (105 miles SE of Da Nang). The exploding round also caused some ammunition being carried by the infantrymen to detonate. Total US casualties were 14 killed and 32 wounded.

- *Toan Thang Offensive* (Tay Ninh Province). At 2145 hours, an element of the 11th Armored Cavalry Regiment at a fire support base 23 miles NW of Tay Ninh City and three miles from the Cambodian border received about 100 rounds of mixed 60mm and 82mm mortar and 107mm rocket fire along with a ground attack by an undetermined size enemy force. The enemy employed small arms, automatic weapons and rocket-grenade fire. The troopers fired back with organic weapons and were supported by artillery, helicopter gunships, and tactical aircraft. Fighting continued until midnight when contact was lost. In a later search of the battle area, the bodies of 55 enemy soldiers were found and three enemy soldiers were detained. In addition, seven crew-served and 17 individual weapons, 100 CHICOM hand-grenades, 5,000 small arms rounds, 20 rocket-grenades, 10 rounds of 57mm recoilless rifle ammunition and 10 bangalore torpedoes were captured. US casualties were seven killed and 20 wounded.
- Camp Enari, the base camp of the Headquarters of the US 4th Infantry Division since the division's arrival in the RVN in September 1966, was turned over to the ARVN in ceremonies today. With the redeployment of the 3rd Brigade, 4th Infantry Division, ARVN forces assumed responsibility for more of the area of operation in the western highlands. The division headquarters relocated to the An Khe area for more effective command and control of its two brigades operating in Binh Dinh Province. The relocation of the 4th Division Headquarters from Camp Enari to Camp Radcliff was completed during the latter part of March 1970.
- The USN will turn over three logistic craft to the RVN Navy in ceremonies tomorrow (April 16, 1970) at the US Naval Support Activity, Da Nang. The three 73-foot LCM will be transferred to the Vietnam Navy as part of the USN Accelerated Turnover to Vietnam program. The program began in February 1969 with the training of crews and subsequent turnover of USN river assault craft to the Vietnam Navy. Tomorrow's turnover will bring the total USN logistic craft turned over to the Vietnam Navy by Naval Support Activity (NAVSUPPACT), Da

Nang, since the start of the Accelerated Turnover to Vietnam program, to 12.

APRIL 16, 1970

- Gia Dinh Province. At 0220 hours, the enemy fired four suspected 122mm rockets into the city of Saigon. The rockets impacted in the 1st and 2nd Precincts one mile NE, ½ mile SE and one mile east of the center of the city. One round impacted near a cemetery on Hai Ba Trung Street, another near the US Army Headquarters Area Command Library on Nguyen Du Street and the remaining two rockets impacted near Nguyen Hue Street two blocks west of the Saigon River. One of the rounds failed to explode. Five VN civilians were reported wounded in the indiscriminate attack. One building was reported heavily damaged. There were no US casualties.

APRIL 18, 1970

- *Toan Thang Offensive* (Binh Tuy Province). At 0300 hours, elements of the 199th Light Infantry Brigade, located in night defensive positions 37 miles NNW of Ham Tan, received an unknown number of rounds of 82mm mortar fire along with rocket-grenade, small arms and automatic weapons fire from an undetermined size enemy force. The infantrymen returned fire with their organic weapons and were supported by artillery and helicopter gunships. At 0435 hours, the enemy withdrew. Twenty-three NVA soldiers were killed and two detained. US casualties were one killed and 35 wounded. In addition, four individual and four crew-served weapons were captured along with a quantity of munitions and individual equipment left scattered in the vicinity. Materiel damage was light to moderate. No enemy were reported to have penetrated the perimeter.
- *Toan Thang Offensive* (Binh Long Province). At 1700 hours, a helicopter from the air cavalry squadron of the 1st Cavalry Division (Airmobile) received small arms and automatic weapons fire from an undetermined number of enemy soldiers 15 miles SW of An Loc and 10 miles from the Cambodian border. The enemy fire was returned with organic aerial machine guns and contact was lost almost immediately. The bodies of 21 enemy soldiers were sighted in the strike area. There were no US casualties.

APRIL 20, 1970

- *Operation Iron Mountain* (Quang Ngai Province). At 1045 hours, helicopter gunships from the Americal Division, while operating in support of an infantry element of the 11th Brigade, Americal Division, observed an estimated enemy company eight miles SW of Quang Ngai City (80 miles ESE of Da Nang). The helicopter crewmen engaged the enemy with aerial machine guns. Contact was lost when the enemy dispersed. The bodies of 19 enemy soldiers were observed in the strike area. Later the infantrymen, while on a sweep of the area, engaged the enemy again with their organic weapons. Contact was lost at an unreported time when the remaining enemy withdrew. An additional five enemy were killed and two individual weapons were captured. Total enemy losses were 24 soldiers killed. There were no US casualties.
- Eight wounded Cambodians presumed to be members of civilian irregular forces in Cambodia presented themselves to US personnel at Ba Xoai in Chau Doc Province on Thursday, April 16, 1970 and requested medical assistance. The Cambodians had been wounded in a firefight in Cambodia and flew to the RVN after being wounded. As a humanitarian measure, they were evacuated to US medical facilities and were being provided treatment.

APRIL 22, 1970

- Quang Nam Province. At 0920 hours, a reconnaissance element of the 1st Marine Division 22 miles WSW of Da Nang engaged an undetermined size enemy force with organic weapons, killing six enemy soldiers. An air observer in support of the reconnaissance element also observed five enemy soldiers and engaged them, killing all five. At an unreported time, contact was lost. At 1430 hours, artillery and tactical aircraft, supporting the reconnaissance element, engaged an undetermined size enemy force, killing 10 of them. A short while later the reconnaissance element was extracted. The cumulative enemy losses were 21 enemy soldiers killed. There were no US casualties.
- *Toan Thang Offensive* (Phuoc Long Province). At 1120 hours, an element of the 2nd Brigade, 1st Cavalry Division (Airmobile),

engaged an undetermined size enemy force 18 miles ENE of Phuoc Binh. Small arms and automatic weapons fire was exchanged and the troopers were supported by artillery and helicopter gunships. In about 15 minutes the enemy withdrew. Three enemy soldiers were killed; and 2,970 pounds of rice and 12 bicycles were destroyed. US casualties were one killed and two wounded.

- Chuong Thien Province. At 1700 hours helicopter gunships from the 164th Combat Aviation Group observed an unknown size enemy force 11 miles SSW of Vi Thanh. The enemy were engaged with aerial machine guns and in about 30 minutes the enemy withdrew, leaving behind 25 dead. There were no US casualties.

APRIL 23, 1970

- *Toan Thang Offensive* (Phuoc Long Province). At 1030 hours, an element of the 2nd Brigade, 1st Cavalry Division (Airmobile), found a cache and grave site in an area 17 miles ENE of Phuoc Binh. The troopers found 23 bicycles, 21 B-40 RPGs, five 75mm recoilless rifle rounds, and two tons of rice in the cache. The items were in good condition and were estimated to have been in place less than one month. The rice was evacuated to the element's command post for distribution. The graves, estimated to be less than 24 hours old, contained nine enemy bodies. There were no US casualties.

APRIL 25, 1970

- Vinh Binh Province. At 1020 hours, helicopter gunships from the 164th Combat Aviation Group in support of an operation accidentally fired into Phuong Thanh Village four miles WSW of Phu Vinh. Six VN civilians were wounded with no fatalities.

APRIL 26, 1970

- *Toan Thang Offensive* (Binh Long Province). At 2315 hours, an element of the 1st Brigade, 25th Infantry Division, located at FSB Pine Ridge, received approximately 25 rounds of 82mm mortar fire and rocket-grenade fire from an undetermined size enemy force. Approximately 10-15 enemy sapper personnel penetrated the perimeter, detonating some satchel charges, but were killed or repulsed. The infantrymen were supported by artillery, helicopter gunships, AC-119 and AC-47 gunships. In about 30 minutes, the enemy withdrew. One enemy soldier was killed. In addition, one individual weapon, 15 satchel charges, and 2½ pounds of C-4 explosives were captured. US casualties were four killed and 12 wounded. The fire support base received moderate materiel damage.

APRL 27, 1970

- Quang Ngai Province. At 1510 hours, two US Marine A-4 aircraft accidentally delivered bombs on CIDG Forces while on a bombing mission in response to a request from ground troops. Friendly casualties were 10 CIDG soldiers killed and 20 CIDG soldiers wounded.
- Binh Dinh Province. At 1000 hours, a reconnaissance element of the 2nd Brigade, US 4th Infantry Division, discovered eight tons of unpolished rice in a hut 11 miles north of An Khe. The rice had been in place approximately two months and was in good condition. The rice was evacuated and the hut was destroyed. There were no US casualties.
- *Toan Thang Offensive* (Phuoc Long Province). At 1030 hours, an element of the 2nd Brigade, 1st Cavalry Division (Airmobile), while operating 13 miles NE of Phuoc Binh, engaged an undetermined number of enemy soldiers. Small arms and automatic weapons fire was exchanged and the troopers were supported by tactical aircraft. Twenty-one enemy soldiers were killed, and four individual weapons were captured. US casualties were three killed and five wounded.

APRIL 28, 1970

- Thua Thien Province. At 0500 hours, an element of the 1st Brigade, 101st Airborne Division (Airmobile), in night defensive positions 19 miles WSW of Hue, received rocket-grenade fire from an estimated five enemy soldiers. The troopers returned fire with organic weapons and were supported by artillery fire. The bodies of 12 enemy soldiers were found in the battle area. US casualties were one killed and 19 wounded. At 1100 hours, while the troopers were continuing a sweep of the area after the 0500 hours contact, they found two bunker complexes containing a total of 75 bunkers with overhead cover. In this area they also found the bodies of 50 enemy soldiers that had been killed by helicopter gunships, artillery, and tactical aircraft within the past three days. In addition, one individual and one crew-served weapon were found in the complex.

- Quang Tri Province. At 0400 hours, an element of XXIV Corps artillery fired on a suspected location eight miles east of Quang Tri City (27 miles NW of Hue). One round landed in Village #88, killing six VN civilians and wounding five VN civilians. The 108th Artillery Group investigated the accident.
- *Toan Thang Offensive* (Phuoc Long Province). At 0755 hours, an element of the 2nd Brigade, 1st Cavalry Division (Airmobile), 14 miles NE of Phuoc Binh, engaged an undetermined number of enemy soldiers. Small arms fire was exchanged and helicopter gunships, artillery, and tactical aircraft supported the troopers. In about 50 minutes the enemy withdrew. Twenty-four enemy soldiers were killed and three individual weapons were captured. US casualties were five wounded with no fatalities.

APRIL 29, 1970

- Thua Thien Province. At 1400 hours, an element of the 1st Brigade, 101st Airborne Division (Airmobile), received an undetermined number and type of mortar and small arms fire from an undetermined size enemy force in a bunker complex 18 miles SW of Hue. The troopers returned fire with organic weapons and were supported by other elements of the brigade, artillery and helicopter gunships. At 1515 hours, the units assaulted the bunker complex causing the enemy to move southeast to a second bunker complex. After being engaged with artillery, helicopter gunships, and tactical aircraft, and another assault by the troopers, the enemy moved to a third bunker complex close by. Again, the enemy were engaged with artillery, helicopter gunships and tactical aircraft. Following this support, the troopers assaulted the third complex and contact was lost at about 1700 hours when the enemy withdrew. The bodies of 15 enemy soldiers were found in the strike area. In addition, two individual and three crew-served weapons were captured. US casualties were 26 wounded with no fatalities.
- Thua Thien Province. At 2000 hours, a helicopter gunship from an air cavalry squadron of the 101st Airborne Division (Airmobile), while in support of an element of the 1st Brigade,

101st Airborne Division (Airmobile), in an area 18 miles SW of Hue, accidentally delivered an undetermined number of rockets into the US positions. US casualties were three wounded with no fatalities. The accident was investigated by the 101st Airborne Division (Airmobile).

APRIL 30, 1970

- Thua Thien Province. At 2140 hours, April 29, 1970, an element of the 2nd Brigade, 101st Airborne Division (Airmobile), located at FSB Granite, 19 miles WSW of Hue, received an undetermined number and type mortar and rocket-grenade fire from an undetermined size enemy force. The US troops returned fire with their organic weapons and were supported by helicopter gunships and artillery. At 0650 hours, this morning, the enemy withdrew. Eighteen enemy soldiers were killed and one suspect was detained. US casualties were seven killed and 41 wounded.
- Thua Thien Province. At 1300 hours, an element of the 1st Brigade, 101st Airborne Division (Airmobile), 18 miles SW of Hue, found a weapons and munitions cache weighing approximately two tons. The cache contained 34 rifles of all types, two shotguns, five 30 caliber machine guns, four 60mm mortars, 80 60mm mortar rounds, 8,000 rounds plus 37 cases of 7.62 ammunition, ninety 57mm recoilless rifle rounds, and 250 M-79 rounds. The cache was in good condition and was evacuated to the command post.
- *Toan Thang Offensive* (Phuoc Long Province). At 0820 hours, an element of the 2nd Brigade, 1st Cavalry Division (Airmobile), 14 miles NE of Phuoc Binh, engaged an estimated enemy platoon. Small arms fire was exchanged and artillery, helicopter gunships, and tactical aircraft supported the troopers. The bodies of 24 enemy soldiers were found in the strike area. In addition, about 660 pounds of rice was captured. US casualties were one killed and six wounded.
- *Toan Thang Offensive* (Tay Ninh Province). At 1530 hours, an element of the 3rd Brigade, 1st Cavalry Division (Airmobile), discovered an enemy munitions cache in an area 21 miles NE of Tay Ninh City. The cache, weighing approximately eight tons, was in a metal box approximately 20 x 10 x 8 feet with walls approximately one inch thick. The cache was in fair

condition and contained: 480 75mm howitzer rounds (US); 722 75mm howitzer rounds (CHICOM); 113 rifle grenades; 10 B-40 rocket-grenade rounds; one individual weapon; 2,200 small arms rounds; and one optical sight for a French 75mm howitzer. The cache was destroyed in place. There were no US casualties.

- In response to the request of the GVN, advisers, air, logistics, medical and artillery support, as required, was provided by COMUSMACV to the RVNAF operating in counter-attacks against NVA and Viet Cong forces deployed in the Parrot's Beak area of Cambodia must cross the border from the RVN. Such support in the form of helicopters, artillery, and tactical air was provided initially by the RVNAF. Supplementary support to help save the lives of FWF and to help accomplish RVNAF objectives was requested by the GVN from the US sources. Authority to provide the requested supplementary support was given in Washington as announced in a statement there.
- US Forces provided the following support to RVNAF engaged in operation against NVA and Viet Cong Forces in the Parrot's Beak area of Cambodia; command and control helicopters; helicopter gunships and advisors. There were no US casualties associated with this support, nor were there any US aircraft losses. At approximately 1100 hours, as a result of undetermined causes, fire was accidentally delivered on friendly troops in the Parrot's Beak area of Cambodia by US gunships responding to a request for fire. Official reports to Headquarters, MACV indicate that 40 ARVN soldiers were wounded.

MAY 1, 1970

- *Toan Thang Offensive* (Tay Ninh Province). At 2315 hours, an element of the 11th Armored Cavalry Regiment, while in night defensive positions in an area 20 miles NW of Tay Ninh City, received rocket-grenade and 82mm mortar fire. A ground probe followed the fire attack by an undermined size of enemy force. Small arms and automatic weapons fire were exchanged and the troopers were supported by helicopter gunships, AC-119 gunships and artillery. Contact was lost at 2345 hours. A few minutes later, one of the helicopter gunships received .51 caliber machine gun fire from two ground positions and returned fire with organic weapons. Enemy losses in both actions were 20 killed, three enemy detained, one .51 caliber gun position destroyed and two 107mm rocket launchers captured. US casualties were seven wounded and light materiel damage.

- At 0730 hours, combined US and RVN forces launched an operation on NVA and Viet Cong positions in the Fish Hook area across the border in Cambodia. Elements of the 1st Cavalry Division (Airmobile) were supported by helicopter gunships. Elements of the RVN Airborne Division also participated in the operation. B-52 missions were flown in the Fish Hook area.

MAY 3, 1970

- Thua Thien Province. At 1130 hours, an element of the 1st Brigade, 101st Airborne Division (Airmobile) while operating in an area 17 miles SW of Hue received small arms and rocket-grenade fire from an undetermined size enemy force. The troopers returned fire with organic weapons and were supported by helicopter gunships and artillery. Contact was lost at 1600 hours when the enemy withdrew and the bodies of 27 enemy soldiers were found in the battle area. US casualties were one killed and 16 wounded.
- Binh Thuan Province. At 0155 hours, an element of the Task Force South located at LZ Betty two miles SW of Phan Thiet received an undetermined number and type of rounds followed by a ground attack by an undetermined size enemy force. The enemy employed satchel charges and small arms fire and penetrated the perimeter. The US forces were supported by artillery and helicopter gunships. The enemy was repulsed. Enemy losses were unknown. US casualties were six killed and 36 wounded. Moderate materiel damage was reported.
- Cambodia. Two significant caches were found today in the Memut area of Cambodia. Fourteen miles of NE of Memut, 1,200 individual weapons, 30 crew-served weapons and 15 55-gallon drums of gasoline were discovered. A 60-ton rice cache along with a munitions cache were found 16 miles ENE of Mamut by an element of the 1st Cavalry Division (Airmobile). Also in the Fish Hook area, USAF pilots flew 109 tactical air strikes. Pilots reported killing 13 enemy soldiers, triggering 20 secondary explosions, igniting one fire and damaging or destroying 125 fortifications and 84 bunkers.

MAY 4, 1970

- Cambodia. Thirteen miles NE of Memut, an arms cache consisting of 907 individual weapons and 100,000 rounds of small arms ammunition was uncovered. In addition, 12 tons of rice in good condition was found eight miles of Memut.

MAY 5, 1970

- Thua Thien Province. At 1315 hours, an element of the 1st Brigade, 101st Airborne Division (Airmobile), observed and engaged an undetermined size enemy force in a bunker complex 18 miles SW of Hue. Initial reports indicate that five enemy soldiers have been killed and three individual weapons captured. US casualties were three killed and 16 wounded.
- *Operation Sea Float* (An Xuyen Province). At 1330 hours, elements of the USN SEAL team while operating in an area 32 miles SSW of Ca Mau, were ambushed by an undetermined size enemy force employing rocket-grenade and small arms fire. The sailors returned fire with organic weapons supported by USN OV-10 aircraft and PBRs.
- Cambodia. At 1230 hours, combined US and RVNAF launched an operation against NVA and Viet Cong sanctuaries in the Se San Base Area across the border in Cambodia, approximately 50 miles west of Pleiku City. Elements of the US Army 4th Division and 22nd ARVN Division participated in the operation. In the combined operations of the US and RVN forces against NVA and Viet Cong positions in the Fish Hook area of Cambodia, the cumulative results to date indicate 685 enemy killed and 118 detained. In addition, 2,193 individual weapons, 65 crew-served weapons, 61 trucks, and 293 tons of rice were captured, destroyed, or damaged. US casualties were 12 killed and 48 wounded. In this operation, elements of the 1st Cavalry Division (Airmobile), 11th Armored Cavalry Regiment and RVN Army Airborne Division were supported by helicopter gunships, tactical air strikes, artillery, AC-119 gunships and B-52 missions.
- Cambodia. In the Fish Hook area, an element of the 11th Armored Cavalry Regiment, in tanks and armored personnel carriers, engaged an undetermined size enemy force while operating in an area 24 miles NE of Memut. The troopers

engaged the enemy with organic weapons and were supported by tactical air strikes and helicopter gunships. The contact continued for about a half hour when the remaining enemy withdrew. Enemy casualties were 88 killed, of which, 63 were killed by air. There were no US casualties.

MAY 6, 1970

- Quang Tri Province. At 0530 hours, an element of the 2nd Infantry Brigade, 101st Airborne Division (Airmobile) and ARVN forces located at FSB Henderson 10 miles SSW of Cam Lo, received an undetermined number of mortar rounds and rocket-grenade fire, combined with a ground attack from an undetermined size enemy force. Another element of the 2nd Brigade was air-assaulted into the area. Contact was lost at an unreported time, and the bodies of 29 enemy soldiers were found in the battle area. In addition, 13 individual weapons were captured. US casualties were 29 killed and 27 wounded. Light materiel damage was reported. ARVN casualties were light. The FSB received an undetermined number of mortar rounds sporadically throughout the day.
- Quang Tin Province. At 0840 hours, two explosive charges believed to have been rigged with a timing device and placed by suspected enemy terrorist, detonated in an outdoor movie area of the headquarters of the 198th Brigade, Americal Division, two miles south of Chu Lai. US casualties were 17 wounded with no fatalities.
- Cambodia. Early this morning, a Brigade Task Force of the US 25th Infantry Division launched an operation into an enemy sanctuary WNW of Tay Ninh City. This action was a continuation of the previously announced action taken by III Corps Forces of the RVNAF to deny the enemy use of supply and training bases in the Parrot's Beak area of Cambodia. The center of the operation was approximately 18 miles from Tay Ninh City. Initial reports indicate nine enemy killed. US losses were one killed and nine wounded. Also this morning, elements of the US 1st Cavalry Division, which was operating in the Fish Hook area of Cambodia along with ARVN forces, commenced operations against enemy sanctuaries in Cambodia 23 miles north of Phuoc Binh, Phuoc Long Province. Also, elements of the US 11th Armored Cavalry Regiment, which was also

involved in the Fish Hook operation, began operations in Cambodia in a combined operation with elements of the 5th ARVN Division in an area 10 miles north of Loc Ninh, Binh Long Province. This was a continuation of the combined US/RVNAF operations initiated in the Fish Hook area of Cambodia to neutralize enemy supplies and base areas, which pose a threat against US and VN forces in III Corps.

MAY 7, 1970

- Thua Thien Province. At 0445 hours, an element of the 3rd Brigade, 101st Airborne Division (Airmobile), while in a night defensive position 19 miles WSW of Hue, received an undetermined number of 60mm mortar rounds along with a ground attack from an undetermined size enemy force employing small arms and satchel charges. The troopers returned fire with organic weapons supported by helicopter gunships. Other elements of the 3rd Brigade, moving into the area to reinforce, also received small arms fire from an undetermined size enemy force. The troopers returned fire with organic weapons and contact was lost almost immediately when the enemy withdrew. Enemy losses were four killed, one individual, and four crew-served weapons captured. US casualties were six killed and nine wounded.
- Cambodia. Shortly after noon, an element of the 2nd Brigade, 1st Cavalry Division, engaged an undetermined size enemy force while operating in Cambodia in an area 24 miles NW of Phuoc Binh. Small arms and automatic weapons fire were exchanged, and the US forces were supported by artillery, helicopter gunships, AC-119 gunships, and tactical air strikes. Enemy losses in the action were 24 killed, five individual weapons, and three trucks captured. US casualties were eight killed.
- Cambodia. At 1030 hours, helicopter crewmen from the aviation element of the 4th Infantry Division observed about 30 to 40 enemy in a large bunker and hut complex, 48 miles WNW of Pleiku City, and about two miles inside Cambodia. The crewmen called in tactical air strikes and following the strikes, observed 15 enemy bodies in the strike area. In addition, 41 structures and 22 bunkers were destroyed.

MAY 8, 1970

- Quang Nam Province. At 1855 hours, a reconnaissance element of the 1st Marine Division received small arms fire from an undetermined size enemy force shortly after being inserted into an area 15 miles west of An Hoa. The Marines engaged the enemy with organic weapons and at about 1945 hours, helicopter gunships killed 13 of the enemy. The Marines were extracted at about 2015 hours and artillery fire killed four more of the enemy for a total of 17 killed in the engagement. There were no US casualties.
- Cambodia. Elements of the 2nd Brigade, 1st Cavalry Division (Airmobile), discovered two significant enemy weapons and munitions cache while operating in an area 17 miles NNE of Phuoc Binh and five miles inside Cambodia. The first cache was discovered at about 1030 hours in a bunker complex and contained the following: Six 122mm rocket launchers, 54 122mm mortar rounds, 60-122mm rockets, 1,150 57mm recoilless rifle rounds, 2,916 B-40 rounds, 1,956 60mm mortar rounds, 350 hand-grenades, 1.4 million rounds of .51 caliber ammunition, and 259,200 rounds of 7.62mm ammunition. The second cache was found at 1545 hours, about half a mile from the first cache and contained 147 individual weapons, 15 crew-served weapons, 478,800 rounds of .51 caliber ammunition, 144,000 rounds of 7.62 ammunition, and 10 CHICOM telephones.

MAY 9, 1970

- Thua Thien Province. At 1030 hours, an element of the 1st Brigade, 101st Airborne Division (Airmobile), while operating in an area 20 miles SW of Hue, engaged an undetermined size enemy force with organic weapons supported by artillery and helicopter gunships. Eighteen enemy soldiers were killed in the engagement. US losses were one killed and 12 wounded.
- Cambodia. US Forces were participating in the RVNAF IV Corps operation into the "Mekong River Corridor" which was initiated this morning. US forces will provide combat support to include resupply, medical evacuation, helicopter gunships and tactical air requested. US advisors will accompany VN units. In addition, approximately 30 USN craft, USN

helicopters, and USN OV-10 Bronco aircraft will participate in the combined US/Vietnam riverine force. The mission of the operation was to neutralize Viet Cong/NVA sanctuary bases located in the area. US Forces were not authorized to proceed into Cambodia beyond the limits authorized by the President. US casualties associated with the operation were one killed and two wounded.

- Cambodia. Further examinations of the large cache discovered on May 8, 1970 by elements of the 2nd Brigade, 1st Cavalry Division (Airmobile) in an area 17 miles NNE of Phuoc Binh and five miles inside Cambodia revealed the following additional weapons and munitions: 316 individual weapons, 53 crew-served weapons, 2,250,000 .50 caliber rounds, 129,600 14.5mm rounds, 3,100 57mm and 75mm recoilless rifle rounds, 1,040 mortar rounds, 13 cases of explosives ad 10 switchboard. Estimated total weight of the cache was over 250 tons, one of the largest weapons and munitions cache discovered in the war.

MAY 10, 1970

- Cambodia. In the combined US and RVNAF operation launched in the Fish Hook area of Cambodia on May 1, 1970 and continuations on this operation launched on May 6, 1970 and to the west, cumulative results indicated 1,368 enemy killed. In addition, 2,165 individual weapons and 338 crew-served weapons have been captured or destroyed. US casualties were 40 killed and one wounded. Additional enemy supplies, munitions and materiel captured or destroyed in this operation include: 3,548 individual weapons; 243 crew-served weapons; 1,034 tons of rice; 181 trucks; 386 122mm rockets; 2,956 B-40 rounds; 3,762 mortar rounds; 4,133,800 .50 and .51 caliber rounds; 2,454,500 small arms rounds; 154,800 14.5mm rounds; 1,400 rifle grenades; 375 hand grenades; 40,000 pounds of explosives; 1,100 gas masks. Forces participating in the operation included elements of the US 1st Cavalry Division (Airmobile); 2nd Brigade, 25th Infantry Division; 11th Armored Cavalry Regiment and the RVN Airborne Division and 5th Infantry Division.
- Fish Hook and Continuations. At about 1230 hours, elements of the 2nd Brigade, 1st Cavalry Division (Airmobile), discovered

another large enemy cache in an area 23 miles NNW of Phuoc Binh and five miles inside Cambodia. Included in the cache were 210 pistols; 2.9 million rounds of .51 caliber ammunition; 152,000 rounds of 20mm anti-aircraft ammunition; 1,760 rounds of mortar ammunition; 1,272 B-40 rounds; 648 75mm recoilless rifle rounds; 3,120 37mm anti-tank rounds; 16 cases of spare parts for small arms and recoilless rifles. Estimated weight of the cache was 36 tons.

- Parrot's Beak and Continuations. At about 0800 hours, elements of the 1st Brigade, 25th Infantry Division, discovered an enemy cache containing an estimated five tons of weapons, munitions and miscellaneous supplies in an area 22 miles NW of Tay Ninh City and four miles inside Cambodia. Included in the cache were more than 200 rifles and pistols, 3,000 pounds of rice, 10,000 rounds of small arms ammunition, 1,600 pounds of miscellaneous clothing, and 90 NVA uniforms.
- Se San Base Area. At about 1500 hours, an airborne infantry element of the 4th Infantry Division engaged an undetermined size enemy force while operating 50 miles WNW of Pleiku City and six miles inside Cambodia. The troopers engaged the enemy with organic weapons and were supported by helicopter gunships and tactical air strikes. Contact was lost at 1800 hours when the enemy withdrew. Enemy losses are unknown. US casualties were five killed and 14 wounded.
- Cambodia. Early this morning, helicopter crewmen of the 1st Cavalry Division's aviation element observed a large complex of tents, bunkers and structures, and an estimated 25 enemy in green and black uniforms in an area 13 miles west of Loc Ninh and three miles inside the Cambodia border. The crewmen engaged the enemy with organic weapons and were supported by helicopter gunships and tactical air strikes. The bodies of 15 enemy soldiers were sighted in the strike area and 14 structures and seven bunkers were destroyed. There were no US casualties.

MAY 11, 1970

- Gia Dinh Province. At about 0150 hours, three 122mm rockets impacted in Saigon. One rocket hit 1200 meters ENE of the center of the city on the Presidential Palace grounds causing no casualties but damaging trees and electrical wires. A second rocket impacted 2000 meters ENE of the center of town causing minor damage to a building with no casualties. The third rocket detonated 1900 meters west of the center of town in a residential area injuring four VN civilians and causing major damage to four houses.

- Fish Hook and continuations. At 1530 hours, elements of the 3rd Brigade, 1st Cavalry Division (Airmobile), discovered a rice cache in an area six miles SE of Memut, two miles inside Cambodia. The cache was estimated to have been in place 30 days, was in good condition and weighed an estimated 13 tons.
- Parrot's Beak and continuations. At 0545 hours, mechanized elements of the 1st Brigade, 25th Infantry Division, while operating in an area 23 miles NW of Tay Ninh City and two and a half miles inside Cambodia, engaged an undetermined size enemy force. Small arms and automatic weapons fire were exchanged and the infantrymen were supported by helicopter gunships and tactical air strikes. Contact was lost at about 1045 hours when the enemy withdrew, leaving 13 of his dead in the battle area. US casualties were five killed and 44 wounded, 30 of these received only minor wounds.
- Parrot's Beak and continuations. Elements of the US 3rd Brigade, 9th Infantry Division, which commenced combined operations with CIDG units in the tip of the Parrot's Beak on May 7, 1970, terminated their role in the operation and were withdrawn to the RVN.
- Se San Base Area. At 1730 hours, an airborne infantry element of the 4th Infantry Division, engaged an estimated three to four enemy soldiers while operating in an area 48 miles WNW of Pleiku City and four miles inside Cambodia. Small arms fire was exchanged and the troopers were supported by artillery. In a search of the battle area, the body of one enemy soldier was found in the vicinity of the weapons cache. In the cache were 200 bolt-action rifles; 15 heavy .50 caliber machine guns; 200 unknown type pistols; 200 rounds of mixed mortar ammunition; 16 60mm mortars; 20 82mm mortars; and a quantity of medical supplies. Estimated weight of the cache was two and a half tons.
- Cambodia. In connection with the operations in the Viet

Cong/NVA sanctuary areas in Southern Cambodia, RVN and US Naval Forces intend to prevent resupply of those areas by NVA/Viet Cong sea borne traffic. Thus, NVA/Viet Cong boats will be intercepted in an area from the Vietnam-Cambodian border on the Gulf of Siam to an area roughly opposite the South Vietnam island of Phu Quoc. There was no intention to interfere with Third-Country or Cambodian traffic or fishing in these waters. This was not a blockade. The Cambodian Government has been informed.

MAY 12, 1970

- Fish Hook and continuations. At about 1730 hours, helicopter crewmen from the aviation element of the 3rd Brigade, 1st Cavalry Division (Airmobile), observed an undetermined size enemy force in an area 28 miles north of Phuoc Binh and nine miles inside Cambodia. The enemy fired at the US forces who then returned fire with organic weapons. The bodies of 37 enemy soldiers were sighted in the area following the strike. There were no US casualties.
- Se San Base Area. Further examination of the large weapons cache discovered earlier today by an airborne infantry element of the 4th Infantry Division following a brief contact in an area four miles inside Cambodia and 48 miles WNW of Pleiku City has uncovered a total of 14.5 tons of enemy materiel. Included in the cache were 486 rifles, 198 pistols, 59 submachine guns, 155 pairs of binoculars, four 60mm mortars, nine 82mm mortars, three grenade launchers, two shotguns, two .51 caliber machine guns, two 57mm recoilless rifles, one minigun, 500 satchel charges, 55 anti-tank mines, and several thousand rounds of mixed small arms, mortar and recoilless rifle ammunition.
- General Officer Casualty. Major General John B. Dillard, USARV Engineer and Commanding General, US Army Engineer Command, Vietnam, was killed at approximately 1500 hours today when the helicopter in which he was flying received hostile fire and crashed. He was 50 years old. The incident took place about 10 miles SW of Pleiku. Nine other personnel aboard the helicopter were killed. An eleventh passenger on board the helicopter was seriously injured. General Dillard was assigned to Vietnam in November 1969

as the USARV Engineer and Commanding General, Engineer Troops, Vietnam, which became the US Army Engineer Command, Vietnam, on February 1, 1970.

MAY 13, 1970

- Gia Dinh Province. At about 0545 hours, an unknown number of terrorists detonated an explosive charge between a US Bachelor Enlisted Quarters (BEQ) and a Vietnam building located about 2200 meters SE of MACV Headquarters. The charge was estimated at between 15 to 20 pounds. One US civilian and four VN civilians were injured by the blast. The BEQ received light damage and the VN building was moderately damaged.
- Fish Hook and continuations. At 0315 hours, an infantry element of the 2nd Brigade, 1st Cavalry Division, located at FSB Brown two miles inside of Cambodia, received an undetermined number of mortar rounds followed by a ground attack from an estimated enemy company. The infantrymen engaged the enemy with unit weapons and were supported by helicopter gunship, artillery, AC-119 gunships and tactical air strikes. The contact lasted until 0545 hours when the remaining enemy withdrew. The bodies of 50 enemy soldiers were discovered in the battle area along with 34 individual weapons, three light machine guns and one 60mm mortar. US casualties were four wounded and no fatalities.
- Fish Hook and continuations. Elements of the 1st Brigade, 1st Cavalry Division, discovered two large rice caches while operating in an area six miles SE of Memut and two miles inside Cambodia. The first cache was discovered at about 1040 hours and contained 23 tons of rice and a half-ton of other food. Both the rice and food were in good condition. The second cache was uncovered at about 1315, a half mile SE of the earlier find. In it were an estimated 30 tons of rice, two motorcycles, two bicycles, and small quantities of munitions and medical supplies.
- Se San Base Area. Approximately one-third of the 4th Infantry Division Task Force, which had been engaged in combined operations with RVNAF against enemy sanctuaries in the Se San Base Area, have completed their mission and have returned to the RVN. The remaining troops of the Division will

continue combined operations with the 22nd ARVN Infantry Division Task force in the Se San area.

- Fish Hook and continuations. At 1500 hours, elements of the 2nd Brigade, 25th Infantry Division, discovered a weapons and munitions cache in an area 18 miles NNW of Katum and five miles inside Cambodia. Included in the cache were 87 individual weapons, five machine guns, three mortars, one rocket launcher, 13,600 rounds of small arms ammunition, 167 60mm rounds, 159 82mm mortar rounds, 66 75mm recoilless rifle rounds, one bicycle, three typewriters and two seven hp generators.

MAY 14, 1970

- Quang Tri Province. At about 1120 hours, a helicopter gunship of the 101st Airborne Division, while engaging a suspected enemy location nines miles WSW of Dam Lo, accidentally delivered fire on a unit of the Army of South Vietnam. ARVN casualties were one killed and six wounded. The 101st Airborne Division investigated the incident.
- Cambodia. Cumulative results of US and combined US/RVNAF operations in Cambodia indicated 2,284 enemy killed. In addition, 6,143 individual weapons, 646 crew-served weapons and 1,986 tons of rice have been captured or destroyed. These total were exclusive of predominantly RVNAF operations continuing or concluded in the Parrot's Beak area and underway in the Mekong River Corridor. US casualties in all Cambodian operations were 110 killed and 469 wounded.
- Fish Hook and continuations. At about 1615 hours, an element of the 11th Armored Cavalry Regiment discovered an estimated 65,000 pounds of rice in an area 14 miles north of Loc Ninh and four miles inside Cambodia. The find was made in a large bunker complex which had evidently been utilized as an enemy medical facility. Surgical lights and blood-soaked bandages were found in the complex, which had an estimated capacity of 500.
- Se San Base Area. US military support of the RVNAF operation launched today in Cambodia south of the Se San River, will include helicopter gunships, helicopter resupply and logistics,

medical evacuation, artillery, tactical air and advisors with the ARVN units. There were no US ground forces involved in the operation.

- Fish Hook and continuations. At about 1055 hours, an element of the 2nd Brigade, 25th Infantry Division, discovered a large rice cache containing an estimated 170 tons in an area 12 miles WNW of Memut and five miles inside Cambodia. Three individual weapons were also discovered in the vicinity of the cache. Thirty tons of rice, which was in good condition, has been evacuated to the RVN.
- Parrot's Peak area and continuations. At about 1500 hours, helicopter crewmen from the 12th Combat Aviation Group, in support of the 1st Brigade, 25th Infantry Division, detected a large cache site in an area 18 mils WNW of Tay Ninh City and one mile inside Cambodia. An infantry element was inserted into the area and discovered 2,500 100-pound sacks of rice totally 125 tons. The rice was in good condition and has been turned over to RVNAF units for disposition.

MAY 15, 1970

- Fish Hook and continuations. The Brigade Task Force of the US 25th Division, which commenced operations in Cambodia WNW of Tay Ninh City on May 6, 1970, terminated operations in the area. The Task Force has been relocated to the Fish Hook area where continued operations against Viet Cong and NVA sanctuaries.
- Fish Hook and continuations. At about 1030 hours, an element of the 2nd Brigade, 25th Infantry Division, discovered a large rice cache in an area 11 miles WNW of Memut, five miles inside Cambodia. The rice was in good condition and was sacked in 1,600 100-kilogram sacks. Total weight of the cache was 176 tons.

MAY 16, 1970

- Quang Tri Province. At about 0630 hours, a helicopter gunship of the 101st Airborne Division, while flying in an area nine miles SSE of Khe Sanh, received fire from an undetermined size enemy force. The gunship was not hit. The crewmen engaged the enemy with onboard ordnance, killing 35 enemy soldiers and destroying two trucks. There were no US casualties.

MAY 17, 1970

- Quang Ngai Province. At about 1715 hours, an element of the 198th Brigade, 23rd Infantry Division, while engaging a suspected company-size enemy position, accidentally delivered two rounds of 4.2 mortar ammunition in the vicinity of the Son Tinh District Headquarters, six miles NE of Quang Ngai City. Two VN civilians were killed and four wounded in the accident. The 23rd Infantry Division investigated the incident.
- Quang Nam Province. At about 1430 hours, an element of the 7th Marine Regiment, 1st Marine Division, operating in an area six miles SSW of An Hoi, discovered 23 tons of rice buried under haystacks and huts. The rice was in good condition and was evacuated.
- Quang Nam Province. At about 0645 hours, an element of the 5th Marine Regiment, 1st Marine Division, engaged an undetermined size enemy force while operating in an area seven miles NE of An Hoi. Contact was lost at an unreported time when the enemy withdrew. The Marines killed six enemy soldiers, detained 39 individuals, and captured two mortar sights and one CHICOM radio. US casualties were one wounded with no fatalities.
- *Operation Iron Mountain* (Quang Ngai Province). At about 1445 hours, an element of the 11th Brigade, 23rd Infantry Division, found nine tons of unpolished rice buried in an area four miles SSE of Duc Pho. The rice was in good condition and was evacuated.
- Fish Hook and continuations. At about 1230 hours, an element of the 1st Brigade, 25th Infantry Division, discovered a large communications equipment cache in a bunker complex five miles SW of Memut and two miles inside Cambodia. Included in the cache were 28 CHICOM generators, eight US manufactured generators, 137 radios of various manufacture and type, and 10 CHICOM field radios. The complex consisted of 135 bunkers and 10 classroom-type structures. Also found in the complex were 20 tons of rice and the bodies of five enemy soldiers killed earlier by air strikes.
- Fish Hook and continuations. At about 1030 hours, an element of the 2nd Brigade, 25th Infantry Division, operating in an area 32 miles NW of Tay Ninh City and two and a half miles inside

Cambodia, engaged an estimated five to six enemy with small arms and automatic weapons. Contact was lost 10 minutes later when the enemy withdrew with unknown losses. There were no US casualties. Shortly after the contact, the infantrymen received an enemy rallier who led the US forces to a large rice cache about a half-mile from the engagement. Included in the cache was 60 tons of rice in good condition. The individual weapon belonging to the rallier was captured.

- Fish Hook and continuations. Elements of the 2nd Brigade, 25th Infantry Division, on ground reconnaissance in an area 11 miles WNW of Memut and seven miles inside Cambodia, discovered the bodies of 151 enemy soldiers killed previously by Allied air strikes.

MAY 18, 1970

- US, RVN and other FWF suspended combat operations in the RVN at 1200 hours today.
- Fish Hook and continuations. At 1400 hours, an element of the 2nd Brigade, 1st Cavalry Division, discovered a large cache containing 210 tons of rice in good condition, in an area 21 miles north of Phuoc Binh and four miles inside Cambodia. Sixty tons of rice will be evacuated today and the remainder will be evacuated during the next few days.
- Fish Hook and continuations. At 1230 hours, a rallier led elements of the 2nd Brigade, 25th Infantry Division, to the scene of a large weapons and munitions cache 11 miles WNW of Mumut and seven miles inside Cambodia. Discovered in the cache were 20 CHICOM machine guns, 66 122mm rockets, 186 60mm mortar rounds, 300 82mm mortar rounds, 11 recoilless rifle rounds, 385 RPG rounds, 183 rifle grenades, 223 blocks of TNT, and a small quantity of small arms ammunition.

MAY 19, 1970

- At 1200 hours, US, RVN and other FWF concluded a 24-hour cessation of combat operations in the RVN. During the 24-hour period, 205 enemy-initiated actions were reported by all forces of which 90 enemy-initiated actions were considered significant (those actions in which casualties occurred). As a result of these significant actions, US casualties were one killed and 25 wounded. RVN and other FWF' casualties were light. Enemy losses resulting from all actions were 196 killed and nine detained.

- Thua Thien Province. At about 2130 hours, a US artillery unit firing in support of an element of the 3rd Brigade, 101st Airborne Division, accidentally delivered one round of friendly troops in an area 20 WSW of Hue. US casualties were one killed and four wounded. The 101st Airborne Division investigated the accident.
- Fish Hook and continuations. At about 1205 hours, an element of the 2nd Brigade, 1st Cavalry Division, discovered a large rice and foodstuff cache in an area 25 miles NNE of Phuoc Binh and four miles inside Cambodia. Included in the cache were 154 tons of rice in 100-kilogram sacks, 30 cases of smoked fish, eight 100-kilogram bags of powdered milk and four tons of corn, all reported in good condition. Sixty tons of rice was evacuated and the remainder of the cache was destroyed.

MAY 20, 1970

- Fish Hook and continuations. At about 1800 hours, an element of the 1st Brigade, 1st Cavalry Division, discovered an enemy weapons and vehicle cache in an area 35 miles NNE of Phuoc Binh 5½ miles inside Cambodia. The cache, which was reported in fair to good condition, contained 50 AK-47 rifles, 24 additional individual weapons, three RPD machine guns, one 2½-ton truck, six passenger trucks, one ¾-ton truck, one ¼-ton truck and three typewriters.
- US military support of the RVNAF operation launched today in Cambodia west of Duc Lap includes helicopter and logistical support, tactical air, artillery and advisors with ARVN units. There were no US ground forces involved in the operation.
- Fish Hook and continuations. At 1030 hours, an element of the 1st Brigade, 1st Cavalry Division, on a ground reconnaissance in an area 33 miles NNE of Phuoc Binh and five miles inside Cambodia, discovered an enemy cache in fair condition. Included in the cache were 34 individual weapons, one 60mm mortar, one radio and a small quantity of small arms ammunition.

MAY 23, 1970

- Fish Hook and continuations. At about 1630 hours, an element of the 3rd Brigade, 1st Cavalry Division, discovered an enemy weapons and munitions cache in a bunker complex 27 miles north of Phuoc Binh and five miles inside Cambodia. The cache, which was in good condition, contained four 7.62mm CHICOM machine guns, two AK-47 rifles, 23 CHICOM flamethrowers, 10 radios, four CHICOM telephones, 244 rounds of mortar ammunition, 158 rounds of recoilless rifle ammunition, 940 rocket-grenade rounds, 380 37mm rounds, 71,570 .51 caliber rounds, and 160,000 small arms rounds. Estimated weight of the cache was 15 tons.

MAY 24, 1970

- Gia Dinh Province. At about 0540 hours, an estimated 15 pounds of C-4 explosives were detonated between a US Bachelor Officers Quarters (BOQ) and a VN building at 36 Huynh Quang Thien Street (1500 meters SE of Tan Son Nhut Air Base). The blast caused no casualties but the Bachelor Officers Quarters (BOQ) sustained minor damage.

MAY 25, 1970

- Thua Thien Province. At about 2235 hours, a US artillery unit firing in support of an element of the 3rd Brigade, 101st Airborne Division accidentally delivered one round on friendly troops in an area 16 miles west of Hue. US casualties were two killed and three wounded. The 101st Airborne Division investigated the accident.
- Binh Thuy Province. At about 1730 hours, an element of the 199th Light Infantry Brigade found an arms cache estimated at two tons in an area 39 miles NNW of Ham Tan. The cache included six CHICOM light machine guns, two .51 machine guns, 22 AK-47 rifles, and 11 60mm mortar tubes. The cache was evacuated.
- Fish Hook and continuations. Two additional caches were discovered by elements of the 2nd Brigade, 1st Cavalry Division. At 1035 hours, the cavalrymen uncovered a cache containing 11.5 tons of salt, in good condition, in an area 24 miles north of Phuoc Binh and a half-mile inside Cambodia. The site was in the vicinity of two munitions caches discovered

earlier today. These caches were in good condition and had been in place for about two months. Contents included 532 60mm mortar rounds, 303 82mm mortar rounds, 78 120mm rounds, 310 57mm recoilless rifle rounds, 680 75mm recoilless rifle rounds, 200 rifle and rocket grenades, 50 bicycles and 100 machine gun ammunition drums. Estimated weight of the cache was 12.6 tons.

- Fish Hook and continuations. At about 1645 hours, helicopter crewmen from the aviation element of the 3rd Brigade, 1st Cavalry Division, observed a group of enemy vehicles containing 55-gallon drums in an area 17 miles of Phuoc Binh, in the vicinity of the RVN/Cambodian border. The crewmen engaged the enemy with unit machine guns and aerial rockets and observed the bodies of two enemy soldiers lying in the strike area. In addition, one 2½ -ton truck and six ¼-ton trucks and an undetermined number of drums were destroyed. There were no US casualties.
- Fish Hook and continuations. At about 1500 hours, an element of the 1st Brigade, 25th Infantry Division, uncovered a cache containing rice and medical supplies in a bunker complex seven miles SE of Memut and two miles inside Cambodia. The cache, which was in good condition, contained 20 tons of rice, 155 one-gallon cans of medical supplies, 4,600 pounds of gauze pads, bandages and cotton, 1,300 pounds of bed linens, a microscope and a small quantity of surgical instruments and seven bicycles.

MAY 26, 1970

- Gia Dinh Province. At about 2015 hours, an undetermined number of terrorists threw an estimated three-pound explosive charge at a bar located at 181 Nguyen Minh Chieu Street (2400 meters NNW of the center of Saigon). The resulting blast injured a US serviceman and two VN civilians. The building sustained minor damage.
- Fish Hook and continuations. At about 1900 hours, an element of the 2nd Brigade, 1st Cavalry Division, discovered a large enemy weapons cache in an area 27 miles NNE of Phuoc Binh an four miles inside Cambodia. The cache, which was in good condition, contained 30 RPD machine guns, 16 60mm mortars, 14 flamethrowers, three individual weapons, 87 82mm mortar

rounds, 210 57mm recoilless rifle rounds, 12 75mm recoilless rifle rounds, 480 B40/41 rounds, 36 85mm rounds, 104,550 12.7mm rounds, 50,840 CHICOM rifle grenades and 396 14.5mm rounds. In addition, 250 sets of web equipment, 924 CHICOM batteries, 20 demolition kits, one CHICOM telephone switchboard, and nearly 17 miles of time fuse were uncovered. Estimated weight of the cache was 67 tons. The materiel was evacuated.

- Fish Hook and continuations. At about 1105 hours, a reconnaissance element of the 1st Brigade, 1st Cavalry Division, discovered an enemy cache in the vicinity of Mondol Kiri City, about eight miles inside Cambodia. The cache, which was in poor condition, contained 63 flintlock rifles, 594 60mm mortar rounds, 304 CHICOM rifle grenades, 2,000 .51 caliber rounds, and 8,000 small arms rounds, and two 90cc motorbikes. The latter were destroyed in place and the remainder of the cache was evacuated.

MAY 27, 1970

- Quang Ngai Province. At about 1230 hours, an element of the 11th Brigade, 23rd Infantry Division, found four tons of unpolished rice in an area 12 miles SSE of Quang Ngai City. At about 1850 hours, the same unit discovered another 3½ ton cache of rice in the same area. The entire 7½ ton cache was evacuated.
- Fish Hook and continuations. Further search of the area in which an element of the 2nd Brigade, 1st Cavalry Division, discovered an enemy cache on May 26, 1970, uncovered additional enemy munitions and supplies. The site was about 27 miles NNE of Phuoc Binh and four miles inside the Cambodian border. The following additional items were discovered: 11 CHICOM flamethrowers, 11 60mm mortar sights, two 60mm mortar tubes, 36 82mm mortar rounds, 195 57mm recoilless rifle rounds, 40 75mm recoilless rifle rounds, 128 RPG anti-tank rounds, 72 B41 rounds, 3,720 CHICOM rifle grenades, 64,760 small arms rounds, 88,740 .51 caliber rounds, one demolition kit, and 100 pickaxes. Estimated weight of the cache, in good condition, was 94 tons.

MAY 28, 1970

- Fish Hook and continuations. Helicopter crewmen from the 2nd Brigade, 1st Cavalry Division, killed 34 enemy in four short engagements over a one-hour period. At 1135 hours, the crewmen observed an estimated 10-12 enemy in an area 17 miles NE of Snuol and 18 miles inside Cambodia. The crewmen engaged the enemy with organic weapons, killing eight. At about 1155 hours, 500 meters to the north of the original contact, the crewmen received small arms fire from an estimated 15-20 enemy. The crewmen again engaged the enemy with organic weapons and the ground fire ceased immediately. The bodies of six enemy soldiers were observed in the strike area. At about 1230 hours, the crewmen observed an undetermined size enemy force in the same general area. Again, the enemy was engaged with organic machine guns and aerial rockets. The bodies of 12 enemy soldiers were observed in the area following this engagement. The final engagement occurred at 1240 hours, a few hundred meters to the south, in the same general area as the first contact. In this engagement, the crewmen with machine guns and aerial rockets took an undetermined size enemy force under fire and the bodies of eight enemy soldiers were found in the strike area. There were no US casualties in any of the engagements.
- Fish Hook and continuations. At about 1215 hours, a US Army helicopter operating in support of ARVN troops in an area seven miles SE of Memut and five miles inside Cambodia, accidentally delivered an undetermined number of aerial rockets onto friendly elements. One US and 39 ARVN personnel were wounded in the accident. There were no fatalities.

MAY 29, 1970

- Binh Tuy Province. At about 2300 hours, an element of the 199th Light Infantry Brigade and Regional Forces elements in a night defensive position at FSB Sun 24 miles NW of Ham Tan, received small arms, automatic weapons, rocket-grenade, 60mm and 82mm mortar fire from an enemy force of undetermined size. The infantrymen returned fire with organic weapons and received support from artillery, an AC-119 gunship, helicopter gunships and flare ship. Contact was lost at about 0500 hours when the enemy withdrew. Thirty-six enemy soldiers were killed in the fight and nine individual weapons were captured. US casualties were 19 wounded and Regional Forces casualties were light.

- Fish Hook and continuations. At about 1015 hours, an element of the 2nd Brigade, 1st Cavalry Division, discovered a rice cache 24 miles north of Phuoc Binh and five miles inside Cambodia. The rice, which weighed an estimated 50 tons, was located in a complex of about 50 huts. The hut complex was destroyed and the rice, reported in good condition, was evacuated.
- Gia Dinh Province. At about 2055 hours, an automobile belonging to a French civilian was destroyed by an estimated 22 pounds of plastic explosive while it was parked at 37 Cach Mang Street (2400 meters NNW of the center of Saigon). The explosion injured a VN civilian and caused major damage to a truck.

MAY 31, 1970

- Cumulative results of US and combined US and RVNAF operations in Cambodia indicate 3,530 enemy killed. In addition, 7,882 individual weapons, 1,144 crew-served weapons, and 3,873 tons of rice have been captured or destroyed. These totals were exclusive of those predominately RVNAF operations continuing or concluded in the Parrot's Beak, Se San Area and the Mekong River Corridor. US casualties in all Cambodian operations were 236 killed and 896 wounded.
- Fish Hook and continuations. At about 1900 hours, an element of the 2nd Brigade, 1st Cavalry Division, uncovered additional weapons and munitions while searching the site of an enemy cache originally discovered by another element of the brigade on May 26, 1970. The cache site was located 27 miles NNE of Phuoc Binh and four miles inside Cambodia. Additional items found today include 31 machine guns, three 60mm mortars, 79,250 .51 caliber rounds, 210 rifle grenades, 426 B40/41 rounds, 48 CHICOM claymore mines, 12 demolition kits, and two CHICOM radios. The cache was reported in good condition, with an estimated weight of more than 21 tons. Estimated weight of the entire cache was 117 tons.
- Fish Hook and continuations. At about 0930 hours, an element

of the 3rd Brigade, 1st Cavalry Division, discovered an enemy munitions cache in an area 18 miles NNE of Loc Ninh and seven miles inside Cambodia. Included in the cache were 315,316 AK-47 rounds, 38 122mm rockets, 400 warheads for 122mm rockets, 185 57mm recoilless rifle rounds, 69 75mm recoilless rifle rounds, 354 B40 rounds, 311 82mm mortar rounds, 70 85mm anti-aircraft rounds, 420 rifle grenades, 450 CHICOM hand grenades and 384 pounds of plastic explosives. Estimated weight of the cache was 20 tons.

JUNE 1, 1970

- Fish Hook and continuations. At about 1430 hours, an element of the 2nd Brigade, 1st Cavalry Division, discovered an enemy vehicular repair facility while on a reconnaissance in an area four miles inside Cambodia and 21 miles NNW of Phuoc Binh. Found at the site were three truck engines, four truck gear boxes, seven generators, four radiators, 12 batteries, two boxes of condensers, coils and distributors, a voltage regulator, a hydraulic jack and a small number of additional parts, including air cleaners, differentials, gear shift levers, mufflers, and shock absorbers. The parts, which were in good condition, were of US, German and Polish manufacture. The items were evacuated.

JUNE 2, 1970

- *Operation Iron Mountain* (Quang Ngai Province). At about 1710 hours, an element of the 11th Brigade, 23rd Infantry Division, found 10 tons of unpolished rice while operating in an area 19 miles SSW of Quang Ngai. The rice was in good condition and was evacuated.
- Binh Dinh Province. At about 1100 hours, an element of the 1st Brigade, 4th Infantry Division, engaged an enemy force of undetermined size while operating in an area 23 miles SW of An Khe. The troopers fired their organic weapons and directed artillery and helicopter gunship fire against the enemy. The enemy withdrew at about 1510 hours, losing 28 killed. There were no US casualties.
- Fish Hook and continuations. At about 1010 hours, an element of the 2nd Brigade, 1st Cavalry Division, on reconnaissance in an area 22 miles north of Phuoc Binh and four miles inside

Cambodia, discovered three bunkers containing an estimated 10 tons of truck parts. Approximately 90 percent of the parts were for 2½ trucks. The parts were new and stored in preservative grease. The items were evacuated.

JUNE 3, 1970

- *Operation Frederick Hill* (Quang Tin Province). At about 1905 hours, an element of the 11th Brigade, 23rd Infantry Division, engaged about 12 enemy in an area 21 miles west of Tam Ky. The troopers returned fire and were supported by artillery. Contact was lost at an unreported time when the enemy withdrew. Ten enemy soldiers were killed in the engagement while there were no US casualties.
- Fish Hook and continuations. This afternoon, an element of the 2nd Brigade, 1st Cavalry Division, discovered additional weapons and munitions estimated at 15 tons while searching the site of an enemy cache originally uncovered on May 26, 1970 by another element of the brigade. The cache was in an area 27 miles NNE of Phuoc Binh and four miles inside Cambodia. Additional items found included two RPD light machine guns, four flamethrowers, a base plate and bipod for a 120mm mortar, 13 machine gun tripods and mounts, 200 AK-47 and RPD magazines, 74 cases of heavy machine gun links, 36 batteries, 53,120 rounds of .51 caliber ammunition, 3,781 14.5mm rounds, 380 37mm rounds, 48 75mm recoilless rifle rounds, 30 bangalore torpedoes, 250 hand grenades, 9,280 rounds of small arms ammunition, 11,600 blasting caps and more than 23 miles of time fuse. All items were in good condition and were evacuated. Estimated weight of the entire cache including today's discoveries was 132 tons.

JUNE 4, 1970

- Quang Tri Province. At approximately 1130 hours, a helicopter gunship of the 101st Airborne Division accidentally delivered fire on an ARVN Ranger unit in an area six miles SE of Khe Sanh. ARVN casualties were two killed and 20 wounded. US casualties were two killed.
- Fish Hook and continuations. At about 1100 hours, an element of the 1st Brigade, 1st Cavalry Division, on reconnaissance in an area 28 miles NNE of Phuoc Binh and five miles inside

Cambodia, discovered a 33-ton rice cache. The rice, which was in good condition, was stored in a hut in 300 100-kilogram bags. The rice was evacuated.

JUNE 5, 1970

- Fish Hook and continuations. At about 1800 hours, helicopter crewmen from the aviation element of the 2nd Brigade, 1st Cavalry Division, observed an estimated 30 enemy in an area 22 miles north of Loc Ninh and 18 miles inside Cambodia. The crewmen engaged the enemy with organic machine guns and aerial rockets and the enemy responded with heavy small arms and automatic weapons fire. The exchange of fire was of brief duration, with the bodies of 13 enemy soldiers observed in the strike area. There were no friendly casualties.
- Fish Hook and continuations. At 1630 hours, an element of the 2nd Brigade, 1st Cavalry Division, discovered an enemy rice and salt cache in a bunker and structure complex 26 miles north of Phuoc Binh and five miles inside Cambodia. Searching some 20 bunker and several structures, the cavalrymen uncovered 33 tons of unpolished rice and five and a half tons of salt. Both the salt and rice were in good condition, had been in place an estimated month and evacuated.
- Fish Hook and continuations. At about 1700 hours, an element of the 3rd Brigade, 1st Cavalry Division, discovered an enemy cache containing communications equipment in an area 18 miles NNE of Loc Ninh and six miles inside Cambodia. In a tin-lined structure measuring 20x5x5 feet, the troopers found 24 radios, two large radio transmitters with hand generators, 19 assorted homemade radio transmitters, seven telegraph keys, 16 speakers, and an assortment of hand sets, microphones and fuses. In an adjoining structure, the troopers also found an undetermined number of bicycles.

JUNE 6, 1970

- *Operation Iron Mountain* (Quang Ngai Province). At about 1455 hours, an element of the 11th Infantry Brigade, 23rd Infantry Division, uncovered an enemy rice cache hidden under the floor of a hut in an area nine miles WNW of Quang Ngai City.

Discovered were 3,000 pounds of unpolished and 2,000 pounds of polished rice, all in good condition. Locally grown, the rice had been in place about a month. The rice was evacuated.

JUNE 7, 1970

- Fish Hook and continuations. At about 1410 hours, an element of the 1st Brigade, 1st Cavalry Division discovered a large enemy rice cache while on reconnaissance in an area six miles SW of O Rang and two miles inside Cambodia. The cache contained an estimated 135 tons of rice, which was reported in good condition. The rice was evacuated.
- Fish Hook and continuations. At about 1505 hours, a helicopter gunship from the 1st Cavalry Division accidentally delivered fire on an ARVN unit while supporting the unit in an area nine miles ESE of Memut and five miles inside Cambodia. Two ARVN soldiers were killed and 16 ARVN and one US were wounded.

JUNE 8, 1970

- Quang Nam. At about 0800 hours, elements of the 5th Regiment, 1st Marine Division, engaged an undetermined size enemy force while operating in an area five miles NE of An Hoa. Small arms and automatic weapons fire was exchanged and contact was lost at an unreported time. Enemy losses were eight killed and four detained. There were no friendly casualties.
- Khanh Hoa Province. The Cam Ranh Army Depot located three miles SSW of Qui Nhon received an unknown number and type of mortar rounds resulting in light materiel damage. There were no casualties.
- Phuoc Long Province. The headquarters of the 1st Cavalry Division at Phuoc Vinh received one 122mm rocket resulting in very light materiel damage. There were no casualties.
- Fish Hook and continuations. At about 1000 hours, an element of the 2nd Brigade, 1st Cavalry Division, discovered an enemy cache in an area 23 miles north of Phuoc Binh and four miles inside Cambodia. Items in the cache included 67 SKS rifles, 25 K-50 sub-machine guns, one B41 rocket launcher, 174 CHICOM

hand grenades, a small quantity of B40/41, mortar and small arms rounds, 24 anti-tank mines and 2,000 pounds of rice. The entire cache was in good condition and was evacuated.

JUNE 9, 1970

- Quang Tin Province. At about 1030 hours, an element of the 196th Brigade, 23rd Infantry Division, while operating in an area 22 miles west of Tam Ky, received small arms and about 30 rounds of mixed 82mm and 60mm mortar fire from an undetermined size enemy force. The infantrymen returned fire with organic weapons and contact was lost at an unreported time when the enemy withdrew. The bodies of five enemy soldiers were found in the area of the fight. US casualties were two killed and eight wounded.
- Cumulative results of US and combined US and RVNAF operations in Cambodia indicated 3,882 enemy killed. In addition, 8,126 individual weapons, 1,147 crew-served weapons and 4,772 tons of rice have been captured or destroyed. These totals were exclusive of those predominately RVNAF operations continuing or concluded in the Parrot's Beak area, Se San Base Areas and the Mekong River Corridor. US casualties in all Cambodia operations were 236 killed and 1,098 rounded.
- Fish Hook and continuations. At about 0345 hours, an element of the 1st Brigade, 25th Infantry Division, received small arms, automatic weapons and rocket-grenade fire from an undetermined size enemy force while operating in an area eight miles NNE of Memut and 12 miles inside Cambodia. The infantrymen returned fire with organic weapons and were supported by artillery, helicopter gunships and USAF AC-119 gunships. Contact was lost at 0445, with enemy losses unknown. US casualties were three killed and 15 wounded.
- Fish Hook and continuations. At about 1330 hours, an element of the 11th Armored Cavalry Regiment uncovered an enemy cache in good condition while reconnoitering an area 14 miles NE of Memut and five miles inside Cambodia. The cache contained more than 40 tons of rice (372 100-kilogram bags), 100 pounds of salt, 10 large cooking pots and a small quantity of eating utensils. All items were destroyed in place.
- Fish Hook area and continuations. Elements of the 2nd Brigade, 1st Cavalry Division, discovered two enemy caches

containing more than 31 tons of rice. The first cache was uncovered at about 0940 hours in an area 23 miles north of Phuoc Binh and four miles inside Cambodia. The cache, containing more than 20 tons (189 100-kilogram bags), was found during a sweep of the area following a contact in which the cavalrymen exchanged small arms and automatic weapons fire with an undetermined size enemy force for less than 10 minutes. The rice was destroyed in place. At 1700 hours, another element of the brigade discovered an additional 11 tons of rice in 100 100-kilogram bags in an area 21 miles NNE of Phuoc Binh and one and a half miles inside Cambodia. The rice, in good condition, was evacuated.

- Fish Hook and continuations. Further exploitation of the cache site originally discovered on May 26, 1970 by an element of the 2nd Brigade, 1st Cavalry Division, resulted in the finding of an additional five tons of munitions. The site was in an area 10 miles SW of O Rang and four miles inside Cambodia. Items found in a complex of 58 bunkers included 139 CHICOM claymore mines, 120 85mm artillery rounds, 860 37mm anti-aircraft rounds, 30 bangalore torpedoes, 22,500 blasting caps and more than seven miles of time fuse. The bunkers were destroyed and the munitions, in good conditions, was evacuated.

JUNE 10, 1970

- Fish Hook area and continuations. At about 1100 hours, an element of the 1st Brigade, 1st Cavalry Division, discovered an enemy munitions cache in an area nine miles SW of O Rang and four miles inside Cambodia. The cache, which weighed more than 21 tons, contained 128,000 rounds of .51-caliber ammunition, 1,550 37mm rounds, and 4,512 14.5mm rounds. The munitions were in good condition and was evacuated.
- Fish Hook area and continuations. At about 1130 hours, an infantry element of the 2nd Brigade, 1st Cavalry Division, discovered an enemy weapons and munitions cache in an area 19 miles SW of O Rang and five and a half miles inside Cambodia. The cache, which was in good condition, contained

81 SKS rifles, 80 rifle grenade adapters, one 60mm mortar, 17 sights for 60mm and 82mm mortars, 1,138 60mm mortar rounds, 45 107mm rockets, 66 75mm recoilless rifle rounds, 2,325 rifle grenades, 160 anti-tank grenades, and 252,000 rounds of AK-47 ammunition. In addition, 6,600 15-volt batteries, 11 unknown-type radios, 25 bicycles and a small quantity of explosives were found. All items were evacuated.

JUNE 11, 1970

- Quang Nam Province. At about 0955 hours, a reconnaissance element of the 1st Marine Division engaged 13 enemy soldiers in an area 20 miles NW of Da Nang. The Marines were supported by helicopter gunships and the 13 enemy were killed. A US casualty from the engagement was one wounded.
- Khanh Hoa Province. At about 0110 hours, an estimated 10 enemy sappers penetrated the perimeter of the Naval Air Facility at Cam Ranh Bay and charged the main gate. Security forces returned fire, killing two of the sappers. One enemy soldier was detained, and one individual weapon and a number of satchel charges were captured. Light materiel damage was sustained in the attack and there were six US wounded.
- FOLLOWING IS THE TEXT OF A MEMORANDUM FOR CORRESPONDENTS PERTAINING TO AN ATTACK ON THANH MAY HAMLET:
- HQ MACV. Da Nang – In the largest terrorist attack in the I Corps of Vietnam since Tet of 1968, an estimated two companies of Viet Cong struck Thanh My Hamlet, located 18 miles SSE of Da Nang, killing 70 VN civilians and wounding 68 others during the early morning June 11, 1970. According to First Lieutenant T.S. Miller, 27, (New Kensington, Pa.) Commander of the Alpha-1 Combined Unit Pacification Program (CUPP), 1st Battalion, 7th Marines, 16-man Marine squad living in the village, "Their main objective was to destroy this village along with the civilian population. They kept my Marines pinned down while they infiltrated the village and then they started the massacre." At 2 A.M., the enemy forces opened up with a murderous barrage of 60mm and 81mm mortar fire upon the Marine command post and the heavily populated areas of the village, with mortar shells landing every

14 seconds with deadly accuracy. The barrage lasted for more than an hour. Lieutenant Miller stated, "The best estimate I could give would be more than 200 mortar rounds exploded in the village. They used a lot of white phosphorus mortar shells to set fire to the houses." Lieutenant Miller called in artillery and Huey gunships on the enemy but the enemy forces were already inside the village. His 16-man force poured out an intense barrage of small arms fire and grenades, trying to keep the enemy from overrunning their small command post. Seven enemy were killed after they penetrated the wire around the Marine position. "After the mortar barrage lifted, they poured into the village in an all-out two-pronged ground assault," Miller explained. "Those villagers who weren't killed in the first mortar barrage had taken cover in their house bunkers. The enemy sappers moved through the village streets destroyed the houses and bunkers where the civilians had taken cover, with numerous satchel charges, CHICOM grenades and small arms fire," Miller continued. "More than half of the civilians who were casualties died in the houses and bunkers, where they had sought cover. Seventy-five percent of the hamlet was completely leveled with 156 homes destroyed and another 37 heavily damaged. Two hours after the attack, the enemy forces broke contact and split up into four and five man teams and scattered to the north," stated Captain C.E. Barnett of the 7th Marine staff. (Operational reports later confirmed damage to the hamlet as 316 homes destroyed and 50 damaged and two offices and two schools destroyed. It was estimated that 85 percent of the hamlet was destroyed in the attack. Civilian casualties were 74 killed and 68 wounded.

- Fish Hook area and continuations. At about 1650 hours, a mechanized element of the 2nd Brigade, 25th Infantry Division, received small arms, automatic weapons and rocket-grenade fire from an undetermined size enemy force while operating in an area five miles WSW of Memut and three miles inside Cambodia. The infantrymen returned fire with their organic weapons and were supported by helicopter gunships. Artillery and tactical air strikes also supported the troopers. Contact was lost at 1700 hours when the enemy withdrew. Enemy losses were one killed. US casualties were three killed and 19 wounded.

JUNE 12, 1970

- *Operation Frederick Hill* (Quang Tin Province). At about 0605 hours, an element of the 196th Brigade, 23rd Infantry Division, received heavy small arms and unknown caliber mortar fire from an enemy force of undetermined size while operating in an area 21 miles west of Tam Ky. The infantrymen returned fire with organic weapons and were supported by tactical air strikes, artillery and helicopter gunships. Contact was lost at 1345 hours when the enemy withdrew. Thirty-three enemy soldiers were killed in the battle; five individual and one crew-served weapons were captured, and five bunkers were destroyed. US casualties were one killed and 15 wounded.
- Fish Hook area and continuations. At about 1400 hours, an element of the 2nd Brigade, 1st Cavalry Division, discovered an enemy medical facility in the hut-bunker complex about 12 miles SW of O Rang and five miles inside Cambodia. Inspection of eight huts revealed that each contained a bunker housing medical equipment and supplies. Each hut also contained a stove and cooking utensils. Among the items found in the complex were a refrigerator, six cases of morphine, eight five-gallon cans of assorted pills, several thousand assorted capsules, 25 pounds of Novocain, 50 pounds of bandages, a sterilizer, and an artificial leg. Also discovered were a CHICOM submachine gun, four bicycles, and a small quantity of training manuals. The supplies and equipment were evacuated and the complex was destroyed.
- Fish Hook area and continuations. At about 1415 hours, an element of the 3rd Brigade, 1st Cavalry Division, found an enemy weapons cache in a bunker complex 15 miles east of Snuol and six miles inside Cambodia. Contents of the bunkers included 51 SKS rifles, 25 Type 43 CHICOM submachine guns, one AK-47 and 225 CHICOM hand grenades. All items were in good condition and have been evacuated. The complex of four bunkers, each measuring approximately 10x10 feet, as destroyed.

JUNE 13, 1970

- Quang Nam Province. At about 0200 hours, a Combined Unit Pacification Program (CUPP) team made up of personnel from an Regional Forces company and Marines of the 5th Regiment, 1st Marine Division, in a position 19 miles SW of Da Nang received a ground attack from an unknown size enemy force. The enemy employed small arms, rocket-grenades and satchel charges. The team returned fire with organic weapons and received fire support from 81mm mortars and artillery. Contact was lost at 0420 hours when the enemy withdrew having suffered unknown losses. Marine casualties were three killed and four wounded. Regional Forces casualties were light.

- Fish Hook and area and continuations. At about 1050 hours, an element of the 1st Brigade, 25th Infantry Division, discovered an enemy weapons cache while on reconnaissance in an area four miles NNE of Memut and nine miles inside Cambodia. The cache, which was found in a bunker, consisted of 94 individual weapons, two crew-served weapons and a small quantity of small arms ammunition. The bunker was destroyed and the weapons and munitions, which were in good condition, were evacuated.

JUNE 14, 1970

- Quang Nam Province. At about 1220 hours, a reconnaissance element of the 1st Marine Division operating in an area 30 miles SSW of Da Nang, received small arms fire from an enemy force of undetermined size. The Marines returned fire with organic weapons and contact was lost at an unreported time. Eighteen enemy soldiers were killed and one individual weapon was captured in the fight. US casualties were one killed and one wounded.
- Fish Hook area and continuations. At about 0250 hours, elements of the 1st Brigade, 1st Cavalry Division, occupying a fire support base about one mile north of O Rang and four miles inside Cambodia, received a ground attack from an estimated enemy company. The cavalrymen returned fire with organic weapons and were supported by artillery, helicopter gunships and a flare ship. Contact continued sporadically until 0630 hours when the enemy withdrew, leaving 28 of his dead in the battle area. US casualties were 12 wounded. In addition,

eight AK-47 rifles, four B40 launchers, one 9mm pistol and 150 CHICOM hand grenades were captured. Also found in the battle area were 21 canvas flack jackets, five pair of wire cutters and a medical kit.

- Fish Hook area and continuations. At about 1610 hours, an element of the 1st Brigade, 25th Infantry Division, discovered an enemy rice cache while on reconnaissance in an area five and a half miles SSW of Memut and a half mile inside Cambodia. The cache contained an estimated 65 tons of rice, in good condition. The rice was evacuated.
- The major portion of the 2nd Brigade, 25th Infantry Division, which has been engaged in operations against enemy sanctuaries in Cambodia west of the Fish Hook, has completed its mission there and has returned to the RVN. The Task Force began operations in Cambodia on May 9, 1970. Less than a battalion-sized element of the force remained in Cambodia.

JUNE 15, 1970

- At about 0830 hours, an undetermined size enemy force fired four rocket-grenades at an MSTS ship in an area 17 miles NE of Vung Tau. Three rounds hit the ship causing minor damage and wounding one civilian crewman (nationality unknown). At about 0925 hours, another MSTS ship was taken under fire by an undetermined size enemy force in the same area. Three rocket-grenades were fired and all missed the ship. A Regional Forces element reacted to the attack killing one enemy soldier and detaining another. There were no friendly casualties. At approximately 1300 hours, an undetermined size enemy force in an area 11 miles south of Saigon fired upon a third MSTS ship. Two rocket-grenade rounds were fired, neither hitting the ship.
- Dinh Tuong Province. At about 2105 hours, three Ranger teams engaged an enemy force of undetermined size in an area 13 miles NNW of My Tho. Small arms and automatic weapons fire was exchanged and the rangers were supported by helicopter gunships, artillery and a flare ship. Sporadic contact continued until about 0325 hours when the enemy withdrew. Ten enemy soldiers were killed in the fight and there were no US casualties.

JUNE 16, 1970

- Fish Hook and continuations. At 1145 hours, an element of the 2nd Brigade, 1st Cavalry Division, discovered an enemy rice cache while on reconnaissance in an area 15 miles SW of O Rang and five miles inside Cambodia. The rice, which was in good condition, and weighed an estimated 22 tons, was found in a complex of four bunkers. The bunkers were destroyed and the rice was evacuated.
- Fish Hook area and continuations. At 0920 hours, an element of the 1st Brigade, 1st Cavalry Division, on reconnaissance in an area five miles SW of O Rang and two miles inside Cambodia, engaged two enemy soldiers with organic weapons. Contact was lost at 0940 hours, after an exchange of small arms fire, with enemy losses unknown and no friendly casualties. In a sweep of the area, the troopers found two huts, approximately 10x20 feet, which contained 11 tons on rice, in 2,220-pound sacks. The huts and rice were destroyed in place.

JUNE 17, 1970

- Fish Hook and continuations. At about 1350 hours, an element of the 1st Brigade, 1st Cavalry Division, discovered two large structures containing enemy munitions and rice while reconnoitering an area six miles SW of O Rang and two miles inside Cambodia. The structures contained 300 60mm mortar rounds, 400 82mm mortar rounds, 70 75mm recoilless rifle rounds, 200 B40 rounds, 500 CHICOM hand grenades, 40 anti-tank mines, 20 satchel charges, 16,800 AK-47 rounds, and 5½ tons of rice. The structures, munitions and rice were destroyed in place.
- Fish Hook and continuations. At about 1200 hours, an element of the 2nd Brigade, 1st Cavalry Division, discovered an enemy cache site while on reconnaissance in an area 20 miles NNW of Phuoc Binh and three miles inside Cambodia. In a complex of seven structures, the cavalrymen uncovered 81 tons of rice. The rice, in poor condition, was estimated to have been in place three to six months. The structures and rice will be destroyed in place.

JUNE 18, 1970

- Fish Hook area and continuations. At 1145 hours, an element of the 2nd Brigade, 1st Cavalry Division, discovered a cache site in a complex of three huts about 20 miles SW of O Rang and six miles inside Cambodia. The cache contained 320 SKS rifles, two miles of communication wire, 1,200 pounds of corn and a small quantity of rice. The weapons were in good condition and were evacuated. The huts and the remaining supplies were destroyed in place.

- Fish Hook area and continuations. At about 1420 hours, an element of the 2nd Brigade, 1st Cavalry Division, discovered four huts containing 61 tons of rice in an area 16 miles SW of O Rang and four miles inside Cambodia. The cache was in good condition and, together with the huts, was destroyed in place.

JUNE 19, 1970

- Cumulative results of US and combined US and RVNAF operations in Cambodia indicated 4,175 enemy killed. In addition, 8,825 individual weapons, 1,164 crew-served weapons, and 5,226 tons of rice have been captured or destroyed. These totals were exclusive of those predominately RVNAF operations continuing or concluded in the Parrot's Beak area, Se San Base Areas and Mekong River Corridor; US casualties in all Cambodian operations were 300 killed and 1,330 wounded.

JUNE 20, 1970

- Quang Nam Province. At about 0530 hours, elements of the 5th Regiment, 1st Marine Division, while operating in an area 16 miles SW of Da Nang, engaged an enemy force of unknown size. The Marines were supported by helicopter gunships and tactical air strikes. The action continued until about 1500 hours when the enemy withdrew. Enemy losses were 15 killed, nine detained, and three individual weapons captured. One Marine was wounded in the fight.
- Quang Tri Province. At about 1315 hours, the crews of helicopter gunships of the 101st Airborne Division engaged an undetermined size enemy force in an area nine miles SSE of Khe Sanh. Ten enemy soldiers were killed by the gunships and there were no friendly casualties.
- Binh Dinh Province. At about 0930 hours, an element of the 2nd Brigade, 4th Infantry Division, operating in an area 24 miles NNE of An Khe, engaged an estimated six enemy.

Sporadic contact continued until about 2240 hours in the evening with enemy elements estimated to be as large as a company. The troopers were supported by artillery and helicopter gunships. Enemy casualties were 25 killed, one detained and two individual weapons captured. US losses resulting from the fight were two killed and two wounded.

- Binh Dinh Province. At about 1500 hours, a cavalry element of the 173rd Airborne Brigade and an Regional Forces element, on a combined operation 14 miles NNE of Phu Cat, engaged an enemy force of undetermined size. Helicopter gunships and tactical air strikes supported the action, which continued sporadically until about 2145 hours when the enemy withdrew. Twenty-one enemy soldiers were killed in the engagement and there were no friendly casualties. In addition, 11 individual and one crew-served weapon was captured. In a sweep of the contact area, the Allies discovered an enemy base camp containing approximately 100 well-constructed bunkers.

JUNE 21, 1970

- Quang Nam Province. Nine 122mm rockets impacted in the city of Da Nang, killing seven VN civilians. Nineteen VN civilians were injured and seven houses were destroyed by the attack.
- Fish Hook and continuations. An element of the 2nd Brigade, 1st Cavalry Division, discovered two enemy rice caches while reconnoitering an area 15 miles SW of O Rang and four miles inside Cambodia. The first find of approximately 12 tons of polished rice was made at 0920 hours while searching an 18x20 foot structure. At 1400 hours, an additional 29 tons were uncovered in the same general area. The rice in the second cache was in good condition and had been in place an estimated two to three weeks. All the rice was destroyed in place.

JUNE 22, 1970

- The USN turned over 273 combat boats to the RVN Navy in ceremonies at Saigon. The craft included 162 PBRs, 75 RACs and 36 PCFs or “Swift Boats”. Today’s turnover brings to 525 the number of USN craft transferred to the Vietnam Navy since June 1968.

- Fish Hook area and continuations. At 1605 hours, an element of the 2nd Brigade, 1st Cavalry Division, engaged an undetermined size enemy force while operating in an area nine miles SW of O Rang and five miles inside Cambodia. The enemy returned fire with small arms, automatic weapons and rocket-grenade fire and the US troops were supported by artillery and helicopter gunships. Contact was lost at 1805 hours but was reestablished at 1830 hours with an exchange of small arms and automatic weapons fire. The contact was terminated at 1835 hours when the remaining enemy withdrew. Enemy losses were six killed and one individual and two crew-served weapons captured. In addition, approximately one ton of rice was destroyed. US casualties were one wounded.
- Fish Hook area and continuations. At 1115 hours, helicopter crewmen from an aviation element of the 1st Cavalry Division received small arms and automatic weapons fire from an undetermined size enemy force in an area 24 miles NW of Phuoc Binh and four miles inside Cambodia. The crewmen returned fire with organic machine guns and aerial rockets and tactical air strikes were called in. The enemy fire ceased almost immediately. The bodies of 10 enemy soldiers were observed in the area following the strike. There were no friendly casualties.

JUNE 25, 1970

- A USN A-7 aircraft escorting unarmed US reconnaissance aircraft over North Vietnam conducted protective reaction against an anti-aircraft installation with unknown results. The protective reaction, the second since the reinforced protective reaction raids in early May, was in response to hostile actions by an enemy radar-controlled anti-aircraft position NW of Vinh in southern Nghe An Province of North Vietnam. There was no damage to US aircraft.
- Fish Hook area and continuations. At 1900 hours, an element of the 3rd Brigade, 1st Cavalry Division, discovered a large enemy weapons and munitions cache in an area 15 miles NE of Snuol and 13 miles inside Cambodia. The cache was uncovered in an

80x80 foot steel-lined bunker and was estimated to weigh more than 150 tons. Thus far, the cache has yielded 103 SKS rifles, 31 .30 caliber CHICOM machine guns, two 75mm recoilless rifles, one 81mm mortar and six CHICOM mine detectors. Munitions include 458,708 small arms and machine gun rounds, 535 57mm recoilless rifle rounds, 92 75mm recoilless rifle rounds, 1,100 85mm rounds, 942 37mm rounds, 1,932 B40 rounds, 216 anti-tank grenades, 4,409 CHICOM hand grenades, 16,000 blasting caps, and more than 1.3 million feet of time fuse.

JUNE 26, 1970

- *Operation Iron Mountain* (Quang Ngai Province). At about 1600 hours, eight tons of locally grown, unpolished rice were found in a hut six miles NNE of Quang Ngai City by an element of the 196th Brigade, 23rd Infantry Division. The rice was in good condition and was evacuated.
- *Operation Frederick Hill* (Quang Tin Province). At about 1355 hours, a Cavalry element of the 11th Brigade, 23rd Infantry Division, while being inserted into an LZ 31 miles WSW of Tam Ky, received small arms and automatic weapons fire from an enemy force of undetermined size. Two UH-1 helicopters were hit by the ground fire, crashed and were destroyed. US casualties were 23 wounded as a result of the helicopter crashes and one enemy soldier was killed.
- Binh Tuy Province. At about 1245 hours, an element of the 199th Light Infantry Brigade, while operating in an area 24 miles NNE of Ham Tan, engaged an estimated 10-15 enemy. Small arms and automatic weapons fire was exchanged and the enemy fired rocket-grenades. The contact lasted about 15 minutes before the enemy withdrew having lost three killed. Three individual weapons were captured. At about 1500 hours, the unit received 30-40 rounds of 82mm mortar fire and then directed tactical air and helicopter gunship strikes against the suspected enemy firing position. US casualties were three killed and 12 wounded. A former enemy soldier operating with the unit was killed in the engagement.
- Fish Hook area and continuations. The withdrawal of US units from Cambodia continued with the return to the RVN of a battalion-size element of the 2nd Brigade, 1st Cavalry Division.

- Fish Hook area and continuations. At about 1200 hours, an element of the 3rd Brigade, 1st Cavalry Division, discovered an enemy weapons and munitions cache in an area 18 miles ESE of Snoul and one mile inside Cambodia. The cache contained 49 SKS rifles, 110 60mm mortar rounds, 324 82mm mortar rounds, 300 57mm recoilless rifle rounds, 549,760 small arms rounds, 25 anti-tank mines and one ton of C4 explosive. All items were in good condition. The weapons were evacuated and the remainder of the cache was destroyed.
- Fish Hook area and continuations. At 1550 hours, an element of the 3rd Brigade, 1st Cavalry Division, uncovered an enemy rice cache in an area 15 miles east of Snoul and six miles inside Cambodia. The rice, which totaled more than 40 tons, was in 370 100-kilogram bags. The rice was destroyed.

JUNE 27, 1970

- Quang Nam Province. At about 1800 hours, a reconnaissance element of the 1st Marine Division observed 10 enemy in an area 20 miles SSW of Da Nang. The 10 enemy soldiers were killed by artillery fire adjusted by the Marines ad there were no friendly casualties.
- Cumulative results of US and combined US and RVNAF operations in Cambodia indicated 4,764 enemy killed. In addition, 9,081 individual weapons, 1,283 crew-served weapons and 5,314 tons of rice have been captured or destroyed. These totals were exclusive of those predominately RVNAF operations continuing or concluded in the Parrot's Beak area, Se San Base Areas and the Mekong River Corridor. US casualties in all Cambodian operations were 339 killed and 1,501 wounded.
- Fish Hook area and continuations. The return of US Forces from Cambodia continued as elements of the 11th Armored Cavalry Regiment and the 1st Cavalry Division completed operations and returned to the RVN.
- Fish Hook area and continuations. The return of US Forces from Cambodia continued as elements of the 1st Cavalry Division, 11th Armored Cavalry Regiment and 25th Infantry Division completed operations and returned to the RVN.

JUNE 29, 1970

- Binh Tuy Province. At about 1305 hours, a 199th Light Infantry

Brigade convoy received small arms, automatic weapons and 10 rounds of 82mm mortar fire from an undetermined size enemy force in an area 30 miles NW of Ham Tan. The infantrymen returned fire with organic weapons and were supported by tactical air strikes, artillery and helicopter gunships. Other elements of the brigade and an Regional Forces company reinforced and swept through the area of contact. The enemy withdrew at about 1405 hours and the bodies of 12 enemy soldiers were found. US casualties were four wounded and Regional Forces casualties were light. Several vehicles in the convoy were lightly damaged.

- Fish Hook area and continuations. The return of US Forces from Cambodia continued. The remaining elements of the 25th Infantry Division and elements of the 11th Armored Cavalry Regiment and 1st Cavalry Division completed operations and returned to the RVN.

JUNE 30, 1970

- Quang Nam Province. At about 0230 hours, an element of the 5th Regiment, 1st Marine Division, observed 15 enemy soldiers crossing the Thu Bon River at a point 19 miles SSW of Da Nang. Seven of the enemy were swimming and the remainder were in a boat. Helicopter gunships took the enemy under fire and killed all 15. There were no US casualties.
- Binh Dinh Province. At about 0830 hours, an element of the 1st Brigade, 4th Infantry Division, found a food and ammunition cache in several large caves located 14 miles south of Bong Son. Included in the cache were 7.5 tons of rice, 6.5 tons of salt, 2,000 AK-47 rounds, 65 CHICOM hand grenades, 50 homemade grenades, 24 B40/B41 rounds, and a rocket-grenade launcher. The disposition of the cache was not reported.
- The return of the US Forces from Cambodia continued as the remaining elements of the 1st Cavalry Division and the 11th Armored Cavalry Regiment terminated operations and returned to the RVN. The return to Vietnam of all combat units was completed yesterday. By 0800 hours this morning, the only US personnel still remaining in Cambodia were advisors to ARVN IV Corps units and a limited number of USAF air

controller and ground control personnel. These personnel will return to Vietnam today. The US advisors to ARVN IV Corps units and USAF air controller and ground control personnel returned to Vietnam today. Their arrival in the RVN completed the return of US personnel from operations in Cambodia.

JULY 1, 1970

- Binh Tuy Province. Two undetermined type high explosive rounds impacted in a VN civilian residence one mile SSE of Ham Tan. Six civilians were killed, eight wounded and the home was destroyed. A US Army unit was firing mortars in the vicinity at approximately the same time.
- The 362nd Tactical Electronic Warfare Squadron was transferred from Pleiku Air Base to Da Nang yesterday. The transfer of the unit, which was equipped with the EC-47 aircraft, made additional facilities available to RVNAF units at Pleiku.

JULY 2, 1970

- Thua Thien Province. An undetermined size enemy force threw satchel charges and fired small arms at a night defensive position occupied by an element of the 3rd Brigade, 101st Airborne Division, 25 miles west of Hue. Fifteen enemy soldiers were killed and US casualties were seven killed and six wounded.
- Admiral John S. McCain, Jr. Commander in Chief, Pacific, announced plans for a five-day conference beginning July 6, 1970 to plan the redeployment of 50,000 US troops from Vietnam to achieve a new authorized strength of 384,000 by October 16, 1970.

JULY 3, 1970

- Tay Ninh Province. An element of the 1st Brigade, 25th Infantry Division, received an undetermined number of 60mm mortar rounds at an FSB 26 miles NNE of Tay Ninh City in Tay Ninh Province. A ground probe of 20 minutes duration followed the mortar attack. Enemy losses were four killed and four detained. In addition, three crew-served weapons, three individual weapons and three rocket launchers were captured.

US losses were two killed and 18 wounded. Light materiel damage was reported.

JULY 5, 1970

- Thua Thien Province. An element of the 2nd Brigade, 101st Airborne Division, received small arms and automatic weapons fire while in a night defensive position 24 miles WSW of Hue. The troopers returned fire with organic weapons, killing five enemy. US losses were one killed and 20 wounded.
- Thua Thien Province. Enemy forces fired four 122mm rockets into Hue City, killing two VN civilians and wounding three.

JULY 7, 1970

- Thua Thien Province. An element of the 2nd Brigade, 101st Airborne Division, engaged an undetermined size enemy force 26 miles west of Hue. Enemy losses were six killed and US casualties were three killed and 19 wounded.

JULY 8, 1970

- Elements of the 101st Airborne Division killed 139 NVN soldiers in an eight-hour battle near Khe Sanh in northern Quang Tri Province. US casualties in the action were four killed and seven wounded. In addition to the 139 enemy killed, seven crew-served weapons and miscellaneous uniform and equipment items and medical supplies were captured.

JULY 9, 1970

- Search and rescue parties located the helicopter in which Major General George W. Casey, Commanding General of the 1st Cavalry Division, and six other members of his command were reported missing on July 7, 1970. The general was enroute in an Army UH-1 helicopter to visit wounded members of his command convalescing in Vietnam medical facilities when contact with the helicopter was lost at 1010 hours Vietnam time.

JULY 14, 1970

- Thua Thien Province. An element of the 3rd Brigade, 101st

Airborne Division, received a ground probe of its night defensive position about 24 miles WSW of Hue. The contact lasted more than an hour when the enemy withdrew with losses of three killed. US casualties were six killed and seven wounded.

JULY 15, 1970

- Binh Tuy Province. An element of the 199th Light Infantry Brigade discovered an enemy cache while on reconnaissance in an area eight miles NNE of Ham Tan in Binh Tuy Province. The cache contained more than 14 tons of wheat flour in 261 50-kilogram bags. The find was in the same general area where the unit had uncovered nine tons of flour earlier in the month. In good condition, the flour was evacuated.

JULY 16, 1970

- *Operation Pickens Forest* (Quang Nam Province). A search and clear operation involving units of two battalions of the US 7th Regiment, 1st Marine Division, began today. The operation was centered 33 miles SW of Da Nang in Quang Nam Province.
- Phuoc Long Province. An element of the 2nd Brigade, 1st Cavalry Division, discovered a significant weapons and munitions cache in Phuoc Long Province and less than a mile from Cambodia. The cache, in good condition, contained 199 SKS rifles, five 7.62mm machine guns, 92,040 rounds of 7.62mm and 8,585 rounds of .51-caliber ammunition, and 1,200 pounds of plastic explosive. The items were evacuated.

JULY 17, 1970

- Phuoc Long Province. An element of the 2nd Brigade, 1st Cavalry Division engaged an undetermined size enemy force 11 miles NNW of Phuoc Binh. Enemy losses were unknown while US casualties were four killed and seven wounded.

JULY 18, 1970

- Phuoc Long Province. An element of the 20th Engineer Brigade, traveling in convoy, received heavy small arms, automatic weapons and rocket-grenade fire while on Highway 14A, 16 miles WNW of Phuoc Binh. Supported by tactical air strikes and an element of the 3rd Brigade, 1st Cavalry Division, the fight continued for about an hour when the enemy withdrew having lost 14 killed. US casualties were one killed and six wounded and the convoy vehicles sustained light damage.

JULY 19, 1970

- Quang Nam Province. A CH-53 helicopter from Marine Group 16, 1st Marine Air Wing, accidentally released an external load of mortar ammunition and gasoline drums while on a resupply mission 16 miles south of Da Nang. Some of the ammunition exploded on impact resulting in minor injuries to three VN civilians, destruction of 22 houses, and damage to 24 other houses and a school.

JULY 20, 1970

- Gia Dinh Province. Two 122mm rockets impacted in Saigon, one in the vicinity of the Presidential Palace grounds, causing no damage, while the other hit about 2,000 meters from the center of the city near the junction of Cong Ly and Thuc Khang Streets causing major damage to one house. There were no casualties caused by either burst.

JULY 21, 1970

- Bien Hoa Province. Three VN civilians were killed and seven others wounded when they detonated a claymore mine in the vicinity of a position occupied by an element of the 11th Armored Cavalry Regiment 14 miles east of Bien Hoa City. The civilians had been warned to stay out of the area by a VN administrative official.
- An unarmed Air Force RF-4 aircraft on aerial reconnaissance over North Vietnam was fired upon by enemy anti-aircraft positions about seven miles west of Dong Hoi. Two USAF F-4's, flying escort for the RF-4, returned fire. None of the US aircraft were damaged and damage to the enemy gun positions was unknown. The Command had previously stated that protective reaction is an inherent right of self-defense.

JULY 22, 1970

- Thua Thien Province. Two elements of the 3rd Brigade,

101st Airborne Division came under enemy attack. The first element at FSB Ripcord in Thua Thien Province, 25 miles west of Hue, received less than five rounds of 60mm mortar fire, which caused light casualties and materiel damage. Later, about 1,300 meters ESE of the earlier attack, another element received small arms, rocket-grenade fire and an undetermined number of 82mm mortar rounds from an undetermined size enemy force. The action continued until early evening when the enemy withdrew having lost 61 killed. US casualties were 12 killed and 51 wounded.

JULY 23, 1970

- Thua Thien Province. The 3rd Brigade, 101st Airborne Division, evacuated FSB Ripcord, 25 miles west of Hue, after three and a half months of operations against NVA and Viet Cong forces in Thua Thien Province. During extraction, the unit came under enemy fire consisting of small arms, automatic weapons and an undetermined type and number of mortar fire. Enemy losses are unknown while US casualties were three killed and 20 wounded.

JULY 25, 1970

- Binh Dinh Province. US Forces killed 39 enemy soldiers in Binh Dinh Province, 19 miles north of An Khe, after losing an OH-6 helicopter to ground fire. The intermittent ground and air action continued for five and a half hours and resulted in unknown casualties to the enemy while US casualties were six wounded and no fatalities.
- Long Khanh Province. An element of the 1st Brigade, 1st Cavalry Division, received small arms, automatic weapons and rocket-grenade fire from an undetermined size enemy force 19 miles NNW of Xuan Loc in Long Khanh Province. Contact was lost an hour later when the enemy withdrew leaving 20 killed. US casualties were one killed.

JULY 26, 1970

- Quang Tin Province. An estimated enemy company while on reconnaissance engaged an element of the 196th Brigade, 23rd Infantry Division, 30 miles SW of Tam Ky in Quang Tin

Province. Enemy losses are unknown while US casualties were four killed and eight wounded.

- Long Khanh Province. An element of the 1st Brigade, 1st Cavalry Division, discovered a weapons and supply cache two miles north of Rang Rang in Long Khanh Province. In good condition, the cache contained 164 SKS rifles, 200 shovels, 200 picks, 164 sets of web gear, 75 pair of wire cutters, 74 bangalore torpedoes and six CHICOM hand grenades. The munitions were destroyed and the remaining items evacuated.

JULY 28, 1970

- Long Khanh Province. A reconnaissance element of the 1st Cavalry Division discovered an enemy cache in a hut complex 40 miles NNE of Xuan Loc in Long Khanh Province. The cache was in good condition and contained 290 SKS rifles, three complete .51 caliber machine guns, 12 boxes of .51-caliber ammunition and an undetermined number of 7.62mm and mixed small arms ammunition.

JULY 29, 1970

- The USN turned over six craft to the RVN in a ceremony at the US Naval Support Facility, Da Nang. Included in the transfer were four landing craft medium, one mini-drydock and one landing craft, utility (LCU).

JULY 31, 1970

- Gia Dinh Province. Two US personnel were wounded along with two VN civilians, when 30 to 40 pounds of plastic explosives detonated immediately adjacent to the Ky Son Bachelor Enlisted Quarters (BEQ) in Saigon. The charge, placed by an undetermined number of enemy terrorists, causing moderate damage to the BEQ, heavy damage to two VN shops and destroyed one US and two VN civilian vehicles.

AUGUST 2, 1970

- Quang Tri Province. At 1220 hours, crewmen from an aviation element of the 1st Brigade, 5th Infantry Division, observed an undetermined size enemy force in a bunker complex 11 miles WSW of Cam Lo. The crewmen called in artillery and tactical air strikes and six enemy soldiers were reported killed and 15 bunkers destroyed. There were no friendly casualties.

AUGUST 3, 1970

- Quang Tri Province. At 0135 hours, an element of the 1st Brigade, 5th Infantry Division, in a night defensive position three miles SSW of Cam Lo, observed an undetermined size enemy force moving toward the friendly position. The troopers engaged the enemy with organic weapons including tank guns and heavy machine guns and received supporting fire from helicopter gunships and artillery. The enemy employed small arms and rocket-grenade fire. A sweep of the battle area revealed the bodies of 15 enemy soldiers, three individual weapons and five crew-served weapons, one radio and a quantity of munitions. There were no friendly casualties although the unit did sustain very light materiel damage.
- Long An Province. At 1605 hours, an element of the 3rd Brigade, 9th Infantry Division, while operating in an area three miles NE of Ben Luc, detonated two bombs rigged as booby traps, killing three US personnel and wounding 18. Light materiel damage was also reported.
- An unarmed USAF RF-4 aircraft on an aerial reconnaissance mission over North Vietnam, was fired upon by enemy anti-aircraft positions located about 25 miles west of Dong Hoi and 10 miles from the Laotian border. The unarmed RF-4 and two armed escort aircraft flew out of range of the enemy fire before receiving any hits or damage and without expending ordnance.
- *Operation Iron Mountain* (Quang Ngai Province). At about 1400 hours, helicopter gunships of the 23rd Infantry Division engaged an undetermined size enemy force 13 miles WNW of Quang Ngai City. A subsequent sweep of the strike area by an element of the ARVN 2nd Division, revealed 16 enemy soldiers killed.

AUGUST 4, 1970

- Quang Nam Province. At about 1830 hours, an element of the 1st Regiment, 1st Marine Division, engaged an enemy force of undetermined size eight miles SSE of Da Nang. Small arms fire was exchanged and the Marines were supported by helicopter gunships. Enemy losses were 12 killed, 12 detained and eight individual weapons captured. There were no Marine casualties.

- Long Khanh Province. At about 0830 hours, an element of the 1st Brigade, 1st Cavalry Division, discovered an enemy weapons cache in a hut seven miles NE of Rang Rang. The cache included 127 submachine guns, 140 SKS rifles, two 75mm recoilless rifles, two 82mm mortar tubes and one .51 caliber machine guns. The weapons were evacuated.

AUGUST 5, 1970

- Quang Tin Province. At 0415 hours, elements of the 196th Brigade, 23rd Infantry Division, and the 23rd artillery, in a night defensive position at Kham Duc, received 50 to 60 rounds of 82mm mortar fire followed by a sapper attack by an estimated enemy platoon. Counter fire was directed at the suspected enemy location and the ground force was engaged with organic weapons. The contact continued until 0610 hours when the enemy withdrew, leaving 15 of his dead. US casualties were two killed and 14 wounded. Light materiel damage was also reported. Also captured were five individual and three crew-served weapons, 16 packs and a small quantity of ammunition.

AUGUST 6, 1970

- Quang Tri Province. At about 1130 hours, a cavalry element of the 101st Airborne Division and the Hoc Bao Company of the 1st Division, ARVN, found an enemy base camp 20 miles SSE of Khe Sanh. The camp contained 55 huts, 10 bunkers, and a munitions cache. Included in the cache were three .51 caliber machine guns, 500 rocket-grenade rounds, 100 82mm rounds, 47,520 7.76mm rounds and 660 pounds of C-4 explosive. Nearly a ton of rice and 500 enemy uniforms were also found. Part of the cache was destroyed and the remainder was evacuated.
- Lam Dong Province. At 1545 hours, an element of the 1st Brigade, 1st Cavalry Division, searched a bunker 22 miles WSW of Bao Loc and discovered eight 60mm and one 82mm mortars, four .30 caliber machine guns, one 75mm recoilless rifle, and small quantities of mortar and machine gun ammunition. The cache was in fair condition and evacuated.

AUGUST 8, 1970

- *Operation Frederick Hill* (Quang Tin Province). At 0830 hours, an element of the 196th Brigade, 23rd Infantry Division, was engaged by an estimated enemy platoon 26 miles SW of Tam Ky. Small arms and automatic weapons fire was exchanged and the infantrymen received supporting fire from artillery and helicopter gunships. Enemy losses are unknown and US casualties were five killed and five wounded.
- Pleiku Province. At 1310 hours, helicopter crewmen from an aviation element of the IFFV, observed an estimated enemy platoon 14 miles NE of Pleiku City. The crewmen engaged the enemy with organic machine guns and aerial rockets, and tactical air strikes were called in. An ARVN Ranger unit was inserted into the area and contact was lost at an unreported time. Enemy losses were 20 killed, five detained, six individual, and three crew-served weapons and captured along with a small quantity of small arms ammunition. There were no friendly casualties but the US forces received very light damage.
- Phuoc Long Province. At noon, an element of the 3rd Brigade, 1st Cavalry Division, engaged an estimated 15 to 20 enemy in bunkers 19 miles NW of Song Be. Small arms and automatic weapons fire was exchanged. While the enemy fired rocket-grenades and mortars, the US troops were supported by artillery, helicopter gunships and tactical air strikes. The results of the three-hour contact were 10 enemy killed and two individual weapons captured. Five US were wounded.

AUGUST 9, 1970

- Binh Tuy Province. At about 2345 hours, an element of the 199th Light Infantry Brigade, located at FSB Gwen, 24 miles NNE of Ham Tan, received less than 10 rounds of 82mm mortar fire followed by a ground probe by an undetermined size enemy force. The enemy employed small arms and rocket-grenade fire and also received supporting fire from .51 caliber machine guns. The infantrymen returned fire with organic weapons and were supported by artillery, an AC-119 gunship and a flare ship. Contact continued until the enemy withdrew with unknown losses. US casualties were two killed and nine wounded.

AUGUST 10, 1970

- Quang Tri Province. At 0345 hours, an element of the 1st Brigade, 5th Infantry Division, in a night defensive position 16 miles SW of Quang Tri City, received an undetermined number of mortar rounds followed by a ground probe from an undetermined size enemy force. The troopers returned fire with organic weapons and were supported by a flare ship. Enemy losses were four killed and one detained while US casualties were two killed and 22 wounded.
- Thua Thien Province. At about 0645 hours, crewmen aboard a helicopter gunship from an aviation element of the 101sts Airborne Division observed small groups of enemy in an area 28 miles west of Hue. The enemy was engaged with organic machine guns and aerial rockets and the bodies of 11 enemy soldiers were observed in the area. Tactical air strikes were conducted in the area and two additional enemy killed were reported by aerial observers. There were no friendly casualties.
- Quang Ngai Province. At 2130 hours, helicopter crewmen from an aviation element of the 23rd Infantry Division received heavy ground fire from an undetermined size enemy force 25 miles WSW of Quang Ngai City. The crewmen engaged the enemy with organic machine guns and aerial rockets. In the next two hours, the crewmen observed several small groups of uniformed enemy in the same general area and received small arms fire on four separate occasions. All enemy locations were taken under fire by the crewmen who called in artillery on the enemy positions. Contact was lost at 2315 hours, with cumulative enemy losses 33 killed. There were no friendly casualties.

AUGUST 12, 1970

- Thua Thien Province. Two USAF F-4 aircraft conducting a close air support mission directed by a forward air controller 31 miles west of Hue, accidentally expended ordnance on an ARVN unit, killing one and wounding 11.
- Quang Nam Province. At 1625 hours, an element of the

1st Marine Division, operating 19 miles SSW of Da Nang, detonated a 155mm shell rigged as a booby trap. The explosion killed four Marines and wounded 18.

AUGUST 14, 1970

- Quang Ngai Province. At 1200 hours, an element of the 198th Brigade, 23rd Infantry Division, while operating in an area 12 miles NE of Quang Ngai City, detonated two booby traps resulting in four US wounded. While evacuating the wounded, the unit received heavy small arms and rocket and rifle grenade fire from an undetermined size enemy force. The troopers returned fire with organic weapons and the contact continued sporadically until 1430 hours. Enemy losses are unknown. Cumulative US casualties were 16 wounded, with no fatalities.
- *Operation Iron Mountain* (Quang Ngai Province). At 1450 hours, an element of the 11th Brigade, 23rd Infantry Division, operating in an area 20 miles SSE of Quang Ngai City, had one of its vehicles detonate an unknown type mine. One American was killed and 30 wounded by the explosion, which destroyed the vehicle.
- Enemy surface-to-air missile sites located approximately six miles south of Vinh fired upon an unarmed USN RF-8 aircraft on an aerial reconnaissance mission over North Vietnam. The unarmed RF-8 and two escort aircraft were not damaged and did not expend ordnance.

AUGUST 15, 1970

- Tay Ninh Province. At 0955 hours, an element of the 1st Brigade, 25th Infantry Division, on reconnaissance in an area 12 miles NE of Tay Ninh City, received small arms and automatic weapons fire from an undetermined size enemy force. The troopers returned fire with organic weapons and were supported by helicopter gunships and artillery. Enemy losses in the brief contact are unknown. US casualties were four killed and five wounded.
- Phuoc Long Province. At 2315 hours, a CIDG had four 155mm artillery rounds impact in its night defensive position 29 miles SW of Bu Dop. A IIFFV artillery unit was conducting fire

missions in the area at approximately the same time. Eight CIDG personnel were killed and seven wounded.

AUGUST 17, 1970

- Quang Tri Province. Between 0600 and 1800 hours, an element of the 1st Brigade, 101st Airborne Division discovered the bodies of 34 enemy soldiers while searching the vicinity of FSB Barnett, 17 miles SW of Quang Tri City. The enemy had been killed approximately 24 hours earlier by small arms, artillery fire, and tactical air strikes. One crew-served weapon was found in the area. There were no friendly casualties.
- Six US personnel flying a US Army UH-1 helicopter were killed when the helicopter crashed from operational causes in Binh Dinh Province and was destroyed. The helicopter was flying in an area of heavy rain at the time of the crash.

AUGUST 19, 1970

- Thua Thien Province. At 0930 hours, an element of the 1st Brigade, 101st Airborne Division, engaged an undetermined size enemy force 17 miles SW of Quang Tri City. The troopers were supported by helicopter gunships and tactical air strikes. Contact was lost at an unreported time when the enemy withdrew, having lost 25 killed and one detained. In addition, 16 AK-47 rifles, two rocket-grenade launchers, one 82mm mortar, one pistol and one radio were captured. US casualties were one killed and eight wounded.

AUGUST 22, 1970

- Phuoc Long Province. At 0940 hours, an element of the 1st Brigade, 1st Cavalry Division, received small arms and automatic weapons fire from a small group of enemy soldiers while operating in an area 18 miles SE of Phuoc Binh. The troopers returned fire with organic weapons and were supported by US artillery and helicopter gunships. Enemy losses were unknown and US casualties were four killed.
- An unarmed USAF RF-4 aircraft on aerial reconnaissance over North Vietnam was fired upon by enemy anti-aircraft positions located about 44 miles south of Vinh. The unarmed RF-4 and two armed escort aircraft were not damaged and did not expend ordnance.

AUGUST 24, 1970

- *Operation Pickens Forest* (Quang Nam Province). *Operation Pickens Forest,* a search and clear operation involving elements of two battalions of the 7th Regiment, 1st Marine Division, terminated today at 1800 hours. The operation, which was centered 33 miles SW of Da Nang, commenced on July 16, 1970. Cumulative results of the operation were 84 enemy killed and 281 detained. Also, 46 individual and 11 crew-served weapons were captured. Marine casualties were two killed and 54 wounded.

AUGUST 25, 1970

- Binh Duong Province. At 1100 hours, an element of the 11th Armored Cavalry Regiment received heavy small arms and automatic weapons fire from an undetermined size enemy force 12 miles SSW of Phuoc Vinh. US artillery, tactical air strikes and helicopter gunships supported the cavalrymen, with contact lost after a short time. Enemy losses are unknown. US casualties were three killed and two wounded.
- Quang Tin Province. At 1315 hours, an element of the 2nd Brigade, 1st Cavalry Division, received small arms and automatic weapons fire from an estimated enemy squad while operating 24 miles NE of Phuoc Binh. Enemy losses in the brief exchange are unknown. US casualties were two killed. A former enemy soldier serving as a guide for the cavalrymen was also killed. US artillery firing in support of the contact had two 105mm rounds impact upon the friendly position, killing an additional two US personnel and wounding five.

AUGUST 26, 1970

- At approximately 1545 hours, a US Army CH-47 helicopter was hit by enemy ground fire and crashed in the vicinity of FSB Judy, 31 miles SW of Tam Ky in Quang Tin Province. Initial reports indicated one crewman and one passenger aboard the aircraft were wounded and four crewmen and 26 passengers missing. Also, flying debris from the crash killed two US and wounded five on the base. After notification of the next of kin, final casualty figures as a result of the crash were a total of nine wounded and 31 killed. These figures included the two killed and five wounded by flying debris on the base.

AUGUST 28, 1970

- Binh Dinh Province. At 0900 hours, a resupply convoy escorted by a mechanized infantry element from the 4th Infantry Division was traveling west on Highway 19 about two and a half miles NE of An Khe when it was ambushed by an undetermined size enemy force employing small arms, automatic weapons and rocket-grenade fire. Helicopter gunships and artillery supported the troopers and an element of the 4th Infantry Divisions, 2nd Brigade was inserted into the area to reinforce the convoy force. During the insertion, a US Army UH-1 helicopter was hit by enemy ground fire, crashed and was destroyed. Two personnel aboard the aircraft were killed and one wounded. In addition, two more US personnel were hit by flying debris from the aircraft and both were killed. The ground contact continued until 1840 hours, with enemy losses two killed and one detained. US casualties in the ground action were two killed and 25 wounded, 11 of these receiving only minor wounds. Very light damage to the convoy vehicles were also reported.
- Binh Dinh Province. At 2120 hours, an element of the 173rd Airborne Brigade engaged an estimated 30 enemy 33 miles NNW of Qui Nhon. Small arms and automatic weapons fire was exchanged and the troopers were supported by helicopter gunships and a USAF AC-119 gunship. Contact was lost at about 0200 hours when the enemy withdrew having lost 12 killed. Also, one enemy soldier was detained and two individual weapons were captured. US casualties were two wounded.
- Long Khanh Province. At 0050 hours, an element of the 2nd Brigade, 25th Infantry Division, received small arms and automatic weapons fire while occupying a night defensive position five and a half miles SSE of Xuan Loc. The infantryman returned fire and approximately 15 rounds of 81mm mortar fire was directed at the suspected enemy location. An early morning sweep of the area revealed that at least one of the mortar rounds had impacted in Trung Hieu Hamlet, killing three VN civilians and wounding 13. Enemy

losses are unknown and there were no US casualties in the earlier exchange of fire.

- Vice President Agnew joined Vice President Ky this morning in a joint US and RVN military ceremony to decorate six Americans and six South Vietnam for gallantry in action during the Cambodian Sanctuary Campaign earlier this year.
- At approximately 1100 hours, a USN A-4 aircraft escorting an unarmed US reconnaissance aircraft over North Vietnam conducted protective reaction against an anti-aircraft installation with unknown results. The protective reaction was in response to hostile actions by enemy radar-controlled anti-aircraft positions located about 23 miles north of Vinh. There was no damage to the US aircraft. As the command has previously announced, this protective reaction is an inherent right of self-defense.

AUGUST 30, 1970

- Khanh Hoa Province. At 0220 hours, an undetermined number of sappers entered a fuel storage area three miles north of Cam Ranh Bay Air Base and detonated an unknown number of satchel charges. A reaction force swept the area and found one undetonated charge. Enemy losses resulting from the attack are unknown while US casualties were three wounded. Light materiel damage was sustained in the attack.

AUGUST 31, 1970

- Binh Thuan Province. At 1045 hours, a Regional Forces unit observed an estimated enemy company attempting to cross Highway 1 about 25 miles NE of Phan Thiet. Regional Forces soldiers engaged the enemy, an element of the 23rd ARVN Division and a US armored cavalry element from Task Force South reinforced the unit in contact. At 1125 hours, the reinforcements made contact with an estimated enemy battalion. Helicopter gunships and tactical air strikes supported the ground troops, with contact continuing sporadically until 1830 hours. Enemy losses were 56 killed. In addition, 12 individual and nine crew-served weapons and one radio were captured. US casualties were one killed and four wounded while ARVN and Regional Forces casualties were light. During the action, a US Army UH-1 helicopter was hit by ground fire, crashed and was destroyed. There were no US casualties but one ARVN soldier aboard the aircraft was killed.

- Long Khanh Province. At 0930 hours, an element of the 2nd Brigade, 25th Infantry Division, engaged an undetermined size enemy force seven miles SE of Xuan Loc. Small arms and automatic weapons fire was exchanged, and the infantrymen received supporting fire from US artillery, helicopter gunships, and tactical air strikes. Contact was lost temporarily at 1100 hours but was regained at noon and continued until 1320 hours. Enemy losses are unknown while US casualties were two killed and six wounded.

SEPTEMBER 1, 1970

- In a ceremony this morning, the US Army's 190th Assault Helicopter Company at Bien Hoa Air Base transferred all its aviation and support assets to the RVN Air Force. The turnover marked the first time in the history of the Vietnam War that the VN Air Force has taken over all assets and operations of a US Army aviation unit. The newly activated 223rd VN Air Force Squadron would utilize the UH-1 helicopters, equipment and facilities turned over today. The transfer of equipment and facilities and the forthcoming inactivation of the 190th Assault Helicopter Company was not a part of the fourth increment of troop redeployment.

SEPTEMBER 2, 1970

- Quang Tin Province. At 1310 hours, an element of the 196th Brigade, 23rd Infantry Division, and a Popular Forces unit received small arms and rocket-grenade fire in an area seven miles SW of Quang Ngai City. The friendly forces returned fire with organic weapons. Enemy losses are unknown. US casualties were two killed and nine wounded. Popular Forces casualties were light, with no fatalities. Very light materiel damage was also reported.

SEPTEMBER 5, 1970

- A USAF F-105 fighter-bomber operating in Laos, conducted protective reaction against an enemy radar-controlled anti-aircraft position located about 21 miles SW of Dong Hoi (five miles from the Laotian border) in North Vietnam. The F-105 was in Laos when the hostile fire was directed against it. The pilot expended his ordnance against the threat with unknown results. There was no damage to US aircraft.

SEPTEMBER 6, 1970

- Phong Dinh Province. At 1520 hours, a US Army aircraft from the 164th Combat Aviation Group engaged a suspected enemy position in a camouflaged building 17 miles SSW of Can Tho. Initial reports indicate that although proper clearance had been obtained for the strike from appropriate officials, the position was in fact occupied by ARVN troops. One ARVN soldier was killed and eight wounded in the incident.
- An Xuyen Province. At about 1300 hours, a US Army helicopter gunship from the 164th Combat Aviation Group was supporting ARVN elements during an operation 11 miles SSW of Cau Mau. While rendering this support, the helicopter accidentally fired on friendly troops, killing one Popular Forces soldier and wounding four.
- Quang Nam Province. At about 1100 hours, an element of the 5th Regiment, 1st Marine Division, discovered an estimated four tons of unpolished rice while on reconnaissance 17 miles SW of Da Nang. The rice was in good condition and was evacuated.

SEPTEMBER 7, 1970

- Binh Dinh Province. At 1330 hours, an element of the 173rd Airborne Brigade and a IFFV aero-rifle unit received small arms, automatic weapons, rocket-grenade and mortar fire from an undetermined size enemy force while on reconnaissance 13 miles SSE of Bong Son. Helicopter gunships, artillery and tactical air strikes supported the US forces. Enemy losses were one killed. US casualties were three killed and nine wounded.

SEPTEMBER 8, 1970

- Long Khanh Province. At 0945 hours, an element of the 2nd Brigade, 25th Infantry Division, engaged an undetermined size enemy forces seven miles SSE of Xuan Loc. The infantrymen were supported by helicopter gunships and artillery, with the enemy employing small arms, automatic weapons and rocket grenades. Enemy losses unknown. There were 11 US wounded.

- The ARVN assumed complete control of all area communications facilities in Go Cong Province, the first to be entirely controlled by the ARVN.
- Quang Ngai Province. At about 1940 hours, an element of the 198th Brigade, 23rd Infantry Division (Americal), at FSB Stinson nine miles NW of Quang Ngai City, received an undetermined number of mixed 60mm and 82mm mortar rounds. A ground probe followed the mortar attack by an undetermined size enemy force. An AC-119 gunship, artillery and helicopter gunships supported the infantrymen. The contact continued until shortly after midnight when the enemy withdrew, having failed to penetrate the unit's perimeter. Enemy losses unknown. There were 13 US wounded.
- Quang Nam Province. At about 1715 hours, three drums of fuel being carried externally by an Air America helicopter were dropped accidentally into a populated area of Hoi An. The accident occurred when the hook, which attached the sling-loaded fuel drums to the aircraft, became disengaged, and the drums fell to the ground. Two of the drums contained gasoline and the third fuel oil. Upon impact, one of the drums burst open and ignited. Three VN houses were destroyed and a fourth heavily damaged. Three VN civilians were killed and seven injured.

SEPTEMBER 9, 1970

- Phuoc Long Province. At 1620 hours, an element of the 1st Brigade, 1st Cavalry Division (Airmobile), uncovered an enemy cache while on reconnaissance 23 miles SSE of Phuoc Binh. Included in the cache were 209 120mm mortar rounds, 386 rocket-grenades, 153 picks, six shovels, three cases of TNT, 1,440 rounds of AK-47 ammunition and 144 rocket-grenade charges. Estimated weight of the cache was more than nine tons. In good condition, the cache was evacuated.
- Tay Ninh Province. At about 1600 hours, helicopter crewmen from the 12th Combat Aviation Group observed two enemy bodies 30 miles north of Tay Ninh City. The crewmen also observed six enemy soldiers in the same general area and

engaged the enemy, killing all six with on-board ordnance. There were no friendly casualties.

- Binh Duong Province. At 1910 hours, an element of the 3rd Brigade, 25th Infantry Division, uncovered a small weapons and ammunition cache about 12 miles SE of Dau Tieng. Included in the cache were one complete 60mm mortar and 10 60mm mortar tubes, seven sub-machine guns, 167 rounds of 60mm mortar ammunition, 13 75mm recoilless rifle rounds, six CHICOM claymore mines, and small quantities of mortar charges, fuses and small arms ammunition. All items were in good condition and were evacuated.

SEPTEMBER 11, 1970

- US SEVENTH FLEET. At about 1330 hours, an explosion occurred in the five-inch mount aboard the destroyer USS LLOYD THOMAS. The ship was providing naval gunfire support for the 1st Australian Task Force at the time of the accident from the South China Sea, about 15 miles SW of Ham Tan and 66 miles ESE of Saigon. Three USN personnel were killed and 10 injured. The injured personnel were evacuated to the 1st Australian Field Hospital in Vung Tau. An investigation conducted to determine the cause of the explosion found that it appeared to have been caused by the premature explosion of a projectile in the left barrel of the ship's forward and causes extensive damage to the remainder of the mount. All munitions of the type being used by the ship at the time of the explosion haves been temporarily suspended from use by Seventh Fleet ships. The suspension had no effect on the ability of naval gunfire support ships to meet their commitments. Repairs to the ship were made at Subic Bay. The USS LLOYD THOMAS was a FRAM II Gearing class destroyer, and was commissioned in March 1947. Home ported at Pearl Harbor, she has a crew of 275.

SEPTEMBER 12, 1970

- Phuoc Long Province. At 1635 hours, helicopter crewman from an aviation element of the 1st Cavalry Division (Airmobile), observed an estimated 50 to 100 enemy soldiers 26 miles NE of Phuoc Binh. The crewmen engaged the enemy with organic machine guns and aerial rockets and the bodies of 16 enemy were observed in the strike area. No friendly casualties.

- Binh Duong Province. At about 0930 hours, a five-ton truck assigned to an element of the US Army's 20th Engineer Brigade, and a VN civilian Lambretta collided on Highway 2A near Tan Dinh Village, 19 miles north of Saigon. Eleven VN civilians were killed and five were injured in the accident.
- Binh Thuan Province. At 1050 hours, helicopter gunships from the 10th Combat Aviation Group observed two sampans in a restricted area seven miles SW of Phan Thiet. One of the sampans was in the water and the second was beached. Upon receiving clearance from proper authorities, the gunships made their initial pass to engage the boats and observed several individuals running from the area. The helicopter crewmen engaged the individual. After the first pass, the individual stopped running and there was no further firing. Two of the helicopters landed and 12 VN females and two males were detained. Four males escaped by swimming to a nearby sampan. The detainees were evacuated to LZ Betty where those requiring medical care were treated. All were later released to the National Police for interrogation. Initial reports indicate that all individuals were aware that the area was restricted and that only one detainee had proper identification. Three VN civilians, all females, were killed and four wounded in the incident.

SEPTEMBER 13, 1970

- Phuoc Long Province. At 1515 hours, an element of the 1st Brigade, 1st Cavalry Division (Airmobile), engaged an undetermined size enemy force 20 miles SSE of Phuoc Binh. Small arms and automatic weapons fire were exchanged, with helicopter gunships and artillery supporting the cavalrymen. During the contact, the enemy fired an undetermined number of 60mm mortar rounds. Enemy losses were 11 killed while one US was killed and seven wounded.
- Binh Dinh Province. At about 0705 hours, an element of the 173rd Airborne Brigade received small arms and grenade fire from an estimated enemy platoon 19 miles SE of Bong Son. The troopers returned fire with organic weapons and were

supported by helicopter gunships. Enemy losses were four killed while US casualties were two killed and one wounded.

- Binh Dinh Province. At about 1800 hours, a reconnaissance element of IFFV received small arms and automatic weapons fire from an undetermined size enemy force 14 miles SSE of Bong Son. Helicopter gunships and artillery supported the US forces. Enemy losses are unknown. Two US were killed and three wounded.
- Bac Lieu Province. At 0915 hours, a US armed spotter aircraft of the 164th Combat Aviation Group engaged an suspected enemy sampan 14 miles NW of Bac Lieu and after obtaining from proper authorities permission to fire. Four civilians were wounded, one of whom later died. .

SEPTEMBER 14, 1970

- Quang Tri Province. At 1340 hours, helicopter crewmen from an aviation element of the 1st Brigade, 5th Infantry Division (Mech), spotted seven enemy soldiers 14 miles WNW of Cam Lo and one mile south of the DMZ. The crewmen engaged the enemy with organic weapons and an aero-rifle element was inserted into the area. Seven enemy were killed and one individual weapon was captured. There were no friendly casualties.

SEPTEMBER 15, 1970

- *Operation Frederick Hill* (Quang Ngai Province). At about 1315 hours, an element of the 196th Brigade, 23rd Infantry Division (Americal), engaged an undetermined size enemy force eight miles WSW of Tam Ky. Helicopter gunships supported the troopers. Twenty enemy were killed, 10 by the gunships. Also, four individual weapons, one radio and one telephone were captured. No friendly casualties. At 1650 hours, the same element established contact with an undetermined size enemy force about 200 meters south of the original contact. In an exchange of small arms and automatic weapons fire, an additional 10 enemy were killed. Again, there were no friendly casualties.
- Quang Nam Province. At about 2000 hours, an element of the

5th Regiment, 1st Marine Division, ambushed an estimated 20 enemy 19 miles SW of Da Nang. Artillery, helicopter gunships and a flare ship supported the Marines. Enemy losses were 20 killed. No Marine casualties.

SEPTEMBER 16, 1970

- Phuoc Long Province. At 0810 hours, a reconnaissance element of the 1st Cavalry Division (Airmobile), engaged an estimated 10 enemy soldiers 21 miles ENE of Phuoc Binh. Six enemy were killed and three individual weapons captured. No friendly casualties.
- *Operation Iron Mountain* (Quang Ngai Province). At about 0215 hours, helicopter crewmen from an aviation element of the 11th Brigade, 23rd Infantry Division (Americal), engaged an estimated 10 enemy soldiers 21 miles SSE of Quang Ngai City. The bodies of the 10 soldiers were observed in the area after strikes. No friendly casualties.

SEPTEMBER 17, 1970

- Thua Thien Province. At 0905 hours, helicopter crewmen from the 101st Airborne Division (Airmobile), engaged an undetermined size enemy force 26 miles west of Hue. The bodies of seven enemy soldiers were observed in the strike area. No friendly casualties.
- Bien Hoa Province. At 1130 hours, an aero-rifle element of the 1st Cavalry Division (Airmobile), while on reconnaissance 13 miles NNE of Bien Hoa City, engaged an undetermined size enemy force. Small arms and automatic weapons fire were exchanged. Ten enemy were killed and five individual weapons, 45 hand-grenades and 35 pounds of medical supplies were captured. There were no US casualties but a former enemy soldier serving as a scout was wounded.

SEPTEMBER 18, 1970

- Thua Thien Province. At 1550 hours, a reconnaissance element of the 1st Brigade, 101st Airborne Division (Airmobile), discovered an enemy cache 11 miles SW of Hue. Included in the cache were four machine guns, one AK-47 and 33 SKS rifles, four radios and a small quantity of ammunition. All items were evacuated to Camp Eagle.

SEPTEMBER 19, 1970

- Quang Tri Province. At about 0300 hours, helicopter crewmen from an aviation element of the 101st Airborne Division (Airmobile), spotted an estimated 40 enemy soldiers 29 miles SW of Quang Tri City and two miles from the Laotian border. The crewmen engaged the enemy with on-board ordnance and the bodies of 18 enemy were observed. There were no friendly casualties.
- Binh Dinh Province. At 0755 hours, an element of the 173rd Airborne Brigade engaged an undetermined size enemy force in a cave complex 19 miles ENE of Bong Son. Small arms, automatic weapons and grenade fire were exchanged. Enemy losses are unknown. Three US were killed and two wounded.

SEPTEMBER 20, 1970

- Quang Nam Province. At about 1900 hours, a reconnaissance element of the 5th Regiment, 1st Marine Division, observed 10 enemy soldiers 16 miles south of Da Nang. The Marines called in artillery and the bodies of seven enemy were observed after the action. There were no friendly casualties.

SEPTEMBER 21, 1970

- *Operation Iron Mountain* (Quang Ngai Province). At about 1900 hours, an element of the 23rd Infantry Division (Americal), discovered four tons of rice in a cache 12 miles SE of Quang Ngai City. Locally grown and in good condition, it had been in place about two weeks and was evacuated.

SEPTEMBER 23, 1970

- Khanh Hoa Province. At about 1030 hours, an explosion occurred aboard the SS QAMERIGO while the ship was unloading ammunition at Cam Ranh Bay. The undetermined type explosion occurred on the cargo ship's right side and thereafter, the ship began leaking oil and listing heavily. The ship was towed away from the pier and brought aground for repairs. Initial reports indicate that an enemy sapper caused the explosion. There were no casualties in the explosion. Damage to the ship was undetermined at this time, as was the time required for repairs. Approximately 70 percent of the ammunition aboard had been off-loaded prior to the explosion.

- Binh Dinh Province. At about 1800 hours, an element of the 2nd Brigade, 4th Infantry Division, received 36 rounds of mixed 81mm and 4.2 inch mortar fire while operating in an area 16 miles south of Bong Son. Field reports indicate that a US Army unit accidentally fired the rounds. Two US were killed and four wounded in the accident.

SEPTEMBER 25, 1970

- Thua Thien Province. At about 1530 hours, an element of the 2nd Brigade, 101st Airborne Division (Airmobile), received small arms fire from an estimated enemy platoon 30 miles SSE of Hue. Enemy losses are unknown while US casualties were two killed and five wounded.

SEPTEMBER 26, 1970

- *Operation Geneva Park* (Quang Ngai Province). At about 1010 hours, an element of the 198th Brigade, 23rd Infantry Division (Americal), received small arms and rifle grenade fire from an undetermined size enemy force 12 miles NW of Quang Ngai City. The troopers returned fire with organic weapons and were supported by helicopter gunships from an element of the 17th Combat Aviation Group. Six enemy were killed and one detained. One US was wounded.
- Binh Dinh Province. At 0820 hours, an element of the 2nd Brigade, 4th Infantry Division, operating 18 miles south of Bong Son, accidentally detonated a claymore anti-personnel weapon. The explosion killed four US personnel and wounded five.

SEPTEMBER 27, 1970

- Binh Tuy Province. At 1830 hours, helicopter crewmen from an aviation element of the 1st Cavalry Division (Airmobile), observed the bodies of 16 enemy soldiers 19 miles NNW of Ham Tan. The enemy had been killed earlier by air strikes.
- Thua Thien Province. At 0745 hours, helicopter crewmen from an aviation element of the 101st Airborne Division (Airmobile), spotted an undetermined size enemy force 32

miles SSE of Hue. The crewmen engaged the enemy with onboard ordnance and called in tactical air strikes. The bodies of 29 enemy soldiers were observed in the area following the strikes. There were no friendly casualties.

SEPTEMBER 29, 1970

- Thua Thien Province. At 0740 hours, helicopter crewmen from an aviation element of the 101st Airborne Division (Airmobile), observed an undetermined size enemy force 33 miles SSE of Hue. The crewmen engaged the enemy with onboard ordnance and called in tactical air strikes. Following the strikes, the crewmen observed the bodies of 13 enemy soldiers in the area. In addition, 10 bunkers were destroyed. There were no friendly casualties.
- Binh Dinh Province. At 1520 hours, an element of the 1st Brigade, 4th Infantry Division, received small arms fire from an undetermined size enemy force 20 miles ENE of An Khe. The infantrymen returned fire with organic weapons and were supported by US artillery. Enemy losses are unknown. Two US were killed and six wounded.
- Kontum Province. At 1130 hours, reconnaissance aircraft from an element of the 17th Combat Aviation Group, spotted an undetermined size enemy force 17 miles NNE of Dak To. The crewmen called in tactical air strikes and later observed the bodies of 14 enemy. There were no friendly casualties.

SEPTEMBER 30, 1970

- Phu Loi Army Airfield. The US Army's 205th Aviation Company turned over 16 CH-47 helicopters to the RVN Air Force this morning. The turnover of the squadron marked the first transfer of the CH-47 Chinook helicopters to the VN Air Force.

OCTOBER 1, 1970

- Soc Trang Air Field. In ceremonies here, the US Army's 121st Assault Helicopter Company transferred its aviation and support assets to the RVN Air Force. The receiving unit was the newly activated VN Air Force 225th Helicopter Squadron. Personnel of the 121st Assault Helicopter Company remained at Soc Trang to assist the VN during the transition program and providing training to the VN Air Force maintenance personnel. Thirty-one UH-1 helicopters were involved in the turnover, which was a part of the Vietnamization Improvement and Modernization Program.

- Bien Hoa Air Base. In ceremonies in the morning, two squadrons of A-37 Dragonfly jet fighter-bombers were turned over to the RVN Air Force. The 40 jets were transferred from the USAF 3rd Tactical Fighter Wing, which was scheduled for inactivation as a part of the fourth increment of US redeployment from the RVN.
- Binh Dinh Province. A reconnaissance element from the 173rd Brigade, operating in the vicinity of FSB Washington, 17 miles south of Bong Son, ambushed an undetermined size enemy force. In a brief 15 minute encounter, 23 of the enemy were killed and two wounded were detained. Twelve individual and four crew-served weapons were captured. US casualties were two wounded. Field reports indicated the enemy unit was a sapper element of the 3rd NVA Division.

OCTOBER 3, 1970

- *Operation Iron Mountain* (Quang Ngai Province). At 1550 hours, elements of the 11th Brigade, 23rd Infantry Division (Americal), engaged an undetermined size enemy force 16 miles SSE of Quang Ngai City. Small arms and automatic weapons fire were exchanged and helicopter gunships from an Americal Division aviation element supported the action. Enemy losses were seven killed, four by the gunships. Three enemy soldiers were detained and one individual weapon was captured. There were no friendly casualties.
- *Operation Frederick Hill* (Quang Tin Province). At 1845 hours, an element of the 196th Brigade, 23rd Infantry Division (Americal), ambushed six enemy soldiers 16 miles WNW of Tam Ky, killing five and detaining one. Five individual weapons were captured. US casualties were two wounded.
- *Operation Frederick Hill* (Quang Tin Province). At 1910 hours, a second element of the 196th Brigade, 23rd Infantry Division (Americal) engaged an estimated enemy squad in the same vicinity. Four enemy were killed and one was detained. There were no friendly casualties.

OCTOBER 4, 1970

- Quang Nam Province. At 1030 hours, a reconnaissance element of the 1st Marine Division engaged an estimated enemy squad 22 miles south of Da Nang. Small arms and automatic weapons fire were exchanged and the Marines were supported by helicopter gunships. Nine enemy were killed, three by the gunships. There were no Marine casualties.
- Binh Dinh Province. At about 1400 hours, a US Army OH-6 helicopter was hit by enemy ground fire, crashed and was destroyed five miles WSW of Bong Son. Three US crewmen were wounded. An element of the 173rd Airborne Brigade was inserted into the area to secure the crash site and crew, and shortly contacted and engaged an undetermined size enemy force. Tactical air strikes supported the action, in which five enemy soldiers were killed. There were no US casualties in the ground action.
- Quang Tin Province. At 0240 hours, an element of the 11th Brigade, 23rd Infantry Division (Americal), and an Regional Forces unit company located six miles WSW of Tam Ky, received an undetermined number of mortar rounds followed by a ground attack by an estimated enemy company. Helicopter gunships supported the action and another element of the 11th Brigade reinforced the units in contact. Contact continued until 0430 hours when the enemy withdrew having lost 11 killed and one individual weapon. US casualties were three killed and four wounded. Regional Forces casualties were light.

OCTOBER 5, 1970

- *Operation Iron Mountain* (Quang Ngai Province). At about 1000 hours, an element of the 11th Brigade, 23rd Infantry Division (Americal), engaged an undetermined size enemy force in bunkers nine miles SE of Quang Ngai City. In an exchange of small arms and automatic weapons fire, five of the enemy were killed. Three individual weapons and a small quantity of medical supplies were also captured. US casualties were two wounded.
- *Operation Iron Mountain* (Quang Ngai Province). Elements of the 11th Brigade, 23rd Infantry Division (Americal), uncovered

two cache sites containing locally grown, unpolished rice. The first cache, containing three tons, was discovered 12 miles SSE of Quang Ngai City. At about same time, and three miles south, the infantrymen found an additional ton and a half stored in crocks and plastic bags inside a hut. All the rice was in good condition and was evacuated.

OCTOBER 6, 1970

- *Operation Geneva Park* (Quang Tin Province). At 1630 hours, helicopter crewmen from an aviation element of the 23rd Infantry Division (Americal), spotted an undetermined size enemy force five miles south of Tam Ky. The crewmen engaged the enemy with on-board ordnance and observed the bodies of 14 enemy soldiers following the strike. There were no friendly casualties.
- *Operation Iron Mountain* (Quang Ngai Province). At 1210 hours, an element of the 11th Brigade, 23rd Infantry Division (Americal), uncovered four and a half tons of rice 12 miles SSE of Quang Ngai City. The locally grown, unpolished rice was in good condition and was evacuated.
- *Operation Geneva Park* (Quang Ngai Province). At 1130 hours, an element of the 11th Brigade, 23rd Infantry Division (AMERICA), discovered a cache containing 15½ tons rice in an area six miles WNW of Quang Ngai City. The rice locally grown and unpolished, was stored underground in tin drums. About 14 tons in good condition and was evacuated while the remainder, which was spoiled, was destroyed.

OCTOBER 7, 1970

- Thua Thien Province. At about 1300 hours, a reconnaissance element of the 1st Brigade, 101st Airborne Division (Airmobile), spotted an enemy squad 20 miles SSE of Hue. Tactical air strikes were called in and the bodies of 11 enemy were observed in the area following the strikes.

OCTOBER 8, 1970

- Quang Tri Province. At 1110 hours, helicopter gunships of the 1st Brigade, 5th Infantry Division (Mech), spotted an unknown size enemy force about five and half miles SW of Khe Sanh, a half mile from Laos. A ground team was inserted and the helicopters engaged the enemy. The contact was lost after seven enemy soldiers were killed by the gunships. About six hours later, an additional contact was established with an unknown size enemy force. The helicopter gunships again engaged the enemy, killing an additional 19 enemy soldiers. Two US Army helicopters were hit by enemy ground fire, crashed and were destroyed in the engagement. An AH-1 crashed with no casualties and an OH-58 crashed, wounding two US personnel. Total results of the engagement were 26 enemy soldiers killed and two US wounded.

OCTOBER 10, 1970

- Quang Ngai Province. At 1715 hours, an element of the 198th Brigade, 23rd Infantry Division (Americal), discovered a cache containing 17½ tons of locally grown, unpolished rice 10 miles NW of Quang Ngai City. The rice was stored in four 6x4x4 foot storage bins and a 55-gallon drum. In good condition, the rice was evacuated.

OCTOBER 11, 1970

- Chuong Thien Province. At about 1700 hours, a US Army helicopter gunship accidentally delivered 12.2.75 rockets on a friendly position while supporting elements of the ARVN. Eight ARVN soldiers were killed and 23 wounded in the accident, which occurred 23 miles SW of Vi Thanh.
- *Operation Iron Mountain* (Quang Ngai Province). At about 1600 hours, helicopter crewmen from the 16th Combat Aviation Group spotted and engaged five enemy soldiers 12 miles west of Quang Ngai City. An aero-rifle unit from the 11th Brigade, 23rd Infantry Division, was inserted into the area and established contact with the enemy. All five enemy were killed and there were no friendly casualties.
- Phu Yen Province. At 1045 hours, helicopter crewmen from the aviation element of the 4th Infantry Division received small arms fire from an undetermined size enemy force 16 miles WNW of Tuy Hoa. The crewmen called in tactical air strikes and the bodies of five enemy soldiers were observed following the strikes. There were no friendly casualties.
- Long Khanh Province. At 1030 hours, an element of the 1st Brigade, 1st Cavalry Division, found an enemy cache site

in a tunnel complex 11 miles NE of Rang Rang. The cache containing the following: 177 SKS/CKC rifles, 12 AK-47 rifles, 20 9mm pistols, 59 .30 caliber machine guns, seven .51 machine guns, 11 60mm mortars, 36 tubes and 20 base plates for 60mm mortars, and eight rocket-grenade launchers. Also discovered were unspecified quantities of spare parts for weapons, tools and foodstuffs. The cache was evacuated.

OCTOBER 12, 1970

- Quang Ngai Province. At 1245 hours, an element of the 11th Brigade, 23rd Infantry Division, received small arms fire from an undetermined size enemy force eight miles south of Quang Ngai City. The infantrymen returned fire with organic weapons and contact was lost at an unreported time. US casualties were four killed and seven wounded. Later, at about 1300 hours, and a half-mile from the contact, helicopter crewmen from the 16th Aviation Group observed an estimated enemy company. The bodies of 27 enemy were observed following the strike. There were no friendly casualties in the air-to-ground engagement.
- *Operation Geneva Park* (Quang Ngai Province). At 1410 hours, an element of the 198th Brigade, 23rd Infantry Division, engaged an estimated enemy platoon 10 miles NNW of Quang Ngai City. Helicopter gunships supported the contact in which 11 enemy were killed. In addition, two crew-served weapons were captured. US casualties were one wounded.
- Quang Nam Province. At about 0100 hours, between 25 and 30 105mm artillery rounds impacted in the vicinity of Hieu Duc District Headquarters, seven miles SW of Da Nang. One US and one Popular Forces soldier were killed and four US and one Popular Forces were wounded. A USMC artillery unit was conducting a fire mission in the area at about the same time.

OCTOBER 13, 1970

- Lam Dong Province. At about 1700 hours, helicopter crewmen from an aviation element of the 1st Cavalry Division spotted an estimated 10 enemy 25 miles NW of Bao Loc. The crewmen engaged the enemy with organic machine guns and aerial rockets and the bodies of eight enemy were observed following the strike. There were no friendly casualties.
- Binh Thuan Province. At about 1445 hours, an IFFV

reconnaissance element engaged an estimated enemy squad 16 miles north of Phan Thiet. Six enemy soldiers were killed. There were no friendly casualties.

- *Operation Geneva Park* (Quang Ngai Province). At about 1940 hours, an element of the 198th Brigade, 23rd Infantry Division, detonated an undetermined type booby trap 12 miles NW of Quang Ngai City. Nine US personnel were killed and six wounded in the explosion.
- Quang Nam Province. At 1430 hours, a reconnaissance element of the 1st Marine Division engaged eight enemy soldiers 22 miles south of Da Nang. A Marine Corps OV-10 aircraft supported the contact in which all eight enemy were killed. There were no friendly casualties.

OCTOBER 14, 1970

- Rung Sat Special Zone. At 1040 hours, helicopter crewmen from the 12th Combat Aviation Group spotted an undetermined size enemy force 12 miles NW of Can Gio. The crewmen engaged the enemy with organic weapons and the bodies of six enemy were observed following the strikes. There were no friendly casualties.

OCTOBER 15, 1970

- Long Binh Province. At about 1210 hours, an element of the 1st Brigade, 1st Cavalry Division, discovered an ammunition cache eight miles NW of Rang Rang. Included in the cache were 142 rounds of 60mm and 14 rounds of 120mm mortar ammunition, 16 75mm recoilless rifle rounds and several mortar and rocket fuses. All items were in poor condition, had been in place an estimated six months, and were destroyed in place.

OCTOBER 16, 1970

- Quang Tri Province. At 0910 hours, an element of the 45th Engineer Group and an ARVN unit were ambushed by an undetermined size enemy force while conducting a mine sweeping operation 10 miles SSE of Quang Tri City. The friendly forces returned fire with organic weapons and 10 enemy soldiers were killed. In addition, three individual and two crew-served weapons were captured. US casualties were two killed and seven wounded while ARVN casualties were light, with no fatalities. Light materiel damage was also reported.

- Lam Dong Province. At about 1800 hours, helicopter crewmen from an aviation element of the 1st Cavalry Division observed a bunker complex 26 miles NW of Bao Loc. Further reconnaissance revealed four structures, a trail leading south and undermined number of enemy soldiers dressed in fatigues and black pajamas and carrying weapons. The crewmen engaged the enemy with organic weapons and tactical air strikes were called in. Following the strikes, the bodies of 14 enemy soldiers were observed in the area. Also, the crewmen reported 10 bunkers and four structures destroyed and the triggering of seven secondary explosions.

OCTOBER 19, 1970

- *Operation Geneva Park* (Quang Ngai Province). At 1340 hours, elements of the 198th Brigade, 23rd Infantry Division, engaged an estimated enemy platoon 11 miles NW of Quang Ngai City. Helicopter gunships supported the action with sporadic contact continuing until 1730 hours. Enemy losses were 26 killed and 10 detained. In addition, 10 individual weapons were captured. There were no friendly casualties.
- Quang Nam Province. At 0930 hours, a reconnaissance element of the 1st Marine Division observed an estimated 30 enemy soldiers 23 miles south of Da Nang. The Marines called in artillery and helicopter gunships and the bodies of 11 enemy were observed following the fire missions. There were no Marine casualties.
- Bien Hoa Province. At 1307 hours, five VN civilians were killed when they accidentally detonated a claymore mine in the vicinity of an element of the 11th Armored Cavalry Regiment, 13 miles NNW of Bien Hoa City. The accident occurred in a restricted area.

OCTOBER 20, 1970

- Binh Duong Province. At 1605 hours, helicopter crewmen from an aviation element of the 1st Cavalry Division received small arms fire from an undetermined size enemy force seven miles ENE of Phuoc Vinh. The crewmen returned fire with organic machine guns and aerial rockets and observed bodies of nine soldiers in the strike area. There were no friendly casualties.

- Binh Dinh Province. At 0840 hours, a convoy of trucks owned and manned by a Korean firm and escorted by an element of the US Army's Qui Nhon Support Command was ambushed by an undetermined size enemy force on Highway 19, 17 miles NW of Qui Nhon. The security element returned fire with organic weapons and was supported by artillery and tactical air strikes. Seven enemy were killed and one individual weapons was captured. US casualties were seven wounded. In addition, the vehicles of the convoy sustained light materiel damage.
- Phuoc Long Province. At 1250 hours, helicopter crewmen from the 1st Cavalry Division received small arms and automatic weapons fire from about 20 enemy soldiers nine miles south of Dong Xoai. The crewmen engaged the enemy with onboard ordnance and an aero-rifle element of the 1st Cavalry Division was inserted into the area. The ground unit made contact with an enemy force in a bunker and the action continued for more than two hours. Enemy losses in the ground action were two killed and the ground unit also confirmed 10 enemy killed by the helicopter strikes. Also, two individual weapons and two packs were captured. There were no friendly casualties.
- An Xuyen Province. At about 2330 hours, an undetermined size enemy force launched a coordinated attack against the USN Advanced Tactical Support Base (ATSB) at New Song Ong Doc, 12 miles WSW of Dong Ong Doc District Town. The enemy employed 57mm and 75mm recoilless rifle, 60mm and 82mm mortars, small arms, rocket-grenades and automatic weapons. The Allied forces at the base returned fire with organic weapons and were supported by helicopter gunships and OV-10 aircraft. Enemy losses unknown. US casualties were one killed and 55 wounded, 29 received light wounds. VN Navy personnel sustained light casualties, with no fatalities. The base suffered heavy damage.

OCTOBER 21, 1970

- Binh Dinh Province. At 0818 hours, an element of the 173rd Airborne Brigade and Regional Forces/Popular Forces units engaged an estimated 25 enemy 25 miles NNW of Qui Nhon.

Small arms and automatic weapons fire were exchanged, with the contact continuing until 0830 hours. Enemy losses were 10 killed. Also, two individual weapons were captured. US casualties were one killed, while Regional Forces/Popular Forces casualties were light with no fatalities.

OCTOBER 22, 1970

- Thua Thien Province. At about 2030 hours, helicopter crewmen from an aviation element of the 101st Airborne Division spotted an undetermined size enemy force nine miles SSW of Hue. The crewmen engaged the enemy with onboard ordnance and observed the bodies of 15 enemy soldiers following the strikes. There were no friendly casualties
- Lam Dong Province. At 1225 hours, an element of the 35th Engineer Group received small arms and rocket-grenade fire from an undetermined size enemy force while on a road repair mission on Highway 20, two miles WSW of Di Linh. The engineers returned fire with organic weapons and were supported by helicopter gunships. Contact was lost after 10 minutes, with enemy losses unknown. US casualties were one killed and four wounded.

OCTOBER 24, 1970

- Quang Nam Province. At 1236 hours, a reconnaissance element of the 1st Marine Division observed five enemy soldiers 19 miles SW of Hoi An. The element called in artillery fire from the 11th Marine Regiment and all five were killed. There were no friendly casualties.
- Quang Tin Province. At about 0700 hours, helicopter crewmen from an aviation element of the 23rd Infantry Division observed and engaged with onboard ordnance, five enemy soldiers 10 miles SSW of Tam Ky. The five enemy were killed in the strike and there were no friendly casualties.

OCTOBER 25, 1970

- Quang Ngai Province. At about 1900 hours, an element of the 11th Brigade, 23rd Infantry Division, discovered a five-ton rice cache two and a half miles SSE of Duc Pho. The locally grown, unpolished rice was in good condition and was evacuated.

OCTOBER 26, 1970

- Quang Nam Province. At 1313 hours, a reconnaissance element of the 1st Marine Division engaged an estimated 10 enemy soldiers 18 miles south of Da Nang. Five enemy were killed in a brief exchange of fire. The Marines who suffered no casualties captured one individual weapon.
- *Operation Frederick Hill* (Quang Tin Province). At 1530 hours, an element of the 196th Brigade, 23rd Infantry Division, engaged an undetermined size enemy force six miles SW of Tam Ky. Four enemy soldiers were killed in the brief action and a fifth was detained. US casualties were one wounded.

OCTOBER 27, 1970

- Quang Nam Province. At 1140 hours, an element of the 5th Marine Regiment, 1st Marine Division, engaged six enemy soldiers 19 miles south of Da Nang. All six enemy were killed in the brief exchange of small arms fire, and the Marines captured two individual weapons. US casualties were one killed and five wounded.

OCTOBER 29, 1970

- Long Khanh Province. At 1115 hours, an element of the 1st Brigade, 1st Cavalry Division, discovered two US 75mm pack howitzers while searching an area six miles NE of Rang Rang. The howitzers, in good condition, were found under heavy vegetation. Later, in the same area, more than five and a half tons of munitions were found. Items found included 309 82mm and 108mm mortar rounds, 21,600 rounds of 7.62mm ammunition and 20,635 .51 caliber rounds. In good condition, the items were evacuated.

OCTOBER 30, 1970

- Pleiku Province. At 0140 hours, an element of the US 52nd Artillery Group and ARVN and Popular Forces units, located at LZ Oasis 16 miles SW of Pleiku City, received about 40 rounds of 82mm mortar fire and rocket-grenade fire followed by a ground attack by an underdetermined size enemy force. The Allied force returned fire with organic weapons and was supported by helicopter gunships. Contact continued until

0650 hours, with enemy losses 14 killed. Also, eight crew-served and seven individual weapons were captured. US casualties were three killed and 21 wounded, while ARVN and Regional Forces casualties were light.

- Long Khanh Province. At about 1100 hours, an element of the 11th Brigade, 1st Cavalry Division, found an estimated four-ton cache six miles NE of Rang Rang. Included in the cache were 4,320 pounds of plastic explosives, 600 TNT blocks, 105 82mm mortar rounds, 1,200 CHICOM grenades and 2,200 rounds of small ammunition. In good condition, the cache was evacuated.

OCTOBER 31, 1970

- Quang Nam Province. At 1152 hours, a forward observer from the 1st Marine Division observed 14 enemy soldiers 19 miles SSW of Da Nang. Artillery from the 11th Marine Regiment was called in, and six of the enemy were killed. There were no friendly casualties.
- Thua Thien Province. At 0905 hours, an element of the 1st Brigade, 101st Airborne Division, discovered a munitions cache 15 miles SW of Hue. The cache contained 132 60mm mortar rounds, 11 82mm mortar rounds, 500 pounds of plastic explosives 1,430 firing devices, five rocket-grenades and 5,000 rounds of small arms ammunition. Estimated weight of the cache was 1,700 pounds. Representative items were evacuated and the remainder of the cache was destroyed.

NOVEMBER 1, 1970

- Long Khanh Province. At 1418 hours, an element of the 1st Brigade, 1st Cavalry Division, exchanged small arms and automatic weapons fire with an undetermined size enemy force 11 miles NE of Rang Rang. US artillery and helicopter gunships supported the contact, which continued until 1500 hours. One enemy soldier was killed and two individual weapons were captured. US casualties were six wounded. A former enemy soldier serving as a scout with the US unit was killed.

NOVEMBER 2, 1970

- *Operation Frederick Hill* (Quang Tin Province). At 1322 hours, an element of the 196th Brigade, 23rd Infantry Division, engaged an undetermined size enemy force 27 miles SW of Tam Ky. Helicopter gunships supported the action in which four enemy were killed. Three individual weapons were captured and US casualties were two wounded.

- Binh Tuy Province. At 1000 hours, an element of the 3rd Brigade, 1st Cavalry Division, discovered a hut containing three tons of polished rice 44 miles NNW of Ham Tan. The rice was in good condition and was evacuated.
- Binh Thuan Province. At 1620 hours, an IFFV reconnaissance element engaged an undetermined size enemy force 18 miles NE of Phan Thiet. Small arms and automatic weapons fire was exchanged and artillery and helicopter gunships supported the action. A mechanized infantry element reinforced the unit, with the contact continuing until 1910 hours. Enemy losses were one killed while US casualties were one killed and three wounded.

NOVEMBER 3, 1970

- Pleiku Province. At 1430 hours, helicopter crewmen from the 17th Combat Aviation group received ground fire from an undetermined size enemy force 30 miles SSE of Pleiku City. Tactical air strikes were called in and the bodies of 10 enemy soldiers were observed in the area following the strikes. There were no friendly casualties.

NOVEMBER 4, 1970

- Soc Trang Army Airfield. In ceremonies at Soc Trang in the southeastern Delta, the former Soc Trang Army Airfield was transferred to the RVN Air Force. Concurrently, the US Army 336th Assault Helicopter Company transferred its aviation and support assets to the VN Air Force. A total of 31 UH-l helicopters were involved in the turnover, the fourth transfer of a complete helicopter company to the VN Air Force in the past two months. Receiving the aircraft today was the newly activated VN Air Force 227th Helicopter Squadron. Some personnel of the US unit remained at Soc Trang, assisting the VN Air Force during the transition period.

- Thua Thien Province. At 1340 hours, an element of the 1st Brigade, 101st Airborne Division, engaged an estimated enemy company 17 miles WSW of Hue. Helicopter gunships from a divisional aviation element supported the action and other elements of the brigade reinforced the troops in contact. Enemy losses were seven killed and one crew-served weapon destroyed. US casualties were three killed and three wounded.
- Quang Nam Province. At 1108 hours, a Combined Unit Pacification Program (CUPP) Team of US Marines and Regional Forces soldiers spotted 15 enemy 17 miles SSE of Da Nang. An element of the 5th Regiment, 1st Marine Division, was inserted into the area as a reaction force and engaged the enemy. Helicopter gunships from Marine Air Group 16 (MAG-16) supported the action, with contact lost at an unreported time. Enemy losses were 20 killed, 11 by the gunships. In addition, four individual weapons, four packs, and 14 grenades were captured. Marine casualties were one killed.

NOVEMBER 5, 1970

- Vinh Binh Province. At 1010 hours, USN OV-10 aircraft crewmen received ground fire from an undetermined size enemy force in a complex of structures five miles WNW of Phu Vinh. The crewmen engaged the enemy with organic weapons and the bodies of nine enemy were observed following the strike. Four structures were also destroyed. There were no friendly casualties.

NOVEMBER 6, 1970

- *Operation Iron Mountain* (Quang Ngai Province). Elements of the 11th Brigade, 23rd Infantry Division, discovered two caches containing three tons of locally grown, unpolished rice. Two tons were found at about 0800, three miles SE of Duc Pho, and a third ton was discovered at 0830 hours, 10 miles south of Quang Ngai City. All the rice was in good condition and was evacuated.
- Quang Nam Province. At about 1200 hours, an element of the 5th Regiment, 1st Marine Division, discovered an enemy rice cache 21 miles south of Da Nang. The unpolished rice, totally 2.75 tons, was stored in bins, partially underground. In poor condition, the rice was destroyed in place.

- *Operation Iron Mountain* (Quang Ngai Province). At about 1100 hours, an element of the 11th Brigade, 23rd Infantry Division, discovered a cache containing almost two tons of rice 10 miles south of Quang Ngai City. The locally grown, unpolished rice was in good condition and was evacuated.
- On the Gulf of Thailand in Military Region 4, the USN transferred control of a combat operation to the RVN Navy. In a ceremony at Rach Soi in Kien Giang Province, the Vietnam Navy assumed control of the former US *Operation "Search and Turn"*. The operation, which was commenced about two years ago, had as its mission the disruption of the infiltration of enemy troops and supplies from Cambodia to the U Minh Forest.

NOVEMBER 7, 1970

- Quang Nam Province. At 1300 hours, an element of the 5th Regiment, 1st Marine Division, found five tons of unpolished rice 21 miles south of Da Nang. Because the rice was found in an area of triple canopy jungle, it could not be extracted and was destroyed. An individual weapon was captured at the site of the cache.

NOVEMBER 8, 1970

- *Operation Geneva Park* (Quang Tin Province). At 1510 hours, an element of the 198th Brigade, 23rd Infantry Division, contacted and engaged an undetermined size enemy force seven miles WSW of Chu Lai. Six enemy were killed and there were no friendly casualties.
- Binh Dinh Province. At 0915 hours, a reconnaissance element of the 173rd Airborne Brigade engaged six enemy soldiers 10 miles north of Bong Son. Five of the enemy were killed in a 10-minute exchange of fire and one individual weapon and a small quantity of munitions were captured. There were no friendly casualties.
- Quang Nam Province. At 1200 hours, elements of the 5th Regiment, 1st Marine Division, found 8½ tons of rice 21 miles south of Da Nang. The locally grown, unpolished rice was discovered stored in bags and bins. Although in good

condition, the rice could not be evacuated and was destroyed in place.

- Quang Ngai Province. At 0820 hours, an element of the 198th Brigade, 23rd Infantry Division, was assembled for a briefing in an area 12 miles NNW of Quang Ngai City when an undetermined type round exploded. Initial field reports indicate that an individual detonating a dud round caused the explosion. Three US personnel were killed and three wounded.
- Phuoc Long Province. At about 1800 hours, an element of the 2nd Brigade, 1st Cavalry Division, discovered five structures containing a total of 12 tons of rice while on reconnaissance 17 miles NNE of Phuoc Binh and about one mile from the Cambodian border. All the rice was in good to excellent condition and had been in place an estimated six to eight months. The rice was evacuated and the structures were destroyed.

NOVEMBER 10, 1970

- Quang Nam Province. At 1715 hours, an element of the 5th Regiment, 1st Marine Division, discovered a cache site containing more than two tons of locally grown rice 18 miles south of Da Nang. Although in good condition, the rice could not be evacuated because of the dense, triple canopy jungle in the area and was destroyed in place.
- Ba Xuyen Province. At 0330 hours, USN SEALs discovered a complex of six huts 15 miles SSE of Soc Trang. The huts contained about 1,500 pounds of rice. While searching the huts, the SEALs received small arms fire from an undetermined size enemy force. The fire was returned and USN OV-10 aircraft supported the action. Six enemy were killed in the engagement and there were no friendly casualties.

NOVEMBER 11, 1970

- Thua Thien Province. At about 1400 hours, an element of the 1st Brigade, 101st Airborne Division, discovered a bunker containing weapons 16 miles west of Hue. Included in the cache were two CHICOM light machine guns, three Browning Automatic Rifles, 23 individual weapons and 540 pounds of TNT. The weapons were evacuated.

- Phuoc Long Province. At 0930 hours, an element of the 2nd Brigade, 1st Cavalry Division, discovered two structures containing 9.4 tons of rice 17 miles NNE of Phuoc Binh and about a mile from Cambodia. The rice was in good condition, had been in place an estimated six to eight months, and was evacuated. The total amount of rice found in this same area during the past four days was more than 21 tons.

NOVEMBER 12, 1970

- *Operation Iron Mountain* (Quang Ngai Province). At 1230 hours, an element of the 11th Brigade, 23rd Infantry Division, detonated an undetermined type mine while traveling in a 2½-ton truck four miles west of Quang Ngai City. Six US personnel were killed, four wounded and the truck was destroyed.

NOVEMBER 13, 1970

- Thua Thien Province. At 1055 hours, an element of the 3rd Brigade, 101st Airborne Division, while operating 23 miles WNW of Hue, was ambushed by an undetermined size force employing small arms and rocket-grenade fire. Artillery and helicopter gunships were called in to support the action. Enemy losses are unknown. US casualties were two killed and 15 wounded.
- Phuoc Long Province. At 1345 hours, an element of the 2nd Brigade, 1st Cavalry Division, discovered an enemy rice cache 18 miles NNE of Phuoc Binh. The rice, in 100-kilogram bags, was found in a structure. The rice totaled more than 11 tons, was in good condition, but was destroyed in place.

NOVEMBER 14, 1970

- Thua Thien Province. At 0240 hours, an element of the 1st Brigade, 101st Airborne Division, received a ground probe from an undetermined size enemy force while occupying a night defensive position 13 miles WSW of Hue. The enemy employed rocket-grenades and satchel charges, with the troopers responding with organic weapons. Artillery and helicopter gunships supported the action, which was terminated after 15 minutes when the enemy withdrew with unknown losses. US casualties were two killed and 10 wounded.
- Phu Yen Province. At 1400 hours, a US Army resupply convoy

traveling on Highway 1, 28 miles NW of Tuy Hoa, received a series of command-detonated mines from an undetermined size enemy force. Four US personnel were killed and six wounded. Very light damage to the vehicles in the convoy was reported.

- Quang Ngai Province. At 0850 hours, helicopter crewmen from the 23rd Infantry Division observed and engaged five enemy soldiers six miles NW of Quang Ngai City. The bodies of all five enemy were observed following the strike. There were no friendly casualties.
- Thua Thien Province. At 0900 hours, a reconnaissance element of the 101st Airborne Division detonated a booby trap while operating 22 miles WNW of Hue. The explosion killed four US personnel and wounded two.

NOVEMBER 15, 1970

- Quang Nam Province. At 2228 hours, an element of the 1st Regiment, 1st Marine Division, operating six miles SE of Da Nang, engaged and killed six enemy soldiers by small arms fire. There were no friendly casualties.

NOVEMBER 16, 1970

- Vinh Binh Province. At 1010 hours, a USN OV-10 aircraft placed strikes on a suspected enemy sapper site and staging area about seven miles NW of Phu Vinh. A subsequent search of the area revealed that seven of the enemy had been killed, and three sampans and two structures destroyed. There were no friendly casualties.

NOVEMBER 17, 1970

- Kontum Province. At 1330 hours, helicopter crewmen from an element of the 17th Combat Aviation Group observed an undetermined number of enemy in a bunker and structure complex 40 miles west of Pleiku City and a half-mile from the Cambodian border. Enemy ground fire received from the area and tactical air strikes were called in. Upon completion of the strikes, the bodies of 18 enemy were observed in the area. In addition, 15 bunkers and 17 structures were destroyed. There were no friendly casualties.

NOVEMBER 18, 1970

- *Operation Frederick Hill* (Quang Tin Province). At 0830 hours, members of an element of the 196th Brigade, 23rd Infantry Division, detonated an unknown type booby trap while operating eight miles SW of Tam Ky. US casualties were six wounded.
- Quang Ngai Province. At about noon, an element of the 198th Brigade, 23rd Infantry Division, engaged seven enemy soldiers nine miles NE of Quang Ngai City. Three enemy soldiers were killed and four others detained. In addition, four individual weapons were captured. US casualties were three wounded.
- Long Khanh Province. At about 1800 hours, an element of the 11th Armored Cavalry Regiment ambushed an undetermined size enemy force 14 miles ESE of Xuan Loc. Five enemy were killed. There were no US casualties.

NOVEMBER 19, 1970

- Binh Dinh Province. At 1905 hours, an element of the 173rd Airborne Brigade ambushed an estimated 10 enemy soldiers 11 miles north of Bong Son. The action lasted about 30 minutes and six enemy were killed. There were no US casualties.
- Long An Province. At 1400 hours, a US Army helicopter gunship accidentally fired into an Regional Forces force while providing support for an element of the ARVN 25th Infantry Division. Regional Forces casualties were two killed and eight wounded. This incident took place 12 miles SE of Tan An.
- Ba Xuyen Province. At about 0140, a USN SEAL team engaged an estimated enemy platoon in a bunker complex while operating 15 miles east of Soc Trang. A short time later, the SEAL team was evacuated and USN OV-10 aircraft placed strikes in the area. Seven enemy soldiers were killed during the air strikes. In addition, the Navy aircraft destroyed seven bunkers, six huts and one sampan. There were no friendly casualties.

NOVEMBER 21, 1970

- HQ MACV – Herbicide Operations in the RVN – Following MEMORANDUM FOR CORRESPONDENTS was released: A recent investigation by the MACV Inspector General confirmed that two brigades (196th and 11th) used Herbicide

Orange on several dates during the months of May, July and August in violation of DOD instructions. The agent was used in May and July for perimeter defoliation of artillery support bases. It was used during the month of August for enemy crop destruction in the vicinity of Kham Duc, a remote uninhabited enemy held location in Quang Tin Province. The decision to use the chemical subsequent to the suspension was made at the staff officer level within the 23rd Infantry Division, and the brigades involved. The investigation revealed that some officers were aware of the restriction but elected to use the defoliant in furtherance of combat operations. The chemical was under temporary suspension from the Department of Defense at the time of its use, pending results of tests being conducted of the agent's effect on animal organisms. The supplies of chemical agent "Orange" were being consolidated at ARVN depots, awaiting final disposition instructions.

- Quang Nam Province. At 1150 hours, an element of the 196th Brigade, 23rd Infantry Division, engaged five enemy soldiers 33 miles SSW of Da Nang. All five of the enemy were killed in the brief action and two individual weapons were captured. There were no friendly casualties.
- *Operation Geneva Park* (Quang Ngai Province). At 1330 hours, an element of the 198th Brigade, 23rd Infantry Division, discovered a cache containing three and half tons of rice 12 miles NW of Quang Ngai City. The locally grown, unpolished rice was stored in a 15x20 foot structure. The rice, which was in poor condition, and the structure was destroyed in place.
- Binh Dinh Province. At about 1100 hours, a US Army convoy traveling west on Highway 19 was ambushed 14 miles WNW of An Khe by an undetermined size enemy force employing small arms and rocket-grenades. Artillery and helicopter gunships supported the action and an element of the 4th Infantry Division reinforced the convoy element. Contact was lost at 1130 hours, with enemy losses unknown. US casualties were two killed and 15 wounded. The vehicles in the convoy sustained light materiel damage.
- Naval Forces. At 2245 hours, a crewmen aboard the USN minesweeper ENDURANCE observed an enemy trawler, presumed to be NVN, in the South China Sea about 37 miles SE of Phu Vinh and 12 miles from the coast. The trawler was

challenged by the ENDURANCE and when the challenge went unanswered, two warning shots were fired across the trawler's bow. The trawler and the ENDURANCE exchanged volleys of fire and the trawler attempted to ram the minesweeper. Two USCGCs, the RUSH and SHERMAN, were in the immediate vicinity of the action and also took the trawler under fire. Navy OV-10 aircraft were scrambled and engaged the ship. At about 0010 hours, the trawler broke the engagement and evaded the coast. Radar contact with the trawler was lost as the ship sank in shallow water about five and half miles off the coast and 13 miles NNW of the original sighting. The wooden-hulled ENDURANCE received superficial damage during the exchange of fire. However, there were no US casualties in the action. Coastal vessels of the Vietnam Navy proceeded to search the area for possible enemy survivors. USN and VN Air Force aircraft assisted in the search.

NOVEMBER 22, 1970

- *Operation Iron Mountain* (Quang Ngai Province). Early in the morning, an element of the 11th Brigade, 23rd Infantry Division, ambushed an undetermined size enemy force 16 miles SSW of Quang Ngai City. A sweep of the ambush area at 0615 hours revealed the bodies of 10 enemy soldiers. In addition, one individual weapon and a small amount of munitions were captured.
- *Operation Geneva Park* (Quang Ngai Province). Between 1622 and 1736 hours, an element of the 198th Brigade, 23rd Infantry Division, exchanged fire with three undetermined size enemy forces in an area centered eight miles NW of Quang Ngai City. The unit was heli-lifted into the area and was supported by helicopter gunships from the 16th Combat Aviation Group. Eleven enemy were killed in the three brief contacts and there were no friendly casualties. The infantrymen also captured seven individual weapons.

NOVEMBER 24, 1970

- Quang Nam Province. At about 0930 hours, helicopter gunships of the 16th Combat Aviation Group engaged an undetermined size enemy force 19 miles SSE of Da Nang. Enemy losses were seven killed. There were no friendly casualties.

NOVEMBER 27, 1970

- Quang Tin Province. At 1400 hours, an element of the 196th Brigade, 23rd Infantry Division, found eight tons of salt in an area eight miles SW of Tam Ky. The cache, stored in bins, was in good condition and was evacuated.
- A USAF C-123 was missing in central South Vietnam with 69 personnel on board (six US and 73 VN). It was last heard from shortly after takeoff when there appeared to be no problems aboard. The search and rescue was hampered by bad weather and the aircraft has not been located.

NOVEMBER 29, 1970

- Binh Dinh Province. At about 1210 hours, an element of the 173rd Airborne Brigade and a Popular Forces platoon engaged an estimated enemy squad with organic weapons 10 miles NNW of Bong Son. Five enemy soldiers were killed in the hour-long contact and four individual weapons were captured. One Popular Forces soldier was wounded. There were no US casualties.
- A USAF C-123 aircraft on a routine passenger and cargo flight was reported overdue and missing in central South Vietnam. An extensive search and rescue effort has not located the aircraft. The search and rescue continued, but low ceilings and heavy cloud cover continued to hamper the search. The C-123 was carrying five US crewmembers, 27 US passengers and 12 VN passengers. The aircraft and personnel were listed as missing.

NOVEMBER 30, 1970

- A USAF F-105 fighter-bomber conducted protective reaction against an enemy radar-controlled anti-aircraft position five and half miles north of the DMZ, near the Laotian border, in North Vietnam. The pilot expended his ordnance with unknown results. There was no damage to US aircraft.
- Long Khanh Province. At 1800 hours, an element of the 2nd Brigade, 25th Infantry Division, received small arms and rocket-grenade fire from an undetermined size enemy force 10 miles west of Xuan Loc. The troopers returned fire with organic weapons and were supported by helicopter gunships.

Five enemy were killed in the 10-minute engagement and there were no friendly casualties.

DECEMBER 1, 1970

- *Operation Geneva Park.* Quang Ngai Province. At about 1900 hours, an element of the 198th Brigade, 23rd Infantry Division, discovered a three-ton enemy cache 11 miles NW of Quang Ngai City. The rice, locally grown, was stored in drums. About half the rice was spoiled and was destroyed in place. The remainder of the cache was evacuated.

DECEMBER 2, 1970

- Quang Ngai Province. At about 1030 hours, an element of the 198th Brigade, 23rd Infantry Division, discovered four tons of rice while operating 11 miles NW of Quang Ngai City. Only one ton of the rice, buried in barrels, was considered usable and was evacuated. The remaining three tons were destroyed.

DECEMBER 5, 1970

- Quang Tri Province. At 0805 hours, an element of the 1st Brigade, 5th Infantry Division, engaged an undetermined size enemy force 18 miles NW of Quang Tri City and a half mile south of the DMZ. The troopers employed organic weapons and were supported by helicopter gunships. Five enemy soldiers were killed and two individual weapons were captured.
- Lam Dong Province. At 1510 hours, a USAF forward air controller spotted an estimated 40 enemy soldiers in an open area 32 miles WNW of Di Linh. US artillery and helicopter gunships were called in and following the strikes and fire missions, the bodies of eight of the enemy were observed. There were no US casualties.

DECEMBER 6, 1970

- The crash site of the second C-123 aircraft, the one that has been missing since November 29, 1970, was found in central South Vietnam. Two US survivors have been recovered and flown to a military hospital. In spite of the treacherous terrain and extremely unfavorable weather, a rescue team of US and VN military personnel were inserted into the crash site. Rescue operations were continuing. Search operations also continued for the C-123 aircraft lost on November 27, 1970.

- *Operation Geneva Park.* Quang Ngai Province. At about 1850 hours, an element of the 198th Brigade, 23rd Infantry Division, supported by an aviation element from the division, engaged an undetermined size enemy force 10 miles SW of Quang Ngai City. Three enemy soldiers were killed by the helicopter gunships and another killed during the ground action. US casualties were one wounded.
- Binh Duong Province. At about 1150 hours, an element of the 11th Armored Cavalry Regiment found seven enemy bodies while on a sweep of an ambush site five miles NE of Lai Khe. In addition, one individual weapon was found in the area.

DECEMBER 7, 1970

- The C-123 aircraft missing since November 27, 1970, was found in the mountainous terrain of central South Vietnam. A para-rescue team was inserted into the area but found no survivors in the immediate area. The aircraft carried six US military personnel and 73 VN personnel and their dependents. Recovery operations continued for both C-123 aircraft.
- Phu Bon Province. At 1615 hours, helicopter crewmen from an element of the 17th Combat Aviation Group spotted an estimated 10 enemy in a bunker complex 29 miles NNW of Cheo Reo. The crewmen engaged the enemy and tactical air strikes were called in. Following the strikes, the bodies of eight enemy were observed. There were no US casualties.
- Kien Hoa Province. At 1010 hours, USN OV-10 aircraft crewmen engaged an undetermined size enemy force eight miles WNW of Phu Vinh. Following the strikes, the bodies of seven enemy were observed. In addition, three structures were destroyed. There were no friendly casualties.
- Quang Tin Province. At 1210 hours, an element of the 11th Brigade, 23rd Infantry Division, while operating four miles west of Tam Ky, had one of its armored personnel carriers detonate a mine. Two US personnel were killed and 22 wounded. The armored personnel carrier was damaged.

DECEMBER 9, 1970

- Quang Nam Province. At 0515 hours, the night defensive

position of a team of US Marines and Regional Forces soldiers, located 24 miles SSE of Da Nang, received about five rounds of 82mm mortar fire and a ground attack from an estimated 40 to 50 enemy. The enemy employed small arms, automatic weapons, rocket-grenades and hand grenades during the attack. The Allies returned fire with organic weapons and were supported by artillery. The attack was repulsed about an hour later with 23 enemy killed. In addition, one crew-served and seven individual weapons and a small quantity of munitions were captured. Regional Forces casualties were light. Marine casualties were five wounded.

- *Operation Frederick Hill* (Quang Nam Province). At about 1400 hours, an element of the 196th Brigade, 23rd Infantry Division, discovered a two and a half ton rice cache 27 miles SSW of Da Nang. The locally grown, unpolished rice was in good condition and was evacuated.

DECEMBER 10, 1970

- Long Khanh Province. At about 1920 hours, an element of the 2nd Brigade, 25th Infantry Division, ambushed an undetermined number of enemy soldiers nine miles west of Xuan Loc. Small arms and automatic weapons fire was exchanged and the troopers were supported by helicopter gunships. Five enemy were killed in the action and four individual weapons were captured. There were no friendly casualties.

DECEMBER 11, 1970

- *Operation Geneva Park* (Quang Ngai Province). At 0350 hours, an element of the 198th Brigade, 23rd Infantry Division, while on a night defensive position 11 miles NW of Quang Ngai City, observed and engaged six enemy soldiers. The troopers were supported by artillery and contact was lost a short time later. Contact was reestablished with an undetermined size enemy force at about 0640 hours and continued until 0915 hours. In the two actions, 13 enemy soldiers were killed, six detained and six individual weapons were captured. Friendly casualties were one US killed and one wounded.
- An Xuyen Province. At about 1650 hours, helicopter crewmen

from the 164th Combat Aviation Group observed and engaged an undetermined size enemy force 27 miles NW of Ca Mau. Twelve enemy soldiers were killed. There were no friendly casualties.

- Khanh Hoa Province. At about 1221 hours, a US Army convoy was ambushed by an estimated enemy company while traveling on Highway 21 about 25 miles NW of Nha Trang. The enemy employed small arms, rocket-grenades and mortar fire. The convoy was supported by an ARVN infantry element and helicopter gunships. Contact was lost at about 1430 hours and enemy casualties were unknown. Seven US soldiers in the convoy were wounded and convoy vehicles sustained light damage.
- *Operation Iron Mountain* (Quang Ngai Province). At about 1520 hours, an element of the 11th Brigade, 23rd Infantry Division, uncovered an enemy weapons cache 17 miles south of Quang Ngai City. The cache contained five machine guns, six submachine guns, three 81mm mortar tubes, two radios and a small amount of munitions. The cache was estimated to have been in place two months, was in good condition, and was evacuated.

DECEMBER 12, 1970

- Binh Dinh Province. At 2002 hours, an element of the 173rd Airborne Brigade ambushed an estimated enemy squad 16 miles south of Bong Son. Helicopter gunships supported the action and contact was lost at 2200 hours. Five enemy soldiers were killed and four individual weapons were captured. US casualties were five wounded.
- Quang Tri Province. At about 1930 hours, a member of a US patrol from the 1st Brigade, 5th Infantry Division, was wounded, either by a booby trap or an anti-personnel mine. The patrol, while evacuating the wounded man in the dark, inadvertently entered an old US mine field one mile south of the DMZ, and detonated an undetermined number of anti-personnel mines. Total US casualties were six killed and two wounded. The two survivors were evacuated to the 18th Surgical Hospital.

DECEMBER 14, 1970

- Vinh Long Province. At about 1015 hours, helicopter crewmen from the 164th Combat Aviation Group observed and engaged an undetermined size enemy force while in an area 14 miles SW of Vinh Long. Ten enemy bodies were observed in the area following the strike. There were no friendly casualties.

DECEMBER 15, 1970

- *Operation Frederick Hill* (Quang Nam Province). At about 0930 hours, an element of the 196th Brigade, 23rd Infantry Division, uncovered a three-ton rice cache while operating in an area four miles SE of An Hoa. The rice, stored in 55 and 30-gallon drums, was in good condition and was evacuated.

DECEMBER 16, 1970

- Binh Dinh Province. An undetermined size enemy force combined small arms, automatic weapons and rocket-grenade fire in a late night ambush against a US convoy traveling east on Highway 19, eight miles east of An Khe. Members of the convoy returned fire and were supported by helicopter gunships and tactical air strikes. Enemy casualties are unknown. US casualties were one killed and eight wounded while materiel damage to the convoy was light.

DECEMBER 18, 1970

- Quang Nam Province. At about 0700 hours, an element of the 5th Regiment, 1st Marine Division, engaged an estimated 30 enemy soldiers in an area 20 miles SSE of Da Nang. The Marines were supported by artillery, and the bodies of eight enemy soldiers were found in the area. In addition, two enemy were detained. US casualties were one wounded.
- Thua Thien Province. A US convoy, traveling on Highway 1 toward Phu Bai, received small arms and mortar fire from an undetermined size enemy force 13 miles NW of Da Nang at 1515 hours. The enemy fire was returned and the convoy was supported by helicopter gunships. Enemy casualties are unknown. US casualties were one killed and four wounded. Light materiel damage was reported to the convoy.

DECEMBER 19, 1970

- Quang Tri Province. At 0145 hours, an element of the 101st Airborne Division engaged an estimated 15 enemy soldiers

28 miles west of Quang Tri City. The troopers were supported by helicopter gunships. Ten enemy soldiers were killed in the action and there were no friendly casualties.

- Thua Thien Province. During a two-hour period, helicopter gunships from the 101st Airborne Division engaged an undetermined size enemy force six different times. The actions took place within a three-mile area centered three miles NE of A Luoi. Thirteen enemy soldiers were killed by the gunships, and four crew-served weapons were destroyed. In addition, two individual weapons were captured. There were no friendly casualties.
- Binh Thuan Province. At about 1235 hours, a US forward air controller, while on a reconnaissance mission 15 miles north of Phan Rang, spotted an undetermined size enemy force in a bunker complex. USAF F-4 aircraft were directed onto the enemy position and six enemy were killed. In addition, five enemy bunkers were damaged or destroyed. There were no friendly casualties.
- Tay Ninh Province. At about 1645 hours, a US convoy traveling south of Highway 4, received rocket-grenade and small arms fire from an undetermined size enemy force about 11 miles NE of Tay Ninh City. The members of the convoy returned fire. One enemy soldier was detained. US casualties were one killed and three wounded. Light materiel damage to the convoy was reported.

DECEMBER 20, 1970

- Quang Tri Province. At about 0800 hours, helicopter crewmen from an aviation element of the 1st Brigade, 5th Infantry Division, observed and engaged an estimated seven enemy soldiers 18 miles NW of Quang Tri City and about two miles south of the DMZ. A short time later, an aerial rifle element was inserted into the area and engaged an undetermined size enemy force. Seven enemy soldiers were killed in the combined action, and one radio was captured. One former enemy soldier, acting as a scout for the rifle element, was killed.
- Quang Nam Province. At about 0545 hours, an element of the 5th Regiment, 1st Marine Division, while in a night defensive position, observed 12 enemy soldiers nine miles SW of Hoi An. The Marines engaged the enemy with small arms fire and were

supported by artillery. Enemy losses in the action were seven killed and one detained. Two US Marines were wounded.

- Quang Tin Province. At about 1100 hours, an element of the 196th Brigade, 23rd Infantry Division, uncovered an enemy rice cache stored in an 8x10 foot structure nine miles WSW of Tam Ky. The six tons of rice, unpolished and in good condition, was evacuated.

DECEMBER 21, 1970

- Phuoc Long Province. At approximately 1215 hours, an element of the 2nd Brigade, 1st Cavalry Division, engaged an estimated enemy squad 26 miles ESE of Phuoc Binh. Two enemy soldiers and two individual weapons were captured. There were no US casualties. The 2nd Brigade also discovered a two-ton enemy rice cache stored in bins at the site. The rice was in good condition and was estimated to have been in place for about two months.
- Kien Hoa Province. At about 0300 hours, a USN SEAL team exchanged small arms fire with an undetermined size enemy force six miles NE of Ben Tre. Enemy losses are unknown. US casualties were two killed and one wounded. In addition, a former enemy soldier acting as a scout was wounded.

DECEMBER 22, 1970

- Phuoc Long Province. At about 0040 hours, an element of the 1st Cavalry Division, operating 22 miles NE of Phuoc Binh, discovered an enemy cache stored in three huts and contained two tons of unpolished rice, 40 pounds of corn, two individual weapons, two radios and a small amount of medical supplies. The cache was in good condition and estimated to have been in place two months. The rice and corn were destroyed and the other items were evacuated.

DECEMBER 23, 1970

- Quang Nam Province. At about 1045 hours, two reconnaissance elements of the 1st Marine Division engaged an undetermined size enemy force at a cave entrance 21 miles WSW of Da Nang. The Marines were supported by helicopter gunships and artillery, and the bodies of six enemy soldiers were found following the action. One Marine was wounded.

- Long Khanh Province. At about 2100 hours, an element of the 2nd Brigade, 25th Infantry Division, received an undetermined number of hand grenades from an undetermined size enemy force nine miles west of Xuan Loc. The troopers returned fire with organic weapons and were supported by helicopter gunships. Five enemy soldiers were killed in the action. There were no friendly casualties.

DECEMBER 24, 1970

- US, RVN and other FWF suspended combat operations at 1800 hours in observance of Christmas. Operations would remain suspended until 1800 hours tomorrow.
- Quang Ngai Province. At 1700 hours, helicopter gunships of the 23rd Infantry Division received small arms fire from an undetermined size enemy force 25 miles WNW of Quang Ngai City. The helicopter crewmen engaged the enemy with onboard ordnance and the bodies of six enemy soldiers were sighted in the strike area following the action. There were no friendly casualties.
- Thua Thien Province. At about 1615 hours, an element of the 1st Brigade, 101st Airborne Division, while in a night defensive position 11 miles SW of Hue, received one round of 105mm artillery from a US artillery position. US casualties were nine killed and nine wounded. In addition, one former enemy soldier serving as a scout was wounded.
- Quang Nam Province. At about 1515 hours, an element of the 5th Regiment, 1st Marine Division, while operating seven miles SE of An Hoa, engaged an estimated enemy squad with organic weapons. Enemy losses were five killed and two detained. In addition, five individual weapons, three radios, 24 backpacks, and about 300 pounds of rice were captured. US casualties were two wounded with no fatalities.

DECEMBER 25, 1970

- US, RVN and other FWF suspended combat operations at 1800 hours, December 24, 1970. As of 1200 hours today, 10 enemy-initiated incidents were reported against US Forces, of which one was significant. US casualties reported for the first 18 hours of the truce period was one wounded.

DECEMBER 26, 1970

- US, RVN and other FWF suspended combat operations from 1800 hours, December 24, 1970 to 1800 hours, December 25, 1970. During the period, 26 enemy-initiated incidents were reported against US Forces, of which, five were considered significant (those incidents in which enemy or friendly casualties occur). As a result of the significant incidents, US casualties were four wounded with no fatalities. Enemy losses were five killed, one detained and three individual weapons captured.
- Quang Nam Province. At about 1220 hours, a US Marine team of the 5th Regiment, 1st Marine Division, engaged an undetermined size enemy force six miles west of Hoi An. The Marines were supported by helicopter gunships and the bodies of three enemy soldiers were found in the action area. In addition, seven enemy soldiers were detained.

DECEMBER 27, 1970

- Kontum Province. At 1150 hours, helicopters on a visual reconnaissance mission, spotted an enemy base camp 15 miles NNE of Kontum. A forward air controller was contacted and tactical air strikes were called in. The forward air controller confirmed 14 enemy killed and the base camp destroyed.

DECEMBER 28, 1970

- Binh Thuan Province. At about 0220 hours, an undetermined size enemy force launched an undetermined number of mortar rounds and a ground attack against IFFV artillery units one mile SW of Phan Thiet. US forces returned fire and contact continued for about 40 minutes. Enemy losses in the attack were unknown, while US casualties were nine wounded.
- Quang Nam Province. At about 1230 hours, a reconnaissance element from the 5th Regiment, 1st Marine Division, found three caves 10 miles NW of An Hoa. The caves contained three tons of unpolished rice in poor condition, four individual weapons and one 500-pound bomb. The rice was destroyed.

- Binh Tuy Province. At about 2045 hours, an element of the 3rd Brigade, 1st Cavalry Division, engaged an undetermined size enemy force 11 miles south of Tanh Linh. Enemy losses in the action were seven killed. In addition, three individual weapons were captured. There were no US wounded.

DECEMBER 30, 1970

- Quang Ngai Province. At about 0900 hours, a USAF forward air controller spotted an unknown size enemy force 23 miles WSW of Quang Ngai City. Tactical air strikes were called in and killed six enemy soldiers.
- The Fifth Increment of Troop Redeployment, which began in mid-October, was completed today with the departure of the USN River Assault Squadron Fifteen from the RVN. Included in this increment were 38,100 Army, 1,300 Navy and 600 Air Force spaces. Major elements of the Fifth Increment were the 25th Infantry Division less one brigade, and the 4th Infantry Division. These redeployments reduced in-country strength authorizations to 344,000, and, as previously announced by President Nixon, would be further reduced to 284,000 by May 1, 1971.

DECEMBER 31, 1970

- The following MEMORANDUM FOR CORRESPONDENTS was released: Subject: Interdiction of Ho Chi Minh Trail. Aircraft of the USAF and USN between December 19 and 28, 1970 struck a large NVN Army truck and storage area located along the Ho Chi Minh Trail in Laos. Pilots reported destroying or damaged over 40 trucks, igniting more than 7,000 secondary explosions, and causing some 225 sustained fires. A USAF forward air controller discovered the target. Fighter-bombers and B-52 aircraft were directed to the supply and truck build-up in the Lower panhandle of Laos. Aircraft encountered heavy NVN anti-aircraft fire to hit the targets but no planes were lost. The ammunition and supplies destroyed were destined for Communist forces operating in Cambodia and the RVN.
- US, RVN, and other FWF suspended combat operations at 1800 hours for a 24-hour period.

- Tay Ninh Province. At about 1400 hours, an element of the 1st Brigade, 1st Cavalry Division received small arms, automatic weapons and rocket-grenade fire from an undetermined size enemy force in a bunker complex 11 miles NE of Tay Ninh City. The troopers returned fire with organic weapons and were supported by helicopter gunships and tactical air strikes. Eight enemy soldiers were killed in the air strikes, and five bunkers and a 20x20 foot structures were destroyed. US casualties were 16 wounded.
- Kien Giang Province. At about 1400 hours, a USN river logistics craft received fire from an undetermined size enemy force 20 miles east of Rach Gia. Enemy casualties are unknown. US casualties were five USN personnel killed.

JANUARY 1, 1971

- US military strength in RVN at the beginning of the year was 335,794; FWF 67,444; RVNAF (includes ARVN, Vietnam Navy, Vietnam Marine Corps, VN Air Force, Regional Forces/ Popular Forces), 1,074,410.
- Sir Robert Thompson, British expert on guerrilla warfare, returned to RVN at President Nixon's request to inspect US and GVN police and public safety programs.
- Two US Coast Guard ocean-going cutters, the YAKUTAT (WHEC-380) and BERING STRAIT (WHEC-382), were turned over to the Vietnam Navy, completing the planned turnover of WHECs.
- *Operation Washington Green* initiated April 15, 1970 in Binh Dinh Province was terminated. Enemy losses were 1,957 killed, 5,152 detained, 123 returnees, 834 individual weapons, 65 crew-served weapons, 65 tons of rice captured. Friendly losses were 227 US killed, 2,237 US wounded, eight Kit Carson Scouts wounded, six individual weapons and two crew-served weapons).

JANUARY 2, 1971

- Two UH-1H helicopter squadrons, the 23rd at Da Nang and the 221st at Bien Hoa, were activated as the fifth and sixth of eight VN Air Force UH-1H squadrons.

JANUARY 4, 1971

- The first group of VN Air Force aircrew members to train in country in US combat aircraft started C-123 flight training.
- US Special Forces end more than five years of operations in RVN border camps with the turnover to GVN forces of the last two outposts, Duc Lap and Ben Het in the central highlands.

JANUARY 6, 1971

- A mortar attack on the ARVN ammunition storage area at Qui Nhon, Binh Dinh Province, destroys an estimated 6,300 tons of munitions.

JANUARY 8, 1971

- *Operation Hiep Dong 5* initiated December 18, 1970 in Quang Tin Province was terminated Enemy losses were 161 killed, 24 detained, 142 returnees, 108 individual weapons and eight crew-served weapons. Friendly losses were 12 killed and 32 wounded.
- Secretary of Defense Melvin R. Laird arrived in RVN to assess the progress of the Vietnam program.

JANUARY 9, 1971

- The first New Zealand Army Training Team (23 personnel) arrived in RVN to become part of the RVN/NZ training team located at Chi Lang National Training Center in Chau Doc Province.
- Elements of the 4th Battalion, 8th ARVN Infantry Battalion on search operations 13 kilometers east of Dau Tieng, Binh Duong Province discovered a weapons and ammunition cache totaling 20 tons of ammunition and two tons of weapons.

JANUARY 10, 1971

- The Special Subcommittee on Alleged Drug Abuse in the Armed Forces, from the House Armed Services Committee, arrived in RVN to assess the drug abuse problem.

JANUARY 11, 1971

- President Park of Korea announced that his government was planning a step-by-step withdrawal of its military forces in RVN.
- A convoy of the 18th ARVN Infantry Division on a resupply mission was ambushed eight kilometers north of Thien Ngon, Tay Ninh Province, by an unknown size enemy unit. Enemy losses were 25 killed, three individual weapons and one B-40 rocket launcher. Friendly losses were seven killed, eight wounded, 15 2½-ton trucks combat loss, eight 2½-ton trucks lightly damaged, one PRC-25 radio lost and one individual weapon.

JANUARY 12, 1971

- The VN Navy initiated *Operation Tran Hung Dao XVIII* to counter the numerous sinkings and attacks on merchant ships carrying fuel and ammunition between the Cambodian/RVN border and Phnom Penh. The convoy escort operation consisted of Vietnam Navy assets and employs both ARVN and Cambodian ground troops for bank security.
- Thai Prime Minister Kittikochorn announced redeployment of all Thai troops from RVN by February 1972. The first 5,000 would leave in July 1971.

JANUARY 14, 1971

- The 416th Regional Forces Company engaged an estimated 50 enemy 11 kilometers southwest of Long My in Chuong Thien Province. Enemy losses were 20 killed, one individual weapon and one crew-served weapon. Friendly losses were one killed, eight wounded, six missing and six individual weapons.

JANUARY 16, 1971

- *Operation Toan Thang 81* initiated July 28, 1970 in Tay Ninh Province was terminated. Enemy losses were 219 killed, 14 detained, 218 individual weapons and one crew-served weapon. Friendly losses were 62 killed and 225 wounded.
- *Operation Toan Thang 72/18* initiated July 22, 1970 in Cambodia was terminated. Enemy losses were 1,194 killed, 42 detained,

295 individual weapons and 47 crew-served weapons. Friendly losses were 174 killed and 639 wounded.

- *Operation Toan Thang 72/25* initiated July 22, 1970 in Cambodia was terminated. Enemy losses were 641 killed, 236 detained, 71 returnees, 256 individual weapons and 22 crew-served weapons. Friendly losses were 68 killed, 266 wounded and one individual weapon.

JANUARY 17, 1971

- Assisted by US gunships, GVN paratroops raided an enemy prisoner of war camp inside Cambodia, where 20 US were believed held. The camp was found to be empty but 30 enemy soldiers were captured.

JANUARY 18, 1971

- The 165th Regional Forces Company on a ground clearing operation 12 kilometers northwest of Tay Ninh, Tay Ninh Province, engaged an estimated enemy platoon. ARVN artillery supported the engagement. Enemy losses were 35 killed, one detained, three crew-served weapons, seven individual weapons and 20 B-40 rockets. Friendly losses were three killed and six wounded.

JANUARY 19, 1971

- *Operation Hoang Dieu 101.* Initiated November 24, 1970 in Quang Nam Province was terminated. Enemy losses were 438 killed, 300 detained, 45 returnees, 144 individual weapons and 27 crew-served weapons. Friendly losses were 43 killed and 279 wounded.

JANUARY 21, 1971

- The GVN announced it was observing a 24-hour cease-fire commemorating the TET Lunar New Year from sundown, January 26, 1971 to sundown, January 27, 1971. The Communists earlier announced a four-day cease-fire to begin on January 26, 1971.
- Communist troops attacked Phnom Penh airport with rockets and mortars, causing heavy damage.
- Cambodia's Prime Minister Lon Nol made courtesy calls on

Ambassador Bunker and General Creighton W. Abrams in Saigon.

JANUARY 23, 1971

- Elements of the 412th F Battalion, supported by VN Air Force tactical air and USN OV-10 air strikes, engaged an unknown size enemy force 11 kilometers northwest of Cai Nuoc in An Xuyen Province. Enemy losses were 38 killed. Friendly losses were Four Regional Forces wounded).

JANUARY 24, 1971

- *Operation Cuu Long 44/02* initiated January 13, 1971 in Cambodia was terminated. Enemy losses were 211 killed, two detained, 45 individual weapons, 16 crew-served weapons. Friendly losses were 16 killed, 87 wounded and four M-113 armored personnel carriers destroyed.
- The GVN returned 37 NVN prisoners of war to North Vietnam during a temporary cease-fire in the DMZ.

JANUARY 25, 1971

- The Viet Cong/NVA begin a four-day TET cease-fire.

JANUARY 26, 1971

- The Department of Defense announced that US would speed delivery of planes and helicopters to Cambodia to replace equipment destroyed in the attack on Phnom Penh airport on January 21, 1971. The equipment would be part of the $255 million in aid provided by the Military Assistance Program (MAP).
- The GVN/US 24-hour cease-fire was observed from 1800 hours, January 26, 1971 to 1800 hours, January 27, 1971.

JANUARY 27, 1971

- The USN transferred custody of eight river patrol boats to the Cambodian Navy, the first such transfer of combat under the Military Assistance Program (MAP). The Vietnam Navy trained the Cambodian crewmen for the boats.

JANUARY 30, 1971

- *Operation Wolfe Mountain* initiated July 22, 1970 in Quang Tri

Province was terminated Enemy losses were 299 killed, 31 detained, 61 individual weapons and 20 crew-served weapons. Friendly losses were 34 killed and 336 wounded.

- *Operation Dewey Canyon II (Lam Son 719, Phase I)* was initiated by US forces in Military Region I to secure western Quang Tri Province and to set up a Logistics Operations Center (lines of communication) in support of the RVN thrust into Laos.

JANUARY 31, 1971

- US military strength in RVN was 334,850. FWMAF strength in RVN was 67,433. RVNAF strength was 1,054,125.

FEBRUARY 2, 1971

- Elements of the 1st Battalion, 46th ARVN Infantry a in night defensive position 10 kilometers NW of Trang Bang, Hau Nghia Province, were attacked by an unknown size enemy force. Enemy losses were 26 killed, six crew-served weapons, nine individual weapons. Friendly losses were four wounded.

FEBRUARY 3, 1971

- MACV announced it was giving full air support, including helicopter gunships, medical evacuation, and aerial supply drops for the new RVN dry season campaign in the Fishhook and Parrot's Beak areas of Cambodia.
- An estimated two enemy companies entered Vinh Hoa Hamlet, 12 kilometers NE of Song Cau, Phu Yen Province, and engaged Rural Development cadre and PSDF units. Enemy losses were 37 killed, 16 detained and two radios. Friendly losses were six killed and 21 wounded.

FEBRUARY 4, 1971

- *Operation Toan Thang 72* initiated July 22, 1970 was terminated. Enemy losses were 1,866 killed, 189 detained, 648 individual weapons and 71 crew-served weapons. Friendly losses were 267 killed and 905 wounded.

FEBRUARY 6, 1971

- The 1st Battalion, 45th ARVN Headquarters received an unknown number of 70mm mortar rounds 18 kilometers south of Ban Me Thuot, Darlac Province. Enemy losses were 25 killed, four individual weapons and two crew-served weapons. Friendly losses were five killed and 23 wounded.

FEBRUARY 8, 1971

- *Operation Lam Son 719, Phase II* began as the RVNAF attack into Laos with the objective of disrupting NVA logistics along the Ho Chi Minh trail in southern Laos. President Nguyen Van Thieu announced the attack.

FEBRUARY 10, 1971

- *Operation Lam Son 719* two VN Air Force UH-1H helicopters received hostile ground fire and crashed 28 kilometers east of Tchepone, Laos. Enemy losses were not available. Friendly losses were 13 killed, including the G-3 and G-4 of I Corps, plus five newsmen and four US).

FEBRUARY 11, 1971

- The US 235th Helicopter Squadron was officially turned over t the VN Air Force and the VN Air Force 530th Fighter and 229th Helicopter Squadrons were designated operationally ready.

FEBRUARY 12, 1971

- The 6th increment of the RTAFV (5,600 officers and men) replaced the 4th increment, completing the last rotation of RTAFV brigades.
- Elements of the 23rd Infantry Division located an enemy prisoner of war camp in the Military Region 2 and recovered nine RVN civilians. No US or FWMAF personnel were at the camp. Two Hoi Chanhs led the recovery forces to the site.

FEBRUARY 13, 1971

- The USS CAMP (DER-21) was transferred to the Vietnam Navy under the USN Accelerated Turnover to Vietnam program. The destroyer escort was renamed TRAN HUNG DAO, HQ 1.
- US military authorities imposed a 24-hour curfew on US

personnel in Qui Nhon in the wake of two days of anti-American rioting resulting from the death of two VN civilians caused by a US military guard accidentally firing an M-79 rocket grenade.

FEBRUARY 15, 1971

- In Qui Nhon US military authorities lifted the 24-hour curfew and US compounds were opened, as the city remained quiet.

FEBRUARY 16, 1971

- The New Zealand Government announced it was withdrawing its Special Air Service troops by the end of the month. The troop of about 30 men has served in a reconnaissance role.
- *Operation Cuu Long 9/9.* Initiated October 5, 1970 in Chau Doc and Kien Giang Province was terminated. Enemy losses were 700 killed, 109 detained, 161 individual weapons, 30 crew-served weapons. Friendly losses were 192 killed, 1,505 wounded, 17 individual weapons and one crew-served weapons.
- Colonel Gerald V. Kehrli, USAF, the highest ranking US officer ever to face a court-martial in RVN, was sentenced to three years hard labor and fined $15,000 after conviction on seven counts of illegal possession and transfer of marijuana.

FEBRUARY 17, 1971

- President Nixon declared he would place no limits on the use of US airpower anywhere in Indochina.
- Terrorists threw firebombs against the US Embassy fence in Saigon on the third successive day of terrorist attacks against US property in the capital.

FEBRUARY 18, 1971

- The China Beach Rest and Recreation (R&R) Center in Da Nang welcomed its 10,000th guest. The center was opened in June 1970 after the R&R facility at Vung Tau closed.

FEBRUARY 19, 1971

- The first tank-vs-tank action of the war took place near Highway 9 in Laos during *Operation Lam Son 719* when an M41A3 (26 tons, 76mm gun) of the 1st Troop, 11th ARVN Cavalry destroyed a Soviet T-34/85 (32 tons, 85mm gun).

FEBRUARY 20, 1971

- MACV announced that herbicides would no longer be used for crop destruction in South Vietnam. Limited herbicide operations, controlled under strict guidance would continue away from heavily populated areas around allied firebases, in order to deny the enemy cover.

FEBRUARY 21, 1971

- A unit of the US 1st Cavalry Division (Airmobile) found $50,000 in US currency and one million piasters among the supplies of an enemy which they routed 26 kilometers NE of Dong Bo, Long Khanh Province.
- Heavy NVN attacks stalled the *Operation Lam Son 719* pushed into Laos for the fourth successive day, with heavy casualties on both sides.
- In Khanh Hoa Province an enemy unit attacked the 136th Regional Forces Company in night defensive position 16 kilometers west of Nha Trang. Enemy losses were 32 killed, 12 individual weapons and five crew-served weapons. Friendly losses were five Regional Forces killed, 12 wounded and one crew-served weapon.

FEBRUARY 22, 1971

- In Chuong Thien Province, a Popular Forces platoon from Thrang Chanh village and one Regional Forces intelligence squad from Duc Long District engaged an unknown size enemy force 10 kilometers NW of Vi Thanh. Enemy losses were 21 killed, eight sampans, 13 grenades. Friendly losses were three wounded.

FEBRUARY 23, 1971

- In Kien Giang Province an enemy unit shelled and attacked the 4th Battalion, 31st Infantry in its night defensive position 29 kilometers SW of Kien An. Enemy losses were 22 killed, one detained, five individual weapons and three crew-served weapon. Friendly losses were three killed, seven wounded and two individual weapons.
- Lieutenant General Do Cao Tri, CG, III Corps, was killed in a

helicopter crash. Also killed were Francois Sully of Newsweek Magazine, four VN officers, and four crewmen.

FEBRUARY 24, 1971

- *Operation Cuu Long/BL/02.* Initiated February 20, 1971 in Bac Lieu Province was terminated. Enemy losses were 127 killed, 68 detained, 27 individual weapons. Friendly losses were two killed and 33 wounded.
- The 711th Regional Forces Company, while searching 11 kilometers SW of Quang Ngai, engaged an unknown size enemy force. US gunships and artillery support. Enemy losses were 47 killed and two detained. Friendly losses were six Regional Forces killed and seven Regional Forces wounded.

FEBRUARY 25, 1971

- The 7th Royal Australian Regiment rotates to Australia and was replaced by the 3rd Royal Australian Regiment.
- *Operation Lam Son 719.* Elements of the 3rd Battalion, 1st ARVN Infantry Battalion checking an *ARC LIGHT* strike area 40 kilometers SE of Tchepone, Laos find 92 killed in action, 11 crew-served weapons, two tons of 37mm ammunition, and six tons of unknown type ammunition.
- *Operation Cuu Long/DK/BX/02.* Initiated February 20, 1971 in Ba Xuyen Province was terminated (Enemy: 104 killed, 16 detained, 30 individual weapons, two crew-served weapons: Friendly: three killed, 46 wounded).
- *Operation Cuu Long/DK/CT/02.* Initiated February 20, 1971 in Chuong Thien Province was terminated (Enemy: 132 killed, four detained, 50 individual weapons; Friendly: 10 killed, 25 wounded, two missing, five individual weapons).
- In Quang Ngai Province, an enemy unit attacks the 713th Regional Forces Company 10 kilometers SW of Binh Son (Enemy: 35 killed, five individual weapons, three crew-served weapons, 90 grenades, four claymore mines; Friendly: one Regional Forces killed, two Regional Forces wounded).

FEBRUARY 26, 1971

- *Operation Toan Thang 1/71.* Elements of the 36th ARVN Ranger Battalion on search operations four kilometers SW of Dambe, Kampuong Cham Province, Cambodia, engaged an estimated enemy battalion. VN Air Force tactical air supported. Enemy losses were 250 killed; Friendly losses were 77 ARVN wounded, seven missing, three 2½-ton trucks, 1¼-ton jeep, one ¾-ton ambulance, two M-113 armored personnel carriers, six individual weapons lost.

FEBRUARY 27, 1971

- *Operation Lam Son 719.* A forward air controller reported sighting 200 killed by air and eight destroyed tanks in an area 23 kilometers east of Tchepone, Laos.
- Elements of the 1st Battalion, 3rd ARVN Infantry on search operations 42 kilometers from Tchepone, Laos in *Operation Lam Son 719* find 157 enemy killed by air, 15 individual weapons, and eight crew-served weapons.
- US military strength in RVN was 323,797. FWMAF strength was 67,791. RVNAF strength was 1,049,163.

MARCH 1, 1971

- *Operation Lam Son 719.* Elements of the 17th Air Cavalry Squadron and the 3rd Airborne Brigade operating 25 kilometers east of Tchepone, Laos received a ground attack from an unknown size enemy force. Enemy losses were 200 killed and 150 individual weapons. Friendly losses were two killed, 50 wounded and six M-113 armored personnel carriers destroyed.
- *Operation Iron Mountain.* Initiated March 18, 1969 in Quang Ngai Province was terminated. Enemy losses were 4,476 killed, 2,724 detained, 1,130 individual weapons and 94 crew-served weapons. Friendly losses were 440 killed and 2,858 wounded.
- *Operation Frederick Hill.* Initiated March 18, 1969 in Quang Tin and Quang Nam Province was terminated. Enemy losses were 5,514 killed, 2,572 detained, 1,848 individual weapons and 192 crew-served weapons. Friendly losses were 572 killed, 3,910 wounded and two missing.
- *Operation Pennsylvania Square.* Initiated June 29, 1970 in Quang Tin Province was terminated. Enemy losses were 261 killed, 228 detained, 96 individual weapons and three crew-served weapons. Friendly losses were 20 killed and 302 wounded.

- *Operation Geneva Park.* Initiated March 18, 1969 in Quang Ngai and Quang Tin Provinces was terminated. Enemy losses were 2,237 killed, 1,458 detained, 532 individual weapons and 49 crew-served weapons. Friendly losses were 231 killed and 1,796 wounded.
- *Operation Nantucket Beach.* Initiated July 20, 1970 in Quang Ngai Province was terminated. Enemy losses were 630 killed, 634 detained, 207 individual weapons and five crew-served weapons. Friendly losses were 57 killed and 651 wounded.

MARCH 2, 1971

- The Cambodian Government and the US Government signed an agreement covering $18.5 million of economic aid. The money was to help Cambodia avoid excessive inflation and other major distortions in its economy.

MARCH 3, 1971

- *Operation Lam Son 719.* Hundreds of US helicopters advanced RVN troops six miles deep in Laos. The advance put RVN forces 24 miles west of the Laos border and ½ mile from Tchepone.
- *Operation Toan Thang 01/71 NB.* In Cambodia, elements of the 1st Battalion, 52nd ARVN Infantry and 15th Armored Cavalry Squadron, 18th Armored Cavalry Squadron and 30th Ranger Battalion on search operations five kilometers SW of Dambe, Kampong Cham Province, engaged an unknown size enemy force in the vicinity of previous *ARC LIGHT* strikes. Enemy losses were 210 killed, 12 B-40 rocket launchers and one 75mm recoilless rifle. Friendly losses were eight wounded and 150 of the enemy was killed by air.
- The Viet Cong announced on Liberation Radio that they would release on March 4, 1971 39 RVN prisoners of war. The prisoners of war were captured May 1, 1971 in fighting in the Central Highlands.

MARCH 4, 1971

- GVN military spokesmen announced that the Viet Cong had not freed any prisoners of war as announced in a radio broadcast on March 3, 1971, and were instead shelling the region of the proposed release.

MARCH 6, 1971

- Elements of the 3rd Battalion, 2nd ARVN Infantry on a search operation seven kilometers east of Tchepone, Laos, find an area hit by air strikes. Enemy losses were 31 killed by air, 1000 tons of rice, 2,000 protective masks, 11 AK-47 rifles, nine B-40 rocket launchers and seven 7.63mm machine guns.

MARCH 7, 1971

- *Operation TRUNG 22/4* initiated February 13, 1971 in Kontum Province was terminated Enemy losses were 329 killed, four individual weapons and two crew-served weapons. Friendly losses were 25 killed, 83 wounded, 274 missing and 393 individual weapons.

MARCH 8, 1971

- The Xa Hiep My village observation post, seven kilometers south of Cau Ngang, Vinh Binh Province, was penetrated by an enemy sapper unit with the aid of a traitor. Enemy losses were two killed and one individual weapon. Friendly losses were 11 killed, nine wounded, 20 VN civilians killed and 13 civilians wounded).

MARCH 9, 1971

- *Operation Hoang Dieu 103* initiated February 3, 1971 in Quan Nam Province was terminated. Enemy losses were 330 killed, 198 detained, 10 returnees, 128 individual weapons, five crew-served weapons. Friendly losses were 46 killed, 359 wounded and two missing.

MARCH 10, 1971

- *Operation Tran Hung Dao I*, the second oldest operation of the *Operation Sea Lords* campaign, initiated November 21, 1968 to interdict enemy infiltration from Cambodia was terminated. Enemy losses were 723 killed and 53 detained. Friendly losses were: 53 killed.

- Elements of the 1st Battalion, 1st ARVN Infantry Battalion searching 22 kilometers SE of Tchepone, Laos, found an open area hit by air strikes. Enemy losses were 144 killed by air, 44 individual weapons, four trucks, 100 122mm rounds and two 37mm guns destroyed.
- Elements of the 4th Battalion, 1st ARVN Infantry on a BDA mission 16 kilometers southeast of Tchepone found 391 enemy killed by air, 18 Russian trucks, 500 barrels of fuel, 30 82mm mortars, 644 AK-47s, eight tons of mixed ammunition, six tons of rice, 64 radios, three 122mm guns, two 122mm rocket launchers, two 37mm guns, four 7mm machine guns, 18 B-40 rocket launchers, eight tracked vehicles, 26 crew-served weapons and 100 rounds of 122 rocket ammunition, and eight wounded prisoners of war.

MARCH 13, 1971

- Secretary of Defense Laird directed a prisoner of war/missing task group be established to improve the direction and coordination of matters relating to these personnel.

MARCH 14, 1971

- *Operation Lam Son 719.* Elements of the 6th ARVN Airborne Battalion on search operations 39 kilometers SE of Tchepone, Laos found an area hit by *ARC LIGHT* strikes. Enemy losses were 70 killed by air, four 82mm mortars, 500 rounds mortar, two 57mm recoilless rifle, 200 rounds of 57mm ammunition, four radios, seven telephones, and 1,000 pounds of rice.
- An American civilian reporter was seriously wounded in Saigon when he failed to stop his vehicle for a RVN National Police checkpoint.

MARCH 15, 1971

- *Operation Dok Soo.* Initiated February 22, 1971 in Phu Yen Province was terminated Enemy losses were 410 killed, five detained, 96 individual weapons, six crew-served weapons. Friendly losses were 23 killed and 74 wounded.

MARCH 16, 1971

- The 145th Regional Forces Company 35 kilometers south of Pleiku, Pleiku Province, receives an attack-by-fire on its compound followed by a ground attack by an estimated enemy company (Enemy: 20 killed, six individual weapons, thee crew-served weapons; Friendly: four killed, eight wounded).

- The Phu Nhon District Headquarters and US Advisory Team 36 in Pleiku Province, 48 kilometers south of Pleiku, receive an unknown number of 82mm mortar rounds and B-40 fire followed by a sapper attack by an estimated enemy company. Gunships and artillery supports the engagement (Enemy: 47 killed, 22 individual weapons; Friendly: 21 killed, 11 wounded).

MARCH 17, 1971

- *Operation Lam Son 719.* 19 kilometers SE of Tchepone, Savannakhet Province, Laos, elements of the 1st ARVN Infantry Regiment report being in heavy contact with an unknown size enemy force in the vicinity of LZ LoLo (Enemy: 1,100 killed, 270 individual weapons, 45 crew-served weapons, eight radios; Friendly: 66 killed, 190 wounded).
- *Operation Cuu Long/DK/CT/03.* Initiated March 13, 1971 in Chuong Thien Province was terminated (Enemy: 165 killed, 46 detained, 35 individual weapons, one crew-served weapons; Friendly: three killed, 32 wounded, three individual weapons).
- *Operation Cuu Long/DK/AX/03.* Initiated March 13, 1971 in An Xuyen Province was terminated (Enemy: 114 killed, 30 detained, two returnees, 26 individual weapons; Friendly: nine killed, 15 wounded).
- *Operation Toan Thang 01/71.* Six kilometers north of Suong, Kampong Cham Province, Cambodia, the 5th ARVN Armored Cavalry Squadron in night defensive position was attacked by an estimated enemy battalion (Enemy: 350 killed; Friendly: eight killed, 50 wounded, three M-113 armored personnel carriers heavy damaged).

MARCH 18, 1971

- Nineteen kilometers SE of Tchepone, Laos, in *Operation Lam Son 719,* elements of the 4th Battalion, 1st ARVN Infantry Battalion report a 24-hour contact with an unknown size enemy force (Enemy: 567 killed, 172 individual weapons, 48 crew-served weapons, 120 blocks of TNT; Friendly: 50 killed, 80 wounded.

- The Honorable John J. Gorton, Australian Minister of Defense, visits RVN for an update on the situation. The New Zealand Prime Minister announces the New Zealand Artillery Battery will commence redeployment beginning May 1, 1971.

MARCH 19, 1971

- *Operation Lam Son 719.* Elements of the 4th Battalion, 2nd Infantry engage an unknown size enemy force 26 kilometers southwest of Tchepone, Laos (Enemy: 195 killed, six individual weapons, 15 crew-served weapons; Friendly: five killed, 91 wounded, 13 missing).
- Elements of the 4th Battalion, 8th ARVN Infantry Intelligence and Reconnaissance Squad on ground reconnaissance 11 kilometers SW of Phuoc Vinh, Binh Duong Province, engage an estimated enemy platoon with small arms. US gunships and ARVN artillery support the contact (Enemy: 36 killed; Friendly: two wounded, two missing, five individual weapons).

MARCH 21, 1971

- *Operation Quang Trung 45/20* initiated March 16, 1971 in Pleiku Province was terminated (Enemy: 130 killed, one individual weapons, two crew-served weapons; Friendly: 28 killed, 47 wounded).
- The 9th ARVN Reconnaissance Company operating four kilometers SW of Snuol, Kratie Province, Cambodia, discovers a cache of unpolished rice weighing approximately 45 tons.
- *Operation Lam Son 719.* Elements of the 4th Battalion, and 2nd Battalion, 2nd Infantry Battalions operating 24 kilometers SE of Tchepone, Laos, receive an attack-by-fire followed by a ground attack from an unknown size enemy force (Enemy: 245 killed, 65 individual weapons, 90 crew-served weapons, eight flame throwers, five radios; Friendly: 37 killed, 58 wounded, 15 missing).

MARCH 22, 1971

- *Operation Quang Trung 47/44.* Initiated March 16, 1971 in Pleiku Province was terminated (Enemy: 178 killed, one detained, 22 individual weapons, nine crew-served weapons; Friendly: 14 killed, 47 wounded).

- Katum Airfield, 30 kilometers northeast of Tay Ninh, Tay Ninh Province, receives five rounds of 82mm mortar which impact in the ammunition and POL storage area resulting in 28,000 gallons JP-4 and 24 tons of assorted ammunition destroyed.

MARCH 24, 1971

- *Operation Lam Son 719.* Elements of the 7th Battalion, 17th US Cavalry operating in Savannakhet Province, Laos, 16 kilometers SW of Khe Sanh sight 21 enemy tanks and engage them with helicopter gunships (Enemy: seven tanks destroyed, two damaged).

MARCH 25, 1971

- Elements of the 22nd ARVN Ranger Battalion in night defensive position 28 kilometers SW of Kontum, Kontum Province, were engaged by an unknown size enemy force (Enemy: 23 killed, two individual weapons; Friendly: four killed, nine wounded).

MARCH 26, 1971

- A Regional Forces supply convoy of three LCM-8s, transporting POL and ammunition, was ambushed 11 kilometers SW of Kien An, Kien Giang Province by two-four enemy using B-40 rockets (Enemy: unknown; Friendly: two VN Navy killed, one US wounded, four missing, 20 VN civilians killed and 33 wounded, 32 houses destroyed by fire from burning POL, one LCM-8 sunk. 9,000 gallons fuel destroyed).
- FSB Vandergrift, 20 kilometers NE of Khe Sanh, Quang Tri Province, received an attack-by-fire consisting of 17 122mm rockets (Enemy: unknown; Friendly: three US wounded, an estimated 242.4 tons of eight-inch ammunition destroyed.

MARCH 28, 1971

- FSB Mary Ann, 42 kilometers SW of Tam Ky, receives an estimated 50 to 60 rounds of 82mm mortar fire followed by a ground attack of sappers, which penetrated the perimeter of the base. The base was manned by an element of the 196th

US Infantry Brigade (Enemy: 12 killed; Friendly: 33 killed, 76 wounded).

- At Cang Long, Vinh Binh Province, Cang Long district town receives a mixed mortar attacked followed by an attack on the 676th Regional Forces Headquarters and the National Police Headquarters (Enemy: six killed, two detained, two individual weapons; Friendly: 45 killed, 72 wounded).

MARCH 29, 1971

- In the An Hoi area of Military Region 1, the Duc Duc District Headquarters and several surrounding villages were overrun by enemy forces (Enemy: 59 killed, 22 individual weapons, six crew-served weapons, three detained; Friendly: 20 killed, 46 wounded, 100 civilians killed, 96 civilians wounded, 1,451 civilian homes destroyed.

MARCH 30, 1971

- USN helicopters sight an enemy SL-6 infiltration trawler, 18 kilometers southeast of Nam Can. SEALs inserted into the area report that the steel-hulled vessel has been stripped and abandoned, apparently due to engineering difficulties. The trawler was estimated to have been in place four to six months.
- The Australian Government announces that between May and November 1971, 1,000 of the 7,000 remaining Australian troops in RVN will be withdrawn.

MARCH 31, 1971

- During March there were 20 recorded mining incidents on the Cua Viet River as the enemy made a determined effort to interdict the flow of supplies in support of *Operation Lam Son 719* in Laos.
- *Operation Hiep Dong 6.* Initiated February 2, 1971 in Quang Tin Province was terminated (Enemy: 591 killed, 50 detained, 90 returnees, 219 individual weapons, 16 crew-served weapons; Friendly: 51 killed, 153 wounded).
- *Operation Quyet Thang 405A.* Initiated January 1, 1971 in Quang Ngai Province was terminated (Enemy: 302 killed, 61 detained, three returnees, 108 individual weapons, 10 crew-served weapons; Friendly: nine killed, 44 wounded).

- *Operation Quyet Thang 504A.* Initiated January 1, 1961 in Quang Tin Province was terminated (Enemy: 179 killed, 21 detained, five returnees, 67 individual weapons; Friendly: two killed, six wounded).
- *Operation Quyet Thang 603A.* Initiated January 1, 1971 in Quang Ngai Province was terminated (Enemy: 469 killed, 134 detained, eight returnees, 183 individual weapons, five crew-served weapons; Friendly: 31 killed, 222 wounded, 14 missing).
- *Operation TRUNG 22/FWD/4.* Initiated March 7, 1971 in Kontum Province was terminated (Enemy: 158 killed, 15 individual weapons, five crew-served weapons; Friendly: 18 killed, 81 wounded).
- US military strength in RVN was 302,097. FWMAF strength was 67,513. RVNAF strength was 1,057,676.

APRIL 1, 1971

- *Operation Solid Anchor. Operation Solid Anchor* was turned over to Vietnam Navy at Vam Can, An Xuyen Province, ending the USN river patrol mission in RVN.
- The curfew in the greater Saigon area for US forces was changed to the period 0100 to 0530 hours, corresponding to the RVN civilian curfew hours.

APRIL 2, 1971

- *Operation Quang Trung 22/FWD/4.* The 2nd Battalion, 41st Infantry moves onto FSB 6, joining the 1st Battalion, 41st Infantry. Heavy contact continued (Enemy: 355 killed, 10 individual weapons, one crew-served weapons, Friendly: seven killed, 54 wounded).

APRIL 4, 1971

- FSB 6, 13 kilometers SW of Tan Canh, Kontum Province, receives an attack-by-fire followed by a ground attack (Enemy: 287 killed, 72 individual weapons, 13 crew-served weapons; Friendly: none).

APRIL 5, 1971

- Nine kilometers northwest of Phu Cat, Binh Dinh Province, the 201st Regional Forces Battalion engages an unknown size enemy force during a search operation. US supports with gunships and tactical air (Enemy: 27 killed; Friendly: eight killed, 29 wounded, eight individual weapons).

- *Operation Toan Thang 01/71 NB.* In Cambodia, three kilometers SW of Snoul, Kratie Province, elements of the 2nd Battalion, 7th ARVN Infantry, 3rd Battalion, 8th Infantry, and 1st Armored Cavalry Squadron engage an enemy force. ARVN artillery and helicopter gunships support (Enemy: 218 killed: Friendly: eight killed, 47 wounded, 82 missing).

APRIL 6, 1971

- The 360th Regional Forces Company observation post, two kilometers SE of Mo Cay, Kien Hoa Province, was attacked by an enemy sapper unit aided by three Regional Forces traitors (former Hoi Chanhs). The outpost was overrun and a nearby bridge 50 percent destroyed (Enemy: unknown; Friendly: 16 Regional Forces killed, three Regional Forces wounded, 14 missing, three RVN civilians wounded, 32 individual weapons, one 60mm mortar, one crew-served weapons).
- Elements of the 2nd Battalion, 42nd ARVN Infantry Regiment operating five kilometers east of Dak To, Kontum Province engage the enemy (Enemy: 56 killed, four detained, 15 individual weapons, seven crew-served weapons; Friendly: two wounded).

APRIL 7, 1971

- President Nixon announces plans for the withdrawal of 100,000 more US troops from RVN by December 1, 1971. This will leave 184,000 personnel on that date.
- New Zealand announces it will withdraw its 130-man artillery battery early in May. This will leave 264 New Zealand troops in RVN.
- Nine kilometers north of An Hoa, Quang Nam Province, a forward observer for the 1st Marine Regiment, observes 25 enemy. Artillery and 81mm mortars were employed. A search of the area reveals 30 enemy killed.
- Elements of the US 7th Squadron, 17th Air Cavalry on a visual reconnaissance mission 25 kilometers NW of Dak To, Kontum Province, observe 15 enemy personnel and five elements loaded with rockets headed south. The enemy unit

was engaged with helicopter gunships (Enemy: eight killed, three elephants killed; Friendly: none). Plei Ring De village, 17 kilometers SW of Pleiku, Pleiku Province, was attacked by an unknown size enemy force (Enemy: unknown; Friendly: 34 missing, 28 individual weapons).

- Elements of the 53rd ARVN Infantry on a search operation six kilometers SE of Ben Het, Kontum Province, contacted a large enemy force (Enemy: 260 killed; Friendly: 12 killed, 38 wounded).

APRIL 8, 1971

- *Operation Lam Son 719.* Initiated January 30, 1971 was terminated. Initial reporting: (Enemy: 13,642 killed, 56 detained, 5,066 individual weapons, 1,935 crew-served weapons, 106 tanks, 422 trucks, 1,250 tons of rice, four tons medical supplies, 98 radios, 20,000 tons ammunition captured or destroyed; Friendly: 1,707 (176 US) killed, 6,466 (1,042 US) wounded, 693 (42 US) missing, 3,060 individual weapons, 198 crew-served weapons, 75 tanks, 103 armored personnel carriers, 152 trucks, 98 artillery pieces, 207,500 gallons POL, 1,498 tons ammunition, 37 bulldozers lost or destroyed).
- At the Paris Peace Talks the GVN offers to intern in a neutral country prisoners of war who have been held for a long period. They identify 1,200 prisoners of war who have been detained four years or more.

APRIL 9, 1971

- Elements of the 4th Battalion, 10th ARVN Infantry engaged an estimated enemy company five kilometers west of Truc Giang, Kien Hoa Province, with organic weapons. OV-10 aircraft and gunships supported. Enemy losses were 20 killed and four individual weapons. There were no friendly losses.

APRIL 10, 1971

- In Cambodia, 10 kilometers SE of Suong, Kampong Cham Province, the 33rd Regiment Battalion, supported by ARVN artillery, engaged an unknown size enemy force (Enemy: 100 killed; Friendly: one killed, five wounded).

- Elements of the 2nd Battalion, 43rd Infantry on search operations engage an unknown size enemy force 14 kilometers SE of Suong Kamponga Cham Province, Cambodia (Enemy: 40 killed, two crew-served weapons, four individual weapons; Friendly: three killed, nine wounded, two trucks destroyed).

APRIL 11, 1971

- *Operation Hiep Dong 7.* Initiated April 7, 1971 in Quang Tin Province was terminated (Enemy: 109 killed, 30 detained, 42 individual weapons, 11 crew-served weapons; Friendly: four killed, 10 wounded).
- The 36th and 52nd Ranger Battalions, supported by the 15th and 18th Armored Cavalry Squadron engage an estimated enemy regiment 14 kilometers SE of Suong, Kampong Cham Province, Cambodia, while operating on *Operation Toan Thang 01/72* (Enemy: 200 killed, two 82mm mortar, 18 .51 caliber machine guns; Friendly: six wounded).

APRIL 12, 1971

- USN elements supported by helicopter gunships and VN Air Force aircraft engage and sink a NVN SL-8 infiltration trawler inside the 12-mile territorial limits of RVN 39 kilometers SE of Ca Mau City. The trawler returned fire before blowing up and sinking.
- US Command announces that its biggest conventional bomb, the 15,000-pound "daisy cutter," has been used for the first time against enemy troops near FSB 6. The bombs explode just above the ground and blast a clearing as big as a ball field.
- The Phuoc Long PRU on a ground operation engages an estimated enemy company 15 kilometers NW of Phuoc Binh, Phuoc Long Province (Enemy: 32 killed, two individual weapons, 15 anti-tank mines, 26 120mm mortar rounds, 30 M-26 grenades, 150 B-40 charges, 40 B-41 charges, 20 82mm mortar rounds, 20 60mm mortar rounds, two radios, 80 B-40 rounds, 50 B-41 rounds captured; Friendly: none).

APRIL 13, 1971

- *Operation Dong Khoi/04.* Initiated April 10, 1971 throughout Military Region 4 was terminated (Enemy: 690 killed, 194 detained, 171 individual weapons, six crew-served weapons; Friendly: 36 killed, 267 wounded, two missing, seven individual weapons).

- Elements of the 3rd Battalion, 44th Regiment on search operations engage an unknown size enemy force 14 kilometers west of Tan Canh, Kontum Province (Enemy: 96 killed, 28 individual weapons, four crew-served weapons; Friendly: four killed, 37 wounded, six missing).
- Elements of the 38th ARVN Ranger Battalion operating seven kilometers SE of Suong, Kampong Cham Province, Cambodia receive an attack by an unknown size enemy force. ARVN artillery and VN Air Force support (Enemy: 148 killed, two crew-served weapons, eight individual weapons, Friendly: 16 killed, 68 wounded).

APRIL 14, 1971

- The III MAF redeployed, leaving the 3rd Marine Amphibious Brigade. Redeploying with the III MAF was the 1st Marine Division and the 1st Marine Aircraft Wing.

APRIL 19, 1971

- Foreign Minister Choi Kyu Hah of South Korea announced his government's plans to withdraw an infantry division from South Vietnam before the end of the year. This would involve 13,000 to 15,000 men.

APRIL 20, 1971

- Prime Minister Lon Nol of Cambodia resigns with his entire cabinet. Lon Nol cites his health and incapacity to resume full duties as the reason.
- *Operation Hoang Dieu 104.* Initiated March 8, 1971 in Quang Nam Province was terminated. Enemy losses were 342 killed, 86 detained, 18 returnees, 122 individual weapons and 15 crew-served weapons. Friendly losses were 51 killed and 152 wounded.
- *Operation Dong Khoi/04, Phase II.* Initiated April 17, 1971 in Military Region 4 was terminated. Enemy losses were 817 killed, 204 detained, 55 returnees, 272 individual weapons and

12 crew-served weapons. Friendly losses were 75 killed, 304 wounded, one missing and 22 individual weapons.

APRIL 21, 1971

- *Operation Hoang Dieu 105.* Initiated March 27, 1971 in Quang Nam Province was terminated. Enemy losses were 121 killed, nine detained, 37 individual weapons and four crew-served weapons. Friendly losses were 27 killed and 98 wounded.
- *Operation Greene Sure.* Initiated March 14, 1971 in Binh Dinh Province was terminated. Enemy losses were 168 killed, four detained, 39 individual weapons and four crew-served weapons. Friendly losses were 17 killed, 157 wounded, three individual weapons and two crew-served weapons).

APRIL 23, 1971

- The USS GARRETT COUNTY (AGP-786), was turned over to the Vietnam Navy as part of the continuing US Accelerated Turnover to Vietnam Program.
- MACV announces the start of the seventh phase *(Keystone Oriole Alpha)* of troop redeployments a week ahead of President Nixon's timetable. The redeployment will account for 29,300 spaces.
- In Cambodia, three kilometers SE of Snuol, Kratie Province, a VN Air Force forward air controller observes an unknown size enemy force and engages them with tactical air strikes (Enemy: 50 killed by air; Friendly: none).

APRIL 24, 1971

- In Quang Ngai Province an enemy unit attacked FSB Honey 21 kilometers NW of Quang Ngai City. Enemy losses were 21 killed and eight individual weapons. Friendly losses were 22 ARVN killed, 49 ARVN and two US wounded.

APRIL 25, 1971

- In Khanh Hoa Province, an enemy unit attacked the Duc My Ranger Training Center, 15 kilometers NW of Ninh Hoa. Enemy losses are unknown. Friendly losses were three killed, 15 wounded, eight VN civilians killed, 24 VN civilians wounded, one bulldozer, one truck, and 100 houses destroyed.

APRIL 26, 1971

- In Binh Dinh Province, elements of the 1st Battalion, 41st ARVN Infantry Battalion on a search operation six kilometers SE of Phu My engaged an unknown size enemy force. Enemy losses were 41 killed by air and four individual weapons. Friendly losses were three killed and 14 wounded.
- In Quang Tin Province the 132nd, 182nd, 199th Popular Forces platoons, while searching 20 kilometers NW of Tam Ky, engaged an unknown size enemy force. Enemy losses were 42 killed, one detained, 16 individual weapons and four crew-served weapons. Friendly losses were two wounded.

APRIL 27, 1971

- Twenty-five kilometers SE of Pleiku, Pleiku Province, the district intelligence platoon ambushed an unknown size enemy force. Enemy losses were 20 killed and five individual weapons. There were no friendly losses.

APRIL 28, 1971

- The Vietnam Navy received its first logistic support base when the USN turned over operation of its Cat Lo facility, 40 miles SE of Saigon near Vung Tau.

APRIL 29, 1971

- The GVN announced at the Paris Peace Talks a proposal for the release of 570 sick and wounded prisoners of war. Also included was an offer to intern temporarily in a neutral country 1,200 NVN prisoners of war who had been imprisoned longer than four years.
- In Binh Dinh Province an enemy unit attacked the 42nd Regional Forces Group Headquarters 10 kilometers NE of Phu My. Enemy losses were 22 killed, four individual weapons and three crew-served weapons. Friendly losses were one killed, 18 wounded, two individual weapons and one radio lost.

APRIL 30, 1971

- US operational headquarters were redesignated. IFFV becomes Second Region Assistance Command; II Field Force becomes Third Regional Assistance Command (TRAC); Delta Military

Assistance Command (DMAC) becomes Delta Regional Assistance Command (DRAC).
- US military strength in RVN was 272,073. FWMAF strength was 66,563. RVNAF strength was 1,058,237.

MAY 1, 1971
- Mr. David S. Thomson, New Zealand Minister of Defence, arrived in the RVN for updating on the situation.
- The hospital ship USS SANCTUARY (AH-17), redeployed to the US ending a four-year tour in RVN.
- The Vietnam Navy assumed all responsibilities from the USN in a ceremony at Cam Ranh Bay.
- The Viet Cong freed Catherine M. Webb, the UPI Phnom Penh bureau manager, after 23 days in captivity. Miss Webb, correspondent Toshiichi Suzuki, and four Cambodian interpreters and photographers were freed about 40 miles SW of Phnom Penh.
- *Operation Cuu Long 9/10.* Initiated February 17, 1971 in Chau Doc and Kien Giang Provinces was terminated. Enemy losses were 355 killed, 222 detained, 189 individual weapons, 29 crew-served weapons. Friendly losses were 60 killed, 457 wounded, three missing, seven individual weapons.
- *Operation Cuu Long 9/10.* Initiated February 17, 1971 in Cambodia was terminated. Enemy losses were 153 killed, 76 detained, 80 individual weapons and eight crew-served weapons. Friendly losses were 26 killed and 113 wounded.

MAY 4, 1971
- *Operation Cuu Long 7/2* initiated January 1, 1971 in Kien Hoa, Vinh Long, Sa Dec, Vinh Binh, Dinh Tuong, and Go Cong Provinces ended. Enemy losses were 1,232 killed, 232 detained, 317 individual weapons and 30 crew-served weapons. Friendly losses were 105 killed, 963 wounded, five missing and seven individual weapons.

MAY 5, 1971
- The Chief of US Bureau of Narcotics and Dangerous Drugs, Mr. Robert Ingersoll, met with President Thieu to discuss the severity of drug abuse among US servicemen and the need

for an unprecedented effort by the RVN to suppress drug availability.

- Seven kilometers NE of Long Phu, Ba Xuyen Province, the Long Phu Regional Forces Company and three Popular Forces platoons engaged an estimated 60 enemy. Enemy losses were 32 killed, 11 individual weapons and one crew-served weapon. Friendly losses were three wounded.

MAY 6, 1971

- The US Customs Bureau ordered intensified inspections of US soldiers returning from Southeast Asia and completed inspection of military mail parcels in a crackdown on the flood of high-grade heroin and other hard narcotics coming into the US.
- *Operation Dong Khoi/05/71.* Initiated May 2, 1971 in all provinces of Military Region 4 was terminated. Enemy losses were 523 killed, 126 detained, 166 individual weapons and 11 crew-served weapons. Friendly losses were 34 killed, 196 wounded, one missing and 10 individual weapons.
- Elements of the 2nd Battalion, 8th Infantry Battalion and the 2nd Battalion, 1st Armored Cavalry Squadron engaged an estimated two enemy companies three kilometers SE of Snuol, Kratie Province, Cambodia. Enemy losses were 72 killed, three individual weapons, two crew-served weapons. Friendly losses were one killed, six wounded.

MAY 8, 1971

- In honor of Buddha's birthday, the GVN announced a temporary cessation of offensive operations from noon May 8, 1971 to noon May 9, 1971. The enemy Provisional Revolutionary Government had previously announced a 48-hour ceasefire to run from 0600 hours May 8, 1971 to 0700 hours May 10, 1971.
- The 161st Battery, Royal New Zealand Artillery, consisting of 10 officers and 121 men, redeployed to New Zealand.
- *Operation Imperial Lake.* Initiated August 20, 1970 in Quang Nam Province was terminated. Enemy losses were 305 killed, 153 detained, 215 individual weapons and 16 crew-served weapons. Friendly losses were 26 killed and 208 wounded.

MAY 9, 1971

- The Royal Thai Navy PGM-12, with 29 personnel assigned, redeployed to Thailand. The PGM had been attached to and operated with the USN Task Force 115 *(Market Time)* since December 17, 1966. The remaining unit of the Sea Horse Element, LST-3, with 155 personnel would redeploy in April 1972.
- Twelve kilometers NW of Quang Tri City, Quang Tri Province, a sampan water taxi with 44 civilians moving from Mai Xa Chanh to Dong Ha was mined resulting in friendly losses of four killed, 26 civilians killed, 18 civilians missing and four civilians injured.
- *Operation Pong Tam 1.* Initiated April 24, 1971 in Quang Ngai Province was terminated. Enemy losses were 106 killed, eight detained, 36 individual weapons and six crew-served weapons. Friendly losses were 17 killed and 18 wounded).

MAY 13, 1971

- Hanoi agreed to formally accept a group of 570 prisoners of war held in South Vietnam. The release was scheduled for June 4, 1971.

MAY 14, 1971

- The Marine Corps announced it would court-martial Sergeant Jon M. Sweeney on charges of aiding the enemy while imprisoned by the North Vietnamese. This was the first case of its kind stemming from the war.
- The 19th Tactical Airlift Squadron, organized at Tan Son Nhut Air Base on October 8, 1964, was deactivated and turned its aircraft and equipment over to the RVNAF. The recently organized 421st Transport Squadron VN Air Force received 16 C-123s, the first VN Air Force unit to operate this aircraft in the RVN.
- *Operation Meng Ho 16.* Initiated April 23, 1971 in Binh Dinh Province was terminated. Enemy losses were 252 killed, one detained, 110 individual weapons and 35 crew-served weapons. Friendly losses were 13 killed and 60 wounded.

MAY 17, 1971

- Approximately 130 policemen, customs officers, and other

officials at Tan Son Nhut Airport were shifted to other jobs as part of a stepped-up GVN drive against smuggling.

- The USCGC BLACKHAW (WLB-390) redeployed from RVN terminating 3½ years duty maintaining maritime navigational aids in the RVN.

MAY 19, 1971

- Secretary of the Army Stanley R. Resor announced that after a review of the My Lai case, Major General Samuel Koster would receive a letter of censure, a vacating of the temporary appointment in his current grade, and withdrawal of a Distinguished Service Medal awarded during the period he served with the 23rd Infantry Division. Brigadier General George Young also received a letter of censure and withdrawal of his Distinguished Service Medal.

MAY 20, 1971

- *Operation Quang Trung 22/1.* Initiated April 1, 1971 in Kontum Province was terminated. Enemy losses were 3,534 killed, seven detained, 511 individual weapons and 142 crew-served weapons. Friendly losses were 220 killed, 624 wounded, 148 missing, 113 individual weapons and 10 crew-served weapons.

MAY 21, 1971

- Secretary of the Army Stanley R. Resor resigned ending six years' service starting from the beginning of the Vietnam buildup in 1965.
- Six kilometers SW of Con Thien, Quang Tri Province, FSB C-2 received an attack-by-fire of 11 rounds of rocket fire. One direct hit on a personnel bunker buried the individuals inside. Enemy losses were unknown and friendly losses were 29 US killed and 33 US wounded.

MAY 22, 1971

- *Operation Cuu Long/DK/05/II.* Initiated May 18, 1971 in Military Region 4 was terminated. Enemy losses were 869 killed, 173 detained, 235 individual weapons and 20 crew-served weapons. Friendly losses were 54 killed, 293 wounded, four missing and 15 individual weapons.

MAY 23, 1971

- An enemy unit shelled and attacked elements of the 2nd Battalion, 42nd Infantry Regiment operating eight kilometers SW of Tan Canh, Kontum Province. Enemy losses were 139 killed, 11 detained, 23 individual weapons, 11 crew-served weapons and one flame thrower. Friendly losses were five wounded.
- At Cam Ranh Bay, Khanh Hoa Province, an enemy sapper attack on the POL Tank Farm Number 1 destroyed 1,680,000 gallons of JP-4 and 210,600 gallons of aviation gasoline.
- Two VN Air Force UH-1H helicopters collided in midair and crashed 38 kilometers SW of Kien An, Kien Giang Province, while approaching an LZ in support of the 2nd Battalion, 32nd ARVN Infantry. Friendly losses were 28 killed.

MAY 25, 1971

- *Operation Quang Trung 23-4.* Initiated May 16, 1971 in Pleiku Province was terminated. Enemy losses were 215 killed, eight detained, 24 individual weapons and seven crew-served weapons. Friendly losses were 30 killed and 100 wounded.

MAY 26, 1971

- The RVN Ministry of Foreign Affairs announced that the North Vietnam conditions for the release of 570 sick and wounded NVA prisoners of war were acceptable. The exchange was to be made June 4, 1971 at Cau Tung on the 17th parallel.
- Terrorists set off an explosion in a crowded market killing three civilians and wounding 32 civilians and 11 Regional Forces soldiers 50 miles south of Qui Nhon.
- Elements of the 2nd Battalion, 8th ARVN Infantry Battalion and the 1st Battalion, 5th Armored Cavalry Squadron operating in *Operation Toan Thang 01/71 NB* in the vicinity of Snuol, Cambodia, engaged an estimated enemy company. Enemy losses were 75 killed. Friendly losses were: 12 killed, 62 killed, 2¾-ton trucks and one M-113 armored personnel carrier damaged.

MAY 27, 1971

- MACV disclosed the use of a new bomb, which sprayed an

explosive mist that produced a blast and concussion when ignited. The new bomb, which was reported to have the blast effect of a 500-pound iron bomb but made no crater, was considered highly effective in clearing LZs of mines and booby traps.

MAY 28, 1971

- The USN turned over its An Thoi logistic support base to the Vietnamese Navy. The base, located in Phu Quoc Island in the Gulf of Thailand, supported coastal surveillance forces assigned to the Vietnam Navy Coastal Flotilla 4. For the past five years the base had been a key base for allied coastal patrol forces.
- ARVN elements participating in *Operation Toan Thang 01/71 NB* engaged an estimated enemy battalion in the vicinity of Snuol, Kratic Province, Cambodia. Enemy losses were 115 killed, two crew-served weapons and three individual weapons. Friendly losses were eight killed and 18 wounded.
- Elements of the 1st Battalion, 52nd US Infantry Battalion operating 15 kilometers NW of Quang Ngai found 21.7 tons of rice.

MAY 30, 1971

- Admiral Elmo R. Zumwalt, Jr. Chief of Naval Operations, while visiting RVN announced the beginning of a 30-day amnesty program for sailors addicted to drugs in RVN.
- Elements of the 2nd Battalion, 17th ARVN Cavalry and 161st Regional Forces Company engaged an estimated enemy battalion 12 kilometers SW of Hoi An, Quang Nam Province. ARVN artillery supported the engagements. Enemy losses were 215 killed, four detained, 15 crew-served weapons, 30 individual weapons and three radios captured; Friendly losses were five killed, 35 wounded, one individual weapon, 19 civilians killed, 30 civilians wounded and 170 homes destroyed.

MAY 31, 1971

- An enemy unit attacked the 54th ARVN Regiment command post 10 kilometers NW of A Luoi, Thua Thien Province. Enemy losses were 56 killed, 15 individual weapons, six crew-served weapons and two radios captured. Friendly losses were 15 killed and 28 wounded.

- Elements of the 5th ARVN Division abandoned Snuol, Cambodia with heavy losses in men and equipment following an enemy attack, which began May 24, 1971. ARVN reinforcements attempted to break through were blocked. The task force of 2,000 men lost 89 killed, 489 wounded, 197 missing. Equipment left behind or destroyed included: 839 individual weapons, 110 crew-served weapons, 14 artillery pieces, nine tanks, 15 armored personnel carriers and 64 trucks.
- US military strength in RVN was 252,210. FWMAF strength was 66,586. RVNAF strength was 1,060.597.

JUNE 1, 1971

- In Kontum Province, the enemy shelled and attacked elements of the 2nd Battalion, 42nd Infantry Regiment at FSB 5, 11 kilometers SW of Tan Can. Enemy losses were 57 killed, 11 individual weapons and five crew-served weapons. Friendly losses were four killed, nine wounded, two 105mm howitzers and one 57mm recoilless rifle damaged.

JUNE 2, 1971

- Brigadier General John W. Donaldson was charged with murdering six VN civilians and assaulting two others while flying over Quang Ngai Province during operations in late 1968. He was the highest ranking officer accused of killing civilians in the Vietnam war and was the first US general to be charged with a war crime in 70 years.
- *Operation Hiep Dong 8-2.* Initiated May 20, 1971 in Quang Tin Province was terminated Enemy losses were 107 killed, 49 detained, 38 individual weapons and three crew-served weapons. Friendly losses were seven killed.

JUNE 3, 1971

- Ten kilometers NW of Krek, Kampong Cham Province, Cambodia, 63 Cambodian Communists rallied to elements of the 3rd Battalion, 52nd ARVN Infantry Battalion.

JUNE 4, 1971

- Thirteen disabled NVN prisoners of war were returned to prison in RVN after North Vietnam announced in Paris they had cancelled an agreement to accept the prisoners of war in a transfer off the coast of the DMZ. Only 13 among 660 prisoners of war interviewed by the International Committee of the Red Cross (ICRC) had agreed to return to North Vietnam.
- Cambodian and RVN sign accord on the suppression of smuggling and transportation of commercial goods. The accord was aimed at clamping down on illegal drug traffic between the two nations.

JUNE 5, 1971

- Elements of the 9th VNMC Battalion operating 16 kilometers SW of Cam Lo, Quang Tri Province were attacked by an unknown size enemy force. Enemy losses were 100 killed. Friendly losses were 10 killed and 20 wounded.
- At Katum, Tay Ninh Province, enemy sappers penetrated Katum Base Camp defenses and destroyed two JP-4 fuel bladders containing 16,000 gallons of fuel.

JUNE 6, 1971

- US OV-10 and helicopter gunships sighted an estimated enemy battalion 13 kilometers SW of Long Toan, Vinh Binh Province. Enemy losses were 22 killed by air, 11 sampans, six structures destroyed and one large secondary fire followed. There were no friendly losses.
- *Operation Cuu Long/KG/21/01.* Initiated May 12, 1971 in Kien Giang Province was terminated. Enemy losses were 238 killed, 10 detained, 56 individual weapons and 21 crew-served weapons. Friendly losses were 26 killed and 27 wounded.
- Elements of the 5th VNMC Battalion operating six kilometers NW of FSB Sarge in Quang Tri Province were attacked by an enemy unit. Enemy losses were 83 killed, one detained, 12 individual weapons and 17 crew-served weapons. Friendly losses were 21 killed and 12 wounded.

JUNE 7, 1971

- *Operation Hoang Dieu 106.* Initiated April 23, 1971 in Quang Nam Province was terminated Enemy losses were 794 killed, 213 detained, 235 individual weapons and 59 crew-served weapons. Friendly losses were 117 killed and 452 wounded.
- *Operation Cuu Long/DK/06/71.* Initiated May 31, 1971 in Military Region 4 was terminated Enemy losses were 583 killed, 102 detained, 35 returnees, 177 individual weapons and six crew-served weapons. Friendly losses were 42 killed, 271 wounded and 14 individual weapons.

JUNE 8, 1971

- An estimated enemy company attacked the Tan Cong Regional Forces observation post four kilometers NE of Don Nhong, Kien Hoa Province. Enemy losses were 30 killed by air. Friendly losses were one Regional Forces killed, 16 Regional Forces wounded and four civilians wounded.
- *Operation Quang Trung 23-4.* Initiated May 25, 1971 in Pleiku Province was terminated Enemy losses were 249 killed, 19 individual weapons and six crew-served weapons. Friendly losses were 17 killed, 85 wounded, 17 missing and 21 individual weapons.

JUNE 9, 1971

- GVN spokesmen in Saigon announced that Major General Nguyen Van Hieu had been relieved as commander of the 5th ARVN Division due to losses by his forces while abandoning Snuol, Cambodia, on May 31, 1971.

JUNE 12, 1971

- Elements of the 4th Battalion, 43rd ARVN Infantry Battalion and 5th Armored Cavalry Squadron received 30 rounds of 82mm mortar fire followed by a ground attack while operating five kilometers NW of Krek, Kampong Cham Province, Cambodia, on *Operation Toan Thang 07/71 NB.* Enemy losses were 45 killed, one detained, 11 individual weapons and one crew-served weapon. Friendly losses were four killed, nine wounded, two individual weapons, one PRC-25 radio lost and two M-113 armored personnel carriers damaged.

JUNE 15, 1971

- MACV announced that US battalion advisory teams, the first units to accompany ARVN troops into combat a decade ago, would be phased out within two weeks. The elimination of the teams, usually made up of about five officers and enlisted men, was another step in the Vietnamization program.
- In Qui Nhon harbor, suspected sappers mined the US merchant ship USS AMERICAN HAWK outside the hull beneath the engine room, flooding the engine room.

JUNE 17, 1971

- President Nixon announced plans for an all-out offensive against drug abuse, including immediate establishment of testing and initial rehabilitation procedures in RVN.
- *Operation Cuu Long/DK/06/II.* Initiated June 13, 1971 in Military Region 4 was terminated Enemy losses were 617 killed, 102 detained, 54 returnees, 214 individual weapons and three crew-served weapons. Friendly losses were 66 killed, 258 wounded, two missing and 18 individual weapons.
- In Quang Tri Province, an enemy unit attacked elements of the 5th VNMC Battalion operating three kilometers north of FSB Sarge. Enemy losses were 63 killed, 14 individual weapons, seven B-40, one flame thrower and one radio captured. Friendly losses were nine killed, 17 wounded and one missing.

JUNE 18, 1971

- MACV announced it would begin a program to identify and provide initial rehabilitation to military personnel who were heroin users prior to their return to the US. All personnel scheduled for return would be given a drug test urinalysis on arrival at out-processing centers.
- In Quang Tri Province, an enemy unit attacked elements of the 5th VNMC Battalion operating 14 kilometers SW of Cam Lo. Enemy losses were 183 killed, 14 individual weapons, 12 crew-served weapons, one flame thrower, radio, 69 RPG rounds and 200 blocks TNT. Friendly losses were 25 killed, 35 wounded and one helicopter damaged.
- At Cung Son, Phu Yen Province, the 2nd Battalion, 53rd Regional Forces Group Headquarters, and 202nd ARVN Artillery Platoon received mortar rounds followed by a

ground attack from an estimated enemy battalion, US helicopter gunships supported. Enemy losses were 87 killed, three detained, 41 individual weapons and four crew-served weapons. Friendly losses were 20 Regional Forces killed, 50 Regional Forces wounded and one US wounded.

JUNE 22, 1971

- The last US Marine combat unit departed the five northernmost provinces, Military Region 1, with the ending of Phase VII redeployments *(Keystone Oriole Alpha)*.
- The commander of the US forces in the Delta region Military Region 4 ordered a crackdown on drug traffic. All servicemen were confined to their compounds except on official business, and extensive searches were held of all personnel and vehicles entering and leaving the compounds.
- Explosions at the ammunition supply point of the Quang Tri Combat Base, believed caused by enemy satchel charges, destroyed 605 tons of assorted munitions.
- An unknown size enemy force entered Soon Trai hamlet, five kilometers west of Cung Son, Phu Yen Province and abducted 70 VN civilians and 30 later returned.

JUNE 23, 1971

- An ARVN ammunition supply point at Qui Nhon was hit by 82mm mortar fire, which destroyed 413 tons of mixed ammunition and mines.

JUNE 26, 1971

- Phase VIII troop withdrawal program, *Keystone Oriole Bravo,* began five days earlier than planned with the stand down of the 35th Tactical Fighter Wing. The redeployment included the 173rd Airborne Brigade and the 1st Brigade, 6th Infantry Division (Mech).
- *Operation Lam Son 720.* Elements of the 4th VNMC Battalion received a ground attack four kilometers NW of FSB Sarge, Quang Tri Province, from an unknown size enemy force. Enemy losses were 79 killed, 18 individual weapons, 11 crew-served weapons, 132 B-40/41 rockets, one flame thrower, 300 blocks of TNT, 15,000 rounds of small arms ammunition were

captured or destroyed. Friendly losses were three killed and 22 wounded.

JUNE 28, 1971

- An estimated enemy battalion attacked and overran the 979th Regional Forces Company observation post seven kilometers NW of Cau Ke, Vinh Binh Province. Enemy losses were three killed by air. Friendly losses were 20 Regional Forces killed, five Regional Forces wounded, two civilians killed, 27 individual weapons, one crew-served weapons, two PRC-25 radios, and assorted ammunition lost, four individual weapons and one M-60 machine gun destroyed.

JUNE 29, 1971

- The US turned over to the Vietnam Navy its intermediate support base at Rach Soi 125 miles SW of Saigon. The base was the second of its type to be transferred to the Vietnam Navy.
- At Qui Nhon, Binh Dinh Province, an ARVN ammunition supply point (ASP) received an estimated six rounds of mortar fire, which ignited five pads of ammunition, destroyed an estimated 2,775 metric tons of ammunition.
- *Operation Quyet Thang 20/B.* Initiated May 3, 1971 in Quang Ngai and Quang Tin and Kontum Provinces was terminated. Enemy losses were 622 killed, 23 detained, 185 individual weapons and 30 crew-served weapons. Friendly losses were 43 killed and 134 wounded.
- *Operation Cuu Long 44/41/10.* In Cambodia, the 67th Ranger Battalion engaged an estimated enemy battalion 21 kilometers SW of Svay Rieng. The VN Air Force tactical air supported. Enemy losses were 58 killed and three individual weapons. Friendly losses were 10 killed, 18 wounded, 18 wounded and one PRC-25 radio destroyed.

JUNE 30, 1971

- Enemy mortars hit the Qui Nhon ammunition dump, the largest in the central region of South Vietnam. More than 10,000 tons of ammunition was destroyed.

- The USN announced that the 30-day trial drug amnesty program in RVN was being extended indefinitely.
- *Operation Quyet Thang 603/B.* Initiated April 1, 1971 in Quang Ngai Province was terminated. Enemy losses were 412 killed, 18 detained, 109 individual weapons and three crew-served weapons. Friendly losses were 44 killed and 147 wounded.
- *Operation Quyet Thang 504/B.* Initiated April 1, 1971 in Quang Tin Province was terminated Enemy losses were 434 killed, 16 detained, 125 individual weapons and 28 crew-served weapons. Friendly losses were 27 killed and 87 wounded.
- *Operation Quyet Thang 405/B.* Initiated April 1, 1971 in Quang Ngai Province was terminated. Enemy losses were 399 killed, 31 detained, one returnee, 125 individual weapons and six crew-served weapons. Friendly losses were 12 killed and 71 wounded.
- US military strength in the RVN was 239, 528. FWMAF strength was 66,842. RVNAF strength was 1,060,129.

JULY 1, 1971

- In Military Region 1, military commanders launched an intensive campaign against drugs and crime. Tight restrictions were put on all personnel entering and leaving compounds.
- *Operation Finney Hill.* Initiated March 2, 1971 in Quang Ngai Province was terminated Enemy losses were 454 killed, 74 detained, one returnee, 241 individual weapons and 33 crew-served weapons. Friendly losses were 32 killed and 280 wounded.
- *Operation Caroline Hill.* Initiated April 29, 1971 in Quang Nam Province was terminated Enemy losses were 161 killed, 66 detained, one returnee, 81 individual weapons and 10 crew-served weapons. Friendly losses were 15 wounded and 162 wounded.
- *Operation Middlesex Peak.* Initiated March 1, 1971 in Quang Tin Province was terminated Enemy losses were 463 killed, 206 detained, six returnee, 122 individual weapons and 16 crew-served weapons. Friendly losses were 50 killed and 473 wounded.
- At the Paris talks, Madame Nguyen Thi Binh made a new seven-point proposal for the Provisional Revolutionary Government which included a provision for the release of all prisoners

captured in the war by Communist forces provided a date was set for the withdrawal of US forces and Allies from the RVN.

JULY 3, 1971

- Dr. Henry Kissinger, assistant to the President for National Security, visited the RVN for discussions on the local situation.

JULY 6, 1971

- Action in South Vietnam came almost to a standstill as Typhoon Harriet inundated the country's northern provinces with up to eight inches of rain.
- *Operation Bak Jue 26.* Initiated June 21, 1971 in Khanh Hoa Province was terminated. Enemy losses were 240 killed, 115 individual weapons and three crew-served weapons. Friendly losses were five killed and seven wounded.
- *Operation Cuu Long 44/41/10.* Conducted in Cambodia, was terminated. Enemy losses were 162 killed, 32 detained, 30 individual weapons and one crew-served weapons. Friendly losses were 22 killed, 46 wounded and three individual weapons.

JULY 8, 1971

- ARVN troops took control of Fire Base Alpha, the northernmost US fire base in RVN.
- The US rejected Communist demands for unconditional withdrawal of US forces contained in the July 1, 1971 seven-point proposal, but moved to negotiate the whole new Viet Cong peace plan in private talks. The Communist delegations, however, rejected the bid for private sessions.
- Thailand began withdrawing its forces from South Vietnam with about 5,000 troops leaving during July and August and all Thai troops withdrawal by the end of 1972. The first Thai troops arrived in Vietnam in September 1967.

JULY 9, 1971

- Secretary of Navy John H. Chafee ordered a one-time-only exemption of USN drug users from punishment if they cooperated in their own rehabilitation. The order stressed volunteering and the disclosure must have been made before arrest or official warning. Persons involuntarily identified by the drug-testing program were also granted exemptions.

- In a ground operation 12 kilometers NE of Thoi Binh, An Xuyen Province, elements of the ARVN 31st Reconnaissance Company engaged an enemy company. ARVN artillery and USN OV-10 aircraft supported the engagement. Enemy losses were 20 killed, one detained, one individual weapons, two crew-served weapons and 20 grenades captured. Friendly losses were two killed and two wounded.
- Fire Base Charlie 2, the last American base along the RVN's northernmost line of defense, was turned over to the ARVN.

JULY 14, 1971

- Three persons were killed and 10 wounded when terrorists tossed two grenades at a militia team patrolling a market in a Mekong Delta town 50 miles southeast of Can Tho.

JULY 15, 1971

- A three-week strike by some 800 South Vietnam dock workers, which tied up thousands of tons of military cargo at the US Army's Newport piers, was settled.

JULY 19, 1971

- Communist gunners hit a US aviation unit less than 16 miles from Saigon with about five 107mm rockets, causing light casualties and damage.

JULY 21, 1971

- Twenty-one South Vietnam Rangers were killed and 31 injured when a US Army Chinook helicopter crashed 50 miles south of Da Nang. Five American crewmen were injured in the crash.
- *Operation Cuu Long/Dong Kho/MR4i.* Initiated July 14, 1971 was terminated. Enemy losses were 269 killed, 80 detained, 83 individual weapons and 14 crew-served weapons. Friendly losses were 39 killed, 140 wounded and 21 individual weapons.

JULY 22, 1971

- MACV announced US combat losses were the lowest since 1965 when the US troop build-up began in Vietnam. US units have suffered more than 345,000 casualties since January 1, 1961 with 45,384 killed; 300,952 wounded and 1,481 captured or missing. An estimated 759,516 enemy soldiers were killed during the same period.

JULY 26, 1971

- Narcotics agents from Thailand, US, and South Vietnam conducted their first combined operation and cracked a major heroin ring supplying soldiers in the RVN. Ninety-seven pounds of pure heroin and 660 pounds of smoking opium were seized.
- *Operation Dong Bo-17.* Initiated July 12, 1971 in Khanh Hoa/ Ninh Thuan Province was terminated. Enemy losses were 245 killed, one detained, 126 individual weapons and 11 crew-served weapons. Friendly losses were one killed and three wounded.

JULY 27, 1971

- Communist sappers armed with satchel charges wounded two Americans and destroyed four helicopters of the 1st Aviation Brigade at Lai Khe, 30 miles north of Saigon.
- *Operation Cuu Long 9/11.* In Cambodia, elements of the 3rd Battalion, 15th Infantry Battalion on search operations engaged an unknown size enemy force six kilometers northwest of Kampong Trabek, Prey Veng Province. Enemy losses were 79 killed, eight individual weapons and five crew-served weapons. Friendly losses were eight killed and 26 wounded.

JULY 28, 1971

- *Operation Hae San Jin 10.* Initiated July 13, 1971 in Phu Yen Province was terminated Enemy losses were 200 killed, 79 individual weapons and three crew-served weapons. Friendly losses were: five killed, 13 wounded.
- *Operation Cuu Long/Dong Khoi/MR 4 Phase III.* Initiated July 23, 1971 in Military Region 4 was terminated. Enemy losses were 359 killed, 79 detained, 130 individual weapons and three crew-served weapons. Friendly losses were 74 killed, 169 wounded, 14 missing and 42 individual weapons.

JULY 29, 1971

- *Operation Toan Thang 01/71.* In Cambodia, elements of the ARVN 50th Regiment and B Company, 3rd Battalion, 17th US Air Cavalry engaged an unknown size enemy force 18 kilometers northwest of Svay Rieng, Svay Rieng Province. Enemy losses were 79 killed, five detained and 13 individual weapons. Friendly losses were one wounded.

JULY 31, 1971

- US military strength in RVN was 225,106. FWMAF strength was 64,762. RVNAF strength was 1,057, 924.

AUGUST 1, 1971

- The MACV program to test all servicemen rotating from RVN for heroin use was expanded to include a check for amphetamines and barbiturate users.

AUGUST 7, 1971

- The 1st Brigade, 5th Infantry Division (Mech) was redeployed after three years of service in the RVN.

AUGUST 8, 1971

- The GVN has ordered the International Voluntary Service (IVS), a Quaker-sponsored group, out of Vietnam by August 31, 1971.

AUGUST 12, 1971

- MACV announces the beginning of *Project Home Run Extended,* a multimillion dollar program to ship war surplus machinery and equipment back to the US in connection with the draw down of US forces in RVN. The program covered civilian goods and supplies, and was separate from *Operation Retrograde,* which sent back military supplies and reconditioned vehicles.
- The Department of Defense announced the total of 66 US battle deaths for July was the lowest monthly figure since May 1965.

AUGUST 15, 1971

- US forces in Vietnam extended the drug testing and treatment program to personnel leaving the country on the 14-day CONUS leave program.

- In Quang Tri Province, 35 kilometers NW of FSB Sarge, an unknown size enemy force attacked elements of the 6th Battalion, 258th VNMC Battalion. Enemy losses were 200 killed and friendly losses were 31 killed.

AUGUST 17, 1971

- In Qui Nhon Harbor, Binh Dinh Province, an explosive device estimated to be 500 to 600 pounds was detonated against the outer hull of the SS GREEN BAY, a cargo ship. The explosion resulted in a 45 to 70 foot hole in the ship's side and injured four individuals.
- *Operation Hiep Dong 9.* Initiated August 10, 1971 was terminated. Enemy losses were 112 killed, seven detained, 28 individual weapons and five crew-served weapons. Friendly losses were seven killed and 25 wounded.

AUGUST 18, 1971

- The Government of Australia and New Zealand announced that they will withdraw all of their combat troops from the RVN, most of them by the end of the year.
- *Operation Hoang Dieu.* Initiated June 28, 1971 in Quang Nam Province was terminated. Enemy losses were 128 killed, 20 detained, 63 individual weapons and seven crew-served weapons. Friendly losses were 19 killed and 152 wounded.

AUGUST 24, 1971

- *Operation Do Kae Bi.* Initiated August 10, 1971 in Phu Yen Province was terminated. Enemy losses were 325 killed, 139 individual weapons and 10 crew-served weapons. Friendly losses were two killed and 15 wounded.

AUGUST 25, 1971

- At Cam Ranh Bay in Khanh Hoa Province an enemy satchel charge caused an explosion in the Tri-Service Ammunition Storage Area and destroyed an estimated 6,000 short tons of munitions.

- Da Nang Air Base and Da Nang City in Quang Nam Province received an attack-by-fire consisting of two 122mm rockets. Enemy losses were unknown. Friendly losses were three civilians killed and 11 civilians wounded. A fire caused by the rockets destroys 137 houses.
- MACV initiated a program of unannounced testing of units by urinalysis.

AUGUST 29, 1971

- Communist gunners fired three 107mm rockets into Tan Son Nhut Air Base as attacks reached a month-month peak in the 24 hours leading up to Vietnam's national assembly elections. Two rockets were duds. The rocket, which exploded inside the base, was the first since December 1969. There were no casualties or damage.

AUGUST 30, 1971

- In Phuong Dinh Province, 22 kilometers southwest of Can Tho, elements of the US 191st Aviation Company on a reconnaissance flight observed an unknown size enemy force in a bunker complex. Enemy losses were 27 killed by air and there were no friendly losses.

AUGUST 31, 1971

- *Operation Lam Son 720.* Initiated April 14, 1971 in Quang Tri and Thua Thien Provinces was terminated. Enemy losses were 3,104 killed, 12 detained, 560 individual weapons and 232 crew-served weapons. Friendly losses were 346 killed, 1,257 wounded, 23 missing and five individual weapons.
- US military strength in RVN was 216,528. FWMAF strength was 61,256. RVNAF strength was 1,052,353.

SEPTEMBER 1, 1971

- MACV announced the beginning of redeployment increment nine. By December 1, 1971, 42,000 spaces would be redeployed including one-third of the 19 maneuver battalions in the 101st Airborne and 23rd Infantry Divisions.

SEPTEMBER 5, 1971

- In Binh Thuan Province, five kilometers northeast of FSB

Sandy, an estimated enemy battalion attacked the 88th Regional Forces Company with small arms and mortars. Enemy losses were 25 killed, one detained, one crew-served weapons and one PRC-10 radio captured. Friendly losses were one Regional Forces killed and four Regional Forces wounded.

SEPTEMBER 10, 1971

- The 81st Regional Forces Platoon operated 10 kilometers north of An Hoa in Quang Nam Province ambushed an estimated enemy company. Enemy losses were 29 killed. There were no friendly losses.

SEPTEMBER 12, 1971

- *Operation Cuu Long/Dong Khoi.* Initiated on September 7, 1971 throughout Military Region 4 was terminated. Enemy losses were 356 killed, 74 detained, 116 individual weapons and four crew-served weapons. Friendly losses were 49 Regional Forces/Popular Forces killed, 186 Regional Forces/Popular Forces were wounded and 112 individual weapons.

SEPTEMBER 13, 1971

- US Senate sources released an announcement that the Central Intelligence Agency (CIA) was training irregulars in Laos and financing additional Thai volunteers supplementing the Laotian Government Forces.

SEPTEMBER 14, 1971

- The GVN announced it was creating another Army division, its first since 1965 to serve along the DMZ defense line vacated by departing US Forces.
- *Operation Ket Hop 12.* Initiated May 7, 1971 in Quang Tri Province was terminated. Enemy losses were 117 killed, 16 detained, 87 individual weapons and 27 crew-served weapons. Friendly losses were 51 killed and 99 wounded.

SEPTEMBER 15, 1971

- The drug testing program was expanded to include all personnel leaving RVN on R&R.
- The Cholon Post Exchange closed in Saigon. At it's peak the

Post Exchange, which first opened in April 1965, had the largest dollar volume of any Post Exchange in the world.

- *Operation Lam Son 810.* Elements of the Hac Bao Company operating 13 kilometers NW of Khe Sanh in Quang Tri Province found and destroyed 20 large storage bunkers containing 100,000 rounds of 37mm ammunition, 300,000 rounds of AK-47 ammunition, 4,000 liters of gasoline, 200 bags of rice containing 50 kilos each, 10,000 meters of communication wire; total approximate weight was 99.3 tons.
- Elements of the 33rd ARVN Infantry on an airmobile operation 35 kilometers south of Kien An in Kien Giang Province engaged an unknown size enemy force. US and VN Air Force helicopters and gunships supported. Enemy losses were 28 killed, 11 individual weapons and five crew-served weapons. Friendly losses were four killed, nine wounded and 24 missing.
- A bomb exploded in a downtown nightclub in Saigon. One US civilian was killed, 14 VN civilians killed, seven US military injured, and 50 VN civilians were injured. The building suffered 70 percent damage.
- Royal Laotian Government forces retook the key town of Pak Song, on the Bolovens Plateau.

SEPTEMBER 16, 1971

- Elements of the 4th Battalion, 32nd ARVN Infantry Battalion at FSB Bien Nhi, 24 kilometers west of Thoi Binh in An Xuyen Province, received a mortar and rocket attack followed by a ground attack by an unknown size enemy force. Enemy losses were 21 killed, 10 individual weapons and thee crew-served weapons. Friendly losses were 26 killed and 69 wounded.
- An ARVN vehicle containing the Tri Tam district S-3 was ambushed on Highway 14, three kilometers south of Tri Tam, Binh Duong Province. The reaction force led by the district chief was also ambushed. Enemy losses were 23 killed and four individual weapons. Friendly losses were 28 ARVN and three US killed including the RVN District Chief, Security Chief, Police Chief, Executive Officer, and S-2, and the US District Senior Advisor; 24 wounded and four missing.

SEPTEMBER 18, 1971

- RVN commanders decided to end *Lam Son 810* ahead of schedule, due to disruption of essential air support because of the onset of monsoon rains.
- Elements of the 2nd Battalion, 31st ARVN Infantry in night defensive position 18 kilometers NW of Dam Doi in An Xuyen Province received a mortar attack followed by a ground attack by an unknown size enemy force. Enemy losses were 19 killed, 11 individual weapons and 11 grenades. Friendly losses were six killed and 10 wounded.
- Saigon police and students battled into the night in anti-government demonstrations.

SEPTEMBER 19, 1971

- *Operation Lam Son 810.* Initiated September 1971 in Quang Tri Province was terminated. The operation was the largest since the invasion of Laos. Final cumulative results of *Operation Lam Son 810*: Enemy losses were 125 killed, one detained, 32 individual weapons and 11 crew-served weapons (includes 122mm field guns). Friendly losses were 13 killed and 90 wounded. An estimated 124 tons of assorted ammunition, 10 tons of rice, 11,000 gallons of fuel, four trucks, one track vehicle, 12,000 meters communication wire, one field phone, one pair of binoculars, two radios, and 45 field packs were captured or destroyed by RVNAF.
- Enemy sappers attacked the 531st ARVN ammunition dump one kilometer north of Gia Ninh in Gia Dinh Province and destroyed three pads of ammunition containing approximately 340 tons of material.

SEPTEMBER 20, 1971

- Elements of the 31st ARVN Regiment on ground operations 27 kilometers southwest of Kien An in Kien Giang Province engaged an unknown size enemy force. Navy OV-10 aircraft and Army helicopter gunships supported the engagement. Enemy losses were 53 killed, six individual weapons and five crew-served weapons. Friendly losses were one killed and one wounded.

- The 18th ARVN Division base camp located two kilometers west of Tay Ninh in Tay Ninh Province received 50 rounds of 82mm mortar and a sapper attack by an estimated enemy battalion. Enemy losses were 52 killed, nine detained, 17 individual weapons, two crew-served weapons, 48 satchel charges, 16 M-26 grenades, 10 mines and one radio. Friendly losses were 21 killed, 63 wounded and one ¼-ton truck destroyed.
- Enemy sappers traveling by sampan under cover of mortar barrage infiltrated the Esso and Shell storage depots in Phnom Penh, Cambodia. The resulting explosions destroyed 18 large storage tanks causing shortages in the city's fuel supply.

SEPTEMBER 22, 1971

- Elements of the 1st Battalion, 43rd ARVN Infantry on ground operations 12 kilometers north of Tay Ninh City in Tay Ninh Province engaged an unknown size enemy force. ARVN and US artillery and US helicopter gunships supported the engagement. Enemy losses were 20 killed, three individual weapons and four crew-served weapons. Friendly losses were 16 wounded.
- *Operation Bun Gae 23.* Initiated September 9, 1971 in Phu Yen Province was terminated. Enemy losses were 173 killed, four detained, 78 individual weapons and four crew-served weapons. Friendly losses were four ROK wounded.
- Captain Ernest L. Medina, the last officer charged in the My Lai Massacre, was cleared of all counts.

SEPTEMBER 24, 1971

- All US Forces in Vietnam were placed on alert because of the pre-election atmosphere.

SEPTEMBER 25, 1971

- The USS FORSTER (DER-334) was turned over to the Vietnam Navy. The ship was renamed the TRAN KHANH DU (HQ-4).
- Students in Saigon firebombed US vehicles and war veterans burned election posters in anti-government and anti-American demonstrations.

SEPTEMBER 26, 1971

- Elements of the 30th ARVN Ranger Battalion and the 172nd

FANK Infantry Battalion were attacked by an unknown size enemy force seven kilometers east of Krek in Kampong Cham Province, Cambodia. Enemy losses were 29 killed, nine individual weapons, five crew-served weapons, 660 pounds TNT, 100 B-4 rocket rounds and 2,000 meters telephone wire. Friendly losses were seven killed and 15 wounded.

SEPTEMBER 28, 1971

- The USN turned over to the VN Navy the Logistics Support Base at Dong Tam and the repair barge YRBM-21 at Tan Chau.

SEPTEMBER 30, 1971

- The USN turned over the Repair Ship USS SATYR (ARL-23) to the Vietnam Navy at Long Xuyen.
- US military strength in RVN was 212,596. FWMAF strength was 60,638. RVNAF strength was 1,047,890.

OCTOBER 1, 1971

- HMAS BRISBANE (DLG-41) ended deployment with the US 7th Fleet closing 4½ years of Australian Naval support in RVN.
- Elements of the 5th ARVN Airborne Battalion engaged an estimated two enemy companies 27 kilometers northwest of Tay Ninh City in Tay Ninh Province. Enemy losses were 35 killed and 11 individual weapons. Friendly losses were eight killed and three wounded.
- *Operations Quyet Thang 405/c, 504/c, and 603/c.* Initiated August 1, 1971 in the provinces of Quang Ngai, Quang Nam, and Quang Tin were terminated. Enemy losses were 1,300 killed, 270 detained, 271 individual weapons and 50 crew-served weapons. Friendly losses were 51 killed and 214 wounded.

OCTOBER 3, 1971

- Saigon received 122mm rocket fire, the first attack on the city since December 19, 1970. A truck in a USN compound and six small VN shops were destroyed.

OCTOBER 4, 1971

- South Vietnam forces reported killing 364 Communists during two hours of fierce fighting near Krek, Cambodia.

OCTOBER 6, 1971

- Hong Kong, an R&R site since mid-1965, closed the center but continued to be a leave site.

OCTOBER 8, 1971

- Army Staff Sergeant (SSG) John C. Sexton, Jr., was returned to US Forces, having been held as a prisoner of war since August 12, 1969. SSG Sexton was the 24th prisoner of war released by the Viet Cong since 1962.

OCTOBER 10, 1971

- Elements of the 1st and 2nd Armored Cavalry Squadron and the 15th Reconnaissance Company engaged an unknown size enemy force nine kilometers NE of Kampong Trabek in Prev Veng Province, Cambodia. Enemy losses were 58 killed, 16 individual weapons and two crew-served weapons. Friendly losses were six killed and 18 wounded.

OCTOBER 13, 1971

- Elements of the 1st Battalion, 33rd ARVN Infantry Battalion engaged an unknown size enemy force 15 kilometers northwest of Hieu Le in Kien Giang Province. Enemy losses were 44 killed, eight individual weapons, one PRC radio and 30 B-40 rounds. There were no friendly losses.
- Elements of the ARVN 30th Ranger Battalion and 2nd Battalion, 18th Armored Cavalry Squadron engaged a company-size force six kilometers east of Krek, in Kampong Cham Province, Cambodia. Enemy losses were 29 killed, three crew-served weapons and 15 anti-tank mines destroyed. There were not friendly losses.
- An unknown number of enemy sappers penetrated the defense of a US helicopter unit at the Di An Base Camp near Saigon, destroying two helicopters and damaging three others.

OCTOBER 15, 1971

- GVN and US uncover agents and police seized 5,100 vials of heroin, valued at more than $10,000, and arrested seven people near the large US military installation at Long Binh.

OCTOBER 18, 1971

- *Operation Quang Trung 44-127.* Initiated October 11, 1971 in Binh Thuan Province was terminated. Enemy losses were 51 killed, nine individual weapons and three crew-served weapons. Friendly losses were six wounded.
- Elements of the 31st ARVN Regiment on ground operations engaged an estimated enemy battalion 17 kilometers north of Thoi Binh in An Xuyen Province. Enemy losses were 40 killed and five individual weapons. Friendly losses were four killed, five wounded and six missing.

OCTOBER 20, 1971

- Cambodian Premier Marshal Lon Nol announced the setting up of a military dictatorship to "combat anarchy" and formed a new government.

OCTOBER 21, 1971

- The US Court of Appeals in Boston decided that the President's conduct of the Indochina war was constitutional, dismissing a suit brought by the state of Massachusetts.

OCTOBER 23, 1971

- Typhoon Hester hit a 200-mile stretch of RVN coast south of the DMZ, causing extensive damage to military equipment and facilities and leaving at least 200,000 persons homeless, about 75 dead, and many injured. The rice crop in Quang Tin Province was estimated to be 90 percent destroyed.

OCTOBER 24, 1971

- *Operation Do Kae Bi 2-3.* Initiated October 10, 1971 in Phu Yen Province was terminated. Enemy losses were 57 killed and 26 individual weapons. There were no friendly losses.

OCTOBER 25, 1971

- *Operation Quang Trung 22.* Initiated October 15, 1971 in Kontum Province was terminated Enemy losses were 93 killed, 14 individual weapons and three crew-served weapons. Friendly losses were two killed, 32 wounded.

- At Qui Nhon in Binh Dinh Province, a fire caused by a ruptured pipeline destroyed 250 VN houses, 100 buildings and 80,000 gallons of gas.

OCTOBER 26, 1971

- Elements of the ARVN 30th Ranger Battalion and 3rd Battalion, 18th Cavalry on a search mission seven kilometers east of Krek in Kampong Cham Province, Cambodia; found 20 enemy bodies. Enemy losses were 20 killed and one 60mm mortar. There were no friendly losses.

OCTOBER 29, 1971

- The US Senate voted to reduce foreign aid, affecting $341 million in aid to Cambodia.
- Elements of the ARVN 53rd Airborne Company on a search mission five kilometers south of Thien Ngon in Tay Ninh Province found nine graves, each with 10 bodies and 70 other bodies scattered around the area. Enemy losses were 160 killed. There were no friendly losses.
- Elements of the ARVN 4th Battalion, 43rd Infantry engaged an estimated enemy battalion seven kilometers SW of Xuan Loc in Long Khanh Province. Enemy losses were 38 killed Friendly losses were five wounded.

OCTOBER 31, 1971

- US military strength in RVN was 198,683. FWMAF strength was 58,813. RVNAF strength was 1,043,232.

NOVEMBER 1, 1971

- A new ARVN Infantry Division, the 3rd ARVN Division, was activated. This division was responsible for tactical operations in northern and northwestern Quang Tri Province.
- Elements of the ARVN 3rd Battalion, 49th Infantry Regiment were attacked eight kilometers SE of Tri Tam in Binh Duong Province. Enemy losses were 30 killed and four individual weapons. Friendly losses were one US killed, six ARVN killed, 41 ARVN wounded, one ARVN missing, four individual weapons and two radios.

NOVEMBER 3, 1971

- US gunships engaged an enemy convoy of 10 2½-ton trucks 16 kilometers west of A Shau Valley in Military Region 1. Enemy losses were one killed and 10 trucks destroyed. There were no friendly losses.
- Secretary of Defense Melvin R. Laird, Chairman of JCS Admiral Thomas H. Moorer, CINCPAC Admin John S. McCain, and various assistants arrived in Vietnam for a visit and update to prepare a report to President Nixon on the progress of Vietnamization.

NOVEMBER 7, 1971

- Australian Forces Vietnam turned over the military installation at Nui Da Dat to the RVNAF.
- The HMAS SYDNEY departed with about 400 Australian Forces Vietnam personnel being redeployed to Australia.
- Elements of the 390th Regional Forces Company ambushed an unknown size enemy force 37 kilometers SW of Quang Ngai City in Quang Ngai Province. Enemy losses were 45 killed, two crew-served weapons and one individual weapon. There were no friendly losses.
- Elements of the 1st Battalion, 3rd ARVN Infantry battalion encountered an unknown size enemy force 15 kilometers SW of Hue in Thua Thien Province. Enemy losses were 25 killed, 14 individual weapons and two crew-served weapons. There were no friendly losses.

NOVEMBER 8, 1971

- *Operation Quang Trung 41/PAC-3.* Initiated June 15, 1971 in Binh Dinh Province was terminated. Enemy losses were 103 killed, 161 detained and two individual weapons. Friendly losses were eight killed, five wounded and one individual weapons lost.

NOVEMBER 10, 1971

- Nguyen Van Bong, A VN politician and a leading candidate for prime minister, was killed when a plastic bomb exploded in his car.

NOVEMBER 11, 1971

- A helicopter gunship belonging to the 17th US Aviation Group, while on a support mission, accidentally fired on the 1st Company 4th Battalion, 41st ARVN Infantry Battalion. Eight ARVN troops were killed and 21 wounded.

NOVEMBER 12, 1971

- President Nixon announced at a press conference that 45,000 US Forces would be withdrawn from Vietnam over the next two months. The troop ceiling for February 1, 1972 would be 139,000.

NOVEMBER 13, 1971

- Elements of the 4th Battalion, 43rd ARVN Infantry Battalion engaged an estimated enemy platoon 30 kilometers SW of Plei Me in Pleiku Province. Enemy losses were 20 killed, four individual weapons and two crew-served weapons. Friendly losses was one wounded.

NOVEMBER 18, 1971

- Elements of the 101st Regional Forces Company with US gunship and tactical air support engaged an unknown size enemy force 25 kilometers east of Dak To in Kontum Province. Enemy losses were 145 killed (estimated 125 killed by air)), three individual weapons, 20 hand grenades and an unknown quantity of equipment captured. There were no friendly losses.

NOVEMBER 19, 1971

- *Operation Kontum 94/71.* Initiated November 15, 1971 in Kontum Province was terminated Enemy losses were 176 killed, two detained and 10 individual weapons. There were no friendly losses.
- *Operation Quang Trung 23-7.* Initiated November 7, 1971 in Pleiku Province was terminated Enemy losses were 182 killed, four detained, 62 individual weapons and 13 crew-served

weapons. Friendly losses were 31 killed, 45 wounded, four missing and 25 individual weapons.

NOVEMBER 25, 1971

- US troop strength in Vietnam was reduced ahead of President Nixon's previously announced schedule, leaving 182,400 US servicemen in Vietnam; other FWMAF totaled 57,800.
- Elements of the 4th Battalion, 33rd ARVN Infantry Battalion, assisted by US helicopters, gunships and ARVN artillery; engaged an unknown size enemy force 15 kilometers west of Kien Long in Chuong Thien Province. Enemy losses were 24 killed, one anti-aircraft gun and two 82mm mortar tubes. There were no friendly losses.
- *Operation Dong Khoi.* Initiated November 20, 1971 in Military Region 4, was terminated Enemy losses were 330 killed, 52 detained, 119 individual weapons and five crew-served weapons. Friendly losses were 65 Regional Forces/Popular Forces killed, 146 Regional Forces/Popular Forces wounded, one Regional Forces missing and 14 individual weapons.
- *Operation Cuu Long HQ/CD/U-Minh* (U Minh Campaign). Initiated November 30, 1970 in An Xuyen, Chuong Thien, and Kien Giang Province was terminated. Enemy losses were 4,903 killed, 524 detained, 1,170 individual weapons and 253 crew-served weapons. Friendly losses were 490 killed, 1,302 wounded, nine missing and 33 individual weapons.

NOVEMBER 26, 1971

- *Operation Hoang Dieu 110.* Initiated October 19, 1971 in Quang Nam Province was terminated. Enemy losses were 382 killed, 201 detained, 132 individual weapons and three crew-served weapons. Friendly losses were 41 killed and 132 wounded.

NOVEMBER 27, 1971

- The 23rd Infantry Division turned over the US base at Chu Lai to the RVNAF. The US Marines originally built the large facility in 1964.

NOVEMBER 28, 1971

- A US CH-47 Chinook helicopter, enroute from Da Nang to

Phu Bai with 28 passengers and a crew of five, crashed with no survivors.

NOVEMBER 29, 1971

- Quach Phat, publisher of the two largest Chinese publications in Saigon, was assassinated.

NOVEMBER 30, 1971

- US military strength in RVN was 178,266. FWMAF strength was 58, 526. RVNAF strength was 1,040, 640.

DECEMBER 2, 1971

- Elements of the 3rd Battalion, 51st Regional Forces Group and the 3rd Battalion, 56th Regional Forces Group on a search operation 19 kilometers SW of Tay Ninh in Tay Ninh Province were engaged by an estimated two company size enemy force employing 82mm mortars and B-40 rockets. A Regional Forces company reinforced and ARVN artillery and US helicopter gunships supported the operation. Enemy losses were 32 killed, 12 individual weapons and three crew-served weapons. Friendly losses were 24 Regional Forces killed, 24 Regional Forces wounded and 12 Regional Forces missing.

DECEMBER 4, 1971

- ROK troops began withdrawing from Vietnam as 1,200 Marines of the "Blue Dragon" Brigade departed, ending the unit's six years of service in RVN.

DECEMBER 8, 1971

- The 4th Battalion, Royal Australian Regiment, the last Australian combat battalion in RVN, redeployed to Australia.

DECEMBER 10, 1971

- The USS ENTERPRISE and a task force of destroyers and amphibious ships were ordered to leave their stations off the coast of Vietnam for positions in the Strait of Malacca off Singapore.

DECEMBER 13, 1971

- Elements of the 2nd Battalion, 1st Regional Forces Group

command post in Quang Tri Province received a ground attack from an unknown size enemy force. The 112th and 188th (-) Regional Forces Company and VN Air Force flare ships assisted. Enemy losses were 23 killed, 15 individual weapons, two crew-served weapons, 30 hand grenades, 30 B-40 rockets and 100 blocks of plastic explosives. Friendly losses were eight Regional Forces killed and six Regional Forces wounded.

DECEMBER 14, 1971

- A US Army U-21aircrft with seven passengers went down in bad weather over water about 18 miles north of Da Nang.

DECEMBER 19, 1971

- The Indochina war was 25 years old, dating from the December 19, 1946 attack against French garrisons in Hanoi by VN revolutionaries under Ho Chi Minh.

DECEMBER 20, 1971

- Communist gunners fired two 122mm rockets into Saigon's waterfront district, the first rocket attack against the capital since October 3, 1971.

DECEMBER 21, 1971

- The US Coast Guard ended active participation in the RVN as it turned over to the VN Navy two high endurance cutters, the CASTLE ROCK (WHEC-383) and COOK INLET (WHEC-384). A total of 957 sea craft have been turned over to Vietnam.

DECEMBER 22, 1971

- The GVN announced plans to free 689 political prisoners on Christmas day.
- The 10th anniversary of the fist US combat death in Vietnam, SP4 James Davis, US Army, of Livingston, Tennessee, was killed December 22, 1961.

DECEMBER 23, 1971

- Admiral John S. McCain, Jr., CINCPAC, arrived in Saigon for this 4th annual Christmas visit to troops throughout the country.
- Part of a small area near Tan Son Nhut Air Base which had

been declared off-limits August 31, 1971 because of drug sales was put back on on-limits.

DECEMBER 25, 1971

- The Allied Christmas cease-fire ended at 1800 hours with reports of three minor incidents against US Forces.

DECEMBER 28, 1971

- Communist terrorists have killed 52 civilians, wounded 13 and kidnapped 70 in 48 incidents reported since December 4, 1971, according to a Vietnam National Police communiqué.

DECEMBER 29, 1971

- James Cardinal Cooke, Archbishop of New York, arrived in Vietnam for a pastoral visit with US servicemen.

DECEMBER 30, 1971

- USAF and USN planes end days of air strikes against North Vietnam, flying 1,000 sorties during the heaviest bombing campaign in more than three years.
- Senator Stuart Symington and party visited Saigon briefly.

DECEMBER 31, 1971

- Two US soldiers were killed, 50 wounded and six missing or captured in Southeast Asia the last week of 1971.
- US military strength in RVN was 158,119; FWMAF strength was 54,497. RVNAF strength was 1,046,254.

JANUARY 1, 1972

- US strength was just over 150,000.

JANUARY 3, 1972

- Military Region 3. Elements of the 1st Cavalry Division made contact with the enemy NE of Xuan Loc in Long Khanh Province. The American reaction force, helicopter gunships, and medevac support all received heavy enemy fire. Results were one American killed, 14 missing, and four helicopters damaged. In Bien Hoa Province American troop elements received an attack-by-fire that wounded 18 American soldiers and one VN.

JANUARY 4, 1972

- Military Region 4. The ARVN 4th Armored Brigade ended a month long operation after having killed 54 of the enemy, captured 42, seized 22 individual and one crew-served weapon. The brigade lost four killed and five wounded.

JANUARY 7, 1972

- Military Region 4. The 42nd Ranger Group began *Operation Cuu Long 44.*

JANUARY 8, 1972

- Military Region 2. In Binh Dinh Province, the 28th Korean Regiment began *Operation Jae 640-1.*
- Qui Nhon City was the target of a major terrorist incident.

JANUARY 11, 1972

- Military Region 2. In Phu Yen Province, the Koreans initiated *Operation Do Kai Bi 2-1* with the 28th Regiment.

JANUARY 12, 1972

- Military Region 2. At Bien Hoa Air Base, a sapper attack in the munitions storage area caused the loss of several hundred tons of ammunition.

JANUARY 13, 1972

- Military Region 4. Territorial Forces throughout Military Region 4 began *Operation Don Khoi.*

JANUARY 15, 1972

- Military Region 4. *Operation Cuu Long 7* terminated. The results were 111 enemy dead, 34 detained, and 26 individual and four crew-served weapons captured. The division losses were 15 killed and 126 wounded. The second phase of the operation continued in Dinh Tuong and Kien Hoa Provinces through January. *Operation Cuu Long 44* terminated. With no friendly casualties, the rangers accounted for 26 enemy killed, 21 captured, and 30 individual and crew-served weapons captured.

JANUARY 16, 1972

- Military Region 2. *Operation Jae 640-1* ended and resulted in 63 enemy killed, one captured, and 36 individual and five crew-served weapons captured. Two Korean soldiers were killed and three were wounded. In Khanh Hoa Province, friendly installations at Cam Ranh Bay received two attacks-by-fire on followed by a sapper attack.
- Military Region 4. *Operation Don Khoi* terminated. 439 enemy were killed, 55 were detained, and 239 individual weapons were captured. The cost of the local forces was 61 were killed, 295 wounded, and four missing.

JANUARY 19, 1972

- Military Region 3. A sapper attack at the ARVN Cu Chi Ranger Camp destroyed 31.5 tons of ordnance. An attack-by-fire followed by a ground attack on a South Vietnam night defense position 11 kilometers NNW of Cu Chi resulted in 15 enemy dead.

JANUARY 23, 1972

- Military Region 2. The Korean initiated *Operation Do Kai Bi 2-1* terminated with 56 enemy killed and 21 individual and two crew-served weapons captured at a loss of 20 Koreans killed and 20 wounded.

JANUARY 26, 1972

- Military Region 2. *Operation Dong Bo 18* ended with one Korean soldier killed. One hundred and twenty-four of the enemy were killed and 80 individual and seven crew-served weapons captured.

JANUARY 30, 1972

- Military Region 2. *Operation Hiep Dong 12* began.

JANUARY 31, 1972

- Military Region 1. The joint Vietnam regular Army, Ranger, and Territorial Force operation terminated and resulted in 462 enemy killed, 190 taken prisoner, and 157 individual and eight crew-served weapons captured. Friendly losses were 59 killed and 244 wounded.

- Military Region 2. The results of *Operation Bac Binh Vuong I* through January were 162 enemy killed, 30 taken prisoner, and 19 individual and three crew-served weapons captured. Friendly forces had lost 24 men killed and 66 wounded.
- Military Region 4. The 4th Ranger Group operation ended. The rangers had accounted for 128 enemy killed, 67 captured, and 54 individual and eight crew-served weapons captured. The group lost nine soldiers killed and 55 wounded.

FEBRUARY 6, 1972

- Military Region 4. ARVN and Regional Forces elements engaged in a 12-hour fight in Chuong Thien Province. Two prisoners identified the enemy force as the 9th Battalion, D-2 Viet Cong Regiment.

FEBRUARY 7, 1972

- Military Region 1. The 3rd ARVN Division conducted a one-day, three battalions into the DMZ north of FSB A-2. Several recently abandoned platoon positions were found in addition to various munitions and weapons.
- Military Region 4. *Operation Dong Khoi commenced.*

FEBRUARY 8, 1972

- Military Region 2. In Binh Dinh Province, allied installations and friendly hamlets near Route 19 were struck by sapper and mortar attacks. In Khanh Hoa Province, a Vietnam Army compound north of Nha Trang received an attack-by-fire followed by a sapper attack.

FEBRUARY 9, 1972

- Military Region 4. *Operation Dong Khoi* ended. The cumulative results were 225 enemy killed and 41 captured; 12 government soldiers were killed and 117 were wounded.

FEBRUARY 10-13, 1972

- Military Region 2. VN Army defenders of an outpost north of Phu My received ground attacks-by-fire.

FEBRUARY 12, 1972

- Military Region 3. Heavy ground-to-air firings indicated the presence of an unknown-size enemy force positioned adjacent to Routes 13, 14, and 15 in the Iron Triangle area; 13 helicopters had been damaged since January 29, 1972 in this area. In Long An Province, RVN hamlet offices were the targets of increased enemy pressure; 17 VN were killed and 25 wounded in these attacks. Phu Loi and Bien Hoa airfields receive attacks-by-fire during February, wounding seven Americans.

FEBRUARY 14, 1972

- Military Region 4. Saigon's announced, 24 hour cease-fire for the Tet holiday started at 1800 hours and the enemy's announced 96 hour cease-fire started the same day at 0100 hours. Enemy activity continued at a low level.

FEBRUARY 16, 1972

- Military Region 4. Four outposts were overrun in the 48 hours immediately after the end of the enemy proclaimed cease-fire period.

FEBRUARY 18, 1972.

- Military Region 2. *Operation Hiep Dong 12* ended. This operation involved all of the Regional Forces/Popular Forces in Quang Tin Province. The final results were 89 enemy troops killed and 19 captured. The local forces lost 16 dead and suffered 38 wounded.

FEBRUARY 19, 1972

- Military Region 2. In Binh Dinh Province, allied installations and friendly hamlets near Route 19 were struck by sapper and mortar attacks.
- Military Region 4. In Chuon Thien Province, an Regional Forces outpost was overrun. There were 59 friendly casualties, 36 of whom were killed.

FEBRUARY 20-21, 1972

- Military Region 4. Hamlets in Vinh Long and Ba Xuyen Provinces were attacked. Two hamlet chiefs and 33 People's Self Defense Force personnel were killed.

FEBRUARY 21, 1972

- Military Region 1. The 2nd ARVN Division began a six-battalion operation in the Que Son mountain region and adjacent areas. By the end of the month, government forces had killed 261 enemy and 27 captured, 22 South Vietnam troops were killed and 39 wounded. On the same day that the 2nd Division operation began, the 69th Ranger Border Defense Battalion executed a hasty ambush against an enemy company in Quang Ngai Province.
- Military Region 2. In Ninh Thuan Province, Phan Rang Air Base was attacked by fire.

FEBRUARY 21-23, 1972

- Military Region 1. Two compounds near Qui Nhon City received ground probes and attacks-by-fire.

FEBRUARY 25, 1972

- Military Region 2. An American convoy was ambushed near Mang Giang Pass.

MARCH 6, 1972

- Military Region 1. The 1st ARVN Division reacted rapidly to the discovery of the enemy in this area by reorienting the planned operation to the south in the vicinity of FSB Veghel and Bastogne on both sides of Route 547. The 3rd Regiment of the division met immediate opposition as the enemy made a determined effort to force the withdrawal of the 1st Division units from this area.

MARCH 7, 1972

- The Royal Australian Task Force withdrew and the Korean forces continued withdrawing the 100th Logistics Command and the 2nd Marine Brigade.
- Military Region 3. ARVN and Regional Forces received attacks-by-fire in two separate incidents.

MARCH 9, 1972

- Military Region 3. The 3rd Armored Brigade and elements of the 3rd Ranger Group moved into the Khmer by way of Route 1 to Svay Rieng. The force then turned north on Route

109. The remaining elements of the 3rd Ranger Group were lifted by helicopter to positions along Route 109. The task force attacked north and seized Kampong Trach without significant enemy contact. The 46th Regiment operated across the border in the vicinity of the Dog's Throat initially, then moved by helicopter to positions west of Kampong Krasang. The 3rd Armored Brigade task force continued NW from Kampong Trach with little enemy resistance and conducted search operations west of the Spean River. B-52 strikes to the east of the Spean River uncovered a substantial bunker and tunnel complex. The 46th Regiment searched portions of the complex. Enemy contact throughout the operation was sporadic. The most significant results were the large caches of rice, salt, and weapons captured, primarily in the vicinity of Kampong Krasang; 748 enemy were killed and 29 captured, 1,114 individual and 36 crew-served weapons were captured, and 871 tons of rice and 48.5 tons of salt were seized. The South Vietnam lost eight killed and 66 wounded.

MARCH 9-30, 1972

- Military Region 3. III Corps conducted a multi-regimental operation across the Khmer border in the enemy Base Area 354 west of the Dog's Head. Units participating included the 3rd Armored Brigade; 3rd, 4th, and 5th Ranger Groups; and the 46th Infantry Regiment.

MARCH 11, 1972

- Military Region 3. A Regional Forces field position nine kilometers SSW of Tay Ninh received an attack-by-fire consisting of 100 rounds of mixed rocket, mortar, and recoilless rifle fire followed by a ground attack by an estimated two companies.

MARCH 13, 1972

- Military Region 2. The airborne brigade from the 22nd ARVN Division engaged part of the 320th NVA Division. The engagement continued intermittently for nine hours. The airborne soldiers were supported by ARVN artillery and VN tactical air.

MARCH 17-18, 1972

- Military Region 1. In two battles fought by the 2nd Battalion, 3rd Regiment, the enemy lost a total of 182 killed; friendly losses were 15 killed and 66 wounded. B-52 strikes were particularly effective, resulting in 131 enemy killed.

MARCH 21, 1972

- Military Region 2. Sapper attacks occurred against the ARVN Trang Lon Base Camp in Tay Ninh City West and a ferry at Ben Soi village, seven kilometers SW of Tay Ninh. Tay Ninh West also received 25 rounds of rocket fire.

MARCH 22, 1972

- Military Region 2. American air cavalry elements on a BDA mission discovered 110 enemy bodies in an area where 70 structures and four bunkers had been destroyed.

MARCH 23, 1972

- The US and South Vietnam suspended the Paris talks due to the Communist refusal to negotiate seriously. Meanwhile, President Thieu was busy visiting the military regions to insure that plans to thwart the enemy were complete.
- Military Region 2. The 23rd Ranger Battalion combat assaulted into the area to conduct further search operations. The battalion remained in the LZ area overnight and the following morning began receiving mortar and small arms fire. The fighting continued throughout the day with South Vietnam artillery and tactical air in support of the rangers. The enemy covered the LZ with antiaircraft fire, making resupply and evacuation of wounded difficult.
- Military Region 3. 440 pounds of TNT were discovered on the Vam Co Don River 1.5 kilometers NW of the Go Dau Ha Bridge.

MARCH 25, 1972

- Military Region 2. The 11th Ranger Battalion began moving toward the battle area to join and reinforce the 23rd Ranger

Battalion. The 23rd Ranger Battalion remained in contact until March 28, 1972 when it left the area overland and moved to link up with the 11th Rangers. The cumulative results for the operation, including those killed by air or artillery, were 180 enemy dead, with 18 rangers killed, 20 missing, and 62 wounded.

- Military Region 3. Vietnam Army forces; four kilometers east of Lai Khe engaged an enemy squad. Later the same day three sappers attempted to penetrate the perimeter of Lai Khe Base Camp.

MARCH 26, 1972

- Military Region 3. Two contacts at the northern and southern extremities of the Song Be River infiltration corridor resulted in 18 enemy killed, two individual weapons, and 11 tons of rice captured.

MARCH 30, 1972

- The long-predicted enemy offensive struck. Despite the North's official denials, there was no doubt that the NVN, not the Viet Cong, were attacking, using weapons never before used in South Vietnam.
- Military Region 1. Beginning this date the enemy initiated heavy attacks-by-fire and ground attacks against all friendly installations in the Gio Linh, Cam Lo and My Loc districts of Quang Tri Province. Friendly combat operations rose to a moderate level over the preceding month until this date, when activity became intense in northern Quang Tri Province.
- Military Region 2. A heavy engagement between ARVN rangers and enemy forces occurred. Sapper and indirect fire attacks increased through the month. A bridge was heavily damaged and an ARVN convoy was ambushed NW of Ninh Hoa City.
- Military Region 3. The 304thB and 308th NVA Divisions, supported by armor and heavy artillery, moved through the DMZ into Quang Tri Province. Concurrently, the 324B NVA Division made an easterly push toward Hue, 90 kilometers below the DMZ, in Thua Thien Province.

MARCH 31, 1972

- US strength was 95,000.

- Military Region 2. In the Central Highlands, the 320th NVA Division launched an attack in Kontum Province.

APRIL-MAY 1972

- Over 30,000 US troops leave Vietnam. In addition, Korea's 2nd Marine Brigade and 100th Logistics Command, and Headquarters, Royal Thai Forces, Vietnam completed their redeployment.

APRIL 2, 1972

- Military Region 1. FSB Carroll was surrendered to North Vietnam after massive artillery and ground attacks. The loss of Carroll left Mai Loc Combat Base vulnerable; the garrison was ordered to withdraw to positions east of Cam Lo.

APRIL 3-5, 1972

- Military Region 4. Corps-wide *Operation Dong Koi* was conducted, resulting in 175 enemy killed, 28 detained and 16 weapons captured. Friendly losses 20 killed, 116 wounded, six missing, and five weapons lost.

APRIL 4, 1972

- A drive was underway in Binh Long Province, 100 kilometers north of Saigon and 600 kilometers below the DMZ. Elements of the 5th and 9th Viet Cong Divisions, again supported by tanks, attacked from the Khmer. This posed an immediate threat to Saigon Route 13 and the Saigon River corridor. The magnitude of the initial invasion was such that six fully equipped divisions entered South Vietnam on three separate fronts in a coordinated attack. They used conventional tactics and introduced weaponry beyond that of a guerrilla campaign. The NVN Army confronted the South Vietnam armed forces with a conventional attack. At the outset, the 13 divisions of the RVN were deployed throughout the country. Major elements of the general reserve, the Marine and Airborne Divisions, were already deployed to Military Regions 1 and 2, where the initial enemy thrusts developed.
- Military Region 1. Continued enemy advances forced the evacuation of Cam Lo and FSB Anne. In the face of the overwhelming enemy assault, I Corps made plans to establish

defensive positions along the Cua Viet River. Marine and Ranger elements from the general reserve began moving north to be employed in the 3rd ARVN Division area.

- Military Region 4. Khmer Republic. The 271st Regiment, C30B NVA Division, encircled a Ranger battalion. Tactical air and artillery enabled the unit to break out of the encirclement on April 5, 1972. Government losses were 16 killed, 124 wounded, and 13 tracked vehicles and 63 weapons lost. Enemy losses were unknown.

APRIL 5, 1972

- Military Region 3. The enemy attacked Loc Ninh in force supported by tanks and artillery. The bulk of RVNAF regular forces at Loc Ninh were enveloped in their forward security positions. Two ARVN infantry battalions, one cavalry squadron, and Ranger border defense battalion, plus the supporting artillery, were rendered ineffective. About 150 individual survivors made their way to An Loc. The two compounds at Loc Ninh were defended for two days by a small force of territorials, few regulars, and US advisors. The skillful employment of US tactical air by the US advisors prevented the immediate fall of the compounds.
- Military Region 3. Tay Ninh Province. Enemy pressure by the 271st NVA Independent Regiment and the 24th NVA Regiment in northern Tay Ninh Province increased. The border Ranger battalion positions received heavy indirect fire and ground attacks. Friendly positions near Tay Ninh City also received attacks-by-fire, and just north of the city a major ambush inflicted heavy casualties on an ARVN battalion. Reacting to this enemy activity, the 25th ARVN Division withdrew its outposts and consolidated defensive positions around Tay Ninh City.

APRIL 6-11, 1972

- Military Region 3. The 3rd Ranger Group reinforced An Loc. On April 10-11, 1972, the 8th Regiment, with two of its battalions, were moved by US helicopters to the city. On April

11, 1972, nine maneuver battalions, some under strength, and miscellaneous support elements were consolidated at An Loc.

APRIL 7, 1972

- Military Region 3. Loc Ninh fell to the enemy.
- A Ranger battalion reported itself surrounded near Kompong Trach. Results were reported as 50 enemy killed against ARVN losses of four killed, 16 wounded, 40 missing, and 44 weapons lost. Activity returned to a low level for several days.

APRIL 8, 1972

- Military Region 4. Enemy initiated activity increased sharply. The reduction of troop density as a result of 21st Division elements moving to III Corps possibly caused the increase. Aggressive action by Territorial Forces prevented the enemy achieving substantial gains. The 7th and 9th ARVN Divisions shifted areas of responsibility to cover the entire IV Corps area. Although contacts were widely scattered, Kien Tuong Province reported the most incidents. Activity increased also in Chuong Thien Province during mid-month as the enemy concentrated his efforts toward disrupting pacification programs. IV Corps committed additional forces in the north-central provinces to meet the increased enemy activity in the Kien Tuong-Kien Phong-Ding Tuong tri-border area. This area continued to report the highest number of incidents, both attacks-by-fire and ground contacts throughout the remainder of the month.

APRIL 8-10, 1972

- Military Region 3. To the south of Loc Ninh, the 52nd Infantry Task Force came under enemy pressure and. was ordered to move south and reinforce An Loc. The task force first encountered an enemy roadblock after which the heavy equipment and vehicles were ordered destroyed by the task force commander and the elements continued on foot around the roadblock. After moving back to Route 13 further south, the column was ambushed and suffered heavy casualties. About 650 men of the 1,000-man task force arrived at An Loc.

APRIL 9, 1972

- Military Region 1. FSB Pedro was heavily engaged by indirect fire and ground attacks by the 203rd Tank Regiment and the 9th Regiment, 304B Division. In two days of battle in the Pedro area, enemy losses were reported at 1,067 killed. Friendly losses were reported as light. However, for the most part, the enemy had accomplished his first phase objectives of forcing the evacuation of South Vietnam-held fire support bases.

APRIL 9-10, 1972

- Military Region 1. After a two-day battle, South Vietnam forces were forced to evacuate FSB West and O'Connor area southwest of Da Nang. Combat activity in southern Military Region 1 was initially light compared to the two provinces in the north. Enemy small unit attacks and light mortar attacks-by-fire were countered by Territorial Forces, Ranger border defense battalions, and the 2nd ARVN Division through the use of increased patrolling and mobile operations. The most significant activity in April 1972 centered in the FSB West and O'Connor area southwest of Da Nang.

APRIL 11, 1972

- Military Region 1. Route 547 between FSBs Bastogne and Birmingham was under enemy control. Intensive antiaircraft fire hampered efforts to resupply by helicopter. A B-52 strike between Bastogne and Birmingham killed over 200 of the enemy, but failed to have any tangible effects on opening supply lines or reducing the enemy pressure. By April 13, 1972, FSBs King and Checkmate were under heavy pressure; the defenders inflicted heavy casualties with each contact. Resupply of Bastogne and King was accomplished by foot when 1st ARVN Division forces continued to be unable to clear Route 547.
- Military Region 2. Significant activity in Binh Dinh Province began when traffic on Route 19 was blocked by an enemy force entrenched at the An Khe Pass. The highway remained closed until April 28, 1972 when elements of the Republic of Korea Cavalry Regiment dislodged the enemy from the high ground overlooking the pass.

APRIL 12, 1972

- Military Region 1. Da Nang Air Base received a 122mm rocket attack that killed 14 VN civilians and wounded 25. American losses were 11 wounded, one aircraft and three trucks destroyed, and three aircraft damaged.
- Military Region 4. Khmer Republic. An estimated four battalions of the C30B Division engaged ARVN Ranger and armored cavalry units. Results of the battle were 163 enemy killed, while ARVN lost eight killed and 42 wounded. The ARVN elements were encircled within Kompong Trach on the following day. Resupply by helicopter was abandoned because of heavy ground fire; air drop became the primary resupply means.

APRIL 14, 1972

- Military Region 1. FSB Bastogne was evacuated.
- Military Region 2. FSB Charlie, manned by the 11th Airborne Battalion, was overrun.

APRIL 16, 1972

- The Military Region 4. The 21st Division's lead regiment reached a position 30 kilometers south of An Loc. The 81st Airborne Ranger Group was later inserted at An Loc, bringing the forces to a peak of 13 battalions.

APRIL 21, 1972

- Military Region 2. FSB Delta fell to the enemy.

APRIL 23, 1972

- Military Region 1. The expected attack on FSB Bastogne began with heavy attacks-by-fire and ground attacks. During the night the South Vietnam defenders were forced to again abandon the position. The evacuation of Bastogne placed Checkmate in an untenable position, and it too was evacuated. The loss of these firebases jeopardized the defense of Hue.

APRIL 23-24, 1972

- Military Region 2. The enemy's armor attacks forced the evacuation of Dak To and Tan Canh.

APRIL 26, 1972

- President Nixon announced another MACV 20,000 space reduction to a level of 49,000, effective July 1, 1972.
- Military Region 1. ARVN forces reoccupied FSB Bastogne, which was evacuated on April 23, 1972.
- Military Region 2. Bong Son Pass fell to the enemy, closing Route 1 and isolating the northeastern corner of the province.

APRIL 27, 1972

- Military Region 1. Dong Ha City came under heavy attack by 130mm guns and 122mm rockets. This was followed by a major attack from the southwest by elements of the 308th NVA Division. The battle began to rage again around Quang Tri City. The province capital was taken under attack by enemy armor and infantry from the northwest, (308th Division), west (304B Division), and southwest (304B Division) following accurate and intensive heavy artillery fire against Quang Tri combat base, La Vang, and Route 1 bridge at the city. Friendly forces were forced back to within three to five kilometers of the city.

APRIL 28, 1972

- Military Region 1. Renewed attacks at Dong Ha and the increasing danger to Quang Tri City led the South Vietnam to decide to withdraw from Dong Ha and reorganize and reinforce the defenses of Quang Tri. Despite the change in defensive posture, the situation deteriorated rapidly around the province capital, as the enemy continued to press his attacks to occupy the city. Troops of the 304th and 308th NVA Divisions, and the 27th, 31st, and 270th NVA Independent Regiments, supported by tanks and heavy artillery, were the enemy forces pressing the attack. Heavy bombardment and sustained ground attacks against all friendly forces around Quang Tri made the continued defense of the city vulnerable and tenuous.

APRIL 28-MAY 2, 1972

- Military Region 3. The enemy buildup in Tay Ninh Province in April culminated in heavy fighting between the 25th ARVN

Division and the 271st NVA Independent Regiment. In several contacts around the Angel's Wing, the ARVN killed 200 and found evidence that over 150 bodies had been evacuated to the Khmer Republic. It was estimated that the 271st Regiment suffered 70 percent casualties dead and wounded. This estimate was borne out during the month by reports indicating that the regiment was attempting to avoid major engagements and was undergoing refitting and retraining the remainder of May. Little major initiated activity was attributed to the 271st Regiment.

APRIL 30, 1972

- Military Region 1. Attacks-by-fire and ground probes against FSBs Birmingham and King continued. All forces north of the Thach Han River were withdrawn to defend Quang Tri City from more tenable positions south of the river line. In the meantime, Route 1 had been interdicted by enemy ambushes and indirect fire between the besieged province capital and Hue to the south, preventing resupply and evacuation convoy operations. Over 4,500 rounds of 130mm artillery, 122mm rockets and mortars heavily bombarded the South Vietnam defenders of Quang Tri. Combined armor and infantry attacks from the north, northwest, and southwest materialized as the invading forces pushed forward. FSB Nancy to the south was also under attack by elements of the 304B Division.
- Military Region 2: The only South Vietnam forces north of the Bon Son Pass were at LZ English and Tam Quan district capital.
- Military Region 4. In cross-border operations activity was at a low level following the *Kompong Trach Operation,* which ended. Final results of that operation were 1,160 enemy killed and 224 friendly dead, 1031 wounded and 153 missing. Government forces also reported 324 weapons and 56 armored personnel carriers lost.

MAY 1, 1972

- US strength was 69,000.
- Military Region 1. Enemy pressure continued to build throughout the morning. US helicopters evacuated most American advisors during the afternoon but 18 advisors

elected to stay with their units. Later that day the Quang Tri defenses collapsed and friendly forces withdrew southward. Some elements were able to maintain control and withdrew in an orderly fashion, while other units became fragmented with the troops exfiltrating toward Hue individually or in small groups. Large amounts of supplies and many major items of equipment were abandoned both in Quang Tri and along Route 1 to the south. Most of the equipment was reported to have been rendered unusable. Since Route 1 had been interdicted by enemy forces and indirect fires, the defeated defenders were repeatedly subjected to attacks-by-fire and sporadically became engaged in ground contacts as they withdrew. In the Da Nang area, two bridges on Route 1 were attacked by the T89 Sapper Battalion. The bridges were heavily damaged but ARVN engineers repaired them and the highway was opened by nightfall.

- Military Region 2. The Territorial Forces defending Tam Quan withdrew to LZ English. The 403rd Sapper Battalion continually increased pressure on LZ English with heavy attacks-by-fire and ground attacks.

MAY 2, 1972

- Military Region 1. FSB Nancy, the last friendly occupied position in Quang Tri Province, was under continuous heavy artillery and ground attack. By early evening, the VN Marine Corps elements there had withdrawn to new position south of the Tach-Ma River. All of Quang Tri Province was then in enemy hands.
- Military Region 2. LZ English was evacuated. The SVN moved overland to the coast, where approximately 2,000 military and civilian personnel were evacuated by LST to Qui Nhon. During the remainder of the month, no significant combat activity was reported in the province, enemy activity decreased and the ARVN 40th Regiment stood down for reorganization and refitting.

MAY 3, 1972

- Military Region 1. Action was taken to organize the battered stragglers from the Quang Tri fighting and to improve the posture of I Corps units. A joint forward command post was established at the Hue Citadel. Straggler control points were established in Hue and Da Nang to assist in the reorganization of units that had been rendered combat ineffective Quang Tri Province battles. The 3rd ARVN Division immediately began to rebuild its forces near Phu Bai under a new commander, Brigadier General Nguyen Duy Hinh.

MAY 4, 1972

- Military Region 3. The 7th NVA Division elements increased pressure on the 21st Division forces attacking north toward An Loc along Route 13. The 21st Division consolidated its forward positions on May 8, 1972 by combat assaulting a 31st Regiment battalion several kilometers to the north. The 3rd Airborne Brigade moved south along Route 13 and linked up with the battalion.

MAY 5, 1972

- Military Region 1. The 1st ARVN Division began limited offensive operations in an area of operations southwest of Hue, where FSB King had been under increasing enemy pressure since May 1, 1972. The division operation was designed to relieve the pressure against FSB King and Birmingham, and to retake those bases to the west and southwest that had been lost to enemy action. The South Vietnam forces were immediately engaged. American and Vietnam tactical air support, together with numerous B-52 strikes, enabled the division elements to make steady progress and inflict heavy casualties on the enemy. Ground combat activity had been light in the Marine area of operations since the fall of FSB Nancy, although rocket and artillery attacks had continued.

MAY 6-7, 1972

- Military Region 1. American installations at Da Nang and Marble Mountain received light rocket attacks, causing minor damage.

MAY 8, 1972

- Military Region 1. Intense firepower consisting of B-52s, tactical aircraft, naval gunfire, and artillery fire was directed against enemy forces in southeastern Quang Tri Province. This program significantly reduced mortar attacks, but attacks by 130mm artillery continued.

MAY 9, 1972

- President Nixon announced that the US had mined the North Vietnam harbors, effectively closing its port.

MAY 9-13, 1972

- Military Region 1. The 2nd Brigade of the VN Airborne Division arrived from Military Region 3 and was placed the operational control of the VN Marine Division. These reinforcements permitted the Marines to start their first offensive operation on May 13, 1972, when the 369th Marine Brigade conducted a limited objective operation 12 kilometers into southeastern Quang Tri Province. Two battalions air assaulted in USMC helicopters, while a third battalion conducted a river crossing operation across the Tach Ma River. Although the plan called for this battalion to link-up with the heli-borne force to the north, immediate heavy contact with the enemy prevented it. The two battalions in the north were inserted without difficulty, affected their link-up, and swept to the south. They reached the defensive line at the province border by nightfall. The results of the operation, supported by American tactical aircraft and naval gunfire, were 243 enemy killed, six enemy soldiers and 109 weapons captured, and three PT-76 tanks and two 130mm guns destroyed. Marine casualties were nine killed and 38 wounded. Meanwhile, 1st ARVN Division patrolling operations continued to engage enemy forces along Route 547 and the outlying fire bases.
- Military Region 2. After heavy attacks-by-fire, the enemy assaulted the Ranger camps of Polei Kleng and Ben Het. The battalion at Polei Kleng was unable to hold and the camp was evacuated. Although the Ben Het defensive perimeter was breached during an enemy tank-infantry attack, the defenders held. By the night of May 10, 1972, the situation had stabilized, and by the following day Ben Het had been cleared of all enemy forces.
- Military Region 3. The ARVN 25th Division area of operations was extended south, taking in all of the Angel's Wing and portions of Hau Nghia and Long An Provinces. This allowed

the division to coordinate and direct the ARVN and Territorial Forces operations throughout the threat area.

- Military Region 4. A contact in western Kien Phong province, with elements of the 275th Regiment, 5th NVA Division, resulted in 46 enemy killed and friendly losses of two killed and six wounded. The contact followed a sapper attack on Moc Hoa airfield that destroyed 43,000 liters of fuel.

MAY 10, 1972

- Inauguration of bombing of North Vietnam (*Operation Linebacker*).
- Military Region 1. A Regional Forces outpost was overrun and the 582nd NVA Battalion blew a bridge in the Hai Van Pass. The bridge was quickly repaired and the outpost reoccupied.
- Military Region 3. Friendly forces at An Loc withstood an all out attack by the 9th Viet Cong Division. Heavy indirect fire started about midnight, followed by tank supported ground attacks from the south, southeast, east, and west. Eight B-52 strikes were placed on the outskirts of the city. By noon, ARVN troops stopped the attack with effective; support from tactical air, gunships, and B-52 strikes. An unknown number of enemy were killed by air strikes and artillery fire while fleeing from the B-52 target areas.
- Military Region 4. The ARVN 7th Division had several battalions operating with Territorial Forces in the three provinces. Activity decreased sharply after B-52 strikes, concentrated tactical air support, and several significant engagements.

MAY 11, 1972

- Military Region 3: Two Regional Forces companies, making contact with probable elements of the 271st NVA Independent Regiment in northern Hau Nghia, killed 62 enemy and captured 46 weapons while sustaining five wounded.

MAY 12, 1972

- Military Region 3. The 9th Viet Cong Division resumed its attack at An Loc, but it lacked the intensity of the day before and by mid-morning had been stopped. Later in the day the enemy attacked again and penetrated the western sector the perimeter. By midnight, ARVN forces had contained the penetration. Heavy indirect fire and direct tank fire continued throughout the night. B-52s were used near the city with six strikes during the night. The South Vietnam restored the perimeter by noon on May 13, 1972. The forces at An Loc conducted an area defense for the remainder of the month.

MAY 13, 1972

- Military Region 1. Enemy rocket and mortar teams of the 575th an 577th NVA Artillery Battalions attacked Da Nang Air Base; 18 122mm rockets hit inside the perimeter, causing damage to the runway and one F-4 aircraft, and destroying a warehouse. The runway was repaired in two hours. One rocket hit the Duy Tan Hospital killing five patients and wounding 16 others. Three Americans were lightly wounded at Marble Mountain in a mixed mortar and rocket attack of 25 to 30 rounds; three helicopters were moderately damaged. A B-52 strike in the Ross area killed 54 enemy and reduced enemy pressure for 10 days.

MAY 14, 1972

- Military Region 1. Twenty-five rockets were found and destroyed by a search operation in the rocket belt. Only one light attack was reported for the remainder of the month. Two regiments of the 2nd Brigade of the Vietnam Airborne Division began an operation to the high ground south of Birmingham and Bastogne. In the first two days, of the operation 172 enemy were killed (probably from the 5th and 6th NVA Regiments) and 20 tons of ammunition and five tons of rice were captured.
- Military Region 2. Following heavy attacks-by-fire against ARVN positions, the enemy conducted a tank-infantry attack against Kontum. The attack was repulsed when enemy forces came under heavy supporting fire and tactical air strikes, destroying eight enemy tanks.

MAY 15, 1972

- Military Region 1. A platoon of ARVN volunteers was air

assaulted into Bastogne. Ground linkup was made the following day against light enemy resistance. In the following two days, heavy fighting at the two firebases cost the enemy 246 dead while South Vietnam casualties were light. The division continued to find large caches of ammunition and supplies. An air strike south of FSB Checkmate caused secondary explosions lasting over an hour.

- Military Region 3. The 271st Regiment was mauled in northwestern Hau Nghia Province. The 1st Battalion, 50th Regiment, 25th Division, made contact and killed 138 while sustaining 19 dead. The next day the 43rd Regiment killed 21 enemy in Hau Nghia in an engagement with an unidentified enemy unit.

MAY 17, 1972

- Military Region 1. Elements of the 2nd Brigade of the Vietnam Airborne Division air assaulted into LZs in the vicinity of FSB Helen, using both Vietnam and American helicopters. Elements of this force moved overland to FSB Rakkasan, encountering only light resistance.
- Military Region 3. A battalion task force of six companies moved to Phuoc Tuy Province to counter increased enemy activity. In a contact six kilometers southwest of Duc Thanh, friendly forces killed 92 enemy, probably members of the 274th Viet Cong Regiment. Friendly forces losses were six killed and 13 wounded.

MAY 18-19, 1972

- Military Region 3. A Regional Forces unit killed 47 enemy in Duc Hue District, western Hau Nghia Province. In three contacts in Hau Nghia on May 19, 1972, 62 enemy were killed with government losses of three dead.
- Military Region 4. In response to reports that elements of the 1st NVA Division were east of Tuk Meas, two Ranger battalions were inserted into the Seven Mountains area. The following day, three additional Ranger battalions and an armored cavalry squadron were deployed to the area with the mission

of spoiling enemy attempts to infiltrate personnel and supplies into western Chau Doc and Kien Giang Provinces.

MAY 18-22, 1972

- Military Region 1. Attacks on Ranger camps at Ba To and Gia Vuc cost the enemy 79 killed and 30 weapons captured, while Ranger losses were light. The enemy renewed his attack on the next day, overrunning two outposts at Gia Vuc and interdicting Route 515 between the two camps. With the support of South Vietnam artillery from FSB Bronco and the assistance of Vietnam tactical air strikes, the rangers retook the outposts and the high ground around the camps on May 22, 1972. Enemy casualties were 272 killed; the rangers reported six killed and 14 wounded.

MAY 19-26, 1972

- Military Region 4. Kien Giang Province. An estimated two companies of the 52nd Regiment, 1st NVA Division, attacked the town of Kien Luong. Three mobile Regional Forces companies and a Ranger battalion were committed to the area. By May 24, 1972 the town had been secured; however, the enemy still held the cement plant and the high ground along the coast. In six days of fighting around Kien Luong, 184 enemy were killed with light ARVN casualties. The cement plant was secured on May 26, 1972 and the high ground along the coast by following day.

MAY 20, 1972

- Military Region 1. An American ship in Da Nang harbor was moderately damaged by an enemy explosive device. Enemy pressure against FSB Ross continued in the form of attacks-by-fire and ground attacks against Regional Forces outposts. Territorial Forces and 2nd Division elements countered with mobile patrolling operations supported by B-52s and American and Vietnam tactical air.
- Military Region 3. The 7th NVA Division persisted in its efforts to prevent the 21st Division from relieving An Loc. Early in

the morning, both the 15th and 31st Regiments repelled tank supported attacks five and seven kilometers south of An Loc, killing 80 enemy and destroying six tanks, while sustaining 15 days The 21st Division made little progress during the month as enemy pressure continued with sporadic indirect fire and ground attacks.

- Military Region 3. One-third of the town of Dat Do in southern Phuoc Tuy Province was lost to the 33rd NVA Regiment. Xuyen Moc and Duc Thanh remained in friendly hands but were isolated and had to be supplied by air.

MAY 21, 1972

- Military Region 1. The enemy initiated a three-pronged attack. The 27th and 31st Regiments, B-5 Front and the 18th Regiment, 325th NVA Division, with armor support from: the 202nd Tank Regiment and artillery support from the 84th Artillery Regiment, moved south along the coast toward FSB Nancy. The 304th NVA Division, with artillery, tanks, and enemy units of the B-5 front, attempted to drive south down the coastline east of Route 1 and one kilometer west of FSB Nancy. The ground attacks, made by enemy tank-infantry teams, succeeded in penetrating three to five kilometers into the South Vietnam defensive positions. Inexplicably, these attacks were not preceded by an artillery and mortar preparation, as was the normal practice of North Vietnam. However, the Marines counterattacked and resorted the original defensive line by nightfall. In the process, an enemy force was trapped behind the lines to the east along the coast.
- Military Region 2. Enemy pressure increased. Several salients developed in the defensive lines; however, ARVN forces were successful in eliminating them before nightfall.
- ARVN forces, consisting of the 2nd Ranger Group, I Ranger Group, and 3rd Armored Cavalry Squadron commenced an operation to clear Kontum Pass and to open Route 14. The first phase of the operation went according to plan and met only light resistance. Two Ranger battalions were air assaulted into the Rock Pile with instructions to link up with units moving north on Route 14 in the pass area.

MAY 22, 1972

- Military Region 1. Heavy fighting continued with elements of the 304B Division penetrating three to four kilometers into Thua Thien Province. The situation stabilized in mid-afternoon. Marine counterattacks once more restored the line by 1900 hours, with the enemy pocket, still trapped. The results of this day's fighting were 302 enemy soldiers dead, 18 tanks destroyed, and two SA-7 missiles captured. This increase in activity influenced South Vietnam commanders to commit the 3rd Airborne Brigade The Airborne Division with two brigades was assigned an area of operation northwest of Hue. The Marine Division assumed control of the 1st Ranger Group, which had just completed reorganizing and refitting at Da Nang. The town of Que Son received a heavy attack-by-fire followed by a ground attack from elements of the 711th Division. Regional Forces, supported by helicopter and fixed wing gunships, repulsed the attack Military Region 3. In a contact east of Dat Do an ARVN battalion killed 31 enemy, possibly from the 33rd Regiment, without friendly casualties.

MAY 24, 1972

- Military Region 1. The Marine Division conducted airmobile and amphibious assault operations into Quang Tri Province. One battalion of Marines, embarked in USN LSTs at Tan My, went ashore in USMC landing vehicles across Wunder Beach. Two hours later another Marine battalion was airlifted by USMC helicopters into a LZ east of Quang Tri. Although both forces were unopposed in their initial landings, contact with the enemy was soon made. These two battalions joined forces and swept toward the south. A third Marine battalion was airlifted by VN Air Force helicopters from Tan My into a LZ along the northeast end of the Thua Thien provincial border. This battalion crossed the Tach Ma River and made contact with the enemy immediately. Tactical aircraft, artillery, and naval gunfire supported the Operation Song Thuan 6-72. In the Hai Van Pass area, the 582nd NVA Battalion heavily damaged the Nam-O Bridge. The bridge was repaired and Route 1 opened on May 26, 1972.
- Military Region 3. The 5th Ranger Group, with three battalions, was deployed to Phuoc Tuy and began conducting operations

in the vicinity of Dat Do. In significant contacts there, the Ranger group killed 75 enemy one kilometer west of Dat Do on May 28, 1972, and on May 29, 1972, in the same area, killed 31, while sustaining light casualties.

MAY 24-25, 1972

- Military Region 3. Elements of the 21st Division suffered heavy casualties in an enemy ambush 12 kilometers south of An Loc along Route 13. ARVN losses were 42 killed, 159 wounded, and 23 armored personnel carriers destroyed.

MAY 25, 1972

- Military Region 1. The two Marine battalions in the north completed their sweep to the south and were joined by the third battalion in the early morning. In this operation, 515 enemy were killed and large caches of food and ammunition were destroyed. Five thousand VN civilians were freed from enemy control. Twelve South Vietnam Marines and four Americans were killed, and 36 Marines were wounded. During the period of the operation, the Marine Division reported heavy fighting all along the northern front. The heaviest contact was northeast of FSB Nancy. In this region, 322 enemy soldiers were killed and six tanks were destroyed. The Marines lost 17 dead and 74 wounded.
- Military Region 2. Enemy sappers penetrated the defense and occupied the southeast portion of the city. The following day the enemy launched attacks along the northern defenses of Kontum and from within the southeast section of the city. Tanks supported the attacks from the north. Twelve enemy tanks were destroyed in this action. Penetration of the ARVN defense allowed the enemy to occupy strong points in the north, northeast, and southeast portions the city. After three days of heavy fighting, the enemy attacks subsided. As the month ended ARVN forces were concentrating on eliminating the enemy strong points within the city.

MAY 26, 1972

- Military Region 1. The Ranger elements that had been airlifted into the Marine area on May 24, 1972 were in heavy contact behind the My Chanh defense line. The Ranger attack was repulsed and an enemy counterattack drove the rangers into secondary positions to the south. When these positions failed to hold, the rangers exfiltrated toward Huong Dinh. Ranger losses were 67 killed, 218, wounded, and 105 missing. Enemy losses were unknown. The 3rd Regiment recaptured Checkmate against moderate enemy resistance.

MAY 27, 1972

- Military Region 1. Contact was reported all along the northern front, but the Marine defenses held. Activity was light in other parts of Thua Thien Province. The ARVN Airborne Division reported light contacts while conducting patrolling operations. In the 1st ARVN Division area, activity was light after the mid-month battles to retake FSB Bastogne. South Vietnam troops occupying Checkmate continued to receive 130mm fire through the rest of the month suffering light casualties.

MAY 30, 1972

- Military Region 1. Ranger border defense elements killed 42 of the enemy in a brief, but intense engagement. The enemy, probably the 70th and 72nd NVA Infantry Battalions, attacked Binh Duong village, east of Route 1 just south of the Quang Nam border. Several Regional Forces outposts were overrun, but these were restored to government control by the end of the month. In Quang Ngai Province activity centered along Route 515 from the highlands to the coast.

JUNE 1, 1972

- Military Region 4. In reaction to intelligence information received on May 31, 1972, ARVN Ranger elements surrounded an enemy force approximately five kilometers south of Tuk Meas. Eight sorties of VN Air Force tactical air supported the engagement, which resulted in 133 enemy killed. Ranger losses were six killed and 17 wounded.

JUNE 4, 1972

- Military Region 3. Territorial Forces, supported by US and South Vietnam tactical air killed 28 enemy, while losing 12 killed themselves. The ARVN 21st Division was reinforced when the 6th Airborne Battalion and a reconnaissance company were air assaulted into a LZ nine kilometers south of An Loc.

JUNE 6, 1972

- Military Region 3. A total of 56 enemy were killed and 22 weapons captured in four separate contacts. The ARVN 6th Airborne Battalion attacked north and on the June 8, 1972 killed 100 enemy as it reached a point 1½ kilometers south of An Loc. Also, the 6th Airborne Battalion linked up with the 8th Airborne Battalion, which was operating from An Loc.

JUNE 8, 1972

- Military Region 1. In northern Thua Thien, the Marine Division began a two-day limited objective operation by attacking north with five battalions, three to five kilometers into Quang Tri Province. The operation accounted for 131 enemy killed, 65 weapons captured (including one SA-7 missile) and three tanks destroyed. The Marines reported two killed and six wounded. Ground activity fell to a low level following this offensive action, but enemy attacks-by-fire increased in number and intensity. Seven to nine attacks of 60 to 100 rounds each were reported.

JUNE 10, 1972

- Military Region 1. A heavy contact developed south of FSB Checkmate as 1st Regiment elements exploited a B-52 strike. Results of the contact were 136 killed and friendly losses of four killed, 52 wounded, and five missing. Just northwest of Bastogne another 68 enemy were killed, while six ARVN were wounded.
- Military Region 3. The enemy's siege of An Loc began to erode as Vietnam helicopters conducted the first substantial air landed operation into the city since the siege began. Over 100 wounded personnel were evacuated and 113 replacements taken in. The next day 119 replacements were taken in and 128 wounded brought out.
- Military Region 4. A sharp increase in enemy activity caused the ARVN to deploy a Ranger battalion to Kien Tuong Province to

counter an attack by elements of the 275th Regiment, 5th NVA Division on the district town of Tuyen Binh. Over 20 tactical air sorties were flown in support of the contact. At the same time, the 12th Regiment commenced operations in the Cai Lay-Cai Be area of Dinh Tuong Province.

JUNE 11-18, 1972

- Military Region 1. B-52 strikes were employed again southeast of Checkmate, followed by ground elements exploitation. The results were 115 enemy killed. Activity increased with an increase in enemy mortar and artillery attacks and ground contacts. The pattern of activity of sharp, brief ground engagements continued. Results for the period were: 485 enemy killed, 228 by air strikes; 26 friendly soldiers killed (one American) and 127 wounded (three Americans). The ARVN also lost over 3,000 rounds of artillery ammunition in an enemy attack-by-fire. Ground activity decreased to a low level as the American installation at Phu Bai received light 122mm rocket attacks causing minor damage. 1st Division elements reported 336 enemy killed (133 by air strikes) for the week, while suffering 23 killed and 80 wounded for the same period. Quang Tin Province reported three Regional Forces contacts that resulted in 69 enemy killed, 24 of who were killed by tactical air strikes. One other contact on June 18, 1972 resulted in 25 enemy killed with light Regional Forces casualties.
- Military Region 3. Phuoc Tuy Province. In contact supported by American tactical aircraft enemy, probably from the 274th Viet Cong Regiment, was reported killed by air strikes. Although the 7th NVA Division still blocked movement along Route 13, its effective isolation of An Loc was broken. On the 13th two additional battalions were inserted and occupied positions on the southern approaches. Forces in the city were reinforced with unit and individual replacements.
- Military Region 4. The 12th Regiment assumed operational control of all forces in Kien Tuong Province. Results were 105 enemy killed with no ARVN casualties. Across the border another 68 were killed. Also, territorial units repulsed an attack

by the D2 Regiment on the district town of Nga Nam, Ba Xuyen Province, killing 53 enemy and capturing 20 weapons.

JUNE 12, 1972

- Military Region 4. The ARVN 12th Regiment reported heavy contact with the 6th Regiment, 5th NVA Division in the Elephant's Foot area of north Kien Tuong Province. In two major contacts 116 enemy were killed.

JUNE 14, 1972

- Military Region 1. Regional Forces element in northeastern Quang Ngai Province repulsed an enemy attack. The next day 37 enemy bodies were found outside the perimeter wire. Two days later, an element of a Ranger border defense battalion at Gia Vuc killed 24 enemy with light casualties to themselves.

JUNE 17, 1972

- Military Region 2. A successful raid was conducted into the Tan Canh area. A reconnaissance company from the 23rd ARVN Division combat assaulted into a LZ immediately north of Tan Canh, and then swept south through the city, seizing limited terrain objectives. Three brief, but sharp, engagements were made with enemy forces, resulting in one ARVN wounded and 24 enemy killed. In addition, five Molatova trucks and two jeeps reported destroyed. After approximately three hours in the area the forces were extracted, along with nine soldiers from the 22nd Division and 37 civilians found in the area. The purpose of the operation was to establish the ARVN's ability to reenter lost territory, exploit the psychological value of the action, and destroy enemy personnel and materiel.

JUNE 18, 1972

- Military Region 1. Thirty enemy were killed four kilometers to the northwest of Quang Ngai City by ARVN Ranger forces. A follow up of the contact yielded 30 additional enemy dead the following day. Ranger losses were four killed and 16 wounded. In the same general area, twenty bodies were found, presumably killed by tactical air strikes. The Vietnam Marines again attacked against objectives five to eight kilometers inside Quang Tri Province. During the first day, the Marines reported

80 enemy killed and 15 rockets and four SA-7 missiles captured. The enemy countered with heavy artillery and mortar attacks, with approximately 500 incoming rounds. The operation terminated late in the day June 19, 1972.

JUNE 20-24, 1972

- Military Region 1. Heavy fighting erupted in the Marine area. North Vietnam attacked with tanks and infantry along the My Chanh defense line, supported by intensive 130mm gunfire. The Marines were supported by American tactical aircraft, B-52 strikes, and naval gunfire, as well as by VN artillery and aircraft. For five days heavy contacts were reported, but the Marines held and inflicted heavy losses on the attackers. When the assault died away after June 24, 1972. 601 enemy soldiers had been killed, and 23 tanks and three 130mm guns were destroyed. The Marines lost 71 killed and 179 wounded.

JUNE 21-24, 1972

- Military Region 1. The airborne troopers became involved in the enemy attack that struck the Marines the day before. The enemy tanks and infantry assaulted across the My Chanh defense line one kilometer southwest of Nancy. The defending forces blocked the penetration two kilometers southeast of the defense line, while American and VN tactical air and artillery pounded the area. By the end of the day, the enemy had lost 51 killed, and 17 tanks and three 130mm guns destroyed. Enemy pressure continued the following day, but the situation remained stable. The VN Air Force reported destroying five enemy, 105mm howitzers and ARVN ground forces accounted for 55 enemy dead. The enemy attempt to renew the attack the next day was spoiled. Sporadic heavy contacts continued on June 24, 1972, but attacks-by-fire were significantly reduced. By nightfall airborne forces had driven the enemy across the river and had restored the My Chanh defense line. Enemy losses for the three-day period were 259 killed, and 34 tanks, 12 artillery pieces, and one anti-aircraft gun destroyed. Friendly casualties were 29 killed, 123 wounded, and16 missing. The South Vietnam also reported that three of their tanks had been destroyed and one 105mm howitzer and four helicopters were damaged.

- Military Region 3. An Loc. The Airborne Brigade was extracted from positions south of An Loc along Route 13 and returned to the Saigon-Bien Hoa area. The 43rd Regiment was airlifted in to replace the airborne brigade.

JUNE 26, 1972

- Military Region 1. Heavy enemy artillery attacks continued throughout the Airborne Division area of operations, but ground attacks were light. The enemy indirect fire inflicted moderate damage to fire support bases. The most severe damage was at FSB Jack where 11 howitzers were destroyed or heavily damaged. Two VN Air Force helicopters and an American Cobra gunship were downed by enemy ground fire; 16 South Vietnam were killed in the crashes. A significant increase in the number and intensity of enemy attacks-by-fire was reported. Particularly hard hit was FSB Checkmate, which also received two ground attacks from elements of the 324B Division and the 5th and 6th Regiments. Several attacks-by-fire of over 100 rounds of mortar and artillery were reported; however, ARVN casualties were light.

JUNE 27, 1972

- Military Region 1. Virtually all bases were hit, with Checkmate reporting 160 rounds of 122mm artillery and Bastogne reporting 142 rounds during the night. Heavy ground contacts, following 430 rounds of mortar and artillery; fire in a two and a half hour period, caused the withdrawal of the ARVN company-size security force from Checkmate on the night of June 29, 1972. Casualties reported for the last week of the month were 267 enemy killed (58 by air strikes) and 45 ARVN killed and 164 wounded.

JUNE 29, 1972

- Military Region 3. In Phuoc Tuy Province, 10 kilometers east of Dat Do, the ARVN 52nd Regiment engaged an enemy force and killed 63 enemy soldiers while losing two dead and 23 wounded.

JUNE 30, 1972

- The offensive redeployments continued on schedule with

eight US maneuver battalions standing down by June 30, 1972, leaving two in country.

JULY 1, 1972

- Military Region 2. Binh Dinh Province. The Korean Cavalry Regiment assumed the security responsibility Route 19 from the An Khe Pass, to the Mang Giang Pass, releasing the 47th Regiment for deployment to northern Binh Dinh Province. The 47th assumed the mission of the 40th Regiment north of Phu My, allowing the 40th to return to Ba Gi for badly needed training.
- Military Region 3. The relay station on Nui Ba Ra Mountain near Song Be in Phuoc Long Province was attacked and destroyed by the E-2 NVA Regiment. Elements of a Ranger border defense battalion counterattacked by air assault and resecured the site late on the same day. ARVN Forces lost 69 killed and 47 wounded. Thirty enemy were killed in subsequent pursuit operations the following day, plus 100 killed by air.

JULY 2, 1972

- Military Region 2. Elements of the ARVN 45th Regiment became engaged for two days with an enemy unit 15 kilometers NE of Kontum City. After suffering heavy casualties, the enemy withdrew and only sporadic, scattered small contacts occurred the remaining of the month.

JULY 3-8, 1972

- Military Region 4. Khmer Republic. The ARVN 7th Division elements attacking north of the Elephant's Foot area made contact with probable units of the 271st NVA Independent Regiment, resulting in 115 enemy killed and ARVN losses of nine killed and 46 wounded.

JULY 4, 1972

- Military Region 4. Khmer Republic. A combined South Vietnam-Khmer operation started with the mission of clearing Route 1 from Neak Luong to Kampong Trabek. Two ARVN Ranger battalions, a cavalry troop, and two FANK brigades attacked east from Neak Luong astride Route 1 towards Kampong Trabek.

JULY 8-18, 1972

- Military Region 4. Dinh Tuong Province. The 215th Regiment made an effort to capture the district town of Sam Giang in Dinh Tuong Province. The fighting continued for five days. On July 9, 1972, four Regional Forces battalions and one Ranger battalion began moving to reinforce the Territorial Force defending the town. On the night of July 9, 1972, the enemy attack reached the market place but was stopped with the support of American and VN gunships and a Cobra fire team. The friendly forces attempting to reinforce made contact two kilometers short of Sam Giang on July 10, 1972 and suffered heavy losses. On July 11, 1972, five ARVN battalions moved to Dinh Tuong as additional reinforcements. The arrival of these units relieved the pressure and subsequently forced the enemy to withdraw on July 12-13, 1972. The 10th Regiment pursued the withdrawing enemy and made contact on July 14, 1972 killing 18. On July 18, 1972, the 67th and 76th Ranger Battalions were attacked early in the evening by the 275th Regiment and sustained 36 killed, 53 wounded, and 53 missing.

JULY 9, 1972

- Military Region 3. The Deputy Commander, Third Regional Assistance Command, Brigadier General Richard J. Tallman, was killed by artillery fire at An Loc during a visit to finalize plans for the two division exchange.
- Military Region 4. Khmer Republic. The 7th Division began to disengage because of pressure in Dinh Tuong Province by the DT1, 218th, and 215th Regiments. One regiment remained in the Khmer and the remainder of the division returned to northern Military Region 4. Through the skillful exploitation of B-52 strikes the operation accounted for over 700 enemy killed during the period June 30-July 9, 1972.

JULY 10, 1972

- Military Region 1. The VN Marines operating east of Route 1 made steady progress toward Quang Tri City against the 27th and 31st Regiments, B-5 Front and the 18th and 325th

Regiments. They had killed over 600 of the enemy, destroyed 10 tanks, and liberated 1,150 VN civilians.

- Military Region 4. Chuong Thien Province. The 2nd Battalion, 14th Regiment was ambushed by an estimated enemy battalion of the 95A Regiment and suffered 87 killed, 102 wounded, and 106 missing, plus heavy losses in weapons and equipment.

JULY 11-24, 1972

- Military Region 1. The VN Marines conducted a combat assault, with USMC helicopters airlifting a reinforced battalion and B-52s, tactical air support, naval gunfire, and VN Marine artillery providing support. The landing was made successfully despite a stout defense on the ground, and the battalion moved toward the other Marine forces advancing from the south. Ground linkup was made on July 15, 1972. Enemy losses were 245 killed, 17 tanks destroyed, and seven artillery pieces captured. On July 22, 1972, the Marines launched another combat assault into a LZ eight kilometers northeast of Quang Tri City and conducted clearing operations in the vicinity for two days.

JULY 13, 1972

- Military Region 1: The Phu Bai ammunition storage area received attacks-by-fire and a sapper attack (probably by the CT2 Sapper Battalion, 5th NVA Regiment) resulting in 2,850 rounds of artillery ammunition destroyed

JULY 16-20, 1972

- Military Region 3. The 25th Division attacked from Route 13 north of Chon Thanh to the west in an envelopment of the 7th NVA Division elements defending the highway. The attack progressed well against light enemy resistance. On July 20, 1972, the enemy strongpoint was neutralized. Considerable minesweeping and road repair was necessary before the road could be opened for traffic.

JULY 19, 1972

- Military Region 2. The first phase of a three phase *Operation*

BAC BINH VUONG 22/8 began. Preceded by B-52, tactical air, and naval gunfire preparations, elements of the 40th Regiment air assaulted into LZs along the high ground at the Bong Son Pass overlooking Route 1. The remainder of the regiment and the 19th Cavalry attacked through the pass along the highway. In Binh Dinh Province, the 45th Regiment and territorial units assumed responsibility for the Kontum Pass area, releasing the 6th Ranger Group for offensive operations. The II Corps Commander directed the 23rd ARVN Division to organize a mobile operation to destroy enemy forces north of Kontum City to a line running east and west of Vo Dinh. This operation did not take place during the month. In addition, he directed the maximum use of Territorial Forces to maintain security and discipline in the city, releasing ARVN units to train and rest. The division rotated two battalions at a time to their home bases for this purpose. A US and ARVN mobile training team was dispatched to Kontum to assist in retraining the division units as replacement personnel and equipment were received. The regiments of the division were reorganized with three battalions per regiment instead of four, a reorganization that had been planned for several months, but was delayed by the enemy offensive.

- Military Region 4. Khmer Republic. In a supporting operation, an ARVN Ranger battalion and an armored cavalry squadron attacked north from Cai Cai toward Kampong Trabek, securing the latter on July 24, 1972. The FANK units consolidated their positions around the town. The South Vietnam left one Ranger battalion in the Kampong Trabek—Neak Luong area and returned the other forces to Military Region 4 to counter the 5th NVA Division buildup in Dinh Tuong Province.

JULY 20, 1972

- Military Region 2. ARVN units pushed through and secured the Bong Son Pass against light resistance.

JULY 21, 1972

- Military Region 2. The second phase of *Operation BAC BINH VUONG 22/8* began. Artillery, tactical air, and naval gunfire preparations were fired in support of battalion air assaults into each of the three LZs: B-11, B-21, and B-22. Two battalions of the 41st Regiment attacked north across the Lai Giang River, near Hoai Nhon, linking up with the battalion at B-11 and raising the South Vietnam flag. The 42nd Regiment elements in the vicinity of LZs B-21 and B-22 consolidated and screened their areas with only light contact.

JULY 22-29, 1972

- Military Region 1. Enemy artillery attacks were heavy in the ARVN 1st Division area when over 10,000 rounds of fire were received in the vicinity of Bastogne, Checkmate, and Birmingham.

JULY 23-31, 1972

- Military Region 1. ARVN 2nd Division elements in the Que Son mountains killed 70 enemy while losing 20 friendly killed. During the next week enemy units continued to threaten, as 2nd Division elements killed 300 enemy while suffering friendly losses of 24 killed and 74 wounded. Enemy probes by the 711th Division elements continued against FSB Ross as the month ended.

JULY 24, 1972

- Military Region 2. The third phase of *Operation BAC BINH VUONG 22/8* began.

JULY 25, 1972

- Military Region 1. Airborne elements breached the northeast wall of the Quang Tri Citadel. After constant heavy fighting inside the fortress airborne elements withdrew as a Corps directed boundary change made the Marines responsible for operations within the city. The 2nd Airborne Brigade assumed a Corps reserve mission, moving to FSB Sally for refitting after participating in some of the heaviest fighting of the counteroffensive.
- Military Region 4. The IV Corps deployment of forces to meet the increased enemy activity in Dinh Tuong Province was

completed. A corps forward command post opened at Dong Tarn and assumed command of the 7th Division in Kien Tuong Province, a Ranger task force of five battalions in western Dinh Tuong Province, and the Dinh Tuong Territorial Forces. The 15th Regiment, 9th Division was placed under operational control of Dinh Tuong Province.

JULY 26, 1972

- Military Region 3. The 18th Division at An Loc began expanding its control to the east to facilitate future operations directed toward Quan Loi and to reoccupy the fire support base there. The 5th Ranger Group secured a hamlet two kilometers west on the approaches to the high ground overlooking the road to Quan Loi.

JULY 27, 1972

- Military Region 1. ARVN 1st Division elements were forced to withdraw from Bastogne. However, the situation stabilized and maintained control of the western approach to Hue. The ARVN 51st Regiment operating in the area south of FSB Birmingham reinforced the ARVN 1st Division.
- Military Region 3. The ARVN 48th Regiment, supported by tactical air strikes, attacked and seized Hill 169 about three kilometers to the southeast of An Loc.

JULY 27-31, 1972

- Military Region 4: On 27 July 1972, a multiple battalion spoiling operation started in the northwestern area of Dinh Tuong. Seven preparatory B-52 strikes were employed on the night of the July 26-27, 1972. This operation inflicted heavy casualties on the 24th Regiment, C30B NVA Division, in both ground engagements and by B-52 strikes. Two Ranger battalions, the 43rd and 44th, engaged suspected elements of the 24th NVA Regiment on July 29, 1972, in a three day battle that accounted for 100 enemy killed with 13 friendly killed. In a small engagement, 23 enemy were killed and 53 additional bodies were found. On July 31, 1972, two battalions of the 12th Regiment combat assaulted into the area southeast of the Ranger operation to exploit B-52 strikes.

JULY 28, 1972

- Military Region 1. I Corps plans for a counteroffensive to regain control of Quang Tri Province and to destroy the enemy forces there were set in motion. Lieutenant General Ngo Quang Truong seized initiative in wake of North Vietnam failure to breach the My Chanh river line defenses, launching a coordinated attack northward with the Marine and Airborne Divisions, supported by Ranger elements and units of the 1st and 2nd ARVN Divisions. The Marine Division was reinforced and then attacked north in a zone bounded by the coastline in the east and Route 1 in the west. The Marine attack began overland and by air assault into a LZ north of Hai Lang with USMC helicopters providing the airlift. Both the troops advancing by ground and those that were airlifted met light to moderate resistance. The Airborne Division attacked north in a zone generally extending from Highway 1 to the high ground on the west. The 4th Regiment, 2nd Division followed reconnaissance company of the 1st Division and the 81st Airborne Ranger Group provided flank security as the Airborne Division pushed three to five kilometers into Quang Tri Province. The airborne reported 280 enemy killed on the first day of the advance, an enemy tank and five 37mm antiaircraft weapons captured, and three enemy tanks destroyed. The offensive gained momentum in the next two days when airborne battalions combat assaulted into LZs eight to ten kilometers north of the Thua Thien provincial boundary. Ground contacts were light; for the moment the enemy forces avoided decisive contact. In the first three days of the attack the Marines reported that 368 enemy were killed, one 130mm gun and two tanks were destroyed, and one tank was captured. Marine losses were light; 25 killed, 55 wounded, and two 155mm howitzers destroyed and one damaged.
- Military Region 2. Elements of the 6th Ranger Group air assaulted in the vicinity of An and secured the town by mid-afternoon.

AUGUST 1, 1972

- Military Region 1. A joint ARVN 2nd and 3rd Division operation was planned against enemy units located northwest of FSB

Ross. I Corps commenced a 48-hour program of preparatory fires to support the VN Marine assault on the Citadel. The program included artillery, naval gunfire, and tactical aircraft targeted at known and suspected enemy positions, particularly 130mm artillery positions in the Dong Ha area.

AUGUST 3, 1972

- Military Region 1. Quang Nam Province. A Da Nang attack consisted of 16 122mm rockets fired, by the 575th NVA Artillery Battalion, resulted in five killed (one American) and 21 wounded (20 Americans).
- Military Region 1. The Citadel. The Marine assault on the Citadel failed to break the enemy defenses, although the assault was supported with over 2,000 rounds of mortar and artillery fire into the Citadel on that day alone; The Marines reported that 140 enemy were killed during the first three days of the month while Marine casualties were reported as light to moderate. Heavy house-to-house fighting continued near the Citadel, while to the north heavy contacts, developed between the Vinh, Dinh and Thach Han Rivers. A B-52 strike four kilometers west, of the city resulted in numerous secondary explosions.
- Military Region 4. The 12th Regiment, while exploiting B-52 strikes, killed 67 of the enemy north of Cai Lay. On the next night in Kien Tuong Province, 7th Division units killed 110 enemy from the 174th Regiment, 5th NVA Division, in a well-executed night attack.

AUGUST 4, 1972

- Military Region 1. FSB Checkmate was reoccupied following pre-emptive B-52 strikes. Enemy pressure continued against Bastogne and Checkmate with 400 to 600 rounds of artillery and mortar fire daily and numerous ground contacts. .

AUGUST 4-6, 1972

- Military Region 4. The ARVN 12th Regiment engaged the 24th NVA Regiment and killed 170.
- Military Region 4. Khmer Republic. The ARVN began an operation 22 kilometers northeast of Cai Cai. An ARVN battalion air-assaulted into the area, in conjunction with a

ground attack by another battalion and cavalry troops. On August 5, 1972, another ARVN Ranger battalion reinforced these units. Sporadic contact was made on August 5-6, 1972 with elements of the 207th Regiment, C30B NVA Division, resulting in 52 enemy killed.

AUGUST 5 and 7, 1972

- Military Region 2. Kontum Province. Significant contacts were reported northwest of Kontum City, resulting in 57 enemy killed. ARVN casualties were four dead and 19 wounded.
- Military Region 3. Friendly forces at the Nui Ba Den Communications facility in Tay Ninh Province repelled ground probes by the D-16 NVA Sapper Battalion, killing 50 enemy and losing four killed and 13 wounded.

AUGUST 6, 1972

- Military Region 1. Quang Nam Province. A Marble Mountain attack consisted of 20 rounds of 82mm mortar fire, wounded six, three of whom were Americans. The enemy carried out light attacks-by-fire, striking an ammunition dump at Camp Evans, and destroying 63 tons of ammunition, mostly 105mm rounds.

AUGUST 7, 1972

- Military Region 1. Elements of the 304B Division launched a combined tank-infantry attack against elements south of FSB Nancy. ARVN defenses held and the enemy withdrew. The following day a lighter attack was reported in the same area, and again the force was repulsed. The enemy lost nine tanks destroyed in the two-day engagement.

AUGUST 8, 1972

- Military Region 1. The Citadel. The west bank of the Thach Han River was struck by B-52s with large secondary explosions lasting 20 to 25 minutes. The same day, US tactical air was employed to breach the Quang Tri Citadel wall and to destroy a large building being used as a fortified position. As a result, enemy mortar fire and recoilless rifle fires, which had been heavy prior to the air strike, were reduced.
- Military Region 1. Quang Ngai Province. The enemy attacked

three villages southwest of Binh Son in Quang Ngai Province before dawn. By the middle of the morning sector forces had blocked the land exits from the area, and the VN Navy was screening the waterways. American helicopters and VN Air Force gunships supported the operation. Regional Forces losses were 24 killed and 59 wounded, while the enemy lost 68 killed.

AUGUST 10, 1972

- Military Region 2. Binh Dinh Province. Combat activity in northeastern part of the province during the month was characterized by sharp, short duration, small unit contacts; scattered attacks-by-fire and ground probes against ARVN and Regional Forces units along Route 1. The 22nd Division conducted multi-battalion operation throughout the month, capitalizing on its mobile and firepower advantage to keep the enemy balance. On August 10, 1972 units of the division began an operation to regain additional territory. For two days, a two-regiment task force moved west into the lower An Lao River Valley. A battalion conducted an air assault onto the high ground northwest of Hoai Nhon, while a regimental-sized force attacked westward along the An Lao River. During the operation numerous light enemy contacts and sightings of small groups of enemy soldiers leaving the area were reported.
- Military Region 3. Friendly forces, at Lai Khe annihilated a sapper company that penetrated the perimeter, killing 40 enemy; while losing two killed and 18 wounded.
- Military Region 4. The 11th Regiment engaged an estimated enemy battalion 15 kilometers north of Moc Hoa in the Elephant's Foot area. The contact with the 174th Regiment, 5th NVA Division continued for two days and resulted in 222 enemy killed and 15 friendly killed. Dinh Tuong Province. Friendly forces, again exploiting B-52 strikes in Dinh Tuong Province reported 128 enemy killed, 68 individual weapons, eight machine guns, and four mortars captured.

AUGUST 11, 1972

- Military Region 1. Quang Nam Province. Regional Forces, nine kilometers southwest of Hoi An, received a heavy ground attack supported by mortar fire. The territorials were quickly reinforced as American helicopter and VN gunships supported. The fighting lasted throughout the day, resulting in 93 enemy killed and 39 weapons captured. Regional Forces suffered 22 killed, 32 wounded, and two 105mm howitzers destroyed. In addition, 25 civilians were wounded, and 80 houses burned. The city of Hoi An also received a light attack-by-fire which wounded nine VN civilians.

MID-AUGUST 1972

- Military Region 1. The Citadel. In defense of the Citadel, the NVA employed a rotation system. The 48B and 64B Regiments, 320B NVA Division, were the first units defending the city. The 325th NVA Division elements began to be rotated in. Ground contacts were mostly friendly initiated and cost the enemy heavily in personnel and equipment. Tactical air and B-52 strikes also took a heavy toll. The 1st ARVN Division patrolling operations supported by tactical air and B-52 strikes gained in momentum and extended farther into enemy held territory.

AUGUST 15, 1972

- Military Region 1. The Citadel. Ground fighting was heavy around the Citadel and in an area four to seven kilometers north-northeast along Phase Line Gold.

AUGUST 16, 1972

- Military Region 4. Khmer Republic. The ARVN 7th Ranger Group was committed to support besieged Khmer units at Kampont Trabek. The attack began from the south against light and scattered resistance. Two days later, significant contact was made eight kilometers south of Kampong Trabek, which resulted in 56 enemy killed and no friendly casualties.

AUGUST 17, 1972

- Military Region 2. The ARVN 22nd Division began a four day, multi-battalion, ground and air assault west of Tam Quan, supported by B-52 strikes. During the operation ARVN forces reported 33 enemy killed. ARVN casualties were one dead and one wounded.

AUGUST 18, 1972

- Military Region 1. Quang Nam Province. Heavy fighting erupted with the 31st and 38th Regiments, 711th NVA Division, in the FSB Ross area, following indirect fire attacks the night before. Enemy forces attacked virtually all friendly positions in the Que Son area and interdicted Route 535 in several places. Da Nang Air Base was also struck with 43 rounds of 122mm rockets, resulting in one American killed, 20 Americans wounded, seven VN civilians killed and 27 wounded; 11 aircraft were destroyed or heavily damaged. Pressure continued throughout the day against Ross and Que Son District headquarters as the enemy assaulted in small units and "hugged" closely to friendly forces, hindering the use of airpower. Ross and Que Son were evacuated late in the day, and 2nd Division elements formed a defensive line midway between Que Son and FSB Baldy.

AUGUST 18-19, 1972

- Military Region 3. Bien Hoa Province. At Trang Bom Village, an ARVN Ranger battalion and Territorial Forces successfully defended against repeated attempts by a company from the 271st NVA Independent Regiment to overrun the village. An estimated 48 enemy were killed.

AUGUST 19, 1972

- Military Region 1. Enemy pressure centered approximately 10 kilometers south of Quang Tri City. Intense fighting, usually of short duration, was reported, as the enemy appeared to be attempting to interdict Route 1. Enemy armor appeared from the Hai Long Forest area moving toward the highway. Tactical air destroyed 10 enemy tanks and the TOW ground missile systems destroyed one. The following day, 50 enemy bodies were found in the same area, presumably killed by the air strikes.

AUGUST 18-20, 1972

- Military Region 1. Quang Nam Province. The situation had which began on August 18, 1972, stabilized with casualties for the two days reported as 180 enemy killed, 31 ARVN killed and

195 wounded, mostly from the 5th Regiment. An unknown number were missing, and many major items of equipment were abandoned during the withdrawal.

AUGUST 21, 1972

- Military Region 3. Friendly forces at the Nui Ba Den Communications facility in Tay Ninh Province repelled a ground probe by the D-16 NVA Sapper Battalion, killing six of the enemy.
- Military Region 4. Khmer Republic. The ARVN 7th Ranger Group linked up with Khmer units southwest of Kampong Trabek. Mass graves containing 141 enemy bodies, apparently killed by tactical air, were found nearby.

AUGUST 23, 1972

- Military Region 4. Dinh Tuong Province. A Regional Forces battalion exploiting a B-52 strike killed 32 enemy and found 30 killed by air. On the same day, the ARVN 14th Regiment became heavily engaged with the DT1 NVA Regiment near the Dinh Tuong—Kien Hoa Province borders and suffered 17 killed and 58 wounded while killing 18 of the enemy.

AUGUST 24, 1972

- Military Region 1. Quang Nam Province. The 4th Regiment joined the 2nd Division and two days later it attacked along Route 535 with the objective of securing Rosa. Late the next day the 60th Ranger Defense Battalion reclaimed the Que Son District Headquarters, although enemy strong points were reported still inside the compound. Enemy forces opposing the southern axis of advance took heavy losses, as tactical air and B-52 strikes supported the 4th Regiment. As the month ended the 2nd Division launched a coordinated attack against Que Son and FSB Ross. The enemy elements of the 270th Regiment, 711th Division were driven from Que Son except for a small pocket on the northwest edge of the town, but the 4th Regiment had not yet retaken Ross.
- Military Region 1. The Citadel. Ground fighting intensified when the enemy launched a series of company-size attacks, supported by mortar and artillery. The contacts, which started

early in the morning, subsided late in the day. The following day the attacks were less intense and focused just south of the Citadel. During these two days the Marines killed 260 of the enemy while sustaining light loses. The Marines continued to fight well throughout August as units were rotated from the front line for rest and fitting.

- Military Region 2. Pleiku Province. The first significant contact was made, seven kilometers west-northwest of Thanh An. Brigadier General Ba then revised his plans in an effort to preempt an expected enemy attack against Thanh An. Instead of continuing operations to the west along Route 19 with the entire regiment, two of the battalions were employed in areas of operations to the south and southeast of the district capital. US air cavalry screened the west and south. Little contact was made for the remainder of the month.

AUGUST 25, 1972

- Dinh Tuong Province. Two companies of the Z15 NVA Regiment attempted to interdict Route 4 west of Cai Lay. By coincidence, an ARVN infantry regiment escorted by a cavalry troop was redeploying from eastern Dinh Tuong to the area northwest of Cai Lay. When the convoy made contact, the regiment deployed and engaged the enemy using the supporting artillery in a direct fire role. After a three-hour battle the road was reopened. As a result of the engagement 51 enemy were killed and two prisoners captured. ARVN losses were four killed, 21 wounded, and one 105mm howitzer destroyed.

AUGUST 27, 1972

- Military Region 1. Ground activity rose sharply as enemy infantry and armor units (probably elements of the 308th Division and the 203rd Tank Regiment) attacked ARVN Airborne elements eight kilometers south of Quang Tri. Just west of the ground battle a South Vietnam forward air controller directed artillery and air strikes against enemy troops in the open and reported 150 enemy killed.

END OF AUGUST 1972

- Military Region 1. Toward the end of the month, Territorial Forces conducted operations to clear Barrier Island southeast of Hoi An. During the operation, 116 enemy were killed while Regional Forces losses were 18 killed and 35 wounded. Enemy forces burned approximately 750 houses withdrawing, before the territorial sweep.

SEPTEMBER 1, 1972

- The logistics facilities transfer progressed as the ARVN assumed the overall responsibility for Cam Ranh port operations.
- Military Region 1. Quang Nam Province. 2nd Division elements continued house-to-house fighting inside Que Son District Town after the occupation of the district headquarters on August 31, 1972. The town was completely retaken on September 1, 1972 against moderate resistance from the 13th Regiment, 711th Division. The 4th Regiment continued its attack south of the town toward FSB Ross, and by September 1, 1972 it had occupied the southern part of base.

SEPTEMBER 2, 1972

- Military Region 1. Quang Ngai Province. The 103rd Regional Forces Battalion killed 50 enemy north of Mo Duc with light losses. VN Ranger border defense battalions at Ba To and Gia Vuc patrolled outward from their base camps, making sporadic contacts with the 52nd Regiment, 320th Division.

SEPTEMBER 2-3, 1972

- Military Region 4. The 7th Ranger Group of four battalions deployed to Military Region 1. Two Ranger battalions and two armored cavalry squadrons launched operations in the Seven Mountains area. On September 3, 1972, the operation was reinforced with an additional Ranger battalion that air assaulted into the area. The 44th Special Tactical Zone forward Command Post at Chi Lang, Chau Doc Province, controlled the operation. Sporadic contact was made as the operation continued throughout the month. The operation was credited by the IV Corps Commander with blunting the infiltration efforts of the 1st NVA Division.

SEPTEMBER 4, 1972

- Military Region 2. Pleiku Province. The Plei Djereng Ranger Border Camp fell to the enemy and activity shifted to the Thanh An area. Numerous daily contacts occurred in this area for the next 10 days as ARVN 23rd Division units and ARVN Ranger border defense battalions continued operations to secure Thanh An and the lines of communications. Light contacts and attacks-by-fire occurred as ARVN units continued clearing operations near Thanh An, Duc Co, and Plei Djereng.
- Military Region 3. The 52nd Regiment, 18th Division, secured an intermediate objective to the northwest of Quan Loi. Its final objective was the dominating high ground north. The attack for the final objective never materialized; the regiment subsequently occupied blocking positions in the area of its intermediate objective. The attacking units were frequently pulled out of the attack and replaced by fresh units. Toward the end of' the month supporting attacks were initiated north and south of Quan Loi, but these had not proven successful as the month ended. The 43rd Regiment breached the perimeter at Quan Loi and secured the southwestern end of the airstrip, which was essentially the limit of advance during the month.

SEPTEMBER 5-7, 1972

- Military Region 1: Kontum Province. Northwest of Kontum City, contacts resulted in 124 enemy killed, while ARVN casualties were 19 killed and 39 wounded.

SEPTEMBER 7, 1972

- Military Region 1. The 1st Ranger Group was attached to the Marine Division and assumed an area of operation north and northeast of Quang Tri City. This action was in preparation for a five-battalion Marine assault on the Citadel which began on September 9, 1972 as part of a coordinated Marine-airborne attack. The Airborne Division, which had seen light action during the first week of the month, was assigned the mission of attacking northwest to secure the east bank of the Thach Han River south of Quang Tri City. The major objectives were to destroy three enemy strongholds south of the river and to prevent use of the river as a resupply route. As part of the coordinated effort, amphibious demonstrations were conducted east of Dong Ha as a diversion from the main attack to retake Quang Tri City. Enemy forces reacted to the operation by increasing the pressure against Ranger units along Phase Line Gold and attacking from the southern Hai Lang Forest area toward Camp Evans and FSB Nancy. Increased sapper activity was also reported in the Marine Airborne Divisions rear areas.

SEPTEMBER 9, 1972

- Military Region 1. The Citadel. Marine elements engaged in heavy fighting as they inflicted heavy casualties on the enemy defending the Quang Tri Citadel. The Airborne Division secured the three enemy strong points to the south of the Citadel.
- Military Region 1. Quang Nam Province. FSB Ross was secured and the major items of equipment previously abandoned were recaptured in an unserviceable condition. Activity decreased sharply in the Que Son area, probably as a result of increased activity at Tien Phuoc Tin Province by the 38th Regiment, 711th Division and the 5th Sapper Battalion.
- A ground attack by elements of the 38th Regiment and 5th NVA Sapper Regiment, supported by heavy artillery and tanks of the 572d Artillery-Tank Regiment, was successful, and Tien Phuoc fell to the enemy. The ARVN initially retained outposts southeast of the town, but enemy heavy artillery, used for the first time in the province, forced evacuation of the outposts.

SEPTEMBER 12, 1972

- Military Region 1. The 2nd Division assumed responsibility for the Tien Phuoc area of operations. Fighting continued around Thien Phouc with heavy casualties on both sides. For the next few days, ARVN forces consolidated defensive positions and realigned forces for a counterattack. The counter-attack was delayed initially by Hurricane Flossie, then later by the upsurge in enemy activity in Quang Ngai Province. Although enemy activity increased in the Quang Tin provincial lowlands, ARVN forces made limited progress toward retaking the high ground around Tien Phuoc. The 4th and 6th Regiments attacked toward the town against light enemy resistance on two separate approaches.

- The Citadel. The Marines had breached the Citadel wall at the north corner, and by the following day a company size force had entered the southeast corner after heavy fighting. The Marine contingent inside the Citadel steadily increased in spite of determined enemy defenses and heavy mortar and artillery fires.

SEPTEMBER 13, 1972

- Military Region 4. The IV Corps mobile force made one of its most successful contacts and killed 116 enemy of the Z18 NVA Regiment in Dinh Tuong Province with light friendly losses.

SEPTEMBER 14, 1972

- Military Region 1. The Citadel. In late afternoon, three Marine battalions were fighting inside the Citadel. The following day the units linked-up along the east wing and conducted a coordinated attack against the remaining enemy forces. By late afternoon the entire Citadel wall was in friendly hands and reports indicated that the remaining disorganized enemy fled north. Enemy losses in the final day of fighting for control of the Citadel were over 700 killed, no prisoners taken and numerous individual and crew-served weapons were captured.

SEPTEMBER 15, 1972

- Military Region 1. Quang Tri City was officially declared recaptured. During the Marine fight for Quang Tri City the Ranger defense along Phase Line Gold withstood daily enemy attacks. The defense was penetrated on one occasion, but the rangers successfully counterattacked, eliminating the penetration. Meanwhile, as anticipated, the 304B Division increased pressure from the Hai Lang Forest against the Airborne Division units, but a counterattack from that area did not materialize. Following the fall of Quang Tri City, activity decreased sharply as the Marine elements eliminated small pockets of enemy resistance remaining in the attacks-by-fire also decreased and Marine units were rotated to rear areas for rest, refitting and to receive replacements. Toward the end of the month enemy attacks-by-fire against the airborne elements increased as they continued their drive toward the east-southeast Thach Han River bank.

- Military Region 1. Quang Ngai Province. A 30-round mortar attack against Mo Duc was carried out, which marked the beginning of the 2nd NVA Division offensive in Quang Ngai Province.

SEPTEMBER 16, 1972

- Military Region 1. Quang Ngai Province. Mo Duc District headquarters came under heavy pressure from the 1st Regiment, 2nd NVA Division with mortar and rocket attacks, followed by ground attacks. An American advisor was among the killed. Over 100 enemy were killed, and the defense held. Territorial reinforcements from the north encountered an enemy roadblock near the Song Ve Bridge and did not reach Mo Duc. LZ Dragon, just south of the town fell into enemy hands by late afternoon. The following day enemy pressure increased at Mo Duc and began at Duc Pho from the 141st Regiment, 2nd Division, and Ba To from the 52nd Regiment. Bridges along Highway 1 were blown, and the strongpoint near the Song Ve remained. American and VN Air Force gunships supported the defenders and were credited with inflicting heavy casualties as bad weather hampered tactical air operations. The following day the Sa Huynh District received a heavy daylong attack, but the defense held. The 2nd Division began preparations to deploy Regular Forces to southern Quang Ngai Province, as it appeared that a major effort would be required there.

SEPTEMBER 18-20, 1972

- Military Region 1. Quang Ngai Province. Government forces, with American tactical air, naval gunfire, and gunship support, accounted for over 600 enemy killed in Quang Ngai Province. VN casualties were 70 killed and 232 wounded.

SEPTEMBER 22-24, 1972

- Military Region 1. Quang Ngai Province. The enemy attacked numerous outposts throughout the province, particularly along Routes 1 and 515, and increased pressure against Duc Pho on September 24, 1972, by gaining control of LZ Bronco.

Also reported in the lowlands were numerous acts of terrorism in various villages and hamlets. The situation resembled a stalemate at the three district towns and along Route 1, for several days; however, American tactical air, naval gunfire, and B-52 strikes were continually hitting enemy positions as ARVN ground troops maneuvered to locate and engage the enemy.

SEPTEMBER 23, 1972

- The Da Nang Air Base was hit with 33 122mm rockets, wounding three USN personnel and causing minor structural and aircraft damage. Rockets, which landed off the base, killed or wounded nine VN.

SEPTEMBER 25 and 28, 1972

- Military Region 1. 122mm rockets hit the Da Nang Air Base. Casualties and damage were light, with two killed (one American and one VN civilian) and 10 wounded (nine Americans and one VN).

SEPTEMBER 28-29, 1972

- Military Region 3. The 25th Division, with the 46th and 50th Regiments, deployed to an area generally astride the Binh Duong-Bien Hoa Province boundary northeast of Tan Uyen. The 25th Division area of operations consisted of Binh Duong Province west of Route 13 and the northwestern corner of Bien Hoa Province, including Tan Uyen. The division mission was to destroy the enemy in its area and block enemy movement into the Bien Hoa area. The division's third organic regiment, the 40th deployed to Tay Ninh under the operational control of the III Corps Mobile Strike Force. Concurrent with the 25th Division redeployment, a combined task force was organized at Chon Thanh under control of the 3d Armored Brigade Headquarters.
- In late September, III Corps forces were shifted south and assumed a defensive posture deployed in an arc covering the northern approaches to Saigon. The general disposition of forces remained the same during the month of October 1972, resulting in a concentration of forces in southern Binh Duong Province.

SEPTEMBER 30, 1972

- Military Region 1. The 3rd Division began an attack westward to seize FSB Anne, with Barbara a secondary objective. The attack into the northern Hai Lang Forest met well-organized positions, heavily defended by the 312th and 304B Divisions elements, supported by mortars and artillery. Progress was slow the first day of the attack, but the airborne soldiers continued to make progress.
- In the Airborne Division area, south of Quang Tri City, the attack initiated to seize FSBs Anne and Barbara met strong enemy resistance. The 209th Regiment, 312th Division, defensive positions along the south bank of the Thach Han River and in the Hai Lang Forest were well-organized and supported by accurate indirect fire. Enemy fire against the Airborne Division elements averaged from 500 to 700 rounds daily. Progress was slow during the first 10 days of the operation; however, forward, elements had reached positions four kilometers east of FSB Anne and two objectives had been secured along the Thach Han River against moderately heavy enemy resistance.
- Military Region 2. Quang Tin Province. Two battalions of the 3d Division conducted a combat assault north of Tien Phuoc District Town. On October 7, 1972, elements of the 6th and 56th Regiments recaptured Tien Phuoc. The enemy suffered heavy losses in his defense of the town. The attack on Tien Phuoc was the first truly offensive operation undertaken by the 3d Division since its retreat from Quang Tri. For the remainder of the month operations were conducted to clear the enemy from the surrounding terrain and return the area to government control.

END OF SEPTEMBER 1972

- Military Region 1. 2nd Division elements were on the offensive. Activity around Duc Pho had decreased to a low level and Ranger units were progressing northward along Route 1 against light resistance. Elements of the 5th Regiment and a Ranger border defense battalion were moving north along Route 1 from Mo Duc, encountering strong resistance near the Song Ve bridge. At Ba To three battalions, under control of the 11th Ranger Group headquarters, were continually under pressure from the 52nd Regiment; however, the rangers were steadily progressing toward taking the dominant terrain around the base camp and the district headquarters compound.

- Military Region 1. Toward the end of the month, in response to increased activity by the 582d NVA Battalion in the Hai Van Pass area, the 51st Regiment conducted operations in Phu Loc District. Although these operations did not result in significant engagements, enemy interdiction of Route 1 was reduced. Meanwhile, the two regiments in the Veghel area continued, to discover small caches of enemy supplies as they expanded control further south and southwest.

OCTOBER 1972-JANUARY 1973

- The enemy used harassing rocket attacks on air installations during the period from October 1972-January 1973, striking Da Nang, Tan Son Nhut, and Bien Hoa on several occasions, resulting in minor damage. The last of these attacks occurred at Tan Son Nhut Air Base exactly 1½ hours before the cease-fire went into effect.

OCTOBER 1, 1972

- The Da Nang port was turned over to the ARVN; the Da Nang Port Authority assumed cargo of general cargo operations and subsequently operations handled all port operations. Similarly, the last two major bulk POL systems at Da Nang and Long Binh were turned over to the RVNAF.

OCTOBER 2-NOVEMBER 11, 1972

- Military Region 2. A corps-wide *Operation Dong Khoi* which began on October 2, 1972 was terminated on November 11, 1972. Enemy losses were 1,433 killed, 78 captured, 80 returnees and Hoi Chanhs, and 692 Viet Cong Infrastructure personnel captured. RVNAF casualties were 163 killed, 430 wounded, and 21 missing.

OCTOBER 4, 1972

- Military Region 1. Quang Nam Province. An unknown size enemy force (probably the 70th NVA Battalion and a Quang Nam Viet Cong Provincial unit) attacked two small villages on Barrier Island. The enemy abducted many of the villagers the next day. Territorial Forces combat assaulted into the area and returned the villagers to government control.

- Military Region 4. In the Seven Mountains area of the Khmer, ARVN Rangers made contact and VN Air Force tactical air, resulting in 54 enemy killed and no ARVN losses were reported.

OCTOBER 5, 1972

- Military Region 2. Kontum Province. Ten kilometers north-northwest of Kontum City, fighting erupted involving elements of the ARVN 44th Regiment of the 23rd Division. The fighting lasted for three days. In this battle, the South Vietnam troops accounted for over 250 of the enemy killed. Government casualties were reported as 40 dead and one wounded.

OCTOBER 6-8, 1972

- Military Region 4. On October 6, 1972, in the Khmer Republic, 13 kilometers southeast of Kampong Trabek, the 3rd Battalion, 10th Regiment, accounted for 109 enemy killed in a combined ground, American air cavalry, and VN tactical air operation. Friendly losses were two killed and 11 wounded. On October 8, 1972, the same ARVN battalion made contact in the same area and killed 69 enemy, while losing nine killed and 48 wounded. Documents from the battlefield identified the enemy in both of these contacts as the 207th NVA Regiment.

OCTOBER 10, 1972

- Military Region 2. Phase I of the ARVN 22nd Division counteroffensive that began in July terminated, and Phase II was initiated. In addition to regaining lost territory during Phase I, the South Vietnam reported 2,653 enemy killed, 258 RVNAF returnees, and 10,306 civilians returned to government control. Friendly casualties were reported as 470 killed, 1,662 wounded, and two missing.

OCTOBER 12, 1972

- Military Region 2. Kontum Province. The Ben Het Ranger Border Camp came under heavy attacks-by-fire followed by a ground attack. American and VN tactical air and gunships supported the camp defenders and one B-52 strike was diverted into the area. However, communications were lost with the camp at 2315 hours when the 95th Ranger Border Defense Battalion evacuated the camp.

OCTOBER 18, 1972

- Military Region 2. Phu Bon Province. Contact between Viet Cong local forces and territorial units was reported. Territorial Forces, reacting to intelligence that the enemy planned to attack a hamlet 10 kilometers northwest of Cheo Reo, set up claymore mines, manned defensive positions, and preplanned artillery fire and tactical air on the approach and egress routes into the area. During the initial ground encounter, 100 enemy were killed, while the territorials sustained one wounded. As the enemy force withdrew, tactical air and artillery were placed along withdrawal routes and 57 additional enemy were killed.

OCTOBER 19, 1972

- Military Region 3. The ARVN 3rd Battalion, 7th Regiment, made contact with elements of the 7th NVA Division southwest of Ben Cat in Binh Duong Province. The enemy was caught in the open and suffered 103 killed from combined USAF and VN Air Force tactical air, ARVN artillery and ground firepower. The 36th Ranger Battalion made contact fifteen kilometers southwest of Xuan Loc and killed 50 enemy while sustaining only nine wounded. A total of 142 enemy were killed during the period October 19-20, 1972.

OCTOBER 20, 1972

- Military Region 1. A VN Marine element launched a reconnaissance-in-force operation along the coast toward Thanh Hoi, north of Phase Line Gold. The attacks met sporadic, enemy resistance, primarily delaying actions. As these operations progressed, the Marine Division was directed to secure and hold Phase Line Brown. Positions near Long Quang were occupied on October 24, 1972. Toward the end of the month heavy rains had inundated the lowlands, and the advance northward was almost at a standstill. A marked increase in enemy attacks-by-fire the last two days of the month indicated enemy knowledge of impending Marine offensive operations as the NVA shifted the majority of its fire from the Airborne Division to the Marine Division area of operations.

- Military Region 2. Pleiku Province. The enemy increased pressure against the villages and Territorial Forces in the vicinity of My Thach, interdicting Route 14 to the south of Pleiku. 23d Division units were deployed to clear the pockets of enemy resistance. Several sharp contacts were reported, but by October 24, 1972, Territorial Forces from Phu Nhon had linked up with 23rd Division elements placing Route 14 south of Pleiku under friendly control.
- Military Region 4. Five ARVN maneuver battalions remained in the Khmer, compared to a high of 16 battalions operating there at the peak of ARVN cross-border operations on October 20, 1972, IV Corps priorities went to operations within Vietnam throughout the month. Screening forces remained along the Khmer border, with the size of the force fluctuating from one to four maneuver battalions.

OCTOBER 23, 1972

- Air operations north of 20 degrees were halted. The assets of the LINEBACKER force thus released were applied mostly to the interdiction campaign in Laos.
- Military Region 4. Thirty-three kilometers SW of Sva Rieng, the 11th ARVN Regiment made contact in an enemy rear service area and captured a large cache containing numerous weapons and supplies. Casualties were 42 enemy killed, 10 friendly killed and 35 friendly wounded.

OCTOBER 24-25, 1972

- Military Region 4. The ARVN 14th Regiment made contact in Dinh Tuong Province with the 6th Regiment, 5th NVA Division, and killed 57 enemy. Friendly losses were 32 killed and 36 wounded.

OCTOBER 25, 1972

- Military Region 1. The ARVN Airborne Division bypassed Annie and Barbara and attack to the rear of these positions to capture enemy materiel. Units on the south flank would then be in a position to attack the firebases from the flank. The

Airborne Division reoccupied Barbara on October 31, 1972 against moderate resistance from the 9th Regiment, 304B Division. Spurred by the 3d Airborne Brigade's success, the 2nd Brigade's attack against FSB Anne gained momentum, but it had not been taken by October 31, 1972. During the Quang Tri counteroffensive, activity continued in the other Military Region 1 provinces.

OCTOBER 26, 1972

- Hanoi announced a peace agreement and set October 31, 1972 for the signing, a date ignored by the US and South Vietnam.

OCTOBER 27, 1972

- Military Region 3. Phuoc Long Province. Near Dong Xoai, Territorial Forces engaged the D-368th Viet Cong Battalion and with VN tactical air support killed 100 enemy while losing two friendly killed and seven wounded.

OCTOBER 29, 1972.

- Military Region 2. Kontum Province. Dak Seang received an attack of approximately 1,000 rounds of mixed artillery and mortar fire followed by a ground attacked by elements of the 66th NVA Regiment. The 337 camp defenders were supported by American and VN tactical air strikes. The camp was evacuated after darkness.

OCTOBER 30, 1972

- Military Region 1. The Ba To Ranger camp received heavy attacks-by-fire, followed by ground attacks by elements of the 52nd Regiment. The 69th Ranger Border Defense Battalion was forced to withdraw from the camp and Ba To was lost to the enemy. The 2nd Ranger Group operation in the vicinity of Duc Pho was aimed at clearing Route 1 north of Duc Pho and linking up with elements of the 4th Regiment moving south from Mo Duc.
- Military Region 2. Kontum Province. Two reconnaissance companies of the 23rd Division combat assaulted into LZs in the vicinity of Dak To and Tan Canh. The mission of these units was to raise the South Vietnam flag over these district headquarters and to remain there for at least five days. Only

light, ineffective attacks-by-fire were reported by the units. In two sharp contacts on October 31, 1972, 62 enemy were reported killed, while ARVN casualties were light.

- Military Region 4. 14 kilometers NW of Cai Lay, a Regional Forces battalion killed 48 enemy from the 6th Regiment, 5th NVA Division, with friendly losses of five wounded.

NOVEMBER-DECEMBER 1972

- Restrictions were lifted over North Vietnam, and a high priority was given to the LINEBACKER II campaign during late December 1972. This was noticeable in the B-52 sortie totals for South Vietnam where, for the first time since the enemy offensive, less than half of the total ARC LIGHT sorties were flown in South Vietnam.

NOVEMBER 1, 1972

- Military Region 1. A battalion of the VN Marine Division crossed the Thach Han River near the Quang Tri Citadel the evening of November 1, 1972. The operation was planned as a limited objective attack as far north as the Ai Tu Combat Base. Enemy resistance was much stronger than anticipated, and the Marines were forced to withdraw the following day after suffering moderate casualties. The Marine Division continued planning for limited objective operations south of Cua Viet River. Indications were that the enemy was aware of these plans, as forward Marine units were continually subjected to heavy indirect fire of 1,500 to 2,500 rounds of mortar, rocket, and artillery daily. In addition, heavy monsoon rains throughout the month hampered ground movements and limited air operations primarily to non-visual bombing methods.
- Military Region 2. Pleiku Province. Route 14 between Kontum and Pleiku was closed by enemy action as the month began. Rangers at Duc Co reported enemy attacks-by-fire and tank supported ground attacks. Although the rangers were supported by helicopter gunships, tactical air, and B-52 strikes, the camp was evacuated late that night.
- Military Region 4. Kien Tuong Province. In Kien Tuong Province, 33 kilometers west of Tuyen Binh on November 1, 1972, element of the 10th Reconnaissance Company and 7th Engineer Battalion contacted an undetermined size enemy

unit and killed 68, with ARVN losses of one wounded. On November 2, 1972 the 10th Reconnaissance Company made contact in the same area and killed 35 enemy without friendly losses.

NOVEMBER 1-5, 1972

- Military Region 4. There were 80 friendly initiated contacts on November 1, 1972.

NOVEMBER 2, 1972

- Military Region 3. One major engagement occurred at An Loc between the 43rd Regiment and an estimated regiment from the 9th NVA Division. In this daylong battle, 192 enemy were killed, and friendly losses were five killed and 25 wounded.
- Military Region 4. Phong Dinh Province. Two Regional Forces battalions engaged possible elements of the D1 Viet Cong Regiment. VN Air Force tactical air supported the operation, which resulted in 26 enemy killed and no friendly losses.

NOVEMBER 5, 1972

- Military Region 3. Elements of the 8th Regiment, 5th Division deployed from Chon Thanh, Binh Long Province to the vicinity of Lai Khe in Binh Duong Province.
- Military Region 4. Dinh Tuong Province. Nine kilometers northeast of My Tho, the 430th Regional Forces Battalion killed 24 enemy, with one Regional Forces soldier killed and two wounded.
- Military Region 4. Kien Phong Province. The 2nd Battalion, 10th Regiment, in a joint operation with forces from Hong Ngu District, conducted a ground and waterborne envelopment of the 207th NVA Regiment elements. This operation broke enemy resistance and resulted in 35 enemy killed, 24 prisoners, and no friendly losses.

NOVEMBER 6, 1972

- Typhoon Pamela hit the RVN.

NOVEMBER 9-14, 1972

- Military Region 1. The 2nd Brigade initiated a coordinated attack to seize Anne. The assaulting elements were in sporadic heavy contact for several days, but by November 13, 1972 the western portion of the firebase was under friendly control. Intensive tactical air support against heavily fortified enemy positions and B-52 strikes to the west enabled the airborne elements to seize Anne on November 14, 1972, and to continue the attack to the north and west. A summary of major equipment captured in the Anne-Barbara area included 30 artillery pieces, four tanks, 41 mortars, 16 recoilless rifles, 54 machine guns, and 55 antiaircraft weapons.

NOVEMBER 10, 1972

- A total of 318 facilities had been transferred, abandoned, or dismantled by US and FWF during 1972, including the multi-million dollar bases at Cam Ranh Bay and Long Binh. An additional 211 facilities were title transferred, but retained until no longer needed.
- Military Region 4. Dinh Tuong Province. Three kilometers southwest of Sam Giang, the 410th Regional Forces Battalion made contact with disastrous results. Friendly losses were 26 killed, 14 missing, and four wounded. Enemy losses were four killed.

NOVEMBER 17-18, 1972

- Military Region 1. In an effort to increase the momentum of a VN Marine offensive, 10 B-52 strikes were employed just south of the Cua Viet River and five strikes were placed in the Dong Ha area on November 17, 1972. Naval gunfire also was increased, and the VN Marine units near the coast reached objectives along Phase Line Brown on November 18, 1972. The momentum was short-lived, as heavy rains and swollen streams severely restricted tactical and logistical movement. Since deteriorating weather had restricted air operations to unobserved delivery techniques, the USN increased gunfire support to approximately 4,000 rounds daily for the week ending November 25, 1972.

NOVEMBER 20, 1972

- Military Region 2. Pleiku Province. In ground contact in the Thanh An area, government elements, with the support of artillery and USAF and VN Air Force tactical air, repulsed an attack killing 91 enemy. B-52s supported the engagement with aircrews reporting three secondary explosions, USAF and VN Air Force gunships were instrumental in stopping the enemy night attack. The following day B-52s again struck enemy positions in the Thanh An-Duc Co area. .

- Military Region 4. Khmer. There was only one significant ARVN cross-border operation during the month. The 3rd Battalion, 10th Regiment, conducted an airmobile assault eight kilometers SW of Svay Rieng and killed 43 enemy, while losing one wounded.

NOVEMBER 22, 1972

- Military Region 4. Elements of the 94th Regional Forces Group were ambushed in Vinh Long Province suffering 26 killed, 20 missing, and four wounded and 56 weapons lost. There were no known enemy losses.

NOVEMBER 24, 1972

- Military Region 1. The VN Airborne Division made several changes in unit deployments. The ARVN 7th Ranger Group replaced the 3rd Airborne Brigade at Barbara, and the 1st Airborne Brigade exchanged its battalions along the Thach Han River. Three days later an estimated battalion-sized enemy force attacked the 2nd Brigade units defending Anne. The attack was repulsed with 34 enemy killed, while airborne losses were 17 killed and 46 wounded.

NOVEMBER 25, 1972

- Military Region 1. The Marine Division committed the 258th Brigade with three battalions to the offensive in an area of operations between the Thach Han and Vinh Dinh Rivers. The 147th Brigade, also with three battalions, retained the area of operations from the river to the coastline, leaving the 369th Brigade to defend Quang Tri City. During a relief of units an enemy attack achieved limited success, following a preparation of approximately 3,000 rounds, which killed 27 Marines and wounded 45. The Marines counterattacked two days later and restored the position against determined enemy resistance. Activity was reduced the last three days of the month as heavy rains and intensive flooding restricted operations.

- Military Region 2. Pleiku Province. The 2nd Battalion, 41st Regiment, reached FSB Thanh Giao, killing 114 enemy in the process, while sustaining 11 killed and 25 wounded. In a supporting operation west of Thanh Giao by elements of the 45th Regiment, an additional 27 enemy were killed.

NOVEMBER 30, 1972

- Military Region 2. Binh Dinh Province. A 10-day *Operation DONG KHOI* was terminated, resulting in 321 enemy killed, 13 prisoners, and 34 Hoi Chanhs. Friendly casualties were 26 killed, 61 wounded, and two missing.

DECEMBER 1, 1972

- The Vietnamization of aerial ports was completed when the VN Air Force assumed responsibility for aerial port activities at Tan Son Nhut. The US maintained small detachments of military and civilian contract personnel at several air bases to handle US secure cargo and mail.

DECEMBER 4, 1972

- Military Region 2. Kontum Province. Heavy USAF tactical air support produced 19 secondary explosions and seven secondary fires. The ARVN 44th Regiment inflicted heavy casualties on 320th NVA Division elements while repulsing several attacks.
- Military Region 4. Dinh Tuong Province. The 3rd Battalion, 16th ARVN Regiment, exploiting a B-52 strike near Cai Lay, killed 25 enemy and captured two, with two ARVN killed and five wounded. A prisoner stated, that possibly 100 enemy had been killed by the ARC LIGHT Strike.

DECEMBER 6, 1972

- Military Region 1. Quang Nam Province. Elements of the ARVN 56th Regiment repulsed an enemy ground attack at Nui Da Ham. The defense was supported by B-52 strikes, tactical air strikes, and ARVN artillery.
- Military Region 2. Pleiku Province. Elements of the ARVN 22nd Division Reconnaissance Company reported contact with elements of the 48th and 64th Regiments, 320th NVA Division following a combat assault into the Duc Co area.

- Military Region 2. Binh Dinh Province. Following a combat assault five kilometers ESE of Haoi An area, the 47th ARVN Reconnaissance Company joined elements of a battalion on the ground and assaulted 3rd NVA Division positions inflicting moderate losses on the enemy. ARVN artillery and USAF aircraft reported as ground forces secured the positions. The arrival of Typhoon Therese further hampered combat operations as sporadic contacts continued with friendly forces receiving light attacks-by-fire. With the 47th ARVN Regiment operation continuing elements of the 40th ARVN Regiment operated along Route 1 near LZ English and Tam Quan, while 64th ARVN Regiment units worked the An Lao Valley in and west of Haoi An without significant contact.

DECEMBER 7, 1972

- Military Region 4. Dinh Tuong Province. The 3rd Battalion, 12th ARVN Regiment killed 30 enemy, while losing seven killed and 22 wounded in a series of contacts.

DECEMBER 9, 1972

- Military Region 1. Quang Tin Province. The 3rd Battalion, 5th ARVN Regiment conducted a coordinated ground attack supported by artillery against enemy positions south of Ky Long. During the day 48 enemy were killed and one captured, with the ARVN suffering light casualties.

DECEMBER 10, 1972

- Military Region 1. Quang Tin Province. A combined Territorial Force-ARVN operation began on Barrier Island with the commitment of three Regional Forces battalions from Quang Tin, two Regional Forces battalions from Quang Nam, and one cavalry squadron from the 3rd Division. Under the control of the Quang Tin Sector Tactical Command Post, the results of the operation were significant and resulted in the destruction of enemy forces on the island.
- Military Region 1. Quang Ngai Province. A combined force of a Ranger border defense battalion, an armored cavalry squadron, and the 4th Regiment Reconnaissance Company attacked an enemy position four kilometers NE of Mo Duc,

killing 29 enemy and suffering light casualties. Activity around Mo Duc for the remainder of the month consisted of sporadic light contacts.

- Military Region 3. The 25th Division started a two-battalion sweep operation in the Hobo Woods area and along the Saigon River. The 5th Division, in coordination with the 25th Division, began a two-battalion operation east of the river west of Ben Cat.

DECEMBER 11, 1972

- Military Region 3. Tay Ninh Province. The 51st Regional Forces Group, acting on information from a Hoi Chanh, made contact with possible elements of the D2 Battalion, C50 Regiment and killed 79 enemy. US and VN Air Force tactical air support was employed. Friendly losses were three wounded.

DECEMBER 14, 1972

- Military Region 4. Kien Giang Province. US cavalry elements attacked an enemy supply base along with US tactical air support, which resulted in 30 enemy killed by air, 27 secondary explosions, and miscellaneous storage facilities and supplies destroyed.

DECEMBER 17, 1972

- Military Region 4. Friendly-initiated contacts increased in number and intensity and were concentrated in Kien Phong, and Dinh Tuong Provinces. There were five significant contacts in Dinh Tuong and three in Kien Phong that accounted for the majority of the 204 total enemy killed.

DECEMBER 19, 1972

- Military Region 1. Quang Tri Province. The 5th Battalion repulsed an enemy counterattack killing 137 enemy. The Airborne Division made significant progress in its attack westward, toward the Thach Han River against elements of the 312th and 325th Divisions. The most significant activity was centered northwest of FSB Anne where a series of coordinated attacks cut enemy escape routes and resulted in a large amount of enemy equipment being captured.

- Military Region 4: A large number of small contacts throughout the region accounted for 195 enemy killed.

DECEMBER 27, 1972

- Military Region 1. Quang Nam Province. The 3rd Division initiated a two-axis attack in the Que Son Valley with the 56th Regiment on the north and the 2nd Regiment on the south.
- Military Region 2. Binh Dinh Province. Elements of the 47th Regiment, supported by artillery, made another significant contact southeast of Hoai An and inflicted heavy casualties on the enemy while suffering only light losses. ARVN artillery was credited with most of the enemy casualties.
- Military Region 3. III Corps initiated a coordinated attack into the Saigon River corridor employing elements of the 5th and 25th Divisions. To the east of the Saigon River, three battalions of the 5th Division attacked into the Iron Triangle. On the west of the river, four battalions of the 25th Division attacked towards the Hobo Woods with objectives near the river. The attack made moderate progress against light resistance.

DECEMBER 31, 1972

- The final logistics port facilities of Newport and Cat Lai were transferred to the ARVN. The US retained control of Newport until March 28, 1973 and the Vung Tau port, although ARVN responsibility continued to be operated by civilian contractors until the same date.

JANUARY 5, 1973

- Military Region 1. Quang Tin Province. In conjunction with the 3rd Division operation in the Que Son Valley, the 5th Regiment occupied blocking positions north of Tien Phuoc. Territorial Forces were also positioned in this area to assist the 6th Regiment in blocking enemy escape routes south of the Que Son Valley. Over a 10-day period, the 5th Regiment accounted for 143 enemy killed, 47 weapons captured, and several tons of enemy equipment, ammunition, and foodstuffs captured or destroyed.

JANUARY 10-20, 1973

- Military Region 3. The *Saigon River Corridor operation* progressed well. Friendly elements reached Tri Tam on January 11, 1973, and a coordinated attack into the Michelin Rubber Plantation was initiated. Two regiment; of the 25th Division and one from the 5th Division pushed northeast of Tri Tam, entering the plantation from the west and southwest.

JANUARY 13, 1973

- Military Region 1. VN Airborne Division elements found 1,000 rounds of 82mm mortar west of FSB Anne while clearing small pockets of enemy resistance.
- Military Region 3. A battalion of the 5th Division made contact with elements of the 209th Regiment. This contact resulted in moderate enemy and light friendly casualties. By mid-January 1973, 15 battalions and the ARVN Ranger Command were involved in the Saigon River operation; contacts were light and scattered, permitting friendly forces to maneuver without great difficulty.
- Military Region 4. Chuong Thien Province. Elements of the 31st Regiment made contact with an estimated enemy regiment and were successful in maintaining sporadic contact for the next several days.

JANUARY 14, 1973

- Military Region 2. Pleiku City was subjected to repeated attacks of 122mm rockets, but the intensity of fire was low with little damage was reported.

JANUARY 15-21, 1973

- Military Region 4. *Operation Dong Khoi.* Numerous small contacts were made throughout the military region, attributed mainly to a corps-wide *Dong Khoi Operation* that began on January 15, 1973. This operation was scheduled to end on January 18, 1973 but was extended three days because of its initial success. On January 21, 1973, when the operation ended, over 500 of the enemy had been killed, with moderate friendly casualties.

JANUARY 17, 1973

- Military Region 1. VN Marine area of operations. The Marine Division launched an attack toward the Cua Viet River east of Route 560, as part of an I Corps plan for the period preceding the cease-fire. The Marines were to seize the area south of the river while other I Corps units conducted security operations to preclude enemy penetration into rear areas and populated areas. The Marine attack met strong resistance and heavy attacks-by-fire, including an estimated 4,000 rounds of mortar and artillery.
- Military Region 1. VN Marine area of operations. The Marines renewed the attack northwest with a feint being conducted by units inland along Phase Line Gold. The following morning a major attack was launched along the coast and met heavy enemy resistance.

JANUARY 21, 1973

- Military Region 3. The *Saigon River Corridor Operation* ended. ARVN forces returned to populated areas to resume security positions and protection of lines of communication. Casualties for this operation during the period January 13-21, 1973, reported by US advisors, were 40 enemy killed, 86 friendly, killed, 207 wounded and 90 missing. This offensive and the intensive supporting air operations were apparently successful in causing substantial enemy casualties, destroying enemy caches and preempting the movement of enemy forces.

JANUARY 24, 1973

- Military Region 2. A battalion of the ARVN 44th Regiment combat assaulted into LZs southwest of Vo Dinh. A fire support base was established along Route 14 two kilometers east of Ngo Trang with two 105mm howitzers for support of the three battalions operating in the Vo Dinh area. In Pleiku Province, the ARVN Ranger company occupying the Duc Co Border Ranger Camp was forced to withdraw after extensive attacks-by-fire and ground attacks. US Spectre and VN Air Force Spooky gunships, US Army Cobras, and USAF and VN Air Force TACAIR supported the defenders.

JANUARY 26, 1973

- Military Region 3. The Bien Hoa Air Base received 28 122mm rockets resulting in one American killed.

JANUARY 27, 1973

- Nearly 59,000 US and Free World personnel remained in Vietnam, including 23,000 Americans 35,000 Koreans, and slightly over one hundred others from Thailand, the Philippines, and the Republic of China.

JANUARY 27-31, 1973

- Military Region 1. VN Marine area of operations. The VN Marines were overrun and forced to consolidate defensive positions along Phase Line Brown. During this operation, the Marines suffered 91 killed, 21 wounded, and 149 missing. Additionally, 24 M-1 tanks, 19 M-41 tanks, and 24 M-113 armored personnel carriers were destroyed.

JANUARY 28, 1973

- The cease-fire hour arrived, 0800 hours, Sunday, January 28, 1973.
- Air Operations. US air operations in South Vietnam ceased at 0800 when the cease-fire began. US operations continued on a limited scale in Laos and the Khmer Republic in response to specific requests of those governments. Targeting for these strikes, which included B-52 and TACAIR, included close air support and an interdiction effort, mostly in Laos.
- Quang Nam Province. Activity in the province consisted of enemy initiated attacks-by-fire against the Da Nang area and attacks-by-fire and ground attacks in the Que Son Valley. These attacks were repulsed and ARVN forces retained the terrain held prior to the ceasefire.
- Military Region 3. The Tan Son Nhut Air Base received 33 122mm rockets. One civilian was killed and 20 were injured at Tan Son Nhut.

JANUARY 28-31, 1973

- Military Region 4. After the cease-fire announcement on January 28, 1973, enemy activity throughout the Delta increased significantly and was directed at villages, territorial outposts and ARVN base areas and outposts.

FEBRUARY 15, 1973

- MACV relinquished the control of air operations in Southeast Asia to the US Support Activities Group (USSAG).

FEBRUARY 27, 1973

- The Civil Operations and Revolutionary Development Support (CORDS) stood down.

MARCH 7, 1973

- "With the end of our direct military involvement in South Vietnam, I am tremendously proud of the overall performance of the several million American military and civilian persons who have had a part to play here. I am equally proud of the results that have flowed from the sacrifices of the millions of South Vietnam, military and civilian alike, who have fought to secure their right of self-determination in the face of massive intimidation by force.

...In the period immediately ahead, the priority of our effort should go to lines of action that will help to insure that all parties recognize the cease-fire agreement for what it is, i.e., the only viable alternative that will lead to the lasting peace that the people of Southeast Asia need and want so desperately."

General Fred C. Weyand
Saigon
March 7, 1973

MARCH 14, 1973

- The majority of the Korean troops had completed their departure from Nha Trang, Phu Cat, and Saigon. Small Korean and Chinese elements remained in Saigon until March 23 and 26, 1973, respectively.

MARCH 27-29, 1973

- The fourth and final US increment departed Saigon within a 72-hour period on March 27, 28, 29, 1973 as the last group of prisoners were released in increments and flown out of Hanoi.

MARCH 29, 1973

- Disestablishment of the MACV.

MARCH 31, 1973

- The US members of the Four Party Joint Military Commission (FPJMC) departed. At 1900 hours, the US Delegation was disestablished.

Glossary

AFRTS	Armed Forces Radio and Television Service
AGP	Motor Torpedo Boat Tender (Auxiliary General Purpose
ANG	Army National Guard
ARVN	Army of the RVN
ASP	Ammunition Supply Point
AUS	Australia or Australian
BDA	Bomb Damage Assessment
BLT	Battalion Landing Team
CG	Commanding General
CHICOM	Chinese Communist
Chieu Hoi	Open Arms Program (RVN)
CIA	Central Intelligence Agency
CIDC	Civilian Irregular Defense Group
CINCPAC	Commander in Chief, Pacific
CNO	Chief of Naval Operations
COMNAVFORV	Commander, Naval Forces, Vietnam
COMUSMACV	Commander, US Military Assistance Command Vietnam
CONUS	Continental United States
CORDS	Civil Operations and Rural Development Support
CRID	Capital Republic of Korea Infantry Division

CTZ	Corps Tactical Zone
DD	Destroyer
DER	Radar Picket Escort Ship
DMAC	Delta Military Assistance Command
DMZ	Demilitarized Zone
DOD	Department of Defense
DRAC	Delta Regional Assistance Command
DRV	Democratic Republic of Vietnam
EOD	Explosive Ordnance Disposal
FANK	Forces Armees Nationales Khmeres (Khmer Armed Forces)
FFV	Field Force Vietnam
FRAC	First Regional Assistance Command
FSA	Forward Support Area
FSB	Fire Support Base
FWF	Free World Forces
FWMAF	Free World Military Assistance Forces
GCA	Ground Control Approach
GVN	Government of Vietnam
Hoi Chanhs	Viet Cong/NVA Rallier
HQ	Headquarters
ICC	International Control Commission
ICRC	International Committee of the Red Cross
IFFV	I Field Force, Vietnam
IIFFV	II Field Force, Vietnam
JCS	Joint Chiefs of Staff
LCM	Landing Craft, Mechanized
LCU	Landing Craft, Utility
LST	Landing Ship, Tank
LZ	Landing Zone
MAAG	Military Assistance Advisory Group
MACV	Military Assistance Command Vietnam
MAF	Marine Amphibious Force
MAG	Marine Air Group
MAP	Military Assistance Program
Market Time	USN anti-infiltration blockade of South Vietnam Coast
Mech	Mechanized
MEDCAP	Medical Civic Action Program
Medevac	Medical evacuation

Mig	Russian Fighter Aircraft
MP	Military Police
MPC	Military Payment Certificate
MR	Military Region
MSB	Minesweeping Boat
MSR	Minesweeper, River
MSTS	Military Sea Transportation Service
NCO	Noncommissioned Officer
NLF	National Liberation Front
NSA	Naval Support Activity
NVN	North Vietnam or North Vietnamese
NZ	New Zealand
PAVN	People's Army of (North) Vietnam
PB	Patrol Boat
PBR	Patrol Boat, River
PCE	Patrol Craft Escort
PCF	Patrol Craft, Fast
PG	Patrol Gunboat
PGM	Patrol Gunboat Medium
PHILCAGV	Philippine Civic Action Group Vietnam
POL	Petroleum, Oil and Lubricants
PSDF	People's Self Defense Force
PSYOP	Psychological Operations
PSYWAR	Psychological Warfare
PT	Patrol Boat, Torpedo
PTSD	Post Traumatic Stress Disorder
RAC	River Assault Craft
RAG	River Assault Group
R&R	Rest & Recuperation
RCT	Regimental Combat Team
RD	Rural Development
ROK	Republic of Korea
ROKFV	Republic of Korea Forces, Vietnam
ROKMC	Republic of Korea Marine Corps
RPD	Enemy light machine gun
RPG	Rocket-propelled grenade
RR	Recoilless Rifle
RVNAF	Republic of Vietnam Armed Forces
SEALS	Sea, Air, Land (Navy special forces)
SKS	Soviet Semiautomatic Carbine

SVN	South Vietnam or South Vietnamese
Swift Boats	PCF (Patrol Craft, Fast)
TAOR	Tactical Area of Responsibility
TET	VN Lunar New Year Holiday
TF	Task Force
TFW	Tactical Fighter Wing
TG	Task Group
TNT	Trinitrooluene
TRAC	Third Regional Assistance Command
USAF	US Air Force
USAID	US Agency for International Development
USARPAC	US Army, Pacific
USARV	US Army, Vietnam
USARYIS	US Army Ryukyu Islands
USCG	US Coast Guard
USCGC	US Coast Guard Cutter
USG	US Government
USMC	US Marine Corps
USN	US Navy
USNS	US Navy Ship
USS	US Ship
USSAG	US Support Activities Group
USSR	Union of Soviet Socialist Republics
VN	Vietnam or Vietnamese
VNMC	VN Marine Corps
VNN	VN Navy
WHEC	Coast Guard High Endurance Cutter
Yankee Station	Carrier Force Area off Coast of VN
YR	Floating Workshop
YRBM	Yard Repair Berthing and Messing

ABOUT THE AUTHOR

Born Canton, Ohio on December 11, 1951. Completed Bachelor of Science Degree from Southern Illinois University. Completed 21 year career in the U.S. Navy. Currently working as a Management Analyst which entails researching military records to verify incidents that occurred in World War II, Korean War, Vietnam War and Desert Storm.

ABOUT GREATUNPUBLISHED.COM

www.greatunpublished.com is a website that exists to serve writers and readers, and to remove some of the commercial barriers between them. When you purchase a GreatUNpublished title, whether you order it in electronic form or in a paperback volume, the author is recceiving a majority of the post-production revenue.

A GreatUNpublished book is never out of stock, and always available, because each book is printed on-demand, as it is ordered.

A portion of the site's share of profits is channeled into literacy programs.

So by purchasing this title from GreatUNpublished, you are helping to revolutionize the publishing industry for the benefit of writers and readers.

And for this we thank you.